THREE YEARS OUR MAYOR

The Urban West Series

Amy L. Scott, Bradley University, *Series Editor*

Urban West examines the development of primary and secondary cities in the Trans-Mississippi West including Texas and California. The series explores issues of class, race, ethnicity, gender, environment, suburbanization, municipal services, public works, community building, culture, and other relevant subjects within an urban context. All types of methodologies are welcome, but special attention will be given to those manuscripts offering important new insights, novel research approaches and sources, and comparative studies of multiple cities.

Urbanism and Empire in the Far West, 1840–1890
Eugene P. Moehring

Class and Gender Politics in Progressive-Era Seattle
John C. Putman

Sacramento and the Catholic Church: Shaping a Capital City
Steven M. Avella

Earning Power: Women, and Work in Los Angeles, 1880–1930
Eileen V. Wallis

Cities and Nature in the American West
Char Miller

City Dreams, Country Schemes: Community and Identity in the American West
Kathleen A. Brosnan and Amy L. Scott

Cities, Sagebrush, and Solitude: Urbanization and Cultural Conflict in the Great Basin
Dennis R. Judd and Stephanie L. Witt

The Coveted Westside: How the Black Homeowners' Rights Movement Shaped Modern Los Angeles
Jennifer Mandel

Three Years Our Mayor: George Moscone and the Making of Modern San Francisco
Lincoln A. Mitchell

Three Years Our Mayor

George Moscone and the Making of Modern San Francisco

Lincoln A. Mitchell

UNIVERSITY OF NEVADA PRESS | *Reno & Las Vegas*

This publication is made possible in part by a grant from The Ettinger Foundation.

University of Nevada Press | Reno, Nevada 89557 USA
www.unpress.nevada.edu

Manufactured in the United States of America

This book has been reproduced as a digital reprint.

Cover design by David Ter-Avanesyan/Ter33Design, LLC
Cover photographs © by SFMTA Photo Archive/sfmta.com/photo (top left), Moscone family (top right), David Glass (bottom)

Library of Congress Cataloging-in-Publication Data available upon request.
ISBN 978-1-64779-249-7 (paper)
ISBN 978-1-64779-188-9 (ebook)
LCCN: 2024038724

The paper used in this book meets the requirements of American National Standard for Information Sciences—Permanence of Paper for Printed Library Materials, ansi/niso z39.48–1992 (r2002).

Contents

List of Illustrations

Figures

Maps

Preface

I FIRST LEARNED OF GEORGE Moscone one day in the fall of 1975 when my brother and I came home from school—he was in fifth grade, and I was in third—talking about John Barbagelata. We heard that name from our Catholic school classmates who had told us that Barbagelata was going to be the next mayor. We thought it was a funny name and shared that opinion with our mother, who responded by telling us that we were supporting "the other guy." The other guy turned out to be George Moscone, who a few weeks later narrowly defeated Barbagelata in a runoff election and became mayor of San Francisco.

When I was an adolescent and young adult in 1980s San Francisco, Moscone's name seemed to be everywhere. By the time I was in high school, my local park, which had two good ballfields where we played baseball and was a short walk from Moscone's childhood home, was renamed in his honor. In 1984, during the Democratic National Convention, I attended Rock Against Reagan concerts and listened to bands like Dead Kennedys perform in the parking lot next to the Moscone Center where the convention was being held. The Moscone Center was San Francisco's newest and best convention facility back then. Thirty-seven years later, many would receive their vaccination against COVID-19 there. For San Franciscans, the name Moscone is with us all the time, but less is remembered about the man himself. Outside of San Francisco, George Moscone is all but forgotten. Scholars of urban politics and American cities rarely pay much attention to him. Visitors and even new migrants to the city Moscone once led now see his name on buildings, parks, and schools and probably assume that he was simply some long-ago civic leader.

Moscone only served as mayor for just short of three years because he was assassinated in his City Hall office on November 27, 1978. Moments after shooting Moscone, Dan White, the disgruntled former San Francisco supervisor who was angry because the mayor would not reappoint him to the job from which he had resigned days earlier, walked down the hall into the office of Supervisor Harvey Milk. White then shot and killed Milk. By doing that, Dan White forever linked Moscone's name to that of a martyred civil rights icon who is known throughout much of the world. In the years since 1978, Milk's legacy has eclipsed that of

Moscone. After all, mayors who serve for only three years are rarely remembered even in their own cities. Moreover, a widely believed, but untrue, story that Milk persuaded Moscone not to reappoint White, leading White to kill both men, has further minimized Moscone in the eyes of many. The Bay Area media now frequently refer to the killings as the Milk-Moscone murders, whereas at the time everybody in San Francisco rightly called the killings the Moscone-Milk murders. It is a small thing, but it shows how Moscone's legacy has faded.

Moscone's 1975 campaign and the years he served as mayor were a political turning point for San Francisco and in many respects for urban America more generally. His election helped electoral politics in San Francisco catch up with the changes that had been enveloping the city for close to a decade. Although Moscone's predecessor in City Hall had appointed several African Americans to high-profile positions, when Moscone became mayor, San Francisco politics went from black-and-white to Kodachrome. Moscone appointed gay community activists and many people of color to important city commissions, successfully assembled a very diverse coalition, and was the kind of politician who received letters of from people such as legendary rock promoter Bill Graham recommending security people who could "bridge the communication gap between the young 'hip' community and City Hall."[1]

Moscone was somebody who, although a product of the old San Francisco, understood the emerging city. He could do things such as throw out the first pitch on opening day of the city's gay softball league, cruise around the city in his purple Alfa Romeo, see his teenage daughter experience San Francisco's punk rock scene, go shopping with the city's charismatic assemblyman Willie Brown, and fully experience and embrace the strange, fun, awesome, frightening place that was San Francisco in the 1970s.

Moscone's three immediate predecessors in City Hall, Joseph Alioto, Jack Shelley, and George Christopher, were all products of an earlier city—socially conservative, ethnic politicians who enjoyed strong support from downtown and real estate interests. They were all born between 1905 and 1916 and grew into adults before World War II. By the time they got to City Hall, all three were middle-aged. It is difficult to imagine any of them wearing anything but a business suit. They were not terribly corrupt or dishonest, and they did some good things. Christopher, for example, helped bring the Giants to San Francisco from New York. Shelley created the Human Rights Commission to address civil rights issues; and Alioto navigated the city through a very volatile period while avoiding the kinds of mass violence that plagued much of urban America in the late 1960s and early 1970s. Nonetheless, they were stuck in an era that by 1975 had passed them by.

That era ended when Moscone got elected mayor. In that extremely close 1975 mayoral election, Moscone brought together a coalition of African Americans,

Latinos, gays and lesbians, progressive whites, and Asian Americans. Today that coalition is central to almost any successful Democratic campaign, but a good argument can be made that Moscone was the first person to successfully assemble that coalition in a high-profile campaign. For example, before Moscone, few, if any, straight politicians proactively campaigned for gay votes and brought gay voters into a coalition with people of color or with labor unions.

During his three years as mayor, Moscone sought to address, ultimately with mixed success, the urban problems and challenges of the 1970s. Rising crime rates, shrinking tax bases, labor unrest, demands from different groups for more rights and access to government, backlash to those groups from more conservative voters, police-community relations, and job creation confronted mayors in most big cities during that era. However, Moscone also confronted issues that were more specific to San Francisco. The gay rights movement was a much bigger part of San Francisco politics than that of any other city. The social upheavals of the 1960s had left a much bigger imprint on Moscone's city than anywhere else in the country. Few mayors find themselves spending their first days and months in office desperately trying to stop their city's big-league baseball team from moving as Moscone did. And no other mayor has ever had to help their city through the aftershocks of anything quite like the Peoples Temple massacre in Jonestown.

Moscone's life is a uniquely San Francisco story as well. Although he was on the left, Moscone had deep roots in an older, more conservative, white ethnic iteration of the city. His ability to move fluidly across both new and old San Francisco was the key to his political success. Moscone was an Italian American who grew up in modest circumstances and became a star athlete and graduate of St. Ignatius, the city's elite Jesuit high school. He was the kind of mayor who when he said Willie McCovey, the great slugging Giants first baseman, was a local institution comparable to the Golden Gate Bridge and the cable cars, sounded like he meant it. Moscone also regularly infuriated those conservative older San Francisco communities by casting his lot with the newer, more radical city. A lot of his more conservative fellow alumni from St. Ignatius were not happy about his supportive attitude toward gay San Franciscans or his efforts to reduce police brutality. Many of those older elite families also opposed Moscone and his efforts to move political and economic power out to the neighborhoods.

A close look at Moscone's life and work provides a glimpse into one of America's most fascinating, important, and beloved cities throughout the middle of the twentieth century. The changes in Moscone's city, changes that in many cases he supported, were extraordinary. Moscone was born in a San Francisco that was 95 percent white, with fewer than 20,000 Chinese Americans and fewer than 5,000 African Americans. The proportion of the city's population that was white had dropped to 59 percent in the 1980 census, taken shortly after Moscone's murder, while the African American and Chinese American populations of San Francisco both exceeded 80,000.[2] Moscone was born into a city that was a major shipping and manufacturing center about to grow even more during World War II, but he spent the last years of his life trying to steer the city's fiscal policy during a time of shrinking resources as manufacturing and shipping jobs had been leaving the city for more than a decade.

When Moscone began his political life, San Francisco politicians were almost entirely white, straight, Christian, and male. In 1978, the year of his death, the president of the San Francisco Board of Supervisors was a Jewish woman. Her colleagues on that body included a gay Jewish man, a radical Jewish woman, a Latino man, an African American woman and a Chinese American man. By the time Moscone became mayor, San Francisco was emerging, or had emerged, as a global center of both the counterculture and the gay liberation movement. Neither of these concepts existed when Moscone was growing up in the city around the time of World War II.

Moscone was able to navigate both the new and old San Francisco in large part because of his enormous personal charisma and charm. Men and women who knew him and are now well into their seventies or eighties still smile when they think of him. They almost all call him George, even those who were his political opponents. Discussions of his politics are still leavened by anecdotes that reveal his decency, humor, and compassion—and his penchant for having a good time and philandering. The boy who grew up playing basketball in the city's many diverse neighborhoods, who also knew the experience of being the only child of a single mother, became a politician who was comfortable in every corner of the city he so obviously loved.

Moscone's legacy is also complex. His association with Jim Jones, the cult leader who murdered more than eight hundred of his followers in the Guyanese jungle, remains troubling, even though it has often been overstated by conservative journalists and historians.[3] We know that Jones supported Moscone in his 1975 election, that the two shared many political positions and allies, and that the mayor appointed Jones to serve on the San Francisco Housing Authority. Moscone knew how to play political hardball, and that sometimes required associating with people such as Jones.

After winning a close election in 1975, Moscone was unable to bring a divided city together and was mired in a political stalemate with the city's legislature. During his brief time as mayor, Moscone had some significant accomplishments—such as the diversity of the people he appointed and his successful effort to keep the Giants in town—but he was never able to implement his broader agenda. He remained a divisive figure, even if he was personally liked by many. Like most big-city mayors before and since, Moscone's ambitious campaign promises ran into the fiscal realities of governing, realities that were made more onerous by the passage of Proposition 13 midway through 1978. The anti-tax bill almost immediately forced cities in California to cut funding for many social programs.

Moscone would have been up for reelection in 1979, and many expected a close race. Because he was perceived as vulnerable, by fall of 1978 several candidates began to either prepare to challenge him or had their names floated as potential challengers. These included conventional politicians such as Quentin Kopp, a respected conservative voice on the board of supervisors, but also people such as Kevin Starr, a well-known conservative columnist and public intellectual who went on to write a multivolume history of California. One candidate who made it clear she was not interested in what would have been her third race for mayor was Dianne Feinstein, the president of the board of supervisors who had come in third in the first round of the 1975 election.

Moscone's final days were spent trying to lead the city through the aftermath of the terrible killings of Peoples Temple members in Jonestown. Jim Jones' jungle madness had devastated our city, particularly its African American community. Moscone also found himself paying attention to political concerns as he prepared to appoint Don Horanzy, a progressive housing activist, to replace Dan White on the board of supervisors.

Two related questions are central to understanding the life and impact of George Moscone. The first is how Moscone became a progressive. The second is what impact he had on his city, his state, and beyond. The first question is the more confounding. Moscone grew up in an Italian Catholic culture in San Francisco that was essentially conservative, particularly on social issues. Many of the leaders of moderate and conservative politics in San Francisco in the 1970s and 1980s, including two of his opponents in his 1975 mayoral race—Jack Ertola and Barbagelata—as well as his predecessor Joseph Alioto and Supervisors John Molinari and Ron Pelosi, all came from similar backgrounds. None were as progressive as Moscone. Nor did any of them embrace the diversity and changes in 1970s San Francisco as Moscone did. In many cities, including San Francisco, Italian Americans were frequently part of conservative backlash movements, but Moscone chose a different path.

There is no easy way to explain Moscone's political evolution. People who knew Moscone attributed his politics to his background as the only son of a single mother without much money, his experiences playing basketball in different parts of the city, the strong labor movement in the San Francisco of his youth, but none of these are entirely convincing and are generally little more than educated guesses. A closer look at Moscone's life inside and outside of politics make it possible to probe this question more thoroughly.

Exploring Moscone's larger impact implicitly raises the question of why write, or read, a biography of him, and why now. Moscone was a fascinating, colorful, charming, politically savvy, and smart man with an extraordinary personal story that has a cinematically horrific ending. That alone does not make Moscone an important political figure worthy of being remembered and studied almost fifty years after his death, but there is more to him than that. As a mayoral candidate in 1975, Moscone brought together a coalition that was groundbreaking at the time and has since become the most important coalition in Democratic politics. After winning that election, Moscone was one of the first big-city mayors to emphasize diversity and remake his city's government to look like the entire city. His progressive vision for San Francisco is still the foundation of left politics in that city. Unfortunately, Moscone's failure to bring about all, or even most, of the progressive change is also evidence of the limitations mayors face because of budget constraints and other challenges of American federalism.

Although Moscone is remembered most for his time as mayor, it was in Sacramento as a state senator where he may have had his greatest policy impact. Moscone's nine years in the senate, almost all as the leader of the Democratic caucus in that legislature, overlapped almost entirely with Ronald Reagan's tenure as governor of California. The two men represented very different visions for the state. While in Sacramento, Moscone was instrumental in numerous pieces of landmark legislation, including things such as decriminalizing marijuana and legalizing sex between consenting adults regardless of gender. He also used his position to try to repeal the death penalty and to advocate for a constitutional amendment guaranteeing the right to privacy. To a great extent, Moscone's work in state government laid the foundations for California's leftward movement, particularly on social issues, over the last half century.

Moscone's life was cut short just after his forty-ninth birthday, but he lived all his life, other than some of his time in the US Navy and his years in college at the University of the Pacific in Stockton, which is a short drive from San Francisco, in the city of his birth. Moscone's love for San Francisco was palpable, so his story is also a tale of San Francisco in the middle half of the twentieth century. You can't understand Moscone without a strong knowledge of the city where he was born, raised, and lived as an adult. Correspondingly, understanding Moscone's life will lead to a much deeper knowledge of San Francisco, and indeed California in the twentieth century and today.

THREE YEARS OUR MAYOR

CHAPTER ONE

Neighborhoods

As the election returns began to come in on the evening of December 11, 1975, most San Franciscans understood just how much was at stake. The incumbent mayor, Joseph Alioto, a charismatic centrist Democrat who had been a trial lawyer and creature of the downtown political interests which had governed the city for decades, was precluded from seeking a third term because of term limits. In November, the first round of the nonpartisan mayoral election had seen centrists such as state Senator Milton Marks Jr. and Supervisor Dianne Feinstein fall to the wayside.

George Moscone and John Barbagelata, the two candidates left standing after the first round, were, at first glance, quite similar. They were both middle-aged Italian American men with deep San Francisco roots. Both had grown up, in part, in the Italian neighborhoods of the northern part of the city, including North Beach and Cow Hollow. One had been educated in the city's Catholic schools, the other in both Catholic and public schools. Both were veterans of the US Navy and had conventional résumés for mayoral candidates at that time, or today. One had spent most of his career in elected office since winning his first election in 1963, serving on the city's board of supervisors, the San Francisco equivalent of the city council, as well as the state senate. The other was a successful realtor who got elected to the board of supervisors in 1969, winning reelection in 1973.

Both men were married with attractive young families; between them they had twelve children—Moscone had four and Barbagelata had eight. Some of the children were close enough in age to know each other and even be friends. Moscone's younger daughter, Rebecca, who was fifteen years old at the time of the election, described how "we were friends, varying ages with the Barbagelata kids. I think her name was Marina Barbagelata. She was around my age. . . .

We weren't best friends, but we were friends." She also added that the election was "kind of hard for me and Marina. We didn't feel very comfortable. . . . There was a lot of tenseness between both my father and John Barbagelata. After that we weren't really great friends anymore."[1] Rebecca's brother Chris recalled that the Barbagelata home was "literally four blocks away," but felt like "enemy territory" and that he and some of Barbagelata's children "were like why do our parents hate each other."[2]

Despite these similarities, Barbagelata and Moscone represented radically different visions of San Francisco. Barbagelata was a conservative Republican who was part of the movement of urban white populism that included Frank Rizzo, who was a right-wing Democrat when he first became mayor of Philadelphia in 1972, and later and more famously, Rudy Giuliani in New York. Like those two mayors, Barbagelata was a product of "a long process shaped by the restructuring urban space and urban politics in the 1950s, forged in the urban crisis of the 1960s and matured during the policy debates of the 1970s."[3] Barbagelata was the kind of politician who despite having served as a city supervisor for six years still claimed to not be a politician. He was a conservative in the truest sense, dedicated to stopping the rapid changes that he saw as ruining his hometown.

Barbagelata's opponent was not an ordinary Democrat seeking to keep the business and real estate interests happy while ensuring enough building and construction to guarantee continued support from organized labor. That coalition had defined the Democratic Party in San Francisco, and most other big cities, for much of the twentieth century. George Moscone had a different idea altogether. Central to Moscone's vision was the radical idea that the people running the city, including the hundreds of commissioners, mid-level political appointees, members of various city-run boards, should look like, and represent, the people who lived in the city. Moscone believed that people of color should have a voice in city government, that the police be held accountable for their actions toward the people they were supposed to serve—even if those people happened to be Chicano, African American, Asian American, or gay. Although Joe Alioto had begun to diversify city government, particularly with respect to African Americans: "I had a Black leader who was on the police commission, a Black leader who was president of the Public Utilities Commission, a Black leader who was president of BART (Bay Area Rapid Transit),"[4] real power in San Francisco had remained in white male hands. Alioto's word choice here is revealing. The phrase "I had" suggests that these appointees had little independence from Alioto.

Moscone's emphasis on diversity was part of his campaign, but if that campaign, and Moscone's vision, could have been summarized in one word, that word would have been "neighborhoods." Moscone's vision for San Francisco was that the neighborhoods where people lived, attended school, raised children, shopped, socialized, ran small businesses, and helped each other out should be at the center of city governance. Barbagelata was also a neighborhood-based candidate, but as a voice for the conservative white neighborhoods in the western part of the city. His blue-collar, white, and heavily Catholic supporters responded to Barbagelata based on what Suleiman Osman described, referring to politics in Brooklyn, New York, during this period, as "an angry and racially charged version of romantic urbanism."[5]

As the polls closed, San Franciscans waited to see if the future would be one of reaction to the preceding eight years that had seen their city undergo so much change, or one that would embrace and accelerate the progressive aspects of that change. Those residents of the city who were following the race knew that it might be a long night as the election was expected to be extremely close. Supporters of Barbagelata gathered at the candidate's campaign headquarters at 1951 Ocean Avenue, an unglamorous address deep in the heart of Barbagelata's western San Francisco base. Barbagelata was not quite the anti-establishment crusader he presented himself as, but he was an unconventional politician whose choice of a victory party venue reflected both his connection with his voters and his frugality.

Moscone's victory party was at a more traditional setting, the San Franciscan Hotel on Market Street, only a few blocks from City Hall. While the crowd at Barbagelata's party, reflecting his electoral base, was largely white, the photographs in the next day's newspapers showed a more diverse and younger crowd celebrating at the San Franciscan. The front-page photo on the *San Francisco Chronicle* that Friday featured a beaming and ecstatic looking Moscone smiling and gesturing with his right hand, surrounded by his family and two well- known San Franciscans, the Reverend Cecil Williams and Congressman Phillip Burton.[6]

Williams and Burton captured the duality of Moscone's mayoral campaign and political persona. The Reverend Williams was an influential and progressive African American minister able to mobilize large numbers of volunteers for candidates he favored. For decades Williams, who died in 2024 at the age of 94, was closely identified with GLIDE Memorial Church, a progressive institution in San Francisco that he led beginning in 1963. GLIDE's deep commitment to social justice includes a homeless shelter and a soup kitchen. The church is in the Tenderloin, a neighborhood that has long been beset with poverty, substance abuse, and homelessness. According to the church's website, "Building on the 50-year legacy of Co-Founders Rev. Cecil Williams and Janice Mirikitani, GLIDE challenges inequities and stands with the poor, people of color and LGBTQ persons, and others facing oppression, isolation and stigma, while offering a holistic, integrated model of programs and services to address the complex needs of the community."[7]

Williams was an African American minister and civil rights leader who fought for equal rights. His enthusiastic support for Moscone was because of the candidate's unambiguous support for African Americans, which included Moscone traveling to the South to register voters in 1965, as well as Moscone's commitment to working people and the poor. Williams was one of dozens of prominent community activists who had supported Moscone in that campaign.

Phil Burton was a politician who had been in elected office since 1957 and had served in the US House of Representatives since 1964. It was Burton, initially through his brother John, who had brought Moscone into politics. Burton was a progressive and an extremely skilled politician adept at redistricting, recruiting candidates, raising and spending money, winning campaigns, and legislating.

In 1975 Moscone was a career politician with strong ties to the Burtons, something for which Barbagelata attacked him during the runoff, frequently referring to Moscone as a "professional politician" while presenting himself as a businessman. However, one of Moscone's greatest political skills was that he could appeal both to community organizers, including many who were much more outsiders than Williams was, and to political operators such as Burton. Thus, Moscone could run for mayor as both the man of the neighborhoods vowing to remake city government, but also the sitting majority leader of the state senate with years of legislative experience.

Moscone's victory demonstrated that the progressive politics of the previous decade had matured. Moscone became the first mayor elected without any real support from downtown business and real estate interests. He was not beholden to the wealthiest and most powerful San Franciscans, something that had been true in varying degrees for most of his predecessors. Instead, Moscone owed his victory to people of color, the city's growing gay community, hundreds of neighborhood activists—and the Burton political operation.

From the perspective of the third decade of the twenty-first century, there is something quaint about the notion that Moscone's victory was one for a radical new San Francisco. After all, Moscone was a straight white man, career politician, and graduate of one of the city's most elite prep schools. Additionally, the political program on which he campaigned—police reform, diversifying city government, and considering the impact of government decisions on neighborhoods—is not radical by today's standards. Some of Moscone's ideas, such as increased diversity on city commissions and the emphasis on neighborhoods, don't even seem particularly progressive anymore. By the 1990s, even right-wing mayors such as New York's Rudy Giuliani had more diverse commissioners and advisors than most big-city mayors did in the 1960s and early 1970s. Giuliani put a right-wing spin on Moscone's neighborhood agenda, called it quality of life, and used it to crack down on petty crime, empower police, defend police brutality, and harass people of color. Osman summarized the approach of the more conservative neighborhood-based politics beginning in the 1970s: "They spoke nostalgically of pastoral Old World urban villages destroyed by public housing, busing programs and state subsidies to African Americans. Attacking downtown power brokers and eulogizing safe enclaves threatened by crime."[8]

This critique misses the point. Moscone was so significant because he was the first major, and winning, candidate to articulate and adapt these positions that have now become almost standard for big-city mayors, even those on the right. His victory was a victory for those ideas and a big step toward moving those ideas into the mainstream. It also helped a create a new progressive coalition politics that arose out of the fracturing of the New Deal coalition, bringing together African Americans, LGBT voters, Latinos, and progressive whites. That coalition no longer seems new or groundbreaking, but it was back in 1975.

Cow Hollow and the Marina

Moscone's successful campaign for mayor in 1975 was possible because it was led by a candidate whose love, and feel, for San Francisco's neighborhoods was genuine. Chris Moscone spoke about his father's understanding of the city's neighborhoods: "My dad grew up in the city. I think he knew the city really well because he would go on buses and walk around and however to get to all these different outdoor playgrounds (to play basketball). . . . So it was a real neighborhood type exposure for him in those days . . . he knew the stairs and the shortcuts."[9]

San Francisco is a city of historic and evocative neighborhoods. Few neighborhoods anywhere were as famous as the Haight-Ashbury during the five or ten years when the 1960s counterculture was in full bloom. The Haight drew young people and hippies from around the country. Decades later, the Haight is still a center of twenty-first century counterculture where the late 1960s and early 1970s have never quite faded away. A few blocks east of the Haight is the Castro, since the 1970s probably the most well-known gay neighborhood in the world.

Neighborhoods are a deep part of the identity of many San Franciscans. As Chester Hartman noted, San Francisco "residents are conscious of being at once part of a neighborhood and a world community."[10] Varying topography and climate help give each neighborhood a unique feel. Different demographics and architecture in many neighborhoods contribute to this as well. This leads to the paradox of San Francisco feeling, frequently at the same time, both larger—because it has so many distinct neighborhoods—and smaller—because it is only forty-seven square miles—than it is.

North Beach is an old Italian American neighborhood that turned into the center of the beatnik movement and later was a hub of West Coast punk rock. Today it is still a stop on the itineraries of most visitors to the city. San Francisco's Chinatown is one of the oldest Chinese communities outside of Asia. It is deeply embedded in the history of the city as well as with the Chinese American experience and remains a popular tourist destination. Pacific Heights, with its beautiful mansions and extraordinary wealth, is a destination for newly minted tech billionaires living side by side with families that have been part of the city's financial and cultural elite since the Gold Rush. The Mission still draws young people, from aspiring coders to interns at tattoo parlors, while the fog-bound Richmond and Sunset Districts, once heavily Irish and now largely Asian, are still romantic in the eyes of a particular kind of San Franciscan.

Cow Hollow, sandwiched between Pacific Heights to the south and the Marina District to the north, is not one of San Francisco's better-known neighborhoods. From most points in Cow Hollow you can look up and see the enormous, beautiful, and expensive mansions of Pacific Heights, but to get there you must walk or drive up several steep hills. Cow Hollow was given its unusual name because in San Francisco's earliest years it was home to many dairies. It is believed that the first of these was started around 1850 by George Hatman.[11]

Cow Hollow is not a famous neighborhood, but there is something very San Francisco about it. The Golden Gate Bridge lies only a few blocks to the north. The Palace of Fine Arts, a reminder of the 1915 Panama Pacific Exposition, is a short walk from Cow Hollow. In the evening, particularly in the summer, Cow Hollow frequently has enough fog to remind you that you are indeed in San Francisco. The neighborhood includes middle class-feeling apartments, usually called flats in San Francisco, on Greenwich and parts of Filbert Street as well as bigger homes to the south as Cow Hollow slowly turns into Pacific Heights. Cow Hollow is downhill from Pacific Heights, thus underscoring the class differences, much stronger in Moscone's youth, between the two neighborhoods. The border between the two neighborhoods is either Union Street or Broadway, depending on whom you ask. Today, all the real estate is expensive, but that was not true until well into the 1980s.

When George Moscone was growing up in Cow Hollow during the 1930s and 1940s, it was still a heavily Italian American and Irish neighborhood. Other, mostly white, ethnic groups lived there as well. The adults worked as police officers, firefighters, small-business owners, waiters, waitresses, and similar jobs. The children went to public or Catholic schools, played on the street, and learned to get around the city by bus or streetcar.

Cow Hollow was a great place to have a San Francisco childhood. For a youth of George Moscone's generation, or even one generation later when I was growing up there, the playground at Marina Middle School, the ballfields at Funston (now Moscone) Park, additional outdoor space in the nearby Marina Green and Presidio, numerous Italian bakeries selling cookies, pastries, and San Francisco's famous sourdough bread, streets full of kids who made it easy to find a pickup ballgame, or occasionally less wholesome fun, and the relative safety of those streets were a great springboard for a lifetime love affair with San Francisco.

The neighborhoods of Cow Hollow and the Marina sometimes blur into each other, but Lombard Street is the generally understood to be the dividing line. The area from Lombard north to the bay is the Marina. South of Lombard is considered Cow Hollow. Another way to determine the dividing line between the two neighborhoods is the architecture. "All that pseudo-Spanish stuff is pure Marina: Cow Hollowans lived in clapboard houses of hybrid Victorian styles. They still do."[12] At the turn of the twentieth century, the area just north of Cow Hollow was a collection of swamps, tidepools, and sand leading into the San Francisco Bay. Over the next two decades, two events changed that—the earthquake of 1906 and the Panama Pacific Exposition of 1915. Much of the city, which had been built largely with wood, burnt to the ground in the 1906 earthquake and fire. Other buildings collapsed, people were displaced, and the economy was badly hurt. Large parts of the city were built or rebuilt after the earthquake, so San Francisco today consists almost entirely of buildings from after 1906.

Not just buildings, but in some cases entire neighborhoods were built. Much of the rubble and debris from the extensive earthquake damage was dumped into those swamps north of Lombard Street. Matthew Morse Booker (2013) describes how "during 1906 and 1907 thousands of carloads of burned brick and twisted steel were carted from downtown to fill the last marshlands on the northern ends of the city. The new neighborhoods built on filled shoreline near Fort Mason were rechristened the 'Marina District.'"[13]

A few years later when it was time to build for the 1915 exposition and show the world that San Francisco had indeed recovered from the earthquake, the land was filled in more. Exposition organizers "poured 300,000 cubic yards of fill into 100 acres of submerged lands."[14] However, this created problems for residents who had still not recovered from the earthquake. "Building the exposition's 'dream city' brought an end to some forms of disaster relief when event construction displaced more than one thousand refugee cottages. Private interests aligned with public health as the San Francisco Real Estate Board encouraged the removal of refugee cottages from the area. . . . Between 1911 and 1915, the local health board and the U.S. Public Health Service condemned and destroyed 1,272 refugee cottages, which accounted for 77 percent of all condemned buildings in this period."[15]

The exposition, despite the displacement of thousands of earthquake survivors, helped reestablish San Francisco as the capital of the West. John McGloin (1978) described how "the opening day witnessed a total attendance of 245,143 people [in a city with a population of just short of 417,000 according to the 1910 census]. The first ten weeks built up to a total of 4,370,000. . . . At the end of the planned ten months, during which little else was talked of in the city . . . an impressive attendance total of 18,756,148 (many of them repeats) had been reached. No doubt, then, that the exposition had been a success . . . and San Francisco had demonstrated to its own satisfaction as well as that of the world, that it had definitely recovered from the wounds inflicted upon it less than ten years before."[16] "The fairgrounds covered 635 acres including almost all of today's Marina district, from Chestnut Street to the bay between Baker and Fillmore Streets. Parts of it spilled over in the Presidio (to the west) and Fort Mason (to the east)."[17]

Today, roughly 10,000 people live in the territory that was once the fairgrounds.[18] Following the exposition, when many of the buildings and exhibition halls were torn down, the residential Marina District arose. Ironically, buildings and homes built on landfill are very unsafe during earthquakes because the "land" is softer and responds to seismic shifts more dramatically than, for example, bedrock. Thus, the Marina District is one of the most dangerous places in San Francisco during an earthquake and was one of the parts of the city most devastated by the Loma Prieta quake in 1989, the biggest in San Francisco since 1906.

Two of the main east-west thoroughfares of Cow Hollow, Filbert, and Greenwich Streets, have long been almost entirely residential. Lombard, Union, and Chestnut, the latter being in the Marina, are streets where residents of Cow Hollow, during Moscone's youth and now shop, eat, and patronize other neighborhood small businesses. Cow Hollow and the Marina are relatively flat. Until about Union Street, the slope south from the bay is quite mild, at least by San Francisco standards. The relative flatness of Cow Hollow and the Marina means that from Moscone's time through the late twentieth century, young people in Cow Hollow played touch football, basketball, running bases, or strikeout (a San Francisco variation of stickball) in the streets.

Through the late 1970s Cow Hollow and the Marina were still working and middle-class neighborhoods, but they were among the first San Francisco neighborhoods to gentrify beginning in the 1980s. Chestnut Street, in particular, was home not to high-end restaurants, expensive boutiques, yoga studios, and the like as it is today, but to the kinds of small businesses that serve working and middle-class communities. Grocery stores, florists, pharmacies, a branch of Bank of America, bookstores, and similar businesses filled the storefronts. Cow Hollow and the Marina back then were better known for good food shops and bakeries rather than great restaurants.

In recent decades Union Street has been an expensive street of shops, boutiques, bars, and restaurants serving residents of Cow Hollow and Pacific Heights, but that was not the case when Moscone was growing up. Beginning in the early twentieth century after the dairies were closed, "Cow Hollow developed into a district of sedate residences and modest stores. . . . By the middle of this (the 20th) century outer Union Street was a nondescript service area running heavily to hardware stores, garages, groceries, five-and-dimes, laundries, barber shops and the like, with a few houses in between. Then things took a Cinderella turn."[19]

The San Francisco into which George Moscone was born in 1929 was on the tail end of a period of extraordinary growth because the gold found in the hills east of San Francisco drew people from all over the world. "In the spring of 1848, the population of San Francisco was 575 men, 177 women and 60 children. Within a year the city had close to twenty-five thousand inhabitants. Doctors and lawyers abandoned practices; tradesmen, laborers and professionals from around the world arrived in California by boat and stagecoach."[20] By the 1930 census, the population had increased to 634,394 for an increase of 78,027 percent in just over eighty years.[21] New York City, which in 1930 had long been the most populous city in the US, had grown from 515,547 people in the 1850 census to 6,930,446 in 1930.[22] That was also a high rate of growth, but New York's 1,244.29 percent population increase over the same period seems almost stagnant compared to San Francisco. However, in 1845 or so, San Francisco was in no meaningful sense a city, while New York was.

Beginning about 1850, new San Francisco neighborhoods had been popping up where only a few decades earlier there had been sand dunes, empty fields, swamps or in the case of the Marina District, no land at all. San Francisco had gone from being a settlement of a few hundred or a thousand people in 1850 to being the eleventh most populous city in the country in 1930. Over the next fifty years, San Francisco's population stabilized.[23]

Italian American North Beach and Cow Hollow

Cow Hollow's western border is Lyon Street abutting the Presidio, a US Army base from 1846 to 1994. The neighborhood's eastern limit is Van Ness Avenue, a few blocks west of North Beach. Today, North Beach is a bit like other older Italian neighborhoods in many American cities. Most of the longtime residents have moved out decades ago to be replaced by newer and younger communities, but they still occasionally return to shop and eat alongside tourists. For several decades North Beach has been an important part of San Francisco's counterculture. During the first third of the twentieth century, North Beach was a crowded and vibrant community of successful and prominent Italian Americans as well as more modest working-class families. By the 1920s, North Beach could no longer contain the city's Italian American population, so many families moved a few blocks west to Cow Hollow.

Italian Americans have made an extraordinary impact on San Francisco. Prominent Italian American politicians such as mayors Angelo Rossi, Joseph Alioto, and Moscone were Italian American. Nancy Pelosi is an Italian American from Baltimore who moved to San Francisco, where she married into a prominent local Italian American family. Countless powerful businesspeople from San Francisco were immigrants, or the children of immigrants, from Italy, including A. P. Giannini, born just south of the city in San Jose. Giannini grew up in San Francisco and founded the Bank of America, first called the Bank of Italy.

Probably the most famous son of North Beach was Joe DiMaggio. The great

Yankees centerfielder who was one of three brothers—the others were Dom and Vince—to play in the big leagues in the 1930s–1950s. DiMaggio was one of the very first major Italian American celebrities and is therefore a significant figure in Italian American history. He was, in many respects, the first Italian American star beloved by all Americans—except perhaps fans of the Boston Red Sox. In addition to the DiMaggio brothers, other Italian American ballplayers from San Francisco who starred in the big leagues in the first half of the twentieth century included two of DiMaggio's teammates, and sometime companions on car rides across the country, infielders Frank Crosetti and Tony Lazzeri. Lazzeri grew up in Cow Hollow, not North Beach. Lazzeri and DiMaggio attended the same high school, Galileo, just northwest of North Beach, although not at the same time.[24] Another Cow Hollow native, Francesco Stephano Pezzolo was a Yankees outfielder in the early 1920s at the tail end of his career. Pezzolo was known as Ping Bodie during his playing days. Cultural institutions such as the San Francisco Opera, landmark tourist attractions such as Ghirardelli Square, the extensive network of Catholic schools and churches, and signature dishes such as cioppino are further evidence of the Italian American influence on San Francisco.

Italians began immigrating to the San Francisco around the time of the Gold Rush. The 1870 census found 1,721 Italians, largely foreign-born, in San Francisco.[25] By the time of the 1930 census, taken shortly after Moscone was born, Italians were among the largest foreign-born group in California. Immigrants from Italy, in the middle to late nineteenth century into the early twentieth century came to San Francisco primarily from Liguria, but later Tuscany and Sicily and by 1930 constituted 16.1 percent of white workers of foreign stock in the city.[26] Only workers of Irish descent (16.5%) were more numerous.[27]

Some Italian Americans in San Francisco had become important and powerful people, but many struggled economically, making their living running modest businesses, as laborers, or around the docks. Today, Fisherman's Wharf is a popular tourist destination with souvenir stores and seafood restaurants, but for much of twentieth century it was very much a working dock where fishermen, many of whom were Italian American, sold their catch to wholesalers and restaurateurs. One of those fishermen was an immigrant from Italy whose son did not inherit the family gene for fishing and, in fact, is reported to have hated everything about fishing on the bay. Fortunately, Joe DiMaggio had other skills that meant he never had to follow in his father's professional footsteps.

At the turn of the twentieth century, 40.8 percent of San Francisco's "fishermen, hucksters and bootblacks" were either immigrants from Italy or first-generation Italian Americans. However, fewer than two percent of the people in "professions" or "bankers and brokers" came from that background.[28]

As an Italian American growing up close to North Beach, young George Moscone would have been part of one of the city's largest ethnic groups, but not in an ethnic enclave. Cow Hollow was a diverse neighborhood, not as the term diversity is meant today—San Francisco at that time was about 95 percent white—but in the early twentieth-century sense of having immigrants from various parts of Europe. However, Chinatown is not that far from Cow Hollow, so Moscone, like most San Franciscans, probably had some interaction with Chinese and Chinese Americans. As he grew older, Moscone's San Francisco naturally got bigger, while the city became more racially diverse.

The Cow Hollow of Moscone's youth would have been familiar to children and grandchildren of immigrants growing up in most major American cities. Moscone's neighborhood was ethnic, but not dominated by immigrants unfamiliar with the language and culture of their new home. It was poor or lower middle class, but not mired in poverty.

The Depression

George Moscone was born on November 24, 1929, a few weeks after the Wall Street crash that led to the Great Depression. The depression devastated the American economy, including that of San Francisco, and contributed to political upheaval domestically and globally. Political radicalism on both the left and the right grew during the depression as the US reckoned with widespread unemployment, reaching as high as 25 percent in the middle of the 1930s, as well as a sense that capitalism had failed.

The decade before the market crashed had been one of great prosperity for San Francisco. Mel Scott described how

> in the 'twenties San Francisco enjoyed another one of those periods of heady prosperity that have recurred at irregular intervals ever since it became a metropolis in the days of the gold rush. So congested were piers along the Embarcadero that many vessels seeking to discharge or take on cargo were diverted to Oakland or Richmond. . . . Within the decade the tonnage handled at the port of San Francisco doubled, and the value of the cargoes moving across its wharves soared in the year 1929 to the unprecedented figure of $1,613,100,000.[29]

Scott, who was very influential in planning and redevelopment in San Francisco, described how San Francisco's economy was hurt by the depression. "The depression that created bread lines throughout the United States in the early 'thirties dealt especially harshly with the San Francisco Bay Area. . . . Indeed in 1939 the value added by manufacturing in the factories of the Bay Area was more than one hundred million dollars less than it had been in 1929. Wholesale and retail trade too suffered serious monetary declines."[30]

This rapid change in the economy contributed to the panic as well as to the growing radicalism in San Francisco, notably the 1934 general strike. The general strike lasted four days in July, bringing the city to its knees. The port, where the strike had begun, remained closed. Deliveries of food into the city were sanctioned by the strike organizers, but other deliveries into the city were halted. Stores were shuttered as union workers walked out, while smaller stores closed in solidarity. This strike established San Francisco as a strong labor town, injecting a radicalism into its politics that still characterizes the city.

The general strike began with the International Longshoremen's Association (ILA) strike at the Port of San Francisco in May 1934, part of a larger West Coast longshoremen's strike. The ILA demands included "coastwide contracts, a union controlled hiring hall, pay raises, a thirty-hour week, the formation of a waterfront federation, unemployment insurance, and a resolution against ships flying the Nazi flag."[31] The hiring hall was essential because it made it more difficult for employers to hire non-union workers, to show favoritism, or buy off some groups of workers. The prohibition against Nazi ships demonstrated an early and principled concern about the rise of fascism and possibly the influence of communist labor organizers who shared Moscow's strong anti-Nazi position at the time.

The ILA believed in racial equality, welcoming African Americans at a time when many labor unions were entirely white and conservative on racial issues. "African Americans were recruited not only to join the new ILA union, but also to occupy positions of power within it. Two African Americans served on the strike committee. The workplace-democracy faction and African-American unionists did outreach on the docks. The rank-and-file strike committee also did outreach to prominent members of the African-American community. They were successful in recruiting union organizer C. L. Dellums of the Sleeping Car Porters Union to help deter strikebreaking."[32]

As the strike continued, the employers pursued various unsuccessful approaches to opening the ports, but the ILA remained steadfast in its demands. Appeals to Washington by employers accomplished little. The new Democratic administration enjoyed the support of organized labor and had supported the National Industrial Relations Act that protected collective bargaining rights in 1933. President Franklin Roosevelt, unlike his three Republican predecessors, was not going to turn his back on working Americans and labor unions.

The ILA was unable to negotiate a settlement with their employers as May turned into June and then July. Shipping companies, anxious about the damage the strike was doing to their businesses, unsuccessfully tried to open ports through using scabs and asking for assistance from the government. The bosses again tried on July 3 to open the ports, as scabs drove trucks filled with cargo that had been sitting in the port. Mayor Rossi provided police protection for this and urged people to stay away. The ILA was not about to give in so easily. This led to violent clashes between striking workers and police who used excessive force against the picketers. The strikers responded in kind with bricks, bats, and whatever else they could find. The battle was one of the most violent of California labor history, but not as severe as what occurred a few days later.

After closing the port on the Fourth of July, the shipping companies again tried to open the port on July 5, but this time the protesting union members and supporters, as well as the police assembled to help keep the ports open, were even more numerous—and the violence even more deadly:

> Several hundred strikers charged a police line at the base of Rincon Hill, located close to the pier. The strikers hurled rocks while the police attacked with tear gas bombs, which some strikers picked up and threw back at them. Other strikers built barricades to block the police. Near ILA headquarters the police shot three men, two of whom died, one instantly. . . . Strikers continued fighting the police as the theme of news stories became "blood-blood-blood." By 2 p.m. the fighting subsided, only to resume within the hour when the strikers stormed down Mission Street in an attempt to gain control of the area next to the ILA headquarters. Here the strikers outnumbered the police. The police again attacked, their bullets hitting the windows of buildings.[33]

July 5, 1934, became known as "Bloody Thursday" in honor of the two union members who were killed by police. Within a few weeks the strike was settled with the ILA winning many of its demands. The ILA evolved into the International Longshore and Warehouse Union (ILWU) and was for years led by the noted radical Harry Bridges, who had been one of the leaders of the ILA strike. Bridges finally stepped down during Moscone's time as mayor. Moscone later appointed him to the Port Commission.

Bridges, an immigrant from Australia, earned a national reputation from his role in the general strike. When Nikita Khruschev, premier of the Soviet Union, visited the US during the height of the Cold War in 1959, Bridges greeted Khruschev warmly. Peter Carlson described how Bridges welcomed Khruschev to the Longshoremen's Hall. "From the platform in the union hall, Khruschev addressed a crowd of three hundred longshoremen. 'We in Russia use the term comrades. . . . May I call all of you here comrades'? The longshoremen cheered. 'The main wish I want to bring to you workers is peace,' Khruschev continued. 'But peace is not enough. There must be enough work—and a good wage. The longshoremen cheered again, louder."[34] This prompted Frank Conniff, a veteran newspaperman to say about San Francisco, "What kind of town is this? They cheer Khruschev and boo Willie Mays."

One of the places from which the strikers encountered opposition was City Hall. The mayor of San Francisco during those years was Angelo Rossi. Rossi was mayor from 1931 to 1944. Although a liberal-to-moderate Republican, he was no friend of organized labor, so he was not sympathetic to the general strike. Rossi was San Francisco's first Italian American mayor. His election, a few years before Fiorello LaGuardia became mayor of New York, marked the first time an Italian American had become chief executive of a major American city. Unlike LaGuardia, who, perhaps because of New York's huge Jewish population, his own Jewish roots, or because of his innate sense of right and wrong, was an early, consistent, and outspoken critic of fascism in the 1930s, Rossi had a more complex relationship with the rise of European fascism, particularly in Italy.

During the period immediately before the US entered World War II, there were some Italian Americans who, most likely as a matter of ethnic pride, were sympathetic to Mussolini. Ettore Patrizi was the influential editor of *L'Italia*, a San Francisco-based newspaper that was widely read by Italian Americans in San Francisco. By the mid-1920s, Patrizi was using *L'Italia* to promote fascist ideas, writing in a 1922 editorial, "It is useful to remember . . . that fascism came at a moment of disorders much worse than the ones taking place now." Sebastian Fichera (2011) described Patrizi as "parrot(ing) the fascist line down to every detail."[35] *L'Italia*, support for Mussolini and his fascist ideas notwithstanding, was influential in the Italian American community because it provided valuable information, promoted local Italian American-owned businesses and reported on events in Italy. An aspiring Italian American politician such as Rossi could not afford to ignore it.

Rossi was appointed mayor in January 1931 when Mayor James Rolph became governor. Rossi won a full term in a close race later in 1931, defeating Adolph Uhl with 52.3 percent of the vote.[36] The Italian American vote, bolstered by strong support from *L'Italia*, was a big reason why Rossi won. "With all the Italian-language newspapers, particularly Patrizi's *L'Italia*, campaigning vigorously for him (Rossi), the Italian vote, running 9 to 1 in his favor, may well have supplied the winning margin. . . . The mayor had reason to be grateful to Patrizi and his Fascist allies: from that day forward, whenever they needed a favor, he was happy to oblige."[37]

Rossi was San Francisco's chief executive for thirteen years and, like most mayors, had a complex record. He remained adamantly anti-communist and never changed his fundamental views on organized labor, particularly the more radical elements of the labor movement such as Harry Bridges and the ILWU. However, Rossi became a strong New Dealer and helped bring Works Progress Administration (WPA) funds to San Francisco for major projects that included repair and construction of numerous roads, renovation of guard houses for the federal penitentiary on Alcatraz Island, and the construction of Lincoln High School in the Sunset District and Washington High School in the Richmond.[38]

Miriam Pawel argues the depression did not hit San Francisco as hard as much of the rest of the country, or state, and that the city benefited from enormous public investment in these years: "San Francisco did not suffer the same relentless degree of relentless poverty and 'Hoovervilles' that plagued the state's vast agricultural valleys during the depression. . . . Yet the geography of the city changed during the 1930s, driven by dozens of federally funded New Deal projects. New parks, schools, sculptures, sidewalks and playgrounds provided short-term employment and long-term recreation and culture."[39]

The most famous public works project built in San Francisco during the depression was only a few blocks from Moscone's Cow Hollow neighborhood. The Golden Gate Bridge was completed in 1937 and is still one of the most famous and beautiful bridges in the world. It is also perhaps the single edifice most associated with San Francisco, appearing in millions of postcards, snapshots, and social media posts. Growing up in the shadow, almost literally, of the Golden Gate Bridge as it was being constructed, as Moscone did, is about the most San Francisco imaginable way to spend one's earliest years. A half a century later, children in Cow Hollow, such as my brother and I, still occasionally had their street games interrupted by tourists asking for directions to the Golden Gate Bridge.

For an Italian American boy growing up in Cow Hollow and the Marina District, San Francisco was a complex, exciting, and inspiring political environment. Rossi remained mayor from the time Moscone was two until he was fifteen. Thus, for his entire childhood, Moscone saw an Italian American man in City Hall, evidence that for Italian Americans in San Francisco there was ample room for political accomplishment.

In the mid-twentieth century, San Francisco was a city of neighborhoods that were a lot like Cow Hollow. Some, like Pacific Heights, were much wealthier, but many were quite similar. Areas such as Bernal Heights, the Mission, Eureka Valley, the western neighborhoods such as the Sunset and Richmond were all largely middle and working class and included many immigrants and their children. Specific demographics varied, but the general feel did not. There were exceptions. Chinatown was also an immigrant neighborhood, but because of decades of racism and racist laws against Chinese Americans, it was more impoverished and isolated from the rest of the city. The Western Addition and the neighboring Fillmore District were home to many of the city's African Americans, who according the 1940 constituted just less than 1 percent of the city's population.[40]

The radical politics of the longshoremen and the general strike of 1934 created a context for progressive politics in San Francisco but was also very polarizing. Nonetheless, for a young boy from a modest background like Moscone, it would have been natural for his sympathies to lie with the working people striking for rights and a better living. Those sympathies influenced Moscone as he grew up and moved into a political life of his own. Similarly, the numerous public works projects in San Francisco demonstrated the power of government to build and improve people's lives. Not everybody took that lesson away from the depression, but Moscone did.

The 1934 general strike was a foundational landmark in the making of modern, progressive San Francisco, but it would be a mistake to draw that line too directly. San Francisco did not become a left-leaning city because of the events of 1934. Those events radicalized some people but did not comprehensively alter city's politics. Moreover, several American cities experienced similar labor uprisings in this period. The general strike of 1934 was joined by Longshoremen in every major western port, including Oakland, Seattle, and Portland. Flint, Michigan, saw a major sit-down strike against General Motors in 1936–1937. Similar strikes occurred in Toledo, Ohio, Minneapolis, Minnesota, and elsewhere.

The War

When the US entered World War II, the sympathies for fascism and Mussolini that a few Italian Americans such as Patrizi held had changed from positive dispositions about a despicable political philosophy into potential sympathy for an enemy of the US, but people such as Patrizi were a minority among Italian Americans. The huge majority of Italian Americans in San Francisco and elsewhere supported the war effort, while more than a million Italian Americans served in the military during the war.[41]

Despite this, wartime hysteria that led to the internment of hundreds of thousands of Japanese Americans, a significant proportion of whom lived in San Francisco, extended to many Italian Americans as well. Sixty years after Pearl Harbor, shortly after the terrorist attacks of September 11, 2001, the *San Francisco Chronicle* discussed this often-forgotten piece of American, and San Franciscan, history:

> During World War II, 600,000 undocumented Italian immigrants in the United States were deemed "enemy aliens" and detained, relocated, stripped of their property or placed under curfew. A couple hundred were even locked in internment camps. . . . In California alone . . . 10,000 were evacuated, mostly from coastal areas and sites near power plants, dams and military installations. Prohibited zones were created. And 257 people—90 from the Golden State—were put in internment camps for up to two years. Fishing boats were seized, and thousands of fishermen lost their jobs. In San Francisco, 1,500 were idled, including Joe DiMaggio's father. Another 52, 000 "enemy aliens" lived under nightly house arrest.[42]

The mistreatment of Italian Americans, despite the presence of powerful members of the community such as Mayor Rossi, was a paradox demonstrating both the best and worst of ethnic relations and politics of the era. On one hand, a first-generation member of a community that was struggling for equality and success in a new country could become mayor of a major city, but despite people such as Rossi and LaGuardia, Italian Americans still confronted state-sponsored bigotry and mistreatment.

The internment of Japanese Americans occurred at a time when Moscone would have been old enough to witness and understand. Arnold Townsend, who moved to the Western Addition in the 1960s after growing up in Los Angeles, described being told about this from older residents of that neighborhood: "The only people that seem to lament their (Japanese Americans) leaving were Black people. The day they left . . . Black church people showed up with bags of fried chicken they had cooked for them and shoebox cake."[43] Some housing left vacant by interred Japanese was filled by African Americans coming north for the war effort, thus turning the postwar Western Addition into an unusual neighborhood where African Americans and Japanese Americans were both present in substantial numbers.

World War II had an enormous impact on San Francisco. The Bay Area became both a place from which soldiers fighting in the Pacific front would embark and a major shipbuilding hub. According to San Francisco historian John Freeman, World War II began to transform the city, particularly the western half, even before the Japanese attacked Pearl Harbor on December 7, 1941:

> This was the part of San Francisco where military defensive preparation had been particularly active in the previous year [before the attack on Pearl Harbor]. Civilians might not have actually seen the concealed gun emplacements and antiaircraft weapons at Fort Funston, Land's End, or the Marin County coastline, but they had been hearing the booming sound of target practice from those weapons. Overhead, squadrons of airplanes from Alameda Naval Air Station or Hamilton Field were regularly spotted in formation. There were increasing numbers of military vessels on the bay, at the ports, and navigating through the Golden Gate. On land, convoys of jeeps and trucks passed through the neighborhoods along 19th Avenue and Park Presidio Boulevard, or down Great Highway from the Coast Artillery Headquarters at Fort Winfield Scott in the Presidio to Fort Funston and on to other defensive positions south to Half Moon Bay. The rest of San Francisco and the Bay Area might have felt some comfort that the Golden Gate strait had mines and a submarine net designed to prevent enemy incursion into the bay, but those who directly faced the Pacific Ocean did not have those reassuring protections. Those on the western slopes of San Francisco felt they were more exposed, staring the enemy in the face.[44]

Hadley Roth, whose family's roots in San Francisco predate the 1906 earthquake and who went on to serve in several mayoral administrations, described how in World War II he could "as a kid, looking down from the top of Coit Tower and there being just a gray cast to the bay because so many ships had anchored all throughout the bay, just this huge array of cargo ships and cruisers and aircraft carriers and what have you."[45]

One of the points of embarkation for troops was Fort Mason, just east of the Marina and Cow Hollow districts. Briefly stationed at Fort Mason in a support capacity was a man half a generation older than Moscone with whom Moscone would clash when they were both serving in Sacramento years later. Ronald Reagan's stint in Fort Mason was brief but was probably the closest he came to combat during World War II.

San Francisco was part of the American industrial effort that was essential to winning the war. Nicholas Veronico (2007) noted that "the Bay Area also had the largest concentration of shipbuilding, reaching from the Golden Gate nearly a hundred miles east to Stockton."[46] The biggest shipyards on the West Coast were the Kaiser shipyards in Richmond, in Contra Costa County, just north of Alameda County, where Berkeley and Oakland can be found. Today Richmond is a BART ride away from downtown San Francisco. As Pawel described it, "At the height of the war, fourteen shipyards in the Bay Area operated twenty-four hours a day in three shifts, a pace that created opportunities for two groups that had been shut out of such work: blacks and women."[47]

During World War II, in the Richmond shipyards, 747 ships were built for the military effort, making it one of the most important industrial hubs in the US. That amount and pace of heavy industrial work created a demand for labor at a time when many working-age men were fighting in the military. Many women moved into the workforce, but Henry Kaiser, the shipbuilder who had never built a boat before the war started, found another group of Americans eager to work in his shipyards. Thousands of African Americans moved from the south to the Bay Area during the war to work in various plants, shipyards, and factories supporting the Allied effort.

The shipyards offered jobs, but African American workers confronted other challenges, some fatal. The Port Chicago Explosion that occurred on July 17, 1944, about thirty miles east of Richmond, killed more than three hundred and injured almost four hundred. Many of the victims were African American. The blast occurred when munitions that were being loaded onto a ship exploded. In addition to this, African American workers were restricted to segregated worker dormitories and faced other forms of racism.

One enduring legacy of this industrial boom in the Bay Area during the war is that the African American presence, particularly in the East Bay cities of Oakland and Richmond, as well as San Francisco, grew. This helped reshape San Francisco from a city that was overwhelmingly white to, within a half century after the end of the war, one where white people constituted only about half the population.

World War II led to other demographic changes in San Francisco. By the mid-1970s San Francisco had become home to a very large gay population and an important center of the gay rights movement. The roots of that were also in World War II. Harvey Milk's biographer Randy Shilts explained how during World War II gay soldiers "heard a new word—a word that not only defined the differences that lurked secretly within, but also indicated that others like themselves existed. . . . Many a California gay had his salad days in San Francisco then, since the city was the major point for debarkation, for the Pacific theater." Shilts also identified a darker side of why San Francisco emerged from World War II with a growing gay population. "The second world war marked the first conflict in which the armed forces tried to systematically identify and then exclude homosexuals. . . . Purge after purge of gays in various branches condemned thousands to the 'blue discharge,' named for the paper upon which the homosexual discharges were written. . . . Most of the men discharged from the Pacific theater were processed out of San Francisco, and that's where they stayed."[48]

The Great Depression and World War II all but remade the demographics, economics, culture, and politics of San Francisco during the first sixteen years of George Moscone's life. These changes were profound, were still largely below the surface, and set the tone for the San Francisco that began to take shape in the 1960s and is still recognizable today. In other words, the tectonic plates were beginning to shift, but the earthquake had not yet occurred.

CHAPTER TWO

Family and Childhood

OAKDALE, CALIFORNIA, IN THE 1910s and 1920s was, in many respects, a typical American small town. Like most of the San Joaquin Valley, Oakdale was, and is, heavily agricultural. Today the population of Oakdale is about 25,000, a substantial increase from the roughly 2,000 living there in the 1920s.[1] Oakdale is about thirty miles from Stockton, a city of about 40,000 in 1920 and more than 300,000 now.[2] Stockton is also home to the University of the Pacific (UoP), one of the oldest universities in California, founded in 1851. Its name was changed to College of the Pacific in 1911, and it went back to its original name in 1961. Sacramento is not too far away, but the nearest big city to Stockton and Oakdale is San Francisco, about one hundred miles to the west.

In the first part of the twentieth century, Oakdale was the kind of town whose local newspapers reported on middle school plays, what recent high school graduates were doing in their adult lives and even when some of those high school graduates came home to visit. Well into the 1970s, the *Oakdale Leader* reported on which alumni came back for their thirty-fifth, fortieth, or even fiftieth high school reunions. One of those alumni who frequently made it back to Oakdale for those events was a woman who had graduated with honors from Oakdale Union High School in 1926. (The twenty-six graduates that year constituted the largest in the school's history.)[3] Lena Monge was born in San Francisco's Mission District on November 18, 1909, but moved to Oakdale as a young girl in about 1919 because her father was opening a vineyard there. The timing of the senior Monge's business decision was not great as Prohibition began in 1920. In fact, the day the *Oakdale Leader* reported young Lena's class graduation on page one and two, another article on page two announced "Monge Pleads Not Guilty." "B. Monge, living near Oakdale, arrested recently when federal dry operatives swooped down on Stanislaus county (sic), pleaded not guilty to maintaining a common nuisance, selling and possession of intoxicating liquor and to a prior conviction."[4] The Monge in that article was almost certainly Lena's father, whose first name was Bartolomeo.

Lena Monge, known to most simply as Lee, did not stay in Oakdale long after graduating from high school. On February 10, 1929, Lee married George Joseph Moscone and took her new husband's last name. Lee Moscone was only a few months past her nineteenth birthday on her wedding day. Her new husband was only a year or so older. The wedding was at the Catholic Church in Oakdale followed by a reception at the Dorada clubhouse. The writeup in the paper the next day described how "to the strains of Lohengrin's Wedding March . . . the bride advanced to the altar on the arm of her father, Mr. B. Monge . . . She wore a beautiful gown of white satin and tulle over which a long veil fell in graceful folds. She carried a shower bouquet of white rosebuds and lilies of the valley." Lena was described as a "beautiful and attractive brunette with many friends here to wish her happiness in her new life." The groom was described simply as "the son of Mr. and Mrs. David Moscone of San Francisco, prominent people in the bay region." The article concluded by noting that the couple would live in San Francisco.[5]

The local paper reported that Lena and George would be making their new home in San Francisco at 732 Cayugh Avenue.[6] This was a misspelling as there is no Cayugh street or avenue in San Francisco. Most likely the street to which the article was referring was Cayuga Avenue. Cayuga Avenue is not in Cow Hollow but is in the far southern part of San Francisco on the border between the Balboa Park and the Excelsior neighborhoods. Almost fifty years later, those working-class neighborhoods would send Dan White to the board of supervisors.

Lee and George Moscone may have been young when they got married, but that did not stop them from very quickly starting a family. Almost exactly forty weeks after the wedding, George and Lena had a son, whom they named after his father. George Richard Moscone was born on November 29, 1929, but all was not well in the Moscone household. Within a few years after the birth of their son, Lee and George J. Moscone split up, leaving Lee alone with a young child. Lee and George would be together the rest of Moscone's childhood and remain close throughout his life. Lee Moscone never had other children, either with Moscone Sr. or another man. For the next half century, Lee would be George's only parent in any meaningful sense of that word, while George would be Lee's only child.

The dynamic between George and his father would be very different. Throughout his life Moscone very infrequently spoke about his father. He continued to rarely mention his father when he became a politician and a public figure. Even Moscone's childhood friends and children indicated that they knew very little about his father. George J. Moscone was not a significant part of his son's life, was sporadically employed, including briefly as a guard at the state prison at San Quentin, and likely struggled with alcoholism.

Moscone's older daughter, Jenifer, only had vague recollections of her father's relationship with her paternal grandfather, whom she never met: "I didn't really learn about my dad's father until (I was) seventeen. We were playing cards in Mexico. He was talking about his father. His father was an alcoholic. He had driven a milk truck, I knew that. . . . Early on in his (Moscone's) marriage, my dad used to go down and spend time with them (Moscone's father) . . . and give them money—until he (Moscone's father) died."[7] The vagueness with which Jenifer Moscone spoke is striking. Throughout the rest of the interview, she recalls her father and her paternal grandmother vividly, but only had those few sentences to say about George J. Moscone. Even those words are not entirely clear. For example, the "they" to which she refers probably means George J. Moscone and a wife whom he married after Lee, but that woman's name was either not known to Moscone or not remembered by his daughter.

George J. Moscone died in 1956 at the age of forty-eight before his son won his first election. There is no evidence that the senior Moscone's parents were involved in the future mayor's childhood either. Moscone's paternal grandfather died in 1931, when Moscone was not yet two years old. His grandmother lived until 1953, but despite living in San Francisco, had little contact with her grandson.

After Moscone's father left the family, Lee opted to remain in San Francisco and raise her son there. By 1933 Lee was no longer living in Balboa Park but had moved from almost the southernmost part of the city to a few blocks from the San Francisco Bay in the Marina District—the northernmost part of the city. Lee and George Jr. had moved to 1535 Chestnut, between Gough and Octavia. That address is in the Marina District but is very close to Cow Hollow. Two blocks to the north was Fort Mason, now a park and cultural center, but for most of the twentieth century a military installation. Two or three blocks west on Chestnut Street was Funston Park, a medium-sized urban park with baseball fields and basketball courts. The latter would become an important part of George's life. Marina Middle School was built in the late 1930s next to Funston Park with WPA money. Generations of children growing up in the Marina would attend middle school there before going on to high school either at the local public high school, Galileo, or to other schools around the city.

After the divorce, Lee might have gone back to Oakdale where her parents could have helped her raise a young son during the Great Depression. This probably would have been easier for Lee while alleviating some of the financial pressure of living in San Francisco alone with her son. It also might have been humbling for her to return to her hometown a divorcée with a young son so soon after her big wedding there. Ultimately, Lee chose not to return to Oakdale, showing the independence and self-sufficiency that would characterize the rest of her life, and in doing that making a decision that would have huge impact on her son and their city.

Although Moscone never lived with his maternal grandparents, he retained a relationship with them through his childhood. Cappy Lavin, Moscone's oldest friend, knew Moscone well and was very close with him from the time they were in high school together. When asked about Moscone's relationship with Lee's family, Lavin responded, "Now my understanding is that George spent some time with his grandparents, and that they would have been Lee's parents, in Santa Rosa on a farm. It's kind of an X factor to me too because he didn't talk that much about it."[8] Lavin's memory was, for the most part, accurate. Moscone spent parts of his boyhood summers at the Monge's ranch in Oakdale, not Santa Rosa, a town about 150 miles northwest of Oakdale.[9]

This is the only reference to the Monges by Cappy during a very long interview. Almost nobody else who knew Moscone well refers to them. This suggests that the time spent on his grandparents' ranch was either not terribly important to Moscone or that for some reason was a source of concern or embarrassment. It is possible there was a rift between Lee and her parents in the middle of which young George was caught, but there is no real evidence for that. However, there is evidence that Lee's relationship with her parents, and with Oakdale, were positive. In addition to her name and photo appearing in the local paper when, every few years, she returned home for a high school reunion, Lena's relationship with her family was good enough that in 1950, when George was only a few years out of high school, Bartolomeo Monge ended his partnership in his winery, known as the Oakdale Winery, with Joseph Rossi and formed a new one with Lee and her sister Anna.[10]

It is more likely that young Moscone was immersed in his life in San Francisco, busy and relatively happy, so time with his grandparents, while perhaps enjoyable was not quite formative. Cow Hollow in the 1940s was distinctly urban, but not the kind of overcrowded dangerous urban community from which a young boy would want to escape—and Moscone was not the kind of youngster who needed to get away from the city. Additionally, it is possible the time Moscone spent with his grandparents was sufficiently incongruent with the rest of his life that he compartmentalized it and did not discuss it much with his San Francisco friends. Moscone's social life in San Francisco was dominated by sports, primarily basketball, and friends from school and the neighborhood. It is hard to imagine that milking cows, picking crops, or shlepping farm equipment was something in which Moscone's San Francisco friends would have been very interested.

Jenifer Moscone suggested that Moscone's grandfather may have indeed been an important figure in his life. In describing her father's childhood, Jenifer noted that "she (Lee) worked constantly. The only male figure in my dad's life was his grandfather, my great grandfather. And that's who he would get his lessons from." The last part of Jenifer Moscone's comment is unclear as she could be referring to either Lee or Monge. It is also not clear to what kind of lessons Jenifer Moscone was referring. Presumably, she was suggesting that Moscone's paternal grandfather was the male role model from whom Moscone learned how to be a man.[11]

There is one more ambiguous clue to this relationship. In the summer of 1972, Bartolomeo Monge died at the age of 88. He lived a good long life, built a business, and raised a family. Monge was born in Costigliole, Italy, in 1884 and had immigrated to the US. The grandson who had spent summers with him in the 1930s and 1940s had become the California State Senate's majority leader. The announcement of Monge's death and of funeral details appeared in the Sunday *Chronicle & Examiner* on August 6, 1972. The announcement described Monge as a beloved father of Lena and her sister, as well as an "idolized" grandfather of "Senator George Moscone" and Robert Bensi, Moscone's cousin. The wording of the article does not make it clear whether Monge was idolized by both his grandsons or just Moscone.[12]

The use of the word "idolized" is striking. Words such as beloved, loving, and devoted are more commonly used to describe the relationship between the recently deceased and his or her survivors. Idolized suggests a relationship that is loving, but also uncritical and worshipful. Overall, it indicates an unusually close relationship between grandfather and grandson. On balance, the notion that Gigi Monge, as he was known, was a sort of surrogate father for young George is not altogether far-fetched, but there is also very little reason, other than that phrase in the funeral announcement, to suggest that.

Moscone's sons had very vague recollections of the great-grandfather who died when they were both quite young. Chris recalled how the older man was known as Padrino (grandfather or godfather in Italian), pronounced "Padring" in the dialect the Monge family spoke. However, Chris added that his father very rarely discussed Padring.[13] Jonathan also had a vague memory of Padrino, adding that he and his siblings called him "Pudding" because they had difficulty pronouncing "Padrino" or "Padring."[14]

Four pillars framed Moscone's life when he was growing up: his mother, the church, his city, and basketball. These themes and subjects reappear in almost every description of his early life. Old friends and early political associates describing the young Moscone, Moscone's own children retelling what their father had told them about his childhood, even early reporting on his political career all focus on four themes.

Cappy Lavin's description of dinners in high school at the Moscone house in Cow Hollow offers some insight into Lee and George's relationship:

> I'll start with beans, because, as it turned out, every time I was over to dinner . . . I kidded her (Lee) a lot and she had a good sense of humor about her. She could look kind of imposing you know, but it was always

> beans . . . I think that as a single parent who worked hard and some of that strength sort of showed in her face. You could even use a stronger word, partly because we got along very well and had a great deal of affection for one another. It was maybe her determination to do everything she could to guide and help George as a kid who was on his own quite a bit, which I was too. Sometimes you would choose to do the right thing, because of a kind of ethical bond, or deeper than that, getting back to that end of thing, that had to do with one's mother. I think George felt that very strongly.[15]

These comments were made more than sixty years after the events in question by a man who had a deep bond to Moscone and his family, so they should be understood in that context. Nonetheless, Lavin's recollection of always being served beans is a reminder that Lee Moscone was struggling financially. She was probably not serving beans because they were a delicacy or because they were anybody's favorite food, but because beans are cheap, filling, and relatively healthy. Lavin was able to look back on the beans with a sense of humor, but serving beans so much probably did not seem funny to Lee or her son at the time.

The jocular relationship that Lavin suggested existed between himself and the mother of his best friend is a reminder that Lee was still in her mid-thirties when George and Cappy first met and not yet forty when Moscone graduated from high school. To Cappy, Lee may have seemed more like an older sister than a mother figure, somebody with whom you could make jokes and laugh, not the parent of a friend to be feared and avoided.

While reminiscing about Lee Moscone, Lavin also mentioned a man named Jerry Brody who was Lee's boyfriend. This is the only reference I found to Lee having any boyfriends or romantic partners after the divorce. Lavin did not describe the precise nature of the relationship or how long they were together, but he indicated that Jerry was still in Lee's life after Moscone got out of law school. Lavin described Brody as having "a twinkle in his eye . . . like a more attractive Norman Mailer . . . without the ego," and as a "stevedore" who "really respected Harry Bridges." Based on Lavin's description, it seems likely that Brody was a union member and, given the mention of Bridges, a longshoreman. Brody may have had an influence on the young Moscone's politics.[16]

Lavin's remarks also make it clear that it was not all joking with Lee. She was, according to Lavin, imposing and determined to do what she could for George. Moreover, Lavin confirms that Lee was a strong presence, literally and metaphorically, in Moscone's life. Lee Moscone always worked hard but made it clear to everybody, most importantly George himself, that he was her top priority. The dedication that Lavin commented upon was clear to others as well. A Mother's

Day profile of Lee Moscone from 1978 described her as "every son's dream of the perfect mom," adding that she was "fiercely independent and self-reliant."[17]

Moscone's four children all remember their grandmother, as she lived until they were all adults. They visited her frequently in her apartment in Cow Hollow. Taken together, their recollections portray a hard-working, serious, sometimes even stern, woman who had a strong sense of family. Moscone's older daughter, Jenifer, spoke of her "Noni Lee (as the Moscone children called their paternal grandmother), who was a single mother at a time when there was a great stigma attached to that. I believe she held down two jobs. She worked at the DMV, and I do believe she worked at a liquor store on weekends. She worked constantly. My dad was her only child."[18] Jenifer's younger sister, Rebecca, recollected "Noni Lee was an extremely strong woman. She was almost so strong you were a little scared of her. She ruled the house. I think she expected a lot of my father. . . . My father was very respectful in the house with her. . . . So I think she had a very rigorous, strict upbringing with my father."[19] Moscone's older son, Chris, recounted how "Noni Lee, I can remember her like it was yesterday. She was really something. You know you think of the Italian grandmother as, like you see in the pictures and movies, as very kind of cooking a lot and very open kissing and everything. My dad's mom was not quite like that. She was very tightfisted. She was very kind of strict. . . . She was always working . . . and she worked, I think, the hardest of anybody I know, every day of her life it seemed like."[20] Moscone's younger son, Jonathan, had similar words about his grandmother: "She was a very rigorous woman. And I suspect he received a lot of rigor from her. You do this? You figure this out? What are you going to do with that? She would always ask questions."[21]

Collectively, Moscone's children's strongest recollection of their grandmother is her stern, rigorous, or tough demeanor. Chris Moscone went so far as to explicitly contrast her to the stereotype of the Italian American grandmother. They also mentioned her reluctance to spend or waste money. That frugality with money, which led her to frequently feed a young Cappy Lavin beans, was probably necessary to make it through the difficult economic times in the 1930s.

Because Lee worked so much, George was on his own a lot as a child. Much of his boyish energy was focused on the basketball court, but this period also began to deepen Moscone's knowledge, understanding of, and passion for San Francisco. His older daughter described the memories Moscone shared with her: "I just think that having not a lot of money and not a lot of supervision—Mom worked hard—gave him a lot of opportunity to run around the city. I really believe he was a product of the streets. . . . He reminisced about the city and what it was like then during the Depression. And it was a good time. He talked about the neighborhood there. They'd go to the movies at the Alhambra . . . and if you answered a certain amount of trivia, you could win bags of groceries."[22]

Basketball

In the 1930s and 1940s, the San Francisco Seals of the Pacific Coast League (PCL) were the most popular professional sports team in the city. The Seals were as good as many American or National League teams. The DiMaggio brothers, Lefty O'Doul, Tony Lazzeri, and Ferris Fain were among those who played on the Seals usually before or after spending time in the American or National League. Many on the West Coast viewed PCL baseball as equivalent to those other two leagues back east. The Seals were the Yankees of the PCL. They had many great players and won more than any other team in the PCL.

Moscone played baseball and was a fan, but his sport was basketball. Basketball remained an important part of Moscone's life from childhood until his death. It was the first thing at which he excelled, giving him a self-confidence that translated to his social and professional life. Moscone's high school basketball teammate Joe Kelly observed that basketball "added to his repertoire and his reputation and gave him more confidence,' because he was good. And I think that enhanced whatever he had going in and, believe me, he had a lot going in, in terms of confidence."[23]

Through basketball, Moscone began to see much more of San Francisco. While most non-San Franciscans have heard of Golden Gate Park, there is much more to the city's network of parks and playgrounds where young people play sports. Today, those activities are more organized and supervised, but in Moscone's time, and for decades after, young people played on formal teams, but also on their own. The latter required athletic skill as well as the ability to navigate new social environments.

Moscone's close friend and political ally John Burton described this:

> When you're kids in San Francisco, at our time, and you played basketball, you played at every playground in town. . . . You played against Black guys, he played against the Chinese, you played against guys from, you know, neighborhoods, and his deal . . . Helen Wills Playground right outside Broadway tunnel. You played at Rossi, you played at Big Rec . . . I grew up in the Sunset . . . a bunch of racist assholes by and large. . . . I went to the YMCA and that's where I met, you know, I didn't go to movies, but I hung out with, you know, with Black guys, the Dukes from the Mission, and all that shit. So, you got to know people.[24]

Moscone's older son, Chris, who also played basketball, explained further: "My dad and some of his buddies would go from playground to playground. They'd have a circuit of maybe three or four playgrounds. . . . They'd go, and they'd play basketball. They'd play pickup games, for hours, for afternoons. . . . They'd play hard. There'd be the same fellows, maybe a couple different guys at each playground. And my sense is that my dad and Cap Lavin and some other guys would go from playground to playground and challenge and just play ball, pickup games."[25]

Chris Moscone explained the social, ethnic, and racial dynamic of these pickup games as well:

> When you go on a playground, there's a lot of things going on. Obviously, you played the game, but within that there's a lot more. There's a little swagger. There's some talking. There's throwing an elbow or two at the right time. You have to act like you're not intimidated. . . . You play against Black guys. You play against Chinese guys, Irish, Italians, Greeks, whoever was out there. . . . So there was a lot of stuff going on I think at these afternoons playing basketball. . . . You get the culture of Chinatown, North Beach, Mission District. I think he loved that. And I think it just started to flow in his veins, in his blood . . . this mixed culture of people.[26]

Catholic School

In 1942 a WPA-sponsored survey on religion in the Bay Area counted fifty Catholic parishes in San Francisco.[27] San Francisco had a population of just less than 635,000 in 1940, so there was one parish for every 12,700 people. Moscone was one of thousands of San Francisco children whose primary school education was at his parish school. In Moscone's case it was St. Brigid, founded in 1888, and in 1928 moved to its current location at the corner of Broadway and Franklin. When Moscone attended St. Brigid, it was run by the Sisters of Charity of the Blessed Virgin Mary. The school was affiliated with the young Moscone's parish church, St. Brigid Church, one block east at Broadway and Van Ness.

St. Brigid was the cornerstone of Moscone's deep and complex relationship with Catholicism. Moscone was born into and raised in the Catholic Church, was a parishioner at St. Brigid and attended Catholic school for many years. His political career was helped by his identity as a Catholic as well. In some respects, Moscone remained close to the church throughout his life. His wife was also Catholic, and a few years behind him at St. Brigid. He raised his children in the Catholic church. He was buried at the Holy Cross Catholic Cemetery.

Despite this, Moscone was not particularly religious. Although his views on helping the poor built on some interpretations of Catholic teaching, he almost never couched his politics or rhetoric in theology and did not bring a Catholic moral code to his own conduct with regards to relationships with women even after he was married. Even his strong opposition to the death penalty was never presented as stemming from his Catholicism. During his political career, Moscone's Catholic bona fides were a strategic asset, but he was frequently out of step with white Catholic San Francisco as many of those voters moved rightward during the 1960s and 1970s.

Moscone's complex relationship with Catholicism also influenced his relationship with his children. For example, when Jonathan Moscone was preparing to go to high school, he wanted to attend University High School. The school was only in its fifth year of existence but had already earned a reputation as the best independent coeducational private high school in the Bay Area. It was, and is, the kind of school that boasts great teachers, a rigorous academic curriculum with a broad range of courses, many extracurricular activities, and, for a small school, a surprisingly good sports program. The top graduates generally go on to Ivy League universities, Stanford, or UC Berkeley; others attend the top liberal arts colleges; and the weaker students frequently still matriculate at various UC campuses.[28] By the late 1970s University High School was becoming the place where San Francisco's elite, particularly its Jewish and Protestant elite, educated their children. According to the younger Moscone, when he shared his preference for this fine school with his father, the mayor's response was "over my dead body."[29]

Moscone reacted so strongly because he wanted his younger son to attend the same high school as he had and where Jonathan's older brother, Chris, was a student. St. Ignatius College Prep (SI) is one of San Francisco's oldest and most venerated educational institutions. For more than a century and a half, its alumni have been extremely visible and successful in business, government, law, and almost every aspect of life in San Francisco. At the time George Moscone became mayor of San Francisco, California's governor and Speaker of the assembly were also graduates of St. Ignatius.

When I asked Jonathan Moscone about the discussion with his father regarding high school, he responded, "It wasn't really a conversation. There was really no option. . . . I remember him saying, 'What's wrong with SI?' I really didn't have much of an answer." The younger Moscone explained, "He (Moscone) was good at ending conversations as quickly as possible when he didn't want to have a conversation."[30]

Chris Moscone, Moscone's older son, wanted to go to St. Ignatius, but his memory, like that of his younger brother, suggests that George Moscone was committed to his alma mater: "Growing up . . . it was always a given that I was going to be at SI and I wanted to be there."[31] Chris told me how "it (St. Ignatius) played a big role in the formation of his life. . . . The people that went there during, just before, and after. A lot of stories about basketball. It all related to that." Chris added that St. Ignatius "probably helped him out. They probably kept him from being thrown in jail or something like that. It was great for my grandmother." Chris's description of St. Ignatius, based his experience and his father's stories: "It's a drinking, smoking, girl-chasing, Jesuit-following school. It's kind of a workingman's private school. . . . A lot of cops' kids went there . . . you're out drinking, fucking around . . . you just get a pass."[32] The description suggests that St. Ignatius was not simply an elite institution but provided opportunities for upward social mobility to young men such as Moscone, while being influenced by those same working-class students. However, Chris Moscone's description of St. Ignatius as a "workingman's private school" is not entirely accurate, despite the presence of some students from working-class backgrounds. The two primary working-class Catholic high schools for boys during these years were Riordan and Sacred Heart.

Moscone's response to Jonathan's desire to go to University High School shows how Moscone was very much a traditional Italian American Catholic of his generation. He worked hard, was a loving father, but wasn't around much and left most of the hands-on childcare and running of the house to his wife, but usually got his way on major family decisions. When I was attending Catholic school in San Francisco during the 1970s, I knew many families like this. In those families, like Moscone's, St. Ignatius was the gold standard for high schools for boys.

The other side of the story is that Jonathan Moscone was a bright young man who was also a gay adolescent at a time when homosexuality was not broadly accepted even in San Francisco. Jonathan Moscone ended up going to St. Ignatius but might have been more comfortable at the secular, more liberal, and bohemian University High School. But his father, who by then had authored groundbreaking gay rights legislation and as mayor had a record on gay rights at that time better than any mayor of any major city in American history, wouldn't allow it.

It is not all that common now, or in the late 1970s, for people who on the left and strongly committed to LGBT equality, tolerance, and civil rights, to have strong loyalties to elite single-sex Catholic High Schools, but Moscone did. His ability to maintain both his political views and his loyalty to St. Ignatius reflected his most valuable political strength, his ability to live and maintain relationships in two San Franciscos, the older and the emerging one, at the same time. For Moscone, there was no contradiction between his political views and his opinion of his alma mater.

St. Ignatius only began admitting girls in 1989, so Rebecca and Jenifer went to the Convent of the Sacred Heart for high school instead. The Convent of the Sacred Heart has long been the city's elite Catholic girls school. Ironically, the most famous graduate of the Convent of the Sacred Heart was a Jewish woman—Dianne Feinstein. The Convent, as many refer to it, is in the heart of Pacific Heights, San Francisco's most expensive and elite neighborhood. The school is part of a three-building complex of former mansions on Broadway between Fillmore and Webster. Many of the classrooms feature extraordinary views of the San Francisco Bay.[33] The westernmost of the three buildings is a boys school called Stuart Hall that until 2000 only went up to eighth grade. Moscone's sons did not attend Stuart Hall. Before high school, Gina and George sent their children to Notre Dame de Victoire, a Catholic school in downtown San Francisco.

Gina attended St. Brigid through high school, and all four Moscone children graduated from Catholic middle and high schools. However, St. Ignatius was the most important of those institutions to Moscone. St. Ignatius was founded in 1855, only seven years after the beginning of the Gold Rush, by Father Anthony Maraschi, a Jesuit born in Italy, who had previously been an educator in Massachusetts.[34] St. Ignatius was initially downtown, on Market between Fourth and Fifth Streets. At that time, St. Ignatius was a college, but in the mid-nineteenth century distinctions between levels of education were often vague.

St. Ignatius's initial location was not big enough for the growing school, so in 1880 St. Ignatius moved a few blocks west to Hayes and Van Ness in what is now the Civic Center area. In 1927 St. Ignatius moved farther west again, this time to Stanyan Street between McAllister and Turk in the Western Addition.[35] St. Ignatius remained in that home through 1969 before moving again to its current location in the Outer Sunset. The Stanyan Street campus was centrally located. Downtown was a quick bus ride away. Golden Gate Park was very close to the school, so students could use the park for athletics. The growing western San Francisco neighborhoods, where many of the city's Catholic population lived, were also easily accessible. The campus was also only a short walk from the University of San Francisco (USF), a well-respected Catholic university. For many St. Ignatius graduates, the journey from high school to college was only a few blocks. Until 1959, the two schools had a formal relationship with many graduates of St. Ignatius seamlessly transitioning to USF, which in turn was originally called St. Ignatius College.

A few blocks south of that campus, Stanyan Street, which runs along the eastern border of Golden Gate Park for several blocks, intersects Haight Street. For the first thirty or more years St. Ignatius was there, this was pretty unremarkable, but by the mid-1960s, because of the Summer of Love and the migration of thousands of young people to the Haight-Ashbury, that had changed. A few blocks away from a school with a tradition dating back for more than a century of excellent, but traditional, education was the center of the 1960s counterculture celebrating, drugs, sexual freedom, and rebellion. The open space around Thirty-Seventh Avenue around Pacheco and Quintara, in the western part of San Francisco, beckoned because by 1969 St. Ignatius needed a larger campus, but it is also likely that the Jesuits were happy to leave the rapidly changing Haight behind.

Moscone's years at St. Ignatius were, by most accounts, happy and very successful. He first drew attention from faculty and fellow students in ninth grade for his academic, rather than athletic, prowess by winning the freshman elocution contest in March 1944. It was noted in the school newspaper that his "stage presence, diction and emotional interpretation was judged the best."[36] According to Joe Kelly, a high school classmate and basketball teammate, the freshman elocution contest was "a big deal for SI" but added of Moscone's high school years. "I don't think he was a great student."[37] A few years later, Jerry Brown would win that same award during his freshman year at St. Ignatius.[38] Cappy Lavin, who met Moscone the summer before they started St. Ignatius together, described Moscone as a high school freshman as having "more confidence and poise than many of his peers. . . . There was a kind of maturity that began to increase, well beyond most young kids, throughout his high school career."[39] Kelly noted similarly that even as a freshman, "he (Moscone) immediately was the standout guy, he was not a quiet citizen, he announced when he was around and everything, and he was quite confident of himself, very self-assured—and the rest of us weren't. . . . The upper-class(men) really looked down on you (when you were a freshman). It was kind of like, you really had to earn your spurs to get in touch with those guys, and he had no trouble with that, fitting in. He was very self-assured, self-confident, loquacious, attractive, good-looking guy, very witty and humorous, so he stood out right away in the freshman class."[40]

Lavin mentioned Moscone's charm and poise in high school: "If you think for a moment of Cary Grant . . . he was one person that George patterned himself after. . . . He was in the same league you might say because he had the same sense of humor. He could be self-deprecating. He was witty. He could laugh at himself, and he had a build, but more than that an intangible feeling about clothes. And he looked better in clothes than most people, the way Cary Grant (did)." These comments were in the context of an older man remembering a dear friend who had been dead for thirty years, but nonetheless reveal something about the young Moscone.[41]

Moscone made a big impression at St. Ignatius on the basketball court where he became an all-city player. Moscone's name appeared in the San Francisco press for basketball long before politics. As his junior season began, the *Chronicle* previewed the upcoming prep basketball season: "St. Ignatius has an evenly balanced crew. Returning vet Roger Farrell, Jim Kenny, Joe Donovan, George Moscone and Larry Rebholz could easily afford the 1946 surprise."[42] A few weeks later, before St. Ignatius prepared to meet Lowell in an important game, the *San Francisco Examiner* reported that "the Ignatians' fate rests pretty much with George Moscone."[43] During the next two seasons, Moscone drew media attention for his play for St. Ignatius as well as for various high school all-star teams.

As seniors, Moscone and Lavin led St. Ignatius to the city basketball championship. Kelly, who was also on that team, said, "My teammates would not like me to say this, we weren't the best team in terms of individual guys, but we did work together. He (Moscone) was a leader, he was a co-captain with Lavin who was the best player in the city, in my opinion. . . . He (Moscone) was a good shooter and not bashful to shoot, by the way. When he got that ball, it didn't come back many times. He was very confident in getting that ball and going for the hoop or shooting or something like that. But he deserved it, he was good."[44]

The 1947 edition of *The Ignatian*, St. Ignatius's yearbook, described the team's up-and-down season: "before sharp-shooting George Moscone, later dropped again under sizzling Lincoln, shoving St. Ignatius into its first championship in four years . . . The victory meant plenty of beer drinking and noise making. But to more conservative Coach Woolpert it was the culmination to prayers and chalk talks, to reading psychology books and teaching new plays."[45] Phil Woolpert left St. Ignatius shortly after Moscone graduated and spent the next decade coaching USF, winning national championships during the 1954–1955 and 1955–56 seasons. The star of those teams was Bill Russell, one of the greatest players ever.

The basketball team's photo page featured individual action, sort of, pictures. The players' photos are arranged around a picture of Coach Woolpert. On the top left is Lavin. Across from him is Don Adams, the team's center described in *The Ignatian* as "sky-scraping." In the center of the top row, the most prominent position, is Moscone. Moscone and Lavin returned to St. Ignatius six years later for an alumni game against the varsity squad. The program for that event misspelled Moscone's name, changing the "e" to an "i," but described him as being the "leading scorer of the College of Pacific Tigers."[46]

In addition to basketball, Moscone played baseball for three years. He apparently had some pop in his bat as his high school yearbook referred to him as "the Bambino."[47] Kelly was Moscone's teammate and more than seventy years later recalled "he (Moscone) was a fairly good baseball player. I think he played second base. . . . He was not an outstanding baseball player, but he made the team."[48] Lavin also noted Moscone played baseball. "He (Moscone) was good size even for basketball in that era. By the time he was a junior, he was probably six one at least, maybe taller, well built. He was a very good baseball player too. I think probably all-city caliber there, but better in basketball, and that was his first love."[49] Moscone was a better basketball than baseball player, but baseball was where George Moscone went on to make the greater impact.

During Moscone's first year at St. Ignatius, the US was still fighting World War II. Many graduates of the school served in the conflict. Some of those returned to St. Ignatius during the war to share their experiences. Jack Grealish, one of the St. Ignatius graduates who enlisted toward the end of the war, described how during one of these visits an alumnus who was in the navy stopped by Latin class "taught by Fr. Lloyd Burns, SJ. Fr. Burns, who was very proud of his Latin class, asked him if Latin had helped him. The officer gave Fr. Burns a funny look and said, 'It hasn't done me any good at all.' That's not what Fr. Burns wanted to hear." On a less light note, ninety-six graduates of St. Ignatius lost their lives fighting in World War II and were recognized for their sacrifice by their alma mater. The specific tragedies of each of the 96 SI alumni deaths were spelled out in *Gold Star Ignatians,* a commemorative pamphlet published in 1947 by the school.[50]

The public high school Moscone would have attended had he stayed in his neighborhood was Galileo High School, known today as the Galileo Academy of Science and Technology. Had Moscone attended Galileo, his high school years would not have exposed him to the larger San Francisco he saw at St. Ignatius. In the 1940s, Galileo was still heavily Italian American with some Chinese Americans as well, drawing students from North Beach, the Marina, Cow Hollow, and Chinatown. At the time the school's most famous alum, Joe DiMaggio, was playing centerfield for the New York Yankees. A few years later, another nationally famous athlete, O. J. Simpson, would graduate from Galileo.

Because St. Ignatius drew students from all corners of Catholic San Francisco, including from affluent Catholic families, Moscone's San Francisco got much bigger at St. Ignatius. The journey from Moscone's childhood home on Octavia Street in Cow Hollow to St. Ignatius's Stanyan Street campus was large enough to take even a young confident George Moscone out of his comfort zone of his neighborhood and St. Brigid school.

St. Ignatius has long been an important San Francisco institution, but in the middle of the twentieth century was still a distinctly Catholic education. Young San Franciscans who were not Catholic generally did not seek out St. Ignatius. Instead, those who had the grades and test scores attended Lowell High School, a top academic public school that is comparable to Stuyvesant or Bronx Science in New York. Others simply went to their local public schools. Thus, while St. Ignatius exposed the young Moscone to a broader San Francisco world, it was still a parochial one.

High schools are formative for most students, but schools such as St. Ignatius can have a tremendous impact. Some take advantage of Jesuit intellectual tradition, soaking in as much as possible from teachers and books. Some may become Jesuits themselves, but most choose the secular world instead. Some carry the love for learning that the Jesuits cultivated as they move through that world. Others come away from the Jesuits with a strong sense of social justice, aspiring to live according to the teachings of Jesus—an aspiration that occasionally got the young person tagged as radical, dangerous, or worse.

St. Ignatius, like many Catholic schools, had, and has, very strong sports programs. Accordingly, some students spend four years as jocks, building their identity around their prowess on the courts and fields. Among those who starred as athletes at St. Ignatius were Dan Fouts, the great San Diego Chargers quarterback and NFL Hall of Famer of the 1970s and 1980s, and Dutch Ruether. Ruether won 137 games between 1917 and 1927 and was one of the top pitchers on the 1927 Yankees, whose star hitters included Babe Ruth and Lou Gehrig. Many still consider the 1927 Yankees the greatest baseball team ever.[51]

Schools such as St. Ignatius offer both intellectual resources and multigenerational relationships and credentials that can ensure ongoing membership in the ruling class. Protecting family wealth and status, making money, and having the right friends and contacts are higher priorities for many students and their families than intellectual ideas or social justice. Some of these students go on to quietly successful careers and lives, while others carry that stench of entitlement throughout their lives. This is true not just of Jesuit schools, but of all elite prep schools, including University High School, the school Moscone did not want his younger son to attend. Other students do not fit in or find themselves upset or angered by the wealth and privilege of some of the students. These students rebel against the institution, do not buy into the culture and traditions of the school, and never feel fully comfortable there.

Moscone became enough of a jock to be an all-city basketball player in high school, and continue with basketball into college and, throughout his adult life. His colleagues from his career in politics frequently tell of first meeting Moscone on the basketball court and of his passion for the game. Even as mayor, Moscone continued to play basketball. In May 1978 he and Eugene Brown, whom Moscone had appointed as the city's sheriff, the first African American to hold that position, played a one-on-one game in front of the media. Brown had played basketball at USF alongside the great Bill Russell and was recognized as an All-American, so Brown likely defeated his political patron.[52]

Moscone's jock credentials were strong, but he was much more than that at St. Ignatius. Although Moscone was never a politician-intellectual, like his fellow Ignatian Jerry Brown, the future mayor was engaged enough academically to attend a good college and then law school. While friends don't describe him as being an avid reader, they nonetheless speak of Moscone reading books and discussing ideas. Moscone's childhood friend Lavin, who spent his career teaching literature and writing, noted one of Moscone's favorite authors as a young man was Saul Bellow. Lavin specified that Moscone preferred Bellow's *Herzog*, "He loved *Herzog*."[53] It is unlikely Moscone, unless he was a very precocious literary mind, would have encountered Bellow at St. Ignatius as Bellow's first book was published while Moscone was in high school. St. Ignatius's curriculum was strong, but it is unlikely literature courses included work by then obscure, young Jewish novelists.

Herzog was published in 1964 when Moscone was already in his mid-thirties and a member of the San Francisco Board of Supervisors. Bellow would have been an unlikely choice of favorite novelist, and *Herzog* of favorite novel for a man like Moscone in the mid-1960s. Bellow was born in 1915, so was a few years older than Moscone. Bellow was neither Italian American nor Catholic but a Jew whose family came from Russia and Lithuania. While Bellow wrote about themes such as the emotional tumult and difficulties in postwar America, he also explored themes that were deeply, and unmistakably Jewish, and post-Holocaust, notably in his short stories and his 1970 novel *Mr. Sammler's Planet*. Bellow, one of the great writers of postwar America, was part of a distinctly white and male group that included writers such as John Updike, Norman Mailer, and Philip Roth. Moscone, according to Lavin, was drawn to Bellow's wonderful writing and particularly his skill at creating and developing emotionally complex characters, including Moses Herzog.

Moses Herzog is a middle-aged Jewish man whose second marriage has recently collapsed and who finds himself unsure of his purpose in life or even what he needs to do to keep making it through each day—not the kind of character with whom Moscone would have been able to identify directly. It is a curious book to captivate a thirtysomething successful politician, but it was, at least for a while, Moscone's favorite. Jon Rubin reflected that "I could see him reading Norman Mailer, but Saul Bellow . . . Saul Bellow was not easy to read."[54] Moscone's younger son, Jonathan, was more direct: "I don't know how much of a book reader he was. He was a moviegoer and a playgoer. He loved musicals. He loved opera."[55]

In a 1976 interview, Lavin fleshed out Moscone's literary tastes more: "He particularly enjoys talking about novelists like Saul Bellow or a work such as Bernard Malamud's *The Natural*."[56] Today many people know *The Natural* because of the 1984 film starring Robert Redford, but the novel was an important literary work. Malamud and Bellow were both Jews who explored themes of becoming American, becoming a man, immigrant struggles, and America in the twentieth century. They were literary novelists who crossed over to a larger audience. Discussing the work of Malamud or Bellow in the mid-1970s was, for a liberal white ethnic man, like Moscone, possibly because of an interest in literature, but also a way to signal sophistication. It is also possible that Moscone had little interest in literature and discussed books with Lavin because of the latter's interests.

A high school diploma from St. Ignatius, particularly for a star athlete such as Moscone, all but guaranteed a young man the college opportunities and a strong network of relationships in Catholic San Francisco that would be helpful to any young professional looking to begin his career in the city. Moscone took advantage of this as he attended college, law school, and began to make his way as an adult in San Francisco, but he did not shift easily into a life of affluence or conservatism.

Although Moscone became a progressive, it was not because he rebelled against the culture of St. Ignatius and rejected the elite and affluent values and environment he encountered there. Kelly recalled at St. Ignatius "politics never came up" in discussions with Moscone.[57] Moscone's experience at St. Ignatius was also framed by his own distinctly non-elite background because as a working-class child of a single mother, Moscone was not a good cultural fit among the elite St. Ignatius families.

Nonetheless, the opportunity to become part of San Francisco's elite that St. Ignatius offered the young Moscone influenced the rest of his life. By the time he was forty, Moscone was one of the most powerful men in California. He worked hard and believed in what he did, but he was also a graduate of an elite private school benefiting from those relationships. As he grew older, Moscone continued to look back happily on those years. "My father had some great times there (St. Ignatius). I know not so much from talking with him but seeing him and his friends together. They always talked about good times. St. Ignatius and some other high schools in San Francisco. But there were fond memories," his son Chris said.[58] Additionally, there is no way to know how many times a conversation between Moscone and a journalist, a fellow attorney, a political staffer, or a government official, an appeal to a judge, or a pitch to a donor was leavened by alluding to a common alma mater. In a small city such as San Francisco, that happened with some frequency.

This is part of both the paradox of Moscone and what made him a good politician. Moscone was, in the context of being an elected official in the 1960s and 1970s, radical. His views on policing, gay rights, diversity, and the role of business in urban governance were years, or decades, ahead of most mayors. However, while his views were radical, the man himself was not. Moscone was a good-looking jock who spent four comfortable years at one of the city's most elite high schools. He was a straight white man who urged his son to attend that same Jesuit school rather than an independent secular school that was academically at least as strong as St. Ignatius. This is not the profile of a radical, but the story of a progressive whose Jesuit education was very formative.

CHAPTER THREE

San Francisco After the War

During the decade and a half following World War II, modern San Francisco began to take shape. In 1950 San Francisco was, like many American cities, essentially conservative, heavily Catholic, and overwhelmingly white. Joe Kelly, Moscone's Irish American teammate from St. Ignatius, who later married into the Brown family—his wife, Cynthia Brown Kelly, was the daughter of one California governor, Pat Brown, and the sister of another, Jerry Brown—was involved in state politics for years. Kelly explained the city during the 1940s and 1950s: "The city was divided into parishes, not into districts, but parishes. Well, that's the way you referred to it, made contact with people, is by their parish, it was very Catholic, very, very Catholic. So, you know, that moderates everybody's political viewpoint. Very, very much Democratic in terms of like Roosevelt Democrats but they were Roosevelt-Truman Democrats, law and order but very pro-union, and the working man was revered."[1]

The US was approaching the height of its hegemony in the mid-twentieth century. World War II had finally gotten the US out of the Great Depression, helping to jump-start industry and dramatically reduce unemployment. The US emerged from World War II as a central part of the winning coalition in both the European and Asian conflicts—and as the only power not devastated by the war. Thus, unlike other Allied powers such as the USSR and Great Britain that had to invest in rebuilding their country, the US did not.

In those years New York City was the most important and powerful city in the US—the leading center of American economic, intellectual, and cultural life. But San Francisco could still claim, at least to itself, to be the most important city on the West Coast. San Francisco could also claim to be a global city, not least because the United Nations was founded there in 1945. Within a few decades, those assertions would no longer be plausible, although true San Franciscans have never stopped believing them.

San Francisco had played an important role in supporting the war effort. Because the Bay Area had been a hub of shipbuilding and major embarkation point for troops going to fight in the Pacific conflict, the local economy grew and changed during and after the war. In the years following the war, the Bay Area experienced other related transformations. For many troops returning from the war, San Francisco was where they were discharged from the military. Many, no doubt taken by the physical beauty, sense of economic opportunity, and feel of the town, decided to stay. Some of these newly returned soldiers were gay and wanted some freedom and distance from their families, but many were straight as well. Accordingly, the 1950 census found that the city's population had increased to 775,357, the highest ever until that point and an increase in population of 140,000 in only ten years. The city's population would not exceed that 1950 figure until the 2000 census.

During roughly a quarter of a century following the war, like all cities at all times, San Francisco was undergoing a period of transformation that would gradually remake the city. It felt slow until it felt sudden. At first San Francisco was a largely conventional and heavily white city enjoying economic growth and relative peace and prosperity. Trends such as the growth of the suburbs, the stirrings of the new left, and the cultural changes of the 1960s were only faintly visible. And then, at some point in the late 1960s, the change accelerated dramatically.

In mid-century, San Francisco was, as always, a city of neighborhoods characterized by distinctive ethnic makeup and, in many cases, weather as well. There were Irish, Italian, Russian, German, and other ethnic communities and areas. However, because of San Francisco's size, relative to bigger cities such as New York or Chicago, and high population density, these communities were never as separate as in many other American cities. In the 1950 census, fully 89.5 percent of the population identified as white. Of those white people, 4.1 percent had Spanish surnames. It is not easy to fit mid-century notions of race into our ideas more than seventy years later, but this clearly shows that at least 85 percent of the city's population was white. While there were African American, Asian (mostly Chinese), and what we would now call Latino populations, the numbers were small. Moreover, because of formal and informal residential segregation and housing policies, most African Americans and Japanese Americans, many of whom were returning from wartime internment, were in the Fillmore and the Western Addition, Chinese in Chinatown, and Mexicans in the Mission or thereabouts.

Most Americans cannot remember a time when major American cities were overwhelmingly white, but, in most cases, that was true until at least 1960. For example, 90 percent of the almost 7.9 million people who lived in New York City in 1950 were white.[2] That was a time when Yiddish and Italian were heard much more frequently on the streets of New York than Spanish, Cantonese, or many other languages one hears today in New York.[3] In Los Angeles, 93 percent of the county's 4.15 million residents were white.[4] In those years racial minorities had almost no voice or representation in local governance. Institutionalized racism including with regard to housing and employment, and other forms of racism were largely unchallenged.

Willie Brown, who moved to San Francisco from Texas in the early 1950s, described the city then:

> This was a segregated town. You didn't integrate at all. You had Chinatown, was its own entity, in the same way as the Western Addition, or (what) we call the Fillmore was. . . . The Mission was, by then, had become where Latinos actually ended up living. Before that the Irish had been populating the Mission. The schools all reflected kind of what that neighborhood happens to be. If you were over in the Chinatown area, Galileo was the high school where Chinese kids went to school, if you were in the Mission, Mission High School shared, was shared by Blacks and, Latinos primarily. On the other hand, the Western part of the city, you had Lincoln High School, you had George Washington High School, and you had Lowell High School, and they were all schools that were, almost without any racial minorities in them, whatsoever . . . But the town was not anywhere near integrated. There were no municipal train operators who were Black, there were no policemen who were Black, there were no firemen who were Black, or Asian. That didn't exist. This was still basically a white town.[5]

Arnold Townsend, the longtime community activist in the Western Addition, was more succinct: "Black men used to tell me that before World War II if you were Black and the police caught you west of Van Ness, they'd bust your head open. The Black neighborhood in the '20s and '30s was down by the Financial District."[6]

The growth in San Francisco's population was made possible by the development of almost all the area in the city. There were still beaches, parks, and industrial areas, but by the 1950s there were very few parts of the city where it was still possible to build. The only direction the city could grow was up. The questions of where and how far up to build have been central to San Francisco politics ever since.

Beginning with the Gold Rush, San Francisco developed roughly from east to west and north to south. The earthquake and fire of 1906 destroyed much of the progress of San Francisco's first half century as a major city, causing much of the city to be built or rebuilt in the following years. As the city's population continued to grow, the city continued to expand to the west.

One of the earliest, important, and famous human-made creations in the western half of San Francisco is Golden Gate Park, a massive and beautiful urban park. Work on Golden Gate Park began in 1871 and was not completed for more than another sixty years when WPA projects such as the Arboretum and the archery field were placed in the park. Golden Gate Park cleaves western San Francisco with the Richmond to the north and the Sunset to the south. The Richmond and Sunset have always been mostly heavily middle- and working-class residential areas with some pockets of affluence. The Sunset was the last horizontal frontier for San Francisco. However, by the 1950s, even the Sunset was fully built out. Lorri Ungaretti described how "the (Sunset) district underwent major change in a short time. In the early 1900s most of it was windswept sand dunes. By the mid-1900s, almost all had been developed."[7]

By 1950 San Francisco was doing well economically and was significantly wealthier than much of the rest of the country. In 1949 the median household income in the US was $3,100.[8] In San Francisco, the median income was $3,923, 26.5 percent higher.[9] In the early part of the decade, shipping and manufacturing were still important parts of the local economy, but professionals, clerical workers, managers, and related white-collar fields accounted for roughly 44 percent of all jobs in San Francisco, with craftsmen, operative, laborers, and related fields constituting about 31 percent of all jobs.[10]

Not all this change occurred during the 1950s. In many ways the politics, economics, and demographics were relatively stable, but by 1960, as in many cities, the seeds of the major changes to come were present. One reason for this is that in the Bay Area, like many metropolitan regions in the postwar period, a growing population and general affluence contributed to the growth of suburbs. Suburban communities offered young families more space and fresh air. Most of these suburbs were also formally or informally restricted to white families. For many who moved there, getting away from a city where the non-white population was growing was also a priority. The growing number of people who commuted into the city by car, and automobile traffic in general, meant a greater demand from the suburbs for freeways. That issue would be central to San Francisco's civic and political life beginning in the 1950s.

Suburban communities in Marin County to the north, Alameda and Contra Costa Counties to the east, and San Mateo County to the south began to expand during these years. To the south, towns such as Daly City and Foster City grew quickly with suburban subdivisions rapidly replacing unused or agricultural land. It was these communities with thousands of relatively modest and almost identical rows of houses that Malvina Reynolds sang about in her 1962 song "Little Boxes." Table 3.1 shows the change in population for each of these suburban counties and San Francisco during the 1950s. All the suburban counties gained population. Two, Contra Costa and Marin, became slightly whiter, while two others, Alameda and San Mateo, saw the white proportion of their population decline slightly. San Francisco lost population and became significantly more racially diverse.

Table 3.1-Population Change 1950-1960[1]

County	1950 Population	1960 Population	Percent White 1950	Percent White 1960
Alameda	740,315	908,209	88.4%	84.7%
Contra Costa	298,984	409,030	91.5%	92.6%
Marin	85,619	146,820	95.6%	96.2%
San Mateo	235,659	447,387	97.7%	95.7%
San Francisco	775,357	740,316	89.5%	81.6%

[1]"Bay Area Census," op. cit.

The paradox of the 1950s for San Francisco was that it was a time of great growth and affluence, but that growth and affluence laid the foundations for conflict and tensions that would define urban America for the remainder of the century. By 1960 the demographics and economics looked only slightly different. Despite the prosperity, the population of San Francisco declined by almost 5 percent over the course of the decade, as the 1960 census showed only 740,316 people living in the city.[11] Much of this was because of people moving to the suburbs as the overall population of the San Francisco-Oakland-San Jose metropolitan area grew from 2,198,000 in 1950 to 3,034,000 in 1960.[12] The region grew substantially while the population of the center city declined. Those who remained in the city included some wealthy families and upper middle-class professionals, but the middle class was smaller. Those trends have continued into the present.

San Francisco was still a relatively affluent city in 1960. The median household income in the city for 1959 was $6,717, an increase of almost $3,000 over 1949. The US median household income had also grown from $3,100 to $5,400 during this period. In both years the US income was about 80 percent that of San Francisco.

The proportion of the population that was made up of white people with non-Spanish surnames dropped slightly to 74.6 percent, while the African American population almost doubled from 43,000 to 74,000. Similarly, the combined total of Japanese Americans and Chinese Americans in San Francisco rose from about 31,000 to about 46,000 over the decade. The number of people in the census category of "White with a Spanish surname" increased by 20,000. Although San Francisco still had a large white majority, the demographics of late twentieth-century city were beginning to emerge by 1960.[13]

Urban Renewal and Urban Revolts

Before the war, the engines of San Francisco's economy were manufacturing and the port. Additionally, aquaculture, based around Fisherman's Wharf, was an important part of the city's economy. Beginning in the 1950s, San Francisco began to shed jobs in the manufacturing and shipping sectors and the city began to pivot to an economy built around the FIRE (Finance, Insurance and Real Estate) and tourism sectors. As a 2002 report by the San Francisco Planning Commission noted:

> By the 1960s, containerization became the new standard for shipping goods. Land constraints, the City's location at the head of a peninsula, and a range of other factors made it extremely difficult for San Francisco to adopt the new technology and compete with Oakland for cargo. Subsequently, many of the City's distribution and warehousing jobs disappeared. At the same time that San Francisco's manufacturing and distribution functions were waning, the City was fast transitioning to an economy based on tourism and the service sector.[14]

In his 1992 book *Left Coast City: Progressive Politics in San Francisco*, Richard DeLeon reflected on how San Francisco's economy had changed over the previous three decades: "Thirty years ago, before the invasion of massive capital and massive builders, San Francisco was a city of neighborhoods with a skyline of low rises. . . . A strong labor town, it had a blue-collar work force, boasted a thriving port. . . . All of that has since changed. . . . The port is sleepy . . . and most of the fishermen have gone. . . . Office workers have replaced many of the blue-collar workers."[15]

The transformation of San Francisco from an economy based around an active port, manufacturing, and small business to one that was based around the FIRE sector, remade the physical geography of San Francisco. Skyscrapers were built downtown, and the port was gradually converted from a working port to a place of recreation, restaurants, tourist attractions, bars, and gift shops. Those changes were more or less complete by the late 1980s, but the tension between those competing visions of San Francisco—on the one hand a quirky, progressive and affordable small city and on the other a center of commerce built around the FIRE and later tech sector—continues to influence politics in San Francisco today. At first glance it may seem the latter vision has won, but on closer inspection it is less apparent.

Brian Godfrey (1997) explained:

> The impetus for the city's transformation lay in post-World War II efforts by planners and developers to transform a quaint West Coast port into an international corporate center of commerce, finance and administration. This strategic effort, which so profoundly influenced urban-renewal efforts, has changed the city's economy from an industrial-commercial emphasis to that of a postindustrial corporate center. As a consequence,

blue-collar activities in the manufacturing and wholesale trades have declined steadily since World War II, while retail, finance, insurance, real estate, transportation, utilities and tourism have generally expanded.[16]

While San Franciscans during the first half of the twentieth century thought of their city as much more than a "quaint West Coast port," Godfrey's argument captures the changes in San Francisco, but, perhaps inadvertently, he touches on an even bigger point. The entire history of San Francisco can be told through a narrative of rapid change and the resistance to that change. That was a key theme in George Moscone's 1975 campaign for mayor and remains a theme anytime longtime San Franciscans gather even today. I expect that if you asked San Franciscans in the early 1850s, they would have said the Gold Rush was bringing in new people who were ruining their town.

The key issues beginning in the 1950s, and now, were how big was San Francisco going to get, for whom the city was going to be developed, and what groups would be able to have meaningful input into land use and development decisions. The threat of San Francisco growing too much was referred to as "Manhattanization." The organization at the center of these debates was the San Francisco Redevelopment Agency (SFRA), created in 1948 after the US Housing Act was passed. The mission of the SFRA sounded benign: to improve cities through upgrading housing and related buildings, streets, parks, and the city's infrastructure. The SFRA's work was never that simple. Areas that were viewed as most blighted and therefore most poised for upgrading and redevelopment were lower-income communities whose residents were frequently not white. In addition, much of the work of the SFRA and those who supported remaking San Francisco contrasted with the slower, neighborhood feel of much of the city that so many residents valued.

The neighborhood feel was also threatened because by the 1960s, San Francisco was fully integrated into California car culture. Many visitors, impressed by the lifestyle and the beauty of the city, have observed that San Francisco is a uniquely European-feeling American city. Those words have never rung true because San Francisco has long been a very car-centered city in a way that was unmistakably American. The steep hills make San Francisco a tougher walking or cycling city than other similarly densely populated cities. The end of a network of street cars and buses that had existed since earlier in the twentieth century also kept many people in their cars. Even BART was always primarily a way to get commuters downtown and San Franciscans to the East Bay, but not a way to move residents around the city. Much of this has begun to change in the last decade or so with the revitalization of cycling culture, many people working from home rather than commuting to downtown, and a growing awareness around climate change, but in 1970, 1980 or 1990 it was different.

As recently as 2016, San Francisco had 1.10 cars per household, the same number as New Haven, Connecticut, very slightly more than Buffalo, Syracuse, and Baltimore (1.08), and just less than Chicago (1.12). Los Angeles, the city San Franciscans rightly like to describe as being freeway bound and dependent on cars, had 1.62 cars per household, but New York only had 0.63.[17]

San Francisco's dependency on the car got a late start as the city was not easily accessible by car until 1937 when the Golden Gate and Oakland Bay Bridges were completed, connecting the city to the north and east. During the 1950s, the US began to facilitate further dependency on cars partially through the creation of what became the Eisenhower Interstate System. The movement of people from all cities to suburbs exacerbated this too. During this period of highway construction, many San Francisco planners got in the spirit of the times, proposing major highways that would have made it easier to get through the city, but would also have disrupted many neighborhoods.

By the 1950s automobiles were raising traffic-, congestion-, and freeway-related challenges for San Francisco. A 1937 proposal by a team "under the direction of Miller McClintock, a nationally known traffic consultant," included "sixty-five miles of these divided free-flow routes throughout the city, including an elevated limited way along the Embarcadero." These "flee-flow routes" included elevated "semidepressed or fully depressed routes, and still others as trafficways at grade or on elevated earth fills with landscaped banks."[18]

Planning for freeways in San Francisco began as World War II was winding down. It was apparent that the number of Americans driving and depending upon cars would increase substantially in the postwar period. In December 1945, the San Francisco Planning Commission approved a proposal that "included plans for freeways, parkways, rapid transit and off-street parking." That plan also called for further study, so two years later the San Francisco Board of Supervisors commissioned a "comprehensive transportation survey" for $200,000. This survey, published in 1948, recommended increasing parking, expanding public transportation, creating secondary urban thoroughfares, but most significantly building numerous highways and freeways in residential parts of San Francisco. The board of supervisors approved it in 1951.[19]

In 1952 California, under the leadership of Governor Earl Warren, a year or so away from being appointed chief justice of the US Supreme Court by President Eisenhower, agreed upon a plan to build freeways in San Francisco. The entirely white and male San Francisco Board of Supervisors relatively quickly approved this plan. The map of the proposed plan shows some freeways, including what are now Highway 280, parts of Highway 101 and the Embarcadero that were eventually built. It also shows several freeways, leading from the eastern edge of Golden Gate Park to downtown, cutting through the Sunset District at Thirty-Fifth Avenue, along Van Ness and Lombard and elsewhere, that were not built. The initial plan went even further. "Approved by the San Francisco Planning Commission in 1951, it called for 25 miles of elevated 'skyways.'"[20]

By 1952 the board of supervisors and city government had approved a series of freeways that would have radically and rapidly remade the physical city. As residents of San Francisco's neighborhoods, including in the heavily residential, and still overwhelmingly white, western parts of the city began to realize the impact this freeway construction would have, they organized opposition to the proposals.

The two freeway proposals that first galvanized San Franciscans into what became the Freeway Revolts threatened to destroy Golden Gate Park. San Francisco has long been a cosmopolitan city with extraordinary natural beauty as well. Beaches on the western and northwestern side of the city, while not great for sunbathing because of the fog and cold, have spectacular views of the Pacific Ocean and Golden Gate Bridge. The Presidio, even when it was a military base, and the Golden Gate National Recreation Area (GGNRA), created in 1972, offer those same great views, hiking and cycling trails, picnic areas, and fresh air for residents of the densely populated city.

Golden Gate Park might be the most beautiful part of the city. The thousand-acre park bisects the western half of San Francisco running from Stanyan Street in the center of the city to the Pacific Ocean in the west. Roughly the shape of and slightly larger than New York City's Central Park, Golden Gate Park is not surrounded by apartment buildings but mostly by residential blocks of smaller buildings usually with fewer than twelve units. Golden Gate Park features a diverse array of flora, wonderful gardens, cycling and walking areas, a golf course, ballfields and even, incongruously, a bison reserve. By the early 1950s, freeway advocates wanted to destroy much of that. Thousands of San Franciscans would not hear of it—and thus began the Freeway Revolts.

The 1951 plan included one proposed freeway connecting Seventh Avenue to Park Presidio, a busy roadway that cuts through the park at what would have been Thirteenth Avenue at Fulton and turning east toward Nineteenth Avenue at the park's southern border. A second proposed freeway was the Western Freeway, sometimes referred to as the Panhandle Freeway. The Panhandle, an area of roughly six blocks from east to west and one from north to south, juts out from the eastern part of Golden Gate Park, a shape that looks like the handle of a pan, the pan being the rest of the park. The Western Freeway would have destroyed the Panhandle by running through the neighborhood just east of that, which by the 1950s was a largely African American area known as the Western Addition. The new freeway would have made it easier to drive from east to west in the city and helped commuters from either Marin or the Peninsula get into downtown more quickly. These two freeways would have altered Golden Gate Park, brought more traffic to several residential areas, increased air and noise pollution in those areas, reduced property values, and destroyed much of the western part of the Western Addition, just as redevelopment was doing in the eastern part of that neighborhood.

Robert Caro's description of the construction of the Cross-Bronx Expressway at about the same time as these freeways were being proposed in San Francisco:

> By 1965 the community's "very good, solid housing stock," the apartment buildings that had been so precious to the people who had lived in them, were ravaged hulks. Windows, glassless except for the jagged edges around their frames, stared out at the street like sightless eyes . . . Of the people who lived in East Tremont, who had found in that neighborhood security, roots, friendship, a community that provided anchor-friends and synagogue and Y—a place where you knew the people and they knew you, where you could make a stand against the swirling, fearsome tides of the sea of life, only the very old, too poor to move, still lived, almost barricaded in their freezing apartments. As for the rest of the people who had lived there, they were gone.[21]

The havoc this wrought on East Tremont, once a working-class Jewish community, was what those involved in the Freeway Revolts feared for San Francisco.

The proposed San Francisco freeways would have physically divided neighborhoods and brought noise and pollution to many residential areas, undermining the city's neighborhood feel. The freeways may have integrated San Francisco into the region more but only by making it easier for drivers going between the peninsula and Marin, or from those areas into San Francisco, without having to really be in the city.

This freeway system, if it had been built, might have relieved some street traffic as cars and commuters would have been concentrated on the freeways rather than city streets, but the twenty-five miles of freeway would have radically changed the geography and culture of San Francisco. This dynamic remains central to San Francisco as the city continues, with deeply mixed success, to seek a balance of facilitating economic growth and maintaining the feel of what so many love about San Francisco. It is not hard to see the echoes of this in today's discourse about housing in San Francisco.

San Francisco never built those freeways; nor did it become a city of quiet streets and few cars. The city split the difference by creating boulevards such as Geary, which runs for most of the breadth of the city from the bay in the east to the ocean in the west, Nineteenth Avenue from the southern border of the city through Golden Gate Park, even Lombard from Van Ness to the Golden Gate Bridge, Van Ness from Market to Lombard, and several others, in many cases along the routes where the freeways were proposed in 1952. These boulevards allow fast-moving traffic, have several lanes in each direction, and are insufficiently safe for pedestrians, cyclists, or any businesses that rely on foot traffic. They almost feel like suburban commercial tracts in the middle of the city but have smaller footprints than freeways.

As Jason Henderson argues, the Freeway Revolts helped create the politics of late twentieth-century San Francisco, but:

> The city's accomplishments should not be overromanticized. In San Francisco the effort to demolish freeways was met with opposing initiatives to have bigger, wider, faster rebuilt freeways, and the debate over how to accommodate cars continues to divide the city. While two freeway segments did eventually come down, they were relatively short in length, and freeways and automobiles today dominate much of San Francisco's urban space. Meanwhile the city's financially strained bus system moves at a snail-paced eight miles per hour on congested streets and, worse, five miles per hour in the downtown, about the same speeds transit moved in the 1920s.[22]

This analysis may be too negative because it overlooks some of the freeway plans that were defeated, but San Francisco has long been dependent on cars and that has changed many neighborhoods. Moreover, it took the 1989 earthquake to finally bring down the Embarcadero Freeway. It had been badly damaged in that quake. Following that, Mayor Art Agnos made the decision to tear the Embarcadero down rather than rebuild it. That decision may have cost Agnos a second term as the Chinese vote went against him—the Embarcadero had been a way for drivers to get to Chinatown quickly. However, Agnos's decision opened the eastern waterfront, making that part of town much more beautiful, accessible, and enjoyable than in the past.

The Freeway Revolts did not simply pit left against right. Nor did it cleave elected officials, or citizens, on partisan lines. Most major business and real estate interests supported the freeways, but so did much of the labor movement. While several neighborhoods with large non-white populations, like the Fillmore, the Western Addition, Bayview/Hunters Point, and Chinatown would have been disrupted by new freeways, the same was true of heavily white neighborhoods such as the Sunset and Richmond. Thus, the Freeway Revolts brought activists from across the political spectrum into politics in a new way. Many progressive activists who became integral to various left-of-center movements in San Francisco, including Moscone's campaign for mayor, got their start during the Freeway Revolts. The language and ideas of the Freeway Revolts were also essential to later conservative neighborhood-based politicians such as Quentin Kopp, John Barbagelata, and Dan White.

Affluent families in the northern part of the city, lower-income African Americans in the Western Addition, and working-class Irish in the western part of the city all envisioned noisy construction, traffic, congestion, and air pollution despoiling their neighborhoods if the freeways were built. This unifying force allowed a broad coalition against the freeways to emerge. William Issel explained: "During the late 1940s and early 1950s conflicts emerged over the basic question of whether automobiles and trucks constituted a promise or a threat to San Francisco. Questions developed about whether freeways addressing the transportation needs of inter-city travelers to and from other Area communities might simultaneously worsen the problems of city residents."[23]

San Franciscans organized at the community and neighborhood level to pressure the board of supervisors and successive mayors to reject hundreds of millions of dollars in state and federal money and decline to build the freeways. The stakes were the future of the city itself. Although the Freeway Revolts were driven by the specter of San Francisco becoming another Manhattan dominated by skyscrapers and finance, the more likely, and worse, outcome was that San Francisco would have become another Los Angeles. Manhattan has a downtown area, actually two, one in midtown and one around Wall Street, that have many skyscrapers and are centers of global business. But it also has cohesive, highly walkable neighborhoods throughout the island. Los Angeles, by contrast, is decentralized and car-dependent with only a few small areas that are walkable. Because San Francisco is so much more compact than Los Angeles, with twice as many people per square mile, walkable neighborhoods have always defined the city. The freeway plan would have destroyed that, and with it a real part of what San Francisco has always been—and still is.[24]

The business community steadfastly advocated for freeway construction throughout the 1950s. A 1959 report from *The Downtowner*, a newsletter representing downtown business interests, expressed that community's support for the freeways:

> Population and traffic projections clearly indicate a need for these planned additional freeways within the near future. Unless this relief is provided, total congestion and restriction to movement will result. To say we do not like freeways elevated, depressed or otherwise, is no solution and is a position which will not be tenable for long . . . the *basic patterns of freeways just must be completed* in order for the other forms of transportation to operate at maximum efficiency. This we have to face up to in San Francisco. The sooner the better for all concerned.[25]

A year and a half later, the San Francisco Chamber of Commerce endorsed the planned freeways in *Trafficways in San Francisco—A Reappraisal*, published late in 1960. It called for some modifications, such as putting the Western Freeway partially underground, but argued more freeways were necessary for the future of the city and to make life more convenient for motorists.[26]

The San Francisco Planning and Urban Renewal Association (SPUR), at the time an "official advisor to the mayor and board of supervisors concerning urban renewal matters," hedged, aware of the possible downsides of freeway construction, but took a strong pro-freeway position:

> Our best residential streets are flooded with the overflow of cars from major streets, jammed to capacity. We need a basic and minimum freeway system which would at the very least carry us around our central core and into surrounding areas. A basic freeway system is an essential part of any well thought out and comprehensive city development program. It is not in itself the complete or satisfactory solution to our transportation problems and can only be effective when carefully integrated with a regional rapid transit system, maximum utilization of existing city streets and local rapid transit system.[27]

SPUR supported the Western Freeway but suggested putting it partially underground: "Regarding the Western Freeway route . . . SPUR believes that careful consideration of aesthetics and of this route's relation to Golden Gate Park and park roads will make this a helpful solution to much of the overwhelming park traffic. . . . SPUR urges: a. Study of the possibility of a subway under the Panhandle . . . Study the possibility of timing freeway construction with urban renewal activities in the area near the Central Freeway."[28]

Resistance to the freeways began with neighborhood civic associations. The Lakeside Property Owners Association, representing a community in the southwestern corner of the city, wrote in a 1961 letter to the City Planning Commission that "our association wishes to be put on record as being opposed to the Western Freeway as presented in the new Trafficways Report. The report makes no mention of on and off ramps in this area, how many homes would be displaced in this section, the effect on our parkway landscaping strip that we at present maintain, and the exact location of the tunnel that is proposed to be built under Ocean Avenue."[29]

In 1961 the Haight-Ashbury was not yet known for its role in the counterculture, but its location at the eastern side of Golden Gate Park just south of the panhandle meant residents were particularly concerned about the Western Freeway. Roger Hulbert, the chairman of the Haight-Ashbury Neighborhood Council wrote a letter to his neighbors March 23, promising that "it appears that, for once, the people of the Haight-Ashbury District will not sit on the sidelines—apathetic, indifferent and complacent—while others far removed from the thinking and desires of neighborhood people make decisions for the area's future. I refer to the intense interest among neighbors about possible freeway construction adjacent to the Panhandle on Oak Street." Hulbert closed his letter asking for volunteers to further work on the issue.[30]

Another neighborhood organization, the Potrero Boosters and Merchants Association, opposed freeway construction in another part of San Francisco: "While we are not 'experts,' we live here, and feel we are better aware of the disruption Plan P-PII will cause our beautiful Hill (sic), with its residential potential. It is difficult to accept the fact that the wishes of the home owners of Potrero Hill could be so ignored, for the sake of expediency, especially so, when concessions have been made, all along the line, for industry."[31]

It was not only neighborhood groups who raised concerns about the 1960 Trafficways Plan. The Northern California chapter of the American Institute of Architects (AIA) warned, "A line on the map, a circle where two of these lines cross, eventually become land-eating, view shocking tangles of steel and concrete structures . . . Views change, neighborhoods change, the whole character of the city changes."[32] The AIA statement in a moment of fanciful futurism added:

> We feel that the true cost of the automobile has never been assayed. Their purchase, maintenance, fuel, insurance, garage space and construction, loss of land in streets and highways which might be put to more productive use; the cost of construction and maintenance has never been totalled (sic). Until these costs have been determined, the costs and benefits of other types of transit cannot be fully weighted.
>
> At a day in history when man has learned to circle the earth in a few minutes, we shouldn't sniff at advanced solutions. Free transit and moving sidewalks may be cheaper than rolling out more miles of red carpet for the 1960 buggy.[33]

Urbanist Lewis Mumford reflected on this in a 1962 interview, describing the San Francisco that many were fighting to protect as "one of the few concentrated cities that are left—and hard to think of another with its variety and charm." He warned ominously of Los Angeles as "the nightmare of the future," adding "the freeway almost ruined San Francisco—but it was stopped in time, before it encircled the city and cut it off from the water."[34]

San Franciscans did allow their city to turn into another Los Angeles. Instead, San Francisco became one of the first big cities in the country where neighborhood activists stopped large-scale development from remaking their city. The Freeway Revolts also pitted community groups interested in preserving their neighborhoods against business, real estate, and big-labor interests that favored more and faster development of different kinds. Suleiman Osman contextualized this conflict in Brownstone Brooklyn and similar neighborhoods as "an existential battle against a new machine—the New Deal pro-growth coalition of real estate agents, planners, business leaders, politicians, civic groups and directors of nonprofit institutions, who since World War II spearheaded a program of urban redevelopment around the country . . . they championed the decentralization of municipal power, replacing the ideal of a regional, integrated city system with a diverse mosaic of local participatory democracies."[35]

During the 1950s and 1960s, the Freeway Revolts led to many victories against freeway construction, including stopping a 1.6-mile underground freeway feeding into the Golden Gate Bridge that would have run through Pacific Heights, numerous elevated freeways, and a freeway that would have bisected the Western Addition leading from Golden Gate Park. Katherine Johnson explained the significance of the Freeway Revolts: "Among the scores of freeway revolts that managed to cancel or reroute the big roads, however, San Francisco's stands out. It was not only the first but also the longest and, in the end, most costly. The price of this revolt was the loss of some $200 million in federal aid—almost $1 billion in today's dollars."[36] Johnson was presumably referring to aid for highway construction, as federal aid to the Bay Area continued and helped pay for, among other things, the construction of BART, the commuter rail that links San Francisco to suburbs to the east and south.

Hadley Roff, a native San Franciscan and longtime government official, explained the impact the Freeway Revolts had on politics and organizing in San Francisco: "One of the principal organizing factors that propelled the neighborhood activists into political prominence was the battle against a crosstown freeway that would have cut across the Panhandle, and across Nob Hill and the Marina. . . . Neighborhood activists . . . really went to work. . . . The city revolted, the freeway was never built . . . The so-called Freeway Revolt demonstrated what could emerge from the neighborhoods. I think led to a belief that neighborhoods could become increasingly influential in larger policies in the city."[37] Roff's comment shows how the Freeway Revolts led to reassessment of the relationship between the neighborhoods and downtown and to how political power could be used and developed in San Francisco.

The Freeway Revolts placed environmental concerns and related quality-of-life issues at the center of San Francisco politics earlier than in many cities. In response to initial concerns raised by activists in 1953, "the Board (of Supervisors) resolved that all future transportation plans had to be compatible with the protection of 'land values, human values, and the preservation of the city's treasured appearance.' The full meaning of this resolution did not become apparent until the end of the decade. In 1966, the Board reaffirmed its 1959 decision when it cancelled the Panhandle and Golden Gate freeways. Then, in 1969, resolution of a protracted conflict over the route of the Junipero Serra Freeway affirmed the power of environmental considerations and grass-roots social movements in modern San Francisco politics."[38]

Redevelopment

The politics of the Freeway Revolts cannot be disaggregated from the racial and economic context of San Francisco in the 1950s. Although, in general, the Freeway Revolts were the first major victory for the neighborhoods over the downtown interests, not all the neighborhoods shared in that victory. The freeways that were proposed but never built largely fell into one of two categories. Either they were in affluent neighborhoods, like the proposed tunnel under Pacific Heights, or they threatened areas of natural beauty, like the Western Freeway and the proposed freeway through Golden Gate Park.

Some of the other proposed freeways were indeed built. The Southern Freeway, now a stretch of Highways 101 and 280, was constructed. That freeway cut through neighborhoods such as Bayview/Hunters Point, Bernal Heights, and Potrero Hill that were lower-income with growing Latino and African American populations. Another freeway, the Embarcadero, would have run alongside of much of the eastern and southeastern part of the city, close to the bay. The Embarcadero Freeway would have been an ugly elevated freeway for commuters to get downtown from the East Bay and down the peninsula from the center of the city, while affecting views and the feel of downtown. The Embarcadero was partially built and remained a source of controversy until 1989 when it was damaged in the Loma Prieta earthquake and then torn down.

This conflict between downtown and the neighborhoods occurred in the context of an electoral system that favored the former. When the Freeway Revolts began, the San Francisco Board of Supervisors was elected by staggered, at-large elections in odd-numbered years. Every election, either five or six of the board's eleven seats were contested. Elections were citywide with the top five or six, depending on the year, finishers in the nonpartisan election, winning seats. Therefore, successful candidates needed enough money and name recognition to run citywide, giving a big advantage to those who either had their own money or affluent supporters. This system was also a barrier for racial minorities because, for example, an African American might do well in African American precincts but would also have to win large numbers of white voters. Accordingly, the eleven members of the board of supervisors in the late 1950s and early 1960s were all white, while ten of the eleven were male. Ideologically, the board consisted largely of pro-business Democrats and a few Republicans. Mayor George Christopher, who served from 1956 to 1964, was also a Republican.

The city's conservative leadership was not only seeking to build freeways but also had an ambitious redevelopment agenda. This was the program to which SPUR alluded in its statement of support for the Western Freeway, as it hoped to link that freeway to the large-scale redevelopment program occurring in the heart of the Fillmore District. The Western Freeway was defeated not because Mayor Christopher or the board of supervisors cared about what people in the

Panhandle and the nearby Fillmore District thought, but because people all around the city wanted to maintain Golden Gate Park's beauty. The African American community was not at the center of the fight, primarily because they were so excluded from politics at that time.

Belva Davis, a groundbreaking African American journalist and media personality, reflected in 2011, about tensions in San Francisco between white neighborhood activists and African Americans: "I don't think the Black community ever really had a voice in the freeway fight although it affected them greatly. They were so busy fighting for a place to live, and that fight seemed to be a fight of middle-class whites, environmentalists, people concerned about historic buildings that would go, infringement on the park and all those kind of things. . . . So those were fights that people who were leading them made friends with the Black community. They had allies there, but I wouldn't say that Blacks were in leadership."[39] Sometimes the goals of white and African American activists overlapped, as in the opposition to the Western Freeway. Other times African Americans had different economic needs and frequently did not get support from neighborhood activists on issues specific to their neighborhoods and communities.

The Fillmore District was once a vibrant African American community in the heart of San Francisco. Fillmore Street itself runs from the bay in the north to Market Street in the south but is only in the Fillmore District for about ten blocks. Occasionally referred as the Harlem of the West, the Fillmore was bordered by Pacific Heights to the north, Van Ness Avenue to the east, Divisadero to the west and Market Street to the south. Today the border with Pacific Heights is several blocks south of where it once was, while neighborhoods such as the Lower Haight, Hayes Valley, Anza Visa, and Alamo Square, in some cases created by the real estate industry, have further shrunk the Fillmore.

The Fillmore District became more important to the city following the 1906 earthquake. Because that neighborhood had been largely undamaged by the earthquake, many who had lost their homes or businesses went there to rebuild their lives. "For the time being, Fillmore Street, in the population swollen Western Addition, became the principal business street of San Francisco . . . It now had the advantage of possessing one of the few undamaged car lines in the city. . . . Every empty lot soon swarmed with workmen hammering together light frame structures to house the leading mercantile establishments of the city. Restaurants, theaters, saloons and hotels opened alongside the stores, giving the streets the lively, tawdry aspects of the main stem of a frontier boom town."[40]

For many the Fillmore does not evoke the Harlem of the West, but a concert venue from the 1960s. The Fillmore Auditorium was on Geary around Steiner Street, in the heart of the Fillmore. It was opened in 1912 as the Majestic Hall and Academy of Dancing. It was owned and operated by Bill Graham, the legendary rock and roll promoter, from 1965 to 1968. Graham was a central player in the San

Francisco music scene for years and was instrumental in promoting bands such as the Grateful Dead, the Jefferson Airplane and others. The Fillmore eventually moved a few blocks east and was renamed the Fillmore West. This was because Graham had opened another venue called the Fillmore East in the East Village in New York, Graham's first adopted hometown. Graham, whose name at birth was Wulf Wolodia Grajonca, was the son of Russian Jews who had immigrated to Germany before he was born. He had come to New York as boy of ten years old after spending much of his first decade of his life finding a way to survive in Nazi Germany and occupied France.

The Fillmore District may be primarily recognized for its position as the heart of San Francisco's African American community, but before World War II, the Fillmore was a very diverse place with Japanese Americans, some African Americans, a Jewish presence, and others. In 1930 there were only 3,803 African Americans in San Francisco. That number grew slightly over the next decade as the 1940 census found 4,846 African Americans in the city, an increase from 0.6 percent to 0.8 percent of San Francisco's population. By 1950 that number had jumped to 43,502, still only 5.7 percent of the city, but a big increase nonetheless. Many of those newer African American migrants settled in the Fillmore. Thus, the efforts to redevelop the Fillmore District beginning in the early 1950s occurred in a community that was only beginning to establish itself.

The Fillmore had also been home to many Japanese Americans who, as late as 1940, outnumbered African Americans in San Francisco. One of the reasons African American migrants to the city settled in the Fillmore was housing that became available when Japanese Americans were sent to internment camps. As Arnold Townsend explained, "When they started inviting Black people to come from the south to work in the war industries, they didn't have a place to put them. They wouldn't have except guess what? It just so happens, they're these vacant buildings that we've got because we just sent a lot of the Japanese folks to the concentration camps."[41]

Almost as soon as the Fillmore District became heavily African American, powerful white San Franciscans viewed it through a racist lens. "At a 1948 Public Hearing, State Senator O'Gara noted that the Fillmore was the city's worst blighted area with metastasizing ramifications for the city's citizenry and other districts: (describing it as) 'where the worst blighted conditions exist . . . the most overcrowded . . . the oldest houses, the most unsanitary conditions, the place where crime and juvenile delinquency and domestic difficulties, and all the other things that grow out of blight and slum(s) exist in the worst degree.'"[42]

Senator Gerald O'Gara's view was not shared by everybody. Elizabeth Pepin and Lewis Watts described the neighborhood in the 1940s and 1950s. "The neighborhood was jumping. Block after block of ornate but slightly worn turn-of-the-century Victorians filled with all matters of fun. Everyone who was anyone could be found there, dressed to the nines, making the scene and strutting their stuff."[43] Two people who grew up in the Fillmore in the postwar era also stressed the racial diversity and tolerance in the neighborhood. Singer Sugar Pie DeSanto, the daughter of a Filipino father and African American mother, described how "that was my childhood. . . . Every race and religion you could think of. We all lived in the neighborhood and were all good friends." Armando Rendon, a Filipino American, described how "the Fillmore during the '40s and '50s was fabulous. A great place to raise kids. The neighborhood was very mixed, and we didn't have any racially motivated outbreaks of violence."[44] Rendon also noted that "once World War II was declared, the neighborhood changed. Overnight, the Japanese families that I had grown up with were gone. . . . There was a quietness over the neighborhood that was unnerving."[45]

Plans to redevelop the Fillmore were first formalized in 1952, only seven years after the end of World War II. The area to be redeveloped was roughly twenty-eight square blocks bound by Eddy Street to the south, Post Street to the north, Broderick to the west and Franklin to the east. This was the heart of the Fillmore and Western Addition Districts. Planning documents described the proposed redevelopment and its goals:

> Redevelopment of the area will start with the widening of Geary Street allowing the channeling of traffic and its removal from minor streets. Some of these streets will be closed for part of their length providing for the creation of superblocks. Land will be made available for privately constructed housing with a variety of building types ranging from row houses to elevator apartments providing dwellings for a population estimated at 7,000. . . . Redevelopment of the area will eliminate more than 2,000 sub-standard dwellings and many hundreds of rooms in dilapidated rooming houses and row dwellings structures, clearing the area representing a substantial part of the total slum and blighted area of the City. This will remove a serious threat to the health, safety and welfare of the people and reduce markedly the costs of city service.[46]

The racism in that document is coded, but phrases like "dilapidated rooming houses" refer to what for many African American men was the only housing they could get in a city where residential segregation was still strong. Similarly, the word "blight," which was used liberally in the report, pathologizes African American neighborhoods and people for being poor.

Redevelopment in the Fillmore and the Western Addition accelerated later in the 1950s. Similar endeavors were undertaken in many American cities. Clement Lai stressed that redevelopment in San Francisco had a unique multiracial component to it because of the presence of large number of African American and Japanese American people in the area being redeveloped: "What differentiates the Fillmore's redevelopment from other cases in mid-twentieth-century U.S. cities is not the project's destructive size, mixture of modernist faith and hubris, or failed good intentions but rather the multiracial nature of the project. . . . African Americans, white and Asian Americans were involved in and affected by the Fillmore's redevelopment. . . . The two communities shared similar histories of segregation, which were enforced through everyday racist violence. . . . The RDA [Redevelopment Agency] treated organizations from these two communities dissimilarly (embracing one and largely dismissing the other) . . . when they approached the agency to protest displacement and make claims to the state."[47]

One difference between how African American and Japanese Americans were treated during this period of redevelopment was that a centerpiece of the redevelopment was the construction of a development known as Japantown. Japantown consists of two neighboring complexes, the Japanese Cultural and Trade Center (JCTC) and the Nihonmachi Mall abutting the JCTC's eastern flank. Japantown was built on a rough approximation of Japanese architecture and consists of some semiofficial government and trade offices as well as numerous Japanese clothing, grocery, other stores, and many bars and restaurants. For many years Japantown Bowl was one of the best, and then one of the only, bowling alleys in the city. Japantown served a purpose in the post-World War II era when the Cold War was in full force because it helped strengthen ties between the US and its new Cold War ally, Japan.

Lai fleshed out how Japanese Americans and African Americans were treated differently in the redevelopment process: "Although the JCTC was a highly problematic development that capitalized on Orientalized images for its appeal and elided differences between Japanese-Americans and Japanese . . . no analogous redevelopment project celebrating black culture existed in the district's African American communities."[48]

The effort to redevelop the Western Addition continued into the 1960s and was met with resistance for much of that and the following decade. Belva Davis described how "the Fillmore was a vital neighborhood with lots of businesses either run or owned by Black people back in those days. Small merchants could make it. Nightlife was blooming and it was almost unthinkable, I thought then, that all of that would somehow be sacrificed for something called urban renewal. But it was happening."[49] Townsend recollected that when he first moved to San Francisco, "the restaurants and the places we had in the Fillmore in the '60s were some awfully nice spots that white people came in, but we didn't give a damn if they ever came in or not."[50] Resistance to redevelopment, unlike the Freeway Revolts, was not a largely middle-class and white movement. The center of that resistance was the city's African American community rather than middle-class white neighborhoods and contributed to the broader leftward shift in San Francisco in the 1960s and 1970s. In both communities, neighborhood activists were gaining experience and occasionally winning. Over time, they began to work together and laid a foundation for a more powerful progressive voice in the city.

New Political and Cultural Movements

The late 1950s brought other changes to San Francisco that began to remake the city's political and cultural profile. North Beach was becoming more than just an old Italian neighborhood and would play a key role in cultural movements from beatniks to punks. Beatniks, like the hippies of the Summer of Love era that came after them, were deeply associated with San Francisco. Beats predated beatniks and, while there was significant overlap between the two groups, they were not quite the same. The beats began in the late 1940s, explored various spiritual, mystic, and religious traditions, were very focused on their art and poetry, and were not a large movement. The beatniks emerged a few years later and were the more popular, accessible, and media- friendly iteration of the beats.

The poet and writer Kenneth Rexroth, writing in *The Nation* in 1958, explained the beats and their relationship to conventional and conservative postwar America:

> An orthodoxy is forming, and like all orthodoxies it is a system of lies and evasions, a ritual of the lazy and greedy. How do you escape It? By reading Marx and Kropotkin? By joining up? Indeed not. *Playboy*, a leading socio-economic authority, says, "Rexroth says, the Anarchists must organize." Excuse me, I mean, ça ira. It is a deliberately fostered delusion of Western Civilization, of the *Old* and *New* Testaments and the *Koran*, that life is hard to understand and harder still to live. It Is only too obvious, every step of the way as the newspapers roll past, what should be-—should have been—done.[51]

Legendary San Francisco newspaper columnist Herb Caen coined the term beatnik, first using it in print on April 2, 1958. Many assume Caen was riffing on the recent Soviet space vessel Sputnik because he came up with the name six months after Sputnik launched.[52] An alternate explanation is that the suffix "nik" in Russian and some related languages means something like "one who" and is somewhat similar to the suffix "er" in English. Caen did not speak Russian, but he was Jewish and reasonably familiar with Yiddish, where the suffix "nik" has the same meaning. Beatniks were a cultural and artistic movement, but unlike, hippies and punks later, it was not the musicians who were the beatnik stars. Instead, the most celebrated beatniks were writers such as Jack Kerouac or poets such as Lawrence Ferlinghetti and Allen Ginsberg.

Christopher Lowen Agee discussed how the beatnik movement evolved in North Beach:

> The postwar growth of the California School of Fine Arts (renamed the San Francisco Art Institute in 1960) on Russian Hill, along with the migration to North Beach of a group of poets trained at the University of California, Berkeley (including Robert Duncan, Jack Spicer, and Robin Blaser), injected vitality into the area's creative circles during the early 1950s. A new beat movement began coalescing in 1953 and 1954 when writers and poets such as Kerouac, Ginsberg, and Gary Snyder arrived on North Beach's already thriving literary scene.
>
> Many beat artists felt that the North Beach community supported their creative work and bohemian lifestyle.
>
> The beats living and working in North Beach also socialized in the neighborhood. The commercial hub of the district's bohemia shifted north during the postwar period, away from the city's expanding financial district and deeper into the Italian-American neighborhood.[53]

Today the beatniks are most frequently remembered, and caricatured, as young men and women in North Beach or New York's Greenwich Village wearing black turtlenecks, sipping wine or coffee, smoking cigarettes—French ones if possible—and listening to, or performing, poetry or folk music. By the late 1950s and early 1960s the beatniks had crept into the larger culture. It was not unusual to see beatnik characters on television shows, most notably Maynard G. Krebs on *The Many Loves of Dobie Gillis*.[54] Jokes were made about beatniks, but there also were efforts to commodify them by companies selling clothes and other beatnik accoutrements.

These stereotypes are, in some vague sense, accurate, but belittle an important social and cultural movement. The beats, and the beatniks, a few years later, were the Ur postwar, albeit largely white, counterculture movement whose influence can still be felt strongly wherever and whenever young, again mostly white, people gather with the understanding society has gone very wrong and the belief that, through radical social, artistic, and even spiritual change it can be made right again.

North Beach haunts such as Vesuvio's, Lawrence Ferlinghetti's City Lights Bookstore, the Hungry I, and others became important touchpoints as American culture evolved over the next decades. City Lights Bookstore still exists today, and Ferlinghetti lived until 2021 when he died at age 101. In 2007, Adler Alley, the small street just north of the store was renamed Jack Kerouac Alley after one of the most famous beatniks. The Jazz Workshop, a club in North Beach, was where comedian and social critic Lenny Bruce was first arrested on obscenity charges, thus contributing to San Francisco's emerging national profile.

Gradually, the rest of the country was beginning to view San Francisco differently. San Francisco was the city most closely identified with cultural figures like Kerouac and Ginsberg and a correspondingly different understanding of life, society, and culture than the postwar consensus. The beatniks were not a particularly political movement, but in those years, San Francisco's progressive tradition was also slowly reemerging.

HUAC Comes to San Francisco

McCarthyism was at its height in the 1950s. Joseph McCarthy, a Republican senator from Wisconsin, began his red-baiting crusade in 1950. His spectacular, and deeply deserved, fall occurred in 1954. By 1957 McCarthy was dead. However, anti-communist crusades did not end with McCarthy, as the House Committee on Un-American Affairs (HUAC) lived on. By early 1960, HUAC had created a traveling road show that went to different cities looking for communists. The HUAC road show came to San Francisco's City Hall in May 1960. The free speech movement, which began at Berkeley, was a few years away, but college students and other activists came to City Hall to protest HUAC's excesses and efforts to limit the freedoms of speech and assembly guaranteed by the First Amendment.

The protesters gathered inside City Hall outside of the board of supervisors chamber, where HUAC was holding its hearing. A news video shows well-dressed and orderly demonstrators chanting, "Open the doors and get out of the city," and then singing the national anthem before resuming their demand to "open the doors." The leader of the demonstrators, seeing the police approaching, says, "Here comes the goon squad." As he and others are being physically removed from the premises by the police, the leader adds, "This is Americanism in action."[55] The well-dressed man, wearing a suit and tie with a flower in his lapel, leading the demonstrators was Archie Brown. Brown was a longshoreman and a member of the International Longshore and Warehouse Union, the union led by Harry Bridges that had initiated the general strike in 1934. Brown was a radical, prominent member of the Communist Party of the USA and veteran of the Abraham Lincoln Brigade.

The police used a range of tactics, including arresting some, using fire hoses, and pushing others out of City Hall, to break up the demonstration. Demonstrators were pushed down the stairs by the force of the fire hoses and manhandled by police. The following day, a few thousand more demonstrators came back to protest HUAC and the police brutality of the previous day. Eventually charges were dropped against everybody who had been arrested except for one man. HUAC, for its part, dismissed the demonstrations as "Communist inspired," and made a propaganda film about the events called *Operation Abolition*.[56]

The demonstrations helped reinvigorate the left and the student movement in the Bay Area. "In response to the events of May 13 and the attacks upon the University and its students resulting therefrom, students quickly organized and prepared themselves to meet the HUAC controversy head on. It must be said that in general the HUAC 'riots' helped generate and revive student organizations throughout the State. TASK at San Jose State and SCOPE at San Francisco State were given shots in the arm by the revival of interest generated by the police riot and the film *Operation Abolition*."[57]

These events did not change the reality that the city was still basically a conservative town where the Republican mayor, George Christopher, worked with business and less radical labor groups to govern from the center. The radicalism of Archie Brown and others represented a small minority of San Franciscans. The previous year when Nikita Khruschev, the Soviet premier, had visited San Francisco, it was Brown's ILWU who had led the cheers for the leader of America's Cold War rival. Nobody then knew how much San Francisco politics, and San Francisco's reputation, would change in the coming decade, but it was soon apparent these rumblings were part of something bigger.

The Giants Come to Town

Another of the most important events in San Francisco in the late 1950s occurred on April 15, 1958, when North Beach native and Galileo High School graduate Dodgers centerfielder Gino Cimoli dug into the batter's box at Seals Stadium against Giants pitcher Ruben Gomez. Gomez struck Cimoli out, and in doing so marked the beginning of the first official Major League Baseball game played in San Francisco, California, the West Coast, or the western half of the United States. Gomez threw a shutout, helping the Giants cruise to an 8–0 win over their longtime rivals, the Dodgers, who had just relocated to Los Angeles from Brooklyn. The *San Francisco Chronicle* marked the beginning of the West Coast version of the rivalry the next day with the huge headline, "WE MURDER THE BUMS."[58] The Giants had moved to San Francisco following the 1957 season after playing in New York, where they had made their home in northern Manhattan, since the nineteenth century, while the Dodgers moved from Brooklyn to Los Angeles at the same time.

The Giants and Dodgers moving to California revolutionized the business of baseball, making what we now think of as Major League Baseball truly national for the first time. The move accelerated the inclusion of Latino ballplayers, opened two huge new markets, and increased attendance at a time when the game was suffering. It also upset many fans in Brooklyn and somewhat fewer fans in northern Manhattan.[59]

The Giants did not make San Franciscans believe their city was finally big league. Rather, the move affirmed their already existing view that San Francisco was big league. The Giants were welcomed with a parade down Market Street, but baseball itself had a very long history in San Francisco. For example, the term "sandlot," part of the vocabulary of every aging baseball fan's sepia-toned childhood memories of playing ball, was first used in San Francisco. The western part of the city, including neighborhoods such as the Richmond and the Sunset as well as Golden Gate Park, was once largely sand dunes. If you were a youngster playing ball out there in the early part of the last century, the sand was inescapable. Even in the 1970s and 1980s, the "dirt" on many of the fields where I played felt more like sand.

Additionally, many great baseball players from the first half of the twentieth century had roots in San Francisco. The DiMaggio brothers and the great Tigers hitter and teammate of Ty Cobb, Harry Heilmann, were from San Francisco. Several of Joe DiMaggio's teammates, such as Tony Lazzeri and Frank Crosetti, were also San Franciscans. Ernie Lombardi, the slugging Hall of Fame Reds backstop of the 1930s and 1940s, considered one of the slowest men ever to play the game at the big-league level, grew up just across the bay in Oakland.

The San Francisco Seals of the old PCL had been San Francisco's team since 1903 and were deeply integrated into the culture of San Francisco. Star players were celebrities in San Francisco, most notably Lefty O'Doul, who played for the team on and off between 1918 and 1940 and managed them from 1935 to 1951. Almost all San Franciscans I know who were old enough to pay attention to baseball before 1957 recount stories of going to Seals games. Some remember the doubleheaders the Seals would play with their cross-bay rivals, the Oakland Oaks. The doubleheader would consist of one game in each team's ballpark as players, media, and fans would travel across the bay by ferry between games. Because of all this, it took the Giants many years to be fully accepted and welcomed in San Francisco. It didn't help that they only won their first World Series on the West Coast in 2010.

During their first two years in San Francisco, the Giants played at Seals Stadium, a beautiful ballpark in the Mission District, accessible to fans from most parts of the city. Seals Stadium was not quite big enough and had insufficient parking, so the city built a new ballpark in southeastern San Francisco, the same Bayview/Hunters Point area that would later play an important role in sending George Moscone to City Hall. The Giants moved into Candlestick Park in 1960. During the forty years the Giants called Candlestick home, the cold and poorly located ballpark was unwelcoming and drove attendance down, leading to revenue problems for the Giants and uncertainty about their future in San Francisco, while contributing to their frequent struggles on the field.

The San Francisco 49ers would join the Giants at Candlestick Park beginning in the 1971–1972 season after having made their home in Kezar Stadium since 1946 when they were part of the All-America Football Conference before joining the NFL in 1950. Kezar is on at the southeastern corner of Golden Gate Park just south of the Panhandle, so during the 1950s the city's major sports teams played more or less in the center of town.

This began to change in the 1960s with the construction of Candlestick Park, a process mired in ethically questionable contracting. The initial plan called for a steam-heating system under the seats that would radiate heat upward on cold nights, but because of budget issues was never built. Robert Garratt, in his history of the San Francisco Giants, summarized the political scandals and corruption surrounding the construction of Candlestick:

> But a closer look at the events leading to the planning and building of Candlestick will show a different picture, one that suggests tension, confusion, shenanigans, (if not duplicity), underhandedness, and backroom deals between city hall and the builder. Candlestick was trouble from its conception, long before any dirt was moved, plans sketched, or pilings sunk. . . . The park's notoriety would also become apparent in veiled backroom deals within city hall, and then in public political squabbling.[60]

The Giants and later the 49ers moved to Candlestick Park because there was no obvious site in the city center and to make the games accessible to suburban fans. While Candlestick may have been difficult to get to from residential parts of northern and western San Francisco, freeways made it easily accessible for fans from the South Bay and the East Bay, although most of the latter switched their allegiance to the A's after they moved to Oakland from Kansas City in 1968.

In the more than sixty years the Giants have played in San Francisco, they have become one of the city's most famous institutions. Despite the mixed welcome, problems of Candlestick Park, and almost leaving the city several times, the Giants have finally won a permanent place in the hearts of San Franciscans and in the city's culture and economics, but in 1958 they were new; and getting a Major League Baseball team was a significant accomplishment for Mayor Christopher.

As the 1950s grew to a close, while George Moscone was beginning to find his way toward an adult life and career, San Francisco was poised for a decade of enormous change that would remake both the city and its image. The stirrings of those changes were present in the late 1950s, but they were not obvious yet.

CHAPTER FOUR

The Navy, College and Law School

When Moscone graduated from St. Ignatius in 1947, the next step for smart, ambitious well-placed young Catholic men from San Francisco was the University of San Francisco (USF), another Jesuit school known both for the fine education it offered and for being a good place to build relationships and to gain access to an alumni network that would be helpful in San Francisco. Unlike many of his classmates, Moscone did not go to USF after high school, nor did he enroll at Saint Mary's, a Catholic college in the East Bay, as suggested by his St. Ignatius yearbook.[1] This was likely at least in part for financial reasons. Had he been offered a basketball scholarship to USF or Saint Mary's, or found some other means to pay the tuition, Moscone probably would have gone right out of high school. Instead, he began a six-year journey that would begin in the US Navy but would lead to a college degree.

Moscone's St. Ignatius teammate Joe Kelly told how Moscone ended up in the navy shortly after high school: "We went up to USF, I went up to USF too. He went up with the freshman team and made it. I don't think he rated very well on the freshman team at USF then. . . . It looked like the father's club, see, they're all returning veterans from WWII. . . . They played in the service, and they played in high school when we were in grammar school, and I don't think he (Moscone) did real great in that school. At about halfway through the freshman year or so, as I recall, he joined the navy."[2]

Growing up during World War II in a city that was central to the war effort and through which many soldiers and sailors passed may have contributed to Moscone's decision to join the navy. Moscone's time in the navy was after World War II and before the Korean War, so he never saw combat. There is little documentation about Moscone's time in the military, but several people who knew him well suggested to me that he spent much of his time in the navy playing basketball.

Many websites and other historical records about Moscone assume that he served after college, but Moscone went almost directly from high school to the navy after only a few months at USF. Moscone made this clear in a 1977 interview with the University of the Pacific student newspaper, the *Pacific Review.* Moscone described the early 1950s as "an unusual time to be on campus. . . . There was the interaction between the veterans and the younger students. . . . I was coming out of the Navy."[3]

After the US Navy, Moscone enrolled at Santa Rosa Junior College in Sonoma County, north of San Francisco, a very rural area at that time. Santa Rosa Community College was not the kind of school that graduates of St. Ignatius typically attended back then—or now. Money and basketball partially explain Moscone's decision to attend a small community college sixty miles away from San Francisco. It is hard to imagine that none of the other schools in San Francisco, including City College of San Francisco or San Francisco State College, now San Francisco State University, could not have found room, and even a little money, for a smart graduate of St. Ignatius who was an all-city basketball player. Given this, Moscone's decision to go to Santa Rosa is puzzling, suggesting for some reason he wanted, or needed, to get out of San Francisco for a while.

While at Santa Rosa, Moscone continued to play basketball, but found time for other activities too. In the spring of 1950, the school paper wrote that "George (Moscone), recently active with the J. C. basketball team, has been prominent on campus this and last semester."[4] The article also announced that Moscone and a student named Barbara Friberg had gotten engaged: "On Wednesday evening, March 15, a group of girls gathered at Barbara's home at 501 East Napa Street in Sonoma to honor Miss Joan Stanley with a surprise birthday dinner . . . The closed dining room held a very special message even more important than the expected celebration. When the girls entered the Friberg dining room they were confronted with a lovely table arrangement of two fluffy pink satin hearts. Not fully grasping the situation the wondering guests rushed to their places to find place card favors and tiny pink paper hearts adorned with doves and the names 'Barbara and George.'"[5]

Friberg had been runner-up for homecoming queen the past two years, the article went on to say, and "Barbara has won the recognition and heart of the campus, (and) she was elected fall president of the Mydan Club last semester, is a member of the Women's Luncheon Club, and is the president of the sophomore class at present. She was a member of the student council as sophomore girl's representative last semester. This engagement climaxes a college romance that has been of much interest to the couple's friends and acquaintances."[6]

Friberg and Moscone never married. Their engagement was probably very brief. Other than the mention in the article from 1950, there is almost no other information about it. However, a month or two later that same paper reported that the couple's song was "This is Always," written by Harry Warren and Mack Gordon but performed by many artists, most notably Chet Baker. More recently, the song, performed by the Junior Mance Trio was part of the soundtrack of the film *The Bridges of Madison County*. None of Moscone's closest associates with whom I spoke knew of Friberg, had heard of the engagement, or knew why it ended. Most were completely surprised to learn Moscone had been engaged to somebody while in college.

After junior college in Santa Rosa, USF might still have been the place where a man like the young Moscone was most likely to go, but instead he opted for a private, essentially secular college outside of San Francisco. It is possible that after four years of Jesuit education at St. Ignatius, Moscone wanted something different or that Stockton, which would have felt like a very small town compared to San Francisco, nonetheless held some appeal for Moscone. His mother's family was nearby; and after a semester at Santa Rosa, Stockton would have felt downright cosmopolitan.

In that 1977 interview with the *Pacific Review*, Moscone explained why he went to the College of the Pacific, "I wanted to go away from home for college, but not too far from San Francisco. . . . I loved San Francisco but knew that to grow as a person I would have to grow and see a different part of life."[7] This interview was given almost twenty-five years after Moscone graduated from college to a college newspaper with a largely student audience, so that may have informed his comments too.

The campus is about seventy miles due east of San Francisco, although it cannot be driven in a straight line, and about fifty miles due south of Sacramento. George Moscone spent much of his life within this triangle. Stockton was where he went to college. Sacramento, the state capital, was where he enjoyed some of his greatest political and legislative successes, but San Francisco was home, the city where he was born and where he would die, and the place that meant the most to him.

Attending the College of the Pacific allowed Moscone to continue playing basketball as a star forward for the school's basketball team. In his junior year, the school paper related his value on the basketball court. "The floor leader of the team, George has a nice long shot and is the team boss, directing all the plays. The colorful San Francisco player is in his second season at COP and is a junior."[8]

Moscone played basketball, majored in sociology, and was involved in student social life at the College of the Pacific. His commitment to basketball sometimes led Moscone to fall behind in his coursework, but Moscone worked hard at academics. In an undated letter to his mother, Moscone wrote, "I had a test this morning and some last week. I know I did well in all of them. I've turned in all my back work (due to ball trips) and I'm all caught up." That letter, written in the beautiful penmanship that was the product of many years of Catholic school,[9] also reveals the closeness between Moscone and Lena. The college-age son began by writing, "I received your letter and I must say it was quite short." A few paragraphs later, Moscone apologized for doing something to his mother's car. "I hope you're not still mad at me for the car. You know I wouldn't be that careless," before adding, "I didn't come home this week-end because I didn't have enough money however I'll be home early Friday." Then, alluding to his one-time fiancé, Moscone wrote to his mother, "I haven't heard from Barbara for some time so I guess that romance is about ended."[10]

Moscone's reputation on the basketball court and as a handsome and charming young man went beyond the College of the Pacific. Gloria Wernsman, who went on to an almost four-decade career in journalism for *The Sacramento Union* and then *The Sacramento Bee* wrote in one of her columns for the Sacramento State College (now Sacramento State University) newspaper, of which she was the editor, "Sidenote: COP beat the University of Nevada TWICE.[11] Isn't that wonderful? Betcha Georgie was really a wow. Talked to a couple of his friends the other day . . . who said they wish we could meet Georgie. Well?"[12]

The early 1950s were certainly not a time of great campus radicalism, particularly at relatively rural schools miles away from the nearest big city. Nonetheless, Moscone had his first direct experience with elections at the College of the Pacific, running for rally commissioner in May 1951, spring of his sophomore year. He won handily, defeating his opponent, 260–165. Moscone served as rally commissioner in his junior year. The position is more or less precisely what it sounds like and involved organizing events around student spirit, support for sports teams, and similar activities. It was not a political position.

At the beginning of his senior year, Moscone was elected president of his fraternity, Rho Lambda Phi, another social position. As he was wrapping up his college education and preparing for his adult life, Moscone seemed like a good-looking athlete whose primary extracurricular interests were social. This was not the profile of a budding progressive leader. However, Moscone was again demonstrating his comfort in many different political, social, and cultural contexts and his ability to move smoothly between these environments, skills that would prove very valuable in his professional life.

While Moscone very likely benefited in a college setting from his looks, charm, and athletic prowess, he was still the son of a single mother of modest means. Being Italian American would also have made him stand out among other college students. Yearbooks and other ephemera from Moscone's years at the College of the Pacific indicate there was not a large Italian American presence there. The student he defeated for rally commissioner, Ted Tiss, was the son of a powerful and wealthy advertising executive. Tiss's contrasting background was most likely not lost on Moscone.

This story looks a little different from the perspective of the third decade of the twenty-first century. The relative difference in lifestyle and economic conditions between, for example, the son of a wealthy executive and the son of a struggling single mother, was a lot less in the early 1950s than it is today. The US was a much more middle-class country then with less of a gap between the wealthy and everybody else, so while Moscone came from a modest background, it was not as defining or as much of a social barrier as it would be today.

Straight white men such as Moscone dominated college campuses, and society in general, in the 1950s. Based on the photos, including of the basketball team on which there was not a single African American player, it is reasonably clear that the College of the Pacific was overwhelmingly white when Moscone was a student there. Competition for leadership positions at schools such as the College of the Pacific was limited almost entirely to white men. This meant both that in general there was less competition and that differences between candidates, students, and social circles were relatively limited. College of the Pacific, unlike St. Ignatius, had women students when Moscone was there, but they rarely ran for leadership positions.

When twenty-three-year-old Moscone graduated from College of the Pacific in 1953, he was firmly on track to a life of professional success and bourgeoise respectability in San Francisco. He had graduated from St. Ignatius, served in the US Navy, and finished college. His choice of college was less conventional and prestigious than USF, the University of California, Berkeley, across the bay from San Francisco, or Stanford University down the peninsula, but the College of the Pacific was nonetheless considered a very good school. The world, and San Francisco, were opening up for young George Moscone.

Hastings

After college, Moscone made a more conventional career decision, particularly for a graduate of St. Ignatius. He returned to San Francisco for law school at Hastings. Hastings, in downtown San Francisco, is part of the University of California (UC) and was renamed UC College of the Law in 2022. San Francisco has never had an undergraduate UC campus but has long been home to both Hastings and UCSF. The former offers graduate programs in law; the latter in medicine. Both are highly respected elite institutions considered among the very best in the country.

In addition to his legal education, while studying at Hastings, Moscone built relationships with people who would be important parts of his political and personal life. Moscone needed money in law school, so he found employment as a custodian at Hastings. One of the other custodians, also a law student at Hastings, was a young African American man who had made his way from east Texas to San Francisco and earned his undergraduate degree at San Francisco State

University. Before going west he had worked picking berries, melons, and cotton, and shined shoes in his hometown.

Racism and de facto segregation, even in northern cities such as San Francisco, was still strong in the 1950s, so close friendships between African Americans and whites were relatively unusual, but Willie Brown and Moscone struck up a friendship that would last the rest of Moscone's life. The two became political allies who helped each other win elections and worked together to pass legislation while representing San Francisco in different houses of the state legislature. But they first became friends because they were financially struggling students who worked as janitors during law school.

Thirty years after Moscone's death, Brown spoke warmly of his good friend. Brown also alluded to John Burton, the mutual friend who introduced Moscone to Brown and who played an important role in the early years of Brown's and Moscone' political careers:

> George Moscone was like almost every other student there, frankly, and he was likeable, and he was unusually friendly. He was very smart, and he was helpful when called upon, and he was clearly dedicated to becoming a good lawyer. . . . He had an unusual interest in the racial and minority populations, which was very small at Hastings and in some cases isolated, but George made sure he knew every one of the people of color attending Hastings, and he was kind of a part of the team. We were on the janitorial crew together; we swept the halls of Hastings.[13]

Moscone's friendship with Willie Brown in the mid-1950s suggested that his commitment to racial equality was genuine and preceded his involvement in politics. This is clear not because Moscone was drawn to Brown, but because of the reverse. In the 1950s and 1960s, the early years of the modern civil rights movement, Brown was a strong advocate for racial equality and unlikely to become close personal friends with somebody who he thought was a bigot.

Brown reflected on Moscone's positions on racial equality and its possible origin: "George was unyielding in his demand for equal treatment of people. . . . I'd not, frankly, come across any non-Black person that was so focused, and, at such a tender age, so focused. But that was George. George saw no color, saw no race, saw no age. And it wasn't a programmed response. . . . It was totally and completely natural, totally and completely natural."[14]

Early in his time at Hastings, in 1954, Moscone married Gina Bondanza. Moscone was twenty-four years old, while Gina was about a year and a half younger. This seems like a young age for a couple to get married, but it was not unusually young in the context of Catholic San Francisco at that time. George and Gina Moscone had known each other since childhood, having both grown up in Italian American families in the Marina and Cow Hollow neighborhoods and even attended St. Brigid's together.

Even by that time, Moscone was beginning to live the paradox that would remain central to his political and personal life. He was an Italian American graduate of St. Ignatius, attending one of the top law schools in California and, by all appearances, preparing for a successful and reasonably conventional career in the law. He had married a young woman from the old neighborhood and within a few years would become a father. Millions of American men in the postwar period followed similar life trajectories, becoming pillars of the rapidly growing middle class while usually moving right in their politics. At the same time as Moscone's adult life was evolving in that conventional path, he had befriended an African American civil rights activist at law school and continued a political trajectory that would land him on the left wing of conventional politics—and deeply out of his step with his ethnic and generational cohort by the time he reached middle age.

A profile of Gina Moscone ran in the Scene section of the Sunday *Chronicle and Examiner* on November 19, 1978, three years into Moscone's mayoralty. The author of that piece, Mildred Hamilton, discussed the couple, who by then had four children and had been married almost twenty-five years: "Both were reared by single mothers who were widowed early, and both attended Catholic schools. Despite one fanciful report, they did not meet when she was 3 and he was 7. 'I knew of him: he and my brother were schoolmates, but we didn't date until he was in law school.'"[15]

Becoming good friends with Willie Brown about the time one is getting married is not great timing. Brown's long career in public service, including thirty years in the assembly, eight years as mayor of San Francisco, and then another more than twenty years as an extremely powerful behind-the-scenes political force in San Francisco and beyond, is only part of Brown's extraordinary life. During the course of a public life that has spanned more than sixty years, Brown has drawn almost as much attention for his cars, clothes, and the female company he kept as for his very impressive record as legislator and later chief executive of San Francisco. Brown, like Moscone, married young. He and Blanche Vitero were wed in 1958. The two never formally divorced, but the marriage was difficult. They were separated by the early 1980s, but the years preceding that separation were not characterized by fidelity or devotion on Brown's part.

George and Gina Moscone remained married for the rest of Moscone's life, but while they built a life together, Moscone behaved like a lot of men, and politicians, of his time. Like Willie Brown, he partied a lot, stayed out late, and philandered. They were both charismatic, stylish, good-looking men, so their actions, while open secrets, were largely seen through the lens of glamour and fun rather than a more sober perspective.

A life in politics takes a toll on one's family life almost no matter what. In recent decades as more women have run for, and won, elective office, there is more awareness of this, but when Moscone began his political career, politics was male-dominated and more beholden to conventional gender norms. This made it easier for men such as Moscone to mix work with socializing in ways that would not be tolerated, at least in Democratic Party circles, today and, naturally, provided more opportunities for infidelity. However, Moscone's philandering, at least according to many who knew him, went well beyond what could possibly pass as typical for a busy politician of his era. For example, Leo McCarthy, another Catholic San Francisco politician and St. Ignatius graduate of Moscone's generation, spent decades in politics, primarily in Sacramento, and was never involved in the kind of rumors and stories that surrounded Moscone.

Moscone's philandering is not widely documented, but those who knew him well or even who lived in San Francisco and paid attention to politics during Moscone's career speak about this as if it was something everybody knew. One political figure asked to speak to me without attribution before stating simply that Moscone was "a philanderer." Another made a similar request to speak without attribution and recounted an odd but humorous anecdote about Moscone and a woman other than Gina. The people who told me these stories said that Moscone was not a sexual predator but was a charming and very handsome man at a time when political and social mores were different than they are today.

This may be true in some respects, but it is also not the entire story. It is too easy to dismiss Moscone as simply a product of his time. There is no real reason to think any of his infidelities were not consensual, but we now know that when it comes to consent, things are not always what they seem. It is almost impossible, and certainly extremely difficult, to really know what the few female staff people at the San Francisco Board of Supervisors felt about working with Moscone in the mid-1960s, or how women who played similar roles in the state senate a few years later felt. A male politician who behaved today the way Moscone, Brown, and so many others did then would very likely find his career threatened by accusations of sexual harassment.

Moscone's career occurred before everybody had a video camera in their back pocket or handbag. There are no known videos of Moscone drinking in bars in San Francisco or Sacramento, carousing with Willie Brown and women other than Gina, or anything like that. Today that would be different. This leaves us with little other than rumors, stories, and anecdotes that have been passed down, sometimes in a tone of admiration, over the years. Moscone was a successful politician and while the time he spent socializing may have helped create an image of him as charming and accessible, it also very likely created problems. Liaisons had to be arranged and concealed; excuses had to be offered to family;

and stories had to be kept out of the media. This required time and effort from both the politician and his staff.

Regardless of Moscone's infidelities, Gina was one of the two most significant women in Moscone's life. The other was his mother, Lena. Moscone's mother was periodically profiled and quoted throughout her son's political career. Moreover, having been raised by a hard-working single mother was a central part of Moscone's political story. Anybody who followed politics closely during Moscone's fifteen-year career as an elected official would have known the basic outlines of Moscone's childhood and his relationship with his mother.

Moscone's father was a different story. Moscone rarely discussed him. His closest associates rarely knew anything definitive about Moscone's father. Even Moscone's own children have only the vaguest recollections of their paternal grandfather. To the extent the senior Moscone was part of his son's political profile, it was through his absence. Moscone's father died when Moscone was finishing law school at Hastings. In a 1976 interview, Moscone told a reporter of the impact his father's death more than twenty years earlier had on him: "Just about the worst thing that ever happened to me personally was, oh, I suppose, the death of my father. . . . I was in my last year of law school. I was 24. . . . My mother and father had been separated since I was a kid. It was that problem. He was an alcoholic." Moscone went on to describe his father as "very handsome—like Errol Flynn, just like a twin. He was smart. He was able. That fact that even he couldn't kick that habit still troubles me so much."[16]

The beginning of Moscone's comment suggests he was responding to a question asking him what the worst thing that ever happened to him had been. That explains the "oh, I suppose" frame for his answer, but nonetheless Moscone identified the death of his father as the worst thing that happened to him. Another way to understand this answer is as an implicit recognition of the extraordinary good fortune that, at the time of the interview, Moscone enjoyed. He gave this interview a few days before becoming San Francisco's new mayor and a few weeks after his forty-sixth birthday. He had an extremely successful career in politics, was married with four healthy children and his mother, who was getting older, still had her health. None of that makes losing a father, even one he barely knew, any easier, but Moscone's "oh, I suppose" suggests an awareness of this.

Because Moscone spoke so rarely about his father, this comment is significant. What Moscone told the reporter about his father did not include what he did for a living, where he lived, whether he ever remarried, or much about his personality, just that he was an alcoholic who was very smart and very handsome. Although Moscone was not an alcoholic, he was no teetotaler. Like his father, Moscone was also very smart and handsome. But Moscone's life, because of a few good breaks, hard work, and a healthier relationship with alcohol, took a very different course.

Absent fathers can still play a big role in the lives of their children. Moscone rarely spoke of his father and unlike another successful politician who was the son of an absent father, Barack Obama, did not write memoirs or essays about his childhood or family. Instead, we have comments that suggest sadness and compassion, not anger and hostility. Moscone probably felt all these things about his father, but he chose to present the father who had not been around and had not provided for the young Moscone in a very sympathetic light.

Like Obama, Moscone shared a name with the father who died while Moscone was finishing law school at Hastings. However, Moscone's middle name was Richard, while his father's middle initial was S. In some of the press coverage of Moscone in the senate, he is identified as George S. Moscone, instead of George R. Moscone. Reporters who wrote this would not have encountered Moscone's father, so they would have gotten this information from Moscone or his office. Moscone's father, while physically absent for most of Moscone's life, was never entirely out of his son's consciousness. Even this question of middle names is murky because in Moscone's parents wedding announcement, the senior Moscone was identified as George J. Moscone.

After Hastings

On November 7, 1956, the *San Francisco Chronicle* had a huge above-the-fold headline in all capital letters, "IKE LANDSLIDE."[17] President Dwight Eisenhower had been reelected with 57 percent of the vote, which translated into an Electoral College margin of 457–73. Ike carried California and its thirty-two electoral votes with 55 percent of the vote. In San Francisco, the margin was even closer as Eisenhower only outpolled Democratic nominee Adlai Stevenson by about 12,000 of the roughly 335,000 votes cast. San Francisco was becoming more liberal than the rest of the country but was still essentially a politically moderate city. Eisenhower won big almost everywhere, including in many big cities. Even in New York City, Stevenson's margin of victory was less than two percentage points.[18]

On the top of page two of that newspaper was a smaller article featuring the headline, "Legislature: Burton Leads Maloney, Busterud Wins."[19] For George Moscone, who had graduated from Hastings just a few months earlier, that assembly race would change his life. While an undergraduate as San Francisco State, Moscone's friend Willie Brown had become friends with a fellow student John Burton who also went on to briefly attend law school at Hastings before transferring to USF and finishing his law degree there. Burton and Moscone had been friendly for years. More than sixty-five years later, Burton told me about first meeting Moscone in high school: "George was a senior. I was a freshman. George had, just the night before or something, they won the city (basketball) championship. Him and some guys were out all night screwing around. I was over at Lowell High School with a friend of mine, and then George came in with a with a guy I knew, Cappy Lavin, who was probably George's best friend. . . . George was like a real important guy, and I was just a fucking freshman. . . . When I was fucking around, George asked Cappy, 'Who the hell's that guy?'"[20]

Burton was three years younger than Moscone, and in his own words, "just a fucking freshman." Additionally, Burton was a student at his local public high school, Lincoln High School, while Moscone was the star basketball player at one of the city's two most prestigious high schools—the other was Lowell—but Moscone still befriended Burton.[21] Another young man might have shunned the younger boy from a more modest background than many of Moscone's St. Ignatius classmates, but Moscone came from an even more humble background and treated Burton nicely.

John Burton was the younger brother of Phillip Burton, whose impact on the politics of San Francisco was massive. Agar Jaicks, a well-known San Francisco Democratic Party activist and leader for more than half a century, described meeting Phil Burton early in the latter's career, probably about 1953: "There was a guy, rough-talking sort of guy, by the name of Phil Burton. It became very clear to me that he was somebody who was pushing for the left in the Democratic Party. . . . He was not a terribly pleasant guy to be around. But anyway, he was somebody that was doing something, so I became aware of him."

Phil Burton was thirty, only a few years older than Moscone, when he was first elected to the state assembly in 1956. Phil and John Burton, along with Willie Brown and Moscone, would be at the nucleus of progressive electoral politics in San Francisco for the rest of Moscone's life. After Moscone died, the remaining three would continue to be powerful figures in the Democratic Party. Phil Burton died in 1983, but Brown and John Burton remained very influential in the party for decades.

Phil Burton had run for the assembly in 1954 and lost the Democratic primary. The defeat was particularly humbling because Burton was trounced by a two-to-one margin by Cliff Berry, who had died a few weeks before the election. Jaicks reflected on this inauspicious start to Burton's political career: "When Phil Burton ran for office the first time around, he lost the election, lost to a dead man. His (opposing) candidate died. It was kind of the laughingstock of the whole political arena. He ran against this guy and even in death the man beat Phil."[22]

Burton sought an assembly seat in a different district two years later, this time against a living Republican incumbent, Tommy Maloney. Jaicks described how after losing in 1954, and in preparation for the 1956 race, "Phil had to step back for a while and build his base a little more. . . . It was the first time that he ran successfully for the state assembly. And then from that point forward, I don't think he ever lost an election."[23] According to Burton's biographer John Jacobs, "San Francisco was undergoing a demographic sea change. Burton was the first politician with the imagination and intelligence to understand it, seize it and give it voice. He ignited these disparate, often at-odds groups, creating constituencies, coalitions and a significant power base that had never before existed. . . . Burton could call on hundreds of issue-oriented white liberals. . . . To Burton and his zealous supporters, this was not just an election, but the triumph of good over evil."[24]

Maloney, although a Republican, was also running for the Democratic nomination. Burton secured the Democratic nomination by beating Maloney and a third candidate, Achille Muschi, in the primary. After a contentious and competitive general election campaign, Burton won with 17,807 votes to 17,148 for Maloney.[25] Burton's manager in that campaign was a young political operative, Rudy Nothenberg, who later went on to be a senior staff person and city official for Brown, Moscone and Dianne Feinstein. Although Moscone was friends with John Burton by the mid-1950s, he was not involved in the older Burton's first successful campaign.

Phil Burton served four terms in the California State Assembly and almost twenty years in the US House of Representatives. John Burton had two stints of about nine years each in the state legislature, first the assembly and later the senate. Between those stints he served almost nine years in the US House of Representatives. Almost a decade after leaving the state legislature, John Burton became chair of the California Democratic Party from 2009 to 2017.

In addition to their years in elected office, the two brothers, with Phil taking the leading role, built an extraordinary political organization with little precedent in American politics. The Burton machine as some called it, was not a conventional urban political machine because it was not based directly on patronage—for example, like the Daley machine in Chicago or the Tammany machine in New York. Instead, the Burton machine was built on politics. Through a network of political favors including fundraising, political dealmaking, smart campaigns, and drawing helpful district lines, the Burtons helped elect numerous politicians who, in turn, made the Burtons stronger.

Phil Burton, as Brown explained, remade San Francisco politics:

> You did not get directly elected to office in San Francisco, you got first appointed to the board of supervisors and then you got reelected, after you had been appointed. There was heavy-duty control by the Irish community, in particular, on the politics of San Francisco. All that began to unravel, though, when this, brazen radical misfit named Phil Burton came along and started challenging each of those entities whenever it was appropriate and convenient. And he began to put together the

> coalition, that, frankly, has led to all of our success or contributed substantially to all of our success.[26]

John Burton provided more detail:

> Phillip, first time he ran, he lost to a dead man. Second time he ran, he beat a guy that nobody should have been able to beat. He wrangled the votes. He showed up. . . . He organized Chinese clubs in my own neighborhood. He had a Slovenian club. He had a Croatian club. He had, maybe, a Caribbean club, and they had the first Chinese Democratic club, and they had Democratic clubs all over the city. And Phillip was the guy who . . . was the leader. . . . I hate the term but, when, all of the sudden, they called it the Burton-Brown machine. I was plucked, plucked up by Phillip and so was Willie. . . . It wasn't a machine. You couldn't give a guy two fucking jobs.[27]

Phil Burton drank and smoked too much, rarely exercised or, according to people who knew him, rarely thought much about anything other than politics. Jaicks summed up Phil's passion for politics: "A few people said that the loneliest day of the year for Phil was Christmas because he couldn't get on the phone and call people and talk politics with them. Phil lived, breathed, and read about politics. . . . In some ways it appeared there was nothing else in his life."[28]

The Burton operation has been extraordinarily enduring. John Burton has been more or less retired from politics since 2017. Phil died in 1983 when he was only fifty-six years old. The Burton operation was at its height from about 1964 to shortly after Phil's death. However, there are still several influential national and local politicians who can trace their political roots directly to the Burton organization.

When Phil Burton died, his wife, Sala, a Poland-born Jew whose family came to the US fleeing the Nazis in 1939, took his seat in the US Congress. Unfortunately, Sala Burton was soon diagnosed with colon cancer. When she was dying, she indicated that her choice to succeed her in Congress was a longtime party activist and fundraiser who had never sought elected office. With the support of the Burton operation Nancy Pelosi went on win a special election against Harry Britt, a member of the San Francisco Board of Supervisors, who had initially been appointed to the board by Mayor Feinstein to fill the Harvey Milk's seat. Milk had indicated that if he were killed, he wanted Britt to replace him. With that victory, Pelosi began a career in Congress that would include serving as Speaker of the House twice, becoming one of the most influential and skilled Speakers in American history. Pelosi did that in part by applying the lessons she learned both from her work with the Burtons as well as from growing up as the daughter of Baltimore Mayor Thomas D'Alesandro Jr.

When Alan Cranston, a liberal Democrat who had represented California in the US Senate since 1969, retired in 1992, he was replaced by Barbara Boxer, whom the Burtons had previously helped. Boxer described the role the Burtons played in her first run for Congress in 1982: "John Burton had been one of my mentors, and I worked for him when he was in Congress and he had helped me my whole career. . . . Out of the blue he calls me and says he's addicted to drugs and alcohol, and he's checking into a rehab facility in Arizona, and would I consider running for his seat. . . . He wanted me there. . . . His brother then called . . . . Phil was so powerful in California at the time. . . . He said, 'I don't want you to worry about it (the money). That I'm gonna do.'"[29]

Boxer served four terms in the Senate, but the Burtons' influence continued beyond Boxer's retirement. In 1996, when Brown was mayor of San Francisco, a vacancy opened up on the board of supervisors. Brown filled that vacancy by appointing a young Gavin Newsom, who went on to become mayor and later governor of California.

Shortly after Brown won the election to become mayor of San Francisco in 1995, Herb Caen, who had been chronicling Brown's political and personal life for decades, reported "'It's all over.' With those words, Mayor-elect Brown let word get around over the weekend that his long affair with Kamala Harris, an Alameda County asst. district attorney, has ended. This news came as a shock to many, including those who found Kamala Harris attractive, intelligent and charming."[30] Harris, whose relationship with Brown was political as well as romantic, went on to the US Senate in 2016 when Boxer retired and was elected vice president in 2020 and was the Democratic nominee for President in 2024. In 2021, almost forty years after Phil Burton's death, two of the most powerful politicians in the country were clear, if indirect, beneficiaries, of the political operation he started in the late 1950s.

Phil Burton's election to the assembly in 1956 was the first electoral rumblings of the political changes that dramatically altered the city in the second half of the twentieth century. John Burton recognized the significance of this, but he gave the credit to his late brother: "If it wasn't for Phillip Burton there would be no George Moscone. There would be no John Burton. There would be no Willie Brown. And without me there would be no Fiona Ma; wouldn't have been no Barbara Boxer. Everything came from Phillip. He's a political genius. Well, they tried to run against the Burton machine . . . and we kicked their ass."[31]

The year before Burton won his assembly seat, San Franciscans had elected a Republican, George Christopher, as mayor. Christopher would serve two terms and govern, much like most of his predecessors and his immediate successors, with a pro-business, pro-development perspective. San Francisco's congressional delegation that was elected in 1956 included one Democrat, Jack Shelley, and one Republican, William Mailliard. There was little in those election outcomes to suggest that anything was changing, but something was. Phil Burton would be at the center of those changes until his death in 1983.

At the time Burton was elected to the assembly, Moscone was beginning to practice law. He and another Hastings graduate Charles O. Morgan, class of 1949, formed the firm Morgan and Moscone. Morgan was about eight years Moscone's senior. Like Moscone, Morgan had been a star athlete, but his sport was football. Morgan had been the quarterback at Lowell and then played at UCLA. Morgan was not the big star on that team. The best player for UCLA when Morgan was there was a punt returner and safety who on offense "led UCLA in rushing, passing, total offense, scoring, and punt returns," during 1940, his senior year."[32] Morgan's star teammate, like many of his generation, served in the military during World War II, but when the war ended, he never played football professionally. Instead, Jackie Robinson became the first African American to play Major League Baseball since the 1880s and earned a place as one of the great heroes of the civil rights struggle.

After college, Morgan spent World War II "with the 485th Bomb Group of the Army Air Force, eventually earning the rank of captain. As a navigator, Mr. Morgan flew 63 missions in the European Theatre and was awarded the Distinguished Flying Cross, the Air Medal [with 3 Oak Leaf Clusters], and a Presidential Unit Citation. The Distinguished Flying Cross was awarded when the B-24 Mr. Morgan was on returned to its home field successfully despite receiving 220 flak holes."[33]

The law firm of Morgan and Moscone was an excellent opportunity for a recent Hastings graduate such as Moscone. Morgan was a good lawyer with the kind of résumé that brought him contacts throughout the legal and political establishment of San Francisco. Much of the middle class that was so rapidly growing in the 1950s consisted of men such as the young Moscone. Overwhelmingly white and frequently a generation or two removed from their family's arrival in the US, these men were able to take advantage of the strong economy, the GI Bill, and expanding educational opportunities to become, like Moscone, the first person in their family to go to college and become a professional.

Moscone began his legal career as a young married man who was about to become a father, but he retained a strong connection to the pillars of his early life. He was still close to his mother and had chosen to attend at law school at Hastings and begin practicing law in his hometown. Moscone also continued to play basketball.

Joe Cotchett, a prominent San Francisco attorney of Moscone's generation, described his first meeting with Moscone:

> I met George at the San Francisco Young Democrats. I think it was the California Club on Polk Street. I played basketball. He played basketball.

> And he was an up-and-coming guy, young lawyer. . . . On the basketball court, I was used to throwing elbows because I came off the streets of Brooklyn. George was not an elbow thrower. He was a real ballplayer. . . . I was very impressed with the fact that this guy was a real ballplayer and I used to muscle him, and he didn't play that way. He was not a muscle guy. He was a mind guy . . . George was a true ballplayer. John Burton was a schlock. I was a schlock.[34]

Cotchett also described Moscone's off-the-court demeanor when they first met. "Well, it was clear to me . . . he had the biggest heart in the world. . . . He was the most sincere guy you've ever met. What you saw is what you got; what he said is what he meant. And he was a hell of a ballplayer and a good-looking guy too. That combination was devastating."[35]

As a graduate of Hastings and St. Ignatius, he probably could have found a good job with a more prestigious and higher-paying law firm, but that did not seem to be what the new law school graduate wanted. Moscone began to practice a different kind of law that was more grounded in the community and seeking to help people. Cotchett described this: "He (Moscone) had a real front-door storefront legal aid office. . . . George Moscone wanted to represent people. George, I don't think ever got paid by a client that I know of because he was always borrowing five or ten bucks from me."[36]

John Vlahos, another San Francisco attorney for many decades who worked with Moscone at the law firm Hanson Bridgett in the 1960s, described Moscone's style as an attorney:

> George as a lawyer had the same characteristics that he did as a politician or government official, in that he was very ambitious, very smart. He wasn't what I would call an intellectual lawyer, the kind that would be writing great briefs that go to the Supreme Court, but he was one that had a lot of savvy, a lot of sort of street savvy about litigation. . . . Although he had the persona of being the handsome athletic sort of fellow . . . really could be impressive 'cause he drove right to the point. . . . George was really good about getting to the heart of it. You could see this guy knows what he's doing.[37]

By the end of the 1950s, Moscone had begun to establish himself, not as a powerful, or even aspiring, politician. Rather, he was evolving into a conventional family man and young attorney. He had graduated from Hastings Law School, gotten married, and begun to have a family. Like millions of others in postwar America, he was already achieving professional success greater than anything his parents had achieved, but from a political perspective, Moscone's work had not yet begun.

CHAPTER FIVE

First Campaigns

By 1960 George Moscone had been practicing law for about three years. The Moscone family, which already included two daughters, Jenifer and Rebecca, was still living in the Cow Hollow neighborhood, at 2735 Gough Street between Union and Filbert, not far from where Moscone had lived as a child and only a few blocks from St. Brigid. Moscone, who had turned thirty during November 1959, was also becoming increasingly interested in politics. There are, and have been, many smart young people thinking about a career in politics, but very few had a good friend who was the younger brother of one of the best political minds of their generation. According to John Burton, it was sometime in 1959 or 1960, when Moscone was spending weekends working at a playground in the Sunset District when the two first discussed politics:

> He (Moscone) was working Sunday at the playground called J. P. Murphy. I went down, just came down, to the playground to shoot some hoops. He had been, I think, in law school, and he asked me, "How do you decide the law? How does a guy get to be a judge?" I said, "I don't know. I'll ask my brother Phillip." So, Phillip, George Moscone, and I met at the cafeteria at the corner of Van Ness and Market. . . . George asked a few questions, then Phillip started asking George, where he was . . . . "Where are you on civil rights? What you'd think of the death penalty? What'd you think of this? What'd you think of that? . . . What'd you think of all of those?" . . . In as far as I knew, George never had a political opinion in his life 'cause we didn't talk about that shit. You talked about basketball. You talked about broads. You talk about other stuff. And then he started answering all the questions . . . Phillip kind of talked him into running for a state assembly seat. It was a Republican seat. He wasn't gonna win, but it will allow him to be a member of

> the county central committee and get three appointments to the state central committee—which was what my brother was more interested in than George's political career. . . . And, so, he ran in that race, but he was attractive guy, attractive candidate."[1]

That meeting occurred in late 1959 or early 1960. Although Phil Burton was serving his second term in the assembly, Moscone had not been interested enough in politics to become involved with any of Phil Burton's campaigns. Similarly, John Burton, who by the late 1950s was a good friend of Moscone, was sufficiently unaware of Moscone's interest in politics that he had not made the introduction between Moscone and Phil Burton earlier.

John Burton's retelling of a discussion that occurred sixty years previously between two men who had been dead for years reflects a couple of truths. While it was certainly the case that having an idle conversation about becoming a judge, which led to a sit-down meeting with Phil Burton, was a good break for Moscone, it is also true that the older Burton brother used that meeting to get a feel for Moscone before determining he would be a good political ally.

Phil Burton would have quickly recognized that the young lawyer would be an extremely appealing candidate for office. Moscone was charming and handsome and had an attractive young wife and a growing family. Black-and-white photos of Moscone from the late 1950s and early 1960s show a smiling and confident face under a full, but closely cut, head of dark brown hair. The former basketball star still had the tall and slender build of most basketball players of the era. For Phil Burton, who was not a native San Franciscan, Moscone's San Francisco story would also have been understood as a major political asset. The humble background, success at the city's top Catholic high school, and fame and stardom on the basketball court made Moscone the perfect political fit for his hometown. It didn't hurt that he was Italian American. Moscone was not just a good-looking young man with the right background and demographic profile. He had the progressive views and instincts that the Burtons valued, as demonstrated by his answers on the death penalty and civil rights, important issues among progressives in the late 1950s and early 1960s.

David Nelson, a longtime reporter for the *San Francisco Chronicle,* described how Phil Burton became interested in Moscone: "I think Phil recognized George as a smart guy that believed in a lot of the same things he did, that he (Moscone) had a future in San Francisco and that he (Burton) would help him if he could." Nelson added that Burton and Moscone understood who had more power in the relationship, at least for the first years. "But, don't push me. I'm still Phil Burton. And George always respected that."[2] Jon Rubin, who was Moscone's field director in 1975, explained, "John and Phil nurtured George. Brought him up . . . both winning and losing. . . . I think he paid a lot of dues. He walked a lot of precincts. . . . George understood retail politics well and Phil understood that George was a viable team player."[3]

Agar Jaicks commented, "George Moscone was a personal friend of John Burton's. They were buddies, I guess, in school. So, George Moscone became a major component to Phil Burton's efforts, but always in the sense that he was indebted to Phil, and he was, to all the efforts to get him to where he eventually went. But, I don't think George had any complaints about that. He was ideologically aligned with Phil. They were all in the same boat together."[4]

Running for the Assembly

As the 1960 election approached, Moscone decided to follow Burton's advice and run for the state assembly in the Twenty-First District. The district was in the northern part of the city, bound by Mason to the east, Geary and California to the south, the bay to the north and the ocean to the west. The district included the Cow Hollow and Marina neighborhoods, where Moscone had grown up, as well as Pacific Heights and the Richmond District. On March 29, 1960, a small article appeared on page eight of the *San Francisco Examiner* announcing that "George R. Moscone, 30 year old San Francisco lawyer, yesterday filed a declaration of candidate for the State Assembly." The article quoted Moscone, "I tend to run on a liberal Democratic platform and, if elected, to be a supporter of the Brown administration."[5] Moscone was seeking to unseat Milton Marks, a Republican serving his first term in the assembly. Before going up against Marks, Moscone faced Edward Blaine in a primary.

With help from the Burtons, Moscone assembled the coalition needed to defeat Blaine. This began with support from the California Democratic Council, a movement of liberal Democratic activists. The California Democratic Council had clubs throughout the state and sought to push the party left. Alan Cranston, who later served four terms in the US Senate, became the first president of the council in 1952. Moscone also won the support of the San Francisco Labor Council and the Chinese American Democratic Club.

Joe Cotchett, who worked on political projects with both Moscone and the Burtons, offered a view of the Democratic Party when Moscone ran his first race: "The Burtons were in the thick of it. Of course, Phil was the guy we looked up to. . . . Well, there were various functions. You had the Irish Democrats, you had Phil Burton's group, you had conservative Democrats, out in the Richmond and the Sunset. So, you had various different factions in the Democratic Party. . . . Then you had Phil, George Moscone, and others. You had a bunch of Italian Democrats who thought that George was a whacked-out liberal."[6]

As Cotchett indicated, the Democratic Party in the late 1950s and early 1960s was very different, nationally and in California, than it has been during this century. During the twenty years or so following World War II, the two major political parties were much more similar ideologically than they have been in the last fifty, and particularly thirty or so, years. After the war, there was a bipartisan consensus around foreign policy and the basic framework of the Cold War. On domestic issues, the Republican opposition to Franklin Roosevelt's New Deal gave way to more agreement about the role of government.

Between 1933 and 1968, there was only one Republican president, Dwight Eisenhower. Eisenhower was a revered war hero who had been courted by both parties as the 1952 election approached. Under President Eisenhower, the marginal tax rate on the wealthiest Americans reached 91 percent. Today any president, Democrat or Republican, who proposed a marginal tax rate on the richest Americans even half of that would be called a communist by the Republicans. Additionally, Eisenhower, to a great extent, continued the spending patterns of his Democratic predecessors, presidents Truman and Roosevelt, most notably through the interstate freeway system.

In those postwar years many of the most important issues facing the country, such as civil rights, created more divisions within rather than between the parties. In the 1960 presidential election, for example, both candidates, John F. Kennedy and Richard Nixon, courted the African American vote in the North—in the South, few African Americans could vote—while seeking civil rights platforms that would not upset those white voters who were less enthused about racial equality. President Johnson passed the Civil Rights Act of 1964 with majorities from parties in both houses of Congress. However, in both houses a higher percentage of Republicans than Democrats voted for the bill because there were many southern segregationists who were still Democrats.

Even the rights of unions and organized labor were not entirely partisan issues. Republicans from the industrial Midwest tended to be more pro-labor than southern Democrats. During these years, the Democratic Party was, on balance, to the left of the GOP, but it was not in general a progressive party. At the national level, liberals led by people such as Adlai Stevenson, who lost presidential elections to Eisenhower in 1952 and 1956, struggled for control of the Democratic Party against a conservative faction led by southern Democrats such as Richard Russell of Georgia. Similarly, the Republican Party was not a cohesive conservative party.

In California beginning in the early and mid-1950s, the Burtons, Cranston, and the California Democratic Council were working to make the Democratic Party reflect the liberal values of the New Deal era and the nascent civil rights movement. In cities such as San Francisco and New York, these ideological issues intersected with reform dynamics, generational change, and stirrings of racial diversity within the party. Attractive young candidates such as George Moscone and a few years later Willie Brown were central parts of this strategy in San Francisco.

In the assembly primary in 1960, Moscone drubbed Blaine 10,089 votes to 2,879. Moscone spent $1,339.79, about $11,700 in 2020 dollars.[7] Moscone then turned his attention to the Republican incumbent. [8] A liberal Republican, the forty-year-old Milton Marks was a bit older than Moscone. He was the grandson of German and English Jewish immigrants who arrived in San Francisco in the mid-nineteenth century. Like many German Jewish San Franciscans of that era, Marks was secular and highly assimilated. He belonged to Temple Emanu-El, San Francisco's most prestigious reform synagogue. Marks had been his class valedictorian at Galileo High School, the same school that Moscone would have attended if he had gone to the neighborhood public school rather than St. Ignatius. After graduation, Marks went to Stanford for a bachelor of arts degree and then to San Francisco Law School.[9] World War II interrupted his law school education at UC Berkeley, as Marks served in the army and saw combat in the Pacific.

As a liberal Republican with strong San Francisco roots, Marks was a tough opponent for Moscone. That is why Phil Burton had urged Moscone to challenge Marks, but he also cautioned the ambitious young lawyer that he probably wouldn't win. Marks's recollection of that race suggested he was not particularly concerned about losing to Moscone, whom Marks viewed as a foot soldier in the Burton political operation. "Phil Burton, I think, put him (Moscone) in the campaign. He was a young lawyer in the Marina somewhere, and he decided he was going to build him up, and he tried to build him up to run against me."[10]

Marks had a very long career in California politics, serving in the state legislature from 1958 to 1996. From 1967 to 1975 Marks and Moscone were San Francisco's two representatives in the California State Senate. During those years, despite their different parties, they were frequently on the same side of proposed legislation. Marks ran for mayor in 1975, finishing a dismal fifth out of five major candidates. He challenged Phil Burton for Congress in 1982 but again lost badly. Six years after that, Marks switched parties and continued winning elections to the state senate as a Democrat. When Marks finally retired from politics at age seventy-six after being term-limited out of the state senate in 1996, he was replaced in that legislature by none other than John Burton. Marks earned the nickname "Uncle Miltie" because "in an age of electronics and sophisticated polling, Marks was a throwback. He believed in the personal touch. A master of old-fashioned, press-the-flesh politics, Marks seemed to be everywhere, hand outstretched, always campaigning. For more than three decades, he was a constant presence at innumerable weddings, birthdays, baptisms, bar mitzvahs, parades, book signings, testimonials, retirement parties, ribbon cuttings, ground breakings, banquets, fund raisers, funerals and public gatherings of every stripe."[11]

A challenge to Marks, who was well-liked, smart, and a good politician, from a relatively unknown attorney did not generate much media attention. The local papers barely covered the race other than an occasional mention that Moscone was the Democrat running against Marks. The most extensive campaign coverage in the *Chronicle* was a description of a Republican gala in the San Francisco Civic Auditorium where "Assemblyman Milton Marks, another respected young legislator went by in a rickshaw. He was wearing a business suit and a slightly self-conscious look. 'Some people said I should be in costume and some said I shouldn't,' he said. 'I think the rickshaw's enough.'"[12]

The presidential election of 1960 was extremely close, even in California, which was then the second-largest electoral college prize. Richard Nixon, the sitting vice president and former senator from California, carried his home state against John F. Kennedy, by only half a percent, or fewer than 39,000 votes. However, in San Francisco, the Democrat Kennedy easily beat the Republican Nixon by 57.8 percent to 41.8 percent.[13] Moscone sought to connect his candidacy to that of the young Democratic presidential nominee. One of his campaign pieces was a card with the two politicians shaking hands under the slogan "Vote for John F. Kennedy and George Moscone, Two Great Democrats." The photo did not flatter either politician. Moscone looks overly earnest and concerned while Kennedy appears uninterested and almost in pain.[14] Six days before the election, the *Chronicle* endorsed Nixon for president and Marks for the Twenty-First District.[15] Marks ended up defeating Moscone. The *Chronicle* described Mark's margin relative to other incumbents who got reelected as "narrower but comfortable," but Mark's victory was more comfortable than narrow. Marks got 29,405 votes to Moscone's 20,959.[16]

Because Moscone's loss to Marks was expected, it did not have a very negative impact on Moscone's political career or future. However, Moscone, and certainly Phil Burton, understood that today's young up-and-coming political star is only a few bad elections away from being yesterday's news, so Moscone had to pick his next electoral battle very carefully to avoid being seen as a two-time loser. This contributed to his wise decision not to run against Marks, who was clearly a formidable opponent, again in 1962.

The 1963 Election in San Francisco

For a young man such as Moscone seeking a career in politics, there were two entry-level electoral positions. The first was the state assembly, the larger of the two houses of the California legislature. Once it became clear that he could not defeat Marks, Moscone's only option to get elected to that body would have been to move to a neighboring district and challenge another incumbent. Of the six assembly districts in San Francisco in the early 1960s, four were held by Democrats. Defeating an incumbent Democrat in a primary would have been very difficult, while moving to another district to run against a popular Republican such as John Busterud would have been equally risky, so Moscone turned his attention to the board of supervisors.

Because the city and county of San Francisco are coterminous, the city legislature and county legislature are the same and known as the board of supervisors. In 1962 the board, which was formally nonpartisan, had seven Democrats and four Republicans—all were white, and ten were men. The dominance of white men, and the presence of four Republicans on the board in a Democratic city reflected the heavily white population of San Francisco at the time. It also reflected the advantage that well-financed and business-supported candidates had in the at-large election system.[17]

Moscone, despite having run once for the assembly, was not well known. But he had the makings of a winning citywide candidate. After losing his 1960 election, he had remained active, continued to build relationships in the Democratic Party and could count on the Burtons' support. Moscone's background as a prep school basketball star, good looks, and attractive family would be assets as well. Italian Americans were still a big constituency in the early '60s, so that would also help him. Additionally, his Hastings and St. Ignatius pedigree gave Moscone a good network and reputation.

Moscone might have run for the board of supervisors in 1961, but another Burton ally was already running and was the focus of the Burtons' efforts. Jack Morrison, a liberal Democrat and Burton ally, came in second overall in the race for five seats in 1961, receiving 99,645 votes.[18] This victory demonstrated the Burtons' ability to compete citywide and helped lay the groundwork for the Burtons next move as 1963 approached. That year, San Francisco voters would be choosing a new mayor as well as six members of the board of supervisors, creating an opportunity for progressive Democrats, led by the Burtons, to begin to make a mark. Since city elections were held in odd-numbered years, turnout was generally lower than in presidential years or midterm elections when the governor and other statewide candidates were on the ballot. But local elections were the city's major electoral story in those years. The twelve months between November 1963 and November 1964 was when the Burton organization became a major force in San Francisco politics. Moscone was part of, but not the key factor in that series of electoral events that would have a dramatic effect on San Francisco.

When 1963 dawned, President Kennedy was starting his third year in office. Some of the glow of the early years of his presidency had faded, but politically Kennedy was doing fine. The 1962 midterm elections had gone well for the Democratic Party. The president's party usually loses seats in the midterm election, but in 1962 the Republicans only gained four House seats while the Democrats picked up an impressive four Senate seats, so Kennedy continued to have majorities in both houses of Congress.

In the US Senate race in California in 1962, incumbent Thomas Kuchel, a moderate Republican, cruised to an easy reelection, defeating Democratic challenger Richard Richards by thirteen points. Howard Jarvis finished third, garnering fewer than 10,000 of the more than 5.5 million votes cast statewide. Jarvis had lost the Republican primary to Kuchel after challenging the senator from the right, but Jarvis received votes as a write-in candidate in the general election. Jarvis would make an indelible mark on policy and politics in California in the 1970s.

The race for governor was the most closely watched and most important campaign in California in 1962. Democratic incumbent Pat Brown had been elected to his first term in 1958. Some thought he would be the first Catholic president, but Kennedy changed that. Brown should have won reelection relatively easily in 1962, but he found himself running against perhaps California's most popular and best-known Republican politician because Richard Nixon wanted to begin his political comeback. Despite losing the presidential race to Kennedy in 1960, the forty-nine-year-old Nixon calculated he was still young enough to have another shot at the White House. He was also smart enough to know 1964 was not the best time for another presidential campaign.

Instead, Nixon decided to begin his comeback by running for governor. Nixon's thinking was Kennedy would likely be reelected in 1964, so there would be no incumbent in 1968. By that time, Nixon would be fifty-five years old with eight years of experience as vice president, six years in Congress and six years, assuming victories in 1962 and again in 1966, as governor of one of the country's biggest and most important states. That résumé would vault him to the top of the Republican primary field and into the presidency.

Unfortunately for Nixon, the 1962 election did not go quite as he planned. After a tough campaign, Brown won reelection by more than five points and almost 300,000 votes. In San Francisco, the Democratic governor's hometown, Brown clobbered Nixon 180,000 to 107,000. The day after the election, Nixon held a bizarre press conference in which he praised and castigated, mostly the latter, the media. The press conference was supposed to be Nixon's farewell to politics as he famously, and falsely, announced, "You won't have Nixon to kick around anymore, because, gentlemen, this is my last press conference."[19]

In the much less heralded Democratic primary for the assembly's Eighteenth District in San Francisco, Willie Brown challenged longtime Democratic incumbent Ed Gaffney. In the racially diverse district, Gaffney, who was white, managed to hold on to his seat, winning by only 116 votes.[20] Had Brown won, it would have been a big breakthrough for African American San Francisco as well as for the Burtons, who had strongly backed Brown. Helping Brown in this way helped the Burtons with San Francisco's African American voters.

The civil rights revolution was accelerating by 1963. In the summer, Martin

Luther King Jr. would make his most famous speech in front of more than a quarter of a million people in Washington, DC. The Montgomery bus boycott, the US Supreme Court's *Brown v. Board of Education* decision, and numerous other landmark actions over the preceding years had raised national awareness around civil rights and also given rise to a backlash against racial equality. Many hoped to see significant federal civil rights legislation soon, while others wanted to keep the old racial order in place.

The Kennedy administration was trying to figure out how to support civil rights without destroying a Democratic coalition that had relied on strong support from southern racists since the Civil War. The Republicans, for their part, counted among their leaders northerners who supported civil rights, such as New York governor, and early front-runner for the 1964 presidential nomination, Nelson Rockefeller. However, there was also strong opposition to civil rights in the GOP, including from Rockefeller's rival for the 1964 nomination, Barry Goldwater, a senator from Arizona. The most powerful racist forces in 1964 were still southern Democrats, but resistance to civil rights was beginning to move some elements of the GOP in an ugly racist direction.

Thus, there was no civil rights consensus in the overwhelmingly white leadership of the Democratic Party. Voting rights restrictions made it almost impossible for African Americans to vote, let alone be elected, in the South, while in the North there were still very few African American elected officials. In San Francisco there was not a single African American elected official. The police and fire departments were almost entirely white. Nationally only five members of the House of Representatives and no members of the US Senate were African American.

This was the national context in which the Burtons, and progressive San Francisco sought to elect a liberal Democratic mayor in 1963, but Phil Burton had something bigger than that in mind. Jack Shelley was a Democrat who, in 1962, had easily won reelection to his eighth term in Congress representing San Francisco, defeating Republican Roland Charles by a margin of four to one. Shelley was Irish American, had grown up in the Mission District, and attended Mission High School, the local public school. Shelley got his political start in organized labor and was president of the San Francisco Labor Council before serving in Congress. He was a conventional labor-machine Democrat, who voted with his party on most issues.

As 1963 approached, Shelley began to explore a run for mayor. Phil Burton understood the opportunity that development raised for his nascent political operation. Shelley getting elected mayor would open up a seat in Congress. Burton would have a good chance at winning that seat. Once Phil Burton was elected to Congress, that would open an assembly seat for his brother John. Additionally, Willie Brown was preparing for another run at Ed Gaffney with the Burtons' support. Bringing a new member or two onto the board of supervisors in 1963 was a secondary part of the plan.

If 1963 and 1964 went well, by the time the dust settled, the Burton operation would have grown from just one assembly member to a member of Congress, at least one member of the assembly, a supervisor and a mayor who, if not part of the organization, would be at least partially indebted to the Burtons for his election. This act of political jiujitsu would have been challenging under any circumstances, but it was made even more difficult by the ill will between Phil Burton and Shelley stemming in part from Burton aggressively pressuring Shelley to run for mayor despite Shelley having some reluctance. Burton's biographer John Jacobs wrote "despite his public declaration of his candidacy, Shelley was ambivalent. He loved being in Congress and was accumulating seniority on the powerful Appropriations Committee. But Burton called on his labor supporters to pressure Shelley to come home."[21]

One of the reasons labor was doing this to an ally such as Shelley was that Burton, who enjoyed very strong labor support too, had made no secret of his desire to get elected to Congress. Jacobs described the relationship between the Burtons and Shelley as the 1963 mayor's race loomed: "Tension between the two men was palpable, and their relationship was tempestuous. One morning, as they shared a breakfast booth at a 1962 California Democratic Council meeting in Fresno, Shelley began screaming at Burton so loudly that acquaintances nearby began discussing in whispers whether Burton was 'trying to give Shelley a heart attack right now so he can take his seat.'"[22]

Bruce Brugmann, the founder and longtime editor of the influential community newspaper the *Bay Guardian*, summarized how Burton leaned on Shelley to run for mayor: "He (Burton) said to Shelley, 'Look. I'm gonna run against ya. And I'll get beat the first time. And then I'll run again and I'll beat ya, and you'll be out of politics.' So, Jack comes back and runs for mayor."[23]

Shelley and Burton were both Democrats but were not political allies. However, as 1963 approached, it was apparent that Shelley, with a good voting record on many issues, was the best mayoral candidate for liberals such as the Burtons. Other than Shelley, the leading candidate was Supervisor Harold Dobbs, a Republican who was first elected to the board of supervisors in 1951 and had been a well-known business and civic leader for years. Dobbs was Jewish and originally from New Jersey, but he moved to San Diego when he was young and attended high school and college there. He settled in San Francisco in 1939.

Dobbs was co-owner of Mel's Drive-In, a popular diner-style restaurant chain in California later made famous in the film *American Graffiti*. Dobbs was a very able candidate running on a conservative platform that included pledges for more police, a slower pace of civil rights reforms, and a network of underground freeways. Absent a strong Democratic candidate such as Shelley and a unified Democratic Party, the city would likely have four more years of a Republican mayor.

Shelley and the Burtons were not close, but making Shelley mayor was important for the Burtons. Phil's ambition for himself and his brother required Shelley to win the mayor's race and vacate his seat in Congress. Thus, while the Democratic Party in San Francisco was not particularly united, there was a commonality of purpose that brought most of the party together behind Shelley.

Six supervisor positions were also on the ballot in 1963. Incumbents Charles Ertola, John Ferdon, Joseph Casey, Clarissa McMahon, and Max Moore were seeking reelection. Dobbs had reached the end of his third term, but he was running for mayor rather than for a fourth term as supervisor. Moore, like Dobbs a Republican, had never been elected to the board, but was appointed by Mayor Christopher after Supervisor James Halley retired in March 1963, so there was one open seat on the board and one new and relatively vulnerable incumbent.

Moscone was thirty when he ran the first time and would turn thirty-four a few weeks after Election Day of 1963, but if he waited even two more years, he would no longer have that aura of being a young man on the rise. Fortunately for him, the stars were lining up the right way as the Burtons were trying to take their game to the next level. If they were going to work so hard to elect a mayor they didn't really like, it made sense for them to also support another citywide candidate who could be helpful to them and with whom they were already allied.

Moscone was not the only aspiring politician who saw an opportunity in 1963. Two other young San Franciscans sought seats on the board of supervisors. One was Percy Moore (not related to Max Moore), who was hoping to become the first African American elected to the board of supervisors. In addition to Moore and Moscone, Leo McCarthy, Moscone's old teammate from St. Ignatius, got in the race. McCarthy was not a Burton supporter, but the protégé of J. Eugene McAteer, a Democratic state senator. McAteer and McCarthy were both more conservative than the Burtons and their allies. One longtime San Francisco political activist described this dynamic: "In the sixties in SF there were basically two groups. One was the Shelley/Burton camp, which represented more the east side of town, the progressive elements of the white community, and African Americans. It was just a different group from the McAteer crowd, which was sort of a moderate group."[24]

McCarthy recalled how McAteer had explored running for mayor in 1963: "Gene McAteer, at the beginning of 1963, intended to run for mayor of San Francisco. But in the January–February period, he received some phone calls from some very highly placed people, and they persuaded him to change his mind and let Congressman Jack Shelley have a free run at mayor in opposition to then supervisor Harold Dobbs. McAteer was deeply disappointed. A lot of people think he could have been elected. He was held in high esteem by the people of San Francisco at the time."[25]

McAteer indeed wanted to be mayor, but as the election approached, it became clear that, as McCarthy called them "very highly placed people," powerful national Democrats, much more influential than Phil Burton, wanted to see Shelley as mayor. One of these was William Malone, a major California Democratic insider. Malone, who was Irish American and Catholic, wanted Shelley, with whom he not only shared an Irish heritage, but a close political relationship, to be mayor. Malone had other Irish American friends in the Democratic Party. John Jacobs explained in his biography of Phil Burton: "Malone re-emerged in a conspicuous way for Irish-Catholic presidential candidate John Kennedy, raising more than one million dollars for him in 1960. Kennedy and Shelley, moreover, were good friends from their days in the House. . . . With the kind of access a million dollars can produce, he (Malone) called the White House and asked Kennedy to intervene on behalf of their mutual good friend Jack Shelley. Unless McAteer could be persuaded to drop out, he and Shelley—two like-minded Democrats—would split the vote, and . . . Harold Dobbs could win. . . . A Dobbs victory could make it harder for Kennedy to capture California in 1964. Kennedy or somebody speaking for him made the phone call. McAteer reluctantly agreed to step aside."[26] Until 1975, the race for mayor was a first past the post system where whoever got the most votes in the first round would win. Thus, there was the real potential for Shelley and McAteer, if they both ran, to make Dobbs the mayor.

With four strong incumbents, Ertola, Ferdon, McMahon, and Casey, who were almost shoo-ins for reelection, one weaker incumbent (Max Moore), and one vacant seat, the race for the final two seats was between McCarthy, Percy Moore, Max Moore, Moscone, and two other challengers, Alan Nichols and Alessandro Baccari. There are also several other minor candidates, but none had much of a chance. Because all candidates were running citywide, they had to appeal to many different neighborhoods, ethnic groups, and other interests to win. Each of the major nonincumbent candidates had some base of support. McCarthy, as a more moderate Democrat, was strong in the western part of the city, including the Sunset, Richmond, and adjoining areas. Percy Moore had a natural base in the heavily African American neighborhoods of the Fillmore and Bayview/Hunters Point. Because Moscone had previously run for the assembly, he had some recognition in that district.

One of the challenges that has confronted African Americans in San Francisco politics has been that the two largest African American neighborhoods are geographically distant from each other. The Fillmore is in the geographical center of the city, a short bus ride or drive from downtown and within easy walking distance of Golden Gate Park, the Haight-Ashbury, Pacific Heights, Japantown, and other central San Francisco communities and landmarks. Bayview/Hunters Point is in the southeast corner of the city, far from much of the rest of San Francisco because it is cordoned off by Highway 280. It is reasonably close to other outlying areas such as Potrero Hill and Bernal Heights, but it is far from the Fillmore. This has made it very difficult to draw even one supervisorial district with a clear African American majority.

The wonderful 2019 film *The Last Black Man in San Francisco* beautifully and subtly captures this. Viewers not familiar with San Francisco may wonder why the two main characters, Jimmie and Mont, ride the bus so much. The answer is that anybody, African American or not, who had reason to spend part of the day in the Fillmore, where the home that Jimmie hopes to own is located, and part of the day in Hunters Point, where Jimmie and Mont live with Mont's grandfather, would spend a lot of time driving across the city, or if they did not have enough money for a car, riding the bus. It is not at all unusual for an African American, particularly one with deep roots in the city, to have family, business, or social connections in both of these mutually distant neighborhoods.

Moscone's base was not as clear as McCarthy's or Percy Moore's. Moscone was a liberal with a commitment to civil rights. However, although there is no data on this from that time, it is almost certain that in early 1963 among African Americans Moscone was less well known than Moore, who was from Hunters Point. Moscone's potential base lay in the labor movement because of his pro-labor positions and relationship with the Burtons. Agar Jaicks summed up Phil Burton's relationship with organized labor in the city: "The assets Phil Burton brought to it were mostly labor. If he endorsed you, then labor would endorse you."[27]

Moscone's relationship with the Burtons, by 1963, went well beyond Phil Burton's ability to deliver organized labor. John Burton was arrested on charges of being a bookmaker and illegal gambling in April 1962. Burton needed a good lawyer and turned to Moscone.[28] Moscone argued in court that Burton had indeed bet on the horse race in question, but he had made the bet after the race was run. "Burton's attorney, George Moscone, made the point that betting on a race that already had been run was not gambling and therefore his client could not be guilty of accepting a bet."[29]

Moscone may not have had a strong base of support, but he was broadly acceptable, even broadly appealing. Moscone was essentially a liberal in a conservative's body. An Italian American family man who was a star athlete at St. Ignatius was not the profile of other progressive San Francisco politicians of the era. Moscone was able to use his identity to assuage conservative concerns while using his record and positions to appeal to progressives, African Americans and others.

Politicians who have the opposite profile, centrist or conservative views and a liberal demographic profile, can also leverage that with the right political skills. While Moscone was preparing to run for supervisor, another San Franciscan was serving on the Women's Parole Board for the state, having been appointed by Governor Pat Brown in 1960. Like Moscone, Dianne Feinstein was just beginning her political career. She was a Jewish woman from San Francisco who was, at heart, a centrist. That profile helped her throughout her political career as liberals, particularly outside of San Francisco, frequently, based on her background, overestimated how liberal she was, while she appealed to more conservative voters based on her voting record in the US Senate.

Moscone formally announced his campaign on March 20, 1963. The *San Francisco Examiner* noted that in addition to declaring his candidacy, "he announced seven goals for the city, ranging from more housing for low and middle income families and racial equality to better parks, public transportation, city planning and a mental health program." The article identified Moscone as "a native San Franciscan, he attended St. Ignatius High School, University of the Pacific and Hastings College of Law. He lives at 1239 42nd Ave. with his wife and three children."[30]

Sone of Moscone's initiatives, such as better parks, were generic good government; others, like his commitment to racial equality and low-income housing, were left of center. Additionally, an *Examiner* reader encountering Moscone's name for the first time would have learned that he was Italian American and a graduate of St. Ignatius, so unlikely to be a radical. While it is not always a great idea to publish the exact address of politicians, readers would have also known that 1239 Forty-Second Avenue was in the Outer Sunset, a neighborhood of primarily working-class Irish and Italian Americans in the far west of the city, about six blocks from the beach and two blocks south of Golden Gate Park. This made Moscone appear less threatening to conservative San Franciscans.

The *San Francisco News, Call & Bulletin* and the *Chronicle* both covered Moscone's announcement and included most of the same information. The *News, Call & Bulletin* included a quote from Moscone: "He promised to fight to 'see that my program of Goals for San Francisco is carried to every voter. . . . The issue is nothing less than the city itself—what we wish it to become, physically, economically and socially.'"[31] This comment amounted to little more than a promise to run a strong campaign.

Moscone was indeed an active campaigner, attending community and neighborhood group meetings, winning support from several local Democratic clubs, and quickly emerging as one of labor's top candidates. In late August, Moscone won the endorsement of the Union Labor Party, which consisted of delegates representing "Teamsters, Bartenders, Park Employees, Machinists, Building Trades and other unions."[32] These were only some of the unions that supported Moscone.

Moscone was sufficiently popular in the labor movement that *Organized Labor*, a union newsletter, featured a very flattering profile of a typical day in his campaign written by the business manager of the tile layers union:

> Mr. Moscone is a 34-year-old attorney who has taken a leave from his law practice to run for Supervisor. At a fund raising party the other day he described a typical campaign day, a Moscone day. George gets up at 5:30 a.m., fixes a quick breakfast and rushes across the city to a busy bus stop. Here he hands out literature and talks to voters until about 9 a.m. when the bus traffic dies down. He then heads for a neighborhood shopping district and works from store to store talking to merchants and shoppers about their problems and his platform. He takes a quick lunch and heads for a big shopping center for the early afternoon shoppers to get his literature and a few words of his platform, if he can slow them down long enough. About 4:30 p.m. the bus traffic picks up and George goes to a busy bus stop again and meets the voters until 6 p.m. After a dinner at home every day, Mr. Moscone starts on the rounds of visits to union meetings, neighborhood improvement clubs and any and all public functions where a candidate can appear before the voter to say a few words, and if lucky, gets time enough to answer a few questions. At about 10 p.m. the meetings are over and the candidate goes home to meet the family and prepare for another day. This goes on with slight variations until November.[33]

Moscone's strong base in organized labor and ties to the Burtons were the foundations of his campaign, but he also built other relationships with powerful San Franciscans outside of the Burton and labor orbits. One of these was with Morris Bernstein, a political insider with particularly strong ties to the city's Jewish community. Their meeting was serendipitous and shows the kind of candidate Moscone was in 1963:

> In front of the Emporium used to be this little guy who was blind, and he had a tray in front of him, he would be making lavender sashays, and sell them for ten cents. . . . He had a police dog lying next to him on a couple of potato sacks. He was there for years and years and years. George was running for supervisor and he was, George is pretty smart. This guy has been a figure in town. He was well liked and tolerated. And so he (Moscone) takes a position next to him. He's got his brochures. He's standing there saying "vote for me in the next election." Rhea (Morris Bernstein's wife) . . . she says to Mo, "Stop the car for a minute. Look at that poor kid out there. He looks like such a nice boy. Let's invite him in to get warm." So Mo rolls down his window and

says, "Hey kid, come over here." And George comes over like a little lamb, climbs in the back seat, and that relationship went on for years and years and years.[34]

As the 1963 campaign season progressed, civil rights became a more central issue both in San Francisco and nationally. Residential segregation, political representation, employment discrimination, mistreatment by police, and other issues were beginning to dominate politics in all cities, including San Francisco. Housing discrimination was a particularly important issue, one that even San Francisco's most well-known African American resident had encountered.

After the Giants moved to San Francisco following the 1957 baseball season, their best and most famous player, Willie Mays, sought to buy a home in St. Francis Wood. This was, and remains, a very affluent planned community. Because of its location in the southwestern part of San Francisco, leafy streets, and lack of commercial activity, St. Francis Wood feels disconnected from the city, almost like a suburb within the city. Wealthy and influential San Franciscans have inhabited the big, beautiful homes there for years.

Mays, one of the best and most beloved players in the game, was an African American who had grown up in the violent segregation of Alabama in the 1930s and 1940s. However, he had spent the first years of his extraordinary career in New York, which had a large African American population and less racism than some big-league towns. Mays could not buy the house he wanted in St. Francis Wood because "the house was mysteriously taken off the market."[35] The racism there was unambiguous. Mays and his wife then tried to buy a home right next to St. Francis Wood.

The seller, Walter A. Gnesdiloff, appeared ready to close the deal until "not long after he received Mays's offer, he and his wife began receiving phone calls from agitated residents in the Miraloma (the street on which the house was located) neighborhood. Their message was the same: Gnesdiloff would be doing a 'terrible thing' if he accepted Mays's offer because a Negro family would lower property values for the entire neighborhood." Gnesdiloff's broker "had told him that his firm would have nothing to do with a sale to a Negro and would not accept Mays's offer."[36] Civil rights organizations, the media, and elected officials soon became involved. The politicians, including Mayor Christopher, did not want this scandal. But they sought to solve it by encouraging Mays to buy another home—in other words, letting the racists win. Mays refused to back down. Eventually, after much ugliness, controversy, and rancor, Mays was able to buy the home.

Mays was not only the highest profile African American in San Francisco, but among the most famous in the whole country. His story of trying to buy a home in San Francisco is illustrative, but not uncommon for the time. Mays sold that home a few years later to move to the suburbs south of the city. The west San Francisco real estate agent for that transaction was John Barbagelata, who had not yet begun his political career.

Civil rights protests and picketing took place in San Francisco as they did throughout the country. Following demonstrations at car dealerships on Van Ness Avenue, one of the first companies targeted by civil rights activists in late 1963 for its racist employment practices was Mel's Drive-In, whose owner happened to be running for mayor in an election that was fast approaching. Harold Dobbs accused the organizers of playing politics, referring to the plans for demonstrations at his restaurant as "politically contrived" and a "shocking reflection on the lack of moral honesty on the part of Negro leaders involved." Shelley responded by asserting that "whatever else is involved, the question is raised whether Mr. Dobbs can effectively handle race problems of the whole city if he cannot handle them in his own business."[37]

The pickets and arrests at Mel's Drive-In were the major news story as Election Day approached. The day before the election, the front page of the *Chronicle* reported that "forty-eight singing, chanting pickets, protesting alleged racial discrimination, were arrested in a wild sit-in demonstration yesterday in Mel's Drive-In. . . . Police dragged the struggling demonstrators bodily out of the restaurant and several scuffles broke out as officers forced them into paddy wagons."[38] On that same front page, the *Chronicle* printed an enthusiastic endorsement for Dobbs for mayor. The paper's endorsements for other offices were also all on the front page. For supervisor the *Chronicle* endorsed four incumbents and Leo McCarthy and Alan Nichols.

It was a challenge for pro-civil rights candidates to campaign in a city that still had a large white majority, while appealing to white and African American voters. Some spoke of the need for reforms to be at the right pace and right time while cautioning against moving too quickly. This was not Moscone's approach. Rather, he ran as an unabashed civil rights advocate who promised African Americans that he would fight for their rights. Moscone's commitment to civil rights caught the attention of Percy Moore, who singled out Moscone in a letter to the *Chronicle* shortly before the election. Moore was not only a candidate for supervisor but also one of the city's most visible African American leaders. The letter provides a glimpse of how civil rights issues were playing out in San Franciscans as they prepared to choose a new mayor and legislature:

> As a Negro campaigning citywide, I have had ample opportunity to sample the feelings of San Franciscans on racial tension and discrimination. There are, of course, pockets of prejudice. By and large, however, San Franciscans are not only aware of the problems, but they have a strong desire to solve them. My own campaign for Supervisor has been

> based in part on the idea that nonwhite citizens have a right to representation. The response of white voters has been encouraging . . . white voters—contrary to the opinions of some campaign professionals—are aware that the problems of minorities are the problems of all citizens. . . . Nonwhites are not the only people who need decent low cost housing. Racial segregation and tension in schools affect the quality of education available to every student, white and nonwhite. . . . I hope, too, that the *Chronicle* will find room for coverage of those few Supervisorial candidates not only myself . . . such as George Moscone, who are speaking out fully and without qualification on these issues.[39]

In addition to Moore, Willie Brown, who was eyeing another run against incumbent Ed Gaffney in the 1964 Democratic primary for an assembly seat, had become a prominent civil rights leader in San Francisco and helped Moscone win African American support. Jack Morrison, the only Burton supporter on the board of supervisors and one of its strongest pro-civil rights voices, also made it clear who he thought were the two strongest civil rights candidates for the board. On October 30 Morrison endorsed Percy Moore and Moscone while not endorsing any of his colleagues seeking reelection. Morrison was an ambitious politician who wanted to consolidate his progressive base and move beyond the board, so his endorsement sent a strong message because by endorsing two challengers and no incumbents he had "broke(n) the unwritten political code of the Board of Supervisors."[40]

Moscone's campaign was broader than civil rights. The 1963 election occurred in the shadow of the Freeway Revolts. Moscone opposed the Hunters Point Freeway, which was planned for that heavily African American neighborhood.[41] Moscone also emphasized his support for neighborhoods against downtown while making a point with which all real San Franciscans will always agree—that San Francisco should never become like Los Angeles. "The unrestricted use of outdoor advertising in our downtown and public places precludes even an attempt at sound city planning. . . . The choice is clear. San Francisco cannot afford to follow Los Angeles into the billboard jungle."[42]

A typical piece of Moscone campaign literature mentioned his focus on keeping San Francisco beautiful, "We must preserve and enhance the beauty of San Francisco and protect ourselves from the blighting effect of poor construction" as well as civil rights, "We must make sure that every one of our citizens, regardless of race, color or creed has equal opportunity for jobs, education and housing." These positions were mentioned after and in smaller print than the text touting Moscone as "born and reared in San Francisco. He attended St. Ignatius High School, University of the Pacific and Hastings College of Law. He is a Navy Veteran . . . He is the LOGICAL CHOICE for election to our Board of Supervisors."[43] The use of the word "logical" also appears on the front of the flyer seems strange today. That word may have even seemed strange in 1963, but it supports the image of a rational, moderate, and educated man that Moscone needed to project to appeal to voters across the city.

Moscone benefited from glowing press coverage during the campaign, but good press coverage doesn't just happen. It is the result of discipline and a good message. About a month before the election, the *Examiner* published profiles of all the candidates. The section on Moscone, began, "George R. Moscone is a tall personable six-footer whose basketball genius at St. Ignatius High School became a legend. He played an All-City forward position in 1946 and 1947." The article went on to suggest that Moscone had been encouraged to run by his friends, making no mention of his unsuccessful bid for office three years earlier. "Moscone's friends thought his background, his awareness of the city's need, and his easy-going charm made him a natural candidate."[44]

In some respects, it is odd that a man in his mid-thirties was still identified by his high school and youthful athletic accomplishments, but those things were important in San Francisco then. As Corey Busch, who did not start working with Moscone until eight years later, observed, "the city that George grew up in, the city that George ran for office in, was still predominantly natives,"[45] and many of those natives cared about things like where people went to high school.

As the election approached, the indicators were good for Shelley and the Democrats. As the candidate of labor, African Americans and liberals in a city that generally voted Democratic, Shelley put together a winning coalition and ended up with just under half of the roughly 244,000 votes cast, while beating Dobbs by more than 27,000 votes.[46] In 1963 the mayor needed only a plurality, not a majority, to win.

The race for the board of supervisors was closer. Incumbents John Ferdon and Charles Ertola finished first and second citywide. Each received more votes than Shelley. Leo McCarthy demonstrated the power of the moderate west-side voting block, coming in a strong third with 114,000 votes. Rounding out the top five were two other incumbents, Joseph Casey and Clarissa McMahon. The race for the sixth and final place on the board was close. Four candidates were within 19,000 votes of each other. Moscone won the sixth seat with almost 103,000, only 9,000 more than seventh-place finisher Max Moore. Percy Moore finished a distant tenth with just under 61,000 votes.[47]

Two days after the election, the *Chronicle* ran a profile of Moscone and McCarthy, the only new members of the board, titled "S. F.'s Rising Young Politicians." The article described McCarthy as having ample "Irish charm and political savvy." Moscone, in language that was already associated with the new supervisor, was portrayed as "look(ing) like an All American boy who has grown up and become a pretty substantial citizen." It mentioned his "trim athletic frame," "dark good looks," and concluded that he "looks, in fact, like a winner." The article went on to recite the schools he had attended, including a mention of his basketball success at St. Ignatius, how hard Moscone had campaigned, and his identity as a liberal Democrat.[48]

The profile concluded with Moscone discussing his relationship with Phil Burton. "It's kind of you to use the word protégé. . . . Some people have used the word 'tool.' I'm not. I've known Phil since 1960. I consulted him on techniques in this campaign. He has introduced a lot of legislation with which I agree, but he has also introduced a lot I would not have introduced."[49] Moscone gave no examples of what kind of legislation would fall into either of those two categories.

It was becoming clear that that Moscone's looks, background, charm, and political skills were assets that made him somebody to watch in progressive San Francisco. It was also evident that Moscone's close relationship with Burton was something that would not endear him to everybody in the city, particularly the more conservative elements. The Moscone brand, the good-looking charmer who could represent the more broadly electable face of the Burton operation, was beginning to take shape.

In the days following the election, the major story in San Francisco was the newly elected mayor. Amazingly, Jack Shelley would be the first Democratic mayor of San Francisco since Edward Taylor, who had left office in 1910. This meant big changes for San Francisco with organized labor, civil rights advocates, and others getting more input into city government, so, 1964 was shaping up as a time of transition.

On the Thursday following the Tuesday election, an article on the front page of the *Examiner* was headlined, "Burton Is Off and Running." It noted Burton "has been unofficially running for months," and posited that the new mayor was likely to back another Democrat against Burton.[50] The special election to fill Shelley's seat in Congress did not become a showdown between the new mayor, who could have supported a candidate of his own, and the aspiring new leader of the left wing of the San Francisco Democratic Party. Burton consolidated support from labor, African Americans, and other progressives, and he won the race easily, netting 52 percent of the vote in an eight-person field. The Burton brothers' plan for 1963 and 1964 was one big step closer to being implemented.

The remaining challenges were in the assembly. The Democratic primary was scheduled for June 2. There was no competitive Democratic presidential primary in 1964, but the GOP battle for the nomination was intense. The far-right Barry Goldwater, senator from Arizona, was vying with the liberal Nelson Rockefeller, governor of New York. On the day after the California primary, the *Examiner* had an above-the-fold headline declaring "ROCKY EDGES INTO LEAD." Just under the masthead was another headline, "W. Brown Upsets Gaffney," that then explained that "Negro attorney Willie L. Brown Jr. apparently defeated veteran assemblyman Edward M. Gaffney for the Democratic nomination at yesterday's primary election in the Eighteenth Assembly District."[51]

Brown's campaign manager was Rudy Nothenberg, who had managed Phil Burton's first winning campaign as well. Nothenberg would work with Brown in the assembly for the next decade. Like Brown, Nothenberg was not a native San Franciscan. He was born in Germany, but his family had fled when Hitler came to power. Like thousands of Jews, they ended up spending the war in China. Nothenberg came to San Francisco after the war when he was sixteen. He and Brown remained close for years.

In the Twentieth District for assembly, John Burton won the nomination by defeating John Delury. Moscone had served as the co-chair of Burton's assembly campaign. With Burton and Brown all but assured victory in November in their heavily Democratic districts, the Burton organization was much stronger going into 1965 than they had been midway through 1963. As expected, Brown and both Burtons won easily in the general election, helped by President Lyndon Johnson's landslide reelection. With Moscone and Morrison on the board of supervisors, and Morrison beginning to think about higher office, John Burton and Willie Brown in the assembly and Phil Burton in Congress, the Burton organization was beginning to change San Francisco politics, but San Francisco itself was beginning to change more rapidly.

CHAPTER SIX

Freeway Fights and Supervisor Moscone

A FEW WEEKS AFTER GEORGE Moscone won his first election, President Kennedy was assassinated. Kennedy had no organic ties to San Francisco, but he had always been very popular there. In 1960 people in that heavily Catholic city cast 57.78 percent of their votes for the man who became the first Catholic president.[1] Kennedy's political operation had also played a quiet role in the machinations that helped facilitate the Burton machine's increased influence in the city. For politicians such as Moscone and the Burtons who placed generational change at the center of their agenda, Kennedy must have been an inspiring figure. He became president when he was forty-three years old, was only twelve years older than Moscone and nine years older than Phil Burton.

Lyndon Johnson became president following Kennedy's assassination. The civil rights movement was the major domestic political issue for the next years and was a key part of Johnson's legislative agenda through 1965. Similarly, the Vietnam War would gradually grow in significance throughout Johnson's time in the White House, becoming the biggest and most divisive issue in the country.

This created a political environment characterized by demands for representation and equality from various groups, including Latinos, Native Americans, women, gays and lesbians, and African Americans; increased radicalism growing out of the anti-war movement; acute generational rifts; and, in some circles, contempt for conventional politics. Phil Burton, George Moscone, Willie Brown, and others who were on the left of the Democratic Party in San Francisco faced the challenge of cultivating progressive support in an increasingly radical environment.

The Burtons, Moscone, and Brown were caught between two generations both demographically and ideologically. Unlike those ten, or even five, years older, they had not fought in World War II, but unlike the baby boomers they were not as comfortable with the burgeoning counterculture. Similarly, while not nearly as conservative as most San Francisco politicians, both Burtons, Moscone, and Brown pursued their progressive goals through the relatively conventional structures around electoral politics.

Moscone was born in 1929, so by the time the Summer of Love came around, he was pushing forty and from a different generation than the many young people who came to San Francisco with flowers in their hair. Jon Rubin contrasted his own experience with the culture of the late 1960s with Moscone's "really good jazz collection" and how Moscone preferred to "go to the jazz clubs on Geary . . . (to hear) people like Dave Brubeck (also a graduate of College of the Pacific) . . . hour after hour in those little clubs." Rubin summarized the generational difference between Moscone and the counterculture: "He (Moscone) was a ring-a-ding-ding Frank Sinatra groovy guy."[2]

When I asked Chris Moscone what music his father liked, he laughingly responded, "It wasn't the Grateful Dead . . . Coltrane a lot of Coltrane . . . Maybe a little Frank. He liked jazz . . . and smoking cigarettes."[3] Ring-a-ding-ding. Chris's brother, Jonathan, had similar recollections: "He loved Stan Getz. He loved Frank Sinatra, Joe Williams, Dinah Washington, Carmen McRae, Blossom Dearie. He loved standards." The younger Moscone son also revealed that in addition to his father's interest in music, "He loved watching TV . . . He was an inveterate TV watcher."[4]

Jeannette Etheredge, a longtime friend of Gina Moscone's, confirmed this: "One of his (Moscone's) favorite TV shows was *The Phil Silvers Show*. It comes on at 11 o'clock at night. If we'd happen to be out, we'd drop whatever we were doing and go to the nearest bar so we could watch *The Phil Silvers Show*."[5] *The Phil Silvers Show*, better known to some by the name of its leading character, Sergeant Bilko, played by Silvers, went off the air in 1959, so if the Moscones and Etheredge were watching it at 11 p.m., it was in reruns.

Transformation of San Francisco

The phrase "San Francisco in the 1960s" brings to mind images of the Summer of Love, the Haight-Ashbury, the civil rights movement, the Black Panthers across the bay in Oakland, unrest at UC Berkeley, the student strike at San Francisco State University, and the political and cultural radicalization of a once relatively normal American city.

There is some truth to that. By the late 1960s San Francisco was a center of the counterculture movement. UC Berkeley and San Francisco State were among campuses with the largest and most powerful student protest movements. Bands such as Quicksilver Messenger Service, the Jefferson Airplane, and Big Brother and the Holding Company were part of an extraordinary music scene. The civil rights movement encompassed numerous ethnic groups as well as women and later gays and lesbians, and the city fundamentally shifted in those years in ways that are still recognizable today.

When George Moscone was first elected to the board of supervisors in 1963, San Francisco was still culturally, politically, and socially the 1950s. Many of the cultural and political touchstones associated with The Sixties, the concept, rather than the 1960s, as a discrete ten-year period, had not occurred. The week of Moscone's election the number-one song in the US was "Sugar Shack" by Jimmy Gilmer and the Fireballs.[6] The Beatles would not make their first trip to the US for a few more months. John F. Kennedy, Robert F. Kennedy, Martin Luther King Jr., and Malcolm X were still alive. College students still dressed and conducted themselves largely the way they had when Moscone was attending College of the Pacific in the early 1950s. In 1963 there were fewer than 17,000 US troops in Vietnam. By the end of 1965, that number would increase tenfold.[7]

Even in San Francisco, where The Sixties lasted well into the 1980s, the gestalt of that decade was not yet evident. Percy Moore's tenth-place finish, in a campaign for six spots on the board of supervisors, meant there would still be no African American elected officials in all of San Francisco. The city spent the months following the election preparing to host the Republican National Convention in 1964. The Haight-Ashbury was still an ordinary middle-class neighborhood with good access to Golden Gate Park and, like most San Francisco neighborhoods, spectacular views from some angles, but the Summer of Love was still almost three years away. On New Year's Eve 1963, a few miles down the peninsula from San Francisco, an aspiring folk musician named Jerry Garcia met and later befriended a fifteen-year-old musician named Bob Weir, but the Grateful Dead had still not played a single note together. Classes were still running smoothly at San Francisco State University. Alcatraz, the craggy island in the middle of the bay that had served as a federal penitentiary since 1933 and as an army prison for decades before that, had shut down earlier in 1963. There was little activity of any kind there.

The years 1964–1966 when Moscone served on the board of supervisors was the period when The Sixties were being born. Some things stayed the same. Out at Candlestick Park, the Giants continued to field excellent teams without ever winning the World Series, finishing within three games of the National League pennant in each of those years. Willie Mays was still playing centerfield with enough excellence and panache to win three Gold Gloves while hitting 136 home runs over that three-year span.

By the middle of the decade, other than Willie Brown and Terry Francois, who was appointed to the board of supervisors by Shelley in 1964, the politicians were still overwhelmingly white and male. Mayor Shelley would have been comfortable in the backrooms of Democratic Party clubhouses in most major cities throughout much of the twentieth century. The immigration from Asia and Latin America that would remake San Francisco was still at least a decade in the future; and San Francisco was not yet a major destination for domestic migrants seeking a less conventional and more tolerant environment. Latino and Asian American San Franciscans had no political representation. It was not until the early 1970s when the first Asian American would hold political office in San Francisco. That occurred in 1973 when Mayor Joseph Alioto appointed George Chinn to fill a vacancy on the board of supervisors. Robert Gonzales, a Mexican American, was appointed to the board in 1969.

In the 1960s San Francisco was still a town where when one native asked another, "Where'd you go to school," they meant high school—and the answer revealed a lot:

> If, for example, the answer is "S.I." you know the man went to St. Ignatius High and was probably raised a Catholic and is from an upper-middle-class family.
>
> If the person says "Mission" or "Bal" (for Balboa High) you know he is from the Mission District, and his father was probably a member of the working class, called "a workin' man" in the San Francisco dialect. If he went to Lowell, he may well be Jewish; if he went to Galileo, he is probably a North Beach Italian, and not a Mission District Italian. One has to be careful, though. Some women, asked where they went to school, will respond that they "went to the madams." A tourist will immediately leap to the conclusion that the poor woman was raised in a whorehouse, but natives understand immediately what this woman means: She attended the Convent of the Sacred Heart, conducted by a ritzy order of nuns, and is doubtless from a wealthy family. She is not necessarily a Catholic, however. Dianne Feinstein went to the madams.[8]

John Burton explained this same idea more succinctly. "San Francisco, you ask a guy where he went to school, if he's a city guy he tells you the high school, if he's some asshole from the outside he tells you some college."[9]

By the end of the Moscone's three years on the board of supervisors, changes were evident in San Francisco. The civil rights movement had gained momentum with the election of Brown, kicking off a long struggle to wrestle control of the city away from the white men who'd been running it for decades. Outside of electoral politics, communities of color began to mobilize against redevelopment, discrimination in housing and employment, and to demand political and economic power.

There were cultural changes as well. For example, the first of Ken Kesey's acid tests—where hippies and others gathered to trip on LSD together usually with the Grateful Dead as the house band—occurred in November 1965.

The escalation of the conflict in Vietnam also had a big impact on San Francisco. By the end of 1966, more than 385,000 American troops were in Vietnam.[10] In 1964, 216 American troops died in the Vietnam War; that number increased to 6,350 by 1966.[11] As those numbers grew, so did protest against the war. San Francisco, and the Bay Area, were among the centers of the national protest movement. By 1966 student radicalism at UC Berkeley became a national issue while activists in San Francisco were organizing the massive national antiwar mobilization that would occur in April 1967, bringing 500,000 people to the streets of New York and San Francisco.

As Moscone's time on the board of supervisors wound down, Vietnam was radicalizing many, tearing some parts of the country, and some families, apart, and ultimately helping bring down a president, but as late as 1965 Vietnam was still fodder for humor on the board. This lighthearted exchange between Moscone and Supervisor William Blake from a June 1965 meeting of the board of supervisors, discussing a proposal to allow troops stationed in the Presidio, the huge army base in the northwestern corner of the city, to ride Muni (the city's public transportation system) for free, could not have occurred even a year later. The repartee between Moscone and Blake, who was only nine years older than Moscone, also shows a bit of how Moscone's colleagues saw him, and how Moscone viewed himself.

Blake: "These are going to be men in uniform. It shouldn't be too difficult to identify them."

Supervisor George Moscone: "It's certainly very innocuous asking the PUC (Public Utilities Commission) to consider this. But you mention Vietnam. What about Santo Domingo?"

Blake: "If there are troops through here on their way to Santo Domingo, all is lost. I'm amazed that you guys are asking questions like this. This is a question of hospitality and offering a courtesy."

Moscone (smiling): "Well, we're concerned because there are some of us here still young enough to be called back."

Blake: "They want fighting men."

Moscone: "Instead of lovers?"

Blake: "There are some here who wouldn't qualify for that either."[12]

Supervisor Moscone

When Moscone took his seat on the San Francisco Board of Supervisors in January 1964, the city had a Democratic mayor and because Moscone and Leo McCarthy had replaced Republicans Harold Dobbs and Max Moore, a 9–2 Democratic majority on the board. Board President John Ferdon made Moscone chair of the Education, Parks, and Recreation Committee while also placing him on the

Judiciary, Legislative, and Civil Service Committee and the Streets and Highways Committee.

Because the board had only eleven members, even new supervisors such as Moscone and McCarthy were made committee chairs. McCarthy was the new chair of the Public Health and Welfare Committee. Neither Moscone nor McCarthy was given a seat on the Finance, Revenue, and Taxation Committee, generally considered the most powerful and important committee. On balance, Moscone's committee appointments were fine. The Streets and Highways Committee was led by William Blake, also a strong opponent of freeway construction, and was likely to draw a lot of attention given the ongoing disputes about freeway construction.

Moscone probably got the position on the Education, Parks, and Recreation Committee because of his youth and history as a sports star, but given his concerns about neighborhoods and racial equality, it was a good place for Moscone. From his position as chair of that committee, Moscone would have oversight about how resources were allocated for youths, including things such as parks, playgrounds, and athletic facilities, and he could ensure lower-income and nonwhite communities got their fair share.

From the time he became a member of the board of supervisors until his death just short of fifteen years later, Moscone remained an elected official. Among the offices he held, the position on the San Francisco Board of Supervisors was where he made the least impact. He was a junior member of the board, served only three years, and spent much of his last year on the board campaigning for higher office. However, as an elected official, he was able to be more active and play a more prominent role in the city's politics. No longer just a foot soldier in the Burton organization, he had become a captain or at least a lieutenant. Although he only served on the board briefly, it gave him experience, perspective, citywide exposure, new contacts throughout San Francisco, and an understanding of city government that would help when he ran for mayor in 1975.

Serving on the board of supervisors was not a full-time job during most of the twentieth century. Moscone, like many other members of the board, had outside employment in addition to his legislative duties. He continued his legal career for several reasons. First, when he was elected to the board, Moscone had three children. His fourth, Jonathan, was born while he was a supervisor. Raising four children required an income well beyond the $400 monthly salary that supervisors were paid.[13] Since neither George nor Gina Moscone had any family money, it was essential that he continue to work. Practicing law also allowed Moscone to continue to build his network of relationships among both powerful San Franciscans and at the community level.

Moscone's tenure on the board of supervisors also marked his transformation into a political insider. He was no longer a bright young man exploring a career in politics, but an elected official unsure of how he wanted to have an impact in San Francisco and what the next step in his political career might be. Moscone was still understood to be part of the Burton machine, but his new position gave him an opportunity to put a little space between himself and the Burtons, and to build political relationships independently of the influential brothers.

Moscone's voting record on the board aligned him with the progressive wing of the Democratic Party, but he solidified his progressive credentials through more than just his voting record. During these years, growing resistance to the Vietnam War and acceleration of civil rights struggles, which in San Francisco included those of African Americans, Chicanos, Asian Americans, Native Americans, women, and a little bit later gays and lesbians, radicalized many young people. Many progressive politicians struggled to connect with this new left. In the early 1960s it was still plausible that a well-groomed white man in a suit could be a progressive leader, but by the end the decade that had begun to change, particularly in San Francisco.

As Moscone sought to build the foundations for what he hoped would be a long and successful political career, he had to do more than simply vote the right way. He also had to show he was attuned to the political and social changes in San Francisco. Sometimes this included relatively small things. For example, in the spring of 1964, a group of entertainers called the San Francisco Mine Troupe was growing in popularity and performing in local parks for free. The San Francisco Mime Troupe quickly became a mainstay in San Francisco, frequently performing at public events and rallies and supporting progressive and radical political causes. Their performances have long been compelling, funny, radical, and bawdy. When they were just getting some momentum in 1964 the *Chronicle* reported: "Instrumental in assisting the growth of the Troupe's summer program were civic leaders such as Supervisor George Moscone, Congressman Phillip Burton, and Democratic candidate for assembly Willie Brown."[14] This is, in the bigger picture, a minor event, but Burton, Brown, and Moscone were staying a little bit ahead of the changes in their city.

In December of that year, Moscone joined with Supervisor Jack Morrison, Terry Francois and fifty-one other labor leaders, academics, lawyers, and intellectuals in supporting the nascent free speech movement across the bay at UC Berkeley and "criticiz(ing) the University of California for failing to recognize the current crisis as a legitimate free speech issue . . . and urged the administration 'to recognize that a fundamental Constitutional question is at the center of the controversy.'"[15]

In Moscone's first years on the board, the most important domestic political issue remained civil rights. The Civil Rights Act passed in 1964; the Voting Rights Act in 1965. All over the country, African Americans and their allies participated in sit-ins, demonstrations, and marches, demanding their rights. During the summer of 1964, one of the most important political battles in the country was fought thousands of miles away in Mississippi, the Deep South state broadly understood as being second to none in its racism and commitment to maintaining segregation and excluding African Americans from political participation. African Americans in Mississippi had been denied the right to vote since the end of the Reconstruction period in the 1870s, but in 1964 civil rights advocates wanted to change that by registering African Americans to vote. Numerous activists came to Mississippi from all over the country, many African American but some white, to support this effort. Progressive lawyers, who could help African Americans in Mississippi, were in great demand during what became known as the Freedom Summer. Real danger was associated with this, given the violent nature of racism, and the commitment to maintaining it in the South.

The Freedom Summer continued into early 1965. Among the lawyers who came to Mississippi were dozens from San Francisco, including two members of the board of supervisors, Moscone and Terry Francois. Francois had been appointed to the board by Mayor Shelley in 1964 when John Ferdon left the board to become district attorney. Francois and Willie Brown were the first African American officeholders in San Francisco. Moscone and Francois spent a lot of time together in Mississippi. They, along with many others from San Francisco and around the country, worked tirelessly and at great personal risk to advance the cause of civil rights. Mel Wax, writing for the *San Francisco Chronicle,* outlined what a typical Mississippi day looked like for the two supervisors. "Francois and Moscone took 39 formal statements working from 9 a.m. to 10:30 p. m. Like all others here (13 more from the Bay Area arrived yesterday), they paid their own way, took time from their private practice, and are convinced, without exception, that this is one of the great experiences of their lives. They send back word that more lawyers are needed. The testimony had a dreary sameness. The stories were shocking, incredible, and vastly remote from San Francisco experience."[16]

Upon his return to San Francisco from Mississippi, Moscone told the *Examiner* that "lawyers obtained 41 statements from would-be Negro voters which show 'a pattern of discrimination, harassment, violence and economic reprisal' by voting officials."[17] He added that lawyers were hoping to gather a thousand or more similar depositions and then challenge the legitimacy of the Mississippi congressional delegation, presumably by arguing that the election that sent them to Congress was not legitimate because African Americans had been denied their right to vote. This was an ambitious, and ultimately unsuccessful, goal.

In progressive circles in San Francisco, this made Moscone and Francois even more popular, but their work in Mississippi also drew some powerful critics. The year 1965 was the height of the Cold War, so inevitably those criticisms included a healthy dose of red-baiting. In February 1965, "Mississippi Sen. James Eastland in a privileged speech on the floor of the Senate . . . contended that two

San Francisco Supervisors and an attorney are connected with 'Communist forces pressing for a Negro revolution in this country.' ... Among the 21 men named by Eastland as being connected with the Freedom Democratic Party—he called it 'a predominantly Negro group to unseat the Democratic House members and a Communist planned attempt'—were Supervisors Terry A. Francois and George Moscone, and Attorney Edward Stern. The three San Francisco lawyers, when informed of Eastland's allegations, were dumbfounded."[18]

A *Chronicle* story discussing Moscone's trip to Mississippi began with a gushing description of Moscone: "He is tall, handsome and young-looking with a friendly smile. It is easy, I thought, looking at him to see why George Moscone won enough votes to be elected Supervisor. His genuine friendliness would appeal to men, to young women he would represent the knight in the shining armor with ideals, and the older women probably feel like mothering him." The article gave Moscone a chance to explain his actions. "It seems obvious that as a lawyer I should become involved in a legal matter—that is part of my work, just as taking care of sick people, no matter who they are, is a doctor's job."[19] The author of that article, Monique Benoit, one of only a handful of female journalists in San Francisco at the time, asked Moscone if he would have done something similar for the suffragist movement. He replied, "Of course I would and I'm not just saying this."

Moscone then offered some thoughts on the challenges of being a woman, reflecting and critiquing the deep sexism of the era. "It's not easy to be a woman ... When she gets married she gives up her choice of life to go along with the one her husband has chosen for himself. His career and life must come first." Moscone's own marriage had followed that pattern. He then raised a problem some women, but not Gina, confronted. "And what if the man she marries wants to live some place other than San Francisco? She has to follow him."[20] This last line was sincere and a smart thing for any San Francisco politician to say. It is also possible that Moscone was revealing something about why his earlier engagement to Barbara Friberg, who was not a San Franciscan, was called off.

During the 1960s it was common for supporters of segregation, such as Senator Eastland, to attack those fighting for racial equality as communists. In general, for the first two decades after World War II anybody whose politics were to the left of Barry Goldwater risked being called a communist. Moscone was a liberal Democrat, what in the twenty-first century would be called a progressive, but he was not a communist. However, his progressive instincts led him to question the excesses of postwar anti-communism.

Four years after the House Committee on Un-American Affairs road show came to San Francisco, Moscone joined many other progressive and patriotic Americans in calling for the abolishment of HUAC. A petition was signed by Moscone and several other Bay Area progressive politicians, writers, religious leaders, and activists. The supporters included John Burton, Jack Morrison, publisher and civil rights activist Carlton Goodlett, writers such as Lawrence Ferlinghetti and Herb Gold, and the philosopher Alan Watts. The petition stated that "the sole power conferred on the Committee is to investigate 'un-American propaganda activities' and 'subversive and un-American propaganda' in the United States. Its jurisdiction is thus limited to inquiring into ideas, opinions, speech and other forms of expression . . . We believe that the existence of a legislative committee with such authority is irreconcilable with a system of free expression in this country."[21]

National sponsors of the petition included Henry Steele Commager, a well-known liberal intellectual, progressive attorney William Kunstler, several law school deans, and other academics. Moscone's support for this initiative placed him relatively clearly on the left-most boundary of mainstream Democratic Party politics. Only a handful of local elected officials—Moscone, Morrison, John Burton, and Assemblyman William Stanton from Santa Clara County— signed on to the petition. Other local elected officials who were seen as liberals, such as Milton Marks, Mayor Shelley and Supervisor Leo McCarthy, decided not to come out so strongly and publicly against HUAC.

More Freeway Revolts

The work of any city's legislature is a mix of politics and governance. Accordingly, much of Moscone's time on the board was spent on land use and budget issues, in which he consistently voted with Morrison, and later Francois, as part of the board's liberal faction. There were discussions about how specific plots of land would be used, how much density would be allowed in parts of San Francisco, and numerous labor related issues. However, from 1964 to 1966, the Freeway Revolts took up the most attention from the board of supervisors. The fight over freeways included public events and rallies, contentious meetings followed by close votes on the board, pressure from various politicians, including the most powerful Democrat in the state, Governor Pat Brown, and efforts to find compromises. The revolts and battles over freeway construction had been part of the politics of San Francisco for several years by the time Moscone was elected to the board, but they only intensified during his time there.

Very early in Moscone's term, the Streets Committee began public hearings primarily regarding the Panhandle Freeway. The freeway would have allowed cars to move quickly from Golden Gate Park and the western part of the city, into downtown, but it would have been a blemish on the park and would have created noise, traffic, and other disturbances in the Haight-Ashbury, the Western Addition, and other neighborhoods. Serving on the Streets Committee gave Moscone a relatively high-profile role in the biggest issue facing the city and the opportunity to build a stronger base, but also to potentially alienate key constituencies. For example, organized labor supported the freeways because it meant good jobs for their members.

Moscone took a strong and clear position against the Panhandle Freeway. In late May 1964, when the mayor proposed crafting a new study of the Panhandle Freeway seeking a compromise between the two sides, the board supported the proposal, 8–1. The one was Moscone who told the *San Francisco Examiner,* "I'm against the Panhandle freeway. . . . This won't pass—ever."[22]

The San Francisco Chamber of Commerce, speaking for the major downtown and business real estate interests, remained among the strongest backers of the freeway. In July the president of the chamber made the business community's views clear: "We have continued to work on the freeway program which is vitally necessary to correct existing deficiencies in San Francisco." Although the chamber and the building trade unions did not agree on everything, they generally supported growth initiatives that meant greater profits for the former and jobs for the latter. This is true of most cities, not just San Francisco, and is one of the reasons why progressive urban governance is so difficult to sustain, but Moscone was trying. That same evening he spoke at an African American church and assured the crowd that "the Board of Supervisors would not approve of a freeway which would interfere with Golden Gate Park and a 'voluntarily integrated neighborhood such as the Haight-Ashbury district.'"[23] A month later, on August 6, the three members of the Streets Committee unanimously rejected the Panhandle Freeway proposal.

The final vote occurred in October when Moscone was, along with Francois and Leo McCarthy part of a narrow 6–5 majority against the Panhandle Freeway. The vote was a triumph for the neighborhoods and activists, who defeated forces that included the Democratic mayor and governor, who was a native San Franciscan. A front-page article in the *San Francisco Chronicle* the day after the vote reflected the historical significance of the vote and placed it in the context of California history. "The railroad barons who dominated California for 30 years were finally overwhelmed in 1910 by a total wave of resentment. . . . Something similar may well be in store for California highway chieftains who have wielded almost unlimited power to send their battalions of bulldozers through towns and cities, across rich farmlands, through parks historic sites and memorial groves of irreplaceable redwoods that the public believed were preserved forever."[24]

A narrow vote against the Panhandle Freeway was not enough to put the issue to rest. Almost immediately following the vote the state highway commission and other advocates of freeway development began making new plans for San Francisco freeways, including trying once again to get their proposal, including the Panhandle Freeway, passed by the board of supervisors. Naturally, this reignited protests, public fora, another round of Freeway Revolts, and by early 1966, more freeway legislation upon which the board had to vote.

Moscone remained a strong opponent of the freeways, framing his views not just as opposition to the freeways, but also as about the need for community input in decision-making. At a January 18, 1966, press conference, Moscone remarked about the state highway commission, "If some of the powers, which I regard as capricious powers, which are presently within the domain of the state highway commission were curtailed, I think there'd be a great deal more community involvement. And so that when we get to these knotty dilemmas that San Francisco certainly questionably enjoys, it's hard to come up with answers."[25] The footage from that press conference is in black-and-white, so like many politicians of the era, Moscone appears as a white guy in a dark suit and tie. His demeanor is earnest as he seems like a young politician still trying to command the room. Moscone also sounded almost mischievous as evinced by, for example, the use of the word "enjoys" and his slight smile when he said that word. At the end of that press conference, Moscone was asked if the thought the board of supervisors would vote to overturn its previous 6–5 vote against the Panhandle Freeway. Moscone responded, "I would say no."

On March 15, 1966, Moscone appeared with Willie Brown at a rally at San Francisco State. The surviving audio of Moscone's speech is unintelligible. However, Brown noted that he opposed the freeway "through Golden Gate Park, through my district and through my living room," adding "if they were putting it through Mr. Mellon or Mr. Shelley's living room, I would be out here on the other side of the issue." The highlight of the rally might have been Malvina Reynolds, of "Little Boxes" fame, singing "Cement Octopus" with lyrics such as "that octopus grows like a science fiction blight . . . the trees that grew for a thousand years, we watched them falling through our tears. Stand by me and protect that tree from the freeway misery."[26] A few days later, on March 20, the board again rejected the new Panhandle Freeway proposal, this time by a margin of 7–4. That same day the board also voted down the Golden Gate Freeway. Reflecting on the defeat, Mayor Shelley, an ardent backer of the freeways, said that "there will be a freeway to the moon before we get one in San Francisco."[27]

The Next Election

By March 1966 it was evident that the defeat of the freeways meant a new kind of politics was emerging in San Francisco. The vote against the freeways was a victory for younger, newer, and more progressive members of the board such as Moscone, McCarthy, Francois, and Morrison over the older leadership. Mayor Shelley and Governor Pat Brown had both backed the freeways. They were also both Irish Americans of the same generation—both had been born in 1905—and had gotten their start in the machine politics of prewar San Francisco. Both were liberal Democrats, but by 1966 they had lost touch with where progressive politics were heading.

As 1966 got underway, both the mayor and the governor were facing political challenges. Brown was a reasonably successful governor seeking a third term but would soon find himself in a very tough campaign. Shelley was in a different position as his first term wound down. He seemed overwhelmed by the rapid transitions in the city. Shelley's strong advocacy for more freeways pushed away a new generation of activists without whose support a liberal Democrat such as Shelley would have a difficult time getting reelected. On balance, Shelley would have been better off had he stayed in the House of Representatives and continued accruing seniority rather than becoming mayor of San Francisco.

Similarly, increased racial tension and civil rights activism raised challenges for old-line white Democrats such as Shelley. Shelley tried to connect with African American voters, most notably by appointing Francois to the board of supervisors in 1964, but that was not enough. In July 1967, when Shelley was still considering seeking reelection, a group of young African American men from Bayview/Hunters Point had what one television broadcaster called an "unscheduled" meeting with Mayor Shelley at City Hall to discuss their dissatisfaction with his lack of action on civil rights and economic opportunity for their community. One man, who appeared to be in his mid-twenties, spelled out the mayor's political problem. "My mother voted for you because she asked me, 'Is this the right man to vote for?' I said, 'Yeah,' but she ain't gonna vote this year." Another added, "You are the mayor of this city, and we expect certain things. If we were a bunch of white boys, you'd have us our jobs. . . . As part of your campaign, you promised new housing. . . . You were elected because of Black people, and don't you forget that."[28]

Larry Simi, a native San Franciscan who worked on the budget in the Alioto and Moscone administrations, explained Shelley's term as mayor: "(Shelley) really thought that he was coming home to SF to retire. . . . And Mayor Shelley was dealing with unbelievable change that neither he nor his bureaucracy were prepared to deal with in terms of civil unrest, riots, the beginnings of the Vietnam protests, the sit-ins on Van Ness Avenue at the car dealership, and the sit-ins at the Palace Hotel, and those things were the kinds of things . . . that launched a whole generation of African American politicians as well as a whole generation of progressives in the city, so he was not very popular when he left office."[29]

By midway through his first term, Shelley's reelection was in doubt. Moscone was still too young and unknown to run for mayor, so he did not explore that possibility. However, the other supervisor affiliated with the Burton organization, Jack Morrison, was eyeing a race for mayor. By 1965 and 1966, it was also clear J. Eugene McAteer, the popular state senator who had decided not to run in 1963, was likely to be a candidate in 1967. McAteer looked like a strong candidate, perhaps even strong enough to push Shelley out of the race.

McAteer represented a senate district that covered the entire city of San Francisco and would be running for his third term in 1966. For Moscone the path to moving up the political ladder seemed to lie in winning reelection to the board in 1967, something he could expect to accomplish relatively easily, and then to run for McAteer's vacated seat in 1968, after the veteran senator was elected mayor. This was a low-risk strategy as Moscone would not have to give up his seat on the board of supervisors to run in a special election.

In the 1960s "seats in the California state senate were apportioned on the basis of counties rather than persons. With 40 seats, 58 counties, and a restriction that no county could have more than one seat, the senate apportionment was approximately 'one-county-one-vote.' The California senate was by many measures the most malapportioned legislative body in the US. The largest senate district contained more than 400 times as many people as the smallest district."[30] Because there were more counties than senate seats, some seats contained two counties, but no county, even the biggest ones like Los Angeles or San Francisco, had more than one seat.

This arrangement not only gave some voters more relative power than others, but it had a racial component as well because by the mid-1960s most African Americans in California lived in a handful of large counties including San Francisco, Los Angeles and Alameda. As the 1966 election approached and arrangements like this were being challenged throughout the country, the courts eventually demanded that California change as well. Rather than move immediately to a districting system based on population and not counties, the short-term solution was for some of the larger counties to get additional senate seats while smaller counties would be forced to further consolidate into multi-county seats.

This meant that San Francisco would get another senate seat beginning in 1967. Voters would choose their second senator during the 1966 election. Since McAteer's seat was up as well, San Francisco would choose both of its state senators in 1966. When McAteer announced that he was going to run for the new seat, meaning a two-year position, as that seat would be for two years before going to the four-year cycle, it made the second seat, for a full four-year term, even more appealing. Naturally, Moscone was eyeing the seat.

Moscone needed to win a Democratic primary before the general election. The Burton operation was strong enough to help Moscone in the primary, but not close to powerful enough to clear the field. Moscone's candidacy contributed to opposition anxious to stop the Burtons from growing even stronger. As 1966 began, Moscone nonetheless was in a good position. He had proven himself during his first two years on the board of supervisors as an able representative, solidified his credentials as a progressive, and continued to benefit from his charm and good looks. John Vlahos, who was a partner at the law firm of

Hanson Bridgett and met Moscone for the first time when he was a supervisor, reflected on why Moscone was a good candidate: "George's reputation at the time was that he was ambitious, smart, savvy, dynamic and a person who also had his heart in the right place."[31]

By October 1965, before it was confirmed that San Francisco would get a second senate seat, *Examiner* political reporter Sydney Kossen mentioned Moscone's interest in the seat. Kossen mentioned John Burton and Leo McCarthy as others looking at the senate race. Kossen alluded to a poll that suggested Burton would be the strongest candidate. If Burton had decided to run, Moscone would have stayed out of the race because running against Burton would have all but guaranteed McCarthy would win. But, more significantly, challenging either Burton brother would have been a terrible career move.

McCarthy was a potentially formidable opponent to Moscone. They had both been elected to the board in 1963, with McCarthy getting more votes than Moscone. On the board, they enjoyed a collegial relationship and frequently voted the same way. However, McCarthy, a liberal Democrat by national standards, was to the right of Moscone with roots in the more conservative western San Francisco wing of the Democratic Party. He had been a protégé of McAteer, but by late 1965 was no longer as close with his political rabbi.

Within a few weeks of Kossen's initial report on the race, John Burton indicated he would run for reelection to the assembly so would not seek the senate seat. John Burton also made it clear that he and his brother would, as expected, support Moscone, clearing the way for a head-to-head matchup between Moscone and McCarthy. The primary between Moscone and McCarthy drew a great deal of attention in San Francisco, because it was one of only a few competitive Democratic primaries on the ballot. There was a sense the direction of the party in San Francisco was at stake in the race. The election was as much about the Burtons as it was about either George Moscone or Leo McCarthy.

Moscone announced his candidacy on January 18, 1966, at the Fairmont Hotel. Neither Burton was there. Instead, he was flanked by two of his co-chairmen, businessman Melvin Swig and insurance broker John P. Figone Jr. By surrounding himself with prominent businesspeople, Moscone was presenting himself as more moderate. During his remarks, Moscone "promised to work for full employment and city beautification . . . (and) to reopen the old legislative battle to reduce the power of the State Highway Commission." When a reporter covering the announcement asked about whether he was part of the Burton organization, Moscone responded, not particularly helpfully, "I know of no Burton organization. . . . I believe in working with them."[32]

Moscone's relationship with the Burtons was, on one level, straightforward. Moscone, the Burtons, and Willie Brown shared political views, including a strong commitment to civil rights, support for neighborhood activists over downtown and business interests, and a belief that government should help working and lower-income people, placing them on the left of the Democratic Party. Other than Phil Burton, they were all younger than most of the politicians who ran San Francisco and were friends dating back to law school, college, or high school. This is also a dramatic oversimplification. Moscone had gotten his start in politics through the Burtons and would not have been elected in 1963 without them. Because San Francisco is a small city where the personal and political frequently mix, the close friendship between John Burton, Willie Brown, and Moscone existed alongside a political relationship that was based on shared views, but it was also transactional. Phil Burton was at the center of that political relationship, but less so on the social side.

Additionally, while Phil Burton's substantive record was very progressive, he didn't support people just because they were good on the issues. A politician supported by Burton was also a resource. Burton could ask that person for help on a piece of legislation, influence on personnel decisions, or help on future campaigns. George Miller, who worked for Moscone in the state senate and went on to represent an East Bay district for twenty terms in the US House of Representatives, explained: "Burton calls to tell you he can get you money. Then he calls to tell you he got you money. Then he calls to tell you the money is on its way. Then he calls to tell you how you should spend it. Then he sends you a note saying he was able to do all that for you."[33]

Regardless of how Moscone presented his relationship with the Burtons, many voters, particularly Democratic insiders, were aware of it. Sometimes this helped. Moscone and McCarthy both had good records on labor issues during their brief tenure on the board of supervisors, but organized labor favored Moscone. That was because of Phil Burton. In mid-December 1965, before Moscone even announced his candidacy, the Bay District Joint Council of Building Service Unions endorsed him.[34] In late April, the Union Labor Party representing a bevy of local unions endorsed him.[35] A week or so later, Moscone won another labor endorsement, this one from the Park Directors Union Local 400. This was no surprise as Moscone had once been a park director.[36] Shortly before the election, Moscone placed an ad in a labor movement newspaper, proclaiming "Backed by Labor-Union Labor Party . . . Building Trades, Machinists, Teamsters and Independent AFL-CIO union locals, ILWU, Railroad Brotherhoods, Building Services, teacher locals and others. AFL-CIO COPE backed Moscone 122 to 65 over his opponent." The AFL-CIO vote was listed instead of an endorsement because Moscone, despite not reaching the two-thirds threshold required for the endorsement, had the support of most of their voting delegates.[37] San Francisco was a considerably more working- class city in 1966 than it is today, so labor support was very important in a Democratic primary.

As the election approached, Moscone began to pick up more support. The Mexican American Political Association (MAPA), the California Democratic Council, and the Chinese American Democratic Club all endorsed Moscone. One endorsement that Moscone did not get was that of the Columbus Civic Club. The city's "oldest Italian-American organization" chose McCarthy. Moscone was rapidly moving to the left of many Italian Americans just as the city was entering a period of greater division.[38]

The race was important for political insiders, but like many primaries, for many voters the differences between the two young, attractive, and smart supervisors were not apparent. For those insiders, the race was substantially about the Burtons' influence. When asked about the Burtons' support during a debate with McCarthy, Moscone responded, "Let me say I'm delighted that I have them. I think my colleague would be equally delighted. I just happened to have gotten them first. They have never in the two and a half years that I've been on the board asked me to do anything on behalf of themselves or anybody who they thought was a constituent of them." McCarthy responded, "I would not (be delighted to be supported by the Burtons) . . . because I feel that although they would not specifically ask me to vote on something before the board of supervisors, unquestionably and no one who is a close viewer of Democratic Party politics in San Francisco can deny this. Unquestionably, it is the goal of Congressman Phil Burton to finally name everybody who seeks elective office in San Francisco or have a great deal to say about naming everyone who seeks elective office in this city."[39]

Neither candidates' position was very believable. Nobody who followed Democratic politics closely at the time would have believed Moscone's assertion that the Burtons had never asked anything of him. However, Moscone was right that McCarthy would have been delighted to get the labor support, financial help, and campaign workers that accompanied support from the Burtons. The McCarthy campaign continued to make the Burtons a major campaign issue. The weekend before the election, McCarthy's campaign co-chair Z. L. Goosby, a prominent African American opponent of the Burtons who had been appointed to the board of education by Mayor Shelley, claimed the Burtons had put $15,000 into Moscone's campaign in the form of campaign literature, posters, and the like. Goosby claimed that "what this means is that Moscone would be nothing more than another cog in the Burton machine."[40] The role of the Burtons may have been important, but it was not the kind of issue that would be on the minds of most voters. Goosby and the McCarthy campaign were unable to distinguish between a question that was on the minds of political insiders and the issues about which ordinary voters cared. With regard to the latter, Moscone had proven to be at least as competent as supervisor as

McCarthy but had earned a citywide reputation because of his visibility on the freeway questions. McCarthy was a good politician and strong campaigner, but Moscone was a better one.

Moscone did not run to the left. Instead, he continued to tout himself in his campaign literature as "the logical choice," highlighting endorsements from both the president of the Central Labor Council and of the Chamber of Commerce. That piece included a picture of Moscone helping a young African American boy who looks to be about seven learn to play basketball. The piece mentioned Moscone's support for "Full Employment" and "Improved Housing." Regarding redevelopment, it also noted that "community participation should be encouraged to the fullest degree possible in the planning of projects" while never explicitly mentioning race.[41] This ambiguity notwithstanding, Moscone was the candidate for most of African American San Francisco. The *Sun-Reporter*, the city's most influential African American newspaper, gave him a very positive endorsement. The "Primary Election Special" edition of the paper had a big above-the-fold headline, "We Stand for George Moscone." The inside pages touted Moscone's support from labor, clergy, and various community leaders. The text of the endorsement was exuberant: "We need a man in government who will equate human rights with property rights. We need a Junior State Senator who has not just recently discovered that votes can be gained from Negro precincts by supporting civil rights. We need a man of the highest degree of intelligence, integrity and social concern who will never yield to political expediency," and it went on to praise Moscone's support for Willie Brown and Percy Moore as well as his work in Mississippi. The endorsement concluded, "We urge our readers to become actively involved in precinct work and the election of our candidate, George Moscone." The endorsement was first published in a February edition of the paper, in time for readers to get involved in the campaign and was reprinted on the eve of the election.[42]

Willie Brown, by 1966 a powerful politician among San Francisco's African Americans, also helped Moscone. Brown's campaign newspaper, *The Mid-City Reporter*, had a front-page story quoting Brown: "The one-man one-vote decision gives us the chance to gain a new seat in the senate. It should be that of Supervisor Moscone. It would be a tragedy to lose our chance by failing to vote." The caption of the photo of Moscone reminded readers that he was "the logical choice." The last page of the paper recounted Moscone's broad community support and reprinted some of the *Sun-Reporter* endorsement.[43]

Moscone built on the reputation as a tireless campaigner he earned in 1963, putting in long days at bus stops, shopping areas, and civic organizations around the city. The *Examiner* recounted: "His 18-hour day starts when he leaves home at exactly 6:35 a.m., as he has every weekday since March 1, and drives downtown for two hours of traffic island and bus stop stumping. He works fast as people alight from the streetcars and buses to go to work. . . . At 9 a.m. Moscone goes to a cafeteria for breakfast and more campaigning. He hands out cards to the counter employees and bus boys and then, after eating, table hops among the diners." The article, which was very similar to the one written during his successful campaign for the board of supervisors, discussed the rest of a typical Moscone campaign day and included a photograph of Moscone displaying the holes in his shoes from all his campaigning.[44]

As primary day approached, Moscone seemed to be in the stronger position. On June 1, six days before the primary, Stanley Kossen wrote a political roundup column for the *Examiner.* He cited two polls: "Pollster Hal Dunleavy said a cross-section of Democratic voters gave Moscone 52 percent, McCarthy 43 percent. . . . Moscone showed up even better in a Research Control poll with 60 percent against 37 percent for McCarthy."[45] On Election Day, the *Chronicle* gave Moscone a concise but unambiguous endorsement. "George Moscone for the Democratic nomination to the Senate from San Francisco, Tenth district. As a Supervisor, Moscone has demonstrated good judgment and courage and will bring energy and ability to the reapportioned senate."[46]

In the end, the race wasn't close. Moscone won easily with 56 percent of the vote. At 36 years old, he was now poised to win his second citywide race in three years. Although McCarthy was still a supervisor and would have other opportunities to run for higher office, Moscone was the rising star of the city's Democratic Party. Moscone's win was evidence the Democratic Party in San Francisco was moving leftward. Moscone's work in Mississippi, role in the Freeway Revolts and consistent votes with progressive forces on the board helped him defeat McCarthy.

While Moscone had been an attractive candidate and a good campaigner, it was impossible not to see his win as a demonstration of the strength of the Burtons. The Burtons did not yet have control of the city's Democratic Party, but it was looking like a possibility. With Willie Brown, John Burton, and Moscone in Sacramento, Phil Burton in Congress, and Jack Morrison looking like if not quite the front-runner, then at least a formidable candidate for mayor, the Burtons were in position to expand their influence in San Francisco. Moscone's victory over McCarthy also was a good omen to the Burtons and their supporters because that race could be interpreted as a proxy or warmup for the 1967 mayoral election. Burton ally and protégé Supervisor Jack Morrison and McCarthy's erstwhile mentor J. Eugene McAteer were emerging as the front-runners in that race, particularly if Shelley decided not to run for reelection.

The Republican Primary and November

In 1966 the race for the Republican nomination for governor was the most closely watched in the state—and the general election in the fall would be one of the most important elections in the country. Pat Brown, the incumbent Democratic governor, was seeking a third term and had managed to persuade assembly Speaker Jesse Unruh to postpone his ambitions for that office to 1970, thus avoiding a difficult primary. Instead, Sam Yorty, the conservative mayor of Los Angeles, challenged Brown from the right. Brown won the primary by a margin of 51 percent to 37 percent. It was not a strong performance for an incumbent and was a warning sign that Brown's path to reelection would not be easy. Brown, a big-government liberal who helped develop the state's highly respected network of public universities and, through the construction of dams, brought more water to Southern California and the Central Valley, was vulnerable. Yorty was also a voice of white racial backlash. His strong showing was evidence that all was not well in California's Democratic coalition.

A growing conservative movement in Southern California, as well as a sense that the UC system, particularly the flagship campus in Berkeley, was becoming a hotbed of radicalism and student unrest, had begun to undermine Governor Brown's popularity. Nationally in 1966, President Lyndon Johnson was leading the Democrats into a tough midterm election as their victory from 1964 was giving way to growing white backlash and disenchantment with the war in Vietnam.

The early favorite to win the Republican gubernatorial nomination and run against Brown was former San Francisco mayor and liberal Republican George Christopher. However, by 1966 the mood in California's Republican Party had moved sharply rightward, energized by the backlash against liberal policies and civil rights that still define the GOP. Christopher's task in the Republican primary was to move an increasingly conservative party back to the center. That was particularly difficult because his right-wing opponent was an extremely charismatic and gifted politician who had honed his communication skills for years as a Hollywood actor and corporate pitchman. Ronald Reagan had never sought or held elective office but by 1965 he was, as conservative historian Jonathan Schoenwald described him, "the most dynamic force in American political conservatism."[47] Christopher was overwhelmed both by Reagan and the direction of the party. Reagan trounced Christopher in the Republican primary by a margin of two to one.

According to Schoenwald, 1966 was the right year for the new conservatism to emerge—and Reagan was the right man for the moment: "Between the Watts riots of 1965, protests at the University of California at Berkeley, air pollution (the newly dubbed smog seemed almost as ubiquitous as the redwoods), a rising crime rate, a yearly influx of nearly 300,000 newcomers, a widening 'morality gap' between the generations, and a growing fiscal crisis in which the state's mounting debt threatened to rage out of control through ever-expanding governmental programs, conservatives could not have chosen a better litmus test for the theories of 1964."[48]

Moscone cruised to victory in the general election, winning more than 66.5 percent of the vote against his Republican opponent James Walker. In the governor's race, Democrat Pat Brown carried his hometown of San Francisco, but the 55 percent of the vote he won there was a lackluster showing from his political base.[49] Unfortunately, San Francisco was Brown's best county. He only carried two other counties in the entire state: Alameda County, where Oakland and Berkeley are located, and tiny Plumas County in the northeast corner of the state where fewer than 6,000 votes were cast. Statewide, Reagan outpaced Brown by more than a million votes and won easily with just short of 58 percent of the vote.[50]

Reagan's win was a shock to California politics and a warning shot from the far right to the rest of America. Pat Brown had been only the second Democrat to serve as California's governor in the twentieth century. However, Reagan was not your typical California Republican. He was much more conservative than other recent Republican governors like Brown's predecessor, Goodwin Knight, a moderate able to work with Democrats. Knight focused less on ideology and more on the economic growth and development of California. Miriam Pawel refers to this commitment across party lines to work for the interest of California during the decades preceding Reagan's election as the "California Party."[51] Reagan was different. He was a right-wing firebrand who captured the hearts of angry white people who thought civil rights were going too far and who believed that the demonstrators at Berkeley and other campuses were ungrateful children and probably communists.

During Reagan's first bid for governor, UC Berkeley was red meat for his right-wing base, playing something of the same role that the welfare queen would play in his presidential campaigns, albeit without the overtly racist component. At a May 1966 speech in San Francisco's Cow Palace, the same venue where the Republican Party had held their convention in 1964, Reagan described how at UC Berkeley, "A small minority of beatniks, radicals and filthy speech advocates have brought shame on a great university. . . . The campus has become a rallying point and a center for sexual misconduct." He then discussed a report by Alameda County's district attorney's office about a dance on the Berkeley campus using the tones of angry disgust and prurient delight that permeated so much of conservative backlash in the 1960s.[52]

Reagan's victory catalyzed a surprisingly enduring shift rightward in California. Other than Jerry Brown, who was elected in 1974 when Watergate contributed to a big Democratic year nationally, the state would not have another Democratic governor until Gray Davis was elected in 1998. Davis served one term, winning reelection in 2002, but was recalled and replaced by Republican

Arnold Schwarzenegger in 2003. After Reagan's victory in 1966, California not only stayed solidly in the Republican column, but it began to dominate national Republican politics. Four times from 1968 to 1984, a California Republican, Richard Nixon and Reagan twice each, won the presidential election. In the twenty-first century, California has become a very Democratic state, but that was not true until relatively recently.

Reagan's victory in 1966 may have been evidence of a rightward shift in California, but that was not so in San Francisco. Not only did Pat Brown carry San Francisco, but all the Democratic candidates for statewide office, except in the race for secretary of state, did as well. Democrats swept both senate seats and all four assembly seats in San Francisco.[53] San Francisco was becoming more Democratic just the state was moving in the opposite direction.

CHAPTER SEVEN

California in the 1960s

As 1967 BEGAN, THE MAJOR political story in California was not the election of a new liberal Democrat to represent San Francisco in the state senate. Rather, it was the new governor. By 1966 Ronald Reagan was a rising star for the conservative wing of the Republican Party. Even before he was elected governor, Reagan was already mentioned as a potential presidential candidate. In 1964 the right wing of the party had managed to win the nomination for Barry Goldwater, but the archconservative senator from Arizona was neither good with media nor a natural campaigner and had the bad fortune to be running against an incumbent during a period of peace and prosperity. Goldwater lost badly to President Johnson, winning only 38.5 percent of the vote and carrying only six states.

Reagan recorded a speech for Goldwater called "A Time for Choosing" that was probably the best thing the Goldwater campaign did. That advertisement helped make Reagan both a candidate for governor in California and national conservative figure. In that speech Reagan captured the sentiment that would be the core of his message throughout his political career, reflecting the Republican Party he helped reshape. "This is the issue of this election: whether we believe in our capacity for self-government or whether we abandon the American revolution and confess that a little intellectual elite in a far-distant capitol can plan our lives for us better than we can plan them ourselves."[1] The through line from the anti-intellectualism and anti-elitism that Reagan expressed to the celebration of ignorance that characterized the presidency of Donald Trump is hard to miss.

Jonathan Schoenwald wrote how the

> reaction to the Speech should have given conservatives some idea of the jewel they had suddenly unearthed, which sparkled before a national audience. Messages to the Goldwater committee urged them to repeat the telecast immediately. Telegrams to Reagan glowed. "Great, Ronnie,

> Great," wrote the film director John Ford. "Phones ringing around the clock here since your telecast. Our deepest thanks and congratulations for a magnificent presentation" was the report from Republican operative F. Clifton White. Goldwater's own senatorial staff, in a tacit acknowledgment that their boss had a tendency to muddy the waters when he spoke, responded, "We heard your great speech last night. A thousand thanks for a tremendous message made so clear." Additionally, some telegrams asked the question that would become commonplace in the next few years: "I heard your talk tonight. I know you're an actor but are you running for President(?)"[2]

The televised "A Time for Choosing" speech demonstrated Reagan's ability to master the medium. James Broussard described how Reagan's successful campaign for governor had been boosted by his ability in front of the camera, honed by working for years in Hollywood: "The contrast between Reagan and Brown almost personified the divide between past and future. The newcomer used television to reach mass audiences; the incumbent relied on traditional handshaking tours and personal appearances. When Brown finally did appear on TV, this only drove home the contrast. One journalist noticed that while the governor might stumble over a word, Reagan's delivery was smooth and capable, and 'Brown never smiles; Reagan has that beautiful smile.'"[3]

In his campaign against Pat Brown, Reagan articulated many of the issues that would define the right for decades but also some positions that would be defined as moderate today. "Campaign issues included the environment and conservation (a topic on which Reagan got himself into trouble when he said, speaking of California's redwood trees, 'I mean, if you've looked at a hundred thousand acres or so of trees—you know, a tree is a tree, how many more do you need to look at?'), education, student protests, taxes and the state budget, and, most of all, race-related issues. Reagan had voiced his opposition to the 1964 Civil Rights Act, and his emphasis on law and order echoed much of Goldwater's race-coded language, especially after the Watts riots of 1965."[4]

Ronald Reagan's political career cannot be separated from the Cold War. Reagan first ran for governor when the Soviet Union had firm control over Eastern Europe and was gaining ground throughout Asia, Africa, and South America. US policy reflected both a healthy concern about Moscow's influence around the world, and a much less healthy tendency to see almost any national liberation movement as communist. Anti-communism was ubiquitous in American politics and was one of the driving forces behind Reagan's rise to power in California and nationally. When Reagan began running for office, despite the worst of the McCarthy era having already occurred, anti-communism was still a powerful political force. Any foreign policy adventure was defended on the grounds that it was necessary to stop communism. This was the logic of the Vietnam War. Anti-communism was also used to stifle domestic discussions around everything from civil rights to almost all programs aimed at helping poor people. Medicare and Medicaid, two of the most important parts of Lyndon Johnson's Great Society were decried as the road to communism by their most vociferous opponents.

Seeing the threat of communism everywhere while synergistically promoting programs that shifted wealth upward was central to Reagan's policies as both president and governor. The link between a higher marginal tax rate on the wealthiest Americans, or providing medical insurance to old people, and the gulag may not have seemed clear to all Americans, but for Reagan and his supporters that link was apparent. The conservative revolution in domestic policy that Reagan led was made possible by shouting down any progressive legislation by calling it communist. Ironically, while his far-right rhetoric was a constant, Reagan did not always govern that way. For example, during his first year as governor, Reagan signed what was at the time the biggest tax increase ever in California as well as a relatively liberal abortion law.

As governor, Reagan began red-baiting right away. During his inaugural address, Reagan told Californians "an increasing number lately have sought to control the means of production as if this could be done without eventually controlling those who produce."[5] Reagan was not referring to Marxist revolution in some faraway country, but to the politics of California and, presumably his predecessor, the noted communist Pat Brown. Reagan saw communism everywhere and viewed every even moderately progressive policy as evidence of creeping communism. Voters in Californians returned Democratic majorities to both houses of the state legislature in 1966, so Reagan's election was more of a personal victory for the new governor, and a rebuke of his predecessor, than clear evidence of a conservative revolution sweeping California.

Reagan and George Moscone began their service in state government at the same time. Other than Moscone's last year in the senate, their time in Sacramento overlapped completely. The two men had very different politics, backgrounds, and life stories, but shared some similarities.

Reagan's media skills are the stuff of political legend. Many Americans old enough to remember Reagan can only recall the later years of his presidency, but when he began his first term as governor, he was a different man. At the time of his first inauguration, Reagan was a few weeks shy of his fifty-sixth birthday. Pat Brown was only six years older than Reagan, but while Brown looked like a caricature of a midcentury big-city politician, Reagan looked like the movie star that he had been. He was in good physical shape, had an easy and friendly smile, and always seemed to be tan. Because of his work in the movies and later as a corporate pitchman, Reagan easily adapted to the age of television. Although Reagan's policies were often cruel and divisive, his personal style was warm and lighthearted. This didn't make his policies any kinder but made them easier to sell. If you were on the left it was easy to hate Reagan, but for most others he seemed like a likable, decent sort.

Reagan's star power paved his way to the White House. Pat Brown, Richard Nixon, Phil Burton, Jack Shelley, and other California politicians of that time may have been hard-working and smart, but they were never media stars the way Reagan was. George Moscone was a first- term state senator in 1967 but had some of that star power as well. Even early in Moscone's career, he had begun to stand out from the other local elected officials and candidates in San Francisco. While running for the board of supervisors in 1963, Moscone was able to arrange for Dizzy Gillespie to perform at one of his fundraisers.[6] Reporters frequently mentioned Moscone's looks, including his height, athletic build, carriage, and handsome face, when writing campaign profiles. His friendship with Willie Brown, who had a reputation as a stylish and sharp dresser, also contributed to this. Just as Reagan was a contrast to his predecessor Pat Brown, Moscone, who was only thirty-eight when he got to Sacramento, seemed younger and more future oriented than most of his fellow legislators. Reagan was almost twenty years older than Moscone, but the differences between them were more than generational. They represented two competing visons that would be at the heart of Californian, and American, politics for the next decades.

Between 1966 and 1992, Democrats and Republicans competed intensely in California, less so at the presidential level, where the Republican candidate carried the state in every election from 1968 to 1988, and the Democrats every election since, but governor's races were generally quite close with the two parties separated by four or fewer points in 1974, 1982, and 1990. For much of this time, 1979–1998, the governor and lieutenant governor were of different parties. The state's US Senate delegation was usually split with one Democrat and one Republican from 1969 to 1992. During these years, the state legislature had Democratic majorities that frequently clashed with Republican governors.

Despite the competition between the parties, California was not a moderate political environment with the two parties competing for a large swath of the center. Reagan's election reflected, and contributed to, the California Republican Party becoming very conservative. Reagan was probably the most conservative non-southern governor in the country and quickly consolidated his position as a national leader of the right wing of his party. Additionally, the tax revolution, which led to severe cuts in taxing and spending and remade domestic policy, began in California during the 1970s. Defense spending, particularly in places such as Orange County also pushed the California GOP rightward. During the 1980s, there were few members of the House of Representatives more conservative than Orange County congressman Bob Dornan, whose support for the defense industry earned him the nickname "B-1 Bob."

Pete Wilson was a Republican mayor of San Diego who got elected to the US Senate in 1982—his opponent in that race was Jerry Brown—and was elected governor in 1990 and again in 1994. His anti-immigrant positions in the mid-1990s, albeit more eloquently and politely expressed, would not be out of place at a Donald Trump rally. Wilson tried to use those positions to make himself a national figure and run for president in 1996. He failed at that and badly hurt the Republican Party among Latino immigrants, a huge and growing constituency in California by the 1990s.

During the years Reagan was governor, many white voters reacted to what they saw in Berkeley, San Francisco, Oakland, and communities of color throughout the state with anger and racism that fueled a backlash. Polarization and partisanship in the 1960s, 1970s, and 1980s do not compare to the divisions of the twenty-first century. Nonetheless, during those years California's Republicans were angrier and more conservative than those in, for example, the Northeast or most other non-southern parts of the country.

Moscone, on the other hand, represented a very different future for California. By 1967 Moscone had gone to Mississippi to register voters and supported civil rights efforts in San Francisco. Reagan had positioned himself as a candidate of white backlash and had run on the promise of not tolerating unrest on college campuses; Moscone had expressed his support for the free speech movement at UC Berkeley. Reagan saw communists everywhere and rarely hesitated to portray policies he did not like as communist; Moscone had already been red-baited because of his civil rights work. During the eight years Moscone and Reagan were in Sacramento together, the social changes that had been just below the surface began to remake California politics and redraw the battle lines, with Reagan and Moscone consistently on opposite sides of those lines.

Before his second year in the senate was over, Moscone emerged as one of the strongest critics of California's conservative Republican governor, attacking Reagan's political operation for what the *Chronicle* described as "helping finance campaigns of distortion against Democratic Assemblymen." Moscone noted, "I think he (Reagan) just shields himself with a little Guard All and sees that the right kind of hatchet men are in charge." Reagan took the bait. "I am sure the people of California are aware that this is silly political season and will judge Senator Moscone's statement on that basis."[7]

Just as Reagan was moving the Republican Party rightward, Moscone was part of a movement that would lead the Democratic Party leftward. From the late 1960s through the 1980s, the California Democrats were frequently to the left of the party nationally. Alan Cranston, who represented California in the US Senate from 1969 to 1992, was one of the most liberal members of the Senate for most of that time. Ron Dellums was elected to the House of Representatives in 1970 from an Alameda County district that included much of Oakland and Berkeley.

He held that seat through the beginning of 1998 and later became mayor of Oakland. Dellums was one of the few truly radical voices in Congress, speaking out against US intervention in Vietnam, Central America, and elsewhere while being an outspoken critic of apartheid in South Africa. San Franciscans may remember Willie Brown primarily as a pro-development centrist mayor, but as Speaker of the assembly from 1980 to 1994, he was a supporter of labor, civil rights, reproductive freedom, and environmentalism. Brown was instrumental in stopping Republican governors George Deukmejian and Wilson from passing their conservative legislative agendas.

When Reagan and Moscone both won their first election for state office in 1967, California was very different from what it became in the twenty-first century. The state that elected Reagan to be its governor in 1966 was still almost 80 percent white.[8] The state legislature was indeed becoming more diverse, and Willie Brown was accumulating more power in the assembly with every passing year. But in the late 1960s in electoral politics, both the left and right were still mostly led by straight white men.

Back in San Francisco

As 1967 began and the mayoral election approached, incumbent Jack Shelley was seen as weak and vulnerable. Several candidates including Harold Dobbs, the Republican whom Shelley had defeated in 1963, and Jack Morrison were thinking about challenging the incumbent. Morrison, who was until then part of the Burton organization, got the support of Phil Burton, but it wasn't easy. Agar Jaicks described the negotiation: "So, when Phil (Burton) called, we got Jack Morrison to the house, and it was back and forth. It was a give-and-take type of discussion, and it was sort of rough politics being played, but in the end, they reached an agreement."[9]

The strongest candidate preparing to oppose Shelley was J. Eugene McAteer, the popular and moderate Democrat whose political base was the west side of San Francisco. McAteer was from a working-class background in the Mission District. Like Moscone, he had been a sports star, primarily on the gridiron, including at UC Berkeley after graduating from Mission High School where he had been all-city.[10] McAteer was considered the favorite to unseat the mayor early in 1967. Nonetheless, an election between McAteer and Shelley, who shared similar positions on many issues, promised to be competitive. That matchup never occurred because on May 26 McAteer died suddenly while playing handball at the Olympic Club, a social club and athletic facility popular among the city's business and social elite. He was only fifty-one years old at the time.

McAteer's death left an opening in the mayor's race for a centrist Democrat. Morrison was too far left, and Dobbs was a Republican in an increasingly Democratic city. However, with the incumbent still in the race, it would take a strong candidate, and most likely a proven vote- getter to win. Shelley was not popular, but he still had the power of the office and could position himself in the center between Dobbs on the right and Morrison on the left.

By the end of summer it looked like Shelley, despite his political troubles, just might find a path to reelection. Then on September 7, a few days after his sixty-second birthday, Shelley announced that he would not run again, claiming he had made this decision under strong advice from his doctor. There was a political angle to it as well. Shelley had never cottoned to being mayor and despite the possibility of being reelected, may not have been looking forward to another four years in City Hall.

This announcement scrambled the race once again, leaving only two candidates—the Republican Dobbs and the progressive Democrat Morrison. McAteer's supporters, only recently over the shock of the death of a relatively young and very popular politician, searched for somebody else to get in what was now a very winnable race for a centrist Democrat. Moreover, McAteer's erstwhile supporters realized that if Morrison, who seemed to be a slight favorite over Dobbs to be elected, the Burton machine would have further consolidated its grip on San Francisco.

McAteer had assembled a coalition of more conservative Democrats from the west side of the city along with downtown business and real estate interests. These voters and business leaders had lost confidence in Shelley because of a perception that under his leadership, demonstrations, crime, and disorder were on the rise. Shelley had tried, and failed, to strike a balance between supporting civil rights while also keeping conservative Democrats, many of whom were union members, in his coalition. With Shelley out of the race, there was space for a more moderate Democrat to appeal to those voters and win the election.

The candidate that emerged from McAteer's circle was a wealthy and prominent attorney named Joseph Alioto. His law clients included Samuel Goldwyn and Walt Disney. Alioto had been the chair of McAteer's finance committee, was deeply integrated into the business and real estate elite of the city and had a reputation as being smart and able. Alioto was a fifty-one-year-old Italian American with deep roots in San Francisco. Like Moscone, he had attended Catholic high school in San Francisco. Alioto had graduated from Sacred Heart, a more working-class school without the academic stature of St. Ignatius. Alioto had grown up in North Beach, not far from Cow Hollow, but unlike Moscone had been around local politics from a very young age. In a 1991 interview, he recalled "my father was the political liaison to the people on Fisherman's Wharf. He got their licenses from the state on the promise that they would build up the Wharf. My mother was active in the Salesian Boys Club Auxiliary."[11] Although Alioto had never held elected office, he was not new to government, having served on the school board and as chair of the city's redevelopment agency. He was a pro-growth and pro-development voice. McAteer's real estate and development supporters quickly got behind Alioto.

According to William Issel, "Alioto's public service from the 1940s to the 1960s reads like a textbook sidebar illustrating the pursuit of postwar 'vital center' Democratic Party urban liberalism. When he returned to San Francisco after wartime work in Washington, Alioto opened a law practice specializing in private antitrust suits. From 1948 to 1954, he was a member and then president of the board of education. Until 1971, school board members were appointed by the mayor, not elected. Alioto also worked in the San Francisco Redevelopment Agency from 1955 to 1959."[12] Another way to say this is that Alioto was inseparable from the political establishment in San Francisco.

Alioto's description of how he became the leading candidate for mayor despite having never run for office and having limited name recognition shows both how Alioto got his start, and that as late as 1967, San Francisco was still a city where labor and big business could quickly make a relatively unknown lawyer become mayor in only a few weeks:

> Anyway, it was announced that Jack Shelley's doctor recommended he get out of the race. And he took that recommendation. That left Harold Dobbs with virtually an election by default. A client of mine had some substantial differences with Harold Dobbs . . . differences led me to think, well, he shouldn't win by default. . . . It was eight weeks, not six weeks, maybe, or seven weeks before the election. I had never been in a campaign before. . . . Yes, the support I had with the McAteer people, who had gone to Shelley, and the Shelley people, who had now nowhere to go. . . . The immediate support I got was from the labor unions, from Joe Mazzola, the Plumbers Union, Harry Bridges, the ILWU. . . . But the Laborers Union, the Electricians Union, the Carpenters Union—the building trades generally were on my side. And when (Ben) Swig became my finance chairman, I sat there in absolute wonderment. There were no maximums or minimums in those days. Ben held a meeting of the so-called checkbook Democrats up in his suite at the Fairmont Hotel.[13]

Labor was not, at first, quite that strongly behind Alioto because many unions continued to support Morrison, but many of the more conservative unions who had supported McAteer quickly rallied behind Alioto. Ben Swig was a very wealthy businessperson who had made most of his money in the real estate business. During the 1960s and 1970s, he was one of the most influential political figures in the city.

Richard DeLeon, a scholar of San Francisco politics, described how Alioto fit into the city's power structure in 1967: "Alioto certainly was for a lot of different reasons a prime candidate to fill in that slot. He served in the Redevelopment

Agency, for example, was generally pro-growth, shared this larger vision and was ready to support it, and had the backing of key downtown business leaders, and the key members of this elite group that formed within the cockpit of the pro-growth coalition."[14]

Larry Simi, who worked on Alioto's reelection campaign in 1971 and then served in the administration during Alioto's second term, was more succinct. "The power elite of San Francisco. The Ben Swigs and the Walter Shorensteins, Cyril Magnin. The big downtown developers had a very strong view—and it was shared, by the way, by the building trades and the African American community, and the leadership of the Latino community, such as it was in those days, and by the Asian community that was basically a Taiwan-based conservative business-oriented group—that San Francisco needed to grow economically."[15]

The article in the *Chronicle* covering Alioto's announcement focused on his personal background rather than political ties: "A North Beach boy who climbed to enviable heights in his native city—millionaire lawyer and controversial figure—now wants to attain the civic peak: the mantle of mayor."[16] The emergence of Joe Alioto as a viable candidate for mayor, ultimately as the front-runner, in September 1967 reflects something very important about San Francisco that makes it fascinating and exciting, but also confounding. San Francisco has long been, and remains, simultaneously one of America's great cities with a political, economic, and cultural footprint that is comparable to or greater than any American city other than New York. However, it is also a relatively small city with a population that is consistently about one-tenth that of New York and about one-third or less that of Chicago and Los Angeles. San Francisco has long been a city where despite its small size, so much seems to be going on at the same time in so many different parts of the city.

The Summer of Love

At the time of Alioto's entrance into the mayor's race, the new school year was beginning and the Summer of Love was winding down. The Summer of Love helped create contemporary San Francisco's image. San Francisco, more than most cities, is the product of major social, economic, and sometimes physical earthquakes that transform the city every few generations. These are in addition to global events such as world wars and depressions that transform every city and country. Beginning in 1849, the Gold Rush radically changed San Francisco within only a very few years. After gold was found in Coloma in the northeast part of the state, an almost unknown, sparsely populated settlement called Yerba Buena until 1847 quickly became an important financial center as people came from all over the US and the world to try to make their fortune.[17] San Francisco's late nineteenth-century status as the biggest and most important city in the West is unimaginable if not for the Gold Rush.

A little more than half a century after the Gold Rush, the earthquake and subsequent fire of April 18, 1906, destroyed much of the city. Thousands of buildings burned, and the disaster's impact is a major reason why San Francisco looks the way it does with very few buildings built before the dawn of the twentieth century. The earthquake, which had a magnitude of 7.9, forced the city to rebuild and to create the structures and institutions that defined modern San Francisco.

The tech boom in the first part of the twenty-first century was the other transformational event for San Francisco. Because of its proximity to Silicon Valley, San Francisco became one of the wealthiest and most expensive cities in the US. This influx of money changed the character of the city as many of its diverse, radical, and avant-garde aspects gave way to gentrification, more conservative politics and conspicuous consumption. Thousands of people of color, working-class San Franciscans, and artists were priced out of San Francisco as affluent tech workers moved in.

Between the 1906 earthquake and fire and the twenty-first-century tech boom, San Francisco's other major transformational event was the late 1960s. The enduring image of San Francisco even today, when it is tempered by the new tech money, was imprinted on the American psyche in the late 1960s, most specifically the Summer of Love in 1967. The Summer of Love was the apex of the hippie counterculture of the 1960s, a largely cultural movement centered on marijuana, LSD, and music. Bands such as the Grateful Dead, the Jefferson Airplane, and Big Brother and the Holding Company made San Francisco a center of the new music scene, briefly exceeding London or New York. Young people from all over the country and sometimes the world made their way to San Francisco to participate in the Summer of Love. Participate is a flattering word to describe what, for many, amounted to getting high, hanging out, and listening to music.

Tour buses drove through the Haight-Ashbury, the neighborhood at the center of the San Francisco hippie scene, so tourists could gawk at the hippies, while conservatives in the rest of the country saw San Francisco as an example of all that was wrong with America and young people. The Summer of Love was also a time when many, particularly the young people themselves, believed they were making real political change and remaking the country's cultural and political life.

The Summer of Love was more than a brief period in San Francisco history that was a festival of drugs, sex, and rock and roll. Growing up in San Francisco of the 1970s and 1980s, I was told countless times how important it was and how unfortunate it was that I wasn't around then. As much as I found that tiresome, it is also in some respects true. However, I had a pretty good excuse for not being in San Francisco for the Summer of Love—I wasn't born until December of that year. By the late 1960s there were hippies in most major cities and college towns, but San Francisco was different. The Animals, one of the noted bands of that era, sang about the beauty and good vibes of San Francisco while urging their fans to "save up all your bread" and move there. Similarly, Scott McKenzie reminded listeners and fans to "wear some flowers in your hair" when they went to San Francisco.

The Reverend John Bernard McGloin, a Jesuit who taught history at the University of San Francisco, only a few blocks from the Haight, close to where St. Ignatius was located in 1967, earnestly observed the first years of the hippie presence. "An increasing number of young men and women, including many blacks began 'dropping out of society' and moving into what they quickly came to call the 'Hashbury District.' By the fall of 1965, there were enough long-haired newcomers for the local press to take notice. . . . By 1967, it was estimated that between 6,000 and 8.000 Hippies, either real or fake, had moved into the area."[18] During the Summer of Love, as John De Luca, a former aide to Mayor Alioto, described it, "all of a sudden the whole country is ascending on us. And I had a call from the then governor of New York, Hugh Carey. He said, 'Privately can you do me a favor? My daughter has moved out to San Francisco. I don't know where she is.' . . . We realized that this was a bigger phenomenon. Runaway kids, people coming from the rest of the country."[19]

The hippies and the Summer of Love startled and frightened many San Franciscans, particularly older ones, who could not understand what was happening in the Haight. But other than in that one neighborhood and in the eastern part of Golden Gate Park that abuts the Haight, it had little impact on the city—at least at first. Tour buses drove through the Haight, telling passengers that this was "the first and only foreign tour within the continental limits (of the US),"[20] but hippies weren't running for office, opening businesses or changing the overall character of the city yet.

The images from the Summer of Love are familiar to anybody who has an interest in American cultural history, listens to the music of that era, or lived in San Francisco for any amount of time since 1967. Young people walking along Haight Street, smoking pot or listening to music in Golden Gate Park, or hanging out at music venues such as the Fillmore or Winterland, are part of the collective visual memory of that summer. However, it is the sounds, not the sights, from the Summer of Love that have been even more enduring because the music from that scene was so memorable.

During the Summer of Love, high school and college kids drawn by the lure of sex, drugs, and rock and roll came to the Haight for the Summer of Love, but so did music royalty. The Beatles were at the height of their popularity and powers in 1967. In April, when the Summer of Love was just getting started, Paul McCartney visited the Haight. A few months later, on August 7, George Harrison stopped by. Between those two trips to the Haight, in May 1967 the Beatles released *Sgt. Pepper's Lonely Hearts Club Band.* That album remains one of the greatest pieces of music of that, or any, era.

For some who were there, the events centered on the Haight in San Francisco during the summer of 1967 represented the beginning of a new human consciousness, "the dawning of the age of Aquarius" as sung in the musical *Hair*, which opened in New York in October 1967. For others it was just a great summerlong party. On the other hand, many of the same Californians who had helped put Ronald Reagan in the Governor's Mansion the previous November, saw the Summer of Love as a festival of decadence, criminality, and probably communist influence.

While the Summer of Love was by far the thing that is most remembered about San Francisco in 1967, it did not really feel that way at the time. The burgeoning civil rights movements, a good Giants team with four future Hall of Famers, the mayor's race, and the other business of the city drew attention away from the Summer of Love. If you found yourself at the corner of Page and Stanyan or Waller and Masonic in August, you felt the Summer of Love all around you, but out on Kirkham on Thirty-Fifth, or down on Bay and Webster near where George Moscone grew up, it mostly felt just like another foggy San Francisco summer.

The cultural transformation symbolized by the long hair, psychedelic rock bands, and drug use associated with the summer of 1967 was linked to political change as well. Although cities across the country were changing, San Francisco was uniquely positioned to be become the center of left-wing politics of the era. First, San Francisco had a long legacy of progressive politics. The general strike of 1934 had not only been one of the biggest of its kind in American history, but it had institutionalized activist labor unions such as the International Longshoremen's Union. More recently, San Francisco had been one of the cities where opposition to the House Committee on Un-American Affairs roadshow had been the most demonstrative. Another factor was the strong military presence in San Francisco. The lighthearted banter about allowing soldiers headed to Vietnam to ride the bus for free from Moscone's days on the board of supervisors occurred because the Presidio occupied prime real estate in the northwest corner of the city from 1847 to 1994 and was considered "the most important Army post on the Pacific Coast."[21] Across the bay in Alameda, the navy base was another major cog in the war effort. San Francisco was a radical city with a huge military presence as soldiers and sailors were departing from and returning to the Bay Area. This had also been the case during World War II, but that conflict had unified the American people while Vietnam divided the country.

The Summer of Love also brought a lot of new residents to the city. Within a few years, many service sector jobs such as driving buses, waiting on tables, and shopkeeping were being performed by people in their twenties and thirties with longish hair, tie-dyes, peasant skirts, and the like, while health food and used-clothing stores began to pop up in previously staid residential neighborhoods. Some who participated in the Summer of Love and then ended up living in the Haight or other affordable neighborhoods in the city may have been local, but many were not. It was not only hippies who came to San Francisco during these years, but other young and middle-aged people who were drawn to San Francisco's growing reputation for tolerance and new ideas. This included a growing number of gay people seeking an easier environment in those embryonic days of the gay liberation movement.

This contributed to a quiet but profound reinvention of San Francisco that continues to shape the city to this day. In the mid-1960s, San Francisco was still a city of natives, but by 1980 or so that had changed. Anybody who has spent time in San Francisco this century knows how rare it is to encounter somebody who grew up there. This is true even in comparison to other global American cities such as New York or Los Angeles. Within a few years of the Summer of Love, the population was overturned in ways that demographic data alone could not capture. For example, most new migrants were more liberal than the white working-class San Franciscans who continued to leave the city during these years. There was a racial component as well. The Haight is a few blocks from the Western Addition. Many who moved to that neighborhood during and after the Summer of Love displaced African Americans. This tension was exacerbated because, as is usually the case, police enforced drug laws more aggressively with regard to the African Americans in the neighborhood.

The Summer of Love was a strange, dramatic, unusual, and for many of the participants, fun and life-changing, event. It led to The Sixties, a period that in San Francisco lasted roughly from 1964 to 1984, having an outsized significance for the city. However, it is not quite that simple because the Summer of Love was an overwhelmingly white phenomenon. There were musicians of color who were part of the scene, including the extraordinary Mexican American guitarist Carlos Santana and the even more extraordinary African American guitarist Jimi Hendrix, as well as the Grateful Dead's Jerry Garcia, who was Spanish American. Many people of color participated, attended concerts, and got high in Golden Gate Park or the Haight, but a large majority of the participants, spectators, and others were white.

The attention focused on the Summer of Love by the national media obscured the extent to which San Francisco's unique racial diversity also contributed to the city's new radical evolution. Beginning in the late 1960s, San Francisco's politics became inextricably tied to questions of racial equality. In 1970 San Francisco was still majority white, but the 43 percent that was nonwhite was divided between Latinos (14.2 percent) African Americans (13.4 percent) and Asian Americans (roughly 12 percent). There were also 2,900 Native Americans in San Francisco.[22] No other major American city had similarly substantial representation of so many racial groups. This led to racial politics that was different from most other cities where the core struggle was the African American civil rights movement. In San Francisco, that movement coexisted alongside Chicano, Asian American, and Native American liberation movements.

Shortly after the Summer of Love, a coalition of student groups led a strike at San Francisco State University (SFSU) that lasted from November 1968 to March 1969. The university's Black Students Union and Third World Liberation Front led the strike. One of the precipitating events of the strike was the university's decision to suspend George Murray, an African American professor in the English department who was a Black Panther. The demands focused on making the university more diverse and responsive to the needs of nonwhite students. African American, Latino, Asian American, and some white students united behind a set of demands aimed at making university policy less determined by white and conservative interests.

About eight months later, Native American groups began an occupation of Alcatraz Island that lasted for a year and a half. The occupation, still among the most well-known acts of Native American resistance in modern American history, drew attention to Native American civil rights. Because Alcatraz is in the middle of the San Francisco Bay and visible (unless shrouded in fog) from most of the northern part of San Francisco as well as from other parts of the Bay Area, for eighteen months all San Franciscans had a powerful reminder of America's deeply troubled history with its indigenous population.

The struggle for the International Hotel was another front in the growing civil rights struggles in San Francisco. The International Hotel was at Jackson and Kearney, an area between the Financial District and Chinatown that had a large Filipino population and was sometimes called Manilatown. The International Hotel was an obstacle to the redevelopment of downtown and became a touchpoint in both the civil rights movements and the anti-Manhattanization efforts. Late in 1968, the mostly elderly Filipino residents of the International Hotel received eviction notices because the building was to be torn down. Over the next decade, there were protests and demonstrations at the International Hotel and the offices of Walter Shorenstein, the wealthy power broker who owned the building. Many progressive and radical groups supported the low-income tenants of the building and sought to defend their right to stay there.[23]

The movement for African American civil rights remained very significant in San Francisco during this period. The African American struggle is more associated with Oakland than San Francisco because Oakland had a larger percentage of African Americans and was home to the Black Panthers. Nonetheless, by the early 1970s the African American civil rights movement was very significant in San Francisco as well, including some groups, like the Black Liberation Army, that were violent and radical.

Mayor Alioto

By November 1967 the strongest challenger to Alioto was Harold Dobbs, who once again failed to get elected as a Republican in an increasingly Democratic city. When the votes were tallied, Dobbs trailed Alioto by a margin of 44 percent to 38 percent. Jack Morrison was unable to consolidate progressive support because neither the Burtons nor labor were fully behind him, and only won 16 percent of the vote. There were no runoffs in those days, so 44 percent was enough to make Alioto mayor.

Alioto began his term in office with an inauguration speech that was eloquent, poetic, and optimistic, allowing Alioto to demonstrate his intellect, charisma, and confidence:

> So while we respect and revere our storied past, the clear fact remains that the world moves much too quickly in our time to permit us the luxury of wandering in the pleasant meadows of the past. It is the discernible future that beckons, and we must seize the hour we have to shape the future we want—or fall by the wayside. . . . No community is an island. If the bell tolls for anyone (sic) of us, it tolls for all of us. It cannot be the best of times for some and the worst for others. It cannot be a season of light for some, a season of darkness for others; a summer of affluence for some, a winter of despair for others; a vision of beauty for some, a nightmare of ugliness for others. It must be like Sandro Botticelli's "Primavera," a new spring of hope for all of us.[24]

The new mayor closed out his inauguration speech with a rhetorical flourish laden with platitudes rather than solutions: "Come join me in a grand urban coalition, involve yourselves deeply with me in a relentless effort to ignite a flame in the breast of this city, a fiery spirit of adventure that soars beyond the ordinary, beyond the complacent, beyond the mediocre, into the heights of the excellent, the daring, and the imaginative."[25]

The 1967 election demonstrated that regardless of what was occurring in the Haight, or how many young people were coming to San Francisco, local politics was, rhetoric and style notwithstanding, largely unchanged. Alioto was younger and more dynamic than Shelley, but ideologically similar. Moreover, Morrison, the most left-of-center candidate, finished a distant third. San Francisco in 1967 was still a moderate political environment where the political center was still strong. The divisions that would threaten the very fabric of the city were still not consolidated. During Alioto's eight years in City Hall, those divisions would grow stronger and come to dominate the city's political life.

To those who look back on San Francisco of 1967 through tie-dyed lenses from the Summer of Love, it is incongruous that Joe Alioto was the kind of mayor San Francisco elected that year. Alioto, despite his personal story, was like Shelley and George Christopher before him, a kind of standard midcentury American mayor. His pro-development views offered growth and profits to big business and jobs to organized labor while paying less attention to the concerns of neighborhoods, ethnic minorities, or the poor. Alioto was not, for his time, racist or angry and contemptuous of the poor like California's new governor, but he was unambiguously a man and a mayor of his time. If the new San Francisco was ascendant, as Moscone's victory in 1966 might have suggested, the emergence of Joe Alioto as mayor indicated that ascent was not happening quite so quickly.

Larry Simi captured how Alioto was a product of the old San Francisco trying to keep up with the new:

> Alioto . . . was like Hubert Humphrey. It was labor and black coalition, and most of the black guys were labor guys, and there were some Latino labor guys, and then he had alliances with the Chinese Six Companies in Chinatown and stuff. But his attitude toward gays was, "Okay, that's fine, but just don't scare the horses, you know. Keep it all behind closed doors. . . . Alioto struggled with anti-Vietnam protests. He struggled with the Haight-Ashbury. . . . (He) came down pretty heavily in terms of a police presence there."[26]

During the 1960s many American cities were governed by mayors that seemed, like Alioto, to be from another era. John Lindsay, the handsome, charismatic Republican mayor of New York, as well as the first group of African American mayors such as Richard Hatcher of Gary, Indiana, were the exceptions. The mayor who best represented the older style of leadership that was still prevalent in big cities was Richard J. Daley of Chicago. Daley first became Chicago's mayor after winning the 1955 election. He remained mayor until his death in 1976. Daley was extremely powerful in Chicago and, for some time, nationally as well. He was a symbol of the old patronage-based and socially conservative way of governance, and in that respect was precisely what the Burton organization, despite their own ability to use some of the same tools, was fighting against.

Alioto, long after he had left office and Daley had died, reminisced about his old friend: "Daley . . . later became one of my best friends. He was a wonderful mayor. Among the mayors he was really about my favorite. . . . He and I were on the same kind of wavelength in many respects." Alioto elaborated that "Daley became one of my best friends. I had great admiration for him in terms of his ability to manage cities and to manage the difficult problems that plagued the major cities at that time. I always had a close, personal, friendly relationship with him."[27]

Larry Del Carlo began working for Joe Alioto in 1972 and remained in city government for the next three decades. He elaborated on the similarities between Daley and Alioto, explaining how Alioto navigated the complex politics of the era: "I observed Alioto using the same kinds of strategies that I saw Mayor Daley use, which involved bringing people into his administration, identifying the leaders, giving them positions in city government . . . I wouldn't say it in a negative sense because it did help communities. . . . He was able to get control (of these communities). . . . He really, I thought, understood power . . . more than other mayors have. . . . Both Daley and Alioto . . . understood how to co-op folks, how to co-op organizations, how to neutralize their power and so on."[28]

Alioto symbolized the enduring power of the older San Francisco, but there was more to him than that. The man who had to navigate San Francisco through these difficult and transformational years was a sophisticated and smart political actor, if not always a progressive one. At a time when the political discourse in many cities pitted progressive supporters of civil rights against representatives of an angry conservative backlash, Alioto did not fit neatly into either camp. He was much more liberal and interested in civil rights than conservative mayors who served during these same years such as Daley in Chicago or Sam Yorty in Los Angeles, but Alioto was not as progressive on racial issues as Lindsay in New York or Carl Stokes, the first African American mayor of Cleveland. Alioto was a big-city liberal trying to balance different factions within his city, open to civil rights, but opposed to radicalism.

Alioto was much more colorful and engaging than Shelley had been. Frances Park-Li Rothman provided some insight this side of Alioto: "He was . . . a man with great charisma. He was always on the move. . . . He would have all these celebrities come in, Tony Bennett. And Joe Alioto would gather all the secretaries together and have Tony Bennett sing to us. And of course he would sing 'I Left My Heart in San Francisco.' Every so often, Joe Alioto would play his violin in the office."[29] Journalist Belva Davis had similar recollections: "Joe Alioto created his own caricatures on purpose. . . . He loved quoting poetry and using romantic language. . . . Sometimes when people were angry with him, he would turn on the Italian charm. . . . He ruled with an iron fist, with charm or with just sheer power."[30]

Alioto's political skills became evident to the whole country early in his first year in office in the days following the assassination of Martin Luther King Jr. San Francisco was one of the few cities where no violence followed King's killing. Following the assassination, instead of finding himself in a confrontational relationship with his city's African American residents, Alioto got ahead of the protests by calling for all flags in San Francisco to be flown at half-mast and for schools to have a two-minute period of silence to honor King. Alioto also called for a public ceremony honoring King at noon on April 5, the day after King was assassinated.[31]

The *San Francisco Chronicle* described the ceremony at City Hall: "Possibly the most moving tribute to the fallen civil rights leader came near the end of the hour-long program when some 7000 black and whites held hands and sang 'We

Shall Overcome.' The huge grief-stricken audience, representing persons from all walks of life had come quietly to the Polk Street side of City Hall from all parts of city. There were housewives from Hunters Point, men in working clothes from BART projects, young secretaries from the nearby State and Federal Buildings and many young students."[32]

That article appeared on the front page below the fold. Above the fold, set off in a square outline, was an article titled simply "Proclamation." It was signed by Mayor Alioto and read in part, "Slightly more than one day ago our nation suffered the loss by violence of one of the truly great Americans of this age. Dr. Martin Luther King had dedicated his work to non-violence. The role he played in the pageant of mankind was to assist his fellow citizens find richer lives. . . . Therefore, as Mayor of San Francisco, I am taking upon myself the opportunity of expressing the shock and numbness that has befallen our entire city caused by the loss of the Reverend Dr. Martin Luther King."[33]

Alioto's deft hand in the days following the assassination caught the attention of at least two powerful politicians. One, Hubert Humphrey, the sitting vice president and the Democratic nominee for president in 1968, seriously considered putting Alioto on the ticket, but ultimately thought that the San Francisco mayor, still in his first year in office, simply did not have enough experience. John De Luca described how Alioto almost became his party's vice presidential nominee:

> During the hotly contested primary battle between Senator Robert Kennedy and Humphrey, Joe forcefully endorsed the Vice President without prodding or inducement. In a series of press interviews and addresses to political audiences Joe was both captivating and eloquent. . . . Humphrey and his advisors took note, and given Joe's West Coast roots and Eastern ethnic and religious appeal, serious consideration was given him as a potential running mate. . . . In the final analysis, the Humphrey inner circle objected that Joe's limited term—barely seven months in office—would negate their planned attack on Nixon's V.P. choice, Spiro Agnew, who was equally unknown to the American public.[34]

Alioto, according to De Luca, carried himself with gravitas and a sense of strength: "Joseph Alioto was a physical and mental force to immediately acknowledge. When he came into a room . . . strong shoulders, balding bullet head, walked with great presence, had a stride that was just fluid. This was a man who had been accustomed to debating in front of the US Supreme Court."[35]

The other powerful politician who took notice of Alioto was Ronald Reagan. As a tough and politically skilled Catholic with a record that was hard to characterize as too liberal, but progressive enough to hold most of the Democratic base, Alioto was poised to be the strongest Democratic opponent against Reagan in 1970. Alioto was showing interest in the race as well. In 1969, as Alioto was preparing to run for governor, an article, better described as a hit piece, titled, "The Web That Links San Francisco's Mayor Alioto and the Mafia," appeared in *Look* magazine. The article tried to show Alioto was connected to the Mafia and was hard-hitting from the first paragraph: "Mayor Joseph L. Alioto of San Francisco, the rising politician who came close to the Democratic nomination for the Vice Presidency in 1968, is enmeshed in a web of alliances with at least six leaders of La Cosa Nostra. He has provided them with bank loans, legal services, business counsel and opportunities, and the protective mantle of his respectability. In return, he has earned fees, profits, political support and campaign contributions."[36]

The article included a diagram that took up almost two pages, in the middle of which was a photo of Alioto surrounded by photos of eight shady-looking men, all of whom had Italian names. The nine people were connected by lines—some dotted, some solid—to suggest Alioto was caught in a Mafia web. The evidence for all these assertions was very flimsy, but the bigoted implication, that Alioto's Italian heritage was proof enough that he was mobbed up, was unambiguous. The author of that article was Richard Carlson, whose son Tucker grew up to become a prominent right-wing propagandist.

The article damaged Alioto enough that he decided not to run for governor. Reagan, who saw an advanced "courtesy" copy of the article, cruised to reelection in 1970.[37] Alioto was, naturally, furious and sued *Look* magazine. He eventually won his libel suit against it and was awarded $350,000. The judge noted in his decision that "plaintiff (Alioto) has sustained the burden of proving by clear and convincing evidence that defendant published the defamatory statements contained in the article with actual malice, that is, with reckless disregard for whether they were true."[38]

Almost two decades after that article was published, and after Reagan had finished serving two terms as president, Alioto still expressed rancor toward both *Look* magazine and Reagan: "I watched Ronald Reagan on television lie about it. He said that he had nothing to do with the article, nor did he have anything to do in publicizing the article. He actually got a copy before the stuff was on the street, had it mimeographed and distributed to a group of Republicans at a statewide convention meeting. . . . It was enough to cost me the governorship of California against Ronald Reagan in 1970 and enough in 1974, the other time I ran, because it wasn't dissipated then."[39]

Alioto was mayor during the strike at SFSU and the occupation of Alcatraz. During his eight years in office, the civil rights struggle began to be more acutely focused on political power. Alioto became a symbol of the white political power structure in the city but tried to balance that with his concern for civil rights. "The dominant concern I had when I became mayor was that there was a growing gap between the black and white communities. And there was no real effort being made at the top to bridge that gap and to close that gap. . . . The primary business of my first year as mayor was to close the gap because without stability on the racial question everything else, it seemed, was threatened."[40] Alioto's civil rights position, as his comments suggest, was primarily about stability.

Alioto's actions were a contrast to Shelley, who had struggled to keep San Francisco peaceful as the civil rights movement accelerated. Shelley had begun his term as a supporter of civil rights, and he was likely a beneficiary of the sit in at Mel's Diner just days before the 1963 election. However, by the end of the term, it seemed as if the fast-changing racial politics of San Francisco, like many other things, were overwhelming Shelley. Shelley was mayor during the period when urban uprisings, almost always referred to as "riots" at the time, occurred in many cities. In most of these cities—such as Newark, New Jersey; Los Angeles; Cleveland; Detroit; and Omaha. Nebraska—the conditions of poverty, inadequate housing, and joblessness were important causal factors, but the most immediate factor was generally some form of police violence against African Americans.

The 1966 uprising in the heavily African American Bayview/Hunters Point section of San Francisco was not much different. The spark that started those uprisings occurred on September 27, when police officer Alvin Johnson, who was white, noticed several youths running from a stolen car they had been driving. The officer, initially unaware the car was stolen but noticing something unusual, gave chase, then shot and killed sixteen-year-old Matthew Johnson, who was African American.[41]

News of Johnson's killing was met with anger and frustration in the community. The next five days saw looting, mostly of stores owned by people from outside of Bayview or Hunters Point, and fighting on the streets between police and residents. Mayor Shelley was unable to stop the violence. By the time calm returned, 898 people, including 102 youths, had been arrested. Matthew Johnson was the only person who died, but 161 people were injured, roughly half of whom were police officers, firefighters, or other city employees. Looting and property damage was estimated to be $135,782, roughly equivalent to $1.2 million in 2023.[42] That number seems too small, but it was partially because of low property values in that part of the city.

Darrell Rogers, who was in his early twenties when he participated in the uprising, said, "What really bothered me the most was the rejection by the City of San Francisco to the outrage of someone being killed in that manner. What I saw them doing was somehow being able to say, 'Enough is enough. This is something we cannot stand. . . . And we spoke on this before and you're not listening. We had people in the streets, and you're not listening. And there's only one alternative—to fight fire with fire.'"[43]

Mayor Jack Shelley's statement of September 30 was, particularly given the time, reasonably good. It was published in full in the *San Francisco Chronicle* and said in part:

> All of these trademarks of violence are but symptoms of social tragedy that is occurring not only in San Francisco, but in all major cities across our land. The tragedy is the fact that a substantial group of American citizens . . . have not yet received all the precious opportunities and rights they deserve according to the sacred guarantees of democracy . . . For the moment, forceful measures have been necessary, simply in order to preserve the tranquility of our city, but the time has come to put an end to the physical violence. The time has come to do something about the things that caused this agony among us.[44]

Shelley seemed to be committing himself to the cause of the African American residents in the Bayview/Hunters Point area while not entirely supporting the city's police force. Shelley's position contrasted starkly with that of Ronald Reagan who, during his campaign for governor, blamed his opponent and unnamed African American leaders. Referring to the Watts riots in 1965, Reagan said of Governor Brown, "It is obvious the Governor has not profited at all from the experience of Watts. . . . The leaders of the Negro community who have urged civil disobedience have forfeited their right to leadership."[45]

Reagan's response to the riots was a clear and unambiguous embrace of the backlash. While Brown's reaction was not as extreme, it was similar to Reagan's. Brown visited San Francisco the day after the riots began and commented that he was "sick and tired of groups and individuals violating the law." When a young African American man told the governor, "I don't understand why that boy got shot." Brown replied with appalling nonchalance, "These things happen. They shouldn't happen but they do." When another African American "made it clear he thought Johnson—whose death sparked the riots—died only because he was a Negro," Brown again displayed insensitivity. "No . . . When I was District Attorney of San Francisco they did it to a little white boy—I don't think it was racial."[46]

Within a month of the shooting of Matthew Johnson, Alvin Johnson, the police officer who shot him, was acquitted. The jury issued a verdict that the shooting was "excusable homicide," which "in effect exonerated" officer Johnson. The trial was held in a coroner's court rather than a more standard courtroom.[47] Police leadership welcomed Johnson, who was back on the beat within a few days, but moved him to the Taraval Station in the western part of the city.[48]

Events in Hunters Point were further evidence Shelley was overmatched as mayor. He said many of the right things, but he was unable to bring calm to the area. Conservatives did not think Shelley was tough enough, while African

Americans did not believe he was doing enough for them. This left little room for Shelley to navigate his way to a viable reelection strategy.

About six weeks after the uprising in Hunters Point, Reagan drubbed Brown in the race for governor. Brown did not lose that race because of his response to the events in Bayview/Hunters Point, but Reagan used the events to mobilize his base, while Brown had no cohesive message.

Alioto and Policing

When Alioto became mayor in 1968, relations between police and African American San Francisco were not good. Beginning in the late 1950s and early 1960s, obscenity, drugs, interracial fraternizing and sexual relations, and just the general unconventionality of the beatniks, and then hippies, drew police ire and harassment.[49] Additionally, police in San Francisco had a history of harassing gay people and shaking down owners of gay bars for bribes. Christopher Lowen Agee described how in the 1950s "on a day-to-day basis, the so-called sex detail waged its harassment program by targeting those areas of the city with the greatest potential for public observation (parks, public bathroom, and bus terminals, for example) . . ." 'The Morals Squad was everywhere,' Robert Duncan, a gay poet, remembered, 'and the entrapment of gay males in the streets, the parks and in the numerous public places was a constant fear and common occurrence.'"[50] This continued into the 1970s.

Alioto's record on policing, like much else about his time as mayor, was mixed. He sought to thread a difficult needle of recognizing that social mores were changing and that civil rights required a different attitude toward policing, while not veering too far from support for law enforcement. For example, Alioto appointed the city's first African American police commissioner, Washington Garner, but his police chiefs, Thomas Cahill, Al Nelder and Donald Scott were, like almost all their predecessors, white Irish Americans.

As the Haight-Ashbury scene became more visible, many San Franciscans, including the police, wanted to crack down aggressively on the hippies. Alioto did not support that approach, asserting that hippies, while odd, were simply exercising personal freedoms. Agee described how Alioto pursued this balance: "Mayor Alioto 'ridiculed the institutionalized indolence of the hippie movement,' but defended 'their right to dress and to speak as they please, no matter how unorthodox, so long as they don't interfere with the rights of others.' When a local conservative exclaimed that hippies had transformed Golden Gate Park into a 'jungle' unsafe for women and children, Alioto sanguinely responded that hippies had a right to the public grounds and then illustrated his confidence in the midst of the counterculture by organizing a made-for-media, tongue-in-cheek picnic in the park."[51] Alioto later fleshed out this position: "In each generation a new set of people demand certain rights. They resorted to violence in some areas and civil disobedience to get attention. . . . I'm not disturbed about things that are going on today."[52]

During the long strike at SFSU, Alioto ran up against the limits of his political skills and used violence, creating tensions between the mayor and many San Franciscans of color. The strike at SFSU began in November 1968 and continued through the following March. On November 13, the San Francisco Police Department Tactical Squad, known as the "Tac" squad, was sent onto campus. The result was a clash between police and demonstrators described in the next day's newspaper as a "Battle on Campus" and "S. F. State Students, Cops in Wild Fight." The latter article described a "savage, rock-throwing battle between police and students."[53]

In an oral history done years later, Alioto explained his decision to send the police to the strike:

> There was a good deal of incitement by Black Panthers and others. This was the thing, you know, that got Sam Hayakawa elected as senator, because of the stand he took there. At one point, Hayakawa didn't think we ought to have policemen on campus. I took a very tough view on that. I said, "I don't care where the violence is within the borders of San Francisco. We're going to stop it." It doesn't make any difference to me whether it's on the university campus or any other place. There's no reason for university campuses to be exempt from police protection when violence breaks out.[54]

Arnold Townsend discussed the strike and the police presence at San Francisco State: "I wasn't enrolled, but I went out there (SFSU) to yell at the police every day. . . . I walked over to the BSU (Black Students Union) and there was Bobby Seale, who I'd seen on TV, using the phone, talking to some other brothers that were out of town . . . talking to Charles Gary. . . . He sat there, made some more phone calls, met with some people, talking about some strike strategy. . . . Next thing you know, he's off the phone, and I'm meeting him, and we're talking, and he's talking about some strategy with the BSU folks. . . . Next thing you know, we're on the picket line. . . . George (Moscone) showed up on campus, Willie Brown, during the strike, Ron Dellums, Carlton Goodlett . . . Terry Francois. . . . All these people came out and supported us during the strike. . . . Brown, Moscone and both the Burtons were supportive." With some understatement, Townsend added, "Joe Alioto was not (supportive), of course, and was pretty much anti-strike. . . . None of the other members of the board of supervisors do I remember being supportive. . . . They were pretty conservative folk." [55] Alioto was neither a culturally conservative voice of racial backlash nor a progressive in any meaningful sense of the word. He, like Dianne Feinstein, would be in the race to succeed him, was trying to inhabit a political middle that was perhaps the best way to hold the city together.

Dianne

In November 1969, two years into Alioto's first term as mayor and a few months after the resolution of the strike at San Francisco State, voters in San Francisco went to the polls to elect five people to the eleven-member board of supervisors. The fifteen candidates included five incumbents who were expected to win and keep their seats: William Blake, Roger Boas, Jack Morrison, Peter Tamaras, and Dorothy von Beroldingen.

There were several other notable candidates. George Chinn, an assistant district attorney who lived in Chinatown, and Gordon Lau, an attorney who lived in the western part of the city, were both seeking to become the first Chinese American member of the board. Because in 1969 supervisors were still elected citywide in a multi-vote, multi-member structure, the two were not competing directly against each other. Two more nonincumbents were making their first bids for elected office. Both would play important roles in George Moscone's future. One was John Barbagelata, who when 1969 began was a relatively anonymous realtor from the western part of the city.

Barbagelata was trying to get elected by the same backlash that helped Reagan become governor a few years earlier. Barbagelata's campaign literature demonstrated the anger, intensity, and penchant for overstatement that would be evident throughout his political career. The inside of one flyer featured the question, in large red font, "Haven't you had enough?" followed by "Our city is in sad shape. . . . Isn't it a fact that almost everyone is dissatisfied with conditions in our City? Crime has reached crisis proportions; property taxes have soared; rents are spiraling in every neighborhood; budget is up (48%)—$200,000,000 in four years!!" The flyer also boasted that "John Barbagelata will strongly support (100%) the needs of the Police Department so that our City may be safe." The photo of Barbagelata, his wife, and their eight children—the girls in matching outfits, none of whom appear to be more than fourteen years old—on a hill with a great view of the city in the background, looks somewhat like a San Francisco version of *The Sound of Music*.[56]

Barbagelata's statement in the voter guide, a book-length pamphlet provided by the city to all voters, made his conservative platform even clearer: "Stop the soaring crime rate by cutting City Hall red tape which binds our fine police department. Slow the spiraling tax rate that forces our families and drives up rents. . . . Turn the tide for San Francisco before the completion of rapid transit brings a wholesale exodus. As a neighborhood businessman, I can bring the fresh look we need."[57] Barbagelata's comments about rapid transit were correctly understood to be an expression of his support for building freeways.

Because Barbagelata was new to politics, an unknown challenger in a race with five incumbents seeking reelection, and because he lived and worked in the western part of the city far away from downtown, he received little attention from the media and the political class during the campaign. The Republican realtor was unburdened by charisma or media savvy and was relatively easy to ignore.

Another first-time candidate was not so easy to ignore. In 1969 Dianne Feinstein was everything that the west-side realtor was not. Feinstein was a woman; Barbagelata a man. Feinstein, about fourteen years younger than Barbagelata, was seeking to become only the second woman elected to the board of supervisors on her own rather than after having been appointed first. Barbagelata was Catholic; Feinstein was Jewish, kind of. Her father had been Jewish. More importantly, from a halachic perspective, her mother was Jewish, but did not tell her children that. Additionally, Feinstein had attended San Francisco's elite Catholic girls school, the Convent of the Sacred Heart. Barbagelata lived in St. Francis Wood, a wealthy enclave in the western part of the city; Feinstein lived in Pacific Heights, the neighborhood that was home to the richest and most powerful San Franciscans. Barbagelata was a conservative Republican; Feinstein a liberal-to-moderate Democrat. Barbagelata was a political outsider with no experience in government; Feinstein was an insider with strong ties to San Francisco's political and business leadership and had served on the California Parole Board for women from 1960 to 1966. She had been appointed to that position by Governor Pat Brown and to the Mayor's Crime Committee by Jack Shelley.

Feinstein was in her mid-thirties and, as the local press frequently commented, was an attractive woman. In 1965, while Feinstein was serving on the parole board but not yet a candidate for office, Joan McKinney, writing in the *Chronicle*, described Feinstein: "Dianne (Mrs. Bert) Feinstein is a raven-haired, blue-eyed beauty who looks more like an actress (which she has been) than an expert on California criminal justice (which she is)."[58] As Feinstein began her campaign, the *Examiner* published a very flattering article about her that began, "Tall and slim with luminous gray eyes and an obvious sense of style—the sort of woman one pictures in the gentle ambience of the drawing room—Dianne Feinstein is paradoxically no stranger to crime and punishment."[59]

Feinstein was also a dynamic, charismatic, and charming politician who had genuine star power. Barbagelata was something of an anti-politician who built his appeal around being angry, grumpy, and no-nonsense. Feinstein's political skill and appeal as a candidate, as well as her contacts in monied San Francisco, were, as described by Feinstein biographer Jerry Roberts, evident in that campaign:

> The Feinstein campaign soon took on a serious and professional dimension beginning with the hiring of a full-time campaign manager named Sandy Weiner. . . . It was his idea to run the candidate as "Dianne," a tactic that instantly separated her from the pack, and to print all her signs and campaign materials with her name boldly splashed in red and her last name less prominently displayed in black.

> Under Weiner's guidance, her campaign had all the earmarks of those that would follow: money, especially family money; skillful use of media; emphasis on themes of effectiveness and independence; and a temperamental candidate.
>
> In the end, Dianne would outraise and outspend all her rivals in the race and forge an impressive network of supporters and donors, skillfully interweaving family and political connections she had made in years of good-government and campaign drudge work.[60]

Feinstein went on to become San Francisco's first female mayor and the first female senator from California, narrowly missed being the first female governor of the state and, in 1984, came close to becoming the first female vice presidential nominee of a major party. The Democratic nominee that year, Walter Mondale, ended up choosing New York congresswoman Geraldine Ferraro instead of Feinstein.

In 1969 Feinstein was a wealthy woman with, as Roberts describes, campaign and government experience, making her first bid for elected office. She was also mother of a young daughter. Feinstein's decision to run while her daughter was only twelve years old is a contrast to another wealthy San Francisco woman who, before running for office for the first time, had a great deal of campaign experience and political acumen. Feinstein was only about seven years older than Nancy Pelosi. However, unlike Feinstein, Pelosi had five children and waited to run for office until 1987 when her youngest had graduated from high school. Their backgrounds were not particularly similar. Pelosi is an Italian American Catholic born into a powerful political family in Baltimore who moved to San Francisco as an adult, but their career paths were similar and illustrate how some upper middle-class women of that generation got their start in politics. These two women went on to become two of the most successful and important female politicians in American history and were perhaps, along with Willie Brown and Kamala Harris, the most important San Francisco politicians of the last half century.

Feinstein and Barbagelata both needed to be among the top five to win a seat on the board. Given that five incumbents were running for reelection, in a city where incumbents usually got reelected easily, this was a difficult challenge for both, more so for Barbagelata, who had fewer resources and less political support. Nonetheless, both first-time candidates had a chance of unseating one of the more vulnerable incumbents. Jack Morrison, only two years removed from finishing a distant third in the mayoral election, and William Blake, who had been in the middle of the fights over freeway development, looked to be the most likely to be defeated.

The race for the final spots on the board was extremely close. Three candidates, separated by fewer than two thousand votes, were vying for only two seats. Barbagelata, demonstrating the potency of his conservative politics during a time when the city appeared to be moving rapidly to the left, finished fourth, while Dorothy von Beroldingen edged out William Blake for the fifth seat by only 585 votes.

The race for first place was also tight. Finishing first in the citywide election for the board was more than just symbolic. The first-place finisher generally, by custom, became president of the board. This position is the equivalent of speaker of a legislature and was the second most powerful elected post in the city. Additionally, according to the city charter, the board president would become acting mayor if the sitting mayor left office, resigned. or died. Popular incumbents Roger Boas and Peter Tamaras were the leading candidates to finish first. Tamaras won 91,715 votes, 1,063 more than Boas. However, those 91,715 votes were only good enough for second place because Feinstein finished in first with 93,092 votes. From the perspective of the 2020s, it is easy to shrug off the importance of this. After all, Feinstein was a centrist and political insider with strong ties to the city's governing class, but at the time it was a very big deal. Feinstein was a young Jewish woman and first-time candidate. Nobody like her had ever led the board of supervisors before.

Finishing in first place changed Feinstein's political fortunes immediately. Instead of being a first-term backbencher, she would lead the board. It was customary for the person with the most votes to become president of the board, but not for that person to have been a first-time candidate, woman, or Jew, so Feinstein still had to get six votes on the board and at least one of her colleagues was not supporting her. The *Chronicle* reported a few days after the election that "the new Supervisor, John Barbagelata will not vote for his fellow freshman, Dianne Feinstein, for President of the Board. John isn't being sneaky about it: he told her face-to-face as they were taping a TV show with Sup. Ron Pelosi. . . . 'Nothing personal,' Barbagelata told her. 'I just don't think you have the experience. Dianne took that with a smile, but when Barbagelata went on to say she'd spent '$120,000 to $130,000 to get elected,' she flipped her pretty top."[61]

This was not reported in the news section of the paper, but in Herb Caen's column. Caen wrote about many subjects, including politics, and had better sources than most reporters, but was he was not the paper's City Hall beat reporter. The interchange showed how Barbagelata was unable to strengthen the appeal of his message with smart politics. Barbagelata was also a first-term supervisor who, although more conservative than Feinstein, needed her help on the board, but decided to begin the relationship by insulting her. This was particularly stupid because by mid-November, Feinstein was likely going to have the votes to be president of the board, so Barbagelata's gambit gained him nothing except perhaps more support from his base. Lastly, Caen's description of Feinstein flipping "her pretty top" shows how even after being elected, Feinstein's gender and looks were still how the media, even a liberal columnist such as Caen, covered her. Barbagelata may have thought he was taking a tough or principled position by opposing Feinstein, but it got him nowhere. Feinstein's election to board president was so automatic that the press did not even bother to report the board's vote making her president. Feinstein responded by leaving Barbagelata off powerful committees like Finance, Fire, and Safety and Police, but made him chair of the Cultural Activities Committee.[62]

With Feinstein now running the board of supervisors, Alioto ensconced as mayor, and Jack Morrison no longer in office, the power of the Burton machine in San Francisco itself seemed contained. The two brothers still had a great deal of influence: John Burton remained in the state assembly and Phil Burton was gaining power in the US House of Representatives, but in their hometown they were not in the inner circles of political power. The overlap between Burton and the progressive faction within the Democratic Party was enough that the failure of the Burtons to gain a foothold in local political office weakened the progressive movement.

Changing San Francisco

Moscone's time in Sacramento was the only period in his postcollegiate life when he spent a significant amount of time away from San Francisco, but even then, he was not absent from the city. Sacramento is only about a two- to three-hour drive from San Francisco depending on traffic. For years, most state legislators representing San Francisco, for political and sometimes personal reasons, have split their time between the two cities, partially because one of the easiest ways for a legislator to lose an election is to be perceived as being disconnected from their district.

Remaining connected to the district, which in his case was the entire city of San Francisco, was particularly important for Moscone because his wife and four young children lived there. Additionally, his time in the state senate overlapped with an extremely impactful, important, and strange nine-year period for San Francisco. The new political movements, trends, and ideas that were just becoming visible and relevant during the early 1960s and during Moscone's three years on the board of supervisors burst into full bloom after he got elected to the senate. Gay rights went from being an obscure, rarely discussed, political issue to a growing part of local politics—one that was not going away. Opposition to the Vietnam War grew quickly during these years as San Francisco became a national center of the anti-war movement. The civil rights struggles of the early and mid-1960s also became bigger and more politically powerful between 1967 and 1975.

These changes gradually broke down the last remnants of the pro-growth, essentially conservative consensus that had dominated San Francisco's electoral politics through most of the postwar period. The energy from the Freeway

Revolts began to be channeled into an anti-development campaign against what was beginning to be called Manhattanization. That term was used by people who did not want San Francisco to be filled with skyscrapers like Manhattan. San Francisco was shifting leftward in earnest, but not without opposition,

For decades people have moved to San Francisco from all over the US and the world. In the 1850s, they came for the Gold Rush. After World War II, soldiers and sailors, including many gay men, stayed after being discharged from the military. The tech sector has been the big draw this century, but, in the late 1960s and 1970s, most of the newer residents were Americans who came to San Francisco not for economic opportunity but because they were drawn to the city's reputation as a center of the counterculture, progressive politics, and gay liberation. In the 1970s and into the 1980s, it was not uncommon, in fact it became almost a cliché, to hear somebody say, "I came to the city in 1970 (or something like that) for spring break (or to see a concert, to follow my girlfriend/boyfriend or for a long weekend) and I never left." I heard that on the bus, in restaurants and cafés, and from people with whom I worked more times than I can count.[63]

Despite so many new people moving to the city, the overall population of San Francisco declined from 740,000 in 1960 to 716,000 in 1970 and 679,000 ten years later, an overall decrease in population of 8.25 percent in twenty years.[64] The same poor economy that made the city affordable facilitated migration to San Francisco. The shrinking population was caused in large part by the city's weak economy that helped keep rent and the cost of living down. While the absence of jobs may have made San Francisco a less appealing place for some, others, willing and able to get by with a little less money and a little less work, were drawn to San Francisco. In the bigger picture during Moscone's time in the senate, as white working-class people left the city, they were replaced by people who were on balance, younger, gayer, less white, more progressive and less conventional.

The city's political leadership was changing too. Willie Brown was accumulating power in the assembly. George Moscone's and Phil Burton's progressive politics kept them in sync with the new San Francisco. A handful of other progressive politicians such as John Burton, still in the assembly, emerged as representatives of the newer San Francisco, but much of the political leadership was still part of the older San Francisco.

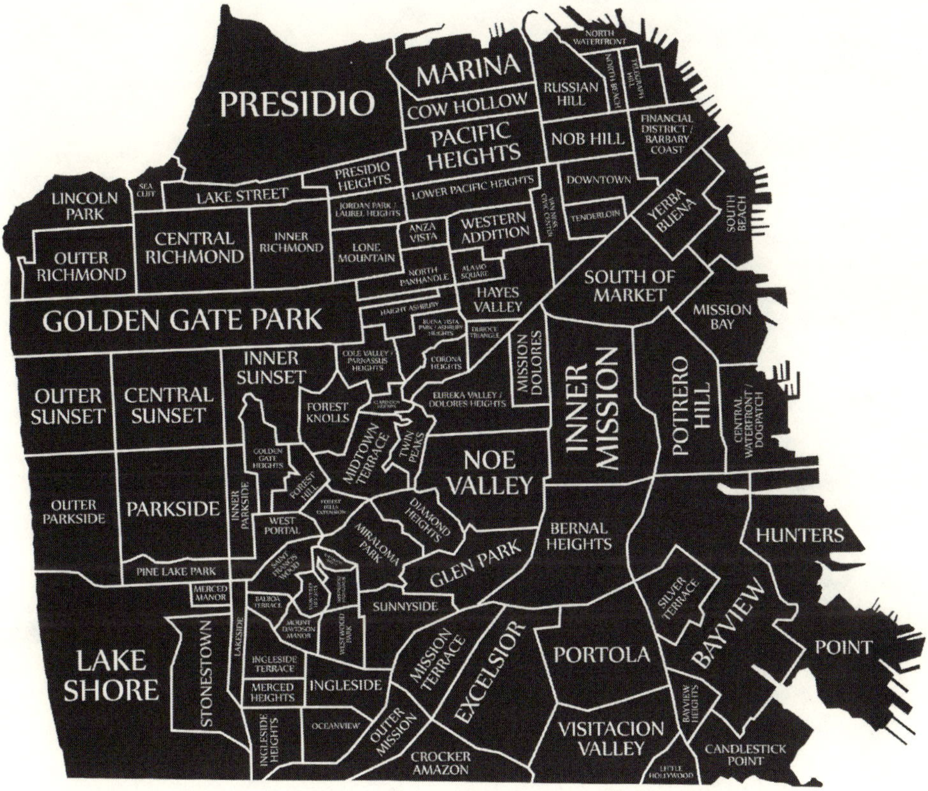

FIGURE 1. Neighborhood map of San Francisco. Courtesy of werbeantrieb.

FIGURE 2. Moscone, wearing number 7, played basketball at Santa Rosa Junior College. Courtesy of Santa Rosa Junior College.

FIGURE 3. Moscone lost his 1960 bid for the California State Assembly. Courtesy of the Moscone family.

FIGURE 4. Moscone was a Kennedy supporter in 1960. Courtesy of the Moscone family.

FIGURE 5. Moscone relaxing at home shortly before his successful campaign for the San Francisco Board of Supervisors. Courtesy of the Moscone family.

FIGURE 6. Moscone's 1974 campaign for governor was short-lived. Courtesy of the Moscone family.

FIGURE 7. Moscone, his wife, Gina, and daughter Jenifer, visit with an unidentified official, *left*, in Israel in 1974. Courtesy of Courtesy of the Israeli Embassy in the United States.

FIGURE 8. Moscone at home in December 1976. Courtesy of the Moscone family.

FIGURE 9. The International Hotel in 1978. Photo by Dave Glass.

FIGURE 10. A home being moved in the Western Addition. Photo by Dave Glass.

FIGURE 11. The Mission District in the 1970s. Photo by Dave Glass.

FIGURE 12. North Beach, as seen from above, in 1978. Photo by Dave Glass.

FIGURE 13. The Richmond District in 1976. Photo by Dave Glass.

FIGURE 14. The Peoples Temple in 1978. Photo by Dave Glass.

FIGURE 15. The Western Addition in 1974. Photo by Dave Glass.

FIGURE 16. Moscone speaking at the opening of the Embarcadero BART station in 1976. Courtesy of SFMTA Photo Archive/sfmta.com/photo.

FIGURE 17. Moscone on the L Taraval shortly before its inaugural run on Market Street in San Francisco. Courtesy of SFMTA Photo Archive/sfmta.com/photo.

FIGURE 18. Moscone with the winner of the 1977 cable car bell-ringing contest. Courtesy of SFMTA Photo Archive/sfmta.com/photo.

FIGURE 19. Moscone at an event celebrating a rebuilt cable car. Courtesy of SFMTA Photo Archive/sfmta.com/photo.

FIGURE 20. Joseph Alioto and Dianne Feinstein served as mayor immediately before and after Moscone. Courtesy of SFMTA Photo Archive/sfmta.com/photo.

CHAPTER EIGHT

In the Senate

MOST FIRST-TERM LEGISLATORS ARE BACKBENCHERS, voting with their party, rarely penning legislation of their own, spending most of their time building relationships with more senior and influential members, focusing on constituency service, and bringing resources and funding back to their district. Moscone's first year in Sacramento was different. Until then, Moscone had proven himself to be a strong vote-getter but an undistinguished legislator. He was identified with the progressive wing of his party but did not yet stand out within that faction. Rather, he seemed to be steadily climbing the political ladder. He was somebody who, it seemed, could look forward to a long career and generally easy reelection campaigns, but not to being a major player in state politics.

That changed in late 1967 when Moscone edged out Alfred Song to become the leader of the senate Democrats. Song was, like Moscone, a first-term senator and progressive. Song represented a district in the southern part of the state that included Monterey Park, and was the first Asian American elected to the California State Senate. Moscone beat Song not just with progressive voters but also by winning support from the more moderate wing of the party.

In a 1988 interview, Song explained that the Democrats in the senate formed a caucus in 1967 and created the position of majority leader. Song believed he had the votes, but Moscone assembled enough support to beat him: "We'd agreed among ourselves, except I wasn't aware of the fact that another guy who was active with us in founding that group had decided that he couldn't compete with me for the votes of my colleagues from the assembly, but he could get the votes of the old-timers who were joining the caucus. And there was George Moscone." When asked if Hugh Burns, the influential conservative Democrat who was senate president, supported Moscone, Song replied, "Yes. They voted for him. They knew they couldn't stop this caucus from forming and so the lesser of the two evils, I guess, they considered to be Moscone. Maybe they found me objectionable, I don't know."[1] Jack McDowell, the *Chronicle*'s Sacramento beat writer, described Moscone's victory: "Today he is Democratic floor leader of the Senate. He was the candidate of the conservative and middle-road veterans who manage the Senate. He defeated a militant liberal who was crusading against this 'establishment' with its bipartisan traditions and its treasured seniority rules."[2]

Moscone managed to win centrist support for his leadership bid while not appearing to waver from his progressive politics. "I feel as strongly about civil rights, housing, educational opportunities, and such as I ever have. . . . I will continue to speak out with my views on a bill—but I know it is not necessary to tell all the senators who oppose you that they're jerks because they disagree."[3] Moscone's rise to Democratic leader also points to the racial politics of the time. It is impossible to prove, but very likely that race was one reason conservative Democrats supported Moscone. Song's reference to some senators finding him "objectionable" suggests that he believed racism hurt him. Moscone's strong civil rights record combined with his identity as a white man allowed him to walk a path to leadership that was much more difficult for an Asian American senator such as Song.

Becoming senate majority leader gave the appearance of some political space between the Burtons and Moscone. Moscone finally had some real legislative power of his own and was not dependent upon the two brothers. His relationship with the Burtons remained complex. The support of the Burtons had been an essential ingredient in both his election victories. It was equally apparent that if Moscone ever sought higher office, he would again need the Burtons' support, but Moscone did not want to be seen as part of a political machine or somehow beholden to the two brothers. His comments to McDowell regarding his relationship with the Burtons conceded that the Burtons were good friends and "a political power . . . but the fact that Phil Burton might choose to support someone in a future election does not mean that I would necessarily support the same candidate. It is quite possible, of course, that we would make the same choice, but I can think of a number of situations in which you would find us on opposite sides of a Democratic primary campaign."[4] The uncertainty in Moscone's tone is hard to miss.

Moscone may have been beginning to carve out an independent political profile, but when John Burton ran for the senate in a special election in 1967 to fill the seat created by the death of Eugene McAteer earlier that year, Moscone was one of Burton's most visible supporters. Moscone was one of the honorary chairmen of the Italian American Committee to Elect John Burton and campaigned with Burton promising to be "a great team" in the senate representing San Francisco.[5] Milton Marks, who had defeated Moscone for the assembly five years earlier, beat Burton in the special election.

Because Moscone represented San Francisco in the senate, the political identity he built in the senate was tied to his city. In early 1967, the Kansas City Athletics baseball team were exploring a possible move to Oakland. This move was opposed by many San Francisco Giants fans who did not want another team in the area to divide the fan base. Moscone, as he explained to *Sports Illustrated* magazine was one of those fans:

> I looked at it this way, we already have the Dodgers in Los Angeles. . . . Then we have the Anaheim Angels, who have the impudence to usurp the state by calling themselves the California Angels. Don't we have enough bush-league teams out here without bringing in one that wears white shoes and green-and-yellow uniforms? The point is, we have the finest food in the San Francisco Bay area. We have the finest culture and the biggest bridges. Must we dilute all this with a team that travels with a mule? Besides . . . I'm a Giant fan.[6]

Moscone's comment, in which he managed to criticize two other team— the Angels and soon to be Oakland A's—was the kind of thing that people in his San Francisco would have chuckled about or cheered, but it was not going to win him friends in Southern California or the East Bay.

Like most legislative leaders, Moscone represented a safe district. Although San Francisco's second senate seat was held by Republican Milton Marks, by the late 1960s San Francisco was increasingly Democratic and out of reach for most Republicans. Marks was different because he was a very liberal Republican who on the issues was much closer to Moscone than to leading California Republicans such as Governor Reagan. Because of their influence and ability to bring pork back to their districts, legislative leaders are generally very difficult to defeat in primaries. This was true of Moscone, who was reelected easily, and without a meaningful primary challenge, in 1970 and 1974. After losing one election and winning two very competitive races early in his career, Moscone finally had some electoral breathing room.

When Moscone became senate majority leader, the assembly was still in Democratic hands, led by Speaker Jesse Unruh, the most powerful Democrat in the state. Unruh, like the Republican governor Ronald Reagan, was from Southern California. Thus, Moscone, in addition to becoming the second most powerful Democrat in state government, was also one of the most powerful San Franciscans in Sacramento. By 1969 Moscone's friend and fellow San Franciscan Willie Brown would be the chair of the powerful Ways and Means Committee in the assembly.

Death Penalty

One of the first issues in which Moscone sought to make his mark in Sacramento was the death penalty. Moscone had not been in the senate more than a few months when Aaron Mitchell was scheduled to be put to death. Mitchell was an African American who had killed a white police officer in a botched robbery in 1963 in Sacramento and been convicted while Pat Brown was still governor. Brown, despite the Catholic roots that led his son to be a strong opponent of the death penalty, had rejected calls for clemency. With Brown out of office, the decision fell to Governor Reagan.

Moscone sought clemency for Mitchell by appealing not to Reagan, whose views on the question were unlikely to change, but to Justice William Douglas of the US Supreme Court. On April 11, 1967, Moscone sent Douglas a telegram: "Justice, may we respectfully request that you exercise your judicial prerogative and ask for a stay of execution for Aaron Mitchell, California. Governor Reagan was not present at the clemency hearing held on Monday April 10. Wednesday April 12 the California senate has a scheduled hearing on the abolition of capital punishment at 10:00 A.M. the hour set for the execution at least until the matter has had a full hearing by the California senate."[7] The hearing Moscone mentioned was a proposal he was sponsoring to abolish the death penalty. Reagan rejected all pleas for clemency, stating, "Here was a case in which every legal avenue had been tried—the U.S. Supreme Court twice, the California Supreme Court twice. . . . The law is the law, and it must be upheld."[8] Mitchell was executed the day after Moscone sent the telegram to Douglas.

Moscone's efforts against the death penalty were not limited to just the Mitchell case. Shortly after, Moscone explained his views on the death penalty in a letter to the *California Reporter*: "It is my firm conviction that vengeance employed by the state is inconsistent with the basic principles of a civilized and compassionate society. . . . Study after study using the most sophisticated statistical methods demonstrates that the death penalty has no effect whatever on the increase or decrease of capital crime. . . . Another important inconsistency incorporated in the exercise of the death penalty is the fact that it is imposed almost exclusively on the indigent, the friendless, the minorities and in many cases, the mentally ill."[9]

Opponents of the death penalty in California won a victory in February 1972 when the California Supreme Court ruled in *People v. Anderson* that the state's death penalty laws were forbidden by California's constitution. Death penalty proponents responded with Proposition 17, a November 1972 ballot initiative that would amend the California Constitution to allow the death penalty. Moscone co-chaired the effort to defeat Proposition 17, stating, "this campaign is crucial because the decision made here will affect the entire nation. Courts and legislatures across the country will cue their own actions on what the electorate in California decides. Every western country outside the Soviet orbit except two has abolished capital punishment. Retention of such an unenlightened practice in the U.S. would signal another confirmation of this nation's uncivilized obsession with violence."[10]

Proposition 17 passed overwhelmingly with support from more than two-thirds of California voters. Proposition 17's huge margin of victory indicated that Moscone's views, at least on this one issue, were out of step with those of the California voters. In general, 1972 was a tough year for progressive causes in California. At the top of the ballot, President Nixon defeated McGovern by fourteen points. Two years earlier, Ronald Reagan had won a relatively easy reelection campaign. Fueling support for both these conservative politicians was concern about crime, so repealing the death penalty, despite Moscone's arguments about its efficacy, was not a popular idea. After 1972, the legislature and courts in the state went back and forth for several years regarding capital punishment, but after Mitchell, nobody was executed by the state in California until Robert Alton Harris in 1992.

His position on the death penalty benefited Moscone politically as San Francisco was becoming increasingly liberal. Additionally, any campaign for statewide office, something that Moscone was considering by the early 1970s, would begin with a Democratic primary. While opposition to the death penalty was not the ideal position for a general election, it would help Moscone in a primary.

Legislating in Sacramento

During Moscone's time as senate majority leader, he was at the center of every major policy dispute in California and became one of the state's leading progressive politicians. Because Reagan was the governor, those years were not a period of great progressive change, but Moscone was a force with whom Governor Reagan had to reckon as he tried to implement his own more conservative policy agenda. One of Moscone's early successes in Sacramento was passing a senate bill to provide school lunches for low-income students in California. The bill, which was also passed in the assembly, was not quite that simple. It did not so much create a school lunch program as provide state support for schools that already had these kinds of programs. The bill called for $5 million in state matching funds to help these schools expand programs and offer lunches to more children. This rather benign proposal, written for the neediest California children, was not consistent with Reagan's free market orthodoxy. In September 1969, Reagan signed it into law, but cut the funding from $5 million to $500,000. Even more than fifty years ago, that was not a lot of money for a school lunch program.

Reagan's press release announcing his support of the bill called Moscone's bill a "poorly drafted program based on an unfair administrative formula that provides no help at all to school districts which do not already have a locally-funded school lunch program. 'These technical defects must be corrected,' the governor said, 'before the state matching fund allocation is expanded beyond a pilot program basis.'"[11] Reagan was not entirely wrong, but the part of the program that Reagan criticized were results of compromises Moscone had to make to win votes from moderate and conservative legislators. A new school lunch program would have been fairer than what Moscone was able to pass, but also would have been bigger, more expensive, and almost certainly vetoed by Reagan.

After 1969 Moscone did not give up on the idea of expanding the school lunch program. Toward the end of his time in the senate, in the middle of a very tough race for mayor, he got a similar bill passed. By 1975 the governor of California was a Democrat, Jerry Brown, who was much more open to Moscone's idea. Senate Bill 120, which Brown signed into law on October 1, 1975, provided $10 million in funding for the school lunch program. On the day of the bill signing, Moscone announced that this was "delightful news to those who are concerned about the plight of hungry school children. . . . This bill pumps needed money into local lunch programs for those who can least afford to purchase what in many cases is the single nourishing meal a child gets during the day. To spend billions of dollars trying to educate children who are hungry is a terrible waste of talent and money."[12]

As Democratic leader of the senate, Moscone worked on some legislation that raised his profile on the left and among important constituencies. He sponsored legislation in 1974 to make acupuncture legal in California. Specifically, the bill made it possible for acupuncturists who were not doctors to get licensed to practice their profession, making it much easier for Chinese American acupuncturists who were not doctors to conduct their work legally. Governor Reagan vetoed the bill, but the next year, after Brown became governor, Moscone again sponsored the bill. Brown signed it into law in July 1975. When Brown signed the law, Moscone commented, "We have had the incredible situation of proven capable acupuncturists having to practice an art 'underground' or face arrest and serious punishment. . . . At the same time licensed physicians, many of whom a possess a great deal less experience in the field, were allowed to practice acupuncture. This new law is going to bring a measure of justice not only to acupuncturists who have perfected the ancient art, but to the thousands of persons who have had to undergo treatment in the 'shadows' for years."[13] It is clear why a senator who represented San Francisco, a city with a large and, even then, increasingly politically powerful, Chinese American community, would work to pass the acupuncture bill, particularly if he was running for mayor.

Overturning racist laws against acupuncture was the right thing to do and had no real downside. Taking the lead on an issue that was important to Chinese Americans in San Francisco was clearly beneficial for Moscone. There was no group of voters in the city, with the exception of perhaps a relatively small number of doctors who were vehemently against acupuncture, who would have opposed the law. Moscone's support for school lunches and similar programs aimed at helping the poor were more divisive but not controversial. These were the kinds of things that liberal Democrats were, and still are, expected to do.

Marijuana

Moscone also took on issues in the senate that aligned more with the new left than with the mainstream of the Democratic Party nationally or in California. This included marijuana decriminalization, bilingual education, and what was then called gay rights. Having progressive positions on these issues today is more or less the cost of entry in contemporary Democratic Party politics, but that was not so when Moscone was in the senate.

Among the issues in which San Francisco and the Bay Area were beginning to separate themselves from most of the rest of the state and country was decriminalization of marijuana. Moscone's time in the senate, from the beginning of 1967 through the end of 1975, was a time when the place of marijuana in American society was changing rapidly. A few years before Moscone took office, marijuana was viewed as a drug taken by jazz musicians, beatniks, and a relatively small number of African Americans, Latinos, and Native Americans, but not something to which most middle-class white Americans gave much thought.

As late as 1969, according to Gallup, only 12 percent of Americans believed in legalizing marijuana, while only 4 percent of American adults had smoked marijuana.[14] That may have been an undercount because some adults would have hesitated to answer that question truthfully.[15] Nonetheless, even if that number were closer to 6 percent or even 8 percent, it was still a small minority. Those numbers may seem low, but by the late 1960s marijuana had taken on a much larger place in the culture relative to the number of people who actually used it. However, the percentage of young people who had smoked marijuana was undoubtedly much higher than 4 percent.

In the late 1950s millions of conservative, middle-aged Americans knew little about marijuana. A decade later many of those same people viewed it as a major problem and, for some, a sign that the youth counterculture was destroying America. In California, this change was dramatic. In 1961 there were 3,794 marijuana arrests in California. By 1967 that number had increased to 37,514, of which "95 to 99 percent of California marijuana arrests were felonies at this time (1967)."[16] By the early 1970s these numbers were not much different. Nationally, still only about 15 percent of the population approved of legalizing marijuana.[17]

By the late 1960s and early 1970s marijuana was strongly associated with the counterculture, hippies, the anti-war movement, African Americans, and radical college campuses such as UC Berkeley. Opposition to marijuana and a belief in the need for law and order and a powerful police response to those who used it were strongly held values among conservatives all over the country, including

Governor Reagan's base. No major force countered this and advocated for reforming punitive marijuana laws.

This became apparent in California in 1972 when advocates for reforming marijuana laws placed an initiative, Proposition 19, on the November ballot. The ambitious and sweeping initiative, if passed, would have "remove(d) state penalties for personal use. Propose(d) a statute which would provide that no person eighteen years or older shall be punished criminally or denied any right or privilege because of his planting, cultivating, harvesting, drying, processing, otherwise preparing, transporting, possessing or using marijuana. Does not repeal existing, or limit future, legislation prohibiting persons under the influence of marijuana from engaging in conduct that endangers others."[18]

Proposition 19 had little chance of winning, but George Moscone was one of only a few elected officials who endorsed Proposition 19.[19] It lost by margin of almost two to one as 66.5 percent of Californians voted against it and only 33.5 percent voted for Proposition 19.[20] In that same November election, President Richard Nixon easily carried his home state of California against Democratic challenger George McGovern, but Nixon only got 55 percent of the vote, so the defeat of Proposition 19 was resounding. In San Francisco, Proposition 19 passed by a narrow margin as just more than 51 percent of the city's residents voted in favor of it. In constituencies that mattered most to Moscone, including African Americans, young liberals and, most importantly, San Franciscans, there was support for the idea of if not legalizing, then at least decriminalizing, marijuana. It was equally clear that as long as Reagan was governor, that was not going to happen.

Yvonne Ryzack, who later went to work for Senator Moscone, described herself as having been a "juvenile delinquent at the age of twelve and thirteen, sort of looking for trouble" during the late 1960s and early 1970s. Ryzack first encountered Moscone at a California Junior Statesmen event in 1972 when she was fifteen and Moscone was the luncheon speaker. According to Ryzack, "In that speech he talked about things we were thinking about but weren't yet ready to talk about—decriminalization of marijuana and universal health care."[21]

Gordon Brownwell, an influential advocate for the legalization of marijuana in California "was a student organizer for Barry Goldwater in '63 and '64. That led to my getting involved in the Nixon campaign in '68. . . . I was fortunate enough that my first job out of law school was to go to work in the White House. . . . I was there less than a year and then came out to California and worked for Reagan in his reelection campaign in 1970. That brought me to California as a Republican." This was not exactly the profile of a pot-smoking hippie or civil rights radical, but Brownwell "started using marijuana when I was in law school in the mid- to late-1960s and realized that making that choice and doing that made me a criminal under the law," which became his "motivation for changing the laws."[22]

According to Brownwell, following the defeat of Proposition 19, Moscone established a Senate Select Committee on the Control of Marijuana. The committee "ended up holding public hearings in late 1973 and early 1974 on the marijuana laws and provided really an important vehicle for educating not just the public but also members of the legislature" about the need to change marijuana laws.[23] One of the other senators on that committee was Milton Marks. The interest that both state senators from San Francisco showed on this issue suggests legalization was more important to voters in that city than the rest of the state.

Within a few years of the failure of Proposition 19, efforts to decriminalize marijuana moved from the initiative process to the state legislature. In the assembly, the chief advocate for this idea was Willie Brown. As with Moscone, for Brown decriminalizing marijuana was both the right and politically expedient position to take. Brown's San Francisco assembly district included most of the African American and progressive parts of the city. Reducing the number of young African Americans who were convicted of low-level marijuana crimes was a civil rights issue important to Brown's constituents. Given the support for decriminalization citywide, there was little political risk for Brown. The assembly was more liberal than the senate back then, so Brown needed a strong ally in the senate to do the harder political work of passing the bill. Naturally, he turned to Moscone. "He (Moscone) carried the bill to decriminalize marijuana, the measure that I was the author of."[24]

The bill to which Brown was referring was SB 195. Moscone began working on the bill in late 1974 and early 1975. According to Brownell, "George's colleagues in the senate knew that this was a bill that he wasn't doing just for show—that he wanted passed." In November 1974, Democrat Jerry Brown narrowly defeated Republican Houston Flournoy to become California's governor, so if Moscone could pass the bill he would have a much more supportive governor than in the previous eight years.

Nonetheless, getting the bill through a state senate where conservatives were very powerful was not going to be easy. In a March 1975 press release, Moscone described the bill as "the kind of realistic legislation that the legislature and the Governor need to approve to show Californians that a government can keep pace with changing public concepts and ideals." The statement added "the Moscone bill would make possession of marijuana a misdemeanor as contrasted to the current situation of a steeper felony charge. In addition, it would stipulate that those accused of possessing an ounce or less would receive a written citation, carrying a maximum $100 fine and no jail sentence."[25]

By 1975 the idea of changing the laws around marijuana use and possession was becoming more popular. Several major California newspapers supported Moscone's efforts. The influential *Sacramento Bee* opined that "California's legislature has the opportunity—and more the obligation—to revise the state's marijuana laws to make it more even-handed and sensible. It ought to do so without qualms. . . . Moscone's SB 95 would insure (sic) against marking the occasional marijuana user who is arrested as a criminal for life."[26] An editorial in the *Los Angeles Times* struck similar chords. "State Sen. George R. Moscone's proposal to liberalize California's marijuana law is a necessary and important step toward addressing this controversial issue in a more sensible and evenhanded way. We support the adoption of SB 95. . . . By including purging of records, the legislation begins to address the crux of the marijuana controversy—that is whether the use of pot should be a crime and whether a marijuana user should be marked for life as a criminal."[27] At least one of Moscone's hometown papers, the *San Francisco Chronicle*, also supported SB 95: "With laudable intent to make the punishment fit the crime, the state Senate has passed a bill that would materially and wisely reduce the overly severe penalties that California law now imposes upon the apprehended users of marijuana. . . . The Moscone bill merits special acclaim for a provision that automatically purges the criminal record of a fine-paying user after two years and permits the courts to purge all past marijuana records."[28]

Getting the bill through the senate was tough and required more than just a political argument. Brownwell again: "I think it was the respect and affection that members of the legislature, particularly members of the senate, had for George that made it possible for the bill to pass the state senate. It was not easy."[29] Democrats had majorities in both houses of the California legislature in 1975 so, despite many conservative Democrats who were reluctant to decriminalize marijuana, Moscone was able to get the votes needed. Willie Brown and his allies were able to do the same in the assembly.

Moscone laid out his argument for passage of SB 95 in a formal letter to the governor asking for his signature on the bill:

> The bill proposes to bring penalties for possession or use of small amounts of marijuana more closely into line with the seriousness of the crime. Frankly, California with regard to marijuana use is out of step with the time. We are one of three states with continues to provide for possible life imprisonment for three-time offenders of the simple possession statute. . . . Under current state law, more than 100,000 Californians will be arrested this year and charged with either a felony or misdemeanor for the possession or use of small amounts of marijuana. This is a costly process not only in terms of state and local dollars, but in terms of human misery.[30]

Brown signed the bill into law, marking California's first legislative step in what became a decades-long struggle to make California's drug laws more rational.

Gay Rights

The early years of the gay rights struggle are central to our collective memory of San Francisco in the 1970s, but it didn't always seem that way then. Nonetheless, even during the first half of the decade, it was clear something was happening as thousands of young gay people moved to San Francisco. Several parts of the city, most notably the Castro, which for most of the previous half century or so had been a working- and middle-class Irish neighborhood, were changing as gay bars, gay-owned businesses, and gay people began to remake those communities.

This outraged conservative San Francisco, but liberal and progressive politicians such as the Burtons, Wille Brown, Moscone, and even Dianne Feinstein were recognizing that anti-gay bigotry was wrong and that gay San Franciscans, like their straight fellow citizens, could vote. However, gay political power was not yet a force in the city. Neither Feinstein nor Alioto had paid much attention to gay rights in the 1971 campaign for mayor. Moscone had cruised to reelection to the senate in 1970 without spending much time talking about gay rights.

During Moscone's years in the senate, there were no out gay elected officials in San Francisco, or anywhere in California. Harvey Milk, an activist and businessman in the Castro, had run for the board of supervisors in 1973 and finished a respectable tenth out of thirty-two candidates in the citywide race but did not make it onto the board. Milk was not notably graceful in defeat. Herb Caen wrote in his November 8 column, "BAD LOSER! Harvey Milk, who went down to defeat in the Supes' race Tues., now has this sign in the front window of his Castro St. camera shop 'Impeach Feinstein, Barbagelata, Nelder, Tamaras, von Beroldingen.'"[31] Although Milk lost, it was apparent even by 1973 or 1974 that gay votes were going to be important in San Francisco and could play a key part in progressive coalitions. It was also apparent to many straight progressives that advocating for civil rights for African Americans, Chicanos, women, or other groups while ignoring discrimination against gays and lesbians was no longer defendable or politically beneficial.

In 1975, as Democrats in Sacramento passed legislation that had been bottled up for years because of Governor Reagan, some turned their attention to gay rights. Naturally, legislators from San Francisco took the lead on this. On the assembly side, John Foran and particularly Willie Brown were the most visible supporters of the proposed legislation. Moscone and Milton Marks also wanted to see gay rights legislation passed. All four of these legislators were straight, but because there were no out gay members of the senate or assembly, liberal San Franciscans were, from a political perspective, the next best thing.

The gay rights agenda in the early 1970s focused on several different issues, including fighting discrimination in housing and the workplace and combating police violence toward gays and lesbians. Instead of addressing these issues, Brown proposed addressing another core issue for gay people—their sex lives. Under California law, sexual acts between consenting adults of the same gender were illegal. As long as these anti-sodomy laws, as they were known, remained on the books, it was not much of an overstatement to claim that gay people's simple existence was illegal. Brown's bill sought to nullify laws criminalizing sodomy, oral sex, and cohabitation between two people of the same gender.

This sounds like basic human rights and common sense today, but in the mid-1970s, this was considered politically radical and even vaguely sleazy or perverse. It was the kind of thing that made San Francisco the target of right-wing ridicule. Getting the votes for anti-sodomy legislation proved even tougher than rounding up support for SB 95, which was winding its way through the legislature at the same time.

In the senate, the May 1, 1975, vote was extremely close as Moscone was unable to get the support of his more conservative Democratic colleagues. Right-wing Republican opposition to the bill was, predictably, also strong. The most vociferous opponent of the bill was probably H. L. Richardson, a senator whose district was centered on Arcadia in Los Angeles County. The *San Francisco Chronicle* described Richardson as almost a cartoonish version of a right-wing homophobe: "(Richardson) waved a sheaf of telegrams, claiming he received 'close to 3000 . . . strongly against this piece of legislation, nine for.' He raised the prospect that homosexuals, if the bill passed, could enjoy sex acts 'under a blanket at the beach' or 'in private automobiles' claiming those as 'private places.' He cited Leviticus in the Bible, denouncing sex between males as 'an abomination,' and counseled the senators they would be judged not only by earthly peers but 'in heaven too.'"[32]

Moscone responded by "thank(ing) his colleagues for the 'gentility and enlightenment of the debate.'" The initial vote in the forty-member senate was 20–14 against. After several more rounds of pressuring his colleagues, Moscone was still unable to get a majority, but he got three more Democrats to support the bill. Ultimately, Moscone could not persuade eight of the twenty-five Democrats in the senate to support the bill. Marks and two other Republican senators joined the seventeen Democrats voting for the bill to deadlock the vote at 20–20.[33]

When Jerry Brown was elected governor, Mervyn Dymally, a Trinidadian immigrant who had served two terms in the state senate alongside Moscone, where the two had become friends, became the state's lieutenant governor and the first Black person to hold statewide office in California. Dymally's responsibilities included casting the deciding vote in case of a tie in the senate, but on the day of the vote he was in Denver at a civil rights event. Moscone, anticipating this possibility of needing Dymally's vote, had asked him to be ready to fly back to Sacramento at short notice. Dymally returned in time to cast the tiebreaking vote, stating he wanted "to get the police out of the demeaning business of regulating victimless acts. The state just has no business poking into the private sexual lives of consenting adults."[34] After the bill passed the senate, it went back to the assembly for one more vote and then to Governor Brown for a signature.

In the spring of 1975, Willie Brown and Moscone worked to passed two bills that were signed into law by Jerry Brown and were instrumental in laying the foundation for California's reputation as a tolerant and progressive place. That year marked Moscone's ninth and final year in the senate. His record there included passing modest liberal legislation when the right-wing Reagan was governor and then moving quickly to pass meaningful progressive legislation once a Democrat became governor. Even as Moscone was passing these key pieces of legislation, he was already looking beyond that chamber.

Governor Moscone?

It is said that every US Senator looks in the mirror in the morning and sees a future president. It is not quite as true that every state senator sees a future governor in the mirror, but many do. Rumors of Moscone's interest in statewide office began before his first term in the senate was over. According to the *Sun-Reporter*, at a conference of the California Democratic Party in the spring of 1969, "the meet turned into campaign openers for Phillip Burton, candidate for governor George Moscone, candidate for Lt. governor. All the aforementioned indicated they were not running, but each was doing the hundred in 9 flat getting their points across and slapping their opponents."[35] That rumor never went much further as Moscone made no effort to run statewide in 1970.

Four years later, Moscone was in a different, and stronger, position. The 1974 election was shaping up to be a good one for the Democrats, and the governorship of California was going to be one of the biggest prizes. Richard Nixon had been reelected in 1972, so 1974 would be the midterm elections of his second term. The sixth year of a presidency is always good for the party that does not occupy the White House. The Watergate scandal made the outlook even bleaker for the GOP. Throughout the country, Democrats anticipated making big gains in the House and the Senate. Ultimately, the Democrats picked up four Senate seats and 49 House seats, substantially increasing their majority in both chambers.

In California, Senator Alan Cranston, a liberal Democrat who would remain in the Senate through 1992, was reelected easily. His Republican opponent was Richardson, who would distinguish himself, so to speak, in that debate around repealing the sodomy laws. The governor's seat was a different story. Ronald Reagan would not be seeking a third term and was beginning to focus on the presidency. The front-runner, who easily won a not very competitive Republican primary was Houston Flournoy, the two-term Republican state controller who had ample experience and looked like the kind of serious man who could steer the state through difficult times. The Democratic field was much more crowded. Candidates initially included assembly Speaker Bob Moretti, Mayor Joseph Alioto, and East Bay congressman Jerome Waldie. That was a tough field, but with no clear front-runner, so in 1973 Moscone began exploring a run.

As early as February 1972, the *Sun-Reporter* reported that Moscone was running for governor, or at least giving the idea a lot of consideration. "More than 1200 friends and supporters of State Senator George Moscone occupied the huge Grand Ballroom of the Fairmont Hotel last Friday evening to help launch his campaign for the Governor's office in 1974. The dinner, which Moscone said added over $175,000 to his campaign budget, will enable him to travel all over the state and assess his political potential for the gubernatorial race."[36] In November, the *Sun-Reporter* informed its readers that Moscone was still in the race, despite rumors to the contrary, and that his running mate for lieutenant governor would be Mervyn Dymally.[37] The *Sun-Reporter*'s political coverage in this era was extraordinary. Led by Edith Austin and Thomas Fleming, it included deep analysis of Bay Area politics, upcoming campaigns, issues and politicians of importance to African Americans, political rumors, and gossip.

Moscone further explored his possible gubernatorial candidacy in early 1973. Other than Alan Cranston, who would be seeking reelection to the US Senate in 1974, there was only one Democratic statewide elected official in California in 1973. In most cases, a thirty-five-year-old serving his first term as secretary of state would not be a clear favorite against the senate majority leader, Speaker of the assembly, or big-city mayor, but this secretary of state was different. Edmund G. Brown Jr. started out with almost universal name recognition because his father, Edmund G. Brown Sr., had been governor from 1959 to 1966 To distinguish between the two, the father was known as Pat and the son as Jerry. Jerry had lived in Southern California and gotten his start in politics there after growing up and attending college and the Jesuit seminary in the Bay Area, so he had statewide political contacts to go with the name recognition and fundraising that his father could help deliver. Like Moscone, Jerry Brown grew up in San Francisco and graduated from St. Ignatius. Before Brown got into the race, the three initial front-runners in the race were all Italian Americans, making it even more difficult for Moscone to distinguish himself to an electorate who could easily confuse Moretti, Moscone, and Alioto.

The race was an uphill battle from the beginning, but Moscone apparently believed that his legislative record, strong political skills, likeability, and progressive vision could help him get past his better-known opponents. A March 1973 poll showed that 79 percent of Democrats either did not know Moscone or had no opinion of him. Only 45 percent of Democrats were similarly unaware of Alioto, and only 35 percent did not know enough about Brown to form an opinion.[38]

Moscone was also contesting the race without one of his closest political allies by his side. Willie Brown was supporting Moretti. The logic of that was clear, because if Moretti dropped out of the race, Brown would need to have a good relationship with the Speaker of the assembly; and if Moretti ran, Brown would need Moretti's help in becoming Speaker himself. Despite Willie Brown's support for Moretti, Moscone was not without allies in the race because at least part of the Burton operation initially supported Moscone. When I asked John Burton about that race, he told me, "Of course I supported him (Moscone). He was my friend."[39]

Six months later, in September 1973, Moscone had closed that polling gap somewhat as only 46 percent of Democrats had not heard of him. However, by then Alioto and Brown were unknown to only 11 percent and 8 percent of the electorate, respectively. The horse-race numbers told a much starker story. Brown had a strong lead with 42 percent. Alioto was a distant second with only 22 percent. Moretti, Waldie, and Moscone were all in single digits with Moscone in fifth place at only 3 percent.[40]

By the late summer of 1973, Moscone was making increasingly frequent trips to Los Angeles to campaign and raise money. On July 29, a Sunday, he took a day trip to Los Angeles for campaign stops that included several receptions as well as hosting a brunch for "potential contributors" at Dodger Stadium and then staying there to see the Giants play the Dodgers. The schedule called for Moscone to leave the game at five o'clock "or the top of the ninth which ever (sic) is sooner."[41] Given that the game took just under two and a half hours to play, Moscone probably left in the top of the ninth, which means he stayed longer than most Dodgers fans. Unfortunately, the Giants lost 6–2 as the Dodgers rallied for four runs in the bottom of the eighth. The big blow was a three-run home run by Steve Garvey.[42] More than fifty years later Garvey would run for the US Senate as a Republican and lose to Adam Schiff.

Moscone enjoyed some support from more liberal elements in Hollywood. An August 7, 1973, fundraiser in Los Angeles was hosted by Leonard Nimoy, best known as Mr. Spock on *Star Trek*.[43] The seminal television show had been off the air for about four years by then. Nimoy had also been an alternate delegate for George McGovern in 1972, but he did not attend the Democratic National Convention in Miami Beach. Moscone was part of that delegation, led by Willie Brown. There was another *Star Trek* connection in that delegation because George Takei, who played Mr. Sulu in the original *Star Trek*, was also a McGovern delegate.[44] Nimoy remained a friend and supporter of Moscone's even after the gubernatorial campaign. On the weekend of August 18–19, Moscone went back to Los Angeles to speak at a National Association for the Advancement of Colored People (NAACP) conference and meet with African American politicians and then some potential contributors. His contact person for that trip was Maxine Waters, then a staff person to a member of the Los Angeles City Council.[45]

By late 1973, Moscone's campaign was gearing up despite the poor poll showings. An undated autumn 1973 issue of his campaign newspaper, *The Moscone Democrat,* featured a cover photo of Moscone and his younger son, Jonathan, who turned nine years old in October 1973. Moscone is smiling and leaning against the hood of a Jeep, his arm around Jonathan, smiling and perched on the hood. On the front bumper is a Moscone for governor sticker. The text of the lead article explained, "Promising a campaign for Governor that will get him out 'among the people' State Senator George Moscone is underway in a border to border tour of California. . . . The Moscone itinerary takes him north to south, including the high north counties, the Sierra, the Mother Lode, the Central Valley, desert areas, parts of Los Angeles and Orange counties and concluding December 15 in San Diego County."[46]

George Miller served forty years in the House of Representatives and was first elected in 1974, but in 1973 he was working for Senator Moscone and helping on the governor's race. Miller recalled the beginning of Moscone's campaign for governor and explained that it was his idea that driving much of the length of California would be a good way to introduce Moscone to voters in various parts of the state:

> We got ourselves a Jeep. I was the designated driver for the most part, and we went up all the way to the Oregon-California border. Jesus, I'm missing the name of the town, but we decided we'd go there, we'd go to the town, I'm haunted by the name, and when we got there, we were entering the town on a dirt road, on sort of the eastern side of highway 5, and it said, "Welcome to Nowhere" painted on a rock, a big rock, "Welcome to Nowhere," and the press was following us. It was the big kickoff, and there was nobody there. The town had been abandoned.

When I asked Miller how Moscone responded to such a disastrous start to his campaign, he responded, "He wasn't thrilled but, you know, he just rode it out, and he says, 'Come on, let's go. We have a long way to go here.'" [47]

After that, they continued down the coast, and Moscone's campaign began to look a little better. Miller described the rest of the drive:

> I think the *LA Times* was following us from beginning to end. . . . Different Democrats were helping him (Moscone) along the way, and we'd meet them at a town square or they'd have a house visit. We'd meet them. . . . He's engaging, so, you know, he would go and engage. He

> wasn't standoffish, you didn't have to come meet him. He was there, he put his hand out, he said who he is. "Jesus, great for you to be here, here's what I'm doing" and I plan on running for governor and do this and do that, and they went up to him and, of course, many of them were Democrats (who told him) nobody's (running for governor) ever been there before.[48]

Moscone's ill-fated Jeep trip did not portend great things for the struggling campaign. Issue two of the campaign newsletter from either November or December 1973 described Moscone's misadventures as the city slicker from San Francisco campaigned in rural California:

> All the candidates have their problems on the campaign trail. . . . But George Moscone has been getting it from both ends—literally. While helping a farmer outside of Redding slop his pigs, Moscone turned his back on one of the more outspoken sows—and was immediately nipped rather painfully in the rear end. Luckily, instant analysis—which naturally follows all major political events—revealed no permanent damage. Nor did it uncover a motive. Moscone, upon limping out of the pen however, confirmed that it was no love peck.
>
> Several days later, our bone-weary campaigners pulled into the Prospector Village Inn in Oroville. The senator and his aide, George Miller, made certain that everyone else was settled down before heading up to their own room. They fiddled around with the key in the lock for a few seconds before the door swung open—revealing two people already in bed in the room.
>
> George Miller, always the gentleman bashfully turned away, George Moscone, always the campaigner, barged on in, Hi! I'm George Moscone and I'm running for . . . .
>
> With a man like that, how can we lose?[49]

Both these anecdotes are funny and charmingly self-deprecating, but they do not suggest a campaign on the cusp of taking California by storm.

Moscone's Jeep trip through California concluded on December 15, 1973, with a rally in San Ysidro, a small border town outside of San Diego. The press release issued by his office at the conclusion of the drive recounted that Moscone's travels "have taken him to nearly 200 communities in 30 California counties. . . . The trip began in a fourwheel (sic) drive vehicle at the Siskiyou County town of Hilt (pop. 6)."[50]

Moscone was a potentially strong candidate for governor, a proven and experienced legislator who knew Sacramento well and had demonstrated an ability to build coalitions and pass legislation. He was also a progressive with strong ties to key Democratic constituencies, but he had the background of the kind of moderate Democrat that Californians had elected in the past. Like the previous Democratic governor of California, Pat Brown, Moscone was a Catholic San Franciscan lawyer, well liked and respected by party leadership. However, Moscone had never run statewide and, by 1974, San Francisco and the Bay Area were increasingly distinct politically from the rest of the state. In 1973 there was little cost for Moscone to run for governor, but in 1974 that began to change. By the spring of 1974, Moscone would have to decide whether to continue to run for governor or run for a third term in the senate. Running for his seat again was the safer option, while running for governor and losing would leave Moscone jobless and likely finished with his once-promising political career at only forty-four years old.

By late 1973, it was apparent Moscone's campaign for governor was going to be a very steep uphill climb, particularly as it was also becoming certain that Jerry Brown was going to run and be very difficult to beat. Moreover, although Moscone was the leader of the Democrats in the state senate, he had never run in a district bigger than the city of San Francisco. He was well known among political insiders who followed events in Sacramento, but despite the influence he had in the capital, not by voters outside of San Francisco. That was particularly true in Southern California.

Moscone's campaign literature boasted of his "100% Labor Record according to the official records of the California Labor Federation, AFL-CIO"[51] and cited myriad accomplishments on women's issues, education, the environment, and similar areas. In an August 1973 campaign newsletter, Moscone spelled out his vision: "I believe the people of California cry out for the kind of leader who can bring together the highest ideals of humanism . . . of quality of life . . . a determination to meet and solve our problems. What I have heard in my travels is that Californians don't want a head of government who has flowed with the tide, who has sometimes wilted under the heat of political expediency. What those same people do want is a leader who has vigorously sought real solutions to the very real problems they face in their lives."[52] That statement was mostly platitudes, but those kinds of platitudes can be effective for candidates, unlike Moscone in that race, whose path to victory looks good.

By late November 1973, Moscone had continued to break through with the electorate but just not enough. He had a 37 percent approval rating from Democrats with only 13 percent disapproving, but that kind of name recognition was not going to be enough to get him past Jerry Brown, who was sailing along with almost twice as many Democrats who had a favorable view of him, 73 percent, and a lower unfavorable rating, 12 percent, than Moscone.[53]

Recognizing that he had little chance of beating Brown, Moscone withdrew from the race on the first day of 1974. He explained his reasoning in a letter to supporters. The letter was an odd mix of sincerity, bitterness, and humility. It began with a cliché: "This is the most difficult letter I have ever written." The second sentence went straight to the point "After three years of almost daily effort I have decided not to seek the Democratic nomination for Governor."[54] This was an overstatement because while Moscone may have been thinking about the race or preparing to run beginning in 1971, the campaign was not his primary focus during most of that time.

The next paragraphs were in a tone that supporters did not see frequently from Moscone. "Campaign financing has been extraordinarily difficult for this race. . . . My problems have been aggravated by my refusal to seek out funds for any special favors. . . . There is a general lack of public interest in the gubernatorial campaign, perhaps due to Watergate, perhaps just general apathy. . . . Additionally, the inattention of the press, as a whole, to the campaign plagued us."[55] Moscone blamed the people and the media for not being sufficiently interested in the campaign, but it is the candidate's job to generate interest. Additionally, the election was more than a year away, so it would be understandable why the media and ordinary voters would be focusing on other things. Moscone's comments about being unable to raise the necessary money are probably best understood as generic excuse-making. Almost all candidates hate fundraising—particularly in those pre-internet days. However, if the senate majority leader cannot raise enough money to run for governor, it is usually because the race just isn't coming together. That was the case for Moscone.

The ending of the letter was humbler and more optimistic, suggesting that Moscone was not thinking of himself as being on the downside of his political career: "The struggle was not without benefits. What I have learned is very valuable. I found myself listening intently to people's ideas, their problems and proposed solutions. I found myself thoroughly understanding the awesome responsibility of representing people as people and not as political units. I am the better for it. . . . I intend to devote my life to public service and count heavily on your continued support."[56] Within a year, Moscone would make good on that pledge and appeal to many of the recipients of the letter for support in another campaign.

The *Sun-Reporter* greeted Moscone's departure from the race with disappointment:

> Senator George Moscone a liberal's liberal, of San Francisco, announced his desire to become governor more than two years ago. Moscone was disenchanted with the performance of Ronald Reagan, who had twice bamboozled enough Californians to win election to the governorship. Of course, there are many sage observers of the politics of the Golden State who will say that California voters love being bamboozled, when

> one looks at the records of such men as Reagan, Max Rafferty, Sam Yorty, and a slew of others who should not even have been elected to the post of dogcatcher. . . . Moscone is a man endowed with fierce independence in which he will not prostitute himself to any groups or individuals who expect to receive special favors from political office holders. This is the reason why he withdrew and the voters of the state will be the real losers in the long run. . . . It is a sad commentary on the American style of democracy that honorable candidates such as Moscone find it difficult to win public elections unless they sell themselves to the highest bidder. The majority of public office seekers not only hustle for votes but they and their closest supporters must hustle for money with the same ardor.[57]

The spin that both Moscone and his supporters put on his withdrawal from the race had some elements of truth, but it was equally true that he simply lacked the name recognition enjoyed by Jerry Brown, the son of the most recent Democratic governor and the sitting secretary of state. Brown used that position to advocate for campaign finance reform, naturally an important issue after Watergate. Additionally, Moscone struggled to distinguish himself from other highly qualified, if somewhat more conservative candidates such as Moretti and Alioto.

Scandal Narrowly Avoided

In early 1970 in Sacramento, Senator George Moscone was involved in an incident that might have derailed his promising career. On the evening of April 13, 1970, Moscone was driving home from Frank Fat's, a Sacramento bar known as a watering hole for legislators, lobbyists, and others involved in state government with a young woman who was not his wife. What happened next was relatively clear. "According to the police report, witnesses said Moscone's car was traveling at excessive speed and went through a stop sign."[58]

Moscone hit a vehicle driven by twenty-year-old John J. Taylor, who called his parents and was then taken to the hospital. Taylor's parents came to the scene of the accident. His mother remarked of Moscone that "he had been drinking. I smelled liquor on his breath." However, she also indicated that Moscone did not seem drunk.[59] The young woman left before the police arrived. Moscone's explanation was not convincing. "He said he did not know the young woman's name, but was giving her a lift from Frank Fat's downtown to the Turf Club."[60]

When the police arrived, Moscone was sent home in a taxi and faced no legal consequences. The police rationale was that the accident happened on private property, the parking area of a strip mall, but there was more to it than that. "Mrs. Taylor told the *Examiner* that when her husband asked police to give

Moscone a sobriety test one of the officers refused 'and threatened to take him (Mr. Taylor) to jail.'"[61]

The extent of Taylor's injuries is not clear. The reporting immediately after the accident said simply that he suffered "head cuts and bruises."[62] However, a few years later, on the day after Moscone was inaugurated as mayor, the *Chronicle* learned of the story and reported that the Taylor family sued Moscone for $250,000 for "medical treatment and permanent disabilities," eventually settling for $25,000. That story also argued that Moscone's conduct at the time of the accident was insensitive and an abuse of his power and position. According to Taylor's father, "He (Moscone) just walked over to my son, hurt there, and handed him a business card. All he said was that he was Senator Moscone and he didn't even ask how my son felt."[63]

Although attitudes were different in 1970, that is not enough of an explanation for why this incident never was very damaging to Moscone. It is also true that state legislators getting drunk, being seen with women who were not their wives, and doing stupid things were dog-bites-man type stories then, and to some extent, even in the twenty-first century. The story went away quickly because of a combination of luck, the times, and Moscone's seeming willingness to take advantage of his power. Even if his explanation, including his assertion that he had just met the woman, whose name was never published, and that he was not drunk, is believed, it is still true that he was sent home in a taxi with few questions from the police and was not given a drunk driving test. That is the way powerful politicians were frequently treated back then and Moscone was okay with that.

Because Moscone's senate district was so strongly Democratic, the incident was never going to hurt his reelection chances. By the time he ran for mayor five years later, enough time had gone by that his opponents never brought it up. The one area in which this had a lasting impact on Moscone was that it gave fuel to the stories of him being a philanderer and somebody who was out on the town too much.[64]

These events occurred only a few months before the 1970 Democratic primary and only about seven months before the November general election. Had he been politically vulnerable, the incident in Sacramento might have been something his opponents could have used against him. However, Moscone was in a very strong political position and could, and did, boast of a strong record in the senate. As he wrote in a letter to supporters asking for their vote and financial contributions, "For the past four years it has been my great privilege to represent San Francisco in the State Senate. During that time I successfully authored over 125 bills, more than any other senator and maintained a perfect attendance record. In this past session of the Legislature (sic) we have made dramatic advances in the fields of consumer protection, environmental quality, bi-lingual education, law enforcement and in providing school lunches to hungry children."[65]

Back in San Francisco

San Francisco's electorate continued to shift leftward during the early 1970s. This gave politicians such as Moscone, who seemed a little more attuned to youth culture and diversity, and were not the old, stodgy, white guys, who had run the state for decades, an electoral advantage. While this dynamic helped Moscone, Brown, and the Burtons avoid any tough reelection fights, it did not have a major influence on city government quite yet. The period of 1969–1972 or so may now be seen as years of tremendous change when the foundations of the more progressive city grew stronger. But many longtime residents saw these events as reflecting the decline of the city they knew into chaos, lawlessness, and redistribution of power way from them. Chris Carlsson identified the role of powerful economic forces in those years: "With a long pedigree of contrarian culture and political radicalism, San Francisco was in the mid-1960s still dominated by the large corporations headquartered in downtown, and the old and newer elites who owned them. . . . The underlying history of San Francisco is one of old monied families dominating property ownership and commercial development."[66]

Some of the changes in the city were continuation of earlier trends. The 1970 census revealed a population of only 715,674, about 25,000 fewer residents than ten years earlier and 60,000 fewer than in 1950. The demographic breakdown, shown in table 8.1, was even more stark.

Table 8.1 Demographic Change 1960–1970[1]

Year	Total Population	White	Hispanic	African American	Asian American	White San Franciscans
1960	740,315	81.6%	7%	10%	7.9%	604,097
1970	715,674	57.2%	14.2%	13.4%	13.3%	409,366

[1]"San Francisco History," SF Genealogy, https://www.sfgenealogy.org/sf/history/hgpop.htm

The numbers for 1960 add up to slightly more than 100 percent because some people were counted as both white and Latino. The data show that during the 1960s, San Francisco become a smaller and less white city. The number of white San Franciscans declined by almost 195,000 during the decade. In San Francisco, as in a lot of cities, white flight changed both the political calculations and contributed to the rise of white backlash politics during the decade. Other changes were more gradual. For example, as Jewish San Franciscans left to the suburbs, Lowell High School, the city's strongest academic public high school, became less Jewish and more Asian, particularly Chinese.

These trends framed the 1971 mayoral election. As the year began, nobody from the progressive Burton faction of the Democratic Party gave much thought to taking on the well-liked incumbent Joseph Alioto. Harold Dobbs, in what had become a quadrennial ritual, decided to run again, challenging Alioto from the right. This left just a faint glimmer of space for a very deft campaign to challenge Alioto from the left and win a slight plurality of the vote. Moscone wisely had no interest in entering the race. Instead, Dianne Feinstein, who had been serving as president of the board of supervisors since her surprise first-place finish in 1969, decided to offer an alternative to Alioto. Although the race was a long shot, Feinstein had little to lose. She would not be up for reelection as a supervisor until 1973, so she did not have to give up her seat. Additionally, by running in 1971 Feinstein could increase her name recognition, demonstrate her knowledge of city affairs and, most importantly, position herself for to run for mayor in 1975 when Alioto would not be eligible to run for reelection because of term limits.

One of Feinstein's challenges was that two years on the board of supervisors, even for somebody who was known to be as smart and well-prepared as Feinstein, is a thin résumé from which to run for mayor. Feinstein's bigger problem was that she had no real path to victory. Dobbs was running to the right of Alioto, but although Feinstein was younger and a woman, she was not a progressive trying to beat Alioto from the left. Because, she had similar politics as the incumbent, Feinstein's campaign was based around being a newish face and being somewhat more liberal on social issues.

Feinstein was seeking to become one of the very first female big-city mayors. San Francisco, along with New York, Los Angeles, Chicago, and almost every other major American city had not yet elected a female mayor. Feinstein used her gender to her advantage by not only differentiating herself from Alioto, and every other previous San Francisco mayor, but also by suggesting that she was compassionate and caring in a way that Alioto was not. This was done primarily through images. Her campaign literature sounded very generic. "Dianne is the City's one real chance for needed change. San Francisco's problems do not defy solution, but they require honest and open leadership to be solved. Dianne's experience in city government and her fresh and candid approach to issues, such as pollution, education, rising crime, unfit housing and high taxes, can move the City ahead." Other than identifying herself only by her first name, that language was decidedly not unique. However, the images Feinstein used, including her speaking with a look of compassion and concern to a Latino child, her leaning in (before that was a popular term) listening to two African American children, and her crouching to speak more easily to two Asian children seemed to try to show that, as a woman, she knew how to listen and cared deeply about children.[67]

Alioto's reelection campaign was upbeat, stressing his accomplishments as mayor and his personal story and background. One piece of campaign literature bore the slogan, "It's Time for a New Day in San Francisco!" The professional-looking flyer used an orange and dark brown color scheme. Baseball fans would not have missed the similarity to the orange and black of the Giants. The front of the flyer summarized Alioto's credentials, "Native San Franciscan . . . Long-Time Civic Leader . . . U.S. Government Official . . . Successful Attorney . . . Successful Businessman . . . Family Man," as well as his five-point plan, "Taxes are bleeding us . . . The transportation mess is choking our system . . . The slums must go! . . . All people must be safe, again . . . 34,000 San Franciscans need jobs." The back listed dozens of Alioto's first-term accomplishments.[68]

Another flyer, this one with the slogan, "He's strong . . . He cares . . . He gets things done," summarized the Alioto reelection argument. "Other Big American Cities are in deep trouble sullen, grim, stagnant and dying. Their streets are crime-ridden, their sidewalks cluttered with garbage. Poverty and joblessness abound. Their ghettos fester, neighborhoods decay. Bitter strikes proliferate, and public services decline. Taxes soar, and the spirits sag. But not in San Francisco." The statement continued lauding Alioto's accomplishments as mayor.[69]

A few things stand out about this flyer. First, Alioto was making an appeal not just on policy but on the feeling in San Francisco. He was a dynamic, optimistic man who wanted to imbue the city with that spirit. Alioto understood that while there were a lot of problems in San Francisco in the early 1970s, it was also, for many, a fun and exciting place. Second, although much of what the flyer said about "Other Big American Cities" could have been applied to Detroit, Cleveland, Pittsburgh, or many others, in San Francisco, most people understood that phrase to refer to one big city in particular, New York. This was also the era when debates raged about whether to build more skyscrapers and more office space in San Francisco. Opponents of that construction referred to that threat as Manhattanization. The possibility of becoming more like New York was something of a bogeyman used by the left, the right, and neighborhood activists.

For many years, in some contexts "New York" has been code for Jewish in San Francisco and elsewhere. For example, phrases such as "pushy New Yorker" were understood to be anti-Semitic. A few years later when Moscone was mayor, *San Francisco Examiner* columnist Kevin Starr, who became a famous historian after writing a seminal, if conservative, multivolume history of California, engaged in this kind of thinly veiled bigotry. Starr described a judicial campaign: "Against the widely respected Richard Figone, the coalition is running dope-lawyer Stephen Perelson a *New York City émigré* who is backed by, among *others of that ilk,* Supervisors Carol Ruth Silver and Harvey Milk."[70] Silver and Milk were both Jews from the East Coast.

Starr's relationship with and views toward Jews were complex. In 1980 he wrote a column about attending his annual Passover seder and remarked that he was "always fascinated with the varieties of belief among Jews. They range from militant orthodox to ethical culturalism to outright disaffinity. And yet, whatever one's theological speculations might mean, when you are a Jew, you are a Jew. That identity has been forged over the millennia in suffering and pain as well as glorious achievement." Starr also had kind words for the woman who hosted him every Passover. "Born and raised in New York, and a Brandeis graduate, Susan Mitchell manages to give a quality of encompassing welcome to her determination to lead her life within the Jewish tradition. . . . I've always felt deeply honored to celebrate Passover with the Mitchells (Susan and sons Jonathan and Lincoln)."[71]

Predictably, Alioto was reelected easily, winning almost 39 percent of the vote in an election where a majority was not needed. Feinstein had not been expected to win, but she ended up in third place with only 21.8 percent of the vote. Dobbs got 27.7 percent of the vote. This was a tough but not career-ending defeat for Feinstein, but not quite a resounding victory for Alioto either. The incumbent could not even manage 40 percent of the vote against a Republican who was quickly becoming San Francisco's answer to Harold Stassen[72] and against a Democrat who had not yet served two full years on the board of supervisors.

In 1971 the board of supervisors was still elected at-large. The same citywide system that had favored the well-funded Feinstein in 1969 had a similar effect in 1971. This time two new supervisors were elected to the board, John Molinari, who at that time was a Republican, and Quentin Kopp, a conservative Democrat. These two new board members were more aligned with the backlash than with the progressive forces in the city. The new president of the board was Ron Pelosi (brother-in-law of Nancy Pelosi), who won the most votes citywide as he secured his second term on the board. Kopp and Molinari would serve on the board well into the 1980s. Each would also run unsuccessfully for mayor before their careers were over.

After the 1971 election, the gap between the trends in San Francisco's political views and its elected leadership was hard to ignore. The city was increasingly racially diverse, becoming a national center of gay and lesbian political life, and a hub of the new left, but the look and feel of its elected leadership lagged. The 1971 vote led to the election of white men as mayor, district attorney, and sheriff; the eleven-member board of supervisors included two people of color and seven white men. The mayor and incoming board president, Pelosi, were both Italian American centrist Democrats. This seemed increasingly incongruous given the changes that were occurring throughout the city.

Migrants and Natives During the Early 1970s

Joseph Alioto began his second term as mayor in 1972 with an inaugural address that was eloquent, poetic, hopeful, and leavened with Catholic theology. He welcomed the changes facing the city and urged his fellow San Franciscans to do the same:

> The City too is a pendulum of joy and sorrow. It has its beautiful things and its ugly things. But the City by its very nature is an amalgam of good and evil. You cannot hope for a sinless city in a sinful world. Now this City, like all big American cities, is engaged in a dramatic struggle to weather a social crisis of disturbing dimensions. Inevitably, change is taking place in the character and personality of San Francisco. There are those who yearn to return to times that never really were except in deceptive recollections of an alleged better day. But only the timid fear change. Everything about us—the universe, the planets, man himself—is in a constant state of alteration and transformation.[73]

By 1972 most of the cultural changes, political awakenings, and policy fights of the 1960s were beginning to have an even larger impact. Although the Summer of Love had occurred a few years before, San Francisco remained a destination for young people from all over the country. Those without much education or job skills were able to live in San Francisco because it was still affordable. They could find work in the service sector, or if they had trouble finding work could live off the reasonably substantial support from the General Assistance program.

My parents were among those migrants, arriving in San Francisco in 1971. They were too old to be hippies, but they came to San Francisco because, like so many others, they needed some change and, for different reasons and in different ways, wanted new starts. Around the time my parents, my older brother, and I boarded a plane from John F. Kennedy Airport in New York for a flight to San Francisco, another Jewish New Yorker was preparing to return to his hometown after a two-year sojourn in San Francisco. The one-time Wall Street banker began that journey as a financial analyst in San Francisco's financial district, but the culture and politics of the time and place began to have an effect on him. He grew his hair, protested against the war in Vietnam, and enjoyed the relative feeling of liberation as a gay man in San Francisco. After he was fired from his finance job, like so many others for whom San Francisco had not worked out, he packed up his car and made his way back to New York.[74] The banker turned hippie had a story that, up till that moment, was not unusual in the tumult of the late 1960s and early 1970s, but this individual was much more significant because Harvey Milk's time in San Francisco did not end when he returned to New York in 1971. It was only just beginning.

Also in 1971, another San Franciscan, this one a native—in general, to qualify as a native San Franciscan, you need to have either been born in the city or to have spent most of your youth there—[75] who had graduated from Woodrow Wilson High School, a neighborhood public school after being expelled from Riordan, a Catholic school. He received his honorary discharge following a stint in the US Army, including serving in Vietnam. Because he was not quite sure what to do after the army, Dan White spent some time working in Alaska. Like Harvey Milk, in 1971 White's San Francisco journey was also far from over.

White, like Moscone, Alioto, McCarthy, and Frank Jordan, who served a term as mayor of San Francisco in the 1990s, all attended Catholic high schools. Until recently, different Catholic high schools occupied distinct places in San Francisco's sociology. White briefly attended Riordan, a much more working-class high school than St. Ignatius, Moscone and McCarthy's alma mater. Alioto and Jordan graduated from Sacred Heart, a school demographically similar to Riordan. Graduates of Riordan and Sacred Heart were much less likely to end up at elite colleges or become attorneys like Moscone and McCarthy. The resentments and intolerance that defined White's politics were strongest in San Francisco among other working-class white Catholics, many of whom had attended Riordan or Sacred Heart. Alioto was a great exception, becoming one of the most powerful lawyers in San Francisco before becoming mayor, but Frank Jordan's path to City Hall began in the police department, where many Riordan graduates could be found.

Riordan, Sacred Heart, and St. Ignatius were only for boys in those years. Naturally, there were girls schools as well. The elite Catholic girls school was, and is, the Convent of the Sacred Heart, in a former mansion in the heart of Pacific Heights. Moscone's daughters went to school there, but the school's most famous graduate is Feinstein.

In the early 1970s, while Moscone was serving his second term in the state senate, both Milk and White made their way back to San Francisco. White came back to his hometown and began a career in the police department. As an Irish American with military experience and conservative political views, White was a strong fit there. As White was beginning his work with the police department, Milk was returning to San Francisco and experiencing the city, where this time he intended to stay, in a very different way. Milk's biographer described how the transplanted New Yorker and his lover, Scott Smith, spent their first year together in California: "Milk and Smith picked up a mutt from the pound, named it The Kid, climbed into Milk's 1967 green Dodge Charger and spent nearly a year driving through California. They lived meagerly off their unemployment checks, usually tossing their sleeping bags under the redwoods of the state park to which they were closest. When the unemployment checks stopped coming, they returned to San Francisco, lived on their income tax refunds, and frittered away afternoons on massive jigsaw puzzles."[76]

This was a radical lifestyle change for the forty-two-year-old former banker, but it had been several years in the making. It is also a reminder of how San Francisco's economy in the 1970s helped create a climate conducive to social change and political activism. The economy was not strong in the 1970s, but San Francisco, particularly with regard to housing, was, correspondingly, not very expensive, so people had time for massive jigsaw puzzles, frittering away time, and even political work. A young, or not so young, childless couple in San Francisco today would fritter away their time driving Uber, working a third job, and trying to find a cheaper place to live.

White, Moscone, and Milk will always be linked together in San Francisco history, but in 1972, the first year they were all in San Francisco at the same time, it would have been hard to imagine them being in the same room, or even being discussed in the same conversation together. White was not yet thirty in 1972, so was roughly half a generation younger than Moscone and Milk. White was a baby boomer, but seemed offended by what fellow boomers were doing to his city. Moscone was seventeen years older than White, but much more comfortable in 1970s San Francisco. Like Moscone, White was Catholic from a modest background and had been educated in San Francisco Catholic schools. Both Milk and Moscone were college graduates who had served in the navy, but most of the similarities ended there. Moscone was already a very accomplished man as he entered early middle age. He was a respected senator and a leader in his party in California. Political insiders saw him as somebody, despite his unsuccessful and short-lived campaign for governor, who had a bright future in politics. Milk was a former stockbroker, hanging out and trying, in the parlance of the time, to find himself.

Like many American cities around 1965, San Francisco was a bit more diverse than the rest of the country, relied heavily on manufacturing and, because of its location on the West Coast, shipping, for its substantially blue-collar economy. The institutionalized racism that was rarely questioned in urban America existed in San Francisco as well. Almost all the city's elected officials were white. African Americans and other minority groups participated in politics primarily as minor players in Irish- and Italian-dominated political machines. Although San Francisco had been a hub of gay activity at least since the end of World War II, gays and lesbians were not involved in politics in any visibly significant way. The old Italian American neighborhood of North Beach had become a center of beatnik activity and culture, but the Haight-Ashbury was still little more than a typical street intersection in a working-class neighborhood near Golden Gate Park. Crime, unemployment, urban redevelopment, racism, and other problems of the mid-1960s could certainly be found in the San Francisco of the period, but in those respects, it looked like most other American cities.

The San Francisco of 1965 was also distinct in some ways. Even sixty years ago, San Francisco was a strikingly beautiful city, nestled in the hills and surrounded by water on three sides. The Golden Gate Bridge, not quite thirty years old then, was already one of the most famous and beautiful bridges in the world. San Francisco was even then renowned for its food and nightlife. These things made San Francisco more cosmopolitan feeling than most similarly sized cities its size, but by 1965, Los Angeles was a more important financial center than San Francisco. Most San Franciscans only recognized that begrudgingly, if at all.

By the early 1970s, San Francisco was growing into the city and identity it would take on through the early twenty-first century when the tech boom and influx of new people and new money remade the city yet again. San Francisco during the decade or so following the Summer of Love saw many of the hippies who had come to the city in or around 1967 with metaphorical flowers in their hair become integrated into San Francisco's life and politics. Those who were still in town a few years later were generally progressive and supported politicians such as George Moscone. The related events of the Summer of Love, the rise of the New Left, anti-war protests, and the myriad civil rights movements that were remaking the city's politics also gave San Francisco a very different feel.

That new feeling frequently went well beyond politics. The anti-war movement continued to grow as San Francisco became one of the centers of radicalism in America. This occasionally led to violence. On the evening of February 16, 1970, a bomb was detonated at the Park Police Station at the western edge of the Haight-Ashbury near Kezar Stadium, the football field on the southeast corner of Golden Gate Park that had been home to the San Francisco 49ers since 1946. The bomb killed Sergeant Brian McDonnell of the San Francisco Police Department. About a month earlier, a bomb had gone off at a police station in Hunters Point. Nobody died in that incident. The Park Police bombing is generally thought to have been done by the Weather Underground; the one in Hunters Point by African American radicals.

In 1973 and 1974 another group of African American radicals murdered fifteen people in San Francisco. These killings, other than the victims all being white, seemed somewhat random and occasionally grisly. The racial nature of the crimes and the suspects being African American led to an extreme form of racial profiling as Mayor Alioto essentially empowered the police to stop and question any African American man they thought might be a suspect. That program was called Operation Zebra, so the killing spree became known as the Zebra Killings. This policy led to the harassment and detainment of many young African Americans. Larry Griffin, who was a young African American man living in the Western Addition at the time recalled, "I never got pulled over once, but I didn't know anybody else who had not been pulled over."[77] The killings began in October 1973 and ended in April 1974 when the killers were apprehended.

Not all victims of these shootings died. On December 13, 1973, a thirty-six-year-old social worker who had lived in San Francisco fewer than five years was shot in the chest twice by the Zebra killers. Amazingly, he survived. Within a few years of that near-death experience, he changed careers. Art Agnos went on to win a seat in the state assembly and in 1987 was elected mayor of San Francisco.

As the Summer of Love wound down, other less benign elements of the 1960s began to make themselves present in San Francisco, and not just in the Haight. Drug use, which had begun for many with the relatively weak marijuana of the 1960s and then on to LSD, morphed into more harmful substances, including heroin and various kinds of amphetamines. The increase in these drugs meant that many people who had come to San Francisco, and the Haight, seeking fun, music, and the months long party that was the Summer of Love, found themselves addicted to potent and more dangerous drugs. These harder drugs brought a different drug culture and different kinds of drug dealers. No distributor of speed or heroin did it in the name of some larger vision or hope. There was no Timothy Leary of heroin. These dealers were in it for the money. Naturally, this led to more street crime, violence, and danger.

One of the starkest indicators of rising crime in the years following the Summer of Love can be seen in the number of murders in San Francisco. Table 8.2 shows the annual number of homicides in San Francisco beginning in 1964 when Moscone joined the board of supervisors, through 1978, the year of Moscone's death. The number of homicides doubled between 1966 and 1969. After a brief decline from 1971 to 1973, it increased again in 1974 and 1975 when Moscone ran

Table 8.2 Homicides per year in San Francisco, 1964–1978

Year	Homicides
1964	47
1965	56
1966	50
1967	63
1968	87
1969	121
1970	112
1971	97
1972	79
1973	96
1974	129
1975	131
1976	132
1977	137
1978	112
2023	55

[1] Data from table https://cjrc.osu.edu/research/interdisciplinary/hvd/united-states/san-francisco

for mayor. By comparison, by 2021 San Francisco had about 50 percent more people than during the early 1970s and fifty-five homicides in 2021, 2022, and 2023.[78]

The Reverend McGloin argued that this had begun as early as 1968 when "the former Flower People or Love Children who had called their area the 'Spiritual Capital of the Love Generation,' had now been replaced by other more sinister elements. . . . By the middle of January 1969 . . . some of the discouraged original residents who had remained through it all spoke of their district in sorrowful terms as 'moribund except for garbage strewn streets, defunct business and assault, rapine and pillage after dark.'"[79]

The drugs and crime around the Haight were only one way that the aftershocks of the Summer of Love changed San Francisco. Because the city had emerged as the center of the early hippie movement, by the 1970s other societal developments related to the counterculture could be found in San Francisco, including cults and radical politics. People such as Phil Burton, Willie Brown, and George Moscone, bolstered by influential community activists, had become powerful San Francisco politicians, but they were unambiguously working within the system on issues such as civil rights, gay rights, moderating drug laws, and opposing the war in Vietnam. At the same time, groups with more radical, violent, and sometimes difficult to understand political agendas began to make their mark in San Francisco.

The Symbionese Liberation Army (SLA) straddled radical politics and cultism in a way that captured a least some of the gestalt of the era. The SLA was most famous for kidnapping the heiress Patty Hearst in 1974. Later that year, Hearst was involved in an SLA bank robbery of a Hibernia Bank in the Sunset District—one of the city's more conservative areas. The SLA drew on Black Liberation and far-left political ideologies and had the unforgettable, and wonderfully 1970s radical, slogan, "Death to the fascist insect that preys upon the life of the people." One of their demands for the release of Hearst was that her wealthy parents contribute $2 million for distribution of food to the hungry in California. When that demand was eventually met, at least in part, one of the organizations that helped distribute the food was Jim Jones's Peoples Temple. Jones had moved his Peoples Temple headquarters from Ukiah, north of San Francisco, to the city earlier in the 1970s. The saga of Patty Hearst dominated the news for roughly a year and was one of the most famous episodes from the period when the ugly and violent hangover from the Summer of Love was at its worst.

Simultaneously, in other respects, the shock of the 1960s had receded somewhat and been replaced by the institutionalization of many of the changes of the period. Men with long hair were no longer gawked at—although many older people still disapproved. The left-wing politics that had felt radical in the 1960s had begun to move slowly into mainstream San Francisco politics, buoying the careers of politicians such as Willie Brown, the Burtons, George Moscone and the man who replaced Ronald Reagan in the Governor's Mansion in 1974, Jerry Brown. Brown may have replaced Reagan, but the new governor never lived in the mansion, preferring a more modest apartment in Sacramento.

In San Francisco, the most significant political changes occurred not in the Haight, but in the Castro, the Mission, the Fillmore, Chinatown, San Francisco State University, Bayview/Hunters Point, and even Alcatraz Island. Those were the places where various minority groups, including gays and lesbians, Chicanos, African Americans, Asian American, and Native Americans demanded that their voices be heard and refused to be marginalized anymore. The activities of those communities, whether it was the strike led by students of color at SFSU, the occupation of Alcatraz by Native Americans that lasted well over a year, or the years of organizing among African American, Chicano, and Asian American communities, remade San Francisco and destroyed the centrist, white-dominated coalition that had been the status quo in San Francisco for much of the twentieth century.

The city continued to be mired in the kind of urban problems usually associated with crime-ridden rust belt cities. Crime had grown rapidly and was a major concern for most San Franciscans. This was partially because the economy, particularly the manufacturing and shipping sectors, that had provided good blue-collar jobs for the first half of the twentieth century, had been in decline for years. This contributed to a shrinking population, down 5.13 percent between the 1970 and 1980 censuses,[80] and budget problems, leading to strikes by city employees, and a general feeling that like many American cities, San Francisco was becoming ungovernable.

Growing Political Tensions

The San Francisco to which Harvey Milk and Dan White returned in the early 1970s was experiencing significant strain on its political institutions and power structures. The downtown and real estate interests that had run the city for decades were still able to do so in the early 1970s, but it was apparent that was not going to last much longer without significant contestation. Cleve Jones described the feeling that many of his generation, particularly gay men, felt when coming to San Francisco, but also noted the divisions in 1973: "It seemed such a magical place. . . . Summer of Love and all of that . . . In my mind before I came to San Francisco, I imagined it as this very liberal progressive town . . . full of hippies, and certainly there was that in certain neighborhoods on the eastern part of the city, but I was really quite struck by what a conservative city it was. . . . The distinct neighborhoods, the identity people had built around their neighborhoods, what school they went to."[81]

Some of the young people who had come to San Francisco in the 1970s returned home, moved away, or struggled to make a new life for themselves in the city, but others had moved into the workforce and civic life of their new home. This was a time when many waiters, bus drivers, teachers, small-business people, and others in a range of professions had some connection to the new left and the new culture that went along with it. Similarly, civil rights movements for Asians, Chicanos, African Americans, women, and gays and lesbians were maturing, while the Freeway Revolts and early years of the civil rights movement during the previous decade had brought neighborhood activists and supporters of civil rights into the political life of the city, although not quite into political office in most cases.

These activists began to cohere around a battery of concerns, issues, and demands. Some were substantive and issue-based: combating police brutality, more city jobs for people of colors, legislation to stop discrimination against gays and lesbians. Other concerns can be better described as thematic, asking people to rethink and redefine what San Francisco was. This was implicitly a rejection of the business leadership that had been so influential for so long in city government. The roots of this were in the Freeway Revolts, which had rejected the notion that economic growth and commerce were the values that should drive city governance. Instead, those who opposed these projects moved toward a view that the goal of city governance should be to make the city livable, even pleasant for its citizens.

As the 1973 elections approached, the new activist San Francisco had an opportunity to demonstrate its political strength. There was no mayoral election that year, but five supervisors: Barbagelata, Feinstein, George Chinn, Peter Tamaras, and Dorothy von Beroldingen were up for reelection. Chinn was the first Chinese American to serve on the board and had been appointed by Alioto in 1973 to fill a vacancy left by Roger Boas. This was an opportunity for progressives, gays and lesbians, African Americans, Asian Americans, and Latinos to get a foothold in city government—but not really. The at-large system for electing supervisors was still a formidable barrier because as long as supervisors needed to get elected citywide, those with the most money and who were most broadly acceptable would win, while candidates who had strong appeal in one part of the city or among one group of voters but did not enjoy the support of the business community had almost no chance.

Among those who tried, and failed, to win a seat on the board in 1973 was Harvey Milk. The support he won in the Castro District and the growing perception that he was a leader of gay San Francisco would made him a strong candidate in the right district, but in the at-large system the 16,900 votes that Milk received were roughly 20 percent of the number that was needed to win a seat.

Four of the five incumbent supervisors were reelected in 1973. The progressive who came the closest to winning was Jack Morrison, who had previously served on the board and still enjoyed good name recognition. He received 84,139 votes, but von Beroldingen secured the fifth seat, and her reelection with 89,319 votes. Another also-ran was Jesus Christ Satan, who only got 4,968 votes.[82]

Milk's 1973 candidacy was one of the early rumblings of the gay rights movement's focus on electoral politics. Milk, who had been back in San Francisco for fewer than two years, ran as the gay candidate campaigning on gay issues. On August 6, Herb Caen, the city's most influential newspaperman, had an item in his column, "SINGLE ENTENDRE of the week honors to Harvey Milk, a homosexual who announces he's running for Supervisor 'because I'm tired of the election year lip service given to the gay community by our officials' (What do these people WANT?)"[83] Caen was a liberal, but his failure to take Milk's campaign seriously reflected the political consensus at the time. Ten days later, Caen weighed in on Milk's candidacy once more. "All those 'Milk Has Something For Every Body' posters in the Castro area are not for Mark Spitz or even Phyllis Diller but for Harvey Milk, running for Supervisor on the homo ticket, and I don't mean homogenized."[84]

Although he was the gay candidate in 1973, Milk's campaign was not yet part of the larger progressive movement in the city. In his efforts to expand his base, Milk did not reach leftward, but instead turned rightward, presenting himself as a businessperson who was concerned about spending. Milk did not mention gay or progressive politics at all in the voter guide. Instead, he stated:

> A Supervisor's responsibility is the thorough understanding and evaluation of how the taxpayer's dollars are spent. My 8 yeas as a security analyst studing (sic) the budgets of major corporations has given me a thorough understanding of the proper use of money by large corporations. In order for a city to make the best use of taxpayer's money it must be extremely efficient. My background has given me a powerful understanding of how to make full use of the taxpayer's money. As the owner of a store, I understand the problems that face the average person in the city each day.[85]

The only incumbent who lost was Chinn, who was replaced by former police chief Al Nelder. Nelder had been a police officer who rose through the ranks and was appointed chief by Mayor Alioto, but stepped down after less than two years. Nelder grew up in San Francisco and played sandlot baseball with, among others, the DiMaggio brothers. While he was not a typical reactionary police chief of the era, he was not a progressive.[86] His election was another victory for the city's political establishment.

Overall, Dianne Feinstein finished first with slightly more than 117,000 votes,

14,000 more than second-place finisher John Barbagelata.[87] Feinstein's unsuccessful run for mayor in 1971 had not done any lasting damage to her standing in the eyes of the voters. Because Feinstein finished first overall, she again became president of the board. Her strong showing in the citywide race immediately positioned her as the front-runner for the 1975 mayoral election. That campaign was still two years away, but Feinstein, particularly given her proven ability to raise money, was establishing a good political position for herself.

By early 1973, there was some discussion in progressive circles of getting rid of at-large elections and replacing them with district elections. But doing that would not be easy. The board of supervisors was not going to make the change themselves because by voting to switch to district elections some supervisors would be voting themselves out of office. This left the initiative process, but passing a citywide initiative required the kind of money that progressives did not have. In other words, the same reason that progressives wanted district elections made it hard to get it passed.

The debate about changing the electoral system was odd because most American cities had some form of district elections. Although San Francisco had been using at-large elections since 1900, Los Angeles had switched to district elections in 1925. Chicago always had district elections, but in 1923, the city switched from two members per district to one. New York had a hybrid system with some members elected by district and others at-large. That system, along with the Board of Estimate, was ruled unconstitutional by the US Supreme Court in 1989 because it was not consistent with the principle of one-person, one-vote. Since then, New York has only had district elections for its city council. At the state and national level, district-based elections have long been the norm.

Feinstein, aware of the pressure from the left for district elections, crafted a hybrid proposal that would have phased in a system where four members of the board were elected at- large and five from individual districts. This idea was cumbersome and never got much political support, but it reflected Feinstein's instinct for the political middle.[88] That instinct was a large part of her appeal in the 1973 campaign for supervisor. While Feinstein may not have had a passionate base, almost nobody hated her. She was youngish and liberal on many social policies that the left liked. For example, in 1973 the Gay Voters League, a group of progressive gay voters, endorsed Harvey Milk, Jack Morrison, and two other challengers, but Feinstein was the only incumbent it endorsed.[89] Her background and close ties to downtown meant that business leadership was happy with her too. This kind of political profile is perfect for winning multi-vote, multi-member elections or elections against any one opponent, but less so in other electoral systems.

As the 1973 election approached, progressives concentrated not on winning seats in what they rightfully considered to be an electoral system that was stacked against them, but in changing the system. They did this through a ballot initiative which was designated Proposition K and would have switched San Francisco to district elections essentially beginning in 1975.

In the voter guide, the argument for the initiative included five major headings: "Yes on 'K' Will Unify the City," "Yes on 'K' to End Big Money Campaigns," "Yes on 'K' for More Democratic Government," "Yes on 'K' for More Accountable Supervisors" and "Yes on 'K' Is the First Step to a Better City." The concluding line under the last heading was "Instead of replacing one unresponsive supervisors (sic) with another unresponsive supervisor, the most ever achieved by at-large elections, it's time for a change."

The author of that summary was Calvin Welch, a well-known San Francisco activist whose work continued well into this century. Endorsers of that statement included the *Bay Area Reporter* (the city's primary gay and lesbian newspaper) and numerous other progressive community organizers, community organizations, and elected officials. Those who endorsed included the well-known activist Sue Bierman, Willie Brown, John Burton, Agar Jaicks, La Raza en Acción Local, Gordon Lau, Local 535 of SEIU, Jack Morrison, the Central City Coalition, the Eureka Valley Promotion Association (the Castro was still known by some as Eureka Valley in 1973), Carlton Goodlett, the Greater Mission Democratic Club, the Haight Ashbury Neighborhood Council, Sue Hestor, SF Tomorrow, Arnold Townsend, and the SF Democratic County Central Committee. Moscone, naturally, was among the endorsers. One of the other endorsers of that statement was an attorney, John E. Benson, who would be appointed to the bench in 1974 and play an important role in San Francisco a few years after that. Additionally, Peter Finnegan, a political activist who had run unsuccessfully for the board in 1971 and would do so again in 1980, also endorsed the statement. Finnegan has an obscure place in San Francisco popular culture because in the 1971 film *Dirty Harry*, there is a scene where a Muni streetcar, presumably the J-Church, passes with a sign on the side saying, "Elect Peter Finnegan"[90]

Opponents of Proposition K filed several statements against the initiative rather than one omnibus statement. Among those filing statements were John F. Crowley from Citizens for a United San Francisco. Crowley, a labor leader close with Mayor Alioto, warned that if the bill passed, "One supervisor would be elected from each district, and he would be concerned with only his district, instead of the entire city." William Dauer, executive vice president of the Greater San Francisco Chamber of Commerce, posed the question, "What happens if the Supervisor from your District (sic) disagrees with you? Where do you go to get a problem solved?" Additionally, Supervisors Francois, Tamaras, Molinari, Chinn, von Beroldingen, Mendelsohn, and Feinstein all signed a statement that concluded with the argument, "Proposition K is bad news for both majority and minority groups in their mutual and continuing struggle to assure election of governmental officials on a basis of representing everyone equally rather than 'representing their own.' . . . Vote 'No' on Proposition K: Insure (sic) equal representation for majority and minority groups."[91]

The question of how to elect a legislature is important, and good arguments can be made for several different structures. The arguments against Proposition K were legitimate. It is true that district-based elections leave a lot of voters who disagree with their representative feeling they lack real representation. It is also true that at-large legislatures incentivize legislators to think about the whole polity rather than their individual districts, but also that, as supporters of Proposition K argued, "district campaigns means that candidates would overcome big money influence by personal contact with voters." Similarly, Proposition K supporters' argument also had a great deal of validity, that the at-large system meant that "supervisors are accountable now to downtown and big money. It's time to give downtown one vote rather than eleven."[92] Both sides made good arguments, but in the context of San Francisco in the early 1970s, it was clear that at-large elections benefited wealthy downtown interests while switching to district elections would benefit progressive neighborhood activists.

Proposition K strengthened some of the battle lines in San Francisco politics that had been forged during the Freeway Revolts and would define the city for the next few years and next few decades. It pitted the left, understood broadly, against the establishment. However, the emerging right was not wedded to the idea of ceding power to the moderate establishment by maintaining at-large elections. Among the four members of the board who did not sign the statement against Proposition K were influential conservatives Quentin Kopp and John Barbagelata. The two men were friends and neighborhood politicians of the right. Their political bases were the old conservative, Catholic voters of western San Francisco. Barbagelata, a native San Franciscan and a Catholic, fit in well with those voters. Kopp was Jewish and from the East Coast, but his politics resonated in conservative western parts of the city.

Overall, the election of 1973 was a win for the political establishment in general and for Dianne Feinstein in particular. By finishing first in the vote citywide, Feinstein would be returning to her role as president of that board, the ideal position from which to run for mayor. Two other election outcomes helped Feinstein position herself for that election. First, Proposition K was soundly defeated. Only 35 percent of the 172,000 San Franciscans who voted on that initiative supported the idea. That was a victory for the center against the left, but it also meant that in 1975 the elections for supervisor would again be citywide. Had the imitative passed, an entirely new board would have been elected by districts in 1975. This would have made it possible for neighborhood progressive activists to align behind a mayoral candidate who could benefit from that newfound political energy. Feinstein had little chance of becoming that candidate.

This also meant that Feinstein would not have to give up her seat in the board to run for mayor in 1975 because the term to which she was elected in 1973 would continue through 1977.

Proposition D received less attention than Proposition K, but it was an attempt to change the structure of San Francisco elections and further empower the center and hurt progressives. Proposition D called for runoff elections for the office of mayor if no candidate received a majority of votes in the first round. This was an effort to ensure that no progressive could get elected with a plurality in a multicandidate race. In the late 1960s and early 1970s, several southern states and localities switched to some form of runoff elections to limit the chances of an African American candidate of winning by splitting the white vote. Proposition D was not a racist initiative, but it was a political one. It was also not, on its face, a bad idea. The idea that the mayor should be elected by a majority of the people is a reasonable and democratic one.

Nonetheless, in 1973 Proposition D mostly pitted the center against the left. In the voter guide, those endorsing the proposition included Mayor Alioto; George Christopher, the liberal Republican who had been mayor in the late 1950s and early 1960s; Leo McCarthy, the powerful assemblyman who was viewed as a centrist; the Downtown Association; the president of the Junior Chamber of Commerce; and nine of the city's supervisors, including Feinstein. Those voicing their opposition to this idea in the voter guide included Terry Francois, the city's only African American supervisor, activists Carlton Goodlett and Carol Ruth Silver, and several progressive Democratic Clubs.

One reason Francois, Goodlett, and several other African American leaders opposed Proposition D was that they believed the runoff system would make it more difficult for an African American to get elected mayor. Their thinking was that an African American could win a plurality of votes in a crowded field but would struggle to win a runoff. Arnold Townsend indicated that Willie Brown considered running for mayor in 1975 but decided not to for precisely this reason.[93]

Proposition D passed by a narrow margin as 52.7 percent of the almost 175,000 San Franciscans who voted on the initiative supported it. The new runoff system meant that if Feinstein ran for mayor and did not win outright, as a centrist she would be able to consolidate her support against a progressive in the runoff by picking up conservative votes and against a conservative by winning support from the left. No other candidate would be able to do that as easily.

The 1973 city elections occurred just as Moscone was beginning to reevaluate his plans to run for governor. Within two months of the election, Moscone would be out of that race. The big win for Feinstein, the defeat of Proposition K, and the failure of Jack Morrison, who finished seventh in the race for five seats, to make it back onto the board were blows for progressive forces and the Burton operation. The plan of switching to district elections by 1975 and leveraging that to a progressive takeover of the city was looking much more difficult, particularly with the emergence of Feinstein as a front-runner to succeed Alioto.

November 1974 was a busy month for Moscone. Shortly after easily winning reelection to the senate, Moscone turned his attention to his first venture into international politics. For many decades in the twentieth century, New York City political lore was that candidates for mayor had to visit the "three Is," Ireland, Italy, and Israel, countries that were of great significance to the city's huge Irish, Italian, and Jewish populations. Moscone did not visit the three Is, but he came close in November 1974 when he took a trip to London, the USSR, Israel, and Rome. He may have neglected Ireland, but as Irish Americans in San Francisco grew more conservative, that was understandable.

This trip was primarily a political gambit. Moscone's trip to the USSR at that time was unusual, but the purpose was "a need to understand more clearly the problems of Soviet Jews both as they relate to American-Russian relations and immigration to Israel."[94] For much of the 1970s and 1980s, the efforts of Jews seeking to leave the Soviet Union and go to Israel or other countries, including the US, was a major source of tension between the two superpowers.

The plight of Soviet Jewry was a genuine human rights issue and was of particular concern to Jews. Moscone, who had good relations with Jewish voters and Jewish organizations throughout his career, was concerned about the issue. It was also a political decision as he prepared to run for mayor against two Jewish candidates, Marks and Feinstein. Similarly, a trip to Italy was not going to hurt Moscone with the large Italian American vote.

The trip to the Soviet Union would also raise Moscone's stature as a statewide and potentially national political figure. In 1974, politicians, particularly state legislators did not frequently visit Moscow. Nor did they focus their trip on issues like Soviet Jewry. Moscone not only did this, but he spent much of that trip talking to Soviet Jews, something that would have drawn the attention of Soviet security forces. Because of how closed the USSR was, Moscone had to be creative about briefings.

One of the people who briefed Moscone for the trip was Herb Gold. A well-known writer and an important figure in beatnik literary history, Gold was not a diplomat and had no experience in international relations. However, he was Jewish and had visited Moscow, so Gold briefed Moscone's aide Corey Busch before the trip. Gold helpfully identified a key contact, Vladimr Slepak, for Moscone, and told him that "if you tell Slepak that you want to see the others, he will arrange it for you."[95] Busch's memo to Moscone included some general tips about carrying papers, being aware of listening devices and other espionage, and ends with the advice, "Have fun. Keep your ass covered and stay warm."[96] That advice would be relevant to most travelers planning a trip to Russia today.

Moscone's trip to Leningrad (now St. Petersburg), Moscow, and Kiev (now Kyiv) was about a week long. He was in Israel for a few days and in Rome only for an afternoon and evening. Overall, Moscone's travels generated little media coverage. His meetings with refuseniks were important but rarely newsworthy. The trip helped Moscone demonstrate his affinity for the struggles of the Jewish people, solidified some relationships within San Francisco's Jewish community, and made him more visible on issues related to Israel and Soviet Jewry. Moscone continued to be a supporter of Soviet Jewry and the State of Israel throughout his life.

Moscone's staff prepared a list of forty-one people to whom he should send postcards during his trip. This list included literary figures such as Gold; the consul general of Israel in San Francisco; religious leaders, including Rabbi Brian Lurie and the Reverend Cecil Williams; newspaper people such as Templeton Peck, Syd Kossen, Abe Melinkoff, Carlton Goodlett, and Caen; prominent Jewish business and civic leaders such as Walter Shorenstein and Naomi Lauter; politicians such as Richard Hongisto; and Moscone's Hollywood friend Leonard Nimoy.[97]

It is not known how many of those people received postcards from Moscone, but his correspondence from Moscow took other forms too. Toward the end of Moscone's trip, Caen reported that "State Senator George Moscone, in Russia to 'observe' the Jewish emigration process, is writing his friends here on toilet tissue 'because that's the thickest paper available in Moscow.'"[98]

CHAPTER NINE

The Race for Mayor—Round One

MOSCONE'S SHORT-LIVED CAMPAIGN FOR GOVERNOR did not slake his ambition for higher office and may have led him to question his future in state government. During Moscone's first eight years in the California State Senate, the governor had been a conservative Republican. The presence of Ronald Reagan in the Governor's Mansion made it difficult for progressive state legislators such as Moscone, but it also raised their profile and influence in Sacramento. When Moscone served as majority leader of the senate, he, along with the four Democrats, Jesse Unruh, Robert Monagan, Bob Moretti, and Leo McCarthy, who served as Speaker of the assembly during those years, were California's most powerful Democrats. That changed immediately once Democrat Jerry Brown took over as governor in 1975 and became the primary agenda-setter for the party. Legislative leaders such as Moscone were still important, but mostly because they were needed to implement the governor's program.

Moscone began to turn his attention to the evolving mayor's race in his hometown. The election to choose a successor to Joseph Alioto, scheduled for November 1975, was drawing interest from several San Francisco politicians including initial front-runner Dianne Feinstein. By early 1974 Moscone was already suggesting he would run too. At an event in San Francisco in March, Moscone told the gathering that "he disagreed with Thomas Wolfe's novel, *You Can't Go Home Again.* 'George Moscone is home and damm (sic) glad of it,' he said. 'That means you and I will be doing things together to make San Francisco the kind of city we know that it can be.'"[1]

San Francisco's nonpartisan election system meant there were no Democratic or Republican primaries. Instead, all candidates would be on the ballot in November 1975. Additionally, for the first time in San Francisco history, because of the passage of Proposition D in 1973, the winning candidate would need 50 percent plus one vote to avoid a runoff. These nonpartisan elections as well as the runoff system sometimes make it easier for moderate Democrats to get elected even in progressive cities because they do not have to make it through Democratic primaries that are frequently dominated by progressives.

This also helps explain why San Francisco so rarely elects progressive mayors. Since 1980, only one real progressive, Art Agnos, has been elected mayor of San Francisco. Almost every other mayor from Feinstein to Daniel Lurie got elected with a coalition of centrist independents, Republicans, and the center and right of the Democratic Party. That coalition works in nonpartisan elections but falters if the candidate has to first win a Democratic primary. New York provides a contrast. In recent years, many Democratic nominees from David Dinkins to Ruth Messinger to Bill de Blasio have been progressives. Michael Bloomberg, at the time a longtime centrist Democrat, abandoned his party and ran, and won, as a Republican in 2001 largely because he would have had a tough time winning a closed Democratic primary. Eric Adams, who won the 2021 Democratic primary for mayor as a moderate, is an exception.

Feinstein possessed some genuine strengths as well as some electoral vulnerabilities. She enjoyed a reputation as a smart and hard-working legislator; and as one of only two women on the board of supervisors, Feinstein easily stood out from most of her peers. In those days, women, particularly mothers of young children, were very unusual in politics. When Feinstein was elected in 1969, her daughter was twelve years old, so she was a teenager during the time her mother was on the board. The media rarely hesitated to comment on this or Feinstein's physical appearance, frequently describing her as "slender" "attractive" or in other possibly complimentary, but definitely sexist, words.

At first cut, Feinstein seemed like a strong candidate. She had twice led all supervisor candidates in votes, demonstrating that she was acceptable to most San Francisco voting blocks and interests. She would likely have the support of the downtown business community because of her pro-business and pro-development positions. As a liberal on social issues, but by no means a radical, Feinstein seemed a good fit for the changing San Francisco.

Like Moscone, Feinstein was a native San Franciscan, albeit from a much more affluent corner of the city. She had attended the Convent of the Sacred Heart, one of the city's best Catholic schools for girls, where Moscone would later send his daughters. Unlike Moscone, Feinstein, the daughter of a successful and prominent doctor, was not one of the lower-income students at her elite school. After high school, Feinstein attended Stanford University. She had lived much of her life in and around Pacific Heights and was deeply integrated into the city's wealthiest communities. Larry Griffin, a Moscone campaign worker in 1975 who knew both politicians. described the contrast. "George was much more working-class. . . . Dianne is like Queen Feinstein."[2] Feinstein was acceptable to most voters, but she was beloved by few. That profile can be very effective in a two-person race but often proves challenging in a multicandidate race where there is no rank order or instant runoff voting. This is particularly true when other candidates with similar ideologies or demographic profiles enter the race. However, because of the passage of Proposition D in 1973, all Feinstein had to do was finish in the top two because her centrist credentials would make her a very strong runoff candidate.

With Jerry Brown the newly elected governor, there would be no opportunity for Moscone to run for governor until 1982 because Brown would be the Democratic nominee again in 1978. Both California's US Senators were Democrats, so that was not an option for Moscone either. The mayor's race was different. Because it would be an open seat, Moscone would have a real shot—and if he didn't run in 1975, he would not have a good chance to run again until probably 1983. Additionally, by December 1974, Moscone had already gone before the voters of the entire city of San Francisco in 1963, 1966, 1970, and 1974, and gotten elected four times.

Chronicle writer Jerry Burns was bullish on Moscone's chances and after talking to political insiders and gamblers in San Francisco, gave Moscone 2–1 odds to be the next mayor, followed by Marks at 3–1 and Feinstein at 5–1. Five other candidates were given much longer odds, but John Barbagelata was not among them.[3] Jack Morrison's defeat in his attempt to return to the board of supervisors pushed Moscone to the front of the line of progressive candidates looking at the mayor's race and meant that Moscone was the best mayoral candidate still in the Burton political orbit. The stakes were high for the Burtons and progressives. If Feinstein became mayor, San Francisco could look forward to eight more years of an administration that would focus on economic growth and the business community, rather than the needs of lower-income San Franciscans and the neighborhoods. Feinstein would be more liberal than Alioto about social issues, notably with regards to gay rights, but her mayoralty would otherwise feel like a third, and then possibly fourth, Alioto term.

A Feinstein mayoralty was not the only threat facing progressive San Francisco. Most of the historiography of the late 1960s and early 1970s focuses on left-leaning political and civil rights movements but frequently overlook the corresponding rise of the right. In San Francisco, the new right did not take the form of conservative evangelical Christianity as it did in other places. Rather, like many major cities, the face of the new right was primarily white ethnics, who were frequently Catholic, resistant to civil rights, and felt they were losing their cities to people of color, gays, liberals, and hippies. These were often working-class people who viewed government as captured by big business and unconcerned about the crime, rising cost of living, and shortage of jobs that were taking a terrible toll on their communities.

As the 1975 race approached, the possibility of a candidate emerging who could ride this backlash sentiment to City Hall loomed. The two candidates positioned to do that were John Barbagelata and Quentin Kopp. Barbagelata had been elected to the board of supervisors in 1969 and reelected in 1973. Kopp was elected for the first time in 1971 so would be up for reelection in 1975. The two were supported by a similar coalition of white working-class and conservative middle-class voters. Both of their political bases were in the western part of the city.

There were also major differences between the two men. Barbagelata was an Italian American San Franciscan who had been born and raised in the city. He was a successful businessman, a realtor who ran an eponymous real estate agency. The firm is still around, but the name has been shortened to Barbco. Kopp was Jewish and from Syracuse, New York. He had moved to San Francisco as an adult with an Ivy League law degree.

By dint of his longer tenure on the board, deeper roots in San Francisco, and being Italian American, Barbagelata looked like the stronger mayoral candidate. Additionally, while Kopp would have to give up his seat on the board after only one term to run for mayor, Barbagelata was not up for reelection until 1977 so would not have to give up his seat to run. Kopp was nine years younger than Barbagelata so would have more chances in the future. One tantalizing possibility for conservative San Francisco was that Barbagelata would get elected mayor and bring out a big enough vote on the west side that Kopp would finish first overall in the at-large supervisorial election, making him president of the new board of supervisors. With Barbagelata as mayor and Kopp leading the board, conservatives would be well positioned to redirect San Francisco rightward.

Progressives could not afford to let the 1975 race devolve into a contest between the center and the right. However, it was not entirely clear who the best progressive candidate might be. By 1975 cities with large African American populations such as Newark, New Jersey, Gary, Indiana, Detroit, and Atlanta had elected African American mayors. In 1973, Los Angeles elected Tom Bradley, for whom Moscone had campaigned, to be its first African American mayor. San Francisco was different; no African American politicians were strong enough to run citywide. The only possible candidates were Supervisor Terry Francois and Willie Brown, but, in part because of the new runoff system, neither gave the 1975 race a real look. Brown would eventually become the city's first African American mayor, but not for another twenty years. No Latino or Asian Americans were thinking of the race. San Francisco was extremely diverse, but white voters still constituted a majority. Any progressive candidate would have to do well with white voters while also winning a big majority from non-white voters. This was a different, and more difficult, political project than the challenge of mobilizing large numbers of African American voters in cities such as Detroit or Gary.

Among white progressives, neither of the Burtons were likely to be strong citywide candidates. However, two other candidates had potential to defeat

Feinstein from the left, and both were state senators. Because of San Francisco's unusual districting history, both George Moscone and Milton Marks represented all of San Francisco, and had each won citywide elections several times. Both were well liked with strong personal skills that served them well on the campaign trail, had similar voting records in the senate, and had strong roots in San Francisco.

Marks was the very liberal Republican who had defeated Moscone in a race for the assembly in 1960. Since then, Marks, an excellent retail politician who was well known throughout the city, had built a political reputation as a reliable liberal. However, Marks did not have deep ties to progressive causes or movements and, despite his personal views, was still a Republican. Progressive Democrats did not want a Republican mayor with whom they had no real relationship, no matter how liberal he was.

This left Moscone as the best hope for progressive San Francisco. Even if Marks got in the race, Moscone would have a chance of consolidating his base among African Americans, Latinos. and white progressives. Feinstein and Marks both had strong records on LGBT issues, but Moscone would be competitive with those voters too. His strong record on labor issues and ties to the Burtons all but guaranteed that he would win most of the major labor endorsements. Feinstein looked like she would be a difficult opponent in a potential runoff, but as an Italian American, with deep ties to Catholic San Francisco, Moscone, despite his political views, could probably compete with Feinstein for the votes of working-class Catholic San Franciscans who might not be ready to vote for a woman.

The Race Takes Shape

On December 19, 1974, Moscone's newly appointed campaign manager, Don Bradley, issued a press release that began, "State Senator George Moscone today announced that he'll seek the office of mayor of San Francisco." The press release continued, "Senator Moscone pledged a campaign—and Mayorship (sic)—dedicated to solving the problems that have beset San Francisco and said the city's future 'hangs in a delicate balance. People don't expect miracles. They only expect, and rightly so, someone to care . . . . someone to try . . . . someone to apply creativity and humanity to our problems.'" The release included several other statements that were more like platitudes than positions, but also included quotes from the candidate such as "San Francisco is not a city of just white males. But rather it is a city of talented women; and blacks and Latinos; of Asians; young and old people, of gays and straights; my campaign will reach into very corner, every segment of the city."[4]

The official announcement on the same day occurred at the Towne House Hotel, a big downtown hotel located at Market and Eighth Street. Moscone's comments revealed a lot about how he was thinking about the race and the campaign. Although the election was nonpartisan, Moscone stressed that he was a

Democrat: "It won't hurt for our mayor to be of the same party as our new governor, our new legislature and to have the unequivocal support of our two San Francisco congressmen." This was a somewhat odd comment because the mayor at the time, Joe Alioto, was also a Democrat, as was Dianne Feinstein. Milton Marks, who according to the report in the *Chronicle* the next day was "considered a sure candidate for mayor,"[5] was the likely target of that comment.

Moscone's speech began modestly, almost jocularly: "I wish I could tell you that my friends and hordes of San Franciscans have been urging me to run for mayor of San Francisco. That after a reluctant denial of my political ambition, I finally succumbed to their plea and am now willing to make this great personal sacrifice in the public interest." He then suggested that was not quite the case and indicated why he decided to run:

> But we are not as confident as we would like to be about the future of San Francisco. The City has problems. While I do not intend to join the chorus that says our cities are dying, the future of our City is hanging in a very delicate balance. To a large extent, the leadership provided, or the lack of leadership provided by the next Mayor of this City will determine whether San Francisco will continue to be a great city or if it will drift toward the sorry fate of Detroit, Buffalo or even New York. This trend will, I assure you, not occur if I am that next mayor.[6]

In 1975, drugs, crime, racial tension, joblessness, and all the urban blights of the era were abundant in San Francisco, but Moscone still described it as a "great city" that was better off than other cities including New York. This was probably true, particularly regarding Buffalo and Detroit, but also reflected the San Francisco myopia, some might say arrogance, that has long been part of that city's vibe. The notion that San Francisco is a great city, and New York is not, has never been true, and was not true in 1975, but this is the kind of thing that San Franciscans always like hearing.

Moscone also used the announcement to flesh out his vision of what neighborhood-based governance would look. "It is not going to be 'business as usual' with the same people minding the store . . . Most of my appointees will consist of names you've never heard of before. It could be someone on your street. You or your neighbor could be the first on your block."[7]

Because he had already shown interest in statewide office, Moscone was asked if he was committed to serving out his term as mayor. This was an odd question because it was not clear what else Moscone would do. He was not going to run in a primary against Governor Brown in 1978 or against Alan Cranston for the US Senate in 1980. Democrat John Tunney, who would be difficult to defeat in a primary, held the other Senate seat. Moscone responded unequivocally—and in retrospect somewhat eerily. "If I am elected . . . I'll serve not only this full term, but I'll try for one more. I'm forty-five. I'm vigorous and healthy. I have some good experience and I want to be mayor, and a good one."

The other tough question Moscone faced was about his personal life. By 1974 Moscone's reputation for philandering, partying, and spending a lot of time out on the town in San Francisco and Sacramento was more or less an open secret. The candidate dismissed this question by stating "my private life won't shake any teacups."[8] The photo accompanying the article was not flattering. Moscone was looking to his right with a countenance of both curiosity and annoyance. Gina was obscured by the podium, while ten-year-old Jonathan was looking at his father, not with admiration, but with his mouth open in a big yawn.

Toward the end of the event, Moscone observed, "I'm the front-runner. The polls show it."[9] As the only announced candidate who already enjoyed the support of Phil Burton, John Burton, and Willie Brown, Moscone was certainly in a strong position as the race was getting started. It was less clear to what poll he was referring. There had been no public polls yet, but in political circles, a poll, taken almost a full year before the election, was being discussed. It showed Moscone leading, followed by Marks, Feinstein, Kopp, Supervisor Al Nelder, and Willie Brown.[10]

The poll supported Moscone's claim that he, not Feinstein, was indeed the early front-runner, but it was still close. Although no numbers were made public, in late October, Herb Caen, referring to the same poll, revealed the state of the race as "Marks and Moscone neck and neck, with Feinstein, Kopp and Nelder close behind."[11] Marks and Feinstein were already hurting each other. They had similar backgrounds and political views despite being members of different political parties, and they appealed to many of the same voters. Within a few years, Willie Brown would become Speaker of the California State Assembly and one of the most powerful legislators in state history, but the poll showed his moment to run for mayor had not yet arrived. Brown's subsequent decision not to run helped Moscone because other than Brown, Moscone was strongest with African American voters. Kopp was in fourth place in the poll, suggesting there was some support for his more conservative message. At that early point in the race, Kopp, not Barbagelata, was considered the most likely candidate to represent this constituency.

Milton Marks was the next candidate to get in the race, followed by Judge Jack Ertola. On the relatively late date of April 22, 1975, Feinstein, as expected, finally announced her candidacy. Feinstein's announcement focused on issues such as increasing economic growth and job development in low-income communities and getting police out of their cars and back onto the streets. Feinstein was positioning herself as the competent, tolerant centrist that she was. She also made another comment that underscored how she stood out from the rest of the field when she said she would "end once and for all the nonsense that a woman is not capable of providing the strength and toughness necessary to lead our city."[12] Feinstein was not quite the front-runner, but she still a very strong candidate. At that point, the race looked to be shaping up as three-person race between Moscone, Marks, and Feinstein, and it seemed likely to be heading toward a runoff.

It was another six weeks before Barbagelata formally got in the race and the field was finalized. During his announcement Barbagelata offered conservative views that one might expect today from a businessman seeking to govern a generally liberal city, asserting that San Francisco needed "strong leadership free of obligation to any particular group and not afraid to make a few enemies. . . . I don't think there is another candidate that represents the type of thinking needed or is forceful enough to get the city turned around."[13] Barbagelata's tone was, as usual, combative. The *Chronicle* reported those comments the day after the announcement, but the Barbagelata comment that the *Examiner* chose to quote was more outrageous and hinted at who would be the focus of Barbagelata's attention. "There isn't a candidate in this race that can do a job. There isn't a businessman. All you have is three attorneys and a housewife."[14] The "housewife" Barbagelata's sexist barb was aimed at was Feinstein, the president of the board of supervisors who had twice received more votes citywide than Barbagelata. It would not be the last time Barbagelata would attack Feinstein during the campaign.

Barbagelata's campaign harvested the not-quite-under-the-surface anger and resentment that was evident throughout San Francisco in the mid-1970s. Although Barbagelata was never quite the nonpolitician he claimed to be, he was not a natural politician. Nor did he have much charisma, a great speaking style, or strong media skills. He was an angry conservative businessman who spoke to the thousands of other largely white and straight voters wanting to return to the peaceful and relatively conservative city they had known a decade ago.

Bruce Brugmann, the longtime editor of the *San Francisco Bay Guardian*, a progressive community newspaper, described both Barbagelata and Kopp as "independent conservatives from the neighborhoods. . . . They were neighborhood conservatives. . . . The problem for him (Barbagelata) was that he was much too conservative for a liberal city like San Francisco."[15] Journalist Jerry Roberts offered a colorful description of Barbagelata: "Barbagelata in Italian means frozen beard, and that in many ways captured what his personality was, but he was an angry guy. . . . He was angry on behalf of these homeowners on the west side of the city who economically saw their taxes going up and saw their money being given to public employees . . . saw the influx of hippies and gays and minorities and really saw the city transforming in a way that they felt power slipping away from them."[16]

Art Agnos also described Barbagelata's approach to politics: "Barbagelata had a lot of the attitudes that we see in Trump. He thought everything was a conspiracy . . . right-wing, a conservative conspiratorial ideology." However, Agnos had a more nuanced view of the realtor turned supervisor's character, noting that Barbagelata was "a very honest, deeply religious man" who respected people if "he sensed you were authentic," citing Barbagelata's decision in 1987 to endorse Agnos for mayor "though I was a screaming lefty . . . He thought Molinari (Agnos's opponent in that runoff) was a dishonest, philandering kind of guy."[17]

It is tempting to see Barbagelata and Moscone as mirror images of each other, with the former being the conservative backlash candidate of white ethnic San Francisco and the latter being the progressive candidate of diverse San Francisco, but that was not quite true. Moscone's base was much bigger. He was the first candidate in the race and immediately became the candidate of progressive and non-white San Francisco, although Marks and particularly Feinstein had some support in gay, African American, Latino and Asian American communities. Barbagelata's base was also large but less diverse with less room for growth. African American, Latino, and LGBT voters were never going to be interested in Barbagelata's conservative politics. Barbagelata had some appeal to the more conservative among Feinstein's supporters, but he was fishing in a much smaller political pool than Moscone was. Additionally, Moscone's was a politician's politician who enjoyed campaigning, was an accomplished legislator, and was at home in the back rooms and bars where so much of politics is done. Barbagelata, on the other hand, boasted of not being a politician, and he backed up that claim by frequently making political mistakes.

Barbagelata and Moscone had lives that were oddly intertwined. They were both Italian American Catholics and native San Franciscans, but the connections were deeper than that. Their wives and children knew each other and were friendly. By the time Moscone was running for mayor he was living in a home that had been purchased with Barbagelata as his realtor. San Francisco, especially native, Catholic San Francisco was still a very small town in many ways in the 1970s.

Barbagelata was not just motivated by backlash politics; he was also a Republican who believed in small government and a free hand for business. A summary of his responses to a questionnaire from the San Francisco Democratic Clubs demonstrates this. Barbagelata responded to the questionnaire despite the presence of two popular Democrats, Feinstein and Moscone, in the race, but his answers were never going to win him the endorsement from that organization. The fact that Barbagelata responded at all suggests that he was trying to have some fun by poking the Democratic clubs and, in today's parlance, was something of a troll. He mentioned his opposition to rent control, opposition to "collective bargaining rights for city employees," support for raising fares on Muni, support for building more freeways, support for redlining, and his desire to repeal the law that Moscone had helped pass legalizing consensual sex between adults of the same gender.[18]

With five legitimate candidates: Barbagelata, Ertola, Feinstein, Marks, and Moscone, the race was very competitive. However, Barbagelata, as the only neighborhood conservative in the race, had a path to victory. The key for Barbagelata was not just to make it into the runoff, but to make it into the runoff against Moscone. Moscone would still probably be the slight favorite against Barbagelata in a hypothetical runoff, but the conservative Republican would have little chance at all against either Marks, who would split the Republican vote with Barbagelata, or moderates such as Ertola or Feinstein. Both of those candidates would hold the center in a runoff against Barbagelata and a win a huge majority of the progressive Moscone vote. There is no way to prove any of this almost half a century after the election. In fact, there was no way to prove any of this at the time, but this is the kind of thinking that multicandidate elections with runoffs require.

Running for Mayor

Few big city mayor's races are genuinely competitive. Since 1975, the only truly competitive races for mayor of San Francisco were in 1991, 2003, 2018, and 2024. Similarly, in New York, the slog between Ed Koch and Mario Cuomo in 1977, when the two men faced off against each other in a primary, a runoff, and then a general election, and the political battles between David Dinkins and Rudy Giuliani in 1989 and 1993 were extremely competitive, but most other races in recent history have not been very close. [19] Moreover, because in big and medium-sized cities, many of the politicians, activists, and consultants know each other, and because retail politics and field campaigns are essential to mayoral elections, close mayoral races, when they occur, take on a high level of intensity and intimacy and can feel oddly personal.

Unlike campaigns for governor or senator which during the 1970s were largely conducted through television, radio, and later, direct mail—and much later, social media—you cannot get elected mayor of San Francisco, Chicago, or even New York, then or now, without getting out and meeting voters. Candidates walk through neighborhoods, attend small gatherings of voters, and shake hands at subway or bus stops or similar public spaces. For the voters and candidates, mayoral elections feel much more personal than statewide or national races.

This kind of retail politics requires specific skills. Some politicians are excellent on television and with media, but they struggle to connect to voters face to face or in small groups. Mitt Romney, the Republican Party nominee for president in 2012, is an example of this. Romney is a handsome and well-spoken man who very much looks the part of a senator, governor, or president. He understands policy well and looks good on camera, but perhaps because he has never run at the local level, does not resonate with voters face to face. Romney is a successful politician who has been the presidential nominee of his party, governor of one state and a senator from another, but would not do well in a mayoral election. Joe Biden was, for much of his career, the opposite. Biden's compassion and empathy made him appealing in face-to-face campaigning with both middle-class white voters and African Americans, key Democratic Party constituents, but never really found his on-camera stride until the 2020 general election.

In diverse cities, the best candidates must be able to strike up relationships with a very diverse electorate. A meet and greet in Pacific Heights, Feinstein's base in that 1975 election, chatting with Italian American seniors in Washington Square Park, greeting voters at a shopping area in heavily white and working-class parts of the Sunset District, and conversing with voters on the streets of the Castro District were very different experiences. Latinos in the Mission District or African Americans in the Fillmore or Bayview/Hunters Point were concerned about different issues and responded to different styles than any of those groups.

Being relatable to a broad range of San Franciscans was Moscone's great strength. No other candidate in the race could compete with him in that regard. Willie Brown, who knew Moscone well and has some knowledge of what it takes get elected mayor of San Francisco, explained this:

> George is probably one of the most popular persons, ever in San Francisco. He really was a dashing figure in San Francisco. He made an impression everywhere, whether it was going to the NAACP events, whether it was going to the Labor Council's events, whether it was interacting with the Church Labor Committee, which was Black Preachers hooking up with primarily with the more left-wing labor movement, whether it was the left-wing lawyers, the National Lawyers Guild, George was involved with all that, at the same time. George exploited, very productively, his Italian heritage and his connection to the people who ran the Scavenger's Association of our city, the garbage people. . . . He also enjoyed a level of credibility with the restaurateurs, the Italian restaurateurs, in a way in which no other politician did.[20]

John Burton shared Brown's assessment: "He's (Moscone) a city guy, he grew up on the . . . playgrounds. . . . George was comfortable with people. He was comfortable anywhere you take him."[21] Moscone's high school teammate and classmate Joe Kelly concurred: "George was more acceptable to the greater community than Willie (Brown) and John and Phil (Burton), just more acceptable out in (the) Richmond, (the) Sunset . . . . He had a great personality, he was a very charming guy, very witty."[22]

Among the limited television footage remaining from that campaign is a clip from December 19, 1974. Moscone is campaigning in what appears to be the Mission District. His upbeat mood is evident as he greets voters amid the grocery stores, take-out pizza places, and Chinese restaurants. He chats easily with voters as he introduces himself. An older Italian American man shakes Moscone's hand and says, "Buon Natale (Merry Christmas)" and then in English, "Good luck." Moscone wishes the last voter to whom he speaks, an elderly Mexican American man, "Feliz Navidad."[23]

Josh Getlin, who wrote speeches and did research for Moscone during the campaign, described how "any time you would spend with him (Moscone) walking various neighborhoods, driving through the city, meeting people at events in San Francisco, it wasn't just that George knew the people who were there, but he had stories connected to them, interfamilial relationships on his end, on their end, going back years. . . . It was like a walking encyclopedia, not just of the city but of the people in the city."[24] Getlin's comments reveal something about San Francisco that natives know intuitively. The city is simultaneously both very big and very small. In Moscone's time, it was diverse with very different neighborhoods, communities, and sometimes climates, but at the same time that if you lived there for close to half a century it was possible to know, or feel like you knew, almost everybody.

Political communities in cities such as San Francisco or bigger cities such as New York or Chicago are small. Most of the consultants, political reporters, operatives, major donors, and politicians all interact with each other frequently. A mayor's race for an open seat can bring people, for example, a longtime city councilperson and a state legislator, into competition for each other for the first time. Feinstein, Marks, Barbagelata, Ertola, and Moscone had all been around San Francisco politics for years, occasionally cooperated, but rarely directly competed with each other. Marks and Moscone had run against each other for the assembly in 1960, but they had both represented the city in the state senate for years, frequently working together and voting the same way. In these races, voters may have to choose between more than one candidate with whom they have an existing, and positive, relationship; voters may feel pulled between several candidates that they basically like. There were undoubtedly voters who had voted for Feinstein for supervisor twice, Moscone and Marks for senate at least once, and possibly even Barbagelata for supervisor at least once.

Marks was probably more effected by this dynamic than the other candidates. He was, like Feinstein and Moscone, left of center, but Marks was competing most directly with Feinstein. Both were tolerant liberals who had good ties to the city's business leadership. Moreover, both were Jewish with deep roots in the city. They would inevitably be going after the same voters and tapping the same fundraising sources. In a 1996 oral history, when asked how the Jewish vote split between the two candidates, Marks responded, "I think it was pretty close. I don't think there was any derivation. There may have been undoubtedly people who were for her who I would have thought would have been for me."[25]

Marks's presence in the race was an obstacle for Feinstein, but Barbagelata's late entrance into the race made a tough campaign much more challenging for her. Moscone and Barbagelata had little in common with regard to ideology, positions on issues, vision for San Francisco, or the coalitions they sought to assemble in their campaign, so Barbagelata getting into the race did not affect Moscone's campaign much. Both Moscone and Barbagelata had loyal bases of support and distinct ideological niches. If only one of these candidates had run, Feinstein might almost certainly would have made it to the runoff and would have had a good shot at winning that runoff, but with both Moscone and Barbagelata in, and with Marks competing with Feinstein in her base, her path got much narrower.

The five major candidates were what, by any measure, was a very accomplished field. According to Art Agnos, "All of them were very first-string candidates. I mean these guys were starters on any political team, all of them, and so it was a bitter contest, but the nastiest campaign."[26] These candidates may have been ideologically diverse, but they did not reflect the city's demographic diversity. That is partially because of the times, but it also speaks to the extent to which racial minorities and gays and lesbians were still struggling to break into political life in San Francisco. All five candidates were straight and white. Three were Italian American, and two were Jewish. San Francisco was moving leftward, but it was still a city where non-white and non-straight people rarely held elected office and where, Willie Brown and Terry Francois notwithstanding, the political class was still overwhelmingly white.

East and West in San Francisco

In the political vernacular of San Francisco, particularly during the 1970s, the city was divided between west and east. The dividing line was Twin Peaks in the middle of the city. As Agnos described it, "the west side of the city was seen as conservative with traditional white Irish Catholics and Italians and that kind of thing, very closely aligned with the Catholic Church. The east side of the city, which was less potent politically because you had many of the smaller populations but the beginnings of a progressive coalition with the minorities and the artists and liberals that lived more on the east side of the city, whether it was in North Beach or in the Mission."[27] Larry Griffin offered a similar analysis: "It was the east side versus the west side in the city. The west side was very conservative. A lot of white homeowners. A lot of Asian homeowners. . . . All what you would call NIMBYs (Not In My Back Yard), and they're still doing that. . . . C'mon guys, this isn't Dennis the Menace's hometown anymore. . . . West Side (people) were about preserving the power they had, and they didn't really want to share it with anybody else . . . Folks on the East Side were looking at the opportunities for change thought it was very possible this time."[28]

Barbagelata was clearly the candidate of the west, with Moscone similarly strong in the east. The west was conservative, mostly white, heavily Catholic and working class, with a few affluent enclaves such as St. Francis Wood. The west was seen as the old San Francisco, resistant to the changes of the 1960s. It included the Richmond, the Sunset, West Portal, Lake Merced, Ingleside, and even neighborhoods such as Parkside and the Excelsior that are more southern than western.

In the 1970s the largest ethnic group in this part of town were Irish Americans, but there was a sizable Italian American population as well. In addition, Jewish Americans, German Americans, and Russian Americans lived in the western part of the city, but there were not a lot of non-whites in that part of town. Today, the western half of San Francisco is heavily Asian American. Western San Francisco, then and now, can be understood as the San Francisco that only natives know. Almost none of the sights and scenes associated with the city in the minds of non-San Franciscans are in western San Francisco. There are no cable cars running through the Sunset District. The Financial District, Chinatown, and North Beach are in the far eastern reaches of the city. Even tourists coming to stare at hippies on Haight Street in the late 1960s or early 1970s would not have made it to western San Francisco. The Golden Gate Bridge, Fisherman's Wharf, and Ghirardelli Square are in the northern San Francisco. This is unfortunate because western San Francisco has always had an extraordinary beauty, including in places such as Golden Gate Park, Land's End and Ocean Beach. The history of that part of the city is also fascinating. Despite what many people who just moved to the city will tell you, you cannot understand San Francisco if you never go west.[29]

The eastern part of San Francisco refers to both the center and eastern parts of the city. Neighborhoods such as the Fillmore, Western Addition, Castro, and Haight-Ashbury are home to large numbers of African American, gay, and progressive San Franciscans, but are in the geographic center of the city. On the other hand, neighborhoods such as Bernal Heights, the Mission, and Potrero Hill are major parts of eastern San Francisco and align with that geographic descriptor. Neighborhoods including Bayview/Hunters Point and particularly Visitation Valley, are for political purposes considered the east, but are at least as southern as eastern.

Northern San Francisco is distinct from both the east and west. Pacific Heights has been the wealthiest part of the city for decades. It is a neighborhood of beautiful mansions with stunning views of the bay. Today it is an ATM neighborhood for liberal politicians from across the country, but in 1975 many people there were powerful San Franciscans who were neither progressives nor angry backlash voters. Just north of there, the Marina and Cow Hollow, where Moscone and I both grew up, particularly in the 1970s, shared some similarities with western San Francisco, but were slightly more liberal.

For Barbagelata, this meant a strategy of working to turn out voters in the working-class white districts primarily in southern and western San Francisco. Barbagelata was the kind of candidate who leaned on his experience in the private sector as a model and as a valuable prerequisite for governing. He explained in a column for the *Examiner* that he reprinted for his campaign literature. "I have over 30 years of business and administrative experience. Seven years out of college (USF), I was the top man in Japan and Korea for the world's largest airline, supervising hundreds of employees. Back home I went into business for myself. . . . The other four major candidates for the job of mayor have no such experience. They have not had to balance budgets, meet payrolls, learn how to cut duplication and waste. They are unequipped to manage departments, supervise thousands of employees, handle the administrative duties which our charter assigns the mayor."[30]

Barbagelata, as suggested in the *Examiner* column, frequently boasted about not being a politician. There was more truth to that claim than the two-term supervisor probably would have liked. Moscone, on the other hand, was a career politician who was very good at his craft. This helped Moscone mobilize more political support than any other candidate.

Moscone had barely entered the race when the 2,800-member Council of Painters, Local Eight endorsed him. "We feel certain that George Moscone will continue the excellent job he started as Supervisor, State Senator and soon to be, Mayor of San Francisco."[31] One of the major unions that enthusiastically endorsed Moscone was the same International Longshore and Warehouse Union that had led the general strike four decades earlier. The union was deeply entrenched in progressive labor politics and believed it was very important to have an ally such as Moscone in City Hall. "George Moscone has shown us the kind of leadership San Francisco needs. His track record shows that he understands and cares about the problems of working people, low-income people, senior citizens and homeowners. And over the years, as a supervisor and as Senate Democratic leader, he's proven that he knows how to get things done." [32] Another article in the ILWU election newspaper noted, "Working people want George Moscone to be the Mayor of San Francisco not only because he has the support of the AFL-CIO, the Teamsters, the Building Trades and the ILWU, but because throughout his career George Moscone has effectively fought for their needs."[33]

Moscone's great strength was that he was a genuine progressive with a corresponding record of accomplishments in Sacramento, a new and even radical vision for how San Francisco should be governed, and who should govern it, while also being a skilled politician whose network of political and labor backers gave him entrée into almost every community in San Francisco. Feinstein, Barbagelata, and Marks had successfully run citywide before and even won broad support from San Francisco's diverse electorate, but with the Burtons, Willie Brown, key labor unions, and influential clergy members such as Amos Brown,

Cecil Williams, and others supporting Moscone, they had limited ability to reach voters in those communities.

Moscone's strength also could have backfired on him. Progressive candidates running on a pledge to govern differently who have spent a career in elected office and enjoy strong ties to powerful political insiders are vulnerable to charges of hypocrisy or worse. However, of the major candidates, only Barbagelata could plausibly make that charge against Moscone because Feinstein and Marks were also both longtime political insiders.

The election brought at least three distinct San Francisco types into competition with each other. Barbagelata was the angry conservative from western San Francisco. His core constituents were, like Barbagelata, longtime San Franciscans, white, Catholic living in the western part of the city. Unlike their candidate, most of Barbagelata's supporters were working class. If Archie Bunker, the grumpy conservative patriarch on the influential 1970s sitcom *All in the Family,* had met Edith at a dance in the Bay Area and settled in San Francisco, rather than in Queens, New York, where the show was set, by 1975 the Bunkers probably would have been living out in the Sunset and voting for Barbagelata.

Feinstein's base was Pacific Heights, Cow Hollow, Nob Hill, the Inner Richmond around Lake Street and Sea Cliff. If Barbagelata was strongest in the west and Moscone in the east, Feinstein and Marks were both strongest in the northern part of the city. While supporters of Barbagelata probably worshipped at their parish church, Feinstein's and Mark's base were more likely to be congregants of Trinity Episcopal, Grace Church or Temple Emanu-El, the large reform synagogue in Presidio Heights. Some affluent San Franciscans did not share Feinstein's liberal views on social issues and may not have been entirely comfortable with a woman as mayor, they knew she was somebody who would not bring too much change and with whom they could do business.

Feinstein was also a known liberal quantity. *The Gay Crusader*, a moderate newspaper focusing on gay voters, endorsed Feinstein and attacked Moscone for his labor support. "Moscone belongs to the big labor bosses. They own him lock stock and barrel. But not so Dianne Feinstein. . . . We must elect Dianne Feinstein the Mayor of San Francisco this year 1975. . . . She has proven herself, time in and time out, the friend of all San Franciscans. We as gay people, can trust Dianne, and we can trust that she will be open to all of us, and not a select few!"[34]

The Final Years of Joseph Alioto's San Francisco

The 1975 mayoral election in San Francisco occurred when the city was experiencing some very specific problems and challenges arising from the tumult of the previous decade. High-profile political crimes such as the kidnapping of Patty Hearst, the bombing of police stations, and, in the middle of the campaign, a bombing of Mayor Alioto's home that fortunately did not take any lives, elevated concerns about crime, but they also heightened the sense that something was going very wrong in San Francisco.

It wasn't all bad news in San Francisco, and it didn't feel that way at the time. For many San Franciscans, the previous ten years had brought greater equality and opportunity and enhanced the city's cultural and social life. Many enjoyed being in a dynamic and progressive city with a great music scene. The slow economy meant that the city was still affordable for young people. San Francisco was also unusual in many ways. Candidates for mayor of Cleveland were not thinking about the political demands of a growing LGBT population; politicians in Dallas were not concerned about the Symbionese Liberation Army; and no city had quite the same diverse demographic mix as San Francisco.

The 1975 election also occurred in the shadow of the fiscal crisis in New York City. This placed budget and fiscal issues at the center of the campaign and probably helped Barbagelata, who presented himself as a businessman. It did not help Moscone, who had a reputation as a tax-and-spend liberal. As Moscone campaign aide Corey Busch noted, "the Barbagelata campaign and the right wing did a pretty good job of saying 'Vote for Moscone and you're gonna end up in New York. And the President of the United States is gonna say to you, drop dead.'"[35]

A particularly bleak article in *The New York Times* described San Francisco in 1975. "There are many tears shed here. Many are poor. Many are threatened. Some are being crowded out. Interests battle interests, and the weak are crushed. Change has come rapidly; it is ill understood, and badly dealt with by community leaders. What once was a city filled with a thriving middle class has been abandoned by families seeking better schools, better homes and the fundamental security of personal safety."[36]

In 1975, there were 1,363.78 violent crimes for every 100,000 people in San Francisco. Some cities, such as Newark, New Jersey, Detroit, New York and, across the bay, Oakland, had even higher crime rates. However, San Francisco had more violent crime per capita in 1975 than Chicago, Pittsburgh, Miami, or Dallas. Houston, San Antonio, and Milwaukee were among the cities where the crime rate was less than half that of San Francisco.[37]

These substantive issues dominated much of the campaign. Barbagelata offered a conservative solution to these problems, promising to cut taxes, reduce spending and, in general, run a tighter fiscal ship. Ertola presented a similar platform. Before the realtor-turned-supervisor got into the race, Ertola sought to be the voice of conservative San Francisco. However, Ertola's temperament was milder than Barbagelata's so he was unable to become the voice of angry white working-class voters.

Moscone's proposed solutions to these problems came from a more progressive place, stressing the need for representation in City Hall, arguing that government, through creating programs and passing laws, could help solve these problems, and that the role of city government was not just to maintain the tax base. Feinstein, predictably, sought to split the difference, stressing her experience as president of the board of supervisors while nodding to the more tolerant views of liberal San Franciscans.

Police and Polls

In 1975, polling was not quite as common as it would become in the following decades. Many mayoral election polls, most likely commissioned by individual candidates, made their way to the public not so much through the hard news sections of the media but through more gossipy and chatty opinion columns. On February 10, before Feinstein got in the race, Caen reported, "On the strength of an elaborate poll that shows her running neck and neck with Moscone and Marks, Dianne Feinstein has made up her mind. She will run for mayor."[38] Caen did not give a source for the poll, nor was his conclusion that Feinstein was running a scoop. She had long been widely expected to run. Although the poll Caen cited indicated the election was going to be very close, he failed to mention Barbagelata, Kopp, Ertola, or any conservative candidate, suggesting that he expected the election to play out on the left and the center.

A few months later, Caen reported another poll. Once again, he did not provide any specific numbers, but wrote that the race was heading to a runoff between Feinstein and Moscone. "A new and probably meaningless poll shows Ms. Feinstein slightly ahead of George, Milton Marks slipping, Barbagelata sliding and Ertola scrambling. At this point, nobody's winning, as usual."[39] Caen might have gotten that information from one of the campaigns, a media colleague, or another political insider. He might just have been passing on rumors he had heard. Regardless of the provenance of that item, it was accurately reflected what had become the conventional wisdom about the race. Because he was so widely read and so influential, Caen was not just reporting the news, he was helping to set a tone about the race and thus decisions that donors and others would make. This was a much bigger problem for slipping Marks, whose supporters were more likely to travel in the same circles as Caen, than those of the sliding Barbagelata.

As the campaign continued into the summer, Moscone was in the unusual position of being the insider, because of his position in Sacramento, and the outsider, because of his political views and lack of support from downtown. He was both the straight white graduate of St. Ignatius and the candidate of the non-white and non-straight. Jerry Adams, who wrote for both the *Chronicle* and *Examiner*, explained the contrast from the perspective of lower-income and progressive San Franciscans between "people regarded as anti-environmental, anti-middle-class, anti-lower income people (and then) here was the champion of the people running for mayor. At last you get a chance."[40] Bruce Brugmann underscored how Moscone put together a very powerful progressive coalition: "George Moscone had labor, he had the Burton machine. He had us at the *Guardian*. He had the Sue Hestors and Calvin Welches (well-known community activists) and the more liberal independent neighborhood types. He had a lot of the Black community, a lot of the Latino community."[41]

Hestor gave her perspective of why so many neighborhood activists supported Moscone: "We were not so stupid as to think that we could have a candidate come out of nowhere and get elected in San Francisco. And, so you looked to see who's around, who'd run, who'd been successful. And George was the one that had the best politics, the most grounding in the community issues, a good guy, and a lot of us went to him and said we'll support you if you run."[42]

Getlin fleshed this out: "George was leading a coalition of people who were clamoring . . . for a seat at the table in terms of power in San Francisco and how the city was going to be governed . . . the gay community, the Blacks, Latinos, Asians, certainly lots of the people in the neighborhoods. . . . George's whole campaign was predicated on the idea that the insider's group was no longer going to continue running the city. The whole process was going to be opened up."[43]

All this progressive support did not guarantee Moscone anything. On October 9, less than a month before Election Day, the *Chronicle* featured a front-page headline, "Feinstein Ahead in S. F. Poll."[44] The article noted that Feinstein led among women, Moscone among men, and that there were still a lot of undecided voters. Underscoring the importance of Feinstein's gender, the article noted, "It is clear from comments made by those questioned in a newly completed telephone poll that the key issue for many voters this fall is whether San Francisco should entrust the office of mayor to a woman." The poll showed Feinstein with 22.9 percent and Moscone close behind with 20.8 percent. Marks, Barbagelata, and Ertola were bunched up, in that order, at around 10 percent. Barbagelata only had 9.2 percent.[45] That poll was consistent with what most of the political class was expecting—a runoff between Moscone and Feinstein with Marks fading from contention, but it, like all polls, was a snapshot in time. That may have been an accurate picture of where things stood with a month to go, but a lot changed in that final month.

At least one candidate had a sense of how the race was shaping up because a week earlier, Milton Marks, who had long had a reputation as personable and friendly politician, changed his approach and attacked the two front-runners. He criticized Moscone for his connection to the Burtons: "If the people of San Francisco want a mayor controlled by the machine, then they most certainly should vote for Senator Moscone." Marks then attacked Feinstein: "The question is can you believe what she promises and if she can make a difference, why hasn't she done so prior to this election. If the voters want things to continue as they have been, then they most certainly should vote for Mrs. Feinstein." Moscone and Feinstein both responded to Marks's attacks by minimizing the liberal Republican's chances. Moscone observed that "Milton's grapes are very sour" and pointed out that Marks had courted the Burtons as well. Feinstein was more patronizing. "I feel sorry for Milton. This is obviously a desperation attempt by a man who the polls show is slipping."[46]

The election changed in August when in a city riven by high crime, budget concerns, and political tensions, the police went on strike. The Police Officers Association (POA) wanted a 13 percent pay raise that would make them paid as much as comparable police officers in Los Angeles. The city countered by offering a 9 percent pay raise, thus leading to an impasse and a strike.[47] Vince Courtney, a longtime San Francisco labor activist, explained: "Although under that system they (the board of supervisors) were authorized to give the police and fire a 13 percent salary increase, they were only going to give them 9 (percent). . . . To tell you the truth, it sounded pretty good back then. But, due to a lot of mistakes that were made both by the POA's leadership and the board of supervisors, the deal didn't come together the way it should have, and as a result you ended up with a police and fire strike, which was real nasty."[48]

Police labor issues frequently scramble political relationships while not fitting into the usual political framework. Supporters of the police are often conservative local elected officials, but these same people are often the most anti-labor. Similarly, the most pro-labor politicians are frequently Democrats who are not always supportive of police unions on other issues. Moreover, in many cities, it is not clear that police officers are allowed to strike. All these factors were in play in San Francisco in 1975. For example, Mayor Alioto was generally pro-police, but as mayor he had to balance the budget and did not want to give police officers such a big raise.

The strike began in the afternoon of August 18 when negotiations between the POA and the board of supervisors broke down. As president of the board, Feinstein was particularly visible in the negotiations. Stephen Brooks (1980) described how when the strike began "cars were called back to the station with the comment that 'Feinstein (board of supervisors president) is doing the arresting from now on.'"[49] The prospect of a major city with virtually no police on duty naturally exacerbated fears of crime but also made many citizens angry at the police, believing the police were abandoning the city. According to Brooks, writing about the middle part of the 1970s, "Crime is a problem for San Francisco. No one can point to those politicians who point to the crime in San Francisco of creating an issue. Violent crimes attracted the most attention. . . . At the end of 1973 and the first half of 1974, streets of San Francisco became barren of activity as residents became more and more concerned about random shootings." He also noted that during this period San Francisco had a much higher crime rate than Chicago or Philadelphia.[50]

Despite the enormous problem of crime, the police demand for a 13 percent pay raise did not sit well with voters, even in a pro-labor city such as San Francisco. This led to a few days of chaos. Picketers were threatened and attacked; a bomb was exploded on the doorstep of Mayor Alioto's house; and there was even a drive-by shooting of police on the picket line. Striking police officers vandalized police cars and the private cars of those officers who crossed the picket line. After the second day of the police strike, the city's firefighters struck as well. The issues were similar and, as with the police strike, city firefighting equipment and vehicles were damaged by the strikers. The violence and disorder were faintly reminiscent of the general strike four decades earlier when George Moscone was a child.

After about three days, the strike was settled. The POA won as Alioto agreed to the 13 percent pay raise and board approved it. This allowed Alioto to quickly resolve the situation before violence and crime increased even more. But the settlement created longer-term budget problems for the city. Alioto only had a few months left in office, so the problems were not ones about which he needed to worry. The political fallout from the strike was complicated and changed the mayor's race. The dramatic strike, the violence around it, and the threat of increasing violence and crime made the city feel more dangerous and frightening for many voters. At the same time, Alioto's quick concession pushed some voters to more hawkish positions on budget-related questions. Both developments helped Barbagelata.

Barbagelata tried to present himself as both tough on crime and a supporter of the police on one hand and a tough negotiator who would stand up to the unions on the other. A piece of Barbagelata's campaign literature during the runoff stated, "BARBAGELATA STANDS FOR TOUGH ENFORCEMENT. He has consistently voted to give the police the tools and manpower to do the job—Barbagelata opposes selective enforcement of laws. Prostitution leads to organized crime . . . gambling . . . heroin . . . and worse."[51]

A few inches down in the same column on the same flyer, the voter was told that "Moscone Supports Strikes by public employees . . . wrote SB 807 this year to give firemen the right to strike. Barbagelata wrote Prop. O to end police/fire strikes. He got to the basic cause of strikes by writing Prop. P . . . fair pay for police and fire without political pressure."[52]

Jim Molinari, a police inspector in 1975, spent many years in the San Francisco Police Department and briefly in other law enforcement bodies. He was part of the security detail for both Moscone and Feinstein when they served as mayor. He noted strike tactics damaged the SFPD's standing in the city and on the board of supervisors, leading to the board taking stronger anti-labor positions.

"There was a bombing at Alioto's house. . . . What that did is set a tone for labor that the POA lost all their support they had on the board, including Feinstein, at the time. And that caused pension reform . . . as a result of that strike."

The board of supervisors placed Propositions B, O, and P on the November 1975 ballot. Barbagelata had been the lead sponsor and author of those initiatives. Together, these three proposals sought to reduce the economic strength of municipal labor unions, including police and firefighter unions. Proposition B gave the board more ability to set wages for city craft workers, rather than have those wages linked to private sector union wages. Proposition O would allow the city to fire any police officer or firefighter who participated in a strike. Proposition Q was less dramatic and sought to restructure the work schedule for firefighters, thus reducing their income. All three passed by large margins in the November election.

As the election approached, the competitive race, fallout from the police strike, the general political climate, and other problems facing the city were on the minds of most San Franciscans, but in the rest of the country 1975 continued more or less normally. On October 21, two weeks before the election, the Boston Red Sox hosted the Cincinnati Reds in game six of the World Series. That game lasted twelve innings, ending with a walk-off home run in the bottom of the twelfth by future Hall of Famer Carlton Fisk. The home run, made even more famous by the cameraman who captured the image of Fisk desperately seeking to wave the ball fair as he took his first steps out of the batter's box toward first base, is one of the most famous in baseball history. The game is widely considered one of the greatest ever.

San Franciscans watching the game were reminded again that in 1975 their Giants finished one game under .500 while drawing fewer than 525,000 fans—the worst attendance in Major League Baseball. The Giants' future was uncertain, and rumors of the team leaving the city were getting louder. The sad shape of the post-Willie Mays Giants was an apt metaphor for the state of San Francisco but was not a campaign issue.

The absence of frequent polling meant that journalists had to rely heavily on their own political instincts to try to dope out the race. *The Bay Guardian*, which generally had excellent political coverage, summarized the race on October 10: "Jack Ertola leads the race to get up campaign signs. George Moscone is out front in the money-raising derby. Milton Marks is getting around more than anyone . . . But Dianne Feinstein has pulled ahead of voters, according to a poll done for Moscone, which Moscone people aren't talking about. The poll reliable sources told the Guardian, shows Feinstein first, Moscone second by about five points. Marks third by an equal distance. . . . The poll projected the Feinstein-Moscone race into the December runoff and showed the race between them too close to call. Both Moscone and Feinstein are running as if they're in the general."[53] The only mention of Barbagelata in the approximately five-hundred-word summary was that he was in fifth place in the poll.

Elsewhere on the Ballot

In addition to the mayoral campaign, there were other important elections in San Francisco in 1975. District Attorney John Jay Ferdon, who had been in office since 1964 and was close with the downtown interests, was being challenged by two progressives—Joseph Freitas Jr. and Carol Ruth Silver. Because there were no runoffs for any office other than mayor, many progressives were concerned that their vote would split and Ferdon would be reelected, but Freitas gradually emerged as the strongest candidate. The race was not close as Freitas narrowly defeated Silver with Ferdon finishing a distant third. This was a big win for progressives in San Francisco.

Terry Francois, Robert Gonzales, Quentin Kopp, Bob Mendelsohn, John Molinari, and Ronald Pelosi were up for reelection on the board of supervisors. In addition to seeking to retain their seats, at least three of these supervisors—Kopp, Molinari and Pelosi—hoped to finish first and become president of the board. Among the notable challengers from the more than twenty candidates were Arnold Townsend, a civil rights activist and strong opponent of the redevelopment plans for the Fillmore, who was trying to become the second African American on the board. Townsend ended up finishing eleventh, winning 31,000 votes, well short of sixth- place finisher Terry Francois's 80,000.

Harvey Milk was also making another run for the board. This time his candidacy was stronger and better organized than two years earlier, but running citywide was still difficult for a gay candidate. Being Jewish and speaking with a heavy New York accent didn't help either. Once again, Milk sought to present himself as an advocate for gay rights but also as essentially a fiscal conservative. "I was a financial analyst for 7 years—I realize the city needs more value for its tax dollars, new sources of revenue that will spare the present taxpayer his heavy burdens—and elected officials who know how to get both."[54] By 1974 and 1975 Milk had emerged as a leader on gay rights in San Francisco, but his political identity was still evolving. He had some progressive views, but also some libertarian tendencies:

> I cannot regard myself as from the extreme Left. I stand with the conservative in this nation who is for freedom of individual! The true conservative—politically, not morally—is for the end of victimless crime laws. I stand in agreement with that . . . The "liberal" that I run into so often wants the government to do everything. I disagree. I think that the government does too much. The government started a war in Viet Nam. The government spends millions of dollars in the war against dope. The

> government spends millions of dollars to put homosexuals in jail for sex crimes. The government runs computer checks on its citizens. I have had enough governmental control in many areas. If that makes me not so far from the Left, well, so be it. Let those on the Left stand up for big daddy doing it all. When you allow the government to get too powerful there are always encroachments. I think that the government should spend more time caring about hospitals, schools and homes and less time caring about the books we read, the movies we go to, the things we put into our own bodies and the acts of sex we may commit.[55]

Milk did a lot better in 1975 than he had two years earlier, but with six incumbents on the ballot, 1975 was a difficult year for any challenger to make it onto the board. Milk ended up in seventh place. No nonincumbent did better than Milk, but he still missed a seat on the board by about 28,000 votes. The forty-five-year-old Milk had already lost two elections and was rapidly approaching the point of crossing over from neighborhood activist to political gadfly.

If the race for district attorney suggested that progressives were in the ascendancy, the results of the campaigns for supervisor indicated the opposite. The conservative Kopp finished first with 115,482 votes, meaning he would be the president of the board regardless of who was elected mayor. Molinari, who was also a conservative and at that time still a Republican, finished second.

CHAPTER TEN

The Runoff

In the hours after the polls closed on November 4, 1975, the question was who would finish second and face Moscone in the runoff. Feinstein, in danger of again underperforming in a mayoral campaign, told the *Examiner* she had "butterflies in my stomach" on election night. Barbagelata moved into second place by a very narrow margin shortly after the beginning of the count, but Feinstein refused to give up. At 12:30 a.m. on Wednesday, Feinstein told her supporters, "I'd like you to go home tonight and get a good night's sleep. And I hope your *Chronicle* newsboy will be on time with some good news. . . . We are not going to concede at this time."[1] The next morning's *Chronicle* did not bring good news for Feinstein or her supporters. Rather, Barbagelata's campaign against her paid off, and he narrowly edged her out for the second spot in the runoff. The final vote for the first round was Moscone, 66,295; Barbagelata 40,540; Feinstein 39,344; Ertola, 30,360; and Marks 27,910. About 6,000 votes went to minor candidates.

In any other mayoral election in San Francisco history before 1975, Moscone would have won in the first round. Moscone's first-place finish was not altogether surprising, but Barbagelata's second-place finish was. The race for second place had been very close as Barbagelata beat Feinstein by a margin of 0.57 percent, or only 1,196 votes. On the surface, this may have been a good thing for Moscone because a runoff against Feinstein, a much smoother politician than Barbagelata, would have been a very tough race. However, the runoff against Barbagelata was not an easy race for Moscone either.

Once he knew he had won a spot in the runoff, Barbagelata explained why he thought he could beat Moscone. "'I do feel,' he explained, 'that votes were split among Mrs. Feinstein, Milton Marks, Judge John Ertola, and myself, and that the majority of the hundred thousand or so that are still sitting out there will go to me.'"[2]

The anger that helped fuel Barbagelata's success and helped derail Feinstein may have surprised some San Franciscans. Many expected the liberal or centrist Feinstein and the progressive Moscone to face each other in the runoff. That matchup, which would have represented a triumph for the new liberal, tolerant San Francisco, almost happened, but Feinstein came up just a little short.

Larry Del Carlo, who was working for Mayor Alioto in 1975 and went on to work for three other mayors and several community organizations described this anger:

> We did think it was gonna be a runoff between Feinstein and Moscone, and we were surprised that Barbagelata did so well. . . . A lot of us thought it probably had to do with George being seen as so left and so liberal that it really activated the most conservative folks in San Francisco and Feinstein was more middle of the road. A lot of us thought she was a bit conservative, but in the west of Twin Peaks neighborhoods, they always thought Feinstein was a little too liberal for them . . . They found the most conservative guy in John Barbagelata and actively supported his campaign, and they did their own grassroots stuff to get John elected."[3]

Josh Getlin explained further: "Let's say you live west of Twin Peaks. And suddenly the police department goes on strike and the fire department goes on strike. In that kind of climate, against that kind of backdrop . . . big cities seem to be going bankrupt and labor is probably a reason for that . . . a lot of people are going to be scared. They're going to say that, what's going on, we've lost control."[4]

Feinstein's disappointing finish could be attributed to several other things. By 1975 Feinstein, who went on to win a district supervisor election in 1977, citywide elections for mayor in 1979 and 1983 and statewide elections in 1992, 1994, 2000, 2006, 2012, and 2018, had demonstrated her ability to win votes citywide. She was the top vote-getter both times she ran for the board. That support did not translate into support for mayor in 1975, just as it had not during her first bid for that office in 1971. Voting for a single chief executive is different than voting for a multimember legislature, so Feinstein was evaluated differently when she ran for mayor. Gender was part of that. In 1975, almost no big cities had female mayors. There had been almost no female governors anywhere in the US, and female candidates for office in general were still relatively rare. Three years earlier, Shirley Chisholm, a congresswoman from Brooklyn, New York, ran for the Democratic presidential nomination but had received little support. Feinstein undoubtedly confronted sexist views, not uncommon at the time, that a woman could not do the job of mayor because women lacked toughness, managerial acumen, or other sexist tropes.

The other challenge facing Feinstein was that her conventional, pro-development, and pro-business vision for San Francisco, linked to a greater tolerance for the city's growing diversity, did not speak to the politics of the city in 1975. In a calmer time, Feinstein might have won by crafting a coalition of downtown business interests, white liberals, and substantial segments of the African American, Asian American, Latino, and gay votes—a more moderate and pro-business version of Moscone's coalition. Feinstein, having been a supervisor for six years, had strong ties in those communities and was viewed as a liberal on civil rights generally. Her charisma and ample political skills might have carried her to victory, but the divisions in 1975 were too sharp; and Feinstein's liberal centrism was squeezed too much. As Feinstein described it, "I suspect I got squished in the middle, and kind of squished out."[5] Feinstein's image was also an obstacle as she courted a newer, more radical San Francisco. A product of wealthy San Francisco with many of the markers of that world, roots in the affluent northern parts of the city, and ties to the city's affluent German Jewish community, including membership in Temple Emanu-El, Feinstein could present an almost aristocratic air, despite being a very smart, hard-working, and in the context of that time, liberal politician.

Mervin Field, a noted California pollster, described the race and the reasons why Barbagelata was able to outpoll Feinstein: "The liberal labor element is receding. The new wave is made up of those with property to protect, older people, the educated, the pessimistic, frustrated by events, the white class. It was a tide, and Barbagelata caught it."[6] Barbagelata, as Field explained, connected with the backlash to the rapid changes of the previous decade, particularly regarding political power shifting away from straight white men and toward ethnic minorities, gays, and liberals.

Feinstein was not a natural retail politician. Journalist Phil Bronstein, who later became editor of the *Chronicle*, described how "she (Feinstein) was a very stiff person. She didn't have that kind of outsized personality at that point anyway. One could see that she was very thin- skinned."[7] Moscone press secretary Corey Busch was more direct in his critique of Feinstein's campaign: "She just ran a god-awful campaign. She ran a horrible campaign."[8]

Another San Francisco journalist, Belva Davis, reflected that in 1975, "People were mystified that Feinstein wasn't walking away with it because she seemed to have it all going for her. . . . Dianne Feinstein never really decided whether she wanted to be mayor or not. She hated campaigning."[9] As Davis suggested, Feinstein was telegenic, smart, and attractive, but unlike Moscone was not a great street campaigner. In a crowded mayor's race in which voters could choose only one candidate, this was a real handicap for the wealthy Feinstein, who had not, like Moscone, spent her youth on the playgrounds and streets of their shared hometown. While many of Barbagelata's voters would probably not have been comfortable supporting a wealthy, liberal, Jewish[10] woman, had Barbagelata not emerged as the conservative candidate, the race would have been different. Feinstein could have appealed to those voters as a moderate, pro-growth alternative to Moscone, but the populist anger that drove Barbagelata's voters was never Feinstein's style.

Similarly, during the previous decade, someone with Feinstein's experience and politics would have been the candidate of liberal San Francisco, but by 1975 many liberals had moved further left, wanting bigger and faster change. Again, Feinstein's cautious, almost patrician, style did not speak to those voters. Despite her institutional advantages, intellect, and impressive résumé, 1975 was not Feinstein's year. She underperformed badly, opening the door to the contentious runoff between Moscone and Barbagelata.

Feinstein paid a political price for being the candidate with whom everybody could live but who was not the favorite of enough voters. Ironically, in a rank order system, which is how San Francisco elects its mayors now, it is possible that enough of fourth- and fifth-place finishers Ertola and Marks's almost 60,000 combined votes would have ranked Feinstein second, that she could have caught up with Barbagelata and possibly even Moscone. Similarly, most Moscone voters would have ranked Feinstein higher than Barbagelata, while most Barbagelata voters would have ranked her ahead of Moscone. We can never know what might have happened if the city had a different electoral system in 1975, but the runoff system that was in place in 1975 led to a divisive election that squeezed out the most broadly acceptable centrist candidate, doing nothing to unify the city.

One person who seemed to understand this was John Barbagelata. Despite facing four opponents, including one fellow Republican, in the first round, Barbagelata focused his campaign efforts almost entirely on Feinstein. Milton Marks was a Republican, but Barbagelata paid almost no attention to him. Similarly, Jack Ertola, an Italian American with ties to the older, more establishment San Francisco, was also ignored by Barbagelata's campaign.

Barbagelata ran a first-round campaign aimed primarily at the woman he probably knew to be the stronger runoff opponent than Moscone. For example, in a campaign mailer titled, "What has Barbagelata done for you?" Barbagelata touted his own record on issues such as "police on the streets" "improving neighborhoods," and "conflict of interest law." There was no mention of Moscone, but there was a section surrounded by a black border with the headline, "Dianne Feinstein's 1969 promises." Below that, five different Feinstein promises were listed followed by the closing line, "We know you won't be misled by glorious campaign promises and slick expensive T.V. ads and media ads disguised to sell you what you want to hear. The above promises were made 6 years ago by Feinstein—not one has been delivered." On the back side of the mailer was a section, "Compare the Candidates," contrasting Barbagelata's record with Feinstein's on "Budget," "Payroll Tax," "Forced Busing," and other topics—again with no mention of Moscone's record or campaign promises anywhere on the flyer.[11] Getlin explained how "John Barbagelata spent virtually all of that general election attacking Dianne Feinstein. He didn't talk about any other candidate running. He never mentioned George . . . attacking Dianne was his ticket into the runoff."[12] Barbagelata's comment describing Feinstein as a "housewife" during his announcement press conference indicated that he may have been motivated by the personal as well as the political.

The Runoff

The runoff between Barbagelata and Moscone offered voters two starkly different visions for San Francisco's future. Feinstein's strong third-place finish and respectable showings for Ertola, 14.9 percent, and Marks, 13.7 percent, meant Moscone and Barbagelata had combined for only about half the first-round votes. Belva Davis described the runoff as being between "two clearly defined characters. There was no muddiness about where Barbagelata stood. There was no muddiness about George's record. So, you could see that San Francisco citizens were going to have to make a choice of direction."[13] According to Marshall Kilduff, an influential reporter who later became an editor for the *Chronicle*, "Moscone was looked at as a softer voice, a guy who was more inclusive, more concerned about neighborhood life, more concerned about growing numbers of minorities who didn't feel looped in at City Hall." Kilduff described Barbagelata as "anti-union, very mistrustful of Democrats, a voice from sort of the west side of town, the Sunset, single-family homeowner, lower city costs . . . a Tea Party voice. He was very galvanizing, could always turn out groups of people for a lot of his causes."[14]

Shortly after the first round, Jerry Roberts wrote an article in the *Bay Guardian* summarizing where the race stood titled, "Who gets the Feinstein/Ertola/Marks vote?" discussing the state of the race and what the candidates needed to do to win:

> Any way you cut up Feinstein's support, it will take roughly 100,000 votes for either Barbagelata or Moscone to win Dec. 11, depending on the size of the voter turnout (question: will voters be electrified or bored beyond belief by the heavy media coverage?). Conceding both candidates the votes they won Nov. 4, Moscone needs only 30,000 to 40,000 "new" votes to win, while Barbagelata must find 55,000 to 65,000. If Moscone wins only half of Feinstein's and half of Milton Marks's general election votes, he can still lose 80% of the Ertola vote and come out ahead. If Barbagelata runs better than expected with either Feinstein or Marks supporters, however, the crucial votes could be the 5,600 votes cast for the six "minor" candidates on election day.[15]

Roberts's overview explained the challenge facing the two candidates, but there was more. Barbagelata was not, like Feinstein or Alioto, a mainstream politician seeking to govern from the center while pushing back a challenge from the left represented by Moscone. He was an extreme conservative seeking to remake San Francisco in that image. His unequivocal support for business, both big and small, put him to the right of the centrist Democrat he was seeking to replace, and out of step in a city that had long been a labor stronghold. An *Examiner* article explained:

> In nearly six years on the Board of Supervisors Barbagelata has been the free enterprise system's most forceful exponent. He's voted consistently for real estate, business and property interests. He voted for a survey of economic activity but against a high rise impact study. He voted no on downsizing in the Haight, no on height limits on Upper Market. Barbagelata supported more freeways. . . . He opposed forcing landlords to take families with children. . . . He voted against gas price posting. . . . To small business and large he proved to be a friend.[16]

These positions helped Barbagelata with the city's Republican voters and business community, but it was not what mobilized his base.[17] For those voters it was his positions on social issues. The *Examiner* profile, printed a few days before the election, continued: "His credentials as a social conservative are well established. He opposed the 18-year-old vote—but supported 18-year-old drinking. He voted against a commission on women and against a resolution prohibiting employment discrimination because of sex or sexual preference. He voted support for the war in Indochina."[18]

Barbagelata was way to the right of San Francisco's sitting Democratic mayor and of all the postwar Republican mayors who preceded him. Had Moscone found himself in the runoff against Feinstein or Marks, the general direction of the city toward being more liberal and tolerant would not have been in doubt. Barbagelata's presence in the runoff elevated the stakes on issues of tolerance and diversity.

A *Bay Guardian* article by Katy Butler from before the first round offered some insight into Barbagelata's constituents, campaign style, and identity as a nonpolitician: "When Barbagelata calls himself a candidate of the people these are the people he has in mind: small businessmen who run grocery stores and small bottling plants, real estate agents, restaurant owners and middle-class people who own their own homes. . . . These are the people who scream most loudly about the payroll tax and the business tax, who want to keep property taxes down and who think city workers are overpaid."[19]

Butler offered insight into Barbagelata's campaign: "Even his campaign is run like a small business enterprise: he and his former administrative assistant thought up the 'boxing bee' symbol on his house signs: his daughter went down to the library to pick up the prototype designs and his college age sons printed them on the printing press in the back of Barbagelata Realty. He goes to his campaign appearances with a single volunteer." Butler's final paragraphs in the long profile showed another side of Barbagelata's character as the candidate tells her "I'm a crusader. I like to sell what's good for people. Otherwise I'd be a phony. . . . And don't write anything phony, all right, Katy?"[20]

Butler's profile showed Barbagelata's far-right views on pretty much every issue and how he styled himself a truth teller and sought to appeal to the forgotten San Franciscan. For Barbagelata, that forgotten San Franciscan was implicitly white, straight, usually Catholic and angry. That was Barbagelata's appeal, but the more emotional reaction to both Feinstein and Moscone was that they, and their supporters, were more sophisticated and cooler than Barbagelata's were. Moscone was the ring-a-ding-ding former all-city basketball player; Feinstein the glamorous daughter of Pacific Heights. Barbagelata had a good high school résumé as well. He had played basketball but was not a star the way Moscone had been. More impressively, Barbagelata had been voted the "Handsomest High Senior Boy" for the class of 1938. However, Barbagelata had done that not at an elite Catholic or public school, but at Galileo, the ordinary public high school a few blocks from North Beach.[21]

Feinstein had the most support from the wealthy Pacific Heights crowd and other affluent parts of the city. Her supporters belonged to the right clubs, had gone to the right schools, and were the kinds of people seen on the society pages—at least that was the perspective of Barbagelata and his supporters. Moscone was not tied in with old San Francisco money and status like Feinstein, but he was the face of cool San Francisco—the handsome, charming ex-jock cruising around town in the purple Alfa-Romeo, ending a night of campaigning holding court at a bar or, according to the rumors, leaving that bar with a woman other than his wife. Veterans of that 1975 Moscone campaign described it as a place where the counterculture and politics met and as a fun scene where a hard-fought campaign was waged and where young people met, became friends, hung out, and slept together. That was a very different vibe than the older San Francisco that gravitated to Barbagelata's campaign. His homemade campaign, based way out in the Sunset, was not cool to most young people. Barbagelata was, according to many, a deeply religious man and a devoted family man who was critical of Moscone's womanizing. Many of the people to whom I spoke for this book said negative things about Barbagelata, but none suggested he ran around on his wife or was not a good father to his children.

These differences between the candidates and the ideological chasm between them contributed to the race becoming nasty. The negativity was not just between the two candidates' campaign ads and the like, but also among supporters. In a 2011 interview, Nancy Pelosi, who was a Democratic activist and fundraiser in 1975, and a Moscone supporter, recalled, "We would be invited to these debates between Barbagelata and Moscone and it was shocking to see how negative—now I know politics—it was shocking to see how negative some of the people who showed up on the other side were in their comments about George Moscone. And I believe much of it was largely because George Moscone was a strong supporter of gay rights."[22]

The strong political differences between the two candidates were mirrored in the culture of their campaigns. Jon Rubin explained, "The whole left coalesced around George, and the whole right coalesced around Barbagelata. . . . George was (seen as) the messiah, and he stood for whatever it was that you wanted him to stand for and Barbagelata was (seen as) a complete fucking lunatic, evil, no-good bastard who stood for exactly what Donald Trump stands for only, if possible, less charmingly. He stood for the Manhattanization of San Francisco, the dowtownization of San Francisco, the extinguishing of arts and color . . . the blue meanies." Rubin also indicated that Moscone had liaisons with more than a few female staff and volunteers during that campaign: "George's campaign (for mayor), it was taken for granted that if some very good-looking young woman wandered into the campaign, she was eventually going to wander off with George."[23]

One week before the election, Herb Caen, who was clearly supporting Moscone, reported a rather odd statement by Barbagelata: "'I married by accident, became a realtor by accident, had eight kids by accident and ran for Supervisor by accident.' . . . He sounds more accident prone than Jerry Ford." Caen then commented, "I don't think John knows about this, but some of his zealous volunteers are losing votes for him by spewing dirt about Moscone during their phone pitches. The reaction I've heard is outrage—not at George but at the tactic."[24]

The negative campaigning went beyond what Pelosi and Caen described. As the runoff approached, the Moscone campaign issued a flyer in the form of an eight-page newspaper broadsheet titled, "The Election News: The Community Edition." In slightly smaller letters after that were the words "Including Hunters Point, Western Addition, Ingleside." Ingleside was a small neighborhood in the southern part of the city that had significant African American and Filipino populations, while Hunters Point and the Western Addition were the heart of San Francisco's two African American neighborhoods.

The newspaper included a nice photo of Moscone and his family, a column contrasting the two candidates' positions on issues such as "tax reform" and "housing," a list of some of Moscone's prominent endorsers, and similar standard campaign fare, but the most jarring images in the newspaper were two black-and-white cartoons more notable for their hard-hitting nastiness than artistic merit.[25] The first featured a poorly drawn, but recognizable because of his big ears and glasses, Barbagelata driving an ominous looking tank-like vehicle. The vehicle is on the top of a hill and is labeled "Republican Machine." It is preparing to run over the words "the neighborhoods." In the background behind the tank, presumably to give it a San Francisco flavor, is the Golden Gate Bridge.[26]

The second cartoon, drawn by Kevin Brady, is equally negative. At the top of the frame is giant hand with the five fingers labeled "Downtown," "G.O.P.," "Real Estate," "Builders," and "Speculators." Each finger has a string tied to it which together are holding up a large-eared, glasses-wearing, suit-clad figure that is unmistakably John Barbagelata. The caption, in case the cartoon was too subtle, reads, "Elect Barbagelata Mayor and watch him dance to the tune of the special interests who have contributed such heavy amounts of money to his campaign."[27]

Barbagelata, for his part, hit back, asking San Franciscans throughout his campaign, "The issue is whose gonna control San Francisco—the people or the labor bosses?"[28] Barbagelata circulated a flyer headlined, "Can You Afford Moscone? George Moscone has the softest record on crime and is the biggest spender in the state legislature. What would Moscone do to San Francisco?" The piece went on to claim that "Moscone's answer to the City budget is MORE TAXES!" and a line about "Forcible Rape. Bill to increase penalties for 'great bodily injury' inflicted during forcible rape. Moscone Opposed," closing with "It's your money . . . your voice. Vote Barbagelata, Dec. 11."[29]

Barbagelata frequently attacked Moscone about his ties to the Burtons. "Part of John J. Barbagelata's campaign strategy is to say publicly at times that his opponent in the mayor's race is supported by what he calls 'the Burton machine.'"[30] Barbagelata began at least one debate by saying, "I happen to be a nonprofessional, and a citizen-politician. . . . George has the backing of the Burton machine."[31] This attack was not false. The Burtons and their political allies were deeply invested in seeing Moscone win and doing whatever they could to make that happen. The question for Barbagelata was whether voters cared. Many San Franciscans liked Phil Burton, John Burton, and Willie Brown. Barbagelata's voters generally hated them, but it was not clear how less politically engaged voters felt.

Throughout the race Moscone remained with close with these allies, even bringing in one of Brown's top advisors to help with the field campaign for the runoff. Rudy Nothenberg left Willie Brown to go to work for Moscone's campaign: "I was sort of the guru of get out-the-vote efforts in those days, and so they asked me, 'Would I come back to the city and run that get-out-the-vote campaign.' A month or so before the election, I did. I quit that job and went back to the city to organize a get-out-the-vote effort, which was probably one of the biggest get-out-the-vote efforts we had ever seen, thousands of people on the streets to get him elected."[32]

Barbagelata also accused Moscone of being corrupt. As a legislator who had been in politics for more than a decade and was in the middle of his sixth race for office, Moscone had raised a lot of money, done many favors, and met with many wealthy insiders. As senate majority leader for eight years, Moscone was in a powerful position from which powerful economic interests needed favors. A few weeks before the election, it was reported that Moscone was entangled in a scandal from his time in the senate. The incident involved wealthy donors, Moscone's friends in Sacramento, and a misuse of senate Democratic campaign funds by Moscone. He had received money from donors supporting assembly candidate Frank Vicencia and funneled that same amount of money back to Vicencia from senate Democratic funds. This allowed the donors to conceal their support to Vicencia. Today this might be illegal, but then it was legal and the kind of thing that politicians did. The scandal bolstered Barbagelata's argument that Moscone was a career politician beholden to big donors and labor, but it was complex, involved relatively small amounts of money, and did not have much of an effect on the campaign.[33]

As the runoff went on, it was clear the race was going to be very close. Every vote would count; and the ability to swing a few votes would be very important. In a race like that, dozens of things might have made the difference. One of those occurred on the other side of the country. On November 10, the United Nations passed Resolution 3379 declaring "Zionism is a form of racism."[34] The US vehemently opposed this resolution. Daniel Patrick Moynihan, the US ambassador to the UN, spelled out the American position in a speech on the floor of the UN. "The United States of America declares that it does not acknowledge, it will not abide by, it will never acquiesce in this infamous act."[35]

Many Americans, including Jewish Americans, were outraged by the UN resolution. The week after the vote, on November 16, the Jewish Community Relations Council of San Francisco organized a rally at Union Square denouncing the resolution. Moscone's high school classmate and sometime political sparring partner Leo McCarthy was one of a handful of politicians to speak, declaring the UN decision "a new form of anti-Semitism." Moscone, whose good relations with San Francisco Jewry had been strengthened by his trip to the Soviet Union and Israel the previous year, "drew the biggest applause at the rally after he declared 'I am a Zionist,'" and "went on to compare the U.N. vote with Adolph Hitler's persecution of Jews in Europe."[36] According to the JCRC website, Moscone also stated "anti-Zionism is anti-Semitism."[37]

This is a stark contrast to today when almost no progressive gentile politician would feel comfortable making a statement like that. It also demonstrates the complexity of mayoral elections. It is obvious that being mayor of San Francisco has nothing to do with Middle East policy, but voters want a mayor whom they like and trust on issues that are important to them, even distant ones. There is reason to believe Moscone's views about the Jewish people were more than a political calculation. When he became mayor, Moscone surrounded himself with many Jewish advisors in a city that has never been particularly Jewish. When I asked one of those advisors, Corey Busch, about that, Busch gave half a laugh and said he had never thought of that before.[38]

In the 1970s, the most elite club for athletic-minded powerful San Franciscans was the Olympic Club. That is where J. Eugene McAteer had been playing squash moments before his death. However, the Olympic Club did not accept Jews. Jonathan Moscone explained to me that "my dad didn't join the Olympic Club for that reason. . . . He wouldn't join. He joined the Concordia Club. . . . We would hang out with him there." The Concordia Club was for many years the Jewish Club in San Francisco.[39]

On December 7, with the election four days away and still very close, each candidate received a major endorsement. Quentin Kopp formalized his support for Barbagelata. The two were friends and shared much of the same base of support, so this endorsement was widely expected. Kopp's endorsement was part of Barbagelata's get-out-the-vote operation more than an effort to persuade voters. However, according to the *Chronicle*, "There had been speculation Kopp was holding back an endorsement becaue (sic) seven board members had come out for Moscone and that he, Kopp, didn't want to lose their votes for him as board president—a traditional, not automatic, privilege accorded the leader in supervisor elections."[40]

That same day, Leo McCarthy, a popular assemblyman whose district included much of Barbagelata's base, endorsed Moscone. This endorsement came with some risk and potential value for McCarthy. Ultimately, McCarthy had to endorse Moscone because as Speaker of the assembly; he could not oppose a Democrat who enjoyed strong support from African American voters against a right-wing Republican. If McCarthy lost support from African American assembly members, his speakership would be in jeopardy, particularly as there was an African American assemblyman one district over eyeing the Speaker's gavel for himself.

The day before the election, McCarthy followed up his endorsement with a letter to voters in his district. It was too late to mail the letter, so it was distributed to voters by volunteers outside polling places, at bus stops, or door-to-door. McCarthy's endorsement of Moscone had a more conservative bent than the rest of the campaign:

> During nine years as your State Senator, George Moscone has shown that fiscal responsibility and humane politics go hand in hand. He knows that government can meet the needs of people, and also live within its means. In this year of skyrocketing taxes and runaway city spending, the election of George Moscone as Mayor (sic) is essential for the fiscal health of San Francisco.
>
> No one knows better than George Moscone that we've got to place

> more policemen on our neighborhood streets, and crack down on murderers, muggers and rapists. As mayor, George Moscone will make it clear to violent criminals that the only place for them in San Francisco is behind bars.[41]

McCarthy's endorsement was helpful, but a few days earlier, Moscone had secured an even more important endorsement from another politician he had beaten in an election, although more recently. Dianne Feinstein's future following two disappointing showings in mayoral elections was not looking too bright, but she was still an influential figure in San Francisco. Corey Busch explained the importance of Feinstein's endorsement: "With John Barbagelata as our opponent in the runoff, Feinstein's endorsement of George was pretty important. Equally, were she to endorse Barbagelata, we were going to be in trouble in the runoff."[42] This is where Barbagelata's lack of political skill again hurt him. Barbagelata's primary strategy of focusing on Feinstein was reasonable, but Barbagelata personalized it unnecessarily. Going after Feinstein as being an insider or too liberal was fine, but referring to her as a housewife was condescending and insulting.

Had Feinstein endorsed Barbagelata, it might have sealed his victory. That calculation was not lost on Moscone, who worked to get Feinstein's endorsement after the first round. Finally with one week to go before the election, Feinstein made her decision, calling a press conference at the Towne House Hotel. Feinstein had waited, but her words were unequivocal. Feinstein began her statement, "It would perhaps be the easy way to go to sit this one out, take a low profile for awhile (sic) and then begin building for another race for mayor in four years. But I cannot do that—I care too much about the future of my city." She explained in great detail why Moscone was better than his opponent and concluded "to my supporters, and to all the people of San Francisco, I urge you to spend the next week, as I will, working hard for the election of George Moscone as our next mayor. We must ring every doorbell between now and next Thursday, and we must walk every precinct on election day if we are to truly see our City returned to the people who for so long have not had their voices and their concerns heard in the Mayor's office."[43]

Busch described the meeting, at Feinstein's second home in Pajaro Dunes, California, that led to her decision: "I don't recall how long the meeting took, but I think it was at least an hour. When George got back in the car, he said to me, 'Well—I've got good news, and I've got bad news. The good news is that she will endorse me. The bad news is that I said you would contact her when she returns to San Francisco to get together to talk about the details." Busch added, "George and Dianne were not very close—not personally nor politically. I don't think Dianne ever had much respect for George for whatever reason. George viewed Dianne as too centrist and too removed from what mattered to people at the grassroots level."[44] Busch added that in his view, "Feinstein was closer in her political views to Barbagelata than she was to Moscone, which is why her endorsement really mattered to us." Feinstein and Moscone were both Democrats, but to many, including one of Moscone's top aides, Feinstein was sufficiently close to the economic powers that she seemed closer to the backlash candidate than to the progressive.[45]

Their chilly relationship would remain the same for the rest of Moscone's life, but at that one moment, Feinstein came through for Moscone. At the time, a rumor was circulating that Moscone would appoint Feinstein as the city's chief administrative officer (CAO). The CAO has a great deal of power, second only to the mayor. The position would have been a good fit for Feinstein, who had strong administrative and management skills, while giving her an opportunity to make a very big impact on the city.

The endorsement, particularly because Moscone did not appoint her CAO, may have saved Feinstein's career. Not only did it, for reasons Feinstein could not have known, set her on course to become mayor without having to run again, but it helped Feinstein shore up her own left flank. Four years later when Feinstein was mayor and running for a full term of her own, what was left of Moscone's political operation helped her defeat Quentin Kopp in a runoff. That probably would not have happened if Feinstein had not endorsed Moscone in 1975.

The Results

As the results began to come in on the evening of December 11, Barbagelata's strategy of campaigning hard in what his campaign referred to as the "golden crescent" seemed to be paying off. The golden crescent was the outer rim of three sides of the roughly rectangle-shaped San Francisco; it included all the western third or so of the city and much of its northern and southern rims. This was a wise approach, but Barbagelata made a mistake by not campaigning much in the rest of the city. That created just the opening Moscone needed. Barbagelata sought to win by cleaning up in the golden crescent; Moscone's strategy was to do very well from the middle of the city to where the San Francisco met the bay in the east.

As the evening progressed, the election results took shape much as expected. Precincts in the Sunset and other parts of western San Francisco returned huge margins for Barbagelata offset by equally big margins for Moscone in the Castro and Hunters Point. As the night wore on, it became clear that the new San Francisco was triumphing over the old San Francisco. Because of the extremely high turnout in African American neighborhoods and Moscone's ability to win over enough voters, based on precinct-level data, who preferred Feinstein in the first round, George Moscone would be the city's next mayor.

During the 1970s, San Francisco was divided into three state assembly districts, the Sixteenth, Seventeenth, and Eighteenth. Barbagelata did very well in

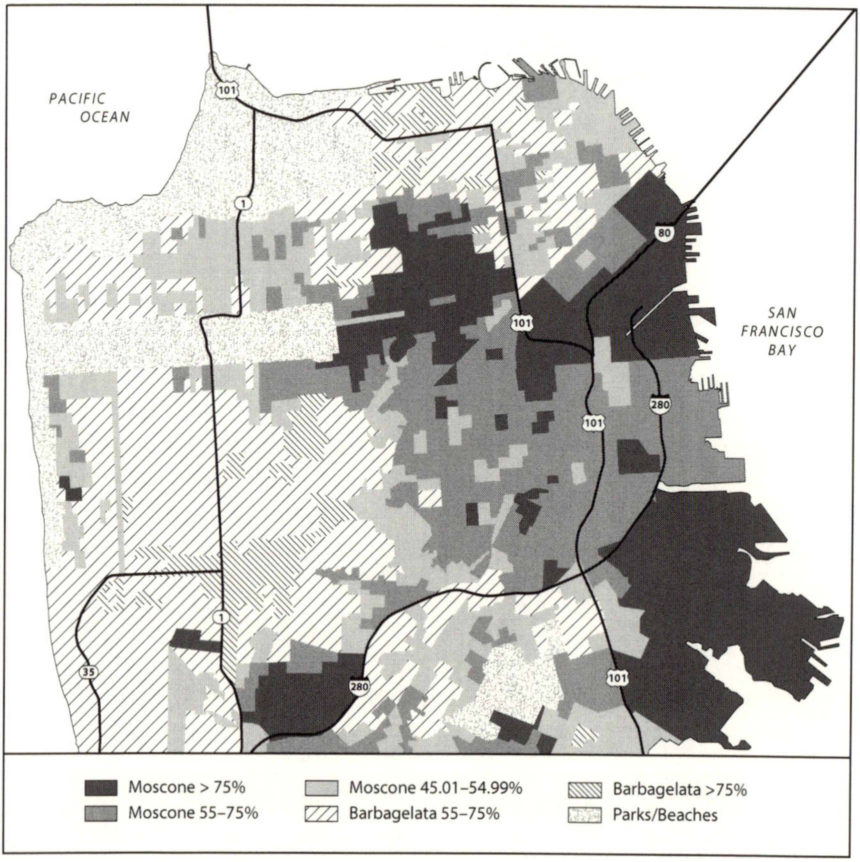

Map 10.1. Results from the 1975 runoff for mayor. Map by Jackson Hasty.

the Eighteenth, where Leo McCarthy was the representative. McCarthy's district went from Golden Gate Park in the north to the city line in the south. Its easternmost point was in the Excelsior District. Barbagelata won the Eighteenth with 56 percent of the vote, but that was not enough to elect make him mayor. The northern and central parts of San Francisco, including the Haight, the Castro, the Civic Center area, the Fillmore, but also Pacific Heights, the Marina and Cow Hollow constituted the Seventeenth District. This district was represented by Willie Brown, who would succeed McCarthy as Speaker, and in 1996 become mayor himself. The race was close there, but Moscone won 52.4 percent of the vote. The Sixteenth District, represented by John Foran, constituted the easternmost third of the city and gave Moscone the votes he needed to win as he drubbed Barbagelata there with 59 percent of the vote.

As Map 10.1 shows, Moscone's strongest neighborhoods were Ingleside in the southern part of the city, Bayview/Hunters Point in the southeast corner, Rincon Valley and South of Market just north of there, and a part of the middle of town that goes from the Fillmore and the Western Addition west to the Haight. The Fillmore, Bayview/Hunters Point, and Ingleside were heavily African American, while the Haight included white progressives as well. The Rincon Valley area was more sparsely populated than it is today. Barbagelata's strongest areas included his longtime bases in the western part of the city as well as Cow Hollow, the Marina, and Pacific Heights in the north.

The election cleaved San Francisco demographically and geographically. Barbagelata did very well with white Catholics; Moscone ran up big margins with African American, Latino, and gay voters while also winning large portions of younger more progressive voters. No exit polls were taken, but a precinct analysis helps demonstrate this. Precinct data is valuable but should be analyzed cautiously. Precincts and most neighborhoods include members of different groups. For example, many of the western precincts where Barbagelata ran well were heavily Irish and Italian but also included some Jews and Asians. The precincts in the Haight that were strongholds for Moscone were primarily younger progressive white voters, but also home to African Americans and some older white voters. Most of the latter had lived in that neighborhood for years and were more conservative than the new migrants to that part of town. Similarly, the affluent community in Pacific Heights that supported Feinstein in the first round also included gay voters who may have been more liberal than their neighbors. Nonetheless, precinct data helps fill in the picture of what happened in the runoff, albeit with a broad brush.

Table 10.1 shows the ten precincts that gave Barbagelata the highest margin of victory. Barbagelata got between 81.2 and 88.8 percent of the vote in each of these precincts. The sixth column lists the streets framing the precinct. Many precincts have more than four sides, but only major streets are listed. The last column is the neighborhood in which the precinct was located. The first thing that is clear from this list is all but 7886 and 6746 are in the western part of the city. Precinct 7886 is in the Marina just north of Cow Hollow—George Moscone's childhood neighborhood; 7886 is a few blocks from Moscone's childhood home and St. Brigid, where he went to grade school. Precinct 6746 is in the northeastern quadrant not far from North Beach. Nob Hill was, and still is, an affluent neighborhood, which includes some of the city's most expensive apartments, many of which have beautiful views.

The other eight precincts are all in the westernmost part of San Francisco, but primarily in the southwest. None are north of Golden Gate Park, but they include wealthy neighborhoods such as St. Francis Wood and Forest Hill as well

Table 10.1-Best Barbagelata Districts

Precinct	Barbagelata	Moscone	Barbagelata %	Moscone %
8421	183	23	88.8%	11.2%
8574	158	24	86.8%	13.2%
8575	177	34	83.9%	16.1%
8407	203	40	83.5%	16.5%
8447	118	24	83.1%	16.9%
8449	263	56	82.4%	17.6%
8425	150	32	82.4%	17.6%
7886	106	24	81.5%	18.5%
8448	238	54	81.5%	18.5%
6746	130	30	81.2%	18.8%

as less affluent areas such as Ingleside Terrace and Park Merced. The data from Table 10.1 show Barbagelata's base as heavily white but are also a reminder that as a Republican, he enjoyed strong support from wealthy San Francisco.

Moscone's ten strongest precincts, shown in 10.2, came from a very different San Francisco. The precincts are concentrated in three neighborhoods, two in the center of the city and one in the southeast. The Western Addition, despite its name, is not in the western San Francisco. It constitutes a few blocks just east of Golden Gate Park and north of Haight Street. The Fillmore District is just to the east of the Western Addition. There is a great deal of physical and social overlap between the two areas, so some regard them as the same neighborhood. Bayview/Hunters Point is not close to these two neighborhoods and in the southeastern part of San Francisco. The most famous San Francisco landmark in that part of town in 1975 was Candlestick Park.

These ten precincts, where Moscone's vote ranged from 91.7 percent to an astounding 97.2 percent were all heavily African American. Those voters who were the strongest part of Moscone's coalition and provided enough support to ensure his victory. Moscone's margin over Barbagelata from these ten precincts alone, out of a total of 935 precincts, was 1,263, well over a quarter of his city-wide winning margin.

Moscone ran up the numbers in African American neighborhoods while Barbagelata performed very well in the predominantly white areas of western San Francisco, but both candidates needed to expand beyond their base. Although San Francisco in 1975 had fewer than 700,000 people, it was still a city with dozens of distinct neighborhoods. A closer look at a handful of specific neighborhoods shows how Barbagelata was almost able to get enough votes, and how

Streets	Neighborhood
Eucalyptus, Sloat, 23rd Ave, 19th Ave	Parkside/Park Merced
Monterey, San Anselmo, Santa Ana	St. Francis Wood
San Anselmo, Santa Paula, Portola	St. Francis Wood
Castaneda, 10th Avenue, Pacheco	Forest Hill
Junipero Serra, 19th Avenue	Ingleside Terrace
Sloat, Winston, Junipero Serra, 19th Avenue	Ingleside Terrace
Merced, Clearfield, Ocean	Park Merced
Lombard, Scott, Alhambra, Steiner, Avila	Marina
19th Avenue, Junipero Serra, Winston Drive	Ingleside Terrace
Jones, Clay, Washington, Leavenworth	Nob Hill

Moscone was able to marry strong African American support to votes from other key demographic groups.

One neighborhood where Barbagelata needed to do well and build upon his first-round strengths was Pacific Heights, where the feel of was more old-money than angry white backlash. The neighborhood was very white and included many of the city's older German Jewish families. The heart of Pacific Heights is a few square blocks bordered by Clay Street to the south, Broadway to the north, Lyon to the west, and Webster to the east. This area, which included the Convent of the Sacred Heart, the prestigious Catholic girls school from which Feinstein graduated, was Feinstein territory in the first round. She carried each of its ten precincts, altogether winning 39.2 percent against four other major opponents.[46] In the second round, Barbagelata beat Moscone there with 57.9 percent of the vote. Most denizens of Pacific Heights, probably believing that Moscone represented a threat to their business and financial interests, ignored Barbagelata's anger and intolerance and cast their collective lot with the Republican pro-business candidate.

Barbagelata also did well among Chinese Americans, at least in some areas. In the absence of exit polls, determining how Chinese Americans, or Asian Americans more broadly, voted in 1975 is difficult. By the mid-1970s, some neighborhoods were substantially Chinese, but Asian Americans, for the most part, were no longer entirely residentially segregated. Many neighborhoods in the western and northern parts of the city had Chinese residents. Nonetheless, some areas were still primarily Chinese American, including Chinatown. Chinatown has a core around Grant Avenue, spreading to the east and north from there. The heart of Chinatown is bound by Broadway to the north, Bush to the south, Powell to

Table 10.2-Best Moscone Districts

Precinct	Barbagelata Vote	Moscone Vote	Barbagelata %	Moscone %
7029	17	189	8.3%	91.7%
7027	12	138	8%	92%
6007	9	111	7.5%	92.5%
8474	14	181	7.2%	92.8%
6024	9	117	7.1%	92.9%
7017	10	155	6.1%	93.9%
6026/7	7	119	5.6%	94.4%
6009	7	163	4.1%	95.9%
7011	3	91	3.2%	96.8%
6028	2	89	2.2%	97.2%

the west, and Kearney to the east. Many people in this area lived in apartments that were often crowded and above the restaurants and stores selling various Chinese tchotchkes that made Chinatown attractive to tourists and visitors. The neighborhood also included numerous small businesses that served the community, such as hardware stores, grocery stores and accountants.

The central area of Chinatown consisted of twelve precincts. Moscone carried three of them, but Barbagelata carried the rest. Overall, Barbagelata won 56.6 percent of the vote. This is not proof that Barbagelata won the Asian American vote citywide but suggests it was likely. The diverse coalition Moscone sought to assemble did not manage to bring in a big majority of the Chinese American vote.

Similar methods suggest that among another key ethnic group, Latinos, the story was different. In 1975, large numbers of Latinos lived in the Mission, Bernal Heights, and Potrero Hill, as well as in many other parts of the city, so analysis based on precinct level data is difficult. However, several precincts in the Inner Mission, an area bound by Mission to the west, Shotwell to the east, Nineteenth Street to the north and Army Street to the south, were heavily Latino. Voters in these nine precincts gave Moscone just over two-thirds of the 1,651 votes they cast as Moscone clobbered Barbagelata with 67.5 percent there. Army Street was renamed Cesar Chavez Street, after the leader of the United Farm Workers in 1995. Moscone and Chavez were contemporaries and allies. Moscone, as *The New York Times* pointed out the day after his assassination, "often marched with the United Farm Workers, led by Cesar Chavez." Mexican Americans in the Mission reciprocated that support on Election Day.[47]

Strong showings among African Americans and Latinos were helpful for Moscone, but in 1975 San Francisco's electorate was still majority white. For Moscone's coalition to be successful, he needed to win some white votes.

Streets	Neighborhood
Fell, Grove, Broderick, Scott	Western Addition
Golden Gate, McAllister, Baker, Scott	Western Addition
Gilman, Hawes	Bayview, Hunters Point
Montana, Lakeview, Capitol, Plymouth	Ingleside
Cashmere, Whitney Young	Bayview, Hunters Point
McAllister, Hayes, Webster, Buchanan	Fillmore
West Point, Middle Point, Hare	Bayview, Hunters Point
Ingalls, Fitch, Palou	Bayview, Hunters Point
Laguna, Buchanan, Turk, Ellis	Fillmore
Ruell, Hudson	Bayview, Hunters Point

Moscone's record as an advocate for gay rights, particularly the key role he played in repealing California's anti-sodomy laws, helped him with gay voters. Barbagelata's angry conservative politics and not very coded language suggesting that the city was being taken over by unwholesome forces made the choice even easier for gay San Franciscans. Barbagelata, according to an internal Moscone campaign document, was "against increasing Human Rights Commission budget to cover all enterprises doing business with the City" and supported an "attempt to repeal Consensual Sex Act of 1975."[48] Dudley Clendinen and Adam Nagourney described Barbagelata as "treat(ing) gay leaders who interviewed him with such obvious discomfort and disdain—'you people' he kept saying in a meeting with twenty-five of them."[49]

Sharyn Saslafsky explained how many people in the gay community viewed Barbagelata: "The more I heard him speak and the more I read his policy statements . . . it was just going backwards . . . the feeling was like the gay community, why do we need these people? We just want to be old San Francisco, the way it was. We're gonna stay the way it was, and that's the right way. . . . He was gonna be the grandfather, the godfather, and he was gonna be in charge and tell us how to be San Franciscans."[50]

The Castro had the highest concentration of gay voters in San Francisco, perhaps in the world, in 1975. It would become the heart of District Five, which would send Harvey Milk to the board of supervisors in 1977. The Castro is a big neighborhood whose hills bleed into Noe Valley to the east and Twin Peaks to the west; its southern boundary is unclear, but Castro and Market is its unambiguous, if not geographic, center. The core of the Castro District was bound by Market and Sixteenth Street to the north and Twentieth Street to the south. Eureka was the western border of this area and Noe to the east. The nine precincts in this area, the heart of gay San Francisco, went for Moscone by a margin of 70.5 percent to 29.5 percent. Voters in these precincts, fewer than 1 percent of the precincts in San Francisco, put Moscone 784 votes ahead of his opponent. The Castro was bigger than these precincts—and gay voters lived elsewhere in the city too, so extrapolating from those numbers it is apparent that Moscone would not have won without gay support.

Another key constituency for Moscone was the people who had moved to San Francisco in the five to ten years leading up to the election, drawn by the city's growing reputation as a place to break out of the conservative culture and economic structures of postwar America. These people were primarily white and had a range of educational and economic backgrounds. They lived in many parts of the city, although they were more comfortable and welcome in some than in others. The neighborhood that was the political and spiritual home for most of the people was the Haight-Ashbury, which San Franciscans always refer to as simply the Haight. The Haight includes the area a few blocks north and south of Haight Street, from Golden Gate Park in the west until about Masonic to the east, but these borders are fluid. The Haight is very close to both the heavily gay Castro and to what was in 1975 the largely African American Western Addition and Fillmore Districts. These four neighborhoods together formed a very progressive voting block almost in the geographical center of San Francisco in 1975—one that still exists today.

Because of the fluidity of these boundaries and the ethnic diversity in the area, it is hard to isolate precisely which groups of voters there are voting for whom, but in 1975, voters in the Haight had a clear preference for mayor. The heart of the Haight, from Page in the north to Frederick in the south, Masonic in the east, and Stanyan in the west was overwhelmingly for Moscone. The progressive candidate carried all nine of those precincts in the runoff with fully 84.5 percent of the vote, running up a 1,002-vote advantage over Barbagelata.

When all the votes were counted, only about 4,400 out of more than 195,000 votes cast separated Moscone from Barbagelata, but it was enough to make Moscone mayor. The new mayor won because of huge support from African Americans, Latinos, gays, and progressive white voters. This new coalition led many to hope or believe a new day was coming for San Francisco, but Moscone's victory could not quite be considered decisive and was unlikely to bring together the deeply divided city. Moscone would devote the rest of his life to pursuing those two goals—bringing harmony to a contested, and indeed angry, San Francisco, and remaking the city on the model of his progressive neighborhood-oriented vision.

Jim Jones and the African American Vote

George Moscone's winning coalition was centered on huge majorities from San Francisco's African American voters. In most African American communities, churches are a central part of the political landscape. Influential African American pastors and church leaders help mobilize voters and volunteers and informally let their community know which candidates they should support. Accordingly, politicians seek to build relationships with powerful African American clergy and major African American churches. San Francisco in the 1970s was no exception to this.

There were many African American churches and church leaders in San Francisco, including people such as Cecil Williams, but one stood out from the rest, not because he was the most powerful or politically connected, but because he was white and because many believed there was something more than a little odd about him. Jim Jones was a white man who had begun to build his church in Indiana before moving to rural Northern California and finally settling in San Francisco in the early 1970s. He built his substantially African American congregation in large part because of his unfailing support for civil rights.

It is very unusual for a white minister to have a large and politically powerful African American congregation and become an important figure in the African American politics of a city. One of the people who probed this question was Edith Austin, an African American journalist who wrote for the *Sun-Reporter*, the city's most influential African American newspaper. She was skeptical about Jones and his Peoples Temple well before the massacre in Guyana. Writing a few weeks after the massacre, Austin commented, "Jim Jones was a mystery man to me. My journalistic instinct had me laboring in the fields to find out just how this man, who claimed he was part Indian and part Black, could arrive in town and in less than a year coopt most of the Black leadership and nearly all of the public officials." She quoted an unnamed community leader explaining Jones's rise to prominence: "'If the Black preachers were doing their job in San Francisco, Rev. Jim Jones could not have lasted five minutes,' one Black leader told me."[51] That unnamed leader was probably half, but not entirely, right. Jones benefited from the absence of strong and unified leadership in San Francisco's African American religious community, which was smaller and newer than those in cities such as New York and Chicago, but he also relentlessly worked at political relationships. That is why Moscone, like many other left-of-center politicians, turned to Jones for election help.

Jones was much more than a preacher and by the mid-1970s had already pretty clearly crossed over from preacher to cult leader. Reports of odd happenings from people in Ukiah, where the Peoples Temple had been headquartered before San Francisco, had been relatively common. Similarly, the strong loyalty from Jones's congregants, Jones's increasing tendency to speak of himself as almost godlike, and less dramatic things, like his tendency to wear sunglasses even when inside, had begun to raise suspicions. On the other hand, many clergy, and not just in the African American community, are involved in politics, and in

America leading a large and successful house of worship requires political savvy and relationships with the relevant political actors. Jones and his Peoples Temple did this very aggressively. Given his political base, Jones had the strongest political ties with African American politicians such as Willie Brown and Lieutenant Governor Mervyn Dymally, both longtime Moscone allies. Jones also had relationships with progressive white politicians and even a handful of Republicans.

In 1975 mayor's race, as Moscone emerged as the candidate of African American San Francisco, Jones had a chance to influence the outcome and get a mayor who would be better for African American San Franciscans and who was potentially more responsive to Jones. For Jones, like any community leader, there were two major goals when supporting a candidate. The first was helping that candidate win through mobilizing voters and volunteers. The second was to receive some credit for the victory.

Jones tried to do both, but he was not politically powerful enough to unilaterally deliver the African American vote to Moscone. Nor did Moscone, who had a long and very good record on civil rights and other issues important to African Americans, support of numerous labor unions with large African American memberships, and personal relationships with many African American leaders, need to rely on Jones. The most significant and influential of those leaders was Willie Brown who, as Busch described it "broke his ass for George in the campaign."[52] Moscone did not need a white pastor, even one with a large heavily African American congregation, to deliver the African American vote to him. Nonetheless, Jones helped Moscone; and Moscone had no problem accepting the help.

This explanation is not quite satisfying. The view that Jim Jones played an instrumental role in electing George Moscone mayor, in part by committing election fraud, has become widely accepted. It is an article of faith for those on the right who know anything about Jonestown or Moscone, and the belief is found in less conservative circles as well.[53] San Francisco of the 1970s is not something that crops up frequently in political conversations, but when it arises—or when people write and discuss what ultimately happened in Jonestown—it is often mentioned, with a metaphorical knowing nod and look of disparagement, that Moscone and Jones were close and that the latter stole the election for the former.

The reality is more ambiguous. However, we know several things for sure about that campaign and particularly the runoff: it was very close; the Peoples Temple and Jones supported Moscone and, were to one degree or another, involved in his campaign; and Moscone appointed Jones to the San Francisco Housing Authority after the election. Derrald Etheley, a longtime African American activist from Hunters Point who worked for Moscone's 1975 campaign, described his first encounters with Jones in during the campaign:

> The first time I met Jim Jones was when Don (Moscone campaign manager Don Bradley) asked me. He said, "George has got to go to this church in the Fillmore, and the pastor's Jim Jones. I want you to go there and make sure he's okay." . . . So George and I go to Jim Jones's church. It was packed. Packed. So, after George gave his spiel, I said, "George, why did he [Jones] keep on doing this and doing that [tugging on his ears]?' And I asked Don when I got back to the office. He says "Jim Jones was giving the people the cue. When to clap, when to laugh when to do this, or when to shout or whatever." . . . Jim Jones's nails were manicured, (Jones was) well-dressed, but the African Americans around him were raggedy, dressed really raggedy, like poor. They looked like they needed food or whatever.[54]

Etheley explained how Jones supported Moscone: "We were going to have our so-called rally, get people to pass out literature and whatnot. . . . I went to the headquarters like at four in the morning. . . . First, Hunters Point. Lines were around the corner. I mean double waiting for the doors to open. . . . So I drove over to the Fillmore, lines all around the corner. They wouldn't sit on the pavement, They were standing. . . . I go over to Oceanview, lines all around the corner. . . . Jim Jones had packed it two hours before. . . . He was muscling, showing his support, so when it was all over he could be a major player."[55]

Larry Griffin, who was organizing in the Western Addition, a neighborhood that included the headquarters of the Peoples Temple, discussed how

> runoff election night, I was told that I would have 150 or 200 people walking precincts, and it was five to five and nobody was there. I was freaking out. . . . All of a sudden, these buses pull up out front. . . . People walked in. Just a glare on their face. No training. We just gave them a walking pamphlet, and they were gone. I think we counted 320, and then started to give up. . . . We had the Western Addition covered. And they were from the Peoples Temple. Peoples Temple buses. Peoples Temple folks. . . . Wow, man. They were like zombies coming in.[56]

Both these anecdotes offer insights into the hold Jones over had over his followers. Given what happened a few years later to many of those volunteers, it has a macabre feel as well. However, it is not election fraud. Conflating hundreds of volunteers showing up at the urging, and probably more, of their minister turned cult leader, with election fraud is simply inaccurate.

Griffin, reflecting more on Jones and the role of the Peoples Temple, recalled his feelings at the time: "This guy's trying to sound like he's Black when he speaks. What is that about? I looked at most of the members of his church, and they were people of color. . . . I personally knew a lot of them. . . . So fucking weird . . . They gave him property. They signed over their homes to him."[57]

We also know that until the end of his life Barbagelata claimed that Jones helped Moscone steal the election. In the late 1980s, Barbagelata wrote, "I was beaten in 1975 by Moscone in a runoff that was the closest mayoral election in modern times. That was the one where (Jim) Jones mobilized his followers and ordered them to vote early and often."[58] Barbagelata was an early critic of Jones, and unlike many progressive San Francisco politicians, Barbagelata was never fooled by the murderous charlatan. However, Barbagelata's assertion about Jones's role in the 1975 election is perhaps half true, but not true enough. Jones was a supporter of Moscone whose followers volunteered for Moscone. Volunteered is probably not the precisely right word as they were undoubtedly compelled by Jones. Barbagelata's claim that the Peoples Temple committed election fraud may have been accurate as well, but the implied idea that therefore the election was stolen is much more difficult to prove and is very probably not true.[59]

While Moscone's final margin of victory was only about 4,400 votes, that is many more than Jones, even if the worst is believed about his role in the campaign, could have had his followers fraudulently cast for Moscone. However, it remains widely believed on the right that Jones made Moscone mayor through election fraud. The accusation rests on some truth—Jones compelled his members to both vote and "volunteer" for Moscone—and some believable assertions—some of those volunteers may have voted illegally and therefore committed voter fraud. However, the conclusion that those nefarious activities had enough of an impact to change the outcome of the election is much less accurate.

In a close race, dozens of factors and people make the difference: a good debate performance, clever ad, an unfortunate UN resolution, fundraising advantages, and key endorsements can turn a loser into a winner—or the reverse. Moscone won by only 4,400 votes. That is close, but in San Francisco, that's an awful lot of votes for one preacher to deliver or steal. If the Peoples Temple had stolen even 1,000 votes through members voting twice or voting even if they lived out of town, it would have required complicity of dozens of campaign staff, election officials, and others. None came forward with plausible evidence of fraud on that scale.

It is indisputable that in the middle and late 1970s Jones enjoyed good relationships with powerful Democratic politicians. According to Marshall Kilduff and Phil Tracy's 1977 article on the Peoples Temple—one of the first that raised concerns about the organization:

> Jim Jones counts among his friends several of California's well-known public officials. San Francisco mayor George Moscone has made several visits to Jones's San Francisco temple . . . as have the city's district attorney Joe Freitas and sheriff Richard Hongisto. And Governor Jerry Brown

> has visited at least once. Also, Los Angeles mayor Tom Bradley has been a guest at Jones's Los Angeles temple. Lieutenant Governor Mervyn Dymally went so far as to visit Jones's 27,000 acre agricultural station in Guyana, South America and he pronounced himself impressed. What's more, when Walter Mondale came campaigning for the vice-presidency in San Francisco last fall, Jim Jones was one of the few people invited aboard his chartered jet for a private business.[60]

During Moscone's first months as mayor, a surreal ecumenical event in occurred in Los Angeles as the Peoples Temple and the Nation of Islam "co-sponsored the first Christian-Muslim Interfaith Rally in American history." The rally, called the Spiritual Jubilee, was at the Los Angeles Convention Center on May 23, 1976.[61] The Nation of Islam at that time was led by Warith Deen Muhammad, whose father had been Nation of Islam founder Elijah Muhammad. Louis Farrakhan, the noted anti-Semite who is believed to have been involved with the murder of Malcolm X, had not yet won control of the Nation of Islam. Moscone did not attend but was listed as an endorser. Mayor Tom Bradley of Los Angeles, Lieutenant Governor Mervyn Dymally, and Kenneth Hahn, an influential Los Angeles County supervisor, were among civic, religious, and political leaders who attended. Jones's relationships and convening power demonstrate that many Democratic leaders did not see, or maybe chose not to see, what was happening at the Peoples Temple, but it does not mean that Jones stole the election for Moscone.

Despite Jones's connections to powerful Democrats, his role in the election was barely mentioned at the time. No contemporaneous reports claimed that Jones delivered a huge block of voters or was central to the outcome. During both the runoff and the first round, Jones and his Peoples Temple were rarely mentioned in the media. Labor unions, the Burtons, Willie Brown, other Democratic elected officials, including people such as Jerry Brown and Mayor Bradley were described as valuable endorsers, but Jones was not. Given what we know about how Jones craved media coverage and wanted to be seen as politically influential, this tells us something.

The African American vote was a top priority for Moscone's campaign. The campaign distributed a newspaper called "The Election News: The Community Edition," focusing on issues and concerns that were important to African American voters. One pre-runoff edition of "The Election News" had a relatively long list of Moscone endorsers on the first page. Among those were numerous African American politicians such as Dymally, East Bay congressman Ron Dellums, Southern California congresswoman Yvonne Brathwaite and Supervisor Terry Francois; several white politicians such as Feinstein, Jerry Brown and US Senator Alan Cranston; community organizers such as Arnold Townsend and Cecil

Williams; several churches; labor unions; and community organizations. Neither the Peoples Temple nor Jim Jones were listed probably because they were not that important. It is possible the campaign was already trying to distance itself from Jones, but there is little evidence of that.

For more than forty years, Jim Jones has been a symbol of evil. His name and that of the Peoples Temple have become a kind of shorthand for the power of cult leaders to lead people into horrific consequences. For several decades, "drinking the Kool-Aid" has become a kind of shorthand for believing somebody or something unquestionably. This phrase is both factually inaccurate—Jones laced mixed cyanide into Flavor Aid, not Kool-Aid—and an insult to the memory of those who perished in Jonestown. Jones forced his parishioners to drink the poison under the threat of being shot. Very few drank it voluntarily.

This story is so deeply etched in the collective memory that it is easy to overlook another part of the history. In 1975, Jones was viewed very differently in San Francisco and beyond. While we now know he had crossed the line from progressive pastor to abusive cult leader years before, this was not widely known by Moscone, Willie Brown, or the local media. At the time of the election, the Peoples Temple was just beginning to draw some negative attention, but it was still not widely viewed as a dangerous cult. Cheryl Coulthard offers a reminder that

> in the early 1970s, most press reports on Peoples Temple emphasized the group's positive contributions. For example, the *Sacramento Observer* reported that Peoples Temple had voted to contribute $2,000 to the ransom fund for Patricia Hearst from the Symbionese Liberation Army and $300 each to families of people murdered in San Francisco, plus a reward for capture of their murderers. The *Sun Reporter* listed Peoples Temple's activities on social justice issues, including raising legal fees for three black men in Washington, DC, who had been accused of rape, donating money to the families of slain law enforcement officers, and sending thousands of dollars and supplies to Biafra, Bangladesh, Sub-Saharan Africa, and Indian reservations in the United States.[62]

The paradox of Jim Jones's impact on the mayor's race is that we know for certain that Jones supported Moscone and that Jones turned out to be a mass murderer. There is also ample reason to believe that Jones either committed election fraud on behalf of Moscone or came very close to doing that. However, that does not, in of itself, render Moscone's election victory fraudulent or illegitimate. The data very strongly suggest Moscone would have won if Jones had not been involved in the election at all. Thus, while it is appropriate to criticize Moscone for his relationship with Jones, it is wrong to think that together the two of them cheated their way to victory in 1975.

The Other Candidates

A voter who just became eligible to vote in time for the 1975 election would be over well sixty years old today. Most of the people who voted in 1975 are dead. The reporters who covered it and activists and campaign staff who worked for the candidates are either not around anymore or in their later years. Those of us with vague childhood memories of that election are now well into middle age.

Dianne Feinstein, who died on September 29, 2023, was the last remaining major candidate in that election. Given her impressive political career, including nine years in the job she sought in 1975 and more than a quarter century in the US Senate, that 1975 defeat is a footnote to Feinstein's political story. Barbagelata died in 1994 after serving on the board of supervisors through 1977 and spending the remaining years of his life running his real estate firm while becoming a conservative political gadfly. Milton Marks remained in the senate until 1996 and died in 1998. He switched parties and became a Democrat in 1992. Jack Ertola died in 2007.

After losing the mayor's race, Barbagelata finished his term on the board of supervisors but never sought elected office again. By the early 1980s, it was clear Barbagelata's moment had been brief. He came within a few thousand votes of becoming mayor in 1975. He claimed victory on election night after learning he lost the runoff, "We won, we won—there's no doubt we won. This gives San Francisco new hope. . . . We are setting an example for the city. And I think we are setting an example for this nation—proving that little people, trying to save . . . can still take over and run this city and this nation."[63] It was no victory at all. Implied in Barbagelata's statement was that despite losing the election, his voters, more conservative, whiter, and older than the rest of San Francisco, had sent an important message. The defeated candidate, it turned out, had badly misread the last gasp of a defeated movement as a reason to be hopeful for the future.

A decade or so after almost becoming mayor, Barbagelata was running his real estate business in San Francisco and publishing, and writing, every word of what he described as "an entertaining newsletter from one neighbor to another," called *Homewards*. One typical edition of *Homewards* was a bizarre combination of conservative political kibitzing about Willie Brown, Richard Hongisto, Rudy Nothenberg, and other San Francisco politicians; comparing San Francisco to the end of the Roman Empire and Barbagelata himself to Gibbon; somewhat random factoids, "Lake Superior is the largest fresh water body in the world in surface area"; household tips about things such as how to remove crayon stains; and a red-baiting cartoon of an unemployed man being consoled by a bearded man wearing a sash labeled "communism" captioned, "It's OK, Son, The State Will Provide." Toward the end of the newsletter is an ad for Barbagelata's firm. The typesetting and printing, most likely done on the printing press Barbagelata kept in his office, look very professional, but otherwise the multipage newsletter reads like something written by somebody who is mentally unstable.[64]

Since Barbagelata, no Republican has made a meaningful bid to become mayor of San Francisco. Few have run competitive races for any office within the city limits. Elections in San Francisco have long been nonpartisan, but the parties of the candidates are generally known by most voters. The white ethnic populism and anger that fueled Barbagelata's campaign more or less disappeared as an electoral force in San Francisco by the mid-1980s. Since then, most mayoral elections have pitted a centrist Democrat, such as Willie Brown, Gavin Newsom, or London Breed, who are ideologically similar to what Dianne Feinstein represented in 1975, against an opponent from the left such as Roberta Achtenberg, Tom Ammiano, Matt Gonzalez, or Mark Leno. The centrist, except in 1987 when Art Agnos was elected mayor, has always won, but the politics shifted away from Barbagelata, making him less relevant, by the end of the 1970s. Even Frank Jordan, a former chief of police who defeated Art Agnos from the right in 1991, was a Democrat and much more moderate than Barbagelata.

CHAPTER ELEVEN

Mayor Moscone

ALTHOUGH MOSCONE WON THE RUNOFF, as 1976 began the mayoral election was still not over. John Barbagelata, in a pique of bitterness and inability to accept defeat that would last well into 1977, demanded a recount. In a close election, the loser has a right to a recount and in many places, including San Francisco, must pay for it himself. That rule did not stop Barbagelata, who was apparently drunk on the illusion that the recount would give him the office he believed he rightfully deserved.

Barbagelata's tactics were proto-Trumpian. On December 13, the Saturday immediately following the Thursday election, Barbagelata led a group of roughly 150 of his supporters into the office of the registrar of voters to review the ballots themselves, claiming to be looking for ballots that had been altered, signatures that didn't match, similar handwriting of voter signatures, and other imagined discrepancies. Barbagelata explained this extraordinary behavior, saying, "We had been told by so many people that there were irregularities, we decided to take a look."[1]

After the Barbagelata's people had been in the office for some time, Superior Court Judge Edward Cragen "held an unprecedented 45-minute telephone hearing before issuing an order to most of Barbagelata's people to leave the registrar's office, adding his concern that the 'integrity of the election' may have already been violated because while the Barbagelata people were in the registrar's office, using pencils in their work, the official election tally sheets were also present. The election results, still unchecked, are written in pencil."[2] During the following days, both Moscone and Barbagelata sent people to the registrar's office—Barbagelata's people to look for evidence of fraud, Moscone's to make sure Barbagelata's people didn't commit any.

Barbagelata continued to demand a recount even though he or his supporters would have to pay the estimated $10,000 that it would cost. The final tally showed Moscone with 101,090 votes, down from 101,528 in the initial tally, and Barbagelata with 96,647, down from 97,213. Barbagelata's concerns caused some ballots to be dismissed, but he was moving no closer to victory. The recount would move forward and begin close to Inauguration Day, January 8. It would not conclude until a few days into Moscone's term. In the extremely small chance that the election was overturned, San Francisco would have faced political chaos.

The recount began on January 7. Over the next few days, it became clear that the numbers were barely changing. After a week, Herb Caen reported "Jeremy Ets-Hokin has pulled out as a 'coordinator' or whatever, of the Barbagelata voter recount. 'A fool's errand,' he sighs heavily. 'It's going nowhere, proves nothing. If John wants to go on spending his money, it's his problem.'" Caen's, and Ets-Hokin's, tones of exasperation were shared by many San Franciscans. The election was over. Moscone had won, and it was time to move on.[3] By the time the recall concluded, few people even noticed. A small item on page three of the Sunday *Examiner & Chronicle* on January 18 proclaimed that "the recount of votes in the mayoral election finally ended yesterday—with the result practically the same as when it began Jan. 7."[4]

Barbagelata had lost the same election twice to Moscone, but even that wasn't enough. He next unsuccessfully challenged Moscone's victory in court, continuing to question the legitimacy of Moscone's victory and his administration. There was another angle here as well. Given the polarizing nature of the election, Barbagelata was spearheading an effort to undermine the victory of a mayor who had been elected by African American, Latino, and gay San Francisco, by throwing out votes from those voters.

This point was not lost on the *Sun-Reporter*:

> John Barbagelata sounds like one of the worst losers ever to appear in local, politics . . . Barbagelata was elected to the Board of Supervisors in his first term because he appealed to . . . baser instinct of the voters, in other words he appealed to white parents that he would serve the interests of those persons who wished to keep San Francisco a city of white only residents.
>
> He did poorly in neighborhoods largely populated by non-white persons in the last election.
>
> It seems that he is seeking to have the Moscone election declared null and void because in his line of reasoning non-white votes are illegal whenever those votes are cast against the candidacy of John Barbagaleta.[5]

The election between Moscone and Barbagelata divided an already polarized and volatile city. Barbagelata's postelection antics only made that worse, making Moscone's fundamental task of unifying the city that much more difficult.

Inauguration

On January 8, 1976, Moscone was sworn in as mayor in a relatively modest ceremony at the City Hall rotunda. There were no speeches other than Moscone's. The event began with the Pledge of Allegiance, the national anthem, an invocation by a Catholic priest, and remarks by outgoing mayor Joseph Alioto. Moscone then made a relatively brief inaugural address followed by the closing prayer by Rabbi Alvin Fine.[6] Fine had been the rabbi at Temple Emanu-El, the city's largest and most prominent reform synagogue, was a member of the city's Human Rights Commission, and an advocate for social justice.

Joining Moscone on the dais were Gina, Lena, Gina's mother Marcella Bondanza, and three of Moscone's children. Jenifer Moscone was studying in France. Among the politicians in attendance were Lieutenant Governor Mervyn Dymally, Alioto, Feinstein, Senator Alan Cranston, John Burton, Quentin Kopp, Willie Brown, Leo McCarthy, Milton Marks and former mayors George Christopher and Elmer Robinson.[7]

Moscone's inaugural address was not marked by soaring oratory, optimism, or an inspiring progressive agenda. Rather it was brief, reflective of a city that had arrived at a difficult moment and was facing tough challenges. The first line of Moscone's speech communicated his desire to get to work solving these problems, but also seemed almost deliberately uninspiring: "I must tell you that I have spent a considerable amount of time trying to decide whether or not I would actually deliver and inaugural address this afternoon because the times cry out for action rather than words."[8]

The speech mixed in generic pledges of good governance that would not have seemed out of place in the inauguration of any chief executive any time in the last hundred years or so: "If we are to regain the confidence of the people of this City, we must insure (sic) that the bureaucracy works—that it is accountable and that it is responsive. It is my job to see to it that that happens. I intend to do that."[9] Moscone made no specific policy related promises but reiterated a campaign theme. "There is no doubt in my mind that the decisions which are born of the widest range of ideas—decisions which come from people with the widest range of backgrounds and philosophies are the best decisions."[10] The speech also included a pledge to bring in a new police chief, get tougher on crime, and a recognition that "the people of our City bear a heavy tax burden. Some of them an unconscionably high one . . . I have advised every Department that I will approve no new position and no new programs unless I am convinced it is cost-effective."[11] Moscone was taking over as mayor at a very difficult time. Although he had a progressive record as a leader in the state senate and had been elected by a groundbreaking progressive coalition, Moscone was already making it clear to San Franciscans that, to a large extent, circumstances and budget realities were tying his hands.

One of those circumstances was his narrow election victory over Barbagelata—a reminder that Moscone only had the slimmest majority of support behind him. It was possible that some San Franciscans would give the new mayor the benefit of the doubt, but there was still a big block of voters who opposed him. Moreover, with Quentin Kopp the incoming president of the board of supervisors, a conservative replacing the more moderate Dianne Feinstein—who would remain on the board—and John Barbagelata, chair of the board's Finance Committee, Moscone would face an uphill battle with the city's legislature. Moscone was aware of the need to build a relationship with Kopp, who had been a strong supporter of Barbagelata in the recently completed election. He began that process on his first Monday in office when the new mayor and the leader of the legislature lunched together.[12] Whatever was discussed at that lunch did not lay the foundation for a great relationship as the two never got along and Kopp prepared to run against Moscone in 1979.

The conservative bent of the board of supervisors was just one of the obstacles Moscone faced. He was also chief executive of a city where, like many in California, executive power was dispersed. San Francisco is often described as a strong mayor city, but that is only true compared to other California cities such as Los Angeles, San Diego, San Jose, or Oakland. Moscone's structural obstacles included the position of chief administrative officer (CAO). The CAO was an appointed position that served for ten years, so when Moscone became mayor, the CAO was Thomas Mellon, who had been appointed by Mayor Shelley in 1966. Fortunately for Moscone, Mellon's term was set to expire in 1976 so Moscone would be able to pick a successor. However, the board of supervisors would have to approve that successor. Moscone's first choice was Rudy Nothenberg, but Moscone did not have the votes on the board of supervisors to confirm the appointment. This was a political defeat for Moscone and reflected the power of the city legislature that did not share his vision. Ironically, Nothenberg would be appointed as CAO a decade later and serve in that capacity for the last months of Dianne Feinstein's mayoralty as well for mayors Art Agnos and Frank Jordan. Instead of Nothenberg, in early 1977, Moscone appointed Roger Boas, a former supervisor and unsuccessful congressional candidate, to be CAO. Boas was confirmed by the board but was not Moscone's first choice for the job.

Executive power in San Francisco was, and is, further dispersed because there are so many citywide elected offices, some of which have responsibilities that in other cities belong to the mayor. In addition to the district attorney and sheriff, which are elected in almost every county, San Francisco elected its city attorney, assessor-recorder, public defender and treasurer-tax collector. This meant that important legal and fiscal roles were done by elected officials independently of the mayor.

The difficulty Moscone faced governing San Francisco given this structure was spelled out by none other than Mayor Richard J. Daley of Chicago, Joseph Alioto's favorite mayor. Corey Busch recalled a discussion Moscone had when he met Mayor Daley:

> Mayor Moscone introduced me as his press secretary . . . Moscone nodded in my direction and said that I was one of only a handful of political appointees that the mayor has in San Francisco and that all the rest are civil service. Daley seemed incredulous . . . "My dear Mr. Mayor," Daley said, "How in the world do you expect to run your city?" These were his exact words. I will never forget them. Moscone shook his head and said that it was certainly going to be a challenge given the notion that many civil servants had the notion that "we were here before him (the mayor), and we'll be here after him" . . . Daley told Moscone that he faced more than just a challenge to his governance, it would end up being a real challenge to his re-election. "If I appoint my brother-in-law, or your brother-in-law, or some guy off the street to be in charge of garbage collection and the garbage isn't collected, the voters will hold me accountable. That's the way it ought to be, otherwise you are not much more than an ornament in the mayor's office." Moscone pointed out that street cleaning in San Francisco, for example, was under the purview of the chief administrative officer . . . If the streets weren't clean, "It won't do me a damn bit of good to run for re-election blaming someone else," Moscone said. . . . Daley just shook his head back and forth and said, "Well, Mr. Mayor, I wish you all the luck in the world."[13]

The mayor's job is primarily about governance, service delivery, and budgeting. Moscone seemed to understand that, but it was less certain how he could achieve those goals while still delivering something to his left-of-center base. Being a legislator and a chief executive are similar jobs that require some overlapping skills, but they are not the same. Legislators craft laws, build coalitions, and vote on legislation. Legislative leaders, like Moscone when he was in the state senate, work with their caucus and other leaders to achieve these goals. Chief executives are responsible for much more. They make appointments, respond to crises, play a larger role in setting the agenda, and must balance budgets. This is less true for presidents because the federal government can borrow enormous amounts of money, but cities and states cannot.

The transition from being a progressive legislator not directly responsible for the budget to being a progressive mayor who must also balance the budget is not easy. One person who had direct experience with this is Art Agnos, who served for more than a decade in the state assembly before becoming mayor of San Francisco in 1988. Agnos supported Moscone for mayor in 1975 and got elected twelve years later with a very similar coalition. Agnos described why being mayor is different and so more difficult than being a progressive legislator:

> That is the major difference, the cataclysmic difference, between being a legislator and an executive in politics because when you're a legislator you have a responsibility to be fiscally prudent, not as a rule. You always figure (you) could take money from here or some other place that you're not as familiar with . . . Let's take money from that and put it here because my idea is far more important and useful than that other idea. When you're the mayor, you're responsible for the total package. You can't slough off any part of it. As a legislator, you can ignore part of it or not value that part of it as much as you do whatever is your priority and get away with it. You can't do that as mayor. You can't say, "I'm going to put more money into the fire department at the expense of the police or the expense of the airport or the port or the health or any of the other important parts of city government in San Francisco where we have a requirement." It must be a balanced budget. You can't do deficit spending, it increases the pressure, but the supervisors don't have the same level of responsibility. They have some, obviously, but they don't have to worry about it because they're not judged by the overall city budget, the mayor is. So, that's the big difference between being an ultra-progressive legislator and an ultra-progressive mayor. The position forces you to make compromises that you wouldn't have to as a legislator but as a mayor you have to in order to balance the budget and take care of all the people. Many times, the legislator says, "You know, I am a legislator for these people, I am an advocate for these issues, not that one." As mayor, you can't do that, and I see that as the biggest difference.[14]

Moscone was aware of this tension, as demonstrated in his inauguration speech, but it did not make his job any easier. Many of the constituencies that elected him expected something in return, but given the city's fiscal conditions, that was never going to be easy. He also became mayor at a time when it was not apparent that big cities, such as San Francisco, could be governed at all. Rising crime rate, loss of jobs, collapse of tax bases, inadequate service delivery, abandoned buildings, deteriorating neighborhoods, and feelings of chaos and danger were part of urban life in the 1970s. In San Francisco, this was overlaid with a sense of the city as being a strange place because of the political and cultural upheavals of the previous ten years.

From a distance, the transition from Alioto to Moscone might have seemed relatively minor. The outgoing mayor, like his replacement, was an Italian American Democrat. Both were close to the leadership of their party and enjoyed reputations for their charm, charisma, and intellect. Despite this, the transition was a real turning point for San Francisco, and not simply because Moscone had campaigned on a distinctly more left-of-center platform than Alioto. The two mayors also differed in style. Moscone was only thirteen years younger than his predecessor, but they were very different kinds of politicians. As Larry Griffin described it, "Alioto was the last mayor that we had that looked like a mayor from central casting. He was the last mayor that rode around town in a limousine." Griffin explained the contrast with Moscone, "When George got elected, he was driving his Alfa Romeo all around town, having a blast."[15]

By the time George Moscone was sworn in, he had been running for mayor for more than a year. He had announced his candidacy in December 1974, won the first round in November, and won the runoff in December. While campaigning in every corner of San Francisco, debating his opponents, attending candidate forums, and doing myriad other campaign activities, Moscone had remained senate majority leader. He had been instrumental in passing legislation decriminalizing sex between adults of the same gender, decriminalizing marijuana, providing money for school lunches, and more. Moscone accomplished a great deal, but it must have been an exhausting thirteen months for the one-time young rising star of San Francisco politics who was elected mayor in a runoff a few days after his forty-sixth birthday.

Moscone was not likely to be any less busy in 1976. The runoff gave him less time to put his administration together than had he won outright in November, something that was unlikely to happen in a competitive five candidate race. He began this process shortly after the election by establishing a committee of forty-eight San Franciscans to advise him on appointments. Moscone announced the committee, chaired by former supervisor Jack Morrison, and indicated that he wanted to follow through on his promise to bring new faces into city government: "I am today asking all organizations, including neighborhood groups, ethnic groups, labor, business and any others to convene their membership for the purpose of submitting to the Morrison Committee their recommendations for appointments."[16]

While Moscone was indeed planning to open city government, he was also continuing to work with the Burtons on appointments. They were not telling Moscone whom to appoint, but the new mayor's decisions about personnel were made, to at least some degree, with an eye toward the Burtons. A memo from Moscone to Busch, undated but clearly from early in the administration said simply, "Would you routinely (automatically?) send copies of our appointment announcement to Congressman Phillip Burton." The note provides the name of the Burton staff member to whom Moscone wanted Busch to send the information.[17] This note was the kind of thing that Moscone's opponents warned about when they attacked the candidate for his ties to the Burtons.

It was not only the Burtons who wanted input on hiring. Some requests for jobs came from unusual places. At the time Moscone became mayor, the culture was shifting again in San Francisco. As the Summer of Love faded into the past, the counterculture dynamism was becoming more apparent in the rumblings of the early years of punk rock. Punks paid homage to the tenth anniversary of the Summer of Love by deeming 1977 the Summer of Hate. Early the next January, the Sex Pistols played their last concert ever in Bill Graham's Winterland. Graham himself never warmed to punk, not least because the genre's liberal use of Nazi imagery did not sit well with the Jewish promoter and Holocaust survivor.

By 1978, the Mabuhay Gardens, in North Beach, had eclipsed any Bill Graham facility, not in size or revenue, but in innovation and buzz. During Moscone's last year, bands such as Dead Kennedys and the Avengers were defining the new San Francisco sound. Hippie bands such as the Grateful Dead, the Jefferson Starship (formerly the Jefferson Airplane), and Santana played and drew good crowds, but were neither innovative nor avant-garde.

Part of a mayor's job is representing and promoting their city. Moscone had to promote a city that, in the eyes of much of the rest of the country, was increasingly strange. For example, shortly before the runoff, Moscone received a letter from Graham recommending a police officer named Stan Damas, who had "taken it upon himself to meet with all of the necessary City officials, ascertain the problems and/or objections that they had and bridged the communication gap between the young, 'hip' community and City Hall."[18] Graham hoped Moscone would find room in his administration for Damas. This was not necessarily a bad recommendation, but not too many big-city mayors receive recommendations for security-related jobs from somebody who had previously hired Hells Angels to provide that service at his own events.

Moscone had cultivated the support of the legendary music promoter, writing him a long letter in April 1975 explaining his background and views on issues. Moscone concluded, "I want your support because I think you represent something to the young people of this City which I would like to have identified with my campaign. You've never cheated anybody and you've always dealt out front with people. I think we need a little bit of that in City Hall. Keep in touch and let's get together soon."[19] No other mayoral candidate could have reached out to Graham in such a way. Barbagelata would not have wanted to, and Marks and Feinstein would not have known how.

Moscone's letter to Graham was written a few weeks after Graham had organized an extraordinary event called the SNACK (Students Need Activities, Culture and Kicks) concert, which raised money for after-school and other activities for San Francisco children. The concert was held on March 23, 1975, at Kezar Stadium, the former home of the 49ers. Among the performers were Bob Dylan, the Band, Neil Young, Jerry Garcia, Carlos Santana and Joan Baez. Special non-musical guests included Marlon Brando and Willie Mays. SNACK was one of the first major benefit concerts of its kind. Moscone helped Graham and offered political and other support for this extraordinary event.

In addition to staffing his administration, Moscone also had to move quickly to follow up on promises he had made, including reforming the police, making city government more diverse, giving neighborhoods more of a voice regarding land use and budget decisions, supporting racial equality, and making the city safer. However, the first crisis of Moscone's mayoralty had nothing to do with any of his campaign promises or even with Kopp and Barbagelata.

The Toronto Giants

By the middle of the twentieth century, Los Angeles had surpassed San Francisco as the financial capital of the West. San Francisco was still hugely influential in state politics—for example, in 1975 both the governor and Speaker of the assembly were, like Moscone, San Franciscans and graduates of St. Ignatius. But Southern California was much more influential in national politics, primarily through people such as Richard Nixon and Ronald Reagan. Nonetheless, San Franciscans continued to see their city as more urban, cosmopolitan, important, and culturally sophisticated than Los Angeles. Given this, San Franciscans were very aware of its big-city bona fides, including the busy Financial District, high-quality local newspapers, opera, symphony, and museums.

Among these bona fides were the presence of big-league sports teams. The San Francisco 49ers had been playing since 1946 and been part of the National Football League since it merged with the All-America football conference in 1949. The Warriors of the National Basketball Association had moved from Philadelphia to San Francisco in 1962, but they left for Oakland, where they became known as the Golden State Warriors, nine years later. This was a loss for the city but was not considered a real blow because at that time the NBA was not as significant as it later became. Decades later, the Warriors moved back to San Francisco and have called the city home since 2019.

San Francisco and Los Angeles both had Major League Baseball teams since 1958 when the Dodgers and Giants both moved from New York to California. By the time Moscone became mayor, the Giants had fallen on bad times both on and off the field. Willie Mays, Willie McCovey, and Juan Marichal, players who had made the Giants one of the best and most recognized teams in baseball during the 1960s, had been sold or traded away. Mays and Marichal were already retired, but McCovey still had a few years left and would spend the last four of those back in San Francisco. The Giants lost more games than they won in both 1974 and 1975. The team struggled to draw fans, finishing last in the league in attendance both years. It didn't help that across the bay, the Oakland A's had turned into a powerhouse, winning the World Series every year from 1972 to 1974. Horace Stoneham, whose family had owned the Giants for decades, long before the move to San Francisco, was frustrated, looking to sell, and didn't care to whom. All this was coming to a head during the mayoral election, but it did not make the headlines or become a real campaign issue.

That changed in the days before Moscone's inauguration when it was announced that the Giants has been sold to the Labatt brewing company, which was going to move the team to Toronto. The sale was presented as a fait accompli and became the first major crisis of Moscone's mayoralty. The departure of the Giants could not reasonably have been blamed on Moscone. To the extent losing the Giants could be blamed on a mayor, it was Alioto who was responsible. However, it was happening on Moscone's watch. If the Giants left, it would be his popularity, and reelection chances, that would be damaged. Additionally, as a lifelong San Franciscan, former athlete, and Giants fan since the team moved west, Moscone did not want to see the Giants leave.

Moscone needed to find a way to slow down the process and to find somebody to buy the team who would meet or exceed Labatt brewery's offer of $8 million and pledge to keep the team in San Francisco. Moscone immediately sought legal recourse and requested an injunction that would buy him some time. It turned out that finding a buyer was easier, sort of. Within hours of the news about the Giants moving to Toronto becoming public, Bob Lurie contacted the mayor's office and expressed his interest in the Giants. Moscone met with Lurie in the mayor's office on Saturday, January 10. Thus, the new progressive mayor's first official meeting was with a wealthy businessman to discuss baseball. It turned out to be a very smart move on Moscone's part, one that would lead to a major part of his legacy and impact on San Francisco.

Lurie, the only child of Louis Lurie, who died in 1972, was the exact kind of buyer Moscone needed. Louis Lurie had built a real estate empire in San Francisco and Chicago, making him one of the wealthiest and best-known business leaders and philanthropists in San Francisco. Bob Lurie had money, liked baseball, was respected in San Francisco, and could be counted upon to keep the Giants in town. However, Lurie was only offering to put up half of the needed money.

Fortunately, San Francisco got a friendly ruling from Judge John Benson of the San Francisco Superior Court. The San Francisco native was amenable to giving the city a bit more time, but Lurie and Moscone were struggling to find a second buyer. The inability of Lurie, a well-connected, respected, and very wealthy businessman, with ample assistance from the mayor, to find anybody who could invest $4 million to buy half of the Giants tells us a lot about the state of the local economy in 1976. The National League was getting impatient and imposed an early March deadline on Lurie. Just as the deadline approached, Arizona businessman Bud Herseth, who made much of his money in the cattle industry, agreed to be Lurie's partner and to keep the team in San Francisco.[20]

This was a major political victory for Moscone, one that unified rather than divided the city. Today the Giants are a successful franchise playing in a beautiful ballpark not far from downtown. They have won three World Series championships this century, after winning none in their first half century in San Francisco. None of that would have been possible without Moscone and Lurie's work in early 1976. The effort to keep the Giants from leaving was the most immediate crisis during the beginning of Moscone's term, but it was also the only one that was resolved so quickly and so happily for San Francisco. Keeping the Giants in San Francisco, along with the convention center that bears his name, are the most tangible parts of Moscone's mayoral legacy. Had Moscone not acted swiftly, picking up the slack from a predecessor who had done nothing to stop the move, a beloved and unifying San Francisco institution would not exist.

On the last day of 1976, the Sunday *Chronicle & Examiner* ran a soft news article asking politicians what their "secret ambition" was. Dianne Feinstein had the best answer. "One is to be the female parallel of the Scarlet Pimpernel or Horatio Hornblower—adventure and swashbuckling. . . . Another is to be a fine ballerina or stage actress. . . . Another is to sail the Pacific on a three-masted schooner and find that island." Feinstein never achieved any of those things, but she did achieve her last secret ambition, "And one was to be mayor of San Francisco."[21]

Moscone's answer was not quite as adventurous. "I would guess that if I could be anything in the world I wanted to be after, of course, completing my tenure as Mayor, I would have to say that covering professional or college athletics, either as a writer or a broadcaster, would be exciting to me. "[22] Ironically, given his passion for sports—his official schedules from his time in the senate and afterward include frequent trips to games and other sports events—Moscone was the rare San Francisco mayor who never had a championship during his time in office. The Warriors won the NBA championship in 1975 but lost in the conference finals in 1976. The Giants never finished higher than third place, and the 49ers never made the playoffs while Moscone was mayor. Dianne Feinstein, Art Agnos, and Frank Jordan all had championship 49er teams during their tenures as mayor. The Giants won the World Series when Gavin Newsom and later Ed Lee were in office.

Sports, particularly baseball, were part of Moscone's public life. In September 1973, baseball legend Henry Aaron was closing in on Babe Ruth's home run record. This was an enormous news story at the time and of interest well beyond fans of Aaron's Atlanta Braves or of baseball fans in general. When the Braves came to San Francisco to play the Giants that month, Moscone, a state senator at the time, held a ceremony honoring Aaron. Moscone and Mervyn Dymally sponsored a resolution recognizing Aaron's accomplishment, and Moscone arranged to present it to him before a game at Candlestick Park on September 1. The resolution stated, "Hank Aaron, who is currently in pursuit of the immortal Babe Ruth's all-time home run record of 714 career home runs, has served throughout his career as a model for youngsters across the country and throughout the world for his untiring dedication to excellence, his integrity as a ballplayer and as a man, and for the complete sportsmanship which has marked his great career."[23] Aaron did not break the record in 1973, but did so early the following season. The record has since been broken by Barry Bonds.

This may have seemed like a baseball fan taking an opportunity to meet and honor one of the game's greatest players ever—but it was more than that. During his pursuit of Ruth's record, Aaron, who was African American, received ugly and racist hate mail and threats. By honoring him, Moscone was showing that he stood with Aaron and against the racists. That was the right thing to do and good politics for somebody who was counting on strong African American support in a future race for governor or mayor.

Four years later, another African American star was closing in on a record that a long-ago white player had held for decades. This time, in 1977, Lou Brock was threatening Ty Cobb's stolen base record. When Brock's St. Louis Cardinals were visiting the Giants June 14–16, Moscone arranged to meet with Brock to congratulate him on closing in on the record. Brock ended up breaking the record on August 29.[24] The meeting gave Moscone another opportunity to be seen with a popular African American baseball player.

There is another explanation for Moscone's interactions with both Brock and Aaron. The clue lies in a thank you note written by Brock's publicist, Ramon Hervey II, to Moscone's staff. The staff person to whom that email was addressed was Corey Busch, who had been a trusted Moscone aide since 1971. Busch was, and remains, a huge baseball fan, although at the time he still rooted for the Dodgers. Busch went on to spend decades as a respected senior executive with the Giants and later with MLB. So, while these meetings may have helped Moscone, it is possible that Busch, then in his mid-20s, simply wanted to meet these baseball legends.

During the last two years of Moscone's mayoralty, no San Francisco ballplayer was more admired than Giants slugger Willie McCovey. McCovey had been a Giant from 1959 to 1973 and then came back to the Giants to finish out his career from 1977 to 1980. In 1977, McCovey was the National League's Comeback Player of the Year as he led his team in home runs and RBIs. Moscone responded by proclaiming September 18, 1977, Willie McCovey Day in San Francisco.

The 1977 proclamation listed some of McCovey's baseball accomplishments and noted that "Willie McCovey's achievements off the field have been equally outstanding, as all of San Francisco has come to respect and admire his selfless devotion of time and energy to numerous private charities and worthy civic concerns, his kindness and his great generosity of spirit; and Willie McCovey has become an inspiration to millions of baseball fans throughout this country, young and old alike, and is surely the most popular and successful individual ever to wear a San Francisco Giants baseball uniform."[25]

Astute baseball fans might question the last words of Moscone's statement because, after all, Willie Mays had been a longtime Giant. Mays was a better ballplayer, but in San Francisco, for many years McCovey was more beloved. His final years with the team, 1977–1980, introduced McCovey to a cohort of fans who never got the chance to see Mays. It was only in this century when Mays replaced McCovey as the top Giants baseball legend in the eyes of many fans. Mays was a presence at Giants games and events until shortly before his death in June 2024.

The following spring, Moscone implored fellow San Franciscans to "launch a massive write-in campaign to get Willie McCovey in the starting line-up for the National League (All-Star team) this July."[26] Moscone kicked off this effort on June 21 at a luncheon with McCovey fans. The sentiment was sincere, but the politics were also apparent. Associating himself with a hugely popular athlete who was particularly popular among African Americans was only going to help the mayor. Moscone's efforts came up short as Steve Garvey of the Dodgers, a player Giants fans broadly despised, was voted the starting first baseman for the National League. Willie Stargell of the Pittsburgh Pirates was selected as the backup.

That evening there was a softball game between the mayor's office and the staff and members of the board of supervisors at a Funston Playground in the Marina District, a few blocks from where Moscone had lived as a boy. Funston would later be renamed after Moscone. Moscone played in the outfield that day and seemed to be enjoying himself, relaxing, and frequently holding a cigarette with his non-glove hand. The board of supervisors team was led by another former high school athletic star, Dan White. White was a good ballplayer but brought an intensity and competitiveness to the game that seemed out of place. By then many of White's colleagues on the board knew that the first-term supervisor from the southern part of town was wound pretty tightly.[27]

Governing San Francisco

During his first week in office, Moscone sent a letter to almost a hundred people who were either working in staff positions at City Hall or as members of city agencies and commissions asking for their resignation. "As you know, I have asked all of the appointees of the Mayor, whether they are on staff or on Boards and Commissions to resign their offices. Your contract contains a 30-day cancellation clause, and I am taking this way to give you notice that we are invoking the cancellation clause, effective 30 days from today." Recipients of the letter included members of the commission on the aging, the criminal justice council, the model cities commission, the community development office, and several other boards and commissions.

The language in the letter was firm and legalistic, but the meaning was quite radical. Moscone was asking the city's permanent government to resign so that he could replace them not only with a much more diverse group of people, but a more diverse group of people of his own choosing who would help Moscone consolidate his power. The duality of Moscone's political identity was reflected in this move. The progressive was seeking to make city government more diverse and representative, while the savvy politician was building a political operation within city government.

For Moscone supporters, this action, which was entirely legal but without precedent, was seen as simply a progressive mayor keeping promises. For his opponents, it was interpreted as a power grab. Opponents often described the Burton political organization as a machine, but the Burtons were always adamant that they were not a political machine because they had no patronage to give out. John Burton's comment about the Burtons being unable to "give . . . two fucking jobs" was no longer quite so true when Moscone became mayor.[28]

By demanding the resignations of so many commission members and others, Moscone was making sure that he had some jobs and appointments to give away. Some commissions were advisory, but others such as the board of permit appeals made decisions that were very impactful. To a less than scrupulously honest person, a position on that commission could be lucrative. There was potential for a network of either corruption or machine politics to emerge from Moscone's appointments. In fact, one of his earliest appointments might have been seen as an attempt to help clear the field for a favored candidate in an upcoming primary campaign, but it didn't quite work out that way.

The board of permit appeals was one of the first commissions to which Moscone appointed people. That commission is a very bureaucratic-sounding body that, at first glance, does not seem powerful, but it has long been an important governing body with the final say on many questions about permits, codes, and other parts of city ordinances. Marshall Kilduff described the board's substantial scope in January 1976 as "the power to reverse or uphold most city decisions pertaining to police permits, building code rules and zoning guidelines on a case by case basis. The appeals board was intended as a little man's court where a citizen could plead his case without the need for a lawyer on equal terms with city bureaucracy." Kilduff added "in recent years personalities both on the board and in the audience have occasionally distracted the informal hearings into rowdy shouting matches that bear little resemblance to reason or fairness."[29]

Moscone reappointed one member of the board of permit appeals, Mattie

Jackson, an African American woman whom he singled out for "even-handed treatment of those who have come before her on the Board." He also appointed Richard Cerbatos, a Filipino American engineer with strong ties to that community; Patrick Hallinan, a progressive attorney; and Claire Pilcher, a lawyer and community activist. The fifth person Moscone appointed was Harvey Milk. By appointing a high-profile gay activist to an important city commission, Moscone repaid a key constituency for helping him win the close runoff while also keeping a campaign promise to make diverse appointments to boards and commissions.

Milk had supported Moscone in his race for mayor and, because of his strong showing in the 1975 race for the board of supervisors, was beginning to be seen as a leader of gay San Francisco, even a potential appointee to the board of supervisors if a seat were to become vacant. Jerry Roberts of the *Bay Guardian* wrote, "If Molinari, Mendelsohn or Gonzales win (the race to succeed Moscone in the senate) Moscone will appoint their successor to the board. Current speculation centers around Harvey Milk, who finished seventh in the race for six supervisor's seats least (sic) month, and who was introduced along with a star-studded cast of incumbent politicians by Willie Brown at Moscone's election night celebration shortly before Moscone offered special thinks to 'the gay community' for supporting him."[30] Jon Rubin added, "Harvey did not play a big role in the Moscone campaign, but he was a force to be reckoned with because he was a power center because he had a camera shop and burning ambition and long hair and he was inoffensive. . . . It was implicit. There's a gay seat here. You guys go and fight with each other and when somebody emerges you guys let me know who it is."[31]

By selecting Milk, the most visible gay or lesbian appointed during the early days of Moscone's administration, Moscone helped resurrect the political career of a politician who was in danger of becoming a gadfly. In 1976 a gay person on the board of permit appeals, rather than a deputy mayor, commissioner, or other higher-ranking position, was considered a political victory for a gay community only beginning to have political power. His appointment to the board of permit appeals was a victory for Milk, but not close to enough to slake his ambition.

A special election was planned for May 11 to fill Moscone's now-vacant senate seat. Milk was not a contender because the district was too big for a candidate who was not popular in conservative parts of the city. The front-runner for the senate seat was John Foran, a six-term assemblyman from the eastern part of San Francisco. Foran won a plurality in the first round in May and on June 8 won the runoff, handily defeating Republican Bruce Makar. None of the supervisors mentioned by Roberts decided to run for that seat.

Foran was a moderate Democrat, but his district included many of the progressive eastern San Francisco neighborhoods that had given Moscone big majorities in 1975. Overall, Moscone had won 59 percent of the vote in Foran's district. The now open assembly seat was opportunity for progressive San Francisco. Milk almost immediately expressed interest in the race. Moscone announced Milk's appointment to the board of permit appeals on January 29, but a few days later, Milk filed papers declaring his intent to run for the assembly. On February 11, Milk formally filed to run.

That decision created a major rift between Milk and the new mayor. Moscone was just beginning his term; and Milk was one of his most significant commission appointments. Regardless of what he did on the board, it would be difficult for Milk to be seen as entirely fair-minded or objective if he was a candidate for office needing to raise money and win support from voters. Accordingly, the mayor made it clear, to Milk as well and the public, that if he ran for the assembly, Milk would be fired. Milk bought some time by not officially announcing until a month after he filed papers. However, shortly after he formally announced his candidacy on March 10, Moscone replaced him on the board with Rick Stokes, a prominent gay attorney. Busch recalled when Moscone learned about Milk's decision from the media: "At one of those Monday meetings a reporter . . . said, 'What do you think about Harvey Milk running for the assembly,' and George had never heard about it, and he said, 'Well, I think he's gonna be the shortest commissioner in San Francisco, and I don't mean his height.' He was pissed. He was livid that Harvey didn't talk to him about it."[32]

There were also political issues behind Moscone's frustration with Milk because he already had a candidate in mind—one that gave him an opportunity to solidify a potentially valuable political relationship and pay back a political debt.

By 1975 Leo McCarthy was the Speaker of the assembly, so the two former classmates and teammates at St. Ignatius had cooperated on passing legislation during Moscone's final year in Sacramento. McCarthy was the leader of the more conservative faction of San Francisco's Democratic Party based in the western part of the city. He had taken over that role after J. Eugene McAteer died in 1967. Had McCarthy gone with Barbagelata in the runoff, Moscone may well have lost. Instead, with about four days to go before the runoff, McCarthy declared that "George Moscone is a doer—not a talker—and no one owns George Moscone. San Francisco needs true leadership, and that means someone at the helm who can weld together the people and their government."[33] It was a strong endorsement, particularly coming from McCarthy, a frequent critic of the Burton political operation.

Politicians as smart as McCarthy don't make endorsements like that without expecting something in return. That something may have been McCarthy's candidate to replace Foran in the assembly—and that candidate was not Milk. Instead, McCarthy wanted his chief of staff to succeed Foran. Under most circumstances, this would have created a conflict for Moscone, who would want somebody more progressive in the assembly—and would be under pressure from the Burtons to support their candidate.

This case was a little different. McCarthy's choice for the seat was the thirty-seven-year-old son of Greek immigrants named Art Agnos who had, like Milk, moved to the city from the East Coast a few years earlier. Agnos had an interesting political profile because his boss and political mentor was McCarthy, but ideologically he was closer to the Burtons, Willie Brown, and Moscone. Agnos was the kind of candidate who had the potential to unify the party and cruise to election, but Milk stood in his way. A defeat for Agnos in his first bid for office would have been a setback but not devastating. For Milk, the stakes were considerably higher. After losing twice for the board of supervisors, Milk had finally been given a reasonably high appointment in city government and given that up after only about six weeks to run for the assembly. A defeat, his third in three years, would have likely meant the end of his political career.

The campaign quickly became nasty. Milk framed the campaign as being Harvey Milk against "The Machine," attacking Agnos as a career bureaucrat and machine politician. "The politicians are trying to determine who is going to run for office. In essence, the right of self-determination is being taken away from the people." This might have worked had Agnos been a product of the Burton operation or if Leo McCarthy had something approaching a political machine. Instead, the charge fell a little flat as both Burton and non-Burton-aligned Democrats supported Agnos. Milk had fewer prominent supporters but was endorsed by Carol Ruth Silver, a friend and progressive who had just lost the race for district attorney, as well as Quentin Kopp.

The Milk against "The Machine" framework also built on the growing view in San Francisco that Moscone, Brown, and the Burtons were indeed a political machine, but Agnos himself did not seem like a machine politician. He was young, good-looking, very progressive, and with no ties to the Burtons. Agnos was not a political insider and had only been in government for about four years. Before that, he was a social worker, working primarily with lower-income African Americans. However, Agnos was endorsed by a huge majority of local politicians as well as groups such as the Central Labor Council. Agnos had a strong record of commitment to gay rights and ran to the left of Milk on most economic and other issues. Agnos defended himself by contrasting his record of public service with Milk's "I don't apologize for being paid to work for the people," while also boasting of his "work on Headstart, police-community relations, helping preserve Ft. Miley from bulldozers, aiding senior citizens and minority groups."[34]

Agnos's political support in the race was overwhelming and certainly would have made Milk feel that the political leadership was making it difficult for anybody but their chosen candidate to win. Agnos looked back on that race and explained very directly, "Well the race with Harvey Milk was a very interesting one. I was the candidate of the political left establishment. Mayor Moscone and Speaker Leo McCarthy, Willie Brown, Congressman Burton, both Congressmen Burton, they were all supporting me, which meant I was gonna get elected."[35]

It seems incongruent given how Milk is remembered, but he was the conservative in that race. Agnos described the discourse in that campaign: "As a candidate against me, his favorite speech, and in the movie about him, there's a scene that depicts this, that he insisted that we needed to government run like a business. Where have you heard that before? And that 'we didn't need any more social workers like Agnos to be developing these social programs,' and he went on from there."[36]

In the end, it wasn't close. Agnos won the primary with 44 percent of the vote. Milk garnered 34 percent with the remaining votes scattered among minor candidates. Milk was unable to defeat what he called "The Machine," particularly when "The Machine" took the form of a handsome young progressive with a strong history of community involvement. However, Milk clearly was expanding his base and gaining name recognition. It was probably cold comfort at the time, but winning a third of the primary vote in a large assembly district was still pretty good for a gay Jewish man with an almost cartoonish outer borough accent and the support of almost no elected officials or Democratic Party organizations.

Milk did not see it that way and was quite bitter following his defeat. He was particularly angry at the city's gay leadership who had largely sided with Agnos, referring to them as "a handful of self-serving people who are utilizing the movement for their own advantage and never support a gay except from their own group. These people have to be weeded out for the sake of the movement." When asked about his future, Milk responded that his "first priority is trying to get this camera store back in shape. I don't know if I'll ever run again." He added that his "next political effort will probably be helping Carol Ruth Silver run for city attorney."[37] The future did not work out that way for Milk or Silver.

Something else about this election reflected how San Francisco was changing. The two leading candidates in this hard-fought Democratic primary both had moved to the city fewer than ten years earlier—Milk from New York and Agnos from Massachusetts. San Francisco was becoming a city where it was beginning to matter a little less where you went to high school, what parish you lived in—neither Milk nor Agnos were Catholic nor had attended Catholic school—or who your parents were.

Appointments

Many of Moscone's staff decisions in early 1976 were easy. Corey Busch came from Moscone's senate office to serve as press secretary. Rudy Nothenberg, who so ably handled Election Day during the runoff, was appointed budget director. Cyr Copertini, who had worked on Moscone's campaign and before that as an aide to Congressman Fortney (Pete) Stark, was appointed Moscone's secretary. Bernard Teitelbaum, who had also been on Moscone's senate staff, was appointed deputy mayor. Josh Getlin was deputy press secretary.

Some appointments were more significant than others. The appointment of Charles Gain as chief of police had an enormous impact on Moscone's term in office. Similarly, Moscone's short-lived appointment of Milk to the board of permit appeals gave new life to Milk's floundering political career. Another Moscone appointee whose role in history is outsized was his choice for chair of the Housing Authority. After the election, Jim Jones believed he had played a big role in electing Moscone, and he wanted a few things in return. Jones and other senior leaders of the Peoples Temple who, given the hierarchical structure of the People Temple, were undoubtedly following Jones's orders, were in frequent contact with Moscone about jobs in his administration.

Moscone first offered Jones a seat on the human rights commission. Guinn (2017) explained, "But in March 1976, when Moscone came through, Jones was bitterly disappointed by his offer of a seat on San Francisco's Human Rights Commission."[38] Jones had set sights on the San Francisco Redevelopment Agency (SFRDA). This was a sensible goal for Jones because a substantial number of Peoples Temple members lived in the Western Addition and Fillmore areas being affected by redevelopment. The SFRDA was also a very high-profile and powerful agency. On May 13, 1976, Jones's aide Michael Prokes wrote to Moscone, "I talked with your aide, Mr. Teitelbaum, regarding an appointment to the Redevelopment Commission which requires that the appointee only be a registered voter . . . I hope you will give serious consideration to such an appointment, mayor." Prokes attached a list of eleven Peoples Temple members whom he hoped the mayor would hire. The list included the professional background and ethnicity of each job seeker.[39]

A few weeks later, Jones wrote to Moscone, "So far, two of the six people we proposed for jobs through your office have been called and interviewed . . . In the meantime, is there anything you can do for another of our members Linda Amos, who has been tested for a position as a hospital social worker in San Francisco?"[40] In another undated letter, which seems to have been written after Moscone offered Jones the position on the Housing Authority, Jones implored, "Some of our members and friends thought I might better serve on the Redevelopment Commission, and I wanted to know if you foresee any problem in passing the Board of Supervisors." Jones then suggests that if Moscone cannot appoint him, he appoint one of Jones's people to the SFRDA, before again asking for more jobs for his congregants. He closed with some flattery. "I sincerely hope that Peoples Temple will be able to play a significant role in helping you to achieve the vital aims of your administration."[41]

Moscone returned this flattery to Jones and the Peoples Temple. In the November 2, 1976, edition of the Peoples Temple newsletter, Moscone congratulated the Peoples Temple for supporting four embattled journalists in Fresno, California, and closed with "The Peoples Temple is a fine institution in our community. As Mayor of San Francisco, I am pleased to commend Rev. Jim Jones and his congregation for taking a stand that reflects such high principles of morality and humanity. We are proud to have the Peoples Temple in San Francisco."[42]

While the idea that Jones somehow was uniquely responsible for Moscone's election is false, there is no getting around that well into his term in office, when concerns were already being raised, Moscone remained very reluctant to criticize Jones. One of the first rules of politics, is that you dance with the one that brung ya. Any politician as successful as Moscone knows that. For Moscone, the primary people who brung him were the Burtons, Willie Brown, organized labor, and African Americans, but Jones was in the mix there too and Moscone remained troublingly loyal to him.

Jones was at the height of his political powers by 1975 and 1976, and he had played a substantial role in Moscone's victory, but the signs that there was something deeply wrong at the Peoples Temple were evident. Members were leaving the Peoples Temple and recounting some of what was occurring there. Jones was prone to increasingly erratic behavior, demanding extreme fealty, bordering on worship, from his congregants and meting out punishment to those who defied him.[43] It was not until October 1976 that Moscone appointed Jones to the Housing Authority. That position gave Jones more governmental power than he had ever enjoyed before, but he did not last long. By late 1976 Jones was already beginning his project in Guyana that would end so horrifically two years later.

The role Jim Jones played in San Francisco politics and his relationship with the city's political leadership, including Moscone, seem shocking and damning of the Bay Area progressive leadership. There is something to this, but it is too easy and intellectually dishonest to suggest that progressive politicians such as Moscone, Willie Brown, and Mervyn Dymally must have known Jones's true colors. After all, when Moscone appointed Jones to the Housing Authority in 1976, Moscone's chief antagonists on the board, Barbagelata and Kopp, voted for the appointment both in committee and at the meeting of the whole board.

Jones and the Peoples Temple must be understood in the context of San Francisco at a time, when, in the aftermath of the 1960s, several groups existed somewhere in the drug rehab-cult-religion nexus. Synanon, for example, straddled the lines between drug rehab program, new age psychological institute, and cult. Although Synanon was based in Southern California, not San Francisco, it had a big presence there including a large, easily recognizable building on 110 Lombard Street in the northeastern corner of the city. Over time, it became known that Synanon was a nasty cult that engaged in violence, financial fraud, child abuse, and verbal abuse.

Some, like Delancey Street, founded by John Maher, who had been part of Synanon, generally did very good work and continue to do so to this day. San Francisco during the last decade or so of Moscone's life was a hotbed of cults, alternative medicines, the new age movement, drug addiction, drug rehabilitation, and religious experimentation. This is the context in which the Peoples Temple and Jim Jones existed and were viewed at the time.

On August 3, 1977, Jones sent Moscone a note on San Francisco Housing Authority letterhead: "It has become increasingly apparent that the needs of my congregation in Guyana necessitate my ongoing presence there which would require my absence from the city for extended periods of time." He then formally resigned and closed the letter, "As you know, I have wanted to resign for months, finding the responsibilities of a city official essentially incompatible with my duties as a pastor of a large congregation both here and in Guyana."[44] Jones had been in the position less than a year and claimed he had wanted to resign for months, raising the question of why he wanted the job in the first place.

The timing of Jones's resignation was neither accidental nor entirely because Jones, as he claimed in the letter, was being stretched too thin. Instead, it was likely a reaction to an article in the August 1 edition of *New West* magazine by journalists Marshall Kilduff and Phil Tracy. Actually published at the end of July, the article showed the Peoples Temple to be something very different from how Jones had presented it to Moscone and others. Basing their reporting on testimony from members who had left the Peoples Temple, Kilduff, whose usual beat was City Hall, and Tracy wrote that "life inside Peoples Temple was a mixture of Spartan regimentation, fear and self-imposed humiliation. . . . In the last two years, we were told, these often humiliating sessions had begun to include physical beatings with a large wooden paddle and boxing matches in which the person on the floor was occasionally knocked out by opponents selected by Jones himself. . . . Church leaders also instructed certain members to write letters incriminating themselves in illegal and immoral acts that never happened. In addition, temple members were encouraged to turn over their money and property to the church." The article documented numerous other abuses committed by Jones and Peoples Temple leadership.[45]

Kilduff and Tracy described close ties between the Peoples Temple and prominent politicians such as Moscone and Dymally. On July 26, Moscone issued a defensive statement in which he confirmed his commitment to Jones remaining on the Housing Authority and indicated he would initiate no investigations of Jones or the Peoples Temple. Moscone went so far as to characterize the well-researched article as "a series of allegations with absolutely no hard evidence that Rev. Jones has violated any laws, either local, state or federal. . . . I will not comment upon the alleged practices of the Temple as it is not my habit to be a religious commentator," implying that blackmail and assault are just another form of religious practice.[46]

This was perhaps Moscone's worst moment in public life. By the summer of 1977, the evidence that Jones was, at best, a sleazy huckster, and at worse a dangerous demagogue, was substantial. Nonetheless, out of either political loyalty or arrogance, Moscone continued to do defend Jones. Had Moscone lived to run for reelection, that release would very likely have haunted him.

The Craft Strike

On April 9, 1976, three months into Moscone's mayoralty, the Giants opened the season at Candlestick Park. Given how three months earlier it looked like the team had moved to Toronto, this was a great relief to baseball fans in San Francisco. Giants fans had more to be happy about as their team, behind home runs by Bobby Murcer and Gary Matthews and some very strong pitching by John "The Count" Montefusco, beat their archrival Los Angeles Dodgers, 4–2.

Opening Day would have been a great opportunity for Moscone to remind San Franciscans about his role in keeping the Giants in town. The former high school ballplayer would have been a natural to throw out the first pitch. However, it was another politician, former mayor George Christopher, who had that honor. Christopher was instrumental in bringing the Giants to San Francisco, but he had not been in office since January 1964. Moscone was not at the ballpark that day because the pro-union Democratic mayor was not going to cross a picket line. The vendors did not cross the picket line either, so the more than 37,000 fans had to bring their own food.[47]

The picket line was part of a strike by the city's craft workers that consumed Moscone's first few months in office. Moscone had been labor's candidate, but as mayor he could not simply side with labor as he might have in the state senate or board of supervisors. The police and fire strike and Mayor Alioto's almost complete capitulation to the demands of those unions had turned many San Franciscans against organized labor. Additionally, the board of supervisors had several strong anti-labor voices, including Barbagelata and board president Kopp.

Anti-labor forces took advantage of the mood by putting an initiative on the 1975 ballot, Proposition B, that weakened the bargaining position of craft workers. Craft workers included a broad range of city workers, including street sweepers, mechanics, carpenters, and others who worked for the city. The initiative passed easily, thus setting the stage for the board of supervisors to renegotiate the contracts with craft workers. As Jerry Roberts wrote in the *Bay Guardian*: "On March 29, the supervisors gave final approval to the salary ordinance for the coming year which cut take-home pay for some crafts workers as much as $5,000 annually."[48]

Naturally, the unions did not like this, calling for more negotiations and raising the possibility of the strike. By March 30, a strike had begun. The key sticking points were both the wage cuts but also the supervisors' insistence that the unions agree to a no-strike clause. This was an extreme position from the legislature of a city that had long been recognized as one of the most pro-labor in the country. This and the salary cut reflected the position of Barbagelata, Kopp, Feinstein, and other supervisors who were unsympathetic to labor, but not that of Moscone, who did not have the power to unilaterally renegotiate the contract.

While there were substantive points of disagreement between labor and the city, the stakes were bigger. As one electrician said in the early days of the strike, "They're trying to wreck all the unions. The handwriting is on the wall if the businessmen and the city win, this in a labor town like San Francisco."[49] San Francisco's progressive reputation was rooted in the general strike of 1934. Now its elected legislature was trying not just to cut union wages, but to take away their right to strike. This occurred as labor's strength nationally was waning. At the middle of this was a progressive, pro-labor mayor who had few options. This is probably not how Moscone had hoped to spend the first months as mayor, but that is the nature of the job.

The strike lasted thirty-nine days, during which everything from bus and cable car service to cleaning city-run spaces such as the airport and the zoo was interrupted. On May 8, the strike was settled. Workers returned to their jobs immediately. The city agreed to remove two anti-labor initiatives from the June ballot and to set up a committee to study wage increases. Moscone had found himself caught between a conservative board of supervisors and the unions that had supported him, but he could not resolve the strike without support from the board.

The compromise was not bad, but the strike had hurt the city. Streets had not been cleaned, city services were poorly delivered and, in general, the idea that San Francisco was in bad shape and perhaps ungovernable was gaining strength. This occurred during Moscone's first few weeks in office and, regardless of whose fault it was, the city's chief executive was inevitably viewed as partially responsible.

Police and Thieves

During the middle of the 1970s, crime was the most important issue facing urban America, including San Francisco. It is not entirely possible to understand urban crime in the 1970s without considering the collapse of manufacturing and shipping-based economies, and the concomitant loss of jobs in many cities. Crime has also long been deeply entwined with race. The perceptions of urban America as dangerous places where African American and Latino criminals terrorize law-abiding white citizens is still a central conservative narrative. This narrative was more potent in the 1970s than today because there was more crime and because the demographics of cities were more in flux.

From roughly 1965 through 1980, the white population of many cities, including San Francisco, dropped dramatically relative to the African American and Latino population, but there were still significant working-class white populations in western San Francisco, south Brooklyn, the north side of Chicago, and other urban neighborhoods. Racial tensions and fear of African Americans committing crimes were more intense in these communities than a decade or so later when the number of white working-class urban dwellers had further declined.

A brief look at some of the data helps form a picture of crime in urban American in 1975 compared to a few decades later. There were 655.4 violent crimes for every 100,000 people in California in 1975. That number remained over 600 for every year from 1974 to 2001, peaking in the early 1990s. By 2019, that number had fallen to 441.2 and has been under 500 every year since 2009. In 1975, the murder rate for the state was 10.4 for every 100,000 Californians. That number remained above 10 through 1995. By 2019, there were only 4.3 murders per 100,000 people. That number had been below 6 since 2008.[50] These numbers cover the entire state, but crime was largely understood to be a problem of cities.

In San Francisco, there were 132 homicides in 1975, an uptick from the 130 of the previous year. It would remain over 100 through 1982.[51] The contrast between those years and more recent years is striking. In 2019 and 2018, the number of San Francisco homicides was 41 and 46, respectively.[52] Those numbers increased to 47 in 2020 and 55 in 2021, 2022 and 2023. There have been fewer than 80 homicides in San Francisco in every year since 2008 and fewer than 100 in all but one year this century.[53] Statistics for other violent crimes across these years are similar. Raw numbers understate how much more dangerous San Francisco was in the 1970s because the population of the city was about two-thirds of what it is now.

Because of crime was such a major issue, Moscone's choice of police chief was extremely important. Police Chief Donald Scott was retiring, so Moscone did not have the option of keeping the incumbent. Moscone's first choice appeared to be Al Nelder. Nelder had been a police officer for decades and served as the chief of police from 1970 to 1971 before being elected to the board of supervisors in 1973. Nelder was well thought of by most San Franciscans and respected by most of the police force. He was not a radical or even a reformer, so his appointment would have signaled Moscone was not the dangerous leftist many feared. Moscone had an additional reason for wanting to appoint Nelder. The appointment would have left a vacancy on the board of supervisors, giving Moscone the opportunity to put a progressive ally on the city's legislature. However, by the time Nelder was elected to the board, he was receiving an annual pension of $33,000 from the City of San Francisco. According to the city charter, Nelder would have had to give up the pension to take a full-time job as police chief. Nelder made it clear that he was "not about to do that," so Moscone had to look elsewhere.[54]

Moscone quickly turned his attention to Charles Gain, the city's undersheriff who had previously been the chief of the Oakland Police Department. Gain had served on presidential and other commissions on crime, civil disorder, and criminal justice. Gain began his career as a police officer in 1947 but became the first police chief in the San Francisco's history who had not served in the SFPD. The *San Francisco Examiner* noted that this led to some "grumbling" within the department. "'Why didn't they pick someone from within the department, someone who knows the territory?' was the typical comment." That article also noted that "liberal policeman—such as those associated with Officers for Justice (the organization of African American police officers) were pleased with the appointment of a man with a liberal reputation."[55]

Gain faced several major challenges. Rising crime and associated fear were only the beginning. The aftermath of the police strike damaged both morale among the police force and police-community relations. Additionally, there was increasing pressure from civil rights groups for the police force to do much more to diversify their hiring practices. Lastly, questions of police violence, particularly toward the city's non-white and gay populations, were major concerns. Given all this, it is easy to understand the seventy-year-old Nelder's decision to keep his pension and remain on the board of supervisors rather than take over the SFPD.

Moscone's appointment of Gain turned out to be one of the most decisive of his career and indeed his life. It was a bold but understandable move. A lifetime San Franciscan and experienced politician such as Moscone would have known that in conservative San Francisco the rank-and-file white police officers, represented by the Police Officers Association (POA), would not be happy with his choice, but by appointing Gain, Moscone reinforced his progressive base, as well as the city's divisions.

Gain was a reformer and activist police chief. Gain focused on fighting crime, but also on issues of equality, diversity, and civil rights. Richard DeLeon, a scholar of San Francisco politics and history, explained the political challenge that Gain faced: "He (Moscone) appointed a new police chief. This is a pretty big deal early in Moscone's tenure. Charles Gain was brought over from Oakland to deal with long-standing problems—the increasing amount of gay bashing and harassing of gay bars (and) racially discriminatory hiring policies within the department. Essentially to change that whole internal culture of the police department against great internal resistance from police."[56]

The battle over integrating the police force had been going on for several years before Moscone became mayor and appointed Gain. A lawsuit filed in 1973 by the Officers for Justice sought federal support for integrating the police force. The suit was decided by the time of Gain's appointment, but the issue was not going away. Lois Salisbury, one of the attorneys in that suit, explained: "The Officers for Justice and public advocates together decided to bring a federal district court action enforcing the Civil Rights Act of 1964 as well as constitutional rights in the Fourteenth Amendment against the San Francisco Police Department . . . on behalf of all people of color as well as women. . . . The case from the beginning raised not only issues of entry-level discrimination from the bottom to the top of the San Francisco Police Department, because while there were very few officers of color, there were even fewer people in the line of command of color, and there were no women."[57]

San Francisco's police force, like many, was still dominated by Irish Americans and Italian Americans, and it was overwhelmingly white. Wallace Turner, writing in *The New York Times,* noted: "In 1968, the department had three black inspectors, one black sergeant and 73 black patrolmen out of 1,755 sworn officers. It had nine women officers."[58] Not much changed in the following eight years. The force Gain led was still overwhelmingly white, conservative, and supportive of law and order, with all the racial connotations of that phrase.

According to Duffy Jennings, a journalist who grew up in San Francisco and covered local news in the 1970s, "the San Francisco Police and Fire Department culture at that time (were) very close-knit, very tight organizations of third- and fourth-generation San Franciscans. It was very clear that outsiders weren't welcome."[59] Another journalist, Barbara Taylor, was more direct: "When George Moscone became mayor, the police department was truly in the old sense of the word, a good old boy network. It was made up of Irish cops, Italian cops, not very many Black cops, not very many women cops."[60]

The lawsuit by the Officers for Justice was pending when Moscone became mayor, but Moscone and Gain wanted to integrate the force and make some changes, The single change older San Franciscans might remember best is that shortly after Gain took over, police cars were changed from an intimidating black-and-white to a friendlier and softer light blue and white. That experiment did not last long as the police returned to using black-and-white cars early in Dianne Feinstein's tenure as mayor. DeLeon fleshed out the impact of this decision: "(Gain) ordered that all the police cars should be painted baby blue, which really was a touchy point with a lot of the police."[61]

Jim Molinari, who was on Moscone's security detail, explained how the rank and file on the force viewed Gain: "Gain comes into office and, of course, (there's) a lot of friction because he's from Oakland for God's sakes, our rival across the bay. How could this ever be? . . . The first thing he does is take the flags out of the chief's office. And then he decides he's gonna paint the cars blue and white instead of black and white. And all of us are thinking, 'What are we doing here?'"[62]

The tension between Gain and Moscone on one side and the POA and its conservative supporters on the other never went away while Moscone was mayor. Given that Moscone was seeking to fundamentally change policing and police attitudes in San Francisco, this was unavoidable. Longtime activist Cleve Jones, who was close with Milk and active in the Castro, described how policing changed when Moscone became mayor: "The cops were the enemy. They were out there to entrap us (gay people), to arrest us, to beat us up. . . . That (treatment by police) was to me the most notable change."[63] While Jones and many others viewed this positively, many police resented civilian authorities reining them in.

Moscone wanted to reform policing in San Francisco while remaining focused on reducing crime. This gave the police some leverage because they could, and frequently did, claim that various reforms would lead to increases in crime, so Moscone's efforts to reduce crime had to be very visible. Statements such as this one from Moscone in late 1976 could have come from any tough-on-crime mayor in America and seemed divorced from Moscone's progressive image and agenda:

> Like so many other problems we face in our city, crime will not be lessened until the people stop looking merely to government for the answers and start working with their leaders and their police in a partnership to prevent crime and to bring criminals to swift apprehension and punishment. We are all familiar with the stories of New York and how people were robbed, beaten and sometimes killed in front of witnesses who were unwilling to "get involved" by calling the police or providing information to the police. We cannot allow that syndrome to happen in San Francisco and we must encourage every resident to our City to join in our efforts to reverse the alarming trend of increased crime."[64]

It was a bit nonsensical for Moscone to urge San Franciscans not to depend on government while simultaneously stressing the importance of working with police who are very much part of the government. The tough-on-crime sentiment of "swift apprehension and punishment" was standard rhetoric. The allusion to New York was expected at a time when New York was a symbol of urban decay, fiscal mismanagement, crime, and chaos—even in cities such as San Francisco that were, by some measures, worse off than New York.

Despite task forces, changes in police tactics, speeches imploring citizens to cooperate more with law enforcement, and other measures, Moscone was unable to reduce crime, so it remained his top priority. A month after those remarks, the mayor announced an increase to the number of police officers on Muni lines and street patrols, senior citizen escort services, better street lighting, and similar measures.[65] A few months later, he bolstered these efforts with more federal money, but crime did not significantly decline.

Moscone's relationship with policing was never simple. The police did not like him or his police chief, but Moscone occasionally took very tough-on-crime actions that empowered police. For example, on November 2, 1977, he executed a massive police raid, because, in part, of the refusal of property owners to pay their taxes, on the block of Haight Street between Steiner and Fillmore in the Western Addition, reputed to have more heroin dealers than any other block in the country. The police "flushed everyone, including children, out of the buildings onto the sidewalks." This was an extremely invasive approach to fighting crime, but forty-seven drug dealers were arrested. Moscone demonstrated a willingness to act against crime. Some claim that this "resulted in this neighborhood's eventual recovery."[66]

As long as the crime rate remained high, Moscone was politically vulnerable. Because race and crime are intertwined in the minds of so many white voters, mayors who are either non-white or whose political base is African American struggle for needed white votes when crime is high. Crime almost certainly cost David Dinkins a second term in 1993 when he was running against Rudy Giuliani in New York City. Dinkins had begun to turn around the decades-long rise in crime in New York midway through his term, but he was unable to communicate that to skeptical white voters who embraced Giuliani's pro-police racial backlash message.

The sentiment toward Dinkins from conservative white New York regarding crime was summed up in a September 7, 1990, headline in the *New York Post*, a right-wing tabloid. The headline in medium letters read, "Crime-ravaged city cries out for help," and in massive letters, "Dave, Do Something." The front page featured lines like "It's time to take off the white gloves," "We are captives in our own homes," and "New York's streets are awash in blood." Dinkins did something, securing state funding to increase the number of police, contributing to a drop in the crime rate, but that was not enough for the *Post* and its readers.

Thirty years later, in the middle of a summer in which New York was experiencing both a pandemic and numerous demonstrations around the resurgent Black Lives Matter movement, the *Post* ran a similar headline targeting another progressive mayor, Bill de Blasio, whose signature campaign issue had been putting an end to the racist "stop and frisk" policy. The headline again said, "Crime-ravaged city cries out for help," but this time the larger print pled, "Bill, Do Something." The article conceded that "(t)oday's crime numbers are nothing like as bad as back on Sept. 7, 1990."[67]

In San Francisco in the late 1970s, the persistence of crime buoyed backlash politics, giving politicians such as John Barbagelata and Quentin Kopp reason to believe Moscone could be defeated. The crime rate meant that Moscone was never entirely secure in his position and that his reelection campaign was going to be a difficult challenge.

Yerba Buena

In 1984, Dianne Feinstein was at the height of her popularity in San Francisco. She had easily won election to a second full term as mayor against no real opposition one year earlier. Feinstein had played an instrumental role in bringing the Democratic National Convention to San Francisco that year. She so impressed Democratic leaders that after presidential nominee Walter Mondale pledged that he would nominate a woman as his running mate, Feinstein landed on his short list. Mondale ultimately chose Geraldine Ferraro, a congresswoman from Queens, New York, instead of Feinstein, but in 1984 Ronald Reagan was cruising to reelection regardless of who Mondale's running mate was.

After choosing San Francisco for their convention, the Democrats naturally convened in the city's newest and best convention center, located in the South of Market District that was beginning a revival that would make it the hub for some of the biggest tech companies in the world in the twenty-first century. Most of the delegates and others attending the convention knew who George Moscone was and why the new convention center was named after him. Construction on what became the Moscone Center began during his time as mayor when it was known as the Yerba Buena Center. The politics around the effort to build that convention center show how Moscone changed governance in San Francisco and the difficulties he confronted balancing competing interests, satisfying his neighborhood activist base, and ensuring budget stability.

At the groundbreaking ceremony for the Yerba Buena Center in August 1978, Moscone declared that the construction of the convention center was

> one of the most important events in the history of the city . . . more than just a shot in the arm for our most important local industry, or the creation of 3,000 jobs. This groundbreaking represents the vindication of the democratic process in San Francisco—and the fact that we have finally arrived at this momentous day is a tribute to the people of our City. . . . For years this important project was delayed by lawsuits, charges of bad faith and the belief that the Yerba Buena was a reality that would never come to pass. . . . The fact that we are commending this groundbreaking today represents one of the greatest—if not the greatest—achievements of this administration to date.[68]

The idea for the Yerba Buena Convention Center originated long before that August 1978 ceremony, beginning about the time Moscone and Willie Brown were sweeping floors at Hastings. According to Richard DeLeon, "the Yerba Buena project was conceived in 1954 by Ben Swig. . . . The original plans called for a convention center, sports stadium, high-rise office building and large parking garage to be constructed in the South of Market area."[69] Swig, who made most of his money in real estate, was a well-known philanthropist and civic leader and very much part of the downtown business leadership.

Swig hoped to locate the Yerba Buena Convention Center in a few square blocks just south of Market Street in a neighborhood called, rather uncreatively, South of Market. It would later, in an odd Huxleyan twist, become known as SOMA. Earlier in the twentieth century, locals had referred to the area as "south of the slot." Market Street is one of the biggest streets in San Francisco, running diagonally from the hills in roughly the center of the city to the bay in the east.

The South of Market district is just south of the Financial District, so it was a reasonable location for a major convention center. However, in the 1950s the area was a residential community of mostly older, single men who were either retired or working in the shipping sector. They lived largely in single resident occupancy (SRO) hotels or similarly modest rental dwellings. Construction of a convention center in that area threatened to displace thousands of those residents.

In addition to displacing these low-income residents, the Yerba Buena Center that Swig envisioned would have accelerated a transformation of San Francisco that, even by the mid-1950s, was already being met with opposition. The Yerba Buena Center would have been a major step in San Francisco's pivot to an economy driven largely by business, finance, and tourism rather than shipping and manufacturing—the engine of San Francisco's economy for the first half of the twentieth century. These competing visions, reframed as the Freeway Revolts, the fights over redevelopment, downtown against the neighborhoods, or the Manhattanization of San Francisco, have long been central to the city's politics. The debates around housing, real estate speculation, gentrification, and affordability in twenty-first century San Francisco are the political descendants of those disputes.

Looking at San Francisco's skyline today, it may be difficult to believe how intense, and enduring the fights over Manhattanization were, but these were also fights about the nature or purpose of San Francisco, pitting those who wanted the city to become a center of finance and business against those who saw it as a city of neighborhoods, diversity, and working-class people. It was a major issue in most competitive mayoral elections in the 1970s and 1980s, and various ballot initiatives were proposed that sought to limit development of office space or limit that kind of development to only a few areas of the city.

The 1950s were a period in San Francisco of both great affluence and the early rumblings of demographic and economic changes. While the Yerba Buena Center, as it was initially planned, may have been a symbol of changes many San Franciscans feared and wanted to avoid, these kinds of projects did not cause those changes. Manufacturing and shipping jobs departed the cities because of globalization and new technology, not because of new convention centers.

Although opponents of the freeways could rightly claim that if the freeway plans were implemented the city would be dramatically changed for the worse for many residents, the impact of a convention center, even a big one like the Yerba Buena Center, would not be as clear. This issue of displacing low-income residents in the area was real and remained a concern over the next decades but believing that a major convention center would reduce manufacturing jobs was misreading the causality. A more accurate understanding of the city's economy would be that because manufacturing and shipping jobs had been declining for years, a convention center could offset that by stimulating tourism and bringing conventions to San Francisco.

The Yerba Buena Center became part of the debate around redevelopment, so no progress was made on it during the decade and a half after Swig's initial proposal. When Alioto became mayor, there was again some movement around the Yerba Buena Center. In his first weeks in office, Alioto requested funding from the Johnson administration for both the Yerba Buena Center and the redevelopment of the Western Addition. He also secured support from organized labor, particularly the building trades. Labor had supported Alioto's campaign but had been hesitant regarding the Yerba Buena Center. Thus, as the 1960s were coming to an end, support from the mayor, the building trades union, and most of the tourism and business community meant the Yerba Buena Center was likely to be built, but there were still people living there who did not want to lose their homes.[70]

Chester Hartman highlighted the contempt with which the planners viewed the residents of the area: "Planners treated the fate of these people to be a minor matter. The area was referred to by the planners, newspapers and City officials as 'skid row,' and the people who lived there were 'bums,' 'drifters,' and 'transients.' Official agencies and the business community played on class prejudices, particularly of suburban commuters."[71] Hartman explained that "residents of South of Market were for the most part single, elderly, male and poor, surviving on the meager proceeds of Social Security and small pensions. . . . Some were alcoholics. Most, however, were retired or disabled working men who had settled in the South of Market to spend the remaining days of their lives."[72]

The neighborhood may have seemed like skid row to outsiders, but many people had lived in the community for decades and did not want to leave. "Standing in the way of the project were some 3000 residential hotel occupants and over 300 families. In 1969, several hundred project-area residents formed Tenants and Owners in Opposition to Redevelopment (TOOR) in order to resist relocation efforts. During their struggle against the Yerba Buena Center redevelopment project, the members of TOOR expressed their identities as workers and unionists, Democrats and citizens, and as members of an established community."[73]

The debate over the Yerba Buena Center pitted the business, labor, and powerful politicians against people in one low-income neighborhood, but there was another side to the question. By the late 1960s the downtown interests had a point. The city was changing and needed a modern convention center to revitalize, diversify, and expand the downtown business core. A San Francisco whose economy was driven by manufacturing and shipping was already by 1967 a thing of the past. Believing it was going to return was to ignore trends and developments that were much bigger than Joe Alioto or the San Francisco Redevelopment Agency.

Additionally, the area where the Yerba Buena Center was to be located was a residential neighborhood, but it was also right next to downtown. It was not as if anybody was proposing a convention center in the heart of the Mission or the Richmond District. The conflict between the residents who wanted to continue living in the South of Market area and the need for the downtown section to expand physically and economically was precisely the kind of dilemma that, when viewed fairly, makes governing big cities so difficult.

This was still a problem when Moscone became mayor in 1976. Most of Moscone's base would have supported the organizers and activists fighting to preserve the South of Market neighborhood, but it was evident to Moscone that while the initial proposal was too big, there was a need for a new convention center. With the right approach a compromise could be reached. In March 1976 Moscone created the Mayor's Select Committee on Yerba Buena Center. The seventeen-member committee was diverse and included Dianne Feinstein, Gordon Lau, who was president of city planning commission, Jack Morrison, John Jacobs from the pro-development group SPUR, and Eugene Coleman from the Canon Kip Community House located South of Market.[74] The committee sought public input, making the draft plan available to interested San Franciscans. The committee proposed a more modest version of the Yerba Buena Center that included a convention center, but no restaurants or hotels, and some vague language about low-income housing. They proposed financing it through a 4 percent hotel tax. Moscone had succeeding in bringing different groups together around a seemingly workable compromise. However, even the committee Moscone had created was not unanimous. Several members, including Coleman, remained opposed to the Yerba Buena Center, while some in the business community were not happy about the scaled-back vision for the facility or the hotel tax.

The recommendations from the Mayor's Select Committee were not implemented immediately. Instead, they were presented, in simplified form, to the voters on the November 1976 ballot. Proposition S asked, "Shall the City construct a convention exhibit hall at Yerba Buena Center using a 4% hotel room tax to finance lease revenue bonds, underground if financially feasible, otherwise above ground." Moscone and much of the political establishment, including Feinstein and a total of ten members of the board of supervisors, supported Proposition S. The only supervisor opposing it was John Barbagelata, still bitter about losing to Moscone. Leo McCarthy, John Burton, Art Agnos, and numerous business and labor groups supported Proposition S in what was an unusual political alliance between downtown and some progressives. However, other progressives including neighborhood groups and neighborhood activists such as Calvin Welch, Sue Hestor, Carol Ruth Silver, Harvey Milk, and Chester Hartman continued to oppose it.[75]

Proposition S passed easily, but the Yerba Buena Center still faced obstacles and legal challenges. The Yerba Buena Center remained a top priority through the remainder of Moscone's term. As late as November 16, 1978, Moscone drafted a letter to the *Chronicle* defending the need for the above-ground section of the convention center: "The City's people, as well as its visitors, would be best served if that important site were devoted to a vibrant recreational-cultural facility combined with a significant commitment to open space. Such development would have to be economically attractive to private entrepreneurs, provide substantial return to our local tax base and provide major employment opportunities in order to maintain my support."[76] That letter was never published because of events in the days following November 16.

Moscone's unpublished letter shows how the Yerba Buena Center, albeit in a scaled- down version but still the brainchild of the business leadership, was a top priority. Some of the sentiments in that letter could have been written by Alioto, Feinstein, or any other pro-business politician. Moscone had ameliorated some of the initial problems associated with the proposal, but it was still anathema to many community organizers. This was the dilemma Moscone faced as he tried to satisfy both his progressive base while addressing the bigger picture economic challenges facing the city. However, it took somebody with Moscone's political skills and background to make the deal. A pro-business mayor would not have been able to diffuse the resistance to the proposal as Moscone did. Moscone did this not just through politics but by making the project smaller and less destructive to the community.

Corey Busch explained why this was one of Moscone's most important accomplishments: "He (Moscone) saw the Convention Center as a win-win for him. . . . The conventional wisdom downtown was that the Convention Center is dead if Moscone's mayor. It was an opportunity for him to show that wasn't true, and it was an opportunity for the activists and the neighborhoods to bring them into the fold."[77]

By the time Mondale accepted the Democratic nomination for president at a convention more remembered for New York governor Mario Cuomo's extraordinary keynote speech than for anything Mondale said, the Moscone Center was three years old and one of the top convention facilities in the US.[78] When it opened in 1981, Feinstein was mayor but there was broad agreement around naming it after the mayor who had the unique political skills to make the project a reality.

The Moscone Center has now been in use for more than forty years and, while still one of the city's most important convention spaces, is no longer a modern or state-of-the-art facility. However, it has been central to the revitalization of SOMA. During the twenty-first-century tech boom, that area became a hub for the tech business, new housing, and other related businesses. Given the complexity of San Francisco housing politics, it remains an area where there are many unhoused people and has become one of the battlegrounds between advocates of affordable housing against those who support the market dictating the kinds of housing to be built.

On balance, the Yerba Buena Center was a major triumph for Moscone, but the International Hotel conflict was more difficult to resolve. The demonstrations and support for the tenants of the I-Hotel, as many knew it, continued into the 1970s. In addition to Asian American organizations and left-wing groups, the demonstrators included prominent clergy who were Moscone supporters such as Cecil Williams and Jim Jones. Moscone proposed using the city's eminent domain powers to create a nonprofit organization (NGO) that would run the I-Hotel, but the courts rejected that and supported the eviction order. Richard Hongisto, the city's progressive sheriff, refused to implement the order and spent five days in jail. The hard-fought battles that followed included physical fights between demonstrators and the deputy sheriffs. Moscone could not stop the eviction of the tenants in August 1977. Once again, Moscone's progressive goals ran up against the mayor's limited power.

While the struggles to build the Yerba Buena Center and resolve the crisis at the International Hotel were major challenges for Mayor Moscone, his time in office was also punctuated by several strange only-in-San Francisco moments. Tourism has long been an important part of the city's economy. This was one of the reasons why Moscone supported the Yerba Buena Center. In 1977, Moscone had the opportunity to meet one of the oddest tourists ever to visit San Francisco. Erwin Kreuz was a middle-aged German man who lived in Bavaria and worked at a brewery. Perhaps the most unusual thing about Kreuz was how much he enjoyed the product he made. He claimed he frequently drank up to seventeen beers a day.

That may explain the miscommunication that led Kreuz to get off his plane from Germany during a layover in Bangor, Maine, and to spend a few days wandering around that very un-San Francisco town before recognizing his mistake. Kreuz, whose story drew some attention, finally made it to San Francisco, did the usual San Francisco tourist things, and saw the usual sights. Unlike most tourists, Kreuz was a media sensation. The *Examiner* paid for his trip from Maine. Moscone met with Kreuz and was a little gobsmacked when the German tourist revealed his heavy drinking ways, but managed to reply, "Well, that beats me."[79]

The House

Unlike a handful of cities such as New York and Los Angeles, San Francisco has no official residence for the mayor. Additionally, Moscone was not wealthy when he became mayor, but he had a big family. Although he had continued to practice law during his political career, Moscone had never made much money in that pursuit and did not come from a wealthy family or have a wealthy spouse.

Moscone had briefly affiliated with a law firm for a few months from late

1976 through early 1977 despite being mayor. This was not illegal but was a rather obvious conflict of interest—which is why he had to leave the firm. W. E. Barnes wrote in the *Examiner* in early 1977: "Since November of last year, the Mayor supplemented his tops-in-The-City $53,106 a year municipal income through a salaried association with the firm of Dobbs, Doyle and Nelson. Sources close to Moscone estimate his income there at about $24,000 a year . . . The mayor's press office explained he had left the firm to avoid any hint or appearance of conflict."[80]

When he took office, Moscone and his family were living at 90 Lansdale Avenue in the western part of San Francisco. The home was close to St. Francis Wood, one of the city's most affluent neighborhoods, but it was really part of the more middle-class Mt. Davidson neighborhood. Mt. Davidson was a pleasant neighborhood in the 1970s—the kind of neighborhood where a Catholic family with four children, particularly if they were Irish or Italian, would have fit in very easily. Mt. Davidson and neighboring West Portal were very much old San Francisco. These neighborhoods were still largely white, substantially working-class, and reasonably conservative. Very few hippies or gay people were running around the neighborhood, other than a few teenage sons or daughters of some of the residents. The precinct that included Moscone's home, 8580 in the Eighteenth District of the California State Assembly, had voted 253–63 for Barbagelata in the runoff.

Moscone, the progressive politician who crafted a historic progressive coalition to get elected mayor, chose to live in a conservative part of town away from the neighborhoods that sent him to City Hall. Even Moscone's old Cow Hollow neighborhood was more diverse and liberal than Mt. Davidson. Moscone and Gina felt comfortable in the Mt. Davidson area, but it was nonetheless a strange choice. However, it worked for someone such as Moscone, who was a product of both old and new San Francisco. It is very difficult to imagine Art Agnos, Harvey Milk, Carol Ruth Silver, or thousands of other progressive migrants to 1970s San Francisco smoothly fitting into that neighborhood, but Moscone could. On the other hand, it was the kind of neighborhood where if Willie Brown stopped by to visit and parked two blocks away, he would have drawn stares, or worse, from many residents. Living in a modest and affordable middle-class neighborhood, even one where the voters supported his opponent with a huge majority, helped Moscone present himself as a man of the people, who valued service more than making money and as somebody who had not grown corrupt during his years in elected office. That would change within a few months of Moscone becoming mayor.

San Francisco's City Hall is large, ornate, and beautiful with ample room for official functions, receptions, and meetings. Accordingly, there is no expectation that the mayor's home be a place for semiofficial events and receptions. This is different than, for example, New York, where Gracie Mansion is used for those purposes as well. Nonetheless, Moscone moved to a larger home in a more upscale neighborhood. Politically, this decision could only hurt him. Perhaps Moscone's sense of what he felt he deserved or even what Gina wanted led the family to move to a bigger house at 45 St. Francis Boulevard in St. Francis Wood.

St. Francis Wood is very close to Mt. Davidson, so the family did not move far. St. Francis Wood has long felt like a wealthy suburb in the middle of San Francisco, featuring big homes and almost no commercial activity—the kind of place that is described as a good place to raise kids but with a subtext that implies distance from the diversity, complexity, and problems of the big city. This was an odd place for Moscone to choose to move. There are other affluent neighborhoods in San Francisco that are less removed from the city itself. Pacific Heights is not far from the Fillmore and the Western Addition. Russian Hill is also home to many wealthy San Franciscans and a stone's throw from Chinatown and North Beach. St. Francis Wood offered none of that, but to a certain segment of Catholic San Francisco, there was a lot of status associated with that community. Corey Busch, who was not a product of Catholic San Francisco, suggested the house in St. Francis Wood "meant something. It showed a different kind of accomplishment."[81]

Chris Moscone expressed a similar view regarding the Moscone family's choice of neighborhoods. Referring to the cost of the house, he called it a "big overreach in St. Francis Wood. I think he (Moscone) thought, 'Wow I made it,' or something. . . . A lot of it too was. 'Hey, check me out.' . . . He was very prideful." Jonathan Moscone told me a story about how all four of the Moscone children got to choose their bedrooms in their new home, which he described as "like a palace. It was huge . . . It was wonderful." Jonathan made the mistake of choosing the first room he saw while his older brother, Christopher, whom Jonathan suspected had scoped out the new place earlier, got the best room—the one with the fireplace. Jonathan explained the choice of neighborhoods. "We weren't a Pacific Heights family. We weren't a Jordan Park family. . . . He (Moscone) was the liberal mayor of San Francisco. He wasn't going to live in Pacific Heights. That wasn't even an option. I don't even know if we could have afforded it." Moscone's younger son then reflected on how the house must have felt to his father: "It was the opposite of what he grew up with."[82]

The Moscone couple's decision to send their girls to the Convent of the Sacred Heart, an extremely affluent-feeling Catholic School in the heart of Pacific Heights, suggests that Jonathan Moscone's observation about his family not being "a Pacific Heights family" is not that simple. It also suggests that Moscone had a different vision for his sons than his daughters. St. Ignatius was an elite school by any measure, but it was in the Sunset District and drew families from all over the city. The Convent of the Sacred Heart was much more embedded in Pacific Heights both geographically and culturally. That was something that was okay for the daughters, but not the sons, in the Moscone family.

Moscone's decision to move to a larger house in St. Francis Wood reflected his desire to feel like, and show others that, he had made it, but also, the complexity of his role in his family. By all accounts Moscone's philandering did not stop when he became mayor, but because he no longer needed to spend time in Sacramento, he was able to be home every night and spend time with his family. Jonathan Moscone explained, "He (Moscone) was home more on weekends than during the week when he was in the senate. . . . I didn't grow up with him consistently. It became consistent when I was about twelve (around the time Moscone became mayor)." Jonathan described the contrast with when his father was in the senate. "He was not so much a visitor, but he was a special guest star."[83] Chris Moscone had a similar perspective on his father's frequent absence. "My dad was away so much throughout all of his kids' lives. . . . I think that really ate away at him," and he emphasized that Moscone "didn't raise us on a regular basis. . . . He didn't raise us. My mother did."[84]

Chris described how his father, despite not being around much, connected with him. By the time Moscone was mayor, Chris, like his father before him was playing basketball for St. Ignatius. Every one of Chris's games appears on the mayor's schedule. When I asked Chris about this, he told me that his father attended most of his games. "He went to almost every one of my games, even when I was in grammar school too . . . Overwhelming amount of them." According to Chris, Moscone "would always be somewhere inconspicuous. I'd look for him. Maybe it was for a quarter. . . . He'd be usually by himself. He'd be sitting up if there was a second deck of stands, or somewhere in the corner. Not front or center. I never heard him yell or anything." Chris told of how Moscone would analyze the games with him afterward. "That was serious stuff between me and him. . . . And then he'd write me notes. . . . He was looking and watching. And then he'd give me notes . . . handwritten. . . . They were critical, rebounds, stuff that he saw. That was our connection. That was our connection."[85]

Moscone's relationship with his younger son was more complex. Jonathan's name appears much less frequently than his brother Chris's on Moscone's official mayoral schedules. When it does, it is frequently for school-related events such as Jonathan's interview at St. Ignatius on December 10, 1977.[86] Jonathan's lack of interest in sports may have puzzled his father. "He just assumed that I would be into sports as he was and as my brother was." Jonathan also explained how, relative to the rest of the children, Moscone "kind of got me wrong the most."[87] Moscone's daughters appear on the mayor's schedules about as much as Jonathan does, mostly for occasional lunches and similar get-togethers.

According to his 1977 financial statement, Moscone became the owner of the home in St. Francis Wood on May 26, 1976, two days before he sold the home on Lansdale Avenue. The transaction was made relatively early in Moscone's term.[88] The form did not indicate any other sources of income or liquidation of assets which would help explain how Moscone was able to, as described in the *Bay Guardian* "move into a house about twice as expensive."[89]

When a powerful politician with no discernible outside source of income or wealth moves into a much larger and more expensive home, questions are raised. David Johnston, writing for the *Bay Guardian,* spelled this out in a 1978 story. "How was Moscone able to buy the splashy new place in St. Francis Wood? Why did he use the vehicle of a contract to do it? Does he pay the property taxes or doesn't he? Does he actually own it? And how is he paying for it?"[90]

The contretemps over his new house was not the only appearance of corruption that threatened to politically damage Moscone. Moscone was finding that the web of businesses that needed favors, campaign fundraising, and the next campaign raised ethical challenges that were increasingly difficult to manage. Moscone's large family, lack of any real money, and expensive tastes did not make things any easier. Although it was his house that drew so much attention, Moscone did not project an image of frugality by driving an Alfa Romeo or frequently being seen in expensive haunts around the city.

By late 1978 the FBI was investigating Moscone's connection to Howard Hughes. Hughes was a hugely successful businessman who is now mostly remembered for his bizarre and reclusive behavior in the later years of his life. Hughes died in early 1976, but the event in question occurred in late 1975, after the election. Allegedly, Hughes operatives D. K. Brown and James Wadsworth donated $10,000 to Moscone in late 1975. The check was to Los Angeles- based political consultant Joseph Cerrell, with whom Moscone had a long relationship, and was meant to either retire campaign debt or help him in his reelection campaign.

Critics alleged the donation was a quid pro quo for Moscone supporting the addition of terminal for Hughes's airline at San Francisco International Airport (SFO). The terminal was never built, but the whiff of malfeasance remained. According to the *Guardian*, a newspaper in Los Angeles had reported that "James Wadsworth, an attorney and former Hughes aide, had told federal investigators last November he had 'personally handed the mayor of a major California city a check from (Hughes affiliated) Summa Corporation for $10,000. . . . The money was given in part for what the mayor could do for a proposed expansion of the city's airport."[91]

The *Guardian* expanded their coverage a week later, noting that "James Wadsworth, ex-Howard Hughes lawyer in Las Vegas, has told FBI agents, that the $10,000 check he wrote to Cerrell Associates in Los Angeles for Mayor George Moscone's expansion at San Francisco International Airport was only a down payment, and that the actual amount paid by Hughes interests for Moscone's support was far more—possibly as much as $50,000."[92] The *Guardian* stayed with the story for the following week, as David Johnston reported that deputy mayor Bernard Teitelbaum had not disclosed $8,000 in income in 1975 from Cerrell's consulting firm, making the Moscone-Hughes-Cerrell relationship even more complex and suspect. As of October 1978, Cerrell had not filed his financial disclosure forms for 1976 or 1977.[93] In a sidebar to that column, Johnston described Moscone as "already badly wounded by the revelations unearthed thus far," and he mentioned eight San Franciscans preparing to challenge him in his bid for reelection. Conspicuously absent from that list was Dianne Feinstein.[94]

With reelection looming only about thirteen months away, Moscone's mayoralty appeared to be in crisis. He still had the powers of incumbency, his substantial political skills, and time to address these problems, but three years into his term, concerns were mounting and the road to reelection was looking rocky. Moscone's reelection required strong support from African American voters, but according to the *Sun-Reporter,* his base was not preparing to save him:

> Since SanFran Mayor George Moscone calls on his Black preachers for everything else, he'd better get to calling on them for prayer, 'cause Lord knows with Howard Hughes haunting him from the grave, he's gonna need it. Mayor George had better call on the Lord, his disciples, and anybody else on duty up there to save him from the huge Hughes mess. . . . Word has it that the vultures have already started swarming over City Hall waiting for the big kill. . . . Further word that somebody is Xeroxing copies of the $10,000 Hughes secret contribution receipt. . . . Furthermore, when they started dabbling into Bernie Teitlebaum's (sic) bank account, the vultures got closer in and started homesteading at the fountain in front of City Hall.[95]

CHAPTER TWELVE

The Changing Board of Supervisors

San Francisco did not easily move on from the Moscone-Barbagelata runoff, so Moscone was drawn into political fights that took time and energy away from his ambitious agenda. Three times between November 1975 and August 1977, the Moscone and Barbagelata forces, directly or indirectly, faced off against each other. Those three campaigns, and the tactics that reactionary forces used after losing at the ballot box three straight times, were absolutely essential to the creation of modern San Francisco and its unique political character. The first showdown was the runoff; the second began shortly after Moscone took office.

The 1976 presidential race between President Gerald Ford and Democrat Jimmy Carter was very close, both nationally, with Carter winning, and in California, which Ford carried by fewer than two points. On the US Senate side, Democratic incumbent John Tunney held off Tom Hayden in the primary but lost a very close general election to S. I. Hayakawa. Hayakawa had been president of San Francisco State University during the student uprisings. California conservatives appreciated how tough he was on demonstrators. Moscone naturally supported both Carter and Tunney.

San Francisco saw no hotly contested local races other than for the state senate in which Milton Marks beat back a tough challenge from Supervisor Robert Mendelsohn. However, community activists made one more attempt at adapting district, rather than at-large, elections for the board of supervisors, this time with an ally in City Hall.

Proposition T

San Francisco has changed its structure for electing its board of supervisors three times in the last half century. The city has had district elections since 2000, but even today many San Franciscans who would like a return to at-large elections. In 1976, advocates for district elections put Proposition T on the ballot. It called for creating an eleven-member board, with each member elected from a district with about 61,000 people. The proposal was detailed and included the boundaries for new districts. The map was drawn so that seven of the eleven incumbent board members lived in two of the districts—five in the proposed District Ten alone—while four districts had no supervisors who were residents. The crafters of Proposition T wanted to leave incumbent supervisors without districts in which to run and find districts for themselves to run, but the proposed map also reflected where the citywide office holders lived. Five lived in or close to St. Francis Wood and three in greater Pacific Heights.[1] Five of the proposed new districts were more than half non-white, while a sixth, District Five, was 59 percent white, but had a very large gay population.[2]

Josh Getlin explained the impetus for Proposition T: "There was this great awakening both in individual communities and certainly in communities and neighborhoods, that they wanted their own say, that the issues facing Pacific Heights were completely different from the issues affecting Hunters Point and the Western Addition. That if you lived in North Beach you couldn't possibly have the same day-to-day concerns as somebody living in the Outer Mission.... There was a growing neighborhood awareness and consciousness, a sense that labor and downtown would not continually just run the city, that neighborhoods had to be heard from—gay community representatives, Blacks, Latinos, Asians, what have you. Chinatown deserved more than just a passing nod from elected politicians."[3]

Journalist Barbara Taylor noted that at-large elections meant "there were major parts of town that felt they had no representation because the majority of the supervisors lived in a very small area . . . and while they functioned, I thought, very well on big issues . . . large issues that affected everyone, if you were talking about a rundown playground in the Excelsior, nobody gave a damn. I mean it was that simple, nobody cared."[4]

Understanding those arguments from Getlin and Taylor requires some familiarity with San Francisco. From the outside, particularly from the perspective of a bigger city such as New York, Los Angeles, or Chicago, San Francisco seems small. When Moscone was mayor, only about 700,000 people lived in its forty-seven square miles. However, by the mid-1970s, San Francisco was a very diverse city with sizable African American, Latino, Asian American, LGBT, white working-class and middle-class populations. Additionally, neighborhoods have always been central to how San Franciscans lived. The Fillmore, the Outer Sunset, North Beach, and many others all had their own schools, churches, restaurants, stores, small businesses, parks, and culture. San Francisco's hills and microclimates make neighborhood boundaries even more distinct. Pacific Heights is not far from the Inner Richmond. North Beach is not far from the Marina, but the hills make both those walks much less inviting than similar distances in other cities. Microclimates mean that on most days the weather in the Mission might be ten degrees warmer than in the Sunset. This all reinforces the neighborhood feel, and neighborhood identities, in San Francisco.

Proposition T was the sequel to the 1975 mayoral race. Racial minorities, gays and lesbians, and neighborhood activists who formed the core of Moscone's support were again the center of the yes on Proposition T effort. Many of the politicians who supported Moscone, such as the Burtons and Willie Brown, supported Proposition T. The opposition to Proposition T in favor of retaining the at-large system was only slightly different than the Barbagelata coalition. Barbagelata himself was one of the most outspoken opponents of Proposition T, but fully ten of the eleven sitting supervisors opposed district elections. The exception was Robert Mendelsohn, who was seeking a state senate seat and hoping to leave the board at the end of the year. The business and real estate interests that had initially supported Feinstein and were mostly with Barbagelata in the runoff recognized that district elections would make it very difficult to maintain their influence on the board of supervisors and were the strongest opponents of district elections.

Progressives believed with Moscone in City Hall and by capturing a majority on the board of supervisors, they could finally begin to make real change in San Francisco. That hope was mirrored by fear among conservatives, the business community, and the people who had essentially run San Francisco for decades. In their view, district elections could take away the only check they had on a mayor, Moscone, who posed a genuine threat to the city's power structure. The business leadership opposed district elections with the same fervency that, twenty years earlier, they had supported freeway construction. Both the *Chronicle* and the *Examiner* were part of the city's business community and opposed Proposition T, urging readers to vote down the proposed change to the city's legislature. An unsigned *Chronicle* article on September 25, 1976, gave a platform to two supervisors, Dianne Feinstein and Al Nelder, to raise concerns that Proposition T would take away the recall option from voters. Feinstein's statement was not rebutted as no supporter of the initiative was quoted in the piece: "Passage of Proposition T could mean an end to the right of voters to recall a supervisor . . . Recall belongs in the charter."[5] This was an obscure—and inaccurate—point on which to oppose the district elections, but it allowed Feinstein and Al Nelder to critique Proposition T from a populist angle.

Abe Mellinkoff, who had been writing for the *Chronicle* for four decades, with a break to serve in the military during World War II, attacked Proposition T in his October 25, 1976, column: "Proposition 'T' on this season's San Francisco ballot should get a close look. . . . The democratic argument for the change runs this way: each supervisor would be elected solely by people in *his* district; he would know *their* desires; and they could lean on his supervisor if he didn't do *their* bidding. Instant democracy! . . . If getting people closer to one supervisor is the answer to San Francisco's major problems, I have something even better than 'T.' Let's abolish the board of supervisors entirely and pass our ordinances at massive weekly town meetings of our own."[6]

A few days before the election in the Sunday *Chronicle and Examiner*, Russ Cone, in a roundup of what was on the ballot, attacked Proposition T as reducing the power and status of the supervisors, giving too much power to the mayor, creating a situation where "conveivab(ly) that 50,000 to 60,000 voters could control a majority on the Board of Supervisors" and warned passage of the initiative would lead to gerrymandering and stronger political machines like "the Burtons."[7]

On October 29, the *Chronicle* urged its readers to reject the initiative, summing up their argument in an editorial: "San Francisco has for more than four decades had an admirable record of government by a Board of Supervisors elected at-large. The city is so small, both geographically and in population, that what happens in one area concerns the entire community. The at-large concept means that every citizen has the opportunity to explain his problem to any one of the supervisors. Proposition 'T' would cut the access to one eleventh and that we find unacceptable. Thus *The Chronicle* urges a 'No' vote on Proposition 'T.'"[8]

The October 29 editorial was not the first time the *Chronicle* weighed in against Proposition T. Three weeks earlier, it ran a stronger editorial denouncing Proposition T, calling it "a time-worn wheeze of a proposal that has cropped up before in the political arena and looks no better this time around. . . . The present board, elected from the entire city, has a lively diversity and has served as good reflection of the city's population as well as its neighborhoods. District elections would be much more likely to foster establishment of entrenched neighborhood political barons with the concomitant temptation for 'log-rolling and vote trade-offs to maintain ward prestige and power. . . . Proposition T would infuse city government with the aroma of ward politics. It should be defeated."[9]

The *Examiner's* views on Proposition T were similarly forceful. On October 12, the paper reported Quentin Kopp's dissatisfaction with the proposal, quoting the president of the board of supervisors asserting supporters of Proposition T wanted to "install themselves or those they can control by the establishment of contrived geographic boundaries. . . . District election of supervisors can only further fragment the City, exacerbate political differences and make this an even more disputatious city government."[10]

An *Examiner* editorial the very next day made the paper's views clearer. The editorial repeated Kopp's statement, adding that "Kopp is 100 per cent (sic) correct. Nothing could be worse for San Francisco municipal government than to transform the board of supervisors into a conglomeration of 11 logrolling wardheelers, each intent on building a political machine in his own fiefdom.... If you want to see a brawling, wheeling and dealing utterly politicized board of supervisors operating, or trying to operate, in City Hall, Proposition T shows you how to do it."[11]

A couple of weeks later, another editorial opposing Proposition T appeared in the *Examiner*, focusing on how passage of the initiative would give each voter only one representative rather than eleven: "One supervisor—that's all you get under T. The other ten would have no compelling personal or political reason to listen to you because you couldn't vote for them. You don't live in the right part of town remember."[12]

The opposition from the two major San Francisco papers, both members in good standing of the city's business elite, was the position of the economic and financial powers in the city. The case they made against Proposition T was a little absurd. Reading these editorials and comments by elected officials such as Kopp, one would think that district-based elections were a foreign concept to San Franciscans, but national and state legislatures were district based. It is true that San Francisco is a relatively small city where at-large representation might work, but the shock at the idea of voters only being to choose one of their city legislators seemed a bit extreme.

The activists supporting Proposition T viewed district elections as the linchpin of progressive change in the city. Their work led the creation of the Community Congress, which evolved from a coalition called Citizens for Representative Government, in 1975. Their mission was to be a "vehicle for San Franciscans to achieve their neighborhood and city-wide aims through political action and issue-oriented campaigns."[13]

Jerry Roberts explained:

> One of the issues that Moscone campaigned on was his support for a push by the neighborhood liberal alliance for a system of district elections.... Seven or eight of them (members of the board of supervisors) basically lived in the same neighborhoods, the same wealthy neighborhoods, so you really had a kind of uniformity, a certain kind of center-right wing views by the supervisors.... So shortly after his (Moscone's) election in early 1976, some of the neighborhood people who had been very prominent in his campaign, notably Calvin Welch from the Haight Ashbury, a guy named Arnold Townsend from the Western Addition, Sue Hestor from SF Tomorrow, put together something called the Community Congress.... One of the key things was really to change this at-large system of election of supervisors to a district system.... So, they put together a measure called Proposition T... and to a certain extent it was kind of a rerun of the Moscone-Barbagelata runoff the year before.[14]

The Community Congress began with neighborhood and issue-based meetings leading up to a gathering of about one thousand community activists in June 1975 at Lone Mountain College.[15] The Community Congress believed in progressive solutions to myriad problems facing San Francisco. The introduction to the organization's program explained:

> The communities of San Francisco, collectively and individually, are plagued by a series of day-to-day problems that are virtually endless, ranging from high unemployment to inadequate park and recreation facilities, from high rents and property taxes to the lack of basic human services, from unjust courts and police practices to unresponsive City government. . . . There is only one place we can look for solutions to our problems: to ourselves, and our own ability to work together for our common good. Every poor and working-class community in San Francisco has learned the hard way that its interests are at the bottom of the list as far as City Hall is concerned. At the top of the list are the banks, real estate interests and large corporations. . . . By using their vast financial resources, they have been able to persuade local government officials that office buildings, hotels and luxury apartments are more important than blue collar industry, low-cost housing and decent public services and facilities. . . . The Community Congress, and its program, is only one step in a very crucial struggle—the struggle to make San Francisco a decent place for people to live and work in."[16]

The program included proposals for restructuring city government, the outline of the district election plan that became Proposition T, and positions on issues such as housing and criminal justice.

Support for Proposition T came from the demographic groups and neighborhoods best positioned to benefit from district elections. African Americans in the Fillmore and Bayview/Hunters Point, Latinos in the Mission, gays and lesbians in the Castro, and progressive whites in the center of the city provided most of the support for Proposition T and the Community Congress. Rachel Brahinsky noted that "the district elections fight became a central plank in Western Addition (the Fillmore) politics. By the mid-'70s residents had decided that electoral reform was necessary to bring real change to the SFRA (Redevelopment Agency)."[17]

The voter guide, again sent to all voters before the election, included two statements supporting Proposition T. The more concise argument was "'YES' vote on Proposition 'T' results in Supervisors who must know about and respond to neighborhood problems to stay in office. It means representation for all San Franciscans and makes Supervisors directly accountable to all of us. It has united a broad spectrum of your neighbors who know it will work for the common benefit. Join us."[18] It was signed by several politicians, including Milton Marks, John

Burton, Robert Mendelsohn, and Willie Brown, and numerous progressive organizations and community activists, including Gordon Lau, Harvey Milk, Ella Hutch, and Carol Silver, all of whom would be elected to the board a year later.

There were three statements against Proposition T—one from Supervisor Peter Tamaras, one from a group of business and civic leaders, most of whom were not terribly well known, and one from John Barbagelata. Barbagelata's statement was hard-hitting and sounds almost unhinged. It began, "The real leaders behind this devious proposal are basically the same people who last year took control of voter registration in our City and conducted a partisan and illegal registration drive," and concluded, "It is a naked power grab. If passed, it will destroy the City."[19]

On Election Day, November 2, just short of 253,000 San Franciscans went to the polls. Turnout was driven by the presidential election and dropped off further down the ballot. Only 219,112 voters weighed in on Proposition T, but a slim majority of 52.46 percent supported it. This was a very slightly higher proportion than the 51.1 percent of voters who chose Moscone over Barbagelata in the 1975 runoff. The losers were less than gracious and immediately began working to repeal Proposition T.

In both the 1975 and 1976 elections in San Francisco, the progressive vote, for Moscone and yes on T, came from the southeast quadrant of the city and from the central neighborhoods around the Western Addition, the Fillmore, the Castro, and the Haight. The conservative vote, for Barbagelata and no on T, was strongest in the west and the north. In other words, most voters cast their votes as if Proposition T was a rematch of the mayor's race. As Map 12.1 shows, the winning voting patterns for Proposition T were very similar to those in the mayoral runoff the previous year.

Propositions A and B

Proposition T was a victory for the new San Francisco, but the city was still divided. Proposition T, while not a creation of the Burtons, dovetailed almost completely with their political agenda, so its passage was a victory for the Burtons as well. The activists behind Proposition T were the same kinds of people who generally voted for the Burtons, Willie Brown, and other progressives, including Moscone. However, the Community Congress was a largely organic political movement that was not initiated by the Burtons, Brown, or Moscone. Opponents of Proposition T nonetheless warned of "naked power grabs," illegal voter registration drives, "Chicago"-style ward politics and big-city corruption while framing the initiative as the product of a political machine. The opposition to district elections combined these good government-based messages with angry backlash politics. It was an odd political marriage, but one that almost worked.

This all meant that for the second time in two years the Feinstein and

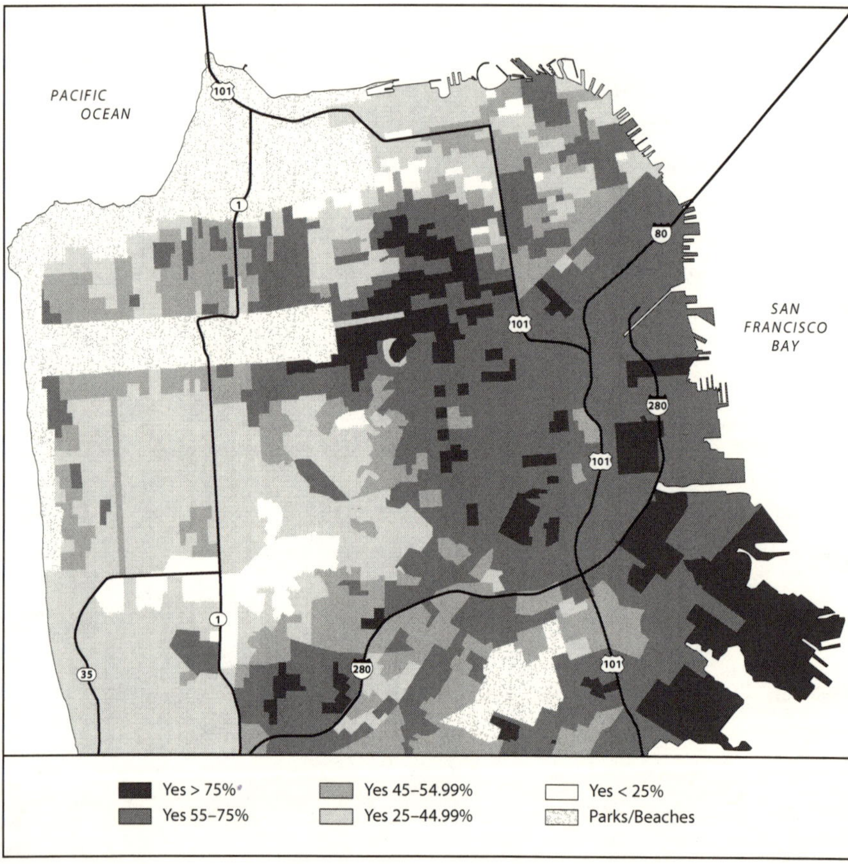

Map 12.1. Results from Proposition T, 1976. Map by Jackson Hasty.

Barbagelata coalitions had lost out to the Burton-Moscone grouping. Both times John Barbagelata was a big part of the reason. The west side realtor's angry, confrontational style, particularly when contrasted to the political skills of Moscone and Willie Brown, pushed voters away. Had Feinstein been the face of that movement, the outcome in 1975 and 1976 might have been different. Because Feinstein served in the US Senate into her nineties, she is often thought of as older and not quite as politically sharp as some of her peers, but Feinstein was for many years a very sharp politician. Although Feinstein was vehemently against Proposition T, she was wise enough not to be the face of the opposition. One reason for that was that she was again drawn to the middle. Another reason was that the district lines in the proposed law worked for her. Feinstein was put in District Two, which included neighborhoods such as Pacific Heights, Cow Hollow, and the Marina in the northern part of the city. That was her political base and as the only incumbent supervisor in the district, she was poised to win easily if the city adapted district elections.

Barbagelata was considerably more visible than Feinstein, but again lost to Moscone in what looked an awful lot like a proxy rematch of the 1975 mayoral runoff. Undaunted, in early 1977, Barbagelata began to organize not one, but two, ballot initiatives aimed at repealing Proposition T. Barbagelata's appetite for combative and divisive politics and enthusiasm for relitigating and refighting the last election elevated political divisions and tensions even higher at an already fraught time. In a city where the transition from a majority white, essentially conservative political community, to a heavily non-white, gay and progressive city, was already contributing to anger, backlash, and hard-fought elections, Barbagelata personally spent several years making things worse.

Barbagelata's approach to the repeal exhibited his instinct for division and conflict. The basis for the repeal was grounded in some vague and patronizing notion that voters didn't really know what they were doing when the approved Proposition T. A November 24 *Chronicle* editorial claimed that "some board members have held that the electorate was unaware what passage of the measure would really mean. . . . it is a benefit of our democracy that what the people have done in one election they can in their wisdom undo in the next."[20] The article quoted two supervisors, Feinstein and Dorothy von Beroldingen, supporting that view. Those remarks, and similar positions by other pro-repeal forces were widely reported in the days following the passage of Proposition T.

A few months later, Channel 7, the local ABC affiliate, joined the chorus clamoring to repeal Proposition T. Before the election, Channel 7 had weighed in against district elections: "The real problem, (with Proposition T) as we now see it, is that control of neighborhoods, or districts, is more and more being taken over by small but active groups who claim to speak for the district, but, in reality, speak only for their own, sometimes far-out, followers. The majority of people in such districts are never consulted or ignored, or are intimidated by these vociferous activists who have been able to foist some incredible things on their neighborhoods."[21] Channel 7's postelection editorial continued this antidemocratic view and contempt for the intellect of voters: "We don't think that many people who supported it, especially organized labor, really knew what they were getting by voting for this proposition."[22] In other words, labor union members who voted for relatively simple piece of legislation that cleaved elite opinion with labor on one side and business on the other were, according to Channel 7, not smart enough to know what they were doing.

The argument that in a compact city of about 700,000 people at-large elections are better than district-based elections was reasonable. The notion that the law should be repealed because voters did not understand what they were doing, given that Proposition T was widely debated and discussed in the city for much of 1976, is strange and deeply antidemocratic. A November 11 letter to the *Examiner* made that point: "Prop. T won by a larger percentage than did Jimmy

Carter. . . . To say that the voters did not know what they were voting on is an insult to the intelligence of the voters. Do the supervisors really think that the voters understood fully every one of the other 34 state and city propositions, but that this one single one they did not understand? The voters made their choice. In a democracy, that's that. . . . If the supervisors continue to express their desire to overturn the will of the voters, then I guess it proves that indeed the voters knew just what they were doing."[23] The writer of that letter was not just a concerned citizen but a three-time failed political candidate eyeing one more run for supervisor because the new districts included the heavily gay District Five where he, Harvey Milk, would have a good chance of winning.

The repeal effort coalesced into two August 1977 ballot initiatives, Propositions A and B. Proposition A was a straightforward repeal. If passed, the city would return to the at-large system that had been in place for the previous decades. In a special election, this initiative might have passed, particularly as the no on T forces from 1976 were highly mobilized, while the pro-T forces were beginning to fracture, partially because many of the organizers were preparing their own campaigns for the new board, which were set to occur in November 1977 but would not occur if either proposition passed.

Proposition B was where Barbagelata badly overplayed his hand. This proposal sought to remake the board through an unwieldy compromise. Supervisors would represent individual districts, but voters could vote on all eleven supervisors. This very strange idea that Jerry Roberts described as "cockamamie,"[24] was only one part of Proposition B. The proposal also called for runoffs for all offices, including supervisor, and recalling the mayor, sheriff, treasurer, and district attorney, and new elections to be held for these offices in November 1977. Because propositions A and B were, with regard to the structure of the board of supervisors, mutually exclusive, the policy was that if either passed, it would become law, but if both passed, only the one with the most votes would become law.

Getlin recounted what anti-district election forces wanted to tell the people of San Francisco: "First of all folks, you really weren't paying that close attention. Obviously, you had other things on your mind. There was a president being elected. Now, you have time to pay attention and we're sure you didn't mean to . . . at the exact same time, John Barbagelata, still clearly smarting from his defeat at George's hands two years before, also put on the ballot a measure which essentially would have recalled George."[25]

As Getlin pointed out, the August ballot was a recall effort against Moscone, Sheriff Richard Hongisto, Treasurer Thomas Scanlon, and District Attorney Joseph Freitas Jr. This was an enormous, and not very smart, gamble by Barbagelata. A repeal of district elections had a chance of winning, but seeking the recall of four elected officials meant that there was much more at stake for the political leadership of the city. The recall effort, despite potentially very broad support, was associated primarily with Barbagelata, and was easily viewed as a power grab by a defeated mayoral candidate.

Proposition B was a sweeping proposal that included some bad ideas such as recalling four citywide elected officials for no particular reason. But is also contained some ideas, such as runoff elections for supervisor and abolishing life tenure for the city's chief administrative officer, that were much more reasonable. Unlike in 1975 when Moscone narrowly defeated Barbagelata for an open seat, this time Moscone had the advantages of incumbency. Nonetheless, the campaign against Proposition B consumed a great deal of Moscone's second year in office.

As the election approached, the Yes on B campaign published a newsletter featuring articles by prominent supporters, including Supervisor Terry Francois and former Chief of Police Thomas Cahill. In the lead column, Barbagelata made the case for Proposition B: "Just look at Moscone's record: Crime has risen 32 per cent since Moscone took office. Moscone has responded to this rise in crime in an odd way. He has cut police manpower rather than increase the police force. With fear dominating people's minds . . . businesses are looking to relocate elsewhere. Homeowners will find their tax bills 20 to 40 per cent higher this year. Police morale is at an all-time low."[26]

Barbagelata's conservative critique of Moscone was the kind of attack that would be expected if Moscone were running for reelection, but Barbagelata was trying to use that as a reason to overhaul all of city government. The conservative supervisor also used the column to reiterate his pledge not to run for mayor if there was a recall and to complain: "From Mayor Moscone's campaign remarks, you'd think Barbagelata was on the August 2 ballot." Given Barbagelata was Moscone's loudest critic on the board of supervisors and the energy behind Proposition B, this was absurd. Among others who supporting Proposition B were the Police Officers Association, who were anxious to rid themselves of the reform-oriented mayor and police chief. Their May 1977 newsletter gleefully reported of the proposal: "It is just what the doctor ordered. The Mayor, the District Attorney, the Sheriff and the entire Board of Supervisors must stand for reelection in November if Prop. 'B' passes on August 2. Who could ask for more."[27]

Moscone rallied his supporters against Propositions A and B, but unlike with Proposition T, he was able to mobilize support from more centrist and business-oriented parts of San Francisco. It also helped that more moderate voters could support A while opposing B. Moscone opposed both, frequently linking them together, but Proposition B concerned and angered him the most. In a statement opposing Propositions A and B, Moscone pointed out "*every single county* in the State of California elects their supervisors by district (with the lone exception of San Francisco)," while also making a strong political critique of Proposition B clearly targeted at Barbagelata. "Proposition B is a thinly veiled scheme by a defeated candidate for mayor to undo the results of an election which he lost.

Proposition B is an insult to the electoral process and should it pass, will become the future model for every defeated and disgruntled politician. Our City could become a series of instant election re-plays, subjecting the people to elections every year, with the resulting chaos, instability and cost to the City ultimately bringing San Francisco to its knees."[28]

Instead of framing his critique of Proposition B as yet another proxy fight between himself and Barbagelata, Moscone's mostly stressed good governance, and that a recall would destabilize the city and make San Francisco look bad to the rest of the country. This probably helped Moscone pick up some support among some wavering political centrists. Getlin noted: "It would have been very easy to paint Barbagelata as this freakish, fringe character who was once again bringing the city to a halt for one reason or another. . . . George's approach in this . . . was to basically say, this is a question for all San Franciscans in terms of the stability and the integrity and the respectability of San Francisco. What kind of city image are we projecting to the outside world."[29]

The No on B campaign also focused on Barbagelata's inability to accept his 1975 loss. A campaign flyer focused on the issue of fairness. The front featured the word "Fairness" in large white letters on a black field with the results from Proposition T in the middle. Below was written, "The American principle of fair elections is being undermined in San Francisco." To make the point more clearly, on the inside were photos of Gerald Ford and Hubert Humphrey, who had lost very close races for president in 1976 and 1968 respectively, below the bold-faced words, "They accepted defeat."[30]

Among Barbagelata's many opponents were organized labor. The San Francisco Labor Council, Longshoremen, and Teamsters summarized their position in a flyer distributed to union members and other voters. The language around Proposition A was somewhat reserved. "District representation gives you a direct voice in your city government. It gives you Supervisors from your own neighborhood who know the problems that face you and will do something about them. Proposition A repeals district representation. Be sure you vote NO!" The language regarding Proposition B was much stronger and more personal. "Proposition B's attack on district representation is hidden behind Supervisor Barbagelata's 'repeal everybody' effort to fire all elected city officials and most members of city boards and commission. It's a senseless attack on orderly government. It's a disaster looking for a place to happen . . . Proposition B is the wild-eyed scheme of Supervisor John Barbagelata to embrace his own political fortunes. Barbagelata boasts that he is responsible for every anti-labor action taken by the Board in recent years . . . Proposition B is his bid for political power, his revenge for the defeat he suffered in his race for mayor. Vote NO on Proposition B!"[31] The tone reflected the difference between the two proposals. Proposition A was simply the powerful moneyed interests trying to hold on to their power and influence by repealing district elections. It was conservative and contemptuous of the voters, but within the bounds of San Francisco politics. Proposition B was a power grab, or tantrum, by a sore loser who was still not over his defeat from 1975.

Herb Caen, a liberal but no radical, also opposed Proposition A and B, using strong but jaunty language. "Nobody asked me, but I'd like to see T given a chance. . . . We've had ward politics for years—one ward run by a powerful politico-economic coalition, pronounced 'Downtown.' . . . So far as I can find out, San Francisco is the only county in California that DOESN'T elect Supes from the district they live in. . . . It's old hat, but the way we have been operating is even older and apparently just fine with those interests who believe they 'control' the Board. They don't like Prop. T for that obvious reason."[32] Caen's words about Proposition B specifically were even stronger:

> Even a cursory reading of history shows this city to be conservative at heart, dominated economically by reactionaries, and studded with such ugly chapters as 'The Chinese Must Go!', vigilantism and hoodlums. . . . The nabobs tolerated, and in fact, profited from, vice as long as it was kept out of sight. . . . Today, the winds of change are blowing hard, and the chill can be felt in high places. That's why Prop. B is instructive, and thus valuable. We will learn a lot about San Francisco. Barbagelata's brainstorm, whether induced by envy or sincerity, will give the ultras a chance to come out of the bushes. They can stand up and be counted in the anonymity of the voting booth—the lawnorder types, the gay-haters, the anti-blacks, those who blame all the ills of the city on the bleeding hearts.[33]

Mike Davis is usually associated with Los Angeles, but in 1977 was writing about San Francisco for left-wing newspaper *Common Sense*. He explained the context of Propositions A and B. "As in all major US cities, San Francisco has been run pretty much in the interests of the big business community, with some input from small business and organized labor. . . . Starting after World War II, and getting into high gear in the late 1950s and 1960s, San Francisco was 'redeveloped' to meet the needs of corporations. Houses, parks, old neighborhoods were destroyed in order to make way for office buildings, parking lots, freeways and tourist facilities." Davis also explained what was at stake in the August election. "Now this hard-won reform (district elections) is under attack as the business community has marshalled its forces and put Prop. A and Prop. B on the special election ballot. A victory for A or B would seriously set back the many years of work in building the unity of progressive forces in SF. . . . If district elections survive August 2, the groundwork will be laid for the next stage of our work."[34]

On the evening of August 2, 1977, Moscone addressed the crowd at the No on A and B victory party. His tone was celebratory and a little gloating. "I think we've won again! I almost feel as though I should apologize to all of you for the fact that your summer was interrupted by the need to become involved in an election which never should have taken place. I know that I had better things to do these past few months than to campaign against two ballot measures, the sole purpose of which was to attempt to overturn the expressed will of the people. I'm sure you all could have found better things to do as well. But that is behind us now, and tonight I feel two very strong emotions: pride and appreciation. . . . Tonight's vote was a resounding defeat for obstructionism in our city."[35]

Unlike the previous two elections that had also pitted, in one form or another, Moscone against Barbagelata, this time it was not close. Proposition A was lost by a margin of 57 percent to 43 percent; Proposition B by an even more decisive margin of 64 percent to 36 percent. The *Chronicle* headline the day after the election was "Both S.F. Propositions Lose—A Big Victory for Moscone," followed by a smaller front-page headline "Barbagelata is Shocked and Bitter."[36]

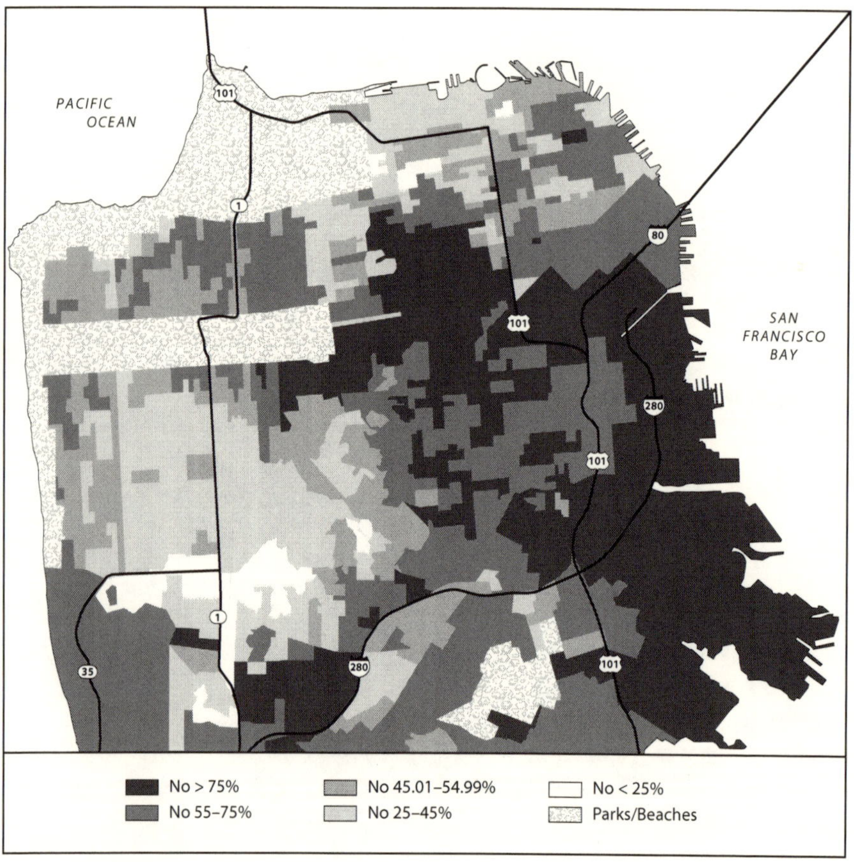

Map 12.2. Results from Proposition A, 1977. Map by Jackson Hasty.

Jerry Roberts described how this victory for those supporting district elections "was really for the third time in the space of two years a confirmation of power of the Moscone coalition that had kind of won over the downtown Chamber of Commerce interests as (over) this sort of small merchant homeowners bloc represented by Barbagelata."[37]

The biggest vote against both Propositions A and B came from the same neighborhoods that supported Moscone in 1975, primarily in the east and central parts of San Francisco, with the west and northern parts of the city—particularly the northwest—continuing to vote more conservatively. Between November 1975 and August 1977, San Francisco voters went to the polls three times to vote in four elections that were in key ways more or less the same. In each case, as shown in maps 12.2 and 12.3, the electoral map looked more or less the same, but the progressive side won by a slightly larger margin as time went by.

The August 2 election was major victory for Moscone, but it came at a cost.

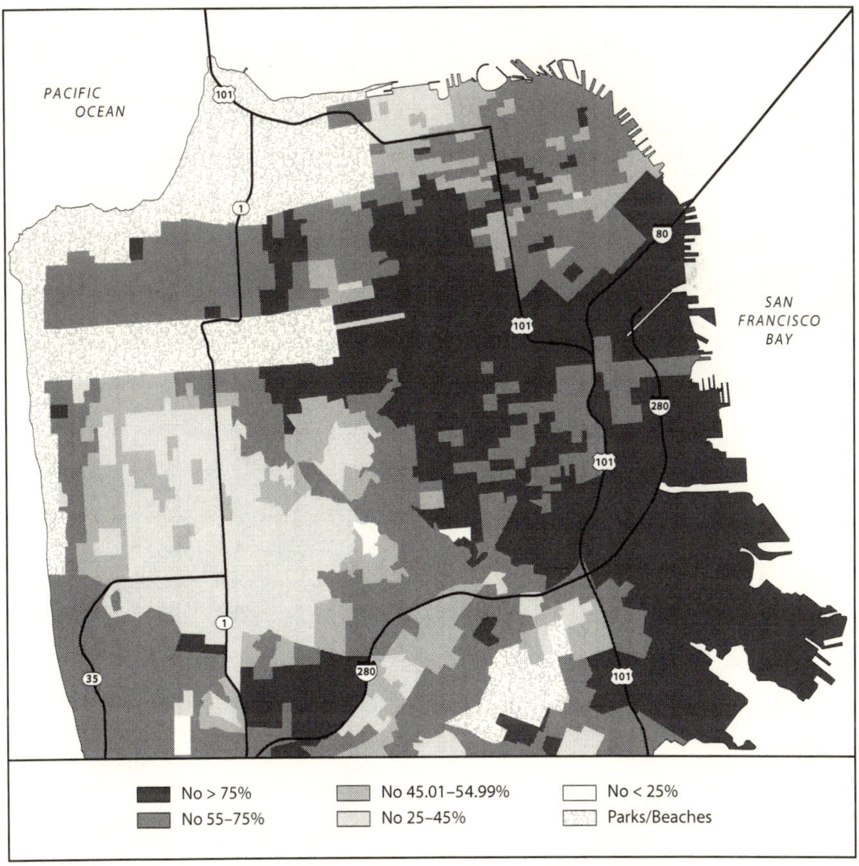

Map 12.3. Results from Proposition B, 1977. Map by Jackson Hasty.

Combating Propositions A and B took a huge amount of Moscone's time during the summer of 1977. Moscone's schedule for those months was filled with events, rallies, and meetings aimed at mobilizing against the two initiatives. During the week of July 18–24 with the vote fast approaching, Moscone had fully seven No on B events, mostly neighborhood meetings, as well as several other events, for example, a picnic at Stern Grove for seniors hosted by the Jewish Community Center, where he urged voters to oppose Propositions A and B.[38] A week or so earlier, July 5–10, Moscone averaged one No on B event per day.[39] In addition to these appearances, Moscone had to spend time working with campaign strategists, crafting and approving language for speeches, press releases, and other statements. Larry Griffin recalled how much time Moscone spent on this: "It was a distraction. How could you not be distracted by people trying to keep you out of office." Griffin added, "Why did they fucking do this? Why did we waste all this time? Why did we waste all this money on something that had already been decided?"[40]

District Elections for Supervisor

After Proposition A and B were defeated, the campaigns for supervisor began in earnest. Jerry Roberts portrayed a "great opening up of fresh air of the city and people being involved in politics who had never been involved, and also with the very very local, micro-local issues they had concerns about. . . . I mean it was just like this circus because all across the city every night there were candidates' nights and debates." Even in even much bigger cities such as New York, district elections lead to very small districts. In New York City, today a city of approximately nine million people, each of the fifty-one city council districts has about 180,000 people. In 1977, San Francisco had roughly 700,000 residents so each of the eleven districts had slightly over 60,000. In a multicandidate race, it would take only a few thousand votes to win.[41]

Well over one hundred people ran for eleven district seats. Some incumbent supervisors immediately found districts in which to run. District Two in the northern part of the city included Dianne Feinstein's home. She ran there and won easily with more than twice as many votes as Lester O'Shea, who finished second in the five-candidate field. Quentin Kopp ran unopposed in his west San Francisco district. Other incumbents, including John Molinari in District Three, Ron Pelosi in District Eleven, and Robert Gonzales in District Seven, were elected in more competitive races. The margin was fewer than one hundred votes in Gonzales's case.

Moscone appointed Gordon Lau to the board in September 1977 to fill the vacancy created by Robert Mendelsohn's departure. Lau then got elected in District One, which was primarily the Richmond in the western part of the city where the Chinese American population had been growing. Lau was the first

Chinese American elected to the board. Ella Hill Hutch won the election in District Four, which included the Western Addition and Fillmore, and became the first African American woman on the board. Most famously, Harvey Milk, in his fourth bid for elected office, finally won an election, becoming the first openly gay person elected to the board. His 30.5 percent of the vote easily outpaced the other sixteen candidates in District Five.

Several incumbents decided not to run for the new board. Most had been opponents of Moscone and district elections, including Peter Tamaras, Al Nelder, and Barbagelata. Had he run, Barbagelata would have had to move a few hundred meters to the east into District Eight to avoid having to run against Kopp. That district included conservative white neighborhoods such as the Excelsior and Portola as well as some pockets of African American voters. Thirteen candidates ran for that open seat. The winner was a handsome young former fireman and policeman who almost immediately became a rising star in the conservative movement in San Francisco.

Dan White won with just shy of 4,300 votes, constituting 30.4 percent of all the votes cast, but he received almost twice as many votes as the second-place candidate, Leonard Heinz. White's election confirmed the fears of the No on T position that a small number of voters would be able to pick supervisors. Dianne Feinstein, with 9,755 votes, and Quentin Kopp, running unopposed with 18,095 votes, were the biggest vote getters, but even they were elected by a fraction of the overall electorate.[42] The eleven new members of the board of supervisors received a combined 69,313 votes.[43] Critics of district elections were right that the new board would appear to be elected by a minority of voters—only Feinstein and Kopp received more than 50 percent of the vote—but that could have been addressed through a runoff system, like there was for mayor or some kind of ranked-choice voting system.

White won in District Eight by embracing the angry backlash that had fueled Barbagelata's support. White, a conservative Democrat, from a largely white working-class part of the city, campaigned on two messages. The first, as seen in a campaign flyer titled simply, "Dan White A Democratic Candidate for Supervisor," featured photos highlighting his deep roots in the community from his parish elementary school and public high school to the military and the police and fire departments. The flyer included campaign promises to "provide them (young people) with meaningful community projects, permanent employment and the possibility to become responsible adults" and to "implement programs that will ease their (seniors) tax burden."[44]

White also took more combative positions. One piece of campaign literature with a title that might be considered a clever rhyme if it had been written by an eleven-year-old was called "Unite and Fight With Dan White." The text urged voters to come together to "eradicate the problems which blight our beautiful city." Adding "I am not going to be forced out of San Francisco by splinter groups of radicals and social deviates. . . . I have committed myself to the confrontation which can no longer be avoided by those who care."[45] The change in power dynamics brought by district elections made a victory like White's possible. He was not supported by most of the institutional powers in the city. The *Chronicle*, long the voice of the political establishment, endorsed Helen Fama, while the San Francisco AFL-CIO opted for Bob Barnes. Even the *Progress,* San Francisco's third paper then, eschewed White in favor of Nick Verreos.[46]

Richard DeLeon explained White's success:

> In District Eight . . . was Dan White. He was a former Vietnam War vet, former firefighter, former police officer who was elected. And partly on the campaign, maybe even mainly on the campaign of addressing, pandering to the fears and concerns of the working class white Irish families in that area . . . the ones who were most feeling threatened and driven to some extent by xenophobic and homophobic reactions to these . . . sudden population shifts and all the other tumult that as going on politically and economically in the city that was changing their world.[47]

White's election proved conservatives would have a presence on the new board and that district elections were not only going to empower progressives.

The new board was ideologically and politically diverse. The previous board included seven white men, one African American man, one Latino man and two women, one of whom was Jewish, but no gays or lesbians. One of those white men was replaced by an Asian American man shortly before the election. The new board included an Asian American man, a Latino, an African American woman, two Jewish women, and six white men, including two Jews—one gay and one straight. The board included a conservative faction led by Kopp and John Molinari, and a left wing that included progressive attorney Carol Ruth Silver, Lau, and Milk, who had steadily moved leftward. Labor leader Larry Del Carlo summed up the feel of the new board: "People got elected that understood the issues because they had lived those issues in those communities. . . . In neighborhoods like the Mission and Castro and others now you had community activists who could actually become members of the board of supervisors. . . . That was a huge change in governmental power in San Francisco."[48]

The election did not determine who would be president of the board of supervisors. The president would wield significant power on the board and succeed the mayor if he died or resigned. During the period of at-large elections, the convention was that whoever finished first in the citywide balloting would be board president. With district elections, this made less sense. Kopp received the most votes, winning 18,095, but he had run unopposed. Instead of this convention, the new board, like most legislatures, would vote on its new leader and whoever could get six votes would become president.

Lau emerged as the candidate of the progressives. According to DeLeon, "Moscone initially pushed Gordon Lau . . . that was his candidate to be board president."[49] Milk, Carol Ruth Silver, a progressive representing District Six in the center of the city, Ella Hill Hutch, Lau, Robert Gonzales, and maybe Ron Pelosi could have formed a progressive majority and elected Lau board president. However, Lau was unable to get the votes and lost out to Dianne Feinstein. Feinstein was able to consolidate the conservative faction of the board in part because Kopp had agreed to support her in exchange, as he claimed for years, for Feinstein supporting him for mayor against Moscone in 1979.

Hutch delivered the decisive vote for Feinstein, breaking with the other progressives. Hutch was African American and had a labor background. Her heavily African American district had supported Moscone for mayor, but Hutch refused to support his choice for board president. Feinstein, although not as popular among African American voters as Moscone, still enjoyed a good reputation among African Americans, which helped her secure Hutch's support. Although Moscone would have preferred a board led by Lau, the new city legislature was better for Moscone. Feinstein and Moscone were never close, but she supported him in the 1975 runoff and was more liberal than her predecessor, Quentin Kopp. Feinstein had little interest in a third campaign for mayor so was not a direct threat to Moscone.

National Politics

During 1968, his first year in office, Joseph Alioto had become a sufficiently prominent national figure that Hubert Humphrey almost put him on the Democratic presidential ticket. Moscone never achieved that status, but many political observers assumed he was eyeing a race for governor in 1982 if he got reelected in 1979. Nonetheless, as mayor of San Francisco, Moscone was becoming slightly more involved in national politics. In early September 1977, New York City was in the midst of an extremely competitive Democratic primary for mayor. There was no candidate in that race who was able to bring together a diverse progressive coalition the way Moscone did, but the candidate who came the closest was Bella Abzug, a former congresswoman and prominent feminist. Abzug's strongest support came from progressive white women, many of whom, like Abzug, were Jewish, but she also did well among progressive white men, African Americans, and gay New Yorkers.[50]

On September 1, only a week before New York's primary, Moscone attended a fundraiser for Abzug hosted by Vivian Hallinan.[51] The Hallinan family was a mainstay of progressive San Francisco politics for decades. At the time of that event, Vivian's son Terrence was running for supervisor in the Fifth District, a race he would lose to Milk. Hallinan would later serve two terms as San Francisco district attorney, losing his bid for a third term in 2003 to Kamala Harris. Had Abzug gotten elected mayor, New York would have had a mayor whose progressive commitment matched, or exceeded, that of Moscone, but in 1977 New York was not ready for that. Instead, primary voters there opted for a liberal congressman who had tacked right in the primary named Ed Koch.

When Moscone became mayor, Republican Gerald Ford was president, but by early 1977 a Democrat was in the White House again. Maintaining a good relationship with the administration was important, but Moscone had no organic or close relationships with the administration. When Carter's vice president, Walter Mondale, came to San Francisco for a fundraising event in June 1977, it was an opportunity for Moscone to strengthen that relationship. Moscone made the opening remarks at the reception at the Hall of Flowers. The visit was coordinated by the California Democratic Party and the party's Northern California chair and Moscone ally, Nancy Pelosi.

Moscone's years as mayor coincided with gay rights continuing to become a national issue at time when there were few prominent politicians for whom supporting gay rights was an easy decision. Most had constituents who were strongly anti-gay while few had large gay constituencies. Moscone was an exception. He had won election with strong gay support and would not be reelected if he could not hold that support. In the polarized politics of San Francisco, there was a strong anti-gay vote, but it was never going for Moscone anyway.

That helps explain why Moscone became involved in a Florida campaign, penning a letter to Dade County Commissioner Ruth Shack supporting her effort to include sexual orientation in the country's anti-discrimination laws. "Our experience has been that our ordinance has enhanced the quality of life and reduced unnecessary friction within our city by extending to the gay community the dignity and respect due to all our citizens. We can only salute your courage in establishing this important legislation and extend our moral support and hope that you will choose to support its continuation."[52]

Shack's efforts failed as voters in Dade Country rejected the initiative. The face of the opposition was beauty queen-turned-orange juice spokesperson Anita Bryant, who was rapidly becoming a symbol of anti-gay prejudice. Gay San Franciscans took to the streets in protest during Mondale's visit to San Francisco. Gay San Franciscans were frustrated with the failure of the Carter administration to take a strong position in favor of gay rights. Moscone had to find a way to balance support for gay San Franciscans with his need to remain in good standing with the administration.

Moscone's statements managed, more or less, to achieve this balance, stating a strong-anti Bryant position, "The results of the Dade County election must not be used by demagogues to unleash a wave of repression upon those whose lifestyles differ from our own. It is only too easy for some to use the emotional appeal of this issue to undo everything we have accomplished in learning to live in some harmony with our neighbors, regardless of the color of their skin, their religious beliefs, their economic status, or their private sexual habits," while condemning at least some of the protesters. "The gay movement must and will be heard, but disruptive, and potentially violent behavior is calculated only to engender the fear and hatred which provides hospitable ground for the success of demagogues and despots. I am confident that will not happen in San Francisco."[53]

Moscone's focus on "private sexual habits" reflected a narrow, by today's standards, notion of the gay rights movement, while also harkening back to Moscone's major legislative accomplishment of 1975. The language in the second part of his statement is extremely strong. Bryant was certainly a demagogue, but despot is an odd word to describe an activist with no governmental power. Lastly his use of the phrase "potentially violent" is eerily prescient while his confidence that will not happen in San Francisco is the kind of thing a politician has to say, particularly when he is indeed concerned about the possibility of violence.

Youth Campus

Land use issues are always at the center of urban policy. This was particularly true during the 1970s in San Francisco when the issues of how much to develop downtown, how many new office buildings were needed and how much the skyline should change, Manhattanization, the Freeway Revolts, the fights over redevelopment, and the struggle to build the Yerba Buena Center were largely about land use. In comparison, the proposed Youth Campus, a facility for fifty to sixty troubled boys and girls between the ages of thirteen and eighteen, to be run by the Sisters of the Good Shepherd and located at 501 Cambridge Street in the Excelsior District, was not a major issue, but the debate around it changed San Francisco.

Facilities such as Youth Campus frequently activate NIMBY impulses. That term had not yet been coined in 1977, but residents of the Excelsior District did not want a home for troubled youths in their backyard. Opponents of Youth Campus from the surrounding neighborhoods had numerous concerns, including: "Youth Campus will house unlimited number of patients with violent and non-violent mental disorders. . . . Inadequate security. . . . Increase of home insurance. . . . Decrease in property values."[54] An unusual wrinkle presented itself because Youth Campus was a project of a Catholic order, and the residents who opposed the project were mostly Catholic. This put the church along with the Moscone administration on one side and the community and the more conservative members of the board of supervisors on the other.

Naturally, Youth Campus became an issue in the race for supervisor in District Eight, where the facility was planned. Candidate Dan White, who was Catholic, cast his lot with those who opposed Youth Campus. White's opposition to the project may have helped him win the election, but it had little impact on the initial debate around Youth Campus because much of that occurred in 1977 before he joined the board in January 1978.

By late November and early December 1977, it appeared Youth Campus was moving forward despite opposition from neighborhood groups and the district's supervisor-elect. On November 30, 1977, the board of permit appeals, the powerful city commission on which Harvey Milk briefly served in 1976, approved the project by a vote of 4–1. The board of permit appeals was led by Patrick Hallinan, who explained his position: "These children have to be helped . . . and that doesn't mean sending them up to Napa and locking them up."[55]

The day the *Chronicle* reported the vote on the board of permit appeals, it also published a letter from Dianne Feinstein, still siding with neighborhood conservatives over the interests of the most needy, that concluded, "why force a mental health facility on a community that is adamantly opposed to it when San Francisco has an excellent site for the treatment of mentally disturbed youngsters in a beautiful rural setting."[56] A few days later, on December 5, the board voted 6–5 against Youth Campus. Feinstein voted with the majority. Dan White testified at that hearing: "The people out there are the life blood of San Francisco . . . Portola residents are already forced to live behind high gates and bars. Injection of a facility for the 'chronically disruptive' would increase the exodus from the city," the supervisor-elect said.[57]

The arguments of Feinstein, White, and others did not persuade Moscone. Instead, he aligned himself with his church, the medical community, and a needy and underserved population. *The Monitor*, the official Catholic newspaper of the Archdiocese of San Francisco, made its views on the question clear in a December editorial. "Rejection by the San Francisco Board of Supervisors of a proposed Youth Campus program at the Good Shepherd Convent in Portola Valley is to be deplored. It was a purely political decision and indicated a complete lack of compassion, concern and responsibility for troubled children in our midst."[58] An editorial in the *Chronicle* a few days earlier pointed out that "the psychiatric treatment plans, innovative and constructive, have been drawn up by the best professionals from St. Mary's, Mount Zion, Presbyterian and Children's Hospitals."[59]

On December 13, the mayor issued a statement explaining his veto of the board's rejection, which meant Youth Campus would move forward. "I am taking this action . . . because the services which this facility will provide to emotionally troubled young boys and girls in San Francisco are absolutely essential, and also because San Francisco has no other comparable facility for dealing with the problems of emotionally disturbed youths providing intermediate, residential care."[60] Given how close the initial vote on the board was, Moscone's veto was unlikely to be overridden. A new board was due to be inaugurated in less than a month, and it looked like Moscone would have the votes. Even though Dan White was not likely to give up quite so easily, Youth Campus appeared to be moving forward.

CHAPTER 13

Moscone's Last Year

George Moscone was starting his third year as mayor in 1978. The new year was almost a reboot of his mayoralty. During the last few months of 1977, the voters of San Francisco had defeated Propositions A and B by substantial margins and a few months later elected a new board of supervisors. Together this meant a much friendlier political environment for Moscone. The defeat of Propositions A and B was a political victory that allowed Moscone to avoid being recalled, but it was a psychological one too. Jonathan Moscone explained, "My dad . . . had a very different demeanor after that defeat (of Proposition A and B). . . . He was like, 'This is mine, fuck you.'"[1]

Youth Campus Redux

In March 1978 the board passed a major gay rights bill authored by Harvey Milk and signed into law by Moscone. *The New York Times* explained that "many here (San Francisco) consider the most stringent and encompassing in the nation . . . the ordinance . . . would ban discrimination in employment, housing and public accommodations based on sexual preference."[2] The gay rights ordinance was a victory for Milk, who delivered on his promise to his new constituents in only his third month in office. It was also allowed Moscone to concretize into law a position he had long supported while delivering for a key constituency. The gay rights ordinance would not have been possible without district elections. Although there had been members of the board of supervisors, possibly a majority, that would have supported this ordinance, it took a gay member to make it a priority—and a gay supervisor was elected because of Proposition T.

Milk's bill passed easily by a margin of 10–1. Feinstein's support sent a signal to the rest of the board that the bill would pass, and several conservative supervisors, including Quentin Kopp, voted for it as well. The only dissenting vote came from Dan White. White explained his concern to *The New York Times*:

"'According to the city attorney's office, if a transvestite shows up at a private school with all the qualifications for teaching, they cannot refuse to hire him for an opening even if they object to having a man dressed as a woman in their school,' Mr. White said he feared that many San Francisco residents who were already upset by the 'demands' of 'large minorities' like the homosexual community would either leave the city or react punitively if the proposed ordinance goes through."[3]

White's sentiments were not just issue-based. By the time of the vote on the gay rights ordinance, White's animus toward Milk and Moscone had deepened largely because of their support of Youth Campus. On the evening of February 28, the Health and Environment Committee of the board of supervisors voted to move ahead with the plan for the facility. The vote was 2–1 with Supervisors Lau and Gonzales for and White against.[4] The committee vote was a victory for Youth Campus, and Moscone, but it did not guarantee that the project would receive the affirmation of the full board. White had one more opportunity to stop the project, and he needed to find a sixth vote. Five members—Feinstein, Kopp, Molinari, Lee Dolson, and White himself—could be counted upon to oppose the project. Feinstein, because of her powerful position on the board had become, along with White, the leading voice opposing Youth Campus. She explained her position to the *Chronicle*: "It's a mistake to press this facility on a fearful community—that will only engender further hostility and misunderstanding."[5] The sixth vote would be more difficult. If the progressive block held together, Youth Campus would be approved. White turned his attention to Milk, believing he would switch sides. Milk and White were on decent terms and were both outsider neighborhood politicians. Perhaps White thought he could find common ground with Milk around that. That strategy speaks to White's lack of political acumen. The chances that Milk, whose politics aligned him much more with troubled youths than angry conservative homeowners, would break with the other progressives and the mayor, whose votes he would soon need for his top legislative priority, were extremely small.

In a 2008 article, *SF Weekly's* Ray Sloan, who had been White's campaign consultant in 1977 and continued to work with him after the election, recounted the vote. "On the Friday before the Youth Campus came before the board, White asked Milk if he had his vote. Sloan, who was taking a head count of likely votes, recalls Milk saying, 'Dan, you've really earned your $9,600 on this one.' White and Sloan took that to mean Milk would side with White, Sloan says."[6] Milk's remark was odd, even cryptic, but certainly was not a clear statement of support for White. The allusion to the $9,600 annual salary members of the board of supervisors earned back then suggests that White may have raised his financial concerns to Milk.

The article continued. "But on Monday, Milk voted *for* the Youth Campus.

White had lost his most important issue, and he was embarrassed in front of a chamber full of Portola residents whom he had invited to witness their victory." Quentin Kopp, a conservative like White, but a much smarter politician is quoted saying, "I knew Harvey wasn't going to vote against the Youth Campus. . . . For crying out loud, it was a liberal vote. White came up to me right afterward and says, 'I guess a leopard never changes its spots.' He was mad. Very mad." Sloan remembered. 'That was it,' he (Sloan) says. 'Harvey was no longer a friend, and it wasn't any fun anymore. It was all 'no' votes on the parades (gay pride parades) and anything else Harvey wanted.'"[7] The Youth Campus vote changed Dan White. It was an early failure and a stark contrast with Milk's big win a few days later. White's vote against Milk's gay rights bill may have solidified his place as the bright young thing of reactionary San Francisco, but it was also a personal reaction to his perception that Milk had wronged him.

The Giants Redux

One of Moscone's major accomplishments was in jeopardy as 1978 began. If Moscone had lost the Giants to Toronto in his first month in office, it would have been politically damaging, but he could have at least partially blamed Joseph Alioto. However, if the Giants left in Moscone's third year, to Denver this time, blame would land squarely on Moscone. While Moscone had been able to stop the sale of the Giants to the Labatt company in Toronto, he could do nothing about the poor attendance and dreadful ballpark the Giants called home. Nor could he do much about the post-Willie Mays mediocrity into which the Giants had descended since trading the Say Hey Kid to the Mets midway through the 1972 season.

While the board of supervisors was debating Youth Campus, gay rights, and other issues, Moscone was fighting off efforts to take the team to Denver or to send the Oakland A's to Denver and have the Giants split their games between Oakland and San Francisco. The question of how to keep the Giants in San Francisco and how to find a better ballpark than Candlestick Park bedeviled each of the three mayors who followed Moscone—Feinstein, Art Agnos, and Frank Jordan—before the work on a new ballpark finally began when Willie Brown was mayor.

Moscone was not as involved in 1978 other than to make it clear that if the Giants played some home games in Oakland, their road uniforms should identify them as "San Francisco."[8] Ultimately, Giants owner Bob Lurie decided to play the 1978 season in San Francisco. While this was happening, Kopp, who preparing to run against Moscone, uncovered a 1976 letter from Moscone to Chub Feeney, president of the National League, in which Moscone agreed that if the Giants did not average one million fans per year from 1976 to 1978, he would not do anything to prevent them from leaving. The Giants had drawn a total of about 1,300,000 in 1976 and 1977, averaging around 650,000 fans a season, so it was widely understood that the Giants would not meet that goal and would probably leave after 1978.

This time the Giants tenure in San Francisco was not saved by a court case or new owner. Instead, Vida Blue, Mike Ivie, Willie McCovey, Darrell Evans, Bill Madlock, and Jack Clark led a surprisingly good Giants team that was in first place most of the summer and drew 1.7 million fans, at that time the second-best attendance in the long history of the team.[9]The Giants finished in third place, six games behind the Dodgers, but it was a very successful season. A new generation of fans, too young to remember Mays, were drawn to this exciting and young team.[10] For older fans, McCovey was a link to earlier Giants teams. By the end of the season, talk about the Giants leaving town subsided. That talk would reappear sporadically for most of the next fifteen years, but the Giants would remain, and in this century become one of the game's most successful franchises on and off the field.

Tax Revolts

On June 6, 1978, California held primary elections as well as votes on a handful of state and local initiatives. One of those initiatives, Proposition 13, changed the course of California and created problems for California's cities, counties, and local jurisdictions that have persisted well into this century. The initiative proposed to limit "ad valorem taxes or real property to 1% of value . . . Establishes 1975–1976 assessed valuation base for property tax purposes. Limits annual increases in value. Provides for reassessment after sale, transfer or construction. Requires 2/3 vote of Legislature to enact any change in state taxes designed to increase revenues. Prohibits imposition by state of new ad valorem, sales or transaction taxes on real property."[11]

Proposition 13 was the brainchild of two Southern Californians, Howard Jarvis, a successful businessman and failed Republican political candidate, and Paul Gann, a conservative political activist. While these two men provided much of the leadership for Proposition 13, the initiative itself was the product of a conservative movement that had been growing since it helped propel Ronald Reagan to the Governor's Mansion in 1966.

The Tax Revolt, as it came to be called, was a conservative movement but also grew out of a concrete economic problem. As property values increased in California throughout the postwar period, property taxes, which were linked to assessments of property, increased correspondingly. For longtime residents, particularly those who were older and had a fixed or modest income, this was a genuine problem. The tax increases were often significant enough that it was difficult for people who had dutifully paid their mortgages for years to remain in their homes. For many, rising taxes were a significant economic burden. The right used this real economic hardship to bolster a broader anti-tax agenda and indeed the Tax Revolt.

While it was necessary to solve the problems created by rising property taxes for some Californians, Proposition 13 was different. By all but freezing property taxes, essentially forever, it locked in a conservative governance framework through the trojan horse of reducing property taxes. If property taxes were frozen, the state would have less money for programs of all kinds. This would have the most impact on cities such as San Francisco that would then have to make up the loss through either cutting programs or raising local taxes, which could push businesses or residents to the suburbs.

This was not lost on urban progressives such as Moscone. In a speech a few weeks before the vote, Moscone spelled out the expected impact of Proposition 13: "The first fact you should know is that if Proposition 13 is approved it means, for starters, that we have a $151 million deficit in our budget. That is the shortage in tax revenue we'll have to balance by cutting services. It represents fifty-seven percent of the local tax share of the city. . . . This does not include the school or community college budgets. Our school budget will have a $72 million deficit. Our community college budget will have a deficit of $25 million." Moscone listed services such as parks and libraries that would be cut, adding, "I can guarantee you that it's inevitable some fire stations will be closed, and some police services will be eliminated."[12] Because Proposition 13 set taxes back to their 1975–1976 rate, its passage would immediately, as Moscone noted, force cities such as San Francisco to cut budgets, with little hope of future assistance from the state.

Although many other liberal elected officials and interest groups shared Moscone's opposition to Proposition 13, it passed easily with just short of 65 percent of the vote.[13] San Francisco voters joined Moscone in rejecting the proposal, but it was one of only three counties to vote no on 13. By 1978 San Francisco was emerging as a liberal corner of a state that was increasingly politically polarized and where the right appeared to be ascending. The anti-tax sentiment in California, particularly among more conservative voters in Southern California, would help Ronald Reagan gain the Republican presidential nomination and defeat President Carter in November 1980.

The passage of Proposition 13 created an immediate crisis for San Francisco that stymied what was left of Moscone's progressive plans. In the following months, Moscone made many of the budget cuts about which he warned San Franciscans before the election. The city also benefited from a one-time infusion of $100 million from the state's budget surplus. All mayors, regardless of ideology or political party, must find a way to keep a tax base in their city. If wealthy families and businesses leave, then the city cannot afford any programs or even to pay basic expenses. Proposition 13 made this even more dramatic because it was such a substantial reduction of state funds.

Meanwhile in Guyana

Because of the events that occurred in November 1978, Jim Jones and George Moscone are connected in history, but by late 1978 their relationship was not close. Jones had sought, and eventually received, a reasonably high-level appointment from Moscone, but he did not stay there long. Jones may not have been entirely forgotten, but after he left town, few in San Francisco paid much attention to him. After Jones resigned from the Housing Authority in early August 1977 because, in Jones's words, "the needs of my congregation in Guyana would necessitate my ongoing presence there which would require my absence from the city for extended periods of time,"[14] his visibility in San Francisco political circles faded relatively quickly. Jones's resignation came the day after Propositions A and B were defeated, which meant not only that Moscone had a renewed confidence, but district elections for the board of supervisors were only a few months away. The supervisor campaigns and the other myriad challenges of governing San Francisco seemed of much greater consequence than Jim Jones, who increasingly looked like one of the many offbeat characters who were part of the city's cultural, political, or religious life for a few years in the late 1960s through the mid-1970s. By late 1977, the Peoples Temple and its leader were receiving less media attention and were almost never mentioned in the coverage of the very hotly contested races for the board of supervisors.

The cult did not disappear from the consciousness of San Franciscans, but it was no longer understood to be a political force. From late 1977 through mid-1978, there were occasional stories of alleged misdoings in the Peoples Temple community in Guyana which, reflecting Jim Jones's immodesty, was called Jonestown. By the end of 1977, it was apparent to anybody paying even a little attention to the Peoples Temple that Jones was taking his congregation in a very dangerous direction, manipulating, abusing, and terrifying many of his congregants, and that his megalomania had only gotten worse. The *New West* article which preceded, and probably contributed to Jones's resignation from the Housing Authority was the most important of these reports, but more trickled out through the rest of the year and into 1978.

By April 1978 many Bay Area residents with family members with the Peoples Temple in Guyana were growing concerned about being unable to contact their relatives, while rumors of abuse and mistreatment by Jones continued to circulate. Several of these concerned relatives, as they called themselves, wrote an open letter to Jones that month: "Sadly, your conduct over the past year has shown such a flagrant and cruel disregard for human rights that we have no choice as responsible people but to make this public accusation and to demand the immediate elimination of these outrageous abuses." The document then accused Jones of making statements indicating the view that it is "better even to die than to be constantly harassed from one continent to the next," of "employing physical intimidation and psychological coercion . . . prohibiting our relatives from leaving Guyana . . . depriving them of their right to privacy, free speech and freedom of association."[15]

Another document a few months later spelled out the horrors occurring in Jonestown. This affidavit, filed on July 15, 1978, by Deborah Layton Blakey, a long-time member of the Peoples Temple who had had managed to flee Jonestown, described the violence and threats that confronted people in Jonestown on daily basis as well as the terrible diet, hunger, sickness, and brutal working conditions they encountered while Jones lived very well. The most chilling passage in the document stated that

> at least once a week, Rev. Jones would declare a "white night," or state of emergency. The entire population of Jonestown would be awakened by blaring sirens. Designated persons, approximately fifty in number, would arm themselves with rifles, move from cabin to cabin, and make certain that all members were responding. A mass meeting would ensue . . . During one "white night" we were informed that our situation had become hopeless and that the only course of action open to us was a mass suicide for the glory of socialism. . . . Everyone including the children was told to line up. As we passed through the line, we were given a small glass of red liquid to drink. We were told that the liquid contained poison and that we would die within 45 minutes. We all did as we were told. When the time came when we should have dropped dead, Rev. Jones explained that the poison was not real. . . . He warned us that the time was not far off when it would become necessary for us to die by our own hands.[16]

Peoples Temple representatives refuted these assertions, but it was becoming evident that what was occurring in Jonestown was very troubling. This was not a front and center concern for Moscone, who was focused on trying to govern San Francisco, adjust to the damage wrought by Proposition 13, and prepare for a reelection campaign that by summer was about sixteen months away. Three years into his term, Moscone was struggling to keep his political head above water and the Peoples Temple was a problem he did not need.

The Next Elections

No high-profile San Francisco ballot initiatives or offices were on the November 1978 ballot. Governor Jerry Brown was in what appeared to be a tight reelection battle, but by early fall he pulled away from his Republican opponent Evelle Younger and cruised to reelection. Neither of California's senators, Alan Cranston or S. I. Hayakawa, were up for reelection. However, the statewide ballot also included an effort by state Senator John Briggs to make himself a player in

California Republican politics. Briggs, a far-right senator from Southern California, was the sponsor of Proposition 6, known as the Briggs Initiative. The Briggs Initiative was a hateful proposal that would have legalized firing any teacher who was gay or was suspected of being gay. Proposition 6 called for "filing charges against school-teachers, teachers' aides, school administrators or counselors for advocating, soliciting, imposing, encouraging or promoting private or public sexual acts . . . between persons of the same sex in a manner likely to come to the attention of other employees or students; or publicly and indiscreetly engaging in said acts."[17]

Harvey Milk played a prominent role in the fight against the Briggs Initiative, including debating Briggs on several occasions. The San Francisco supervisor's intellect and wit were no match for Briggs. Many other politicians joined the fight against the bigoted initiative, including Governor Brown, most of the state's Democratic leadership and, extremely significantly, former governor Ronald Reagan—probably the most popular Republican politician in the state and perhaps the country. Reagan published an opinion column in the *Los Angeles Herald Examiner* on November 1, 1978, opposing Proposition 6 primarily through an argument about "the potential of infringing on basic rights of privacy and perhaps even constitutional rights."[18] Moscone also opposed Proposition 6, calling it "the most outrageous distortion of what this country stands for I've ever seen" at a September 28 fundraiser for the No on 6 campaign. Among the attendees at that event were progressives such as actor Ed Asner, liberal politicians such as Supervisors Lau and Feinstein and even conservative legislators like Dan White.[19]

Although Proposition 6 had a good chance of passing at first, by the time the election approached, Democratic opposition had consolidated and been bolstered by conservatives such as Reagan and anti-tax crusader Howard Jarvis. Briggs was reduced to stunts such as wagging his finger at the Halloween revelry in San Francisco's gay neighborhoods. On Election Day, Proposition 6 was drubbed by a margin of 58–42 percent. San Francisco delivered the biggest defeat to the Briggs Initiative as fully 75 percent of voters in the city voted no.[20] Moscone noted that the defeat of Proposition 6 "is not a victory over a lightweight like John Briggs. It is a victory over the despair that has fallen on gay people. It's a victory of intellect over emotion."[21]

Shortly after the election, Quentin Kopp, the leading conservative on the board, announced, as widely expected, that he would run against Moscone in 1979. Kopp had been on the board of supervisors since his first election in 1971 and was the legislature's loudest and most consistent critic of Moscone. Others considering running against Moscone included nonpoliticians such as attorney Fred Furth and Kevin Starr, a public intellectual and columnist for the *San Francisco Examiner*. Kopp seemed a stronger candidate than either of them since he won two citywide elections for the board before winning in his district, running unopposed, in 1977. One candidate whose name was not rarely mentioned in these discussions was Dianne Feinstein, who appeared to have little appetite for a third run for mayor. A Moscone-Kopp election, or a Moscone-Kopp runoff after the lesser candidates had been eliminated, would have almost been rematch of the 1975 race. Although Kopp shared Barbagelata's conservative views on many issues, he was smarter, understood governance better, and had more political sense. However, as a Jew from the East Coast with a fancy education, Kopp's San Francisco story was not as good as Barbagelata's.

Moscone was preparing a different campaign than 1975 when he had put together an historic coalition and promised progressive change. In 1979 he would be running on his record while Kopp would attack him for the persistently high crime rate, the city's economic and budget problems, and for being too liberal on social issues. Moscone needed to persuade voters he had significant accomplishments during his first term and would do even more if reelected. An undated internal memo from 1978 outlines what Moscone's administration viewed as his most impressive accomplishments as the election approached, including

> bringing in more representatives from previously "outcast" S. F. communities to serve on S. F. Boards and Commissions, positions of power and trust in local government than ever before . . . Resolving the Yerba Buena Center logjam once and for all . . . removing the threat of a building ban (and bringing the city) in compliance with clean water standards . . . instituting more austere fiscal policies in S.F . . . hir(ing) as many as 200 additional cops . . . devised and implanted a 103 person security guard force to ride MUNI vehicles . . . funded and expanded an escort program for senior citizens, so they can walk the streets day and night without fear of violent crime . . . pumped over $1 million in federal funds to restore and maintain the beautiful park system in SF . . . inaugurated an ambitious, citywide anti-litter campaign.[22]

This may or may not have been enough to get Moscone reelected, but, except for the first, the accomplishments are not notably progressive. Building a convention center, removing a building ban, cutting expenses from the budget, and hiring more police may have been good for San Francisco, but are the kind of things that most mayors, regardless of party or ideology, try to do. Overall, other than diversifying city government, this list would not have looked out of place in a piece of literature for Joe Alioto's reelection campaign in 1971.

The hiring of two hundred additional police officers was particularly significant because during Moscone's first three years as mayor, crime was a huge problem, further complicated because Moscone never established good relations with the police, particularly with a Police Officers Association (POA) that opposed any police reform. After being in office for about a year, Moscone issued a press release proclaiming "significant decreases in crime in San Francisco as measured by the monthly FBI crime index."[23] A little more than a year later, in a May 1978 press release announcing funding for hiring more police, Moscone boasted of his record while taking a political shot at Kopp. "Now Supervisor Quentin Kopp, who says he is interested in cutting crime, and in cutting budgets, says crime was up in April in San Francisco and yet opposes me in my efforts to add the strength of 100 additional officers. . . . The fact is, overall crime in San Francisco down 7.9 percent for the first quarter of this year, including April, and Quentin knows it."[24]

Moscone cited statistics, found money for more police, invested in community-based anti-crime programs, and put together commissions to address crime in San Francisco, but got little credit for his efforts for two main reasons. First, during the 1970s crime in San Francisco, like most major cities, was a persistent problem. Slight variations in the year-to-year crime rate did not change the reality that San Franciscans were, for good reason, very concerned about crime. Additionally older San Franciscans could remember a time when the city was much safer. They were not comparing the crime problem of 1977 to 1974, but to 1967 or even 1957, when conditions were very different.

The POA never did anything quite as dramatic as the "Welcome to Fear City" pamphlets distributed by police in 1975 when New York Mayor Abe Beame was planning to lay off thousands of police officers because of the city's fiscal crisis. Nonetheless, the POA's criticism of Moscone was constant and included enthusiastically backing Propositions A and B in 1977. An article in the POA newsletter shortly before that vote described Moscone as "a man who apparently does not have the capacity to lead a great city out of its vexing urban problems."[25] A POA press release accused Moscone and Police Chief Gain of "playing a public relations game with the citizens of the city . . . continu(ing) to demoralize our police officers by implementing radical proposals" and warning obliquely that "until this administration responds to what is really needed, we will continue to astonish the nation with our crime rate."[26] The POA also reported the data from a survey of their members. This survey, "complied (sic) from a questionaire (sic) that was distributed to our 1500 member organization." According to the survey, only 4 percent of respondents believed "morale is on the rise within the Police Department, while only 11 percent believed "the criminal justice administrators (are) acting in the best interest of the citizens."[27]

The POA's resistance to reforms contributed to their dislike for Moscone and Chief Gain. Gain was a reformer, but he was often tone-deaf and spent too much of his limited political capital on things like changing the colors of police cars and moving a flag out of his office while not doing the harder work of building relationships with the rank and file in the department. That task was never going to be easy, but Gain rarely seemed to try.

November 1978

The ongoing tension with the police, early noise from Quentin Kopp's mayoral campaign, continued fallout from Proposition 13, and a handful of scandals around the provenance of the money Moscone spent to buy his home, contributions from Howard Hughes to allies of Moscone, and Deputy Mayor Bernard Teitelbaum failing to properly disclose some of his income, meant that November 1978, like most of the previous thirty-four months since he had become mayor, was not going to be an easy one for Moscone. However, Moscone had navigated difficult times before and still had strong support in some quarters of the city, political skill, and no lack of self-confidence. Additionally, the defeat of Proposition 6 was a victory for Moscone and progressive San Francisco, and maybe even evidence that the consensus in the city was moving toward tolerance, while the reactionary politics of John Briggs and, in San Francisco, John Barbagelata, were waning. The passage of Proposition 13, while terrible for San Francisco from a fiscal perspective, gave Moscone some cover because he could blame the newly passed state law for some of San Francisco's problems.

The three weeks between the defeat of Proposition 6 and November 27 have been written about extensively.[28] In those weeks, two stories dominated the news, politics, and events in Guyana. The first began in earnest when, in response to concerns about what has happening in Jonestown, which had only grown since the spring and early summer, Representative Leo Ryan, a Democrat representing a district just south of San Francisco, decided to visit the Peoples Temple's Guyana encampment to see for himself what was going on and to offer assistance to those who wanted to leave.

At the same time, Dan White, the favorite son of conservative San Francisco, decided that he could not make enough money on his salary as a supervisor and was leaving the board. He was planning to help manage the french fry stand for which he had been given rights at Pier 39, a new development offering entertainment, shopping, and food for tourists and San Franciscans. It was not widely known, but the FBI was investigating White because it looked like he had received the rights to sell fries in exchange for his vote on the board to move forward with the creation of Pier 39. White's departure from the board reflected the peripatetic nature of his career to date. The former fireman and former policeman was now a former supervisor, but the financial pressure was legitimate. Unlike most members of the board, White neither came from money nor had any outside income. Given that, the difficulties he faced supporting his wife and young child on his $9,600 salary were real.

White's resignation was an opportunity for Moscone that was not lost on the former state senate majority leader who understood legislation, coalition building and political math. According to the city charter, if a supervisor resigned, the mayor would pick the replacement.[29] White's resignation meant that Moscone could pick a progressive replacement for the most conservative supervisor. There was also a chance there would be enough votes replace Feinstein with a more progressive board president. This was a huge political break for the mayor who had struggled with an uncooperative legislature since taking office.

White announced his resignation from the board on November 10, but within a few days he regretted his decision and wanted his job back, and a few days after that asserted that his resignation had not been processed properly so was not official. That argument got no traction, so White then pivoted and asked Moscone to reject the resignation, allowing White to remain on the board. But City Attorney George Agnost ruled that was not allowed by the city charter. This left White with the long-shot hope that Moscone would appoint him to his former seat. This was legal but was never going to happen because for the mayor the opportunity to replace White with a progressive ally was too good to pass up. It was political not personal, but that is not how White saw it.

White decided he wanted his job back not because he suddenly thought he could provide for his family on his $9,600 supervisor salary or because he decided to devote himself to serving the people. Rather, his conservative backers, including real estate interests and the police unions, made it clear that they wanted him on the board and that they would find a way to help him make some more money. The police unions were particularly interested in getting White back on the board because they needed his vote to stop the ratification of a federal consent decree backed by Moscone that would have forced the police to substantially accelerate the integration of the force. This fight had been going for a decade, but progressives won a victory earlier in the year when the consent decree was handed down by the courts. The police wanted to stop it and to do that they needed White on the board.

If the city approved the federal consent decree, the San Francisco Police Department would have had to rapidly integrate. The consent decree would break up one of the centers of reactionary backlash politics—the SFPD—and force it to modernize its racial politics while making it more difficult for white police officers to bring their friends and relatives, who were almost always white, into the force. The decree was anathema to the conservative and overwhelmingly white force. The POA was committed to stopping the consent decree and needed six votes on the board to do that. If there was one vote on which they could have counted, it was that of the conservative former police officer Dan White, but then White left the board. Ironically, White left the board when he finally was in a strong bargaining position because by then the POA needed his vote more than he needed them. However, White lacked the political skills to take advantage of that.

White's lack of political skills made him susceptible to the urging from police and other interests who wanted him back on the board, but his temperament led him to this quandary in the first place. Cleve Jones described White as "a petulant child. He was in way over his head. He did not have the intellectual prowess or the political instincts. . . . He was clueless. He was resentful. . . . He struck me as someone who was uncomfortable in his own skin. . . . Everybody knew there was something wrong with him. The guy was a mess, and it showed. . . . To him, the normal process of politics, because he couldn't figure out how to play, he just thought it was all crooked. When people were making deals, he didn't know how to do that, so he would have temper tantrums about it."[30]

The contretemps around White's resignation occurred in the week or so after the election. During that same period, newly reelected Representative Leo Ryan was preparing for and embarking upon his fact-finding journey to Guyana. Ryan's trip and White's political shenanigans were occurring on parallel tracks and were not related, but within a few days, the former would overtake the latter in the minds of San Franciscans. By November 17, news was trickling back from Guyana. On that day, a below-the-fold article in the *Chronicle*—the headlines concerned inflation; a feud between Paul Gann and Howard Jarvis; and residents of the small town of Clayton, California, trying to quit smoking—described "thirteen troubled relatives held a shouting, angry and tearful meeting with the U.S. ambassador to Guyana, seeking his help in their quest for a meeting with their own family members who are living in a remote communal settlement in the country's interior."[31] Although the article, by Ron Javers, was studiously neutral, readers could easily infer that something was amiss in Jonestown but could not have known what was coming next.

Ryan initially persuaded Jones to let several Peoples Temple members leave Guyana and return to the US. But because Ryan had seen the truth about Jonestown and was prepared to report that back to media, government, and law enforcement in the US, Jones changed his position. As Ryan and his traveling party prepared to leave Jonestown by plane, security forces from the Peoples Temple opened fire, killing Ryan and four others while injuring nine

The massacre at Jonestown occurred on Saturday, November 18, but was discovered later and only reached the American media the night of November 19 and morning of November 20. On that Saturday, the "white nights" drills about which Layton had warned became a reality. Jonestown congregants were made to drink cyanide-laced Flavor-Aid. The Jonestown massacre is frequently understood as a mass suicide, but that is misleading. The victims were forced, in many cases, at gunpoint, to take the poison, so the killing in Jonestown can be more accurately described as a mass murder. The final death toll was more than nine hundred. The horrors that occurred in Jonestown sent San Francisco into a kind of collective shock. Not only had Jones been a public figure in San Francisco during much of the 1970s, but many of the victims of the massacre had roots in San Francisco and the Bay Area. The Peoples Temple headquarters was in the middle of the city—an unmissable reminder of the horrors that occurred in Guyana.

Traumatic events such as the Jonestown killings generally turn the spotlight on political leaders. Mayor Rudy Giuliani of New York City briefly became America's Mayor because of his perceived leadership following the terrorist attacks of September 11, 2001. In 1989, when a major earthquake hit San Francisco, Mayor Art Agnos was lauded for his leadership—although not enough to prevent him from losing his bid for reelection two years later. Jonestown was different for many reasons. First, the events were so ghastly, grisly, and downright strange that the story overtook the sense of loss and grieving. The media focused more on Jones, the Peoples Temple, and cults in general rather than Moscone or the people of San Francisco.

Second, Jones's political relationships in San Francisco could not be ignored. This made it difficult for Moscone to simply lead the city through a difficult time of grieving. The same day news of the massacre was widely reported in the US, the *Chronicle* was already reminding voters of these relationships and ran a story titled, "What Politicians Say Now About Jim Jones," that began "some of California's top political leaders labored yesterday to explain their past alliances with the Rev. Jim Jones and his People's (sic) Temple. Jones has been a potent political force in San Francisco, courted by top officeholders for the help his loyal following could bring to an election campaign." These kinds of stories created, or exposed, problems for many elected officials. Among the politicians named in that article were Milton Marks, Willie Brown, Jerry Brown, District Attorney Joe Freitas, and Moscone. They all stumbled to explain their relationship with Jones, while seeming to still be in denial about who he really was. Moscone's comments, "If Jones was harboring some deep-seated evil intention at that time (when Moscone appointed him to the housing authority) . . . I didn't know about it, and I don't think [my] political colleagues did," were unconvincing. Moscone then offered that when he appointed Jones, he viewed the cult leader as "a peacemaker . . . who had the ability to work with people."[32]

Kopp, who never benefited from Jones's support, distanced himself from Jones while criticizing the city's liberal leadership. "Every one of them went over there and bragged about how they were getting support from the People's Temple (sic) . . . They ought to feel awful good about it today."[33] The nastiness of Kopp's comments and the defensiveness of Moscone and others in the same article all seem a little insensitive given the scope of the killings, but that shows how quickly the horrors in Guyana was politicized in San Francisco.

Looking toward the upcoming campaign, Moscone staffer Josh Getlin did some research and sent a memo to Mel Wax, Moscone's press secretary, pointing out that Kopp had voted twice, in committee and in a meeting of the whole board, to confirm Jones to the Housing Authority.[34] That found its way to Herb

Caen, who preferred Moscone to Kopp. That Friday, November 24, Caen opened his very widely read column with this item. "Sup. Quentin Kopp, already running hard for Mayor, has been the most vocal of all City Hall figures in blaming 'local politicians,' such as Rivals (sic) Moscone and Milton Marks, for their early support of Rev. Jim Jones and his People's (sic) Temple. Yet it was Kopp's own Rules Committee that approved Jones for the job of chief of the Housing Authority, and the full Board (Quentin Kopp, President) that voted the final okay on Dec. 3, 1976. Quentin's Koppout: 'I thought all nominations by the Mayor had been thoroughly screened by the time they reached us.'"[35]

The politics surrounding Jim Jones precluded Moscone from spending the week of November 20 consoling a grieving city. Meanwhile, Moscone had made up his mind not to reappoint White. After and initially considering Helen Fama, who had finished third in the 1977 election in that district, to replace White, Moscone decided to appoint another activist Don Horanzy, but White still had not given up.

Moscone's Last Day

The mayor's press release, dated November 27, 1978, has the words "Never Issued" written in red block letters diagonally across it and underlined once. The release was going to announce Moscone's appointment of Don Horanzy to the board of supervisors. Horanzy is described as "a longtime community leader" and "a founder and President of the All Peoples Coalition." The release quotes Moscone saying, "My first concern was to find somebody who could represent all the people of District 8. I have found that person in Don Horanzy. He comes to office with a superb record of community leadership, and a proven ability not only to get along well with all the diverse ethnic populations of District 8, but with merchants, tenants and other social and economic classes as well."[36]

Moscone never appointed Horanzy, and that release was never made public because Dan White, believing he could change the mayor's mind at the last minute, insisted on one more meeting with Moscone. Moscone took the meeting even though his mind was made up. That was a reasonable political decision. White was a young politician who, at that moment, still had a possible future in politics. There was no reason why Moscone needed to further antagonize White by refusing to meet with him. The same skills that made Moscone a very effective legislator led him to meet with White.

Jon Rubin hypothesized that for White the meeting with Moscone was a matter of pride as much as politics: "The reason that he (White) thought he could get his seat back was because these guys were telling him that he could. . . . that he deserves to get his seat back. . . . When these guys tell him to man up and go down there and get that seat back, he doesn't say, 'Fuck you, you go down there and get the seat back, asshole. I want to live to fight another day.'"[37]

John Burton, one of Moscone's closest friends, shared Rubin's view: "Dan White quit, and then the cops got on his ass 'cause he was the swing vote on affirmative action or something about a consent decree to get more Blacks in (the police force), so the cops talked him into going back. He made an appointment to go see George." Burton explained that when White learned that Moscone was not going to reappoint, "he (White) figures, 'What a lying son of a bitch!' And, that's what did it." Burton described how White and Moscone might have handled this if the former had been a bit more politically savvy and mentally stable. "He would've been alive, George would've said, 'Hey, I can't do it, but here's what I'm going to do for you. You're on the bridge District, that gives you Health Care . . . You're a cop, I'll get all my lawyers to use you, so your investigators will be making more money than you'd be making on the board' and he would have charmed him and done that."

Art Agnos attributed White's actions to the mayor and the former supervisor having different communication styles. "He (Moscone) wasn't dishonest, but he did more gray, and the ultimate gray thing he did killed him with Dan White because he couldn't give it to him straight. He tried to be gray about it to soften the impact of saying 'No,' and White couldn't handle it. He thought he was being manipulated and ultimately it enraged him to do the insane things he did."[38]

Another close friend and political ally of Moscone's, Willie Brown, had a somewhat similar view, stressing Moscone' desire to let White down softly: "Moscone . . . being the gentle person that he always was, being the respectful person, he wanted to give him (White) one more shot of saying why he thought he should; although, clearly, he already was gonna swear in Don (Horanzy) at noon that day or thereabouts that would replace Dan White."[39]

Moscone and White met in the small room behind the mayor's office after White, armed with his .38 caliber Smith & Wesson revolver from his days as a police officer, had entered City Hall through an open window to evade security. Moscone brought White to that room seeking to create a more warm and informal atmosphere. The meeting was very brief as the former supervisor wasted little time before shooting the mayor at point-blank range three times, once in the chest and twice more in the head. Rudy Nothenberg described how he, and then all of San Francisco, learned of Moscone's death:

> I was waiting for George in the outer office. I knew that White was there because those of us on the inside were privy to George's calendar and . . . I waited for a while . . . There was a door to George's private office which led out in the hall where people would generally leave so they wouldn't come by me in the outer office. So I assumed White had left . . . So I went and took the opportunity to go into the office to see whether George was free so I could have my meeting . . . George was

not in the main office. I went to the back room which he'd like to talk to people one-on-one, and that's where I found the body."[40]

Harvey Milk

Almost half a century after his death, the person most frequently associated with Moscone is not the woman to whom he was married for more than twenty years, the mother who dedicated herself to her only child, any of his four children, the powerful politicians who were also close friends, or even the man who killed him. Instead, Moscone's name will always be linked to that of Harvey Milk.

Milk was finishing his eleventh month on the board of supervisors and emerging as an influential legislator able to deliver on his promise of a major gay rights ordinance, a savvy political actor with a bright future in politics, and a statewide, and even national, figure in the gay rights movement when Dan White killed him. White killed Moscone out of anger, frustration, a deeply misplaced sense of machismo and self-righteousness combined with some psychological instability. His motivations for killing Milk are less apparent, even now.

The 2008 film *Milk* includes a scene that explains why White decided to kill Milk after shooting Moscone. The scene shows Milk and Moscone in the mayor's office discussing whether the mayor should reappoint White to the board of supervisors. Milk is pacing while Moscone sits at his desk:

> Moscone: "A man has the right to change his mind. Give me some peace."
> Milk: "How many of our propositions has Dan shut down? We could finally settle this police desegregation nonsense. Cement rent control. It's his vote on this board that stands in our way."
> Moscone: "I get it, Harvey. I've been lobbied all week. Enough."
> Milk: "Let me just remind you that you're up for re-election. If you reappoint Dan, you lose the gay vote. They listen to me. You won't get elected dogcatcher."[41]

In his very influential 2012 books *Season of the Witch*, David Talbot provides a similar explanation for White's motivation for killing Milk. "Meanwhile, Harvey Milk began using Jonestown to pressure Moscone from the left, telling the mayor that he was now going to need the gay vote more than ever to get reelected the following year. 'You reappoint Dan White to the board, and you won't get elected dogcatcher,' Milk told Moscone—a political threat loaded with chutzpah, considering Milk's own Jonestown vulnerabilities. On Monday, November 21, Moscone signaled that he was backing away from reappointing White."[42] Talbot's book was published after the film *Milk*, so it is possible that he was influenced by the film, but he may have done his research before seeing the film.

The likely source for this description of Milk's role in keeping White from being reappointed was a July 4, 1979, article in *The Village Voice* by Randy Shilts, who later became Milk's biographer. In that column Shilts wrote, "White shot Moscone because the mayor refused to re-appoint him to his seat on the Board of Supervisors. Milk had warned Moscone that any gesture towards White, the city's most anti-gay politician, would cost Moscone gay support and, therefore his upcoming election."[43]

It is a good political story offering a neat explanation why White killed Milk, while showing how Milk was a clever politician able to manipulate a less sophisticated mayor. However, if the scene from *Milk* and the explanation by Talbot are to be believed, we must accept that a supervisor who had not yet served a full year in elected office lectured the former majority leader of the state senate, three years into his term as mayor, about how to count votes. This also suggests that Milk was willing to threaten the mayor and that he could withhold the gay vote from a politician who had passed landmark gay rights legislation in Sacramento when Milk was still trying to find an election he could win.

Ironically, this explanation, in seeking to elevate Milk's role in Moscone's decision not to reappoint White, makes the slain civil rights leader seem less sophisticated and politically astute than he was. By late 1978 Milk was aware enough of events and thinking at City Hall to know that he and Moscone were on the same page regarding Dan White, as they had been on so many other issues in 1978. Accordingly, while Milk might have benefited from letting his opinion on White's reappointment be known, threatening the powerful mayor would have been badly overplaying his hand—and Milk was too smart for that.

In my research for this book as well as for my 2019 book, *San Francisco Year Zero: Political Upheaval, Punk Rock, and a Third-Place Baseball Team*, I spoke to numerous people close to Moscone, Milk, or both, and none believed this story was true. Some, like former supervisor Carol Ruth Silver, a friend of Milk's who served alongside him and White on the board, explained that White may have blamed Milk for persuading Moscone not to reappoint White, but Milk never threatened Moscone. Aides to Moscone, like Nothenberg, made it very clear that Moscone understood the political opportunity presented by White's initial resignation and was never going to reappoint the conservative supervisor.

White may have believed, falsely, that Milk had been instrumental in stopping his return to the board of supervisors, but the relationship between the two onetime colleagues had not been good since Milk sided against White, and with Moscone and other progressives, on the Youth Campus question. Additionally, White was, by most accounts a bigot and a homophobe who had many reasons not to like Milk.

Rubin suggested that White simply did not like Milk and felt that Milk and Silver had persistently mocked him: "He's (White) going to these meetings and here's Carol on one side and Harvey on the other. These two Jewish people . . .

And the two of them are going," Rubin then made gestures suggesting two people mocking a third. "I think he killed Harvey as an afterthought."[44]

Sharyn Saslafsky focused on who Dan White was: "It was Dan White. . . . Dan White wanted to get rid of Harvey, and he just thought George won't reappoint me, he doesn't care for me, he's against my principles as a San Franciscan." John Burton also offered a succinct explanation: "He (White) was just a fucked-up, troubled young man." Burton commented on White's dislike for Milk as well: "You really were kind of fucked in a way if you didn't like Harvey, you know Harvey was full of shit . . . he couldn't take himself seriously . . . If you're in politics and you can't get along with people with whom you disagree, you're in the wrong business."[45]

Moscone's older son, Chris, focused less on White and on the bigger picture of his father's life and death. "What killed my dad was that he did swim upstream. He wasn't afraid. He was on a mission to cause shit, in a good way . . . He got stuff done. All the stuff he did . . . I'm so proud of . . . He was on the right side."[46]

We can never know for certain why White killed either Moscone or Milk, but by the middle of the day they were both dead and Dianne Feinstein, who had started the day by telling the City Hall press corps that she was not going to seek reelection and was therefore likely retiring from politics when her supervisorial term expired, was mayor. She would stay in that job longer than any San Francisco mayor since Angelo Rossi, who had been in City Hall during most of Moscone's childhood.

After the Assassinations

The assassinations occurred only a week after the news from Jonestown broke. This put a temporary end to the political fighting over the Peoples Temple massacre as the city collectively grieved both tragedies. Saslafsky's feelings when she learned about the assassinations were shared by many San Franciscans: "Between Jonestown and this with Harvey and George, like it broke my heart. I mean, one I couldn't believe it, two I wouldn't believe it, three I was so heartbroken, and I think I represent a lot of people that I know. . . . I was heartbroken and so angry and so mad."[47]

On November 29 the City of San Francisco had an official memorial for Moscone and Milk. The San Francisco Symphony performed "Ave Maria" as well as a movement from Bach's Suite Number Three. Acting Mayor Dianne Feinstein and Lieutenant Governor Mervyn Dymally were the only politicians who spoke. The other speakers were Rabbi Albert Fine, Bishop Kilmer Myers, Joan Baez, Milk's friend and advisor Anne Kronenberg, and Moscone's oldest friend Cappy Lavin.[48]

Ever the son of Catholic San Francisco, Moscone's funeral was held at St. Mary's Cathedral. In addition, mass cards were sent to his family from Catholic organizations such as the Sacred Heart Spiritual Society, the Perpetual Mass Association of the SMA (Society of African Missions) Father, and the Don Bosco Sacred Heart Association. The San Francisco Giants, who would no longer have been in San Francisco if not for Moscone, had a special tribute to the slain mayor at their 1979 home opener. Bob Lurie, the owner of the team, and his newest front office hire, former Moscone press secretary Corey Busch, invited Christopher and Jonathan Moscone to throw out the ceremonial first pitch. The Giants beat the San Diego Padres, 4–2, that day on a dramatic pinch-hit ninth inning home run by backup catcher John Tamargo.

The bereavement was not universal. Segments of the city celebrated the deaths of Moscone and Milk and either treated White as a folk hero or sought to minimize his crimes. Many police officers fell into this category. According to Talbot, upon hearing the news, "cheers broke out . . . among the police inspectors who felt betrayed by Moscone. The Notre Dame Fighting Irish song crackled on the police radio, then Danny Boy."[49]

It was not just the police who seemed to celebrate, or at least sympathize, with Dan White. An appalling article in the *Palo Alto Times*, which appeared the day after the assassinations, began, "Daniel White was always serving people, whether it be in elected office, public safety departments or dishing out French fries. A few weeks ago when Mayor George Moscone was out of town it was White's turn to be acting mayor. It didn't faze the pleasant supervisor. That weekend like the others, 'there he was shoveling French fries,' a friend recalled after seeing White working at his fast-food stand, The Hot Potato."[50] The newspaper from a few miles down the road from San Francisco was covering the man who had just murdered the mayor as if he was some cheerful and quirky public servant.

A few days later the same newspaper ran an even more pro-Dan White headline, "White: 'The brightest thing on the (political) horizon.'" The article absurdly suggested White's actions were justified because of his strict sense of his moral code. "Dan White was a man adhering to such a strict code of right and wrong that when he saw no one else was living that way, he felt betrayed and could not cope, a close friend and political co-worker said Thursday. The close friend is Dennis De Silva, a photographer, who regarded White as 'the brightest thing on the (political) horizon.'"[51] The logic, if that word can be applied here, is that the fault lay with Moscone and Milk, who by doing something wrong pushed the morally superior White to kill them.

A more balanced article in the *San Francisco Chronicle* described how White received better treatment in jail than others, but also restated his military record and All-American boy image. It quoted a friend of White's family, saying, "(h)e is the warm gentle Danny I have always known. A man who could not hurt anyone unless he had lost his mind."[52]

These articles, and the strong dislike toward both Moscone and Milk in conservative quarters of the still-divided city, had an impact on public opinion. For example, in November 1978, my brother and I were in eighth and sixth grades, respectively, and attending Catholic school. Among our classmates, it was a common, perhaps even consensus, opinion that White was a good man who had made one mistake and therefore should not be punished too harshly. Our mother made it clear to us that was not our family's position.

Other than the two politicians who were killed on November 27 and the erstwhile supervisor who shot them, the politician whose life changed the most that day was the president of the board of supervisors who had begun that Monday telling the City Hall press that she was winding down her political career. By the end of the day Dianne Feinstein was acting mayor. She would go on to serve out the rest of Moscone's term and win two full terms of her own, leaving an indelible mark on San Francisco.

Few mayors have taken over their city at such a traumatic time. The terrible murders at City Hall, coming only about a week after the massacre at Jonestown, left the city in psychological shambles and with widespread concern about its future. By any measure, Feinstein rose to the occasion.

Willie Brown summarized how Feinstein guided the city through the aftermath of the assassinations. "Dianne stepped up and did her acceptance of the responsibility to run the city . . . and she did such a magnificent job, and that was right on top of the nonsense and horror that Jim Jones had perpetrated on the city in Guyana a few days earlier. A combination of all those things caused whatever disagreements many people in the city had with each other to be at least muted for a short period of time while the city got itself back together."[53]

Feinstein was more conservative than Moscone, but, in addition to her leadership in the weeks after the assassinations, Feinstein made political decisions that respected Moscone's legacy. When Feinstein became mayor, White's former seat was still open; somebody needed to replace Harvey Milk; and her own seat was now vacant as well. Three open seats on the board gave Feinstein an opportunity to remake the city's legislature in her image, but she chose another approach.

Feinstein appointed Louise Renne to succeed herself on the board. Renne was something of a Feinstein protégé, a smart centrist who distinguished herself with her hard work and preparation. After serving on the board for seven years, Renne went on to serve fifteen years as city attorney. The appointment of Renne was a smart and easily defendable move. Nobody could criticize Feinstein for appointing a political ally with similar views to her old seat on the board.

The other two vacancies left Feinstein with more complex political decisions. Feinstein, who was the first person to see Harvey Milk's body after White killed him, had a mixed relationship with Milk. She supported Milk's two major legislative proposals, the gay rights ordinance and a September law requiring people to pick up after their dogs, but on many important legislative fights, including the consent decree and Youth Campus, Milk and Feinstein had been on different sides. Additionally, Feinstein had a good record on gay rights issues and gay supporters whom she might have appointed to Milk's seat. Instead, Feinstein appointed Milk political ally Harry Britt, whom Milk had indicated was his choice to replace him if necessary. Similarly, Feinstein quickly appointed Don Horanzy, Moscone's choice as well, to replace White on the board of supervisors.

Those decisions helped stabilize the political situation and showed Feinstein was not simply interested in solidifying her political power—at least not yet. The other major decision that Feinstein made was to keep in place the diverse appointments that Moscone had made. Gradually, particularly after she was elected to a full term of her own after defeating Kopp in a 1979 runoff, Feinstein started replacing Moscone's people with her own choices. But she never went back to the heavily white straight male San Francisco leadership of the pre-Moscone era. In doing that, Feinstein made permanent one of Moscone's biggest accomplishments and permanently ended the days when San Francisco was run overwhelmingly by straight white men.

The assassinations lingered over San Francisco well into 1979. White's trial is mostly remembered because of the so-called Twinkie Defense—a phrase that was never used in the trial. Nonetheless, White's claims of stress, mental instability, and a chemical imbalance brought on by too much sugar that day fell on sympathetic ears, and he was only convicted of manslaughter and given a sentence seven years and eight months. District Attorney Joe Freitas wanted the death penalty for White. That led him to make the major mistake of choosing conservative San Franciscans who he believed would be more likely to support capital punishment to sit on the jury. Freitas's miscalculation was that those same jurors were also likely be more sympathetic to White and considerably less so toward Moscone and particularly Milk.[54]

When the verdict was announced on May 21, 1979, the day before what would have been Harvey Milk's forty-ninth birthday, violent demonstrations erupted in San Francisco. Angry gay people clashed with police, overturned cars, broke windows at City Hall, and expressed their frustration with a system that treated killing Harvey Milk as a minor offense. Those demonstrations, known with an eerie Jonestown resonance as the "White Nights Riots," are an important moment in the struggle for LGBT equality. Even by then, Moscone was beginning to fade into history as Milk's story was beginning to eclipse his. White ended up serving eight years in prison, before being released in January 1984. Twenty-one months later, he killed himself in Los Angeles. Upon hearing the news, many in the Castro and other parts of San Francisco celebrated.

Epilogue

THE ASSASSINATIONS OF GEORGE MOSCONE and Harvey Milk are a fault line that bisects San Francisco history. Like the Gold Rush, the earthquake of 1906 and the Summer of Love, the assassinations are one of the few San Francisco historical events that newer residents and people outside the city know about San Francisco. November 27, 1978, was, to a great extent, the moment when a modern, tolerant and, yes, business-friendly, San Francisco emerged from the chaos, contestation, and backlash of the previous fifteen years. On that day, the progressive idealism that had emerged during those years was dealt, from the perspective of almost half a century later, a permanent setback.

The constituency Dan White represented—angry white voters who felt they were losing control of their city—had lost three elections in a row by 1978. That anger and defeat finally and brutally, in the cruel and disturbed person of Dan White, made their mark on San Francisco. The horrors of that day led Dianne Feinstein, an eminently centrist and sensible politician, to understand that tolerance had to become a core value if the city was going to survive and thrive. Feinstein was no progressive, but during the nine years she was mayor, she navigated San Francisco through the tail end of a very rough period into a much more tolerant, although certainly flawed, incarnation. This narrative is appealing in its simplicity and, in broad strokes, its accuracy. However, a city like San Francisco and an event as momentous as the City Hall assassinations, and indeed a life like George Moscone's, merit more than a broad brush. The nuance and context give a fuller picture, and indeed meaning, to those events, beginning with the relationship between the two men who were killed that day.

Harvey Milk, who long ago became more prominent than George Moscone in the collective memory, inside and outside of San Francisco, is now remembered for his powerful oratory, winning an election, passage of landmark civil rights legislation, and his tragic assassination. However, the fuller story of Milk's struggles to be taken seriously in San Francisco in the years before he got elected helps explain the struggles of those early years of the gay rights movement. After losing his second bid for the board of supervisors in 1975, Milk was one of many community activists in San Francisco, albeit one with a sharp intellect, fierce sense of justice, *Yiddishe kop* and charming, to some, outer borough accent.

Moscone rescued Milk from that fate by giving him a high-profile appointment on the board of permit appeals. Milk's decision to repay Moscone by turning around and running a quixotic campaign for state assembly, which he was never going to win, speaks to the challenge of a gay man who needed to win on his own rather than gain power through being appointed by a straight white man.

For some progressive San Franciscans, the assassinations marked the end of the left's ascendancy in San Francisco. This opinion recognizes the tragedy of Moscone's murder but overstates the extent that Moscone's term in office led to broad progressive change. Some flesh out this position to assert that if Moscone had lived he would have served two terms and been succeeded by Harvey Milk.[1] It is certain if San Francisco had been governed from 1976 through 1991 by mayors Moscone and Milk, the trajectory of the city would have been very different, but to assume this is how history would have played out if the assassinations had not happened may be a triumph of progressive fantasy over political reality.

We cannot know what would have occurred if Moscone and Milk had not been assassinated. Imagining or fantasizing about an alternate political history of San Francisco may be fun for some, but it is not useful political analysis. It also obscures something important about Moscone's tenure as mayor and urban governance generally. Moscone was mayor when there was a growing concern that San Francisco, New York, Detroit, and other big, diverse cities with rising crime rates and shrinking tax bases were ungovernable. San Francisco may or may not have been ungovernable in the late 1970s, but time and again during his term as mayor, Moscone's progressive vision ran up against the fiscal and political realities facing the city. Proposition 13 made those constraints stronger for Moscone and all his successors. Moscone's three years as mayor are, among other things, the story of a progressive candidate finding himself governing from the center and touting his austerity and crime-fighting credentials out of political necessity. In other words, even before Feinstein became mayor, Moscone was moving to what we would now think of as a Feinstein or even Michael Bloomberg approach to the job of being a big-city mayor—balancing tolerance with the need to keep the tax base strong by supporting business and bolstering police efforts to reduce crime.

Almost a century after his birth, George Moscone's life is remembered, other than by those who were close to him and by a few older San Franciscans, for the days immediately preceding and immediately following his murder. However, his life was much more than that. Moscone was an extraordinary son of an extraordinary city, one that had already undergone massive changes in the decade before Moscone became mayor and that today is almost unrecognizable to anybody who was fortunate enough to have lived there during the three years Moscone was our mayor.

Of all the important, famous powerful national political figures of the last half century or so who, in one way or another, came out of San Francisco, few were of the city to the extent that Moscone was. Willie Brown, Phil Burton, Harvey Milk, and Nancy Pelosi moved to the city as adults. Kamala Harris grew up across the bay and did not begin her legal career in San Francisco. The only national politician who was comparable to Moscone in this sense was the woman who became mayor after he was murdered.

Dianne Feinstein, the most influential mayor of San Francisco since at least Angelo Rossi, was a native daughter of the city who retained strong ties to San Francisco throughout her life. However, Feinstein's San Francisco was a much different and more rarified version of the city than the one that created George Moscone, and that he loved so much. Her background in Pacific Heights, the Convent of the Sacred Heart, and Stanford University is less relatable for many San Franciscans, even those who were of her and Moscone's generation.

Moscone grew up almost literally in the shadow of the construction of the Golden Gate Bridge, spent his youth on the streets and playing basketball in playgrounds throughout San Francisco's neighborhoods, and was educated through high school in its vast network of Catholic schools. Moscone's mother was a working woman who spent her career primarily in the Department of Motor Vehicles, an honest and important but unglamorous way to make a living. As a man, Moscone frequented restaurants, bars, and nightclubs, but also playgrounds and parks to pursue his lifelong passion for basketball. He was also part of the last generation of Italian Americans in San Francisco that could claim to be part of the city's largest and most politically powerful ethnic group.

During the years Moscone was mayor, it was still relatively easy to meet men and women in San Francisco whose life story was very similar to his. Many of the parents of my Catholic school classmates had childhoods that were not too different from that of Moscone. Most were politically to the right of Moscone, but they had gone to Catholic school and grown up on the streets and playgrounds of the city. Moscone was a representative of that San Francisco, but in the last years of his life he was no longer embraced by that older version of the city. Instead, his political support came from those who had either not been in San Francisco in the middle third of the twentieth century or had been pushed to the political, social, and economic periphery of San Francisco during those years.

Moscone's life was deeply tied to place and time. The period when Moscone was a powerful state senator and later mayor was the last moment in American history when politics, even left-of-center politics, was still dominated by conventional men who struggled to maintain their roles in a rapidly changing culture. Nowhere were these changes more acute than San Francisco; and no politician navigated those changes better than George Moscone, despite, or perhaps because of, the paradoxes that defined him. Within a few years of his death, the idea of a straight white jock being the face of a radical San Francisco political movement would be difficult to imagine, but it is equally difficult to imagine anybody who did not have the demographic profile of a George Moscone getting elected mayor in 1975 while leading the progressive coalition that eventually remade San Francisco.

Moscone was a political creature of both the new and old worlds. A huge part of Moscone's significance was that he was able to leverage his old San Francisco credentials to help forge a newer, more progressive city and state responsive to the social, cultural, and political changes during his fifteen years in elected office. Moscone was one of a handful of California politicians, including Phillip and John Burton, Willie Brown, Jerry Brown, Mervyn Dymally, and a few others who played that role. Those were all standout politicians, but other than Jerry Brown, none had as strong ties to the old San Francisco; other than Willie Brown, no legislator played as important a role in passing legislation in Sacramento.

Moscone's adult life reflects his grounding in both San Franciscos. He fought for decriminalizing marijuana possession, acupuncture, and gay sex, but was also the Catholic father of four who insisted that his son, who he may have known was gay, attend his own Jesuit alma mater rather than a more secular and liberal independent high school, and who sent his daughters to an elite Catholic school in the city's toniest neighborhood. Moscone was a man whose reputation for philandering has outlived him by more than four decades and would destroy a political career today, yet he remained married to his wife and was a loving, if not always present, father.

Moscone had a sense of style in a city, and media environment, where that kind of thing was appreciated. Both Moscone and Willie Brown were known for the sports cars they drove, the restaurants and bars which they frequented, and their womanizing, although Moscone was never as sharp a dresser as Brown. That sense of style won Moscone years of positive coverage from Herb Caen, the most influential newspaperman in San Francisco during Moscone's adult life. Moscone's image belied the reality that he had little money and left his widow and four children almost nothing. Even the house in which they lived had very likely not been bought by Moscone, but by wealthy political patrons.

Had Moscone not been assassinated in late 1978, he would have been up for reelection in 1979. His most likely opponent in that race would have been the conservative supervisor, and close friend of John Barbagelata, Quentin Kopp. Kopp was a better politician than Barbagelata, but Moscone would have had the advantage of incumbency. If Moscone had been able to serve two full terms, he would have had a much bigger role in the making of modern San Francisco. However, even in that scenario, he would have been constrained by the passage of Proposition 13 in June 1978, the election of Ronald Reagan to the presidency a year and a half later, and the AIDS plague that had such a terrible and profound impact on San Francisco. On the other hand, if Moscone had lost to Kopp,

Moscone would have been viewed as part of a failed effort to shift the city's politics leftward before San Francisco was ready for that.

Dwelling too much on these questions obscures the real impact Moscone made as a politician and his centrality to the evolution of San Francisco during the middle half of the twentieth century. Moscone was more than simply a transitional figure. He helped craft and guide the enormous changes his city underwent during his life and career. Growing up in the aftermath of the 1934 general strike and spending much of his youth on the playgrounds and basketball courts of what was then a very working-class town gave Moscone a deep and enduring empathy for labor and working people as well as an understanding of the city's neighborhoods as the foundation of life in San Francisco.

On the board of supervisors, Moscone cast decisive votes against freeway construction that would have in a very meaningful way destroyed San Francisco. His position was a natural outgrowth of the value he placed on neighborhood. During his years as a supervisor, Moscone rounded out his positions by beginning to embrace what became the new left. In addition to traveling to Mississippi to help register voters, he used his position as a supervisor to give his support, and a measure of protection, to the free speech movement and other political and cultural benchmarks that helped define modern and progressive San Francisco. In doing this, Moscone carved out space in the city's political institutions for positions that, within a few years after his death, would be mainstream in most of San Francisco.

During his nine years in the state senate, Moscone began to forge the future of progressive California. As the Democratic leader in the senate, Moscone, along with colleagues in Sacramento including Willie Brown and John Burton, as well as Southern Californians such as Mervyn Dymally and Jim Mills, invigorated progressive politics in Sacramento. They fought and won some of the earliest skirmishes in the efforts to decriminalize drugs and for LGBT equality. They also passed important civil rights legislation and supported the United Farm Workers, civil rights advocates, and anti-war activists at a time when they were under assault from a right-wing governor with national political aspirations.

Moscone's term as mayor represented an important transition in San Francisco. Although the woman who became mayor after Moscone was assassinated left a far greater mark on San Francisco, it was made possible by Moscone. Moscone's three years as mayor take on a different feel when viewed not through the prism of just San Francisco, but of urban America more generally. The contrast between the 1975 election in San Francisco and the mayoral election in New York two years later where, as in San Francisco, a large field of candidates was winnowed down to a contest between two white men, demonstrates how unusual San Francisco was at the time.

Unlike George Moscone in 1975, neither Ed Koch nor Mario Cuomo, the two leading candidates, embraced gay rights in that election. Koch, who never married, pretended to be romantically involved with Bess Myerson, the first Jewish Miss America, to counter rumors that he was gay. The Cuomo campaign sought to exploit this perception in the runoff as unofficial campaign channels used the slogan "vote for Cuomo not the homo." The candidate himself was not directly involved in the use of that homophobic slur, but many believe the person behind that was Cuomo's oldest son and close confidante, Andrew. The candidate most associated with gay rights in that campaign was Bella Abzug, but she finished in fourth place in the first round of the Democratic primary with only about 16.5 percent of the vote.

Mario Cuomo was, like Moscone, a Catholic school-educated Italian American. Cuomo, who was three years younger than Moscone, ran as a centrist but represented the more liberal elements within New York's Italian American community. Cuomo lost that election, but he went on to serve three terms as the governor of New York. By 1994 when he was finishing his twelfth year in that office, he had moved close to where Moscone was on social issues back in 1975.

Koch served three terms as mayor of New York, but in 1989 lost the Democratic primary to David Dinkins. Dinkins was the first African American mayor of New York and a true progressive. He won by building a coalition that included progressive white voters, Latinos, gay and lesbian voters, and massive margins and turnout among African American voters. Throughout the campaign and his time in office, Dinkins referred to his coalition and to his city's diversity in general as a "gorgeous mosaic."

Dinkins's victory in that 1989 primary drew heavily on the previous year's Democratic primary for president in which Jesse Jackson outpolled eventual nominee Michael Dukakis in New York City. Jackson's multiracial coalition as well as his outreach to LGBT New Yorkers lay the groundwork for Dinkins's defeat of Koch the following year. Dinkins recognized this by noting, "I know what Jesse did for me."[2] Jackson's New York coalition was the same as Dinkins a year later, but also the same as George Moscone's fourteen years earlier and three thousand miles away. This progressive coalition may seem obvious in retrospect, but that was certainly not the case in 1989 much less 1975.[3] Dinkins is just one example, but the Moscone coalition, which led to the Barack Obama coalition, is now the only way progressives win elections in big diverse cities or states.

More than forty years after his death, Moscone does not seem quite so far left. By 1990 or so, it had become extremely rare for cities to be governed entirely by white men, but when Moscone came into office in January 1976 he became the first white big-city mayor to make a commitment to diversity. Similarly, positions on LGBT rights and marijuana use that made Moscone seem like a quirky San Francisco liberal while he was alive are now mainstream opinions held by even some Republicans.

Since Moscone's death, several other progressive big-city mayors have assembled Moscone-like coalitions and made similar promises on issues such as empowering neighborhoods, giving a voice to a diverse group of activists, reigning in police, and making City Hall a counterweight to the business community. In San Francisco, Art Agnos is the only post-Moscone mayor who fits this mold. But New York's Dinkins and Bill de Blasio, Chicago's Harold Washington, and a handful of others built similar coalitions, made similar promises, and took similar positions to those of Moscone. During the last several decades, Moscone's radical San Francisco politics have been at the core of progressive cities.

While mayor, Moscone's progressive vision for the city always had to be balanced against what was necessary to keep the business leadership reasonably happy and to prevent them from leaving the city. This dynamic limited what Moscone was able to do, but was made worse because midway through his third, and final, year in office, Moscone had to reckon with the fallout from Proposition 13. The balance between progressive goals and maintaining a tax base remains a challenge for all progressive mayors. Few, if any, genuinely succeed at this. Moscone did not either and was unable to realize his more ambitious programs for the city and its neighborhoods. In one of his last interviews, when asked what his major accomplishments were, Moscone cited his ability to balance the city's budget.[4]

The challenges Moscone faced as mayor underscore central questions about Moscone—why he became a progressive committed to helping the poor and the underrepresented rather than an affluent conservative attorney, and why he reacted to the cultural and political changes in his city the way that he did? These questions may not ever be answered fully, but it is critical to give it some rigorous thought.

Because Moscone was killed shortly after his forty-ninth birthday, our only images of him, whether through old photographs and video or actual memories are that of a young person or a very vibrant and youthful looking middle-aged man. Because Moscone is always youthful in our memories, with time it is more difficult to place him generationally, but it's essential to do that. Moscone was born in 1929, so was in his mid-thirties when he registered voters in Mississippi in 1964, and almost forty when the Summer of Love was happening in his hometown. Moscone was more than fifteen years older than the oldest baby boomers, so his politics were not a product of the youth culture of his college or early career years. He was of that generation too old to have been hippies and too young to have fought in World War II.

By the time Moscone ran for mayor, his politics were out of step with his demographic cohort. Straight, middle-aged, Italian American men were not appreciably on the cutting edge of San Francisco's progressive politics in the 1970s. In fact, the opposite was true. People who shared those characteristics were the backbone of conservative politics in most cities, including San Francisco. His four years at St. Ignatius could have pushed Moscone more firmly into the conservative camp. A young lawyer with Moscone's people skills and a high school diploma from St. Ignatius—these things mattered a lot in San Francisco then—would have been welcomed at any corporate conservative law firm in the city and all but guaranteed a successful and lucrative legal career.

There are many possible explanations for why Moscone did not follow that path, but all are gnawingly unsatisfactory. Several people cited Moscone's years as an adolescent growing up in Cow Hollow, traveling throughout the city to play basketball in various playgrounds against other young men from those neighborhoods as having formed his worldview. Jonathan Moscone explained, "Every neighborhood could be equal. . . . He was playing the same game with different people in different parts of the city. To him, the city was made up of very different people who could play on the court. . . . If you gave everybody the same court, the same platform, everybody in the city would thrive."[5] The idea of a young George Moscone playing in a pickup game in Potrero Hill, the Mission, the Sunset or Hunters Point is appealing, even romantic. We can imagine the future mayor visiting different parts of the city, being exposed to its human and meteorological diversity, and falling in love with San Francisco. However, the connection between that and being drawn to progressive politics is unclear. I grew up in Cow Hollow and played ball, in my case baseball, throughout the city in both middle school and high school. Like Moscone, it helped me learn about and love San Francisco, but it did not change my politics. More pertinently, it did not change the politics of many of my more conservative friends and teammates.

It is possible to play ball in an African American or Latino neighborhood and come to appreciate the obstacles, off the court, that the people in those communities face because of their skin color, or heritage, but it is just as possible to play in those games and look down on the people there because the neighborhoods aren't as clean or have higher crime rates. The conclusions may have a lot more to do with the biases and opinions that are brought into the playground rather than the playground itself.

People who knew Moscone frequently allude to the future mayor being raised by a hard-working, single mother in a household where money was scarce. Lena Moscone was hugely influential in her son's life as is frequently the case with only children of single mothers. Their bond by all accounts was very intense, but little is known about his mother's work experiences or politics that would clearly point Moscone in a particular ideological direction. Even Lena Moscone's own grandchildren have trouble remembering precisely what her political opinions were. She worked for decades at the Department of Motor Vehicles in a modest-paying, but not exactly radicalizing, environment. Similarly, while the experience of being raised by a single mother may have helped Moscone present a more compelling story to voters, millions of Americans are raised by single mothers and not all become great progressives.

Larry Griffin was a young volunteer when Moscone ran for mayor in 1975. Griffin's work included organizing and getting out the vote in the heavily African American Western Addition. Griffin got to know Moscone well during that campaign and during his time as mayor. He described Moscone as "a really caring guy and you could see it." Griffin also believed that Lena Moscone was instrumental in Moscone's political view: "His mom was a single mother. She had a hard time. . . . Whether Lee instilled it or whether George just got it, saw what his mom was going through," but Griffin also conceded, "I'm just guessing. I don't know for sure."[6]

Jon Rubin preferred a more mystical explanation: "Every once a while the right guy comes to the plate with the bases loaded and gets his pitch and hits it out of the park. It happens, so we have to acknowledge it. . . . If it's this batter at this moment, it happens. If it's some other batter at this moment . . . it doesn't happen. This synthesis is a spark in a universe that is inexplicable."[7]

A related and more persuasive point here is that Moscone was not just raised in any city at any time, but in San Francisco during the 1930s and 1940s, a time of radical politics and then mobilization against fascism. During the general strike of 1934, Moscone was only four years old, so he could not have had strong memories of the event itself. But in the event's aftermath, the presence of the powerful and triumphant International Longshore and Warehouse Union, whose members worked only a short walk away from Moscone's home, other strong labor unions, and pro-labor politics throughout much of the city were part of the background of his childhood. Moscone may have embraced the radicalism of the time and place as a young boy and stuck with it into adulthood.

St. Ignatius was one of the most important institutions in Moscone's life. Attending the prestigious all-boys Jesuit high school brought Moscone into contact with a much broader range of young people than he had known at St. Brigid and made it possible for Moscone to build relationships with the sons of the city's Catholic elite. St. Ignatius was, and remains, a complex place. It has long been the high school of choice for San Francisco's wealthiest and most powerful Catholic families. It has never been a hotbed of radicalism, but nor is it a bastion of reaction. St. Ignatius was, and is, a Jesuit school where academic excellence, intellectual curiosity, service and, importantly for Moscone, athletics, are all important parts of the pedagogical approach. For generations, graduates of St. Ignatius have joined the ranks of San Francisco's most prestigious businesses, banks, law firms and establishments, but that is not all they have done. Among those who have gone on to public service are Jerry Brown, who got to St. Ignatius a few years after Moscone, Leo McCarthy, who played basketball with Moscone at St. Ignatius, and other successful politicians.

The night Moscone defeated John Barbagelata in the runoff, one of the men who stood closest to him on that stage alongside his family was Phil Burton. Moscone had long been associated with what many referred to as the Burton machine, but it was not Phil who provided the future mayor's political entrée into this powerful political family. Moscone's initial contact with the Burtons was through Phil's brother John. John Burton was an impressive politician in his own right, spending more than thirty years in the California State Senate and Assembly and US House of Representatives. He and Moscone met first not as politicians, but as high school students. The Burtons helped bring Moscone into politics and remained close political supporters during the early years of Moscone's political career, backing him beginning with his unsuccessful campaign for the assembly in 1960. The Burtons were on the left wing of the Democratic Party even in the 1950s. While they alone did not bring Moscone to that same political place, they certainly made it a lot easier for him to stay there.

Phil Burton may have been Moscone's primary political patron, but Willie Brown was his closest friend in politics. The two met as students working their way through law school and were friends and political allies until Moscone's death. In Sacramento, they worked together on numerous pieces of legislation and supported each other's political endeavors. They also came from different backgrounds. Brown was not from Italian American San Francisco but was African American and had grown up in segregation-era Texas. He also played an instrumental role in sharpening Moscone's concerns about racial injustice and commitment to racial equality. Arnold Townsend, the longtime San Francisco civil rights activist, told me that Brown had "of course" influenced Moscone and the Burtons in this regard as well and explained that "Willie Brown had as much or more influence on their politics than they had on Willie's.[8]

There is no one reason, event, institution or person that set Moscone on a course that would lead to a life working for progressive causes, but it was a combination of these things. The only son of a hard-working single mother whose prowess on the basketball court allowed him to experience the San Francisco of the 1930s and 1940s through the lens of its neighborhood playgrounds later had the good fortune to study at a Jesuit high school, where academic excellence and service were part of the culture. He then found his way to a pair of brothers who became pillars of progressive politics in San Francisco and nationally and whose influence is still felt in the third decade of the twenty-first century.

That is a compelling narrative of George Moscone's journey to progressive politics, but again it is a correlation, a retelling of events, with little evidence of causality. Those events could have led to different outcomes. Many children who grow up in tough circumstances and then make it to good Jesuit schools end up subscribing to right-wing worldviews that see the less fortunate as undeserving and refuse to accept the reality of how deep-seated bigotry is in American life, but that was not George Moscone. Those who knew Moscone spoke of his kindness, humor, decency, and belief that all of us are equal. That view into Moscone's character also helps explain why his life experience led him in a particular political direction.

From 1930 to 1980, that is from a few weeks after Moscone's birth to about a year after his death, the demographics, politics, culture, and economics of San Francisco changed almost beyond recognition. Few people were at the center of that, and played as big a role, as George Moscone. The story of his life cannot be told other than in the context of San Francisco during those five decades, but it is also the case that San Francisco during those years cannot be fully appreciated without understanding who George Moscone was and how he helped shape the city.

The journey from working-class son of a single mother to all-city athlete at an elite private school to progressive attorney to powerful elected official is a bit like a San Francisco Horatio Alger story, albeit one with a tragic ending. However, Moscone's impact was much greater than that. In today's San Francisco, with its enormous wealth, corresponding income inequality, and declining African American population, it may seem like the impact of the progressive mayor who served for only three years has faded, but it is still there. His significance is felt not just in a few places that now bear his name such as a ballfield in his old neighborhood and a school in the Mission District. Moscone's enduring influence on San Francisco can be felt far beyond the Giants still playing in San Francisco or the convention center that he helped make a reality—and where in 2021 thousands of San Franciscans, including one middle-aged friend of mine who as a young Catholic school boy snuck into St Mary's Cathedral to attend Moscone's funeral, were vaccinated against COVID-19.

Despite the now twenty-year-long influx of new tech money and the more than forty continuous years of centrist mayors in City Hall, broken up only by Art Agnos's one term, much of the progressive and neighborhood-based vision that drove Moscone and mobilized so many San Franciscans to support him can still be felt. The LGBTQ movement has made enormous strides since Moscone became the first big-city mayor to successfully campaign on a pro-gay rights platform and then to sign a new law banning discrimination against LGBTQ people. San Francisco continues to play a central role in that movement and is still one of the most pro-LGBTQ cities in the world. That cannot all be attributed to Moscone obviously, but his role in making that happen in the mid-1970s should not be overlooked.

The Harvey Milk Center for the Arts is in Duboce Park, just north of the Castro District, and is part of the San Francisco Recreation and Parks Department. It is a city-run facility with programs in the visual and performing arts. On the front of the modernist building that was built in 1954 is a Milk quote from a 1977 speech that reads, "The American Dream starts with the neighborhoods. . . ."[9] Milk's phrasing reflects both his skills as a leader and speaker, but also the politics of San Francisco during the Moscone era.

Milk's comment, like Moscone's emphasis on neighborhoods, still drives much of San Francisco politics, but in different ways. Moscone's San Francisco was a largely middle- and working-class city with declining populations and diverse neighborhoods struggling against a business community that had run San Francisco for generations. The neighborhoods organized for more representation in city government and more services, but they also opposed freeway construction and Manhattanization that threatened to turn San Francisco into a financial hub that would destroy much of the city's beauty and feel. It is apparent now that the neighborhood movement succeeded in the first area but failed in the second.

Today, in a city that has seen population growth, a transformed economy, and a massive homelessness problem, neighborhood politics in San Francisco cannot be separated from the intense debates around housing. Neighborhood politics are frequently caricatured as NIMBYism, but many of these alleged NIMBYs are calling for building affordable, rather than market-rate and luxury housing. In some senses, Manhattanization has moved to the neighborhoods, and the neighborhoods are fighting back. The politics of this are very complicated: some neighborhoods are fighting to keep out development that would bring in affluent tech workers, but some say limiting housing in this way drives costs up and contributes to the housing crisis. Moscone never confronted this particular problem, but his emphasis on neighborhoods is an antecedent that informs the housing debates of today.

The San Francisco that Moscone knew, where most residents were natives and frequently judged by where they went to high school, where it was possible for a mayoral candidate to know people throughout the city, has given way to an extremely transient city with very little institutional memory and many residents who cannot trace their roots there for more than two decades, and even fewer for more than two generations. Given that, it is very easy in the San Francisco of today to dismiss history, even relatively recent history, as irrelevant or not to know it at all. However, you cannot fully understand the current debate about housing if you don't know about the Freeway Revolts. The 2022 recall of District Attorney Chesa Boudin looks somewhat different when the long and destructive role the Police Officers Association, one of the major forces behind the recall, has played in San Francisco, particularly during the 1970s, is remembered. Similarly, the displacement of low-income renters, who are primarily people of color, over the last two decades or so is part of the longer story of redevelopment in the city. More broadly, understanding George Moscone's life and his San Francisco allows for deeper insight into how San Francisco grew into the unique, deeply paradoxical, extraordinarily diverse city it is today.

Acknowledgments

THIS BOOK WOULD NOT HAVE been possible without the support, advice, and assistance of several people and institutes. The team at the San Francisco History Center at the main branch of the San Francisco Public Library as well as at the George Moscone Collection at the University of the Pacific helped me find enormous amounts of archival and other material that were essential for writing this book. The Bay Area Television Archive at San Francisco State University is a wonderful video archive where I found most of the videos cited in the book. This is not a baseball book, but the excellent Baseball Reference site was, as usual, essential for checking baseball facts.

Many people who knew George Moscone very generously spent time doing lengthy interviews with me. Among those people were Art Agnos, Willie Brown, John Burton, Corey Busch, Jeannette Etheredge, the late Larry Griffin, Cleve Jones, the late Joe Kelly, George Miller, Christopher Moscone, Jonathan Moscone, Rudy Nothenberg, Jon Rubin, Sharyn Saslafsky, Larry Simi, and the late Arnold Townsend.

In addition to those interviews, Rubin shared with me a collection of interviews he had coordinated in 2009–2011 for a currently unfinished documentary film on the life of George Moscone. Those interviews are now at the University of the Pacific's George Moscone Collection. They are referred to as the George Moscone Oral History Project in the endnotes and bibliography of this book. Busch was also extremely helpful as I was writing this book. He put me in touch with several people for interviews and made his personal Moscone archive available to me. Additionally, the countless hours I spent talking baseball with Corey were a fun, healthy, and sometimes necessary diversion from my writing and academic work.

This book is about one San Franciscan and San Francisco more broadly, but much of it was written in New York. Several people in New York offered important support for me. Ester Fuchs from Columbia University, Mitchell Moss from New York University, and the late Ken Sherrill from Hunter College have all played instrumental roles in my thinking about urban history, urban politics, and George Moscone. All three of them encouraged me to write this book and to continue writing about San Francisco. Robert W. Bailey passed away in 2001, but when I was a young graduate student at Columbia University, Bob was the first academic who showed interest in my knowledge of the politics of San Francisco. His work continues to frame much of my views of urban politics.

Jackson Langford Hasty was an undergraduate student of mine who is much better with mapping software then I am. He created maps that helped me understand the persistence of neighborhood-based voting in San Francisco.

While Jackson was a fantastic research assistant, my two nonhuman research assistants also were essential to this book. Isis and then Penny Lane slept on the job a bit but also got me out of the house for breaks and walks. I don't know if I would have made it through working on this book during the early months of the pandemic if not for those breaks with Isis, which were frequently the only times I left the house for days. Isis died in 2021, and Penny Lane now has those responsibilities.

I am very grateful to the University of Nevada Press. It has been a pleasure working with JoAnne Banducci, Curtis Vickers, Caddie Dufurrena, Paul Szydelko, and their colleagues. I am appreciative of the work they have done to make this book a reality. Two anonymous reviewers for the University of Nevada Press helped make this book better. One of those reviewers had an encyclopedic knowledge of San Francisco political history. That reviewer's painstaking work was a great contribution to the process and the final version of the book. Additionally, Christian Ettinger from the Ettinger Foundation provided a grant that helped me complete this book.

My support network in San Francisco includes many people with whom I have been discussing San Francisco politics for a long time. None have informed my thinking about the city more than Will Lowry. The conversations we began in the early 1980s continue today. Charles A. Fracchia Sr. died in 2021, but the hours we spent discussing San Francisco still help guide my thinking about the city. Charles A. Fracchia Jr. remains one of my closest friends. Charles Jr. is the biggest San Francisco Giants fan I have ever known and for decades has reminded many of us that George Moscone saved the Giants from moving to Toronto.

During the three years Moscone was mayor, there was nobody with whom I spent more time than my late brother, Jonathan Mitchell. San Francisco has not been the same for me since he died in 2014. My mother, Susan Mitchell, has always supported my work in any way she can. I am deeply grateful for everything she has done for me. Like pretty much everything I do, this book would not have been possible without my wife, Marta, and my sons Asher and Reuben.

I'm not sure it is possible to acknowledge a city, but this book reflects my deep fascination, some might say obsession, with San Francisco. It is my hope that people who read this book will not only learn about George Moscone's life and the important role he played in forging modern San Francisco but will also gain a deeper understanding of what remains, in my view the most beautiful, fascinating, complex, and important small city in the world.

Notes

Preface

1 Letter from Bill Graham to George Moscone, December 4, 2021, courtesy of Corey Busch/George Moscone archive.

2 US Census.

3 One extreme example of this is Daniel Flynn's (2018) *Cult City: Jim Jones, Harvey Milk, and 10 Days That Shook San Francisco*, Wilmington, DE: Intercollegiate Studies Institute.

Chapter 1. Neighborhoods

1 Interview with Rebecca Moscone, George Moscone Oral History Project, November 30, 2009.

2 Christopher Moscone, interview with author, November 4, 2021.

3 Lombardo, Timothy J. (2018), *Blue-Collar Conservatism: Frank Rizzo's Philadelphia and Populist Politics*, Philadelphia: University of Pennsylvania Press, 243.

4 Joseph L. Alioto, "Changing the Face of San Francisco: Mayor 1968–1976, and Antitrust Trial Lawyer," an oral history conducted in 1991 by Carole Hicke, Regional Oral History Office, The Bancroft Library, University of California, Berkeley, 1999, 151, parentheses mine.

5 Osman, Suleiman (2011), *The Invention of Brownstone Brooklyn*, London: Oxford University Press, 246–247.

6 The 1975 mayor's race was the first in San Francisco where if no candidate got 50 percent of the vote, the top two candidates would go to a runoff. Moreover, the runoff was held on a Thursday, rather than a Tuesday as in most years. This made turnout in the runoff a particular challenge for both candidates.

7 GLIDE Memorial Church, About, https://www.glide.org/about/, accessed December 17, 2018.

8 Osman, *The Invention of Brownstone Brooklyn*, 247.

9 Interview with Chris Moscone, circa 2010, George Moscone Oral History Project, parentheses mine. Because of San Francisco's steep hills, hidden stairways around the city function as shortcuts for pedestrians.

10 Hartman, Chester (2002), *City for Sale: The Transformation of San Francisco*, Berkeley: University of California Press, 6.

11 Larry D. Hatfield, "Cow Hollow—Chic New Tourist Mecca," *San Francisco Examiner*, August 3, 1970, 38.

12 George Dushek, "The Early Days of Cow Hollow," *San Francisco Chronicle & Examiner*, February 6, 1966, Section 11, 2.
13 Booker, Matthew Morse (2013), *Down by the Bay*, Berkeley and Los Angeles: University of California Press, 6,
14 Davies, Andrea Rees (2012), *Saving San Francisco: Relief and Recovery after the 1906 Disaster*, Philadelphia: Temple University Press, 140.
15 Davies, 140.
16 McGloin, John Bernard (1978), *San Francisco: The Story of a City*, San Rafael, CA: Presidio Press, 159–160, parentheses in original, brackets mine.
17 Rand Richards, "Neighborhood Historic Sites," *The Marina Times*, January 2003, 8, parentheses in original.
18 "San Francisco Neighborhoods: Socio-Economic Profiles," American Community Surveys, 40. This document uses a larger definition of the Marina in which the population is 25,000, so the 10,000 is an estimate based on that, parentheses in original.
19 "Cow Hollow," undated pamphlet, probably circa 1980, from a series promoting various San Francisco neighborhoods. "Outer" in this context means western because Union Street, like much of San Francisco, developed from east to west, parentheses mine.
20 Pawel, Miriam (2019), *The Browns of California*, New York: Bloomsbury, 5
21 Bay Area Census, http://www.bayareacensus.ca.gov/historical/copop18602000.htm, accessed December 13, 2018.
22 World Population Review, http://worldpopulationreview.com/us-cities/new-york-city-population/, accessed February 5, 2019.
23 Yglesias, Matthew, "America's 10 biggest cities, in every decade going back to 1790," Vox, July 5, 2015.
24 Another famous athlete who graduated from Galileo was O. J. Simpson.
25 Gumina, Deanna Paoli (1978), *The Italians of San Francisco 1850–1930*, Center for Migration Studies, New York, 5.
26 Gumina, Epilogue.
27 Issel, William and Robert W. Cherny (1986), *San Francisco 1865–1932: Politics, Power and Urban Development*, Berkeley and Los Angeles, University of California Press, 56.
28 Gumina, 57.
29 Scott, Mel (1959), *The San Francisco Bay Area: A Metropolis in Perspective*, Berkeley, University of California Press, 202.
30 Scott, 224.
31 Johnson, Victoria L., *How Many Machine Guns Does It Take to Cook One Meal?: The Seattle and San Francisco General Strikes*, Seattle: University of Washington Press, 2008, 79.
32 Johnson, 82. C. L. Dellums was the brother of Verney Dellums, who was also a member of the ILA. Verney Dellums was the father of Ron Dellums, who served in Congress from the East Bay from 1971 to 1998 and later became mayor of Oakland.
33 Johnson, 94.
34 Carlson, Peter (2009), *K Blows Top: A Cold War Comic Interlude, Starring Nikita Khruschev, America's Most Unlikely Tourist*, New York: Public Affairs, 192.
35 Fichera, Sebastian (2011), *Italy on the Pacific: San Francisco's Italian Americans*, New York: Palgrave Macmillan, 134–135.

36 Our Campaigns, https://www.ourcampaigns.com/ContainerHistory.html?ContainerID=16198, accessed March 28, 2023.
37 Fischera, *Italy on the Pacific*, 149.
38 "The Living New Deal," https://livingnewdeal.org/us/ca/san-francisco/page/4/, accessed January 7, 2019.
39 Pawel, *The Browns of California*, 45.
40 US Census, http://www.bayareacensus.ca.gov/counties/SanFranciscoCounty40.htm.
41 Belmonte, Peter (2001), *Italian Americans in World War II*, Illinois, Arcadia Publishing.
42 Patricia Yollin "A SECRET HISTORY / The harassment of Italians during World War II has particular relevance today and serves as a warning of what could happen," *San Francisco Chronicle*, October 21, 2001.
43 Arnold Townsend, interview with author, February 24, 2021.
44 Freeman, John, "War Anxiety in San Francisco's Western Neighborhoods," *Outside Lands: San Francisco History from the Western Neighborhoods Project*, Vol. 13, No.1, 2017, 7.
45 Interview with Hadley Roth, George Moscone Oral History Project, July 19, 2011.
46 Veronico, Nicholas (2007), *Images of America: World War II: Shipyards by the Bay*, San Francisco: Arcadia, 7.
47 Pawel, *The Browns of California*, 49.
48 Shilts, Randy (1982), *The Mayor of Castro Street: The Life and Times of Harvey Milk*, New York: St. Martin's Press, 50–51.

Chapter 2. Family and Childhood

1 World Population Review, http://worldpopulationreview.com/us-cities/oakdale-ca-population/, accessed February 13, 2019.
2 World Population Review, https://worldpopulationreview.com/us-cities/stockton-ca-population, accessed April 8, 2021.
3 "Large High School Class Graduates," *Oakdale Leader*, June 17, 1926, 1.
4 "Monge Pleads Guilty," *Oakdale Leader*, June 17, 1926, 2.
5 "Local Girl Weds S. F. Man Sunday," *Oakdale Leader*, February 14, 1929, p. 4.
6 "Local Girl Weds," *Oakdale Leader*, 4.
7 Interview with Jennifer Moscone, George Moscone Oral History Project, parentheses mine.
8 Interview with Cappy Lavin, George Moscone Oral History Project, July 2, circa 2011.
9 "We Wonder Why," *Oakdale Leader*, November 29, 1978.
10 *Oakdale Leader*, May 4, 1950, 4
11 Interview with Jennifer Moscone, George Moscone Oral History Project.
12 "Funerals," *San Francisco Examiner & Chronicle*, August 2, 1972.
13 Chris Moscone, interview with author, November 4, 2021.
14 Jonathan Moscone, interview with author, November 6, 2021.
15 Lavin interview, circa 2011.
16 Lavin interview, circa 2011.
17 Morch, Albert, "Lee Moscone: Every Son's Dream of the Perfect Mom," *San Francisco Examiner and Chronicle*, May 14, 1978, Scene, 3.
18 Interview with Jennifer Moscone, George Moscone Oral History Project, parentheses mine.

19 Interview with Rebecca Moscone Rodolph, George Moscone Oral History Project, November 30, 2009.
20 Interview with Christopher Moscone, George Moscone Oral History Project, date unknown.
21 Interview with Jonathan Moscone, George Moscone Oral History Project, May 4, 2011.
22 Interview with Jennifer Moscone, George Moscone Oral History Project, parentheses mine.
23 Joe Kelly, interview with author, October, 20, 2021.
24 John Burton, interview with author, September 11, 2020.
25 Interview with Christopher Moscone, George Moscone Oral History Project, circa 2011.
26 Christopher Moscone, Oral History Project, circa 2011,
27 *A Guide to Church Vital Statistics Records in California, San Francisco and Alameda Counties: Six Denominations*, The Northern California Historical Records Survey Project, Service Division, Work Projects Administration; San Francisco, May 1942.
28 I attended University High School, graduated in 1985, and was in the fourth category of students. Among my fellow students were a daughter of Nancy Pelosi; son of John Molinari, who was a powerful member of the board of supervisors; son of a top aide to former President Richard Nixon; the son of an influential federal judge; and many other sons and daughters of wealthy and powerful San Franciscans.
29 Interview with Jonathan Moscone, George Moscone Oral History Project, May 4, 2011.
30 Jonathan Moscone, interview with author, November 6, 2021
31 Interview with Christopher Moscone, George Moscone Oral History Project, date unknown.
32 Christopher Moscone, interview with author, November 4, 2021.
33 I attended Stuart Hall from kindergarten through eighth grade and graduated in 1981. My math teacher in sixth-eighth grade would occasionally pause class to admire a ship in the bay and explain the history or design of the ship.
34 *Traditions of Excellence: The History of St. Ignatius College Preparatory 1855–Present*, undated 1970s, 2.
35 *Traditions of Excellence*, 9.
36 "George Moscone Wins Frosh Elocution Medal," *The Red and Blue: Official Organ of the Student Body*, Saint Ignatius College Prep March, 1944.
37 Joe Kelly, interview with author, October 30, 2020.
38 Pawel, Miriam (2019), *The Browns of California*, 68.
39 Lavin interview, circa 2011.
40 Kelly, interview, October 30, 2020.
41 Lavin interview, circa 2011.
42 Marcus, Bob, "Lowell, Sacred Heart Draw Cage Inaugural," *San Francisco Chronicle*, January 6, 1946, 28.
43 "Prep Rivals Vie Tonight," *San Francisco Examiner*, February 4, 1946, 18.
44 Kelly, interview, October 30, 2020.

45 *The Ignatian*, 1947.

46 Basketball program: S. I All-City All-Stars vs. S.I. Varsity (1953).

47 Our History—War & Valor: 1940–1949, St. Ignatius website, https://www.siprep.org/about-us/our-history/war-valor-1940–1949.

48 Kelly, interview, October 30, 2020.

49 Lavin interview, circa 2011.

50 "Our History—War & Valor: 1940–1949, St. Ignatius website, https://www.siprep.org/about-us/our-history/war-valor-1940-1949, accessed March 28, 2023.

51 Fouts and Ruether should be seen in a context. Galileo counts O. J. Simpson and Joe DiMaggio as its most famous alumni athletes.

52 Mayor George Moscone schedule, May 3, 1978.

53 Lavin interview, circa 2011.

54 Jon Rubin, interview with author, October 27, 2021.

55 Jonathan Moscone, interview with author, November 6, 2021.

56 Michael Grieg, "George Moscone—Who He Is, What He's Like," *San Francisco Chronicle*, January 8, 1976, 6.

57 Kelly, interview, October 30, 2020.

58 Christopher Moscone interview, November 4, 2021.

Chapter 3. San Francisco After the War

1 Kelly, interview with author, October 30, 2020.

2 US Census.

3 Some older New Yorkers felt dismayed by this development. Others responded differently. For example, my maternal grandfather, who was a lifelong New Yorker, was born in 1907 and grew up speaking Yiddish as a first language, but at in the early 1970s learned Spanish to communicate more easily in his city.

4 Los Angeles Almanac, http://www.laalmanac.com/population/po20.php, accessed March 28, 2023.

5 Interview with Willie Brown, George Moscone Oral History Project.

6 Arnold Townsend, interview with author, February 24, 2021.

7 Ungaretti, Lori,"The Sunset District: From Dunes to Cityscape," undated, FoundSF, http://www.foundsf.org/index.php?title=The_Sunset_District:_From_Dunes_to_Cityscape, accessed March 28, 2023.

8 "Income of Families and Persons in the United States: 1949," US Census Bureau, February 18, 1951 https://www.census.gov/library/publications/1951/demo/p60-007.html, accessed March 28, 2023.

9 "Bay Area Census," San Francisco City and County, http://www.bayareacensus.ca.gov/counties/SanFranciscoCounty50.htm, accessed March 28, 2023.

10 "Bay Area Census."

11 "Bay Area Census."

12 "Urban Areas in the United States: 1950 to 2010," Demographia, http://www.demographia.com/db-uza2000.htm, accessed March 28, 2023.

13 "Bay Area Census"

14 "Industrial Land in San Francisco: Understanding Production, Distribution, and Repair," San Francisco Planning Department, July 2002, https://sfplanning.org/sites/

default/files/resources/201906/Industrial_Land_in_San_Francisco_PDR_SF_2002.pdf , accessed March 28, 2023. Note how the word "city" is capitalized. That is very common in San Francisco when referring to the city.

15 DeLeon, Richard (1992), *Left Coast City: Progressive Politics in San Francisco, 1975–1992*, Lawrence: University of Kansas Press, 13.

16 Godfrey, Brian (1997), "Urban Development and Redevelopment in San Francisco," *Geographical Review*, Vol. 87, No. 3 (309–333), 316.

17 "Vehicle Ownership in US Cities Data and Map," Mike Maciag, Governing, December 9, 2014 (updated 2017), https://www.governing.com/archive/car-ownership-numbers-of-vehicles-by-city-map.html, accessed March 28, 2023.

18 Scott, Mel (1959), *The San Francisco Bay Area: A Metropolis in Perspective*, Berkeley, University of California Press, 238

19 The quotation in the beginning of this paragraph and the information throughout the paragraph draws on William Lathrop's 1969 paper, "The San Francisco Freeway Revolt," which is in the archives at the San Francisco History Center at the San Francisco Public Library. A final version of that essay appeared in *The Transportation Engineering Journal*, (1971) 97/1, 133–144.

20 Johnson, Katherine M., "Captain Blake versus the Highwaymen: Or, How San Francisco Won the Freeway Revolt," *Journal of Planning History*, Vol. 8, No. 1, February 2009, 56–83, 61,

21 Caro, Robert (1974), *The Power Broker: Robert Moses and the Fall of New York*, New York: Vintage Books.

22 Henderson, Jason Mark. (2013), *Street Fight: The Politics of Mobility in San Francisco*, Amherst: University of Massachusetts Press, 3,

23 Issel, William, "Land Values, Human Values, and the Preservation of the City's Treasured Appearance": Environmentalism, Politics, and the San Francisco Freeway Revolt, *Pacific Historical Review*, Vol. 68, No. 4 (November 1999), 611–646, 622.

24 "Population for U.S. Cities Statistics," Governing.com, accessed March 28, 2023.

25 *The Downtowner*, Progress Report, December 2, 1959. Boldface in original. This was a one-page document.

26 Report from San Francisco Chamber of Commerce to San Francisco Planning Commission, April 14, 1961

27 SPUR, "Report on the Proposed Freeway and Trafficways Plan for the City and County of San Francisco," April 1961, 1.

28 SPUR, 3.

29 Lakeside Property Owners Association, letter to San Francisco City Planning Commission, March 24, 1961.

30 Haight Ashbury Neighborhood Council, dear neighbor letter, March 23, 1961.

31 Potrero Boosters and Merchants Association, letter to Mayor George Christopher, April 19, 1961.

32 Board of Directors of the Northern California Chapter of the American Institute of Architects, Statement Made at City Planning Commission Hearing on Trafficways Report, April 13, 1961.

33 Board of Directors of the Northern California Chapter of the American Institute of Architects, April 13, 1961.

34 "Parting Advice from Mumford," *San Francisco Chronicle*, January 16, 1962, 2.

35 Osman, Suleiman (2011) *The Invention of Brownstone Brooklyn: Gentrification and the Search for Authenticity in Postwar New York*, Oxford: Oxford University Press, 13.

36 Johnson, *Journal of Planning History*, 56–57.

37 Hadley Roth interview, George Moscone Oral History Project, July 19, 2011.

38 Issel, *Pacific Historical Review*, 617

39 Interview with Belva Davis, George Moscone Oral History Project, May 4, 2011.

40 Scott, Mel (1959), *The San Francisco Bay Area: A Metropolis in Perspective*, Berkeley, University of California Press, 111.

41 Townsend, interview with author, February 24, 2021.

42 Lai, Clement (2012), "The Racial Triangulation of Space: The Case of Urban Renewal in San Francisco's Fillmore District," *Annals of the Association of American Geographers*, Vol. 102, No. 1, 157.

43 Pepin, Elizabeth and Lewis Watts (2006), *Harlem of the West: The San Francisco Fillmore Jazz Era*, San Francisco, *Chronicle* Books, 13.

44 Pepin and Watts, 37.

45 Pepin and Watts, 56.

46 San Francisco Department of Planning, "The Tentative Plan for the Redevelopment of Western Addition Project Area Number One," February 29, 1952, A-1.

47 Lai, *Annals of the Association of American Geographers*, parentheses mine, italics in original, 153.

48 Lai, 153.

49 Interview with Belva Davis, George Moscone Oral History Project, May 4, 2011.

50 Townsend, interview with author, February 24, 2021.

51 Rexroth, Kenneth "Revolt: True and False," *The Nation*, April 26, 1958, 379.

52 See, for example, Jesse Hamlin, "How Herb Caen Named a Generation," *San Francisco Chronicle*, November 26, 1995. No page number.

53 Agee, Christopher Lowen, "The Emergence of the North Beach Beat Scene," FoundSF, undated. http://www.foundsf.org/index.php?title=The_Emergence_of_the_North_Beach_Beat_Scene.

54 Krebs was played by Bob Denver, who is better known for his role as Gilligan on *Gilligan's Island*.

55 "HUAC Hearing at City Hall," (1960), KPIX News, Bay Area Television Archive, https://diva.sfsu.edu/collections/sfbatv/bundles/190424.

56 "HUAC: May 1960, The Events; The Aftermath," Free Speech Movement Archives, http://www.fsm-a.org/stacks/AP_files/APHUAC60.html.

57 "HUAC: May 1960, The Events; The Aftermath."

58 *San Francisco Chronicle*, April 16, 1958, 1.

59 For more on the changes to the game brought about by this move, see Mitchell, Lincoln (2018), *Baseball Goes West: the Dodgers, the Giants, and the Shaping of the Major Leagues*, Kent, OH: The Kent State University Press.

60 Garratt, Robert F., *Home Team: The Turbulent History of the San Francisco Giants*, Lincoln: University of Nebraska Press, 51.

Chapter 4. The Navy, College and Law School

1 Our History—War & Valor: 1940–1949, St. Ignatius website, https://www.siprep.org/about-us/our-history/war-valor-1940–1949.

2 Joe Kelly, interview with author, October 30, 2020.

3 Doty, Richard, "George Moscone: A Visit with the Mayor of San Francisco, Class of 1953," *Pacific Review*, November 1977, 2.

4 "Surprise Party Announces Friberg, Moscone Betrothal," *Oak Leaf*, March 22, 1950, 7.

5 "Surprise Party," *Oak Leaf*, March 22, 1950, 7.

6 "Surprise Party," *Oak Leaf*, March 22, 1950, 7.

7 "Surprise Party," *Oak Leaf*, March 22, 1950, 1.

8 "Player Sketches of Basketball Tigers," Rod Detrick, *Pacific Weekly*, December 7, 1951, 4.

9 Based on my experience, left-handed Jews, even if they attend Catholic school for a decade, fail to learn good penmanship.

10 Letter from George to Lena Moscone, undated.

11 Gloria Wernsman Glyer obituary, *The Sacramento Bee* from July 19 to July 23, 2017.

12 "Buzz of the Hornet," Gloria Wernsman, *Sacramento State College Hornet*, February 8, 1952, 8, capitals in original. Moscone was the only player named George on the College of the Pacific roster.

13 Willie Brown, interview with author, September 15, 2020.

14 Brown, interview.

15 Hamilton, Mildred, "Gina Moscone: The Private First Lady," *San Francisco Chronicle and Examiner*, November 19, 1978, Scene, 1. The profile of Gina Moscone was essentially a nonpolitical article that sought to give readers of sense of what the mayor's family life was like. It came at an auspicious moment. The headline in that day's newspapers was "Rep. Ryan Shot: Ambush at Guyana Airport," referring to the killing of Representative Leo Ryan at the end of his fact-finding trip. The next ten days would be in turn, horrific, traumatic, and hugely important for the future of San Francisco and the Moscone family.

16 "Moscone's Self-Appraisal," Michael Grieg, *San Francisco Chronicle*, January 9, 1976, 4. First ellipses is not in original.

17 *San Francisco Chronicle*, November 7, 1956, 1.

18 US Election Atlas, https://uselectionatlas.org/RESULTS/state.php?year=1956&fips=36&f=0&off=0&elect=0, accessed March 29, 2023.

19 US Election Atlas, 2.

20 John Burton, interview with author, September 11, 2020.

21 Burton was hanging out at Lowell High School the night he met Moscone, but he attended Lincoln High School, not Lowell.

22 Interview with Agar Jaicks, George Moscone Oral History Project, undated.

23 Interview with Agar Jaicks.

24 Jacobs, John (1995), *Rage for Justice: The Passion and Politics of Phillip Burton*, University of California: Berkeley, 41–42.

25 Jacobs, 41–42.

26 Interview with Willie Brown, George Moscone Oral History Project.

27 John Burton, interview with author, September 11, 2020.

28 Interview with Agar Jaicks.

29 C-Span User Clip (2016), "Barbara Boxer (D-CA) on Phil and John Burton," https://www.c-span.org/video/?c4605655/user-clip-barbara-boxer-phil-john-burton, accessed March 29, 2023.

30 Herb Caen, "'Twas the Day After," *San Francisco Chronicle*, December 26, 1995.

31 John Burton, interview with author, September 11, 2020. Fiona Ma served on the San Francisco Board of Supervisors and in the California State Assembly. She was elected treasurer of California in 2018 and reelected in 2022.

32 Jason Lewis, "Black History: Jackie Robinson excelled at a higher level in other sports," *Los Angeles Sentinel*, July 14, 2011. https://lasentinel.net/black-history-jackie-robinson-excelled-at-a-higher-level-in-other-sports.html, accessed March 29, 2023.

33 "Charles O. Morgan Obituary," *San Francisco Chronicle*, June 10, 2012.

34 Interview with Joe Cotchett, George Moscone Oral History Project, August 26, 2009.

35 Interview with Cotchett.

36 Interview with Cotchett.

37 Interview with John Vlahos, George Moscone Oral History Project, January 24, 2011.

Chapter 5. First Campaigns

1 John Burton, interview with author, September 11, 2020. Somewhat striking is Burton's recollection that when he and Moscone got together they talked about, among other things, "broads" at a time when the latter was a married man with two children. Many married men with two children spend less time talking about "broads" with their friends and more time, for example, with their children.

2 Interview with David Nelson, George Moscone Oral History Project, November 2012, parentheses mine.

3 Jon Rubin, interview with author, October 27, 2021.

4 Interview with Agar Jaicks, George Moscone Oral History Project, undated.

5 "Moscone Seeks Office," *San Francisco Examiner*, March 29, 1960, 8. For much of the period between 1959 and 2018, California had a member of the Brown family as governor. The Brown to which Moscone was referring was Pat Brown, Jerry's father.

6 Interview with Joe Cotchett, George Moscone Oral History, August 26, 2009.

7 "5 S. F. Winners Fail to File Campaign Fund Reports," *San Francisco Chronicle*, July 14, 1960, 26.

8 Elmont Waite, "City Vote: Prop. A 'in'; Underwood Ahead," *San Francisco Chronicle*, June 8, 1960, 11.

9 "State Government Oral History Program, Oral History with Milton Marks," California State Archives (1996) ii.

10 "Oral History with Milton Marks," 102.

11 Pimsleur, J. L, and Kevin Leary "S. F.'s 'Uncle Miltie' Dies—Inveterate Campaigner/Milton Marks served 4 decades in office," *San Francisco Chronicle*, December 5, 1998.

12 Hoppe, Art "GOP Ousts Tuna—No Surprise," *San Francisco Chronicle*, May 16, 1960, 32. This incident demonstrates the casual anti-Chinese racism of the era. The "costume" to which Marks referred, in this context, clearly suggests that some thought it would be good idea to dress Marks, a white politician, in traditional (or their idea of traditional) Chinese clothing.

13 Our Campaigns, https://www.ourcampaigns.com/RaceDetail.html?RaceID=2562, accessed March 29, 2023.
14 "Vote for Two Great Democrats," George Moscone for Assembly, 1960.
15 "The *Chronicle* Recommends," *San Francisco Chronicle*, November 2, 1960, 1.
16 "California Legislature," "S. F. Vote For All Offices," *San Francisco Chronicle*, November 9, 1960, 1a.
17 According to the 1960 census, fully 81.6 percent of San Francisco's population were non-Hispanic whites. http://www.bayareacensus.ca.gov/counties/SanFranciscoCounty50.htmm, accessed March 29, 2023.
18 "Final S. F. Vote," *San Francisco Chronicle*, November 8, 1961, 1.
19 Richard Nixon, press conference, November 7, 1962, http://languagelog.ldc.upenn.edu/myl/RichardNixonConcession.html, accessed March 29, 2023.
20 Richardson, James (1996), *Willie Brown: A Biography*, Berkeley: University of California, 80.
21 Jacobs, John (1995), *A Rage for Justice: The Passion and Politics of Phillip Burton*, Berkeley: University of California Press, 123.
22 Jacobs, 123.
23 Interview with Bruce Brugmann, George Moscone Oral History Project, undated.
24 Interview with Larry Simi, George Moscone Oral History Project, undated.
25 Interview with Leo McCarthy, California State Archives, State Oral History Program, 20.
26 Jacobs, *A Rage for Justice*, 123–124, parentheses mine. I.
27 Interview with Agar Jaicks, George Moscone Oral History, undated.
28 "Lawyer Arraigned As Bookmaker," *San Francisco Chronicle*, April 7, 1962, 3.
29 "Burton Acquitted In Bookie Charge," *San Francisco Chronicle*, November 30, 1962, 3.
30 "Moscone To Run for Board Seat," *San Francisco Examiner*, March 21, 1963, 9.
31 "Atty. Moscone Will Seek Post As Supervisor, *San Francisco News, Call & Bulletin*, March 21, 1963.
32 "Union Body for Shelley," *San Francisco Examiner*, August 27, 1963.
33 Sundahl, Carl, "Tile Layers 19 Notes," *Organized Labor*, August 12, 1963.
34 Interview with David Nelson, George Moscone Oral History Project, November 2012, parentheses mine.
35 Hirsch, James (2010), *Willie Mays: The Life, the Legend*, New York: Scribner, 274, parentheses mine.
36 Hirsch, 274–275.
37 Robertson, Bob, "Dobbs Says Picket Plan Has Political Motive," *San Francisco Chronicle*, October 18, 1963, 4.
38 "Melee at S. F. Drive-in," *San Francisco Chronicle*, November 4, 1963, 1.
39 "The Kind of People We Are," Percy Moore, letter to the editor, *San Francisco Chronicle*, October 31, 1963, 38.
40 Cone, Russ, "Morrison Backs Two for Board," *San Francisco Examiner*, October 31, 1963, 6.
41 "Political Notes," *San Francisco Examiner*, September 5, 1963, 19.
42 "Moscone Blast at Billboards," *San Francisco Chronicle*, October 20, 1963, 23.
43 "George Moscone for Supervisor," campaign flyer, 1963.
44 "George Moscone," *San Francisco Examiner*, October 11, 1963.

45 Corey Busch, interview with author, October 29, 2021.

46 "The Election Returns," *San Francisco Chronicle*, November 6, 1963, 8.

47 "Election Returns," *Chronicle*.

48 Jerry Belcher (Moscone) and Rich Jordan (McCarthy), "S. F.'s Young Rising Politicians," *San Francisco Chronicle*, November 7, 1963, 68.

49 Belcher and Jordan, *Chronicle*.

50 Peter Trimble, "Burton Is Off and Running," *San Francisco Examiner*, November 7, 1963, 1.

51 Harry Johanesen, "W. Brown Upsets Gaffney," *San Francisco Examiner*, June 3, 1964, 1.

Chapter 6. Freeway Fights and Supervisor Moscone

1 "1960 Presidential General Election Results—California," Dave Leip's Atlas of U.S. Elections, https://uselectionatlas.org/RESULTS/state.php?year=1960&fips=6&f=1&off=0&elect=0&minper=0, accessed March 29, 2023.

2 Jon Rubin, interview with author, October 27, 2021. Brubeck was also a graduate of University of the Pacific.

3 Chris Moscone, interview with author, November 4, 2021.

4 Jonathan Moscone, interview with author, November 6, 2021.

5 Jeannette Etheredge, interview with author, January 13, 2022.

6 Breihan, Tom "The Number Ones: Jimmy Gilmer And The Fireballs' 'Sugar Shack,'" https://www.stereogum.com/1999603/the-number-ones-jimmy-gilmer-and-the-fireballs-sugar-shack/franchises/the-number-ones/. accessed March 29, 2023.

7 "Vietnam War Allied Troop Levels 1960–73," American War Library, https://www.americanwarlibrary.com/vietnam/vwatl.htm, accessed March 29, 2023.

8 "How to Talk Like a San Franciscan," Carl Nolte, *San Francisco Chronicle*, February 26, 1984.

9 John Burton, interview with author, September 11, 2021.

10 https://www.americanwarlibrary.com/vietnam/vwatl.htm, accessed March 29, 2023.

11 "Vietnam War U.S. Military Fatal Casualties," National Archives, https://www.archives.gov/research/military/vietnam-war/casualty-statistics, accessed March 29, 2023.

12 Bob Robertson, "The Board, GIs and the Dentist," *San Francisco Chronicle*, June 11, 1965, 4. Brackets mine, parentheses in original.

13 "Pay Hike? Don't Give a Hoot," *San Francisco Examiner*, August 25, 1964, 8.

14 Davis, R. G., "Bawdy Bravado in City Parks," *San Francisco Chronicle*, June 21, 1964, 149.

15 "Day of Secret Talks by Brown, UC Brass," *San Francisco Chronicle*, December 7, 1964, 1.

16 Wax, Mel, "Voice In Nowhere Mississippi," *San Francisco Chronicle*, January 21, 1965, 22.

17 "S. F. Lawyer Squad Returns from Miss." *San Francisco Examiner*, January 27, 1965, 5c.

18 "Eastland Blasts S. F. Supervisors," *San Francisco Examiner*, February 4, 1965, 1.

19 Benoit, Monique, "On the Side of the Underdog," *San Francisco Chronicle*, March 9, 1965.

20 Benoit, *Chronicle*.

21 "A Petition to Bay Area Congressmen," *San Francisco Chronicle*, December 28, 1964, 14.

22 Cone, Russ, "New Study of the Parkway," *San Francisco Examiner*, May 19, 1964, 1.
23 "Chamber To Boost Panhandle," *San Francisco Examiner*, July 8, 1964, 8.
24 Gilliam, Harold, "Many Seeds of Rebellion," *San Francisco Chronicle*, October 14, 1964, 1, 14.
25 "George Moscone on the California State Highway Commission," KRON, January 18, 1966, Bay Area Television Archive, https://diva.sfsu.edu/collections/sfbatv/bundles/227863, accessed March 29, 2023.
26 Rally at San Francisco State Against Freeway, March 15, 1966, Bay Area Television Archive, https://diva.sfsu.edu/collections/sfbatv/bundles/239151, accessed March 29, 2023.
27 Cone, Russ, "Shelley Concedes It's Over for Freeways," *San Francisco Examiner*, March 22, 1966, 12.
28 "Mayor Shelley Answers to Bayview Delegation," KPIX, July 5, 1967, Bay Area Television Archive, https://diva.sfsu.edu/collections/sfbatv/bundles/228185, accessed March 29, 2023.
29 Interview with Larry Simi, George Moscone Oral History Project, undated.
30 Ansolabehere, Stephen, James Snyder, and Jonathan Woon (1999), "Why did a majority of Californians vote to limit their own power?" Presentation at meeting of American Political Science Association, 1
31 Interview with John Vlahos, George Moscone Oral History Project, January 24, 2011.
32 "Moscone To Run for State Seat," *San Francisco Examiner*, January 18, 1964, 5.
33 Jacobs, *A Rage for Justice*, 254.
34 "Labor Group Backs Moscone," *San Francisco Chronicle*, December 17, 1965, 19.
35 "A Roundup of Political Activity," *San Francisco Chronicle*, April 27, 1966, 21.
36 "A Roundup of Political Activity," *San Francisco Chronicle*, May 9, 1966, 50.
37 "Backed by Labor," *Organized Labor*, May 23, 1966.
38 "Silent Treatment," Jack Rosenbaum, *San Francisco Examiner*, May 6, 1966, 35.
39 "Moscone and McCarthy in State Senate Primary Debate," Bay Area Television Archive, undated, https://diva.sfsu.edu/collections/sfbatv/bundles/190885, parentheses mine, accessed March 29, 2023.
40 "Burton Cash for Moscone," *San Francisco Examiner*, June 5, 1966, 1.
41 "Moscone for State Senator," campaign flyer, 1966.
42 "Moscone for State Senator," *The Sun-Reporter*, Primary Election Special, May-June 1966, 2
43 *Mid-City Reporter*, May 20, 1966, 1, 4. The "one-man one-vote" to which Brown referred was the decision to try to equalize the size of senate districts by giving San Francisco a second district. Campaign newspapers of this kind were not uncommon in the 1960s and 1970s in San Francisco.
44 Sam Blumenfeld, "Moscone Campaigns With His Heart and Sole," *San Francisco Examiner*, May 19, 1966, 32.
45 Sydney Kossen, "Bitter S. F. Battle for State Senate Seat," *San Francisco Examiner*, June 1, 1966.
46 *San Francisco Chronicle*, June 7, 1966, 44.
47 Schoenwald, Jonathan M., *A Time for Choosing: the Rise of Modern American Conservatism*. e-book, New York: Oxford University Press, 2003, 190.

48 Schoenwald, 191.

49 "How S. F. Voted," *San Francisco Examiner*, November 9, 1966, 6

50 Anderson, Totton J.; Lee, Eugene C. (June 1967). "The 1966 Election in California," The Western Political Quarterly. 20 (2): 535–554.

51 Pawel, Miriam (2018) *The Browns of California: The Family Dynasty that Transformed a State and Shaped a Nation*, New York: Bloomsbury.

52 "Ronald Reagan's 'Morality Gap' Speech," 1966, Bay Area Television Archive, https://diva.sfsu.edu/collections/sfbatv/bundles/229317, accessed March 29, 2023.

53 "How S. F. Voted," *San Francisco Examiner*, November 9, 1966, c.

Chapter 7. California in the 1960s

1 Reagan, Ronald, "A Time for Choosing," October 27, 1964.

2 Schoenwald, *A Time for Choosing*, 197.

3 Broussard, James H. (2014), "Ronald Reagan: Champion of Conservative America," New York: Routledge, 65–66.

4 Schoenwald, *A Time for Choosing*, 208–209, parentheses in original.

5 Reagan, Ronald, (1967), first inaugural address.

6 Schaefer, Hal, "The Owl Steps Out," *San Francisco Chronicle*, September 28, 2963, 28.

7 Jackson, Doyle, "Reagan Funds for 'Campaign Lies,'" *San Francisco Chronicle*, November 1, 1978, 14.

8 US Census.

9 Interview with Agar Jaicks, George Moscone Oral History Project, undated.

10 James Goodfellow, "His Beloved City Mourns Gene McAteer," James Goodfellow, *San Francisco Examiner*, May 27, 1967, 5.

11 Alioto, Joseph, "Changing the Face of San Francisco: Mayor 1968–1976, and Antitrust Trial Lawyer," Bancroft Oral History Project University of California, Berkeley, 7–8.

12 Issel, William "'The Catholic International' Mayor Joseph L. Alioto's Urban Liberalism and San Francisco Catholicism," *U. S. Catholic Historian*, Vol. 22, No. 2, Urbanism and American Religion (Spring, 2004), 99–120.

13 Alioto, Oral History Project, 121.

14 Interview with Richard DeLeon, George Moscone Oral History Project, March 30, 2011.

15 Interview with Larry Simi, George Moscone Oral History Project, undated.

16 Campbell, Bruce J., "Millionaire Lawyer Aims for Top," *San Francisco Chronicle*, September 9, 1967, 8.

17 This gold was first discovered in 1848, but the Gold Rush began in earnest in 1849.

18 McGloin, John Bernard, S. J., *San Francisco The Story of a City*, San Rafael, CA, and London: Presidio Press (1978), 354–355.

19 Interview with John De Luca, George Moscone Oral History Project, August 24, 2011. De Luca's memory was not quite accurate. In 1967 Hugh Carey was a member of the House of Representatives. Nelson Rockefeller was the governor of New York at that time.

20 "Hippie Funeral in San Francisco ," KRON TV San Francisco, October 6, 1967, accessed through the Bay Area Television Archive, https://diva.sfsu.edu/collections/sfbatv/bundles/189595, accessed March 29, 2023.

21 "History of the Presidio," The Presidio, https://www.presidio.gov/visit/history-of-the-presidio, accessed March 29, 2023.

22 US Census.

23 Sobredo, James, "The Battle for the International Hotel," FoundSF, undated.

24 "Inaugural Address by the Honorable Joseph L. Alioto: Mayor of San Francisco," January 8, 1968.

25 "Inaugural Address," Alioto.

26 Larry Simi, interview with author, October 28, 2021.

27 Alioto, Oral History Project, 129, 148.

28 Interview with Larry Del Carlo, George Moscone Oral History Project, undated.

29 Interview with Frances Park-Li Rothman, George Moscone Oral History Project, October 18, 2011.

30 Interview with Belva Davis, George Moscone Oral History Project, May 4, 2011.

31 "Alioto on the death of Rev. Dr. Martin Luther King Jr.," Bay Area Television Archive, https://diva.sfsu.edu/collections/sfbatv/bundles/191484, accessed March 29, 2023.

32 Draper, George, "Thousands at City Hall Tribute," *San Francisco Chronicle*, April 6, 1968, 1.

33 "Proclamation," *San Francisco Chronicle*, April 6, 1968, 1.

34 Alioto, Oral History Project, 5.

35 Interview with John De Luca, George Moscone Oral History Project, August 24, 2011.

36 Carlson, Richard and Lance Brison, "The Web that Links San Francisco's Mayor Alioto and the Mafia," Look, September 23, 1969, 17.

37 Mullaney, Alexander, "Look: San Francisco Mayor Joseph Alioto and the Press," undated https://escholarship.org/content/qt8qg8r6xg/qt8qg8r6xg_noSplash_b7011e90a9164f7f6114be07700cb1c9.pdf?t=no8law, accessed March 29, 2023.

38 Alioto v. Cowles Communications, Inc., (1977) https://casetext.com/case/alioto-v-cowles-communications-inc-3, accessed March 29, 2023.

39 Alioto, Oral History Project, 126–128.

40 McGruder, Robert, "Alioto's Spirit is Catching in San Francisco," *Cleveland Plain Dealer*, February 20, 1969.

41 Although they shared a last name, Alvin, who was white, and Matthew, who was African American, were not related.

42 "128 Hours: A Report on the Civil Disturbance in the City & County of San Francisco" (1966), compiled by Sgt. Ford E. Long, director, Planning and Research, and Sgt. Richard Trueb, Office of Assistant Deputy Chief, San Francisco Police Department, iii, 76.

43 Carlsson, Chris, "Hunters Point Uprising," Found SF, undated.

44 "The Mayor's Message," *San Francisco Chronicle*, September 30, 1966.

45 Harris, Michael, "Reagan's Views of Riots," *San Francisco Chronicle*, September 30, 1966. The Watts uprising to which Reagan referred occurred in August of the previous year.

46 Belcher, Jerry, "Gov. Brown Walks On Riot Street," *San Francisco Examiner*, September 29, 1966.

47 Anspacher, Carolyn,"Cop Cleared in Slaying at Hunters Pt.," *San Francisco Chronicle*, October 21, 1966, 1.

48 Melnick, Norman, "Riot Cop Back on New Beat," Norman Melnick, *San Francisco Examiner*, October 22, 1966.

49 Agee, Christopher Lowen, *The Streets of San Francisco: Policing and the Creation of a Cosmopolitan Liberal Politics, 1950–1972*, Chicago: University of Chicago Press, 76.

50 Agee, 76.
51 Agee, 76.
52 McGruder, *Cleveland Plain Dealer*, February 20, 1969
53 *San Francisco Chronicle*, November 14, 1968, 1.
54 Joseph L. Alioto, op. cit.
55 Arnold Townsend, interview with author, February 24, 2021.
56 "Haven't You Had Enough," Barbagelata for Supervisor, 1969.
57 Barbagelata, John (1969) "For Supervisor, John Barbagelata," *Statements of Qualifications of Candidates and Propositions*, 9.
58 McKinney, Joan, "A Pretty Expert on Crime," *San Francisco Chronicle*, July 11, 1965, 4, parentheses in original.
59 Drewes, Caroline, "The Dedicated Dianne," *San Francisco Examiner*, March 9, 1969, 111.
60 Roberts, Jerry (1994), Dianne Feinstein: Never Let Them See You Cry, San Francisco: HarperCollinsWest, 70–71.
61 Caen, Herb, "All the News That Fits," *San Francisco Chronicle*, November 14, 1969, 25.
62 "Dianne Chooses Her Committees," *San Francisco Chronicle*, January 9, 1970, 4.
63 For an example of one of these people, see my essay, "Ruby the Pizza Guy" in John van der Zee (2011), *San Francisco Childhood, Memories of a Great City Seen Through the Eyes of Its Children*, Kensington, CA: Grizzly Peak Press.
64 "San Francisco Population," San Francisco History, https://www.sfgenealogy.org/sf/history/hgpop.htm, accessed March 29, 2023.

Chapter 8. In the Senate

1 Alfred H. Song, Oral History Interview, conducted by Raphael J. Sonenshein (1986), History Department, California State University, Fullerton, for the California State Archives State Government Oral History Program, 56–58.
2 McDowell, Jack S., *San Francisco Chronicle*, "Has Moscone Changed His Views," September 10, 1967, 12.
3 McDowell, *Chronicle*, 12.
4 McDowell, *Chronicle*, 12.
5 "Italian American Committee to Elect John Burton" John Burton for Senate campaign flyer, 1967.
6 *Sports Illustrated*, August 21, 1967, Vol. 27, No. 8, 11. The iconoclastic baseball scholar Darren Viola brought this comment to my attention.
7 Telegram from George Moscone to Justice William Douglas, April 11, 1967.
8 "Crime: Stirrings on Death Row," *Time*, April 21, 1967.
9 George Moscone, letter to the *California Reporter*, June 28, 1967. This letter was in Corey Busch's archives. It is not clear if it was ever published.
10 State Senator George Moscone, press release, September 8, 1972.
11 Press release, Office of the Governor, September 5, 1969, https://www.reaganlibrary.gov/sites/default/files/digitallibrary/gubernatorial/pressunit/p10/40-840-7408623-p10-003-2017.pdf, accessed March 29, 2023.
12 Senator George Moscone, press release, October 1, 1975.

13 Senator George Moscone, press release, July 10, 1975.
14 Gieger, A. W. and John Gramlich, "6 Facts About Marijuana," Pew Research Center, November 22, 2019.
15 Robison, Jennifer, "Decades of Drug Use Data from the '60s and '70s," Gallup, July 2, 2002, https://news.gallup.com/poll/6331/decades-drug-use-data-from-60s-70s.aspx, accessed March 29, 2023.
16 "A Fiscal Analysis of Marijuana Decriminalization," Schaffer Library of Drug Policy, undated. http://druglibrary.org/schaffer/hemp/moscone/chap1.htm, accessed March 29, 2023.
17 "Illegal Drugs," Gallup, https://news.gallup.com/poll/1657/illegal-drugs.aspx.
18 "California Marijuana Legalization, Proposition 19 (1972)," Ballotpedia. https://ballotpedia.org/California_Marijuana_Legalization,_Proposition_19_, accessed March 29, 2023.
19 Brownwell, Gordon, George Moscone Oral History Project, June 15, 2011.
20 Anderson, Patrick (1981), *High in America: The True Story Behind NORML and the Politics of Marijuana*, chapter 5, http://www.druglibrary.org/special/anderson/highinamerica5.htm, accessed March 29, 2023.
21 Interview with Yvonne Ryzack, (2010) George Moscone Oral History Project.
22 Interview with Gordon Brownwell, George Moscone Oral History Project, June 15, 2011.
23 Brownwell, Oral History Project, June 15, 2011.
24 Willie Brown, interview with author, September 15, 2020.
25 George Moscone, press release, March 3, 1975.
26 "Sensible Pot Laws Change," *Sacramento Bee*, March 11, 1975.
27 "Pot and the Law," *Los Angeles Times*, March 5, 1975, B6
28 "Sensibly Easing Penalty for Pot," *San Francisco Chronicle*, March 24, 1975.
29 Brownwell, Oral History Project, June 15, 2011.
30 Letter from George Moscone to Governor Brown, June 27, 1975.
31 Herb Caen, "From Here to Absurdity," *San Francisco Chronicle*, November 8, 1973, 30.
32 Weisser, Peter "Senate Oks Sex Bill: Liberalized Law for State Adults," *San Francisco Chronicle*, May 2, 1975, 24.
33 Weisser, *Chronicle*, 24.
34 Weisser, *Chronicle*, 24.
35 Edith Austin, "Demos Failed To Tell It Like It Is," *Sun-Reporter*, April 19, 1969, 2.
36 "Moscone Begins Early Campaign," *Sun-Reporter* February 5, 1972, 4.
37 "Bay Bits," Edith Austin, *Sun-Reporter*, November 25, 1972, 6.
38 California Field Poll, March 7, 1973.
39 John Burton, interview with author, November 10, 2020.
40 California Field Poll, September 5, 1973.
41 Senator George Moscone schedule, July 29, 1973.
42 Baseball Reference, https://www.baseball-reference.com/boxes/LAN/LAN197307290.shtml, accessed March 29, 2023.
43 Senator George Moscone schedule, August 7–8, 1973.
44 Richardson, *Willie Brown: A Biography*, 200.
45 Senator George Moscone schedule, August 18–19, 1973.
46 "Moscone bid for Governor opens with statewide tour," *The Moscone Democrat*, 1973. 1.

47 George Miller, interview with author, November 5, 2020. The town was, based on other campaign materials, in Siskiyou County, which is in the northeastern corner of the state, just south of Oregon.

48 Miller, interview, November 5, 2020.

49 "The Jeep Trip: Bit! By a Pig! Where?!" *The Moscone Insider*, Issue 2, 1973, 1, Ellipses in original.

50 State Senator George R. Moscone, press release, December 10, 1973, parentheses in original.

51 "100% Voting Record," Moscone for Governor Campaign literature, 1973.

52 "Moscone Newsmaker," George Moscone for Governor, August 1973.

53 California Field Poll, November 29, 1973.

54 George Moscone, letter to supporters, January 1, 1974.

55 Moscone, letter, January 1, 1974.

56 Moscone, letter, January 1, 1974.

57 Thomas Fleming "Thomas Fleming's Weekly Report," *Sun-Reporter*, January 12, 1974, 7.

58 "Moscone Involved in Auto Mishap," *Examiner* Capitol Bureau, *San Francisco Examiner*, April 14, 1970, 12.

59 *Examiner*, 1.

60 *Examiner*, 12.

61 *Examiner*, 1.

62 *Examiner*.

63 "Unhappy Incident in Moscone's Past," *San Francisco Chronicle*, January 9, 1976, 4.

64 At the time of the event, it was reported that the woman in the car with Moscone was African American. This may have also contributed to the rumors in conservative San Francisco that Moscone had several liaisons with African American women. I heard this sotto voce from several elderly San Francisco conservatives while doing research for this book.

65 Letter from Senator George R. Moscone to supporters, October 24, 1970.

66 Carlsson, Chris, *Ten Years that Shook the City*, 9.

67 Dianne Feinstein for mayor, campaign flyer, 1971.

68 Alioto for Mayor, campaign flyer, 1971.

69 Alioto for Mayor, campaign flyer 1971, grammar in original.

70 "The show-biz campaign," Kevin Starr, *San Francisco Examiner*, June 3, 1978, italics mine.

71 "Two traditions," Kevin Starr, *San Francisco Examiner*, April 3, 1980, 24, parentheses in original.

72 Harold Stassen was a Republican governor of Minnesota from 1939 to 1943. He was a strong candidate to be his party's nominee for president in 1944 but was defeated in that endeavor by Tom Dewey. Stassen went on to seek, but never win, the GOP presidential nomination in 1948, 1952, 1964, 1968, 1980, 1984, 1988. and 1992. He also ran unsuccessfully in for several other offices in Minnesota and Pennsylvania.

73 "For American Cities—A Declaration of Independence," inaugural address by the Honorable Joseph L. Alioto, January 8, 1972. Capitals in original.

74 Shilts, *The Mayor of Castro Street*, 40–41.

75 White was born in Southern California but moved to San Francisco as a young boy.

76 Shilts, *The Mayor of Castro Street*, 46
77 Larry Griffin, interview with author, July 24, 2021.
78 Barmann, Jay, "SF Sees Exact Same Number of Homicides In 2022 as Previous Year, While Burglaries Are Down," SFist, January 3, 2023. San Francisco Police Department, crime dashboard, https://www.sanfranciscopolice.org/stay-safe/crime-data/crime-dashboard.
79 McGloin, *San Francisco The Story of a City*, 356–357.
80 US Census.
81 Cleve Jones, interview with author, March 9, 2021.
82 S. F. Vote Tally, *San Francisco Chronicle*, November 7, 1973, 4.
83 Caen, Herb, "About This Town," *San Francisco Chronicle*, August 6, 1973, 24, parentheses and capitalization in original.
84 Caen, Herb, "Pocketful of Notes," *San Francisco Chronicle*, August 16, 1973, 33.
85 "Voter Handbook, General Municipal Election November 6, 1973," City and County of San Francisco, 1973, 21.
86 Marinucci, Carla, "ALFRED J. NELDER / 1915–2002 / Former S. F. police chief a lifelong public servant," *San Francisco Chronicle*, January 31, 2012.
87 "S. F. Vote Tally," *San Francisco Chronicle*, November 7, 1973, 4
88 "The Five-Four Plan," Undated memo from the Office of Supervisor Dianne Feinstein.
89 "Gay Voters Endorse Seven Candidates," *San Francisco Chronicle*, October 27, 1973. The headline was misleading because the group only endorsed six candidates, May Haynes for treasurer and five for the board of supervisors.
90 "Voter Handbook, General Municipal Election November 6, 1973," City and County of San Francisco, 1973, 101–102, parentheses mine.
91 Voter Handbook, 102–105.
92 Voter Handbook, 102–105.
93 Arnold Townsend, interview with author, February 24, 2021.
94 Senator George Moscone, press release, November 5, 1974.
95 Senator George Moscone, briefing memo, November 4, 1974.
96 Moscone, memo, November 4, 1974.
97 Postcard list, George Moscone Schedule, November 1974.
98 "One Thing After Another, Herb Caen, *San Francisco Chronicle*, November 29, 1974, 31.

Chapter 9. The Race for Mayor—Round One

1 Thomas Fleming, "Political Potpourri: Moscone Almost Announces for Mayor," *Sun-Reporter*, March 23, 1974, 11.
2 Larry Griffin, interview with author, July 24, 2021.
3 Jerry Burns "Morning Line On Next Mayor," *San Francisco Chronicle*, November 25, 1974, 6.
4 Don Bradley and associates, press release, December 19, 1974, four-dot ellipses in original.
5 Murphy, George "Moscone's Hat First in Ring," *San Francisco Chronicle*, December 20, 1974, 2.

6 George Moscone, announcement for Mayor, December 19, 1974. The capitalizations and grammar are from the original.
7 Moscone, announcement for mayor. Ellipses and quotation marks in original.
8 Moscone, announcement for mayor. Ellipses mine.
9 Moscone, announcement for mayor.
10 "Race for Mayor: Moscone to Announce," *San Francisco Chronicle*, December 6, 1974, 5. The article alluded to the poll, but did not provide any numbers.
11 Caen, Herb, "This Old Town," *San Francisco Chronicle*, October 24, 1974, 27.
12 Wegars, Don, "Feinstein Announces She's Running for Mayor," *San Francisco Chronicle*, April 23, 1975, 2.
13 "Barbagelata Files to Run For Mayor," *San Francisco Chronicle*, June 11, 1975, 2.
14 "Barbagelata files as mayor candidate," *San Francisco Examiner*, June 10, 1975, 6.
15 Bruce Brugmann, George Moscone Oral History Project, undated.
16 Jerry Roberts, George Moscone Oral History Project, April 26, 2011.
17 Roberts, Oral History, April 26, 2011
18 "Barbagelata," George Moscone for Mayor internal memo, 1975.
19 Cuomo was the nominee of the Liberal Party so remained on that ballot line for the general election after Koch had secured the Democratic nomination in the runoff.
20 Willie Brown, interview with author, September 15, 2020
21 John Burton, interview with author, September 11, 2020. Burton's point about San Franciscans is indeed accurate. Several native San Franciscans whom I interviewed for this and other books have asked me where I went to school. Burton went further with this line of questioning. When I mentioned I had grown up playing baseball in San Francisco, he quizzed me about the playgrounds and ballfields where I had played ball in the 1970s and 1980s.
22 Joe Kelly, interview with author, October 30, 2020.
23 "George Moscone Announces for Mayor," KPIX Eyewitness News, December 19, 1974, Bay Area Television Archive.
24 Interview with Josh Getlin, George Moscone Oral History Project, undated.
25 Interview with Milton Marks, California State Archives State Government Oral History Project, The Bancroft Library, University of California, Berkeley, conducted February 27, 1996, 310.
26 Art Agnos, interview with author, November 11, 2020.
27 Agnos, interview, November 11, 2020.
28 Larry Griffin, interview with author, July 24, 2021.
29 The Western Neighborhoods Project of Outsidelands.org does great work teaching people the history of that part of the city. My October 2014 essay, "Towards Land's End" in *Roads and Kingdoms*, is a good introduction to the western half of San Francisco in the twenty-first century.
30 "Businessman mayor needed to run City," Johh Barbagelata, *San Francisco Examiner*, November 29, 1975, 37.
31 Moscone for Mayor, press release, "Moscone Endorsed By Painters Union," January 16, 1975.
32 "Why the ILWU Backs Moscone for Mayor," *The Dispatcher*, November 28, 1975, 1.
33 "He's Labor's Choice," *The Dispatcher*, November 28, 1975, 1

34 “Dianne: First Woman Mayor of San Francisco,” *The Gay Crusader*, 1975 Election Special, 5.
35 Corey Busch, interview with author, October 29, 2021.
36 Turner, Wallace, “Magical, ‘Happy’ San Francisco Also Has Problems and Tears,” *The New York Times*, December 11, 1975, 47.
37 Dance, Gabriel and Tom Meagher, “Crime in Context,” The Marchall Project, August 18, 2016, https://www.themarshallproject.org/2016/08/18/crime-in-context, accessed March 29, 2023.
38 Caen, Herb, “Pocketful of Caenfetti,” *San Francisco Chronicle*, February 10, 1975, 17.
39 Caen, Herb, “One Thing After Another, *San Francisco Chronicle*, July 17, 1975, 23.
40 Interview with Jerry Adams, George Moscone Oral History Project, date unknown.
41 Brugmann, Oral History Project, undated, italics mine.
42 Sue Hestor, George Moscone Oral History Project, July 20, 2009.
43 Getlin, Oral History Project, undated,
44 “Feinstein Ahead in S. F. Poll, ” *San Francisco Chronicle*, October 9, 1975, 1.
45 Harris, Michael, “Feinstein Ahead in S. F. Poll,” *San Francisco Chronicle*, October 9, 1975, 1, 30.
46 Murphy, George, “The New Milton Marks,” *San Francisco Chronicle*, October 2, 1975, 22.
47 Malcolm, Andrew H., “Police Out, San Francisco Faces Fire and Transit Strikes,” *The New York Times*, August 20, 2975, 1.
48 Interview with Vince Courtney, George Moscone Oral History Project, January 10, 2011.
49 Brooks, Stephen C., (1980) “Politics of Crime in the 1970s: A Two City Comparison,” Reactions to Crime Project, http://www.skogan.org/files/Brooks.Politics_of_Crime_in_the_1970s_A_Two_City_Comparison.1980.pdf, accessed March 29, 2023.
50 Brooks, “Politics of Crime in the 1970s.”
51 “One New York City Is Enough,” Barbagelata for Mayor Committee, 1975. Hyphens mine. Ellipses in original.
52 Jim Molinari, George Moscone Oral History Project, undated circa 2010–2011.
53 “SF Election Intelligencer: ‘Feinstein's ahead, but … ,’” *Bay Guardian*, October 10, 1975.
54 San Francisco Voter Guide, November 4, 1975, 40.
55 Black, Jason Edward and Charles E. Morris, eds., *Milk, Harvey. An Archive of Hope: Harvey Milk's Speeches and Writings*, Berkeley: University of California Press, 2013.

Chapter 10. The Runoff

1 Dexter Waugh, “Butterflies … dashed hopes,” *San Francisco Examiner*, November 2, 1975.
2 Waugh, *Examiner*, November 2, 1975.
3 Interview with Larry Del Carlo, George Moscone Oral History Project, undated.
4 Getlin, Oral History Project, undated.
5 Interview with Dianne Feinstein, George Moscone Oral History Project, undated.
6 Joe Scott, “The Political Animal,” newsletter, December 24, 1975.
7 Interview with Phil Bronstein, George Moscone Oral History Project, undated.

8 Corey Busch, interview with author, October 29, 2021.

9 Interview with Belva Davis, George Moscone Oral History Project, May 4, 2011.

10 Dianne Feinstein was indeed Jewish, but she almost never made this a campaign issue, nor did any of her opponents try to use her Judaism against her. Nonetheless, in a heavily Catholic city such as San Francisco, Feinstein's religion cannot be overlooked. San Francisco had elected Jewish politicians in the past, including Adolph Sutro, who served as mayor from 1894 to 1896. During the 1970s, San Francisco's Jewish community was changing as thousands of Jews from the Midwest and the East, particularly New York City, moved to San Francisco. These Jews frequently had roots in Russia, Ukraine, and similar places, unlike the German Jews who had been the largest part of the Jewish community in San Francisco until then. The newer Jewish migrants, whose most memorable representative was Harvey Milk, tended to encounter more anti-Semitism.

11 John Barbagelata campaign flyer, "What has Barbagelata done for you?" undated, 1975. Bold in original.

12 Getlin, Oral History Project, undated.

13 Belva Davis, op. cit.

14 Marshall Kilduff, George Moscone Oral History Project, August 2010.

15 "Who gets the Feinstein/Ertola/Marks vote?" Jerry Roberts, *Bay Guardian*, November 28, 1975, parentheses in original.

16 "Closeup: The Candidates, Part Three: Their style and stands," James Finefrock and Robert Hollis, *San Francisco Examiner*, December 3, 1975, 9.

17 In the twenty-first century, San Francisco has been a very strongly Democratic city, but that was not the case in the mid-1970s. Data from presidential elections demonstrate this. In 2020, Democrat Joe Biden defeated Republican Donald Trump in San Francisco by a margin of 85 percent to 13 percent. However, in the 1976 presidential election—one year after Moscone defeated Barbagelata—Republican Gerald Ford managed to win 44 percent of the vote in San Francisco. Democrat Jimmy Carter carried the city, but only with 56 percent of the vote.

18 Finefrock and Hollis, *Examiner*, December 3, 1975, 9.

19 "S. F. mayor's race in the stretch," Katy Butler, *Bay Guardian*, October 10, 1975.

20 Butler, *Bay Guardian*, October 10, 1975.

21 "They Were a Couple of Sweethearts," *San Francisco Examiner*, November 15, 1975, 1.

22 Interview with Nancy Pelosi, George Moscone Oral History Project, circa 2010.

23 Jon Rubin, interview with author, October 27, 2021.

24 "The Rambling Wreck," Herb Caen, *San Francisco Chronicle*, December 4, 1975, 25.

25 "The Election News: The Community Edition," George Moscone for Mayor, November 1975, 1–4.

26 "The Election News," 3.

27 "The Election News," 4

28 Jerry Roberts, op. cit.

29 "Can You Afford Moscone?" John Barbagelata for Mayor, 1975. Capitals and elipses in original.

30 Johanesen, Harry, "Moscone's ties to the Burtons," *San Francisco Chronicle*, November 23, 1975, 4.

31 Harris, op. cit.
32 Rudy Nothenberg, interview with author, November 17, 2020.
33 Welter, Jack, "A Moscone contributions tangle," *San Francisco Examiner and Chronicle*, November 23, 1975, 4.
34 United Nations Resolution 3379, November 10, 1975.
35 Daniel Patrick Moynihan, speech opposing UN Resolution 3379, November 10, 1975.
36 "Rally Against U.N on Zionism," *San Francisco Chronicle*, November 17, 1975, 8.
37 Jewish Community Relations Council, "Our History," https://jcrc.org/who-we-are/our-history/, accessed September 13, 2021.
38 Corey Busch, interview with author, October 29, 2021.
39 Jonathan Moscone, interview with author, November 6, 2021.
40 George Murphy "Kopp Backs Barbagelata for Mayor," *San Francisco Chronicle*, December 8, 1975, 5.
41 Letter from Assembly Speaker Leo McCarthy, December 10, 1975.
42 Corey Busch, email correspondence with author, September 27, 2021.
43 Statement by Supervisor Dianne Feinstein, December 4, 1975,
44 Busch, email, September 27, 2021.
45 Busch, email, September 27, 2021.
46 University High School, the school that Jonathan Moscone wanted to attend, is also in this area.
47 Saxon, Wolfgang, "George Moscone, A Firm Mayor Who Stressed Anticrime Effort," *The New York Times*, November 28, 1978.
48 "Barbagelata," George Moscone for Mayor internal memo, 1975.
49 Clendinen, Dudley, and Adam Nagourney (1999) *Out For Good: The Struggle to Build a Gay Rights Movement in America*, New York: Touchstone, 344.
50 Sharyn Saslafsky, interview with author, November 10, 2020.
51 Edith Austin, "Bay Bits," *Sun Reporter*, November 30, 1978, 9.
52 Corey Busch, interview with author, October 29, 2021,
53 Flynn, Daniel J. (2018) *Cult City: Jim Jones, Harvey Milk, and 10 Days That Shook San Francisco*, Wilmington, DE: Flynn ISI:, and Delgado, A. J. "The Unburied Truth About Jim Jones," *National Review*, May 6, 2014, are examples of conservatives linking Moscone and Jones.
54 Interview with Derrald Etheley, George Moscone Oral History Project, May 4, 2011, parentheses mine; brackets in original.
55 Derrald Etheley, Oral History Project.
56 Larry Griffin, interview with author, July 24, 2021.
57 Griffin, interview, July 24, 2021.
58 *Homewards*, John Barbagelata, 1987. The newsletter is undated, but based on the political items, it was clear it was written sometime in 1987.
59 In my 2019 book, *San Francisco Year Zero: Political Upheaval, Punk Rock, and a Third-Place Baseball Team* (Rutgers University Press), I break down the numbers and show that it was almost impossible for the Peoples Temple to have had enough of an impact to have changed the outcome of the election.
60 Kilduff, Marshall, and Phil Tracy, "Inside Peoples Temple," New West, August 1, 1977, 30.

61 "'One Brotherhood': Muslims, People's (sic) Temple Get It Together in L. A.," *Sun Reporter*, June 5, 1976, 4.
62 Coulthard, Cheryl (2018), "The Peoples Press: The Evolution of the Media's Treatment of Jim Jones and the Peoples Temple," *Communal Societies*, Vol. 38, No. 2, 202.
63 "Barbagelata Tells his Supporters 'We Won," *San Francisco Chronicle*, December 12, 1975, 2.
64 *Homewards*, John Barbagelata, 1987. The newsletter is undated, but based on the political items, it was clear it was written sometime in 1987.

Chapter 11. Mayor Moscone

1 Kramer, Larry, "Tampering charges in mayor race," *San Francisco Examiner*, December 14, 1975, 1.
2 Kramer, *Examiner*, December 14, 1975, 1.
3 "One Man's San Francisco," Herb Caen, *San Francisco Chronicle*, January 15, 1976, 25.
4 "Recount over—no change," *San Francisco Examiner & Chronicle*, January 18, 1975, 3.
5 "Supervisor's Barbagelata's Self-Deception," *Sun-Reporter*, January 24, 1976, 7.
6 Program, Inauguration of George R. Moscone as Mayor of San Francisco,
7 Program, Inauguration.
8 "Inaugural Address," George R. Moscone, January 8, 1976.
9 "Inaugural Address."
10 "Inaugural Address."
11 "Inaugural Address." Capitals and hyphen in original.
12 Mayor's schedule, January 10–12, 1976
13 Corey Busch, email, December 6, 2021, parentheses in original.
14 Art Agnos, interview with author, November 11, 2020.
15 Larry Griffin, interview with author, July 24, 2021.
16 Press release, George Moscone, mayor-elect of San Francisco, undated.
17 Memorandum from Mayor George Moscone to Corey Busch, undated, parentheses and question mark in original.
18 Letter from Bill Graham to Senator George Moscone, December 4, 1975.
19 Letter from George Moscone to Bill Graham, April 7, 1975.
20 For more on this, see chapter of one of my books *The Giants and Their City: Major League Baseball in San Francisco, 1976–1992* (Kent State University Press, 2021).
21 Flynn, William, "My secret ambition ..." *San Francisco Chronicle* & *Examiner*, December 31, 1976.
22 Flynn, *Chronicle* & *Examiner*, December 31, 1976.
23 "Moscone To Honor Aaron," *Sun-Reporter*, September 1, 1973, 4.
24 Rickey Henderson is now the all-time stolen base leader.
25 Willie McCovey Day Proclamation, Mayor George Moscone, September 1977.
26 Statement from Mayor George Moscone, May 1978, parentheses mine; National League in lower case in original.
27 For more on this game, see my book *San Francisco Year Zero: Political Upheaval, Punk Rock and a Third- Place Baseball Team*, Rutgers University Press, 2019.
28 John Burton, interview with author, September 11, 2020.

29 Marshall Kilduff, "Moscone Names New Permit Appeals Board," *San Francisco Chronicle*, January 30, 1976.

30 "The first glimpses of the New Mayor," Jerry Roberts, *Bay Guardian*, December 24, 1975, 3, parentheses mine.

31 Jon Rubin, interview with author, October 29, 2021.

32 Corey Busch, interview with author, October 27, 2021.

33 Murphy, George, "Kopp Backs Barbagelata for Mayor," *San Francisco Chronicle*, December 8, 1975, 5.

34 Carroll, Jerry, "Milk, Agnos Slugging It Out for the Assembly," *San Francisco Chronicle*, June 1, 1976, 5.

35 Interview with Art Agnos, George Moscone Oral History Project, circa 2010.

36 Interview with Agnos, Oral History Project, circa 2010.

37 Ron Moskowitz, "Harvey Milk Blames 2 Factors for Defeat," *San Francisco Chronicle*, June 10, 1976, 7.

38 Guinn, Jeff (2017), *The Road to Jonestown: Jim Jones and Peoples Temple*, New York: Simon and Schuster, 324.

39 Letter from Michael Prokes to George Moscone, July 13, 1976.

40 Letter from Jim Jones to George Moscone, July 12, 1976.

41 Undated letter from Jim Jones to George Moscone, 1976.

42 *Peoples Forum*, November 2, 1086, 2.

43 See for example, Reiterman, Tim and John Jacobs (1982), *Raven: The Untold Story of the Rev. Jim Jones and His People*, Boston: E. P. Dutton; and Gunn, Jeff (2017), *The Road to Jonestown: Jim Jones and the Peoples Temple*, New York: Simon and Schuster.

44 Letter from Jim Jones to Mayor George Moscone, August 3, 1977.

45 Marshall Kilduff and Phil Tracy, "Inside Peoples Temple," *New West*, August 1, 1977, 34.

46 Press release, Mayor George Moscone, July 26, 1977.

47 Rosenbaum, Art, "A Picnic at Candlestick Park," *San Francisco Chronicle*, April 10, 1976, 1. Given the quality of food at Candlestick Park in the 1970s, having to bring food from home cannot be considered a hardship.

48 Roberts, Jerry, "City Strike: yellow dogs, red herrings and blue munis," *The Bay Guardian*, April 9, 1976.

49 Roberts, *Bay Guardian*, April 9, 1976.

50 "California Crime Rates 1960–2019," Disaster Center. The data on the site was compiled from California Law Enforcement Agency Uniform Crime Reports 1980 to 2005, http://www.disastercenter.com/crime/cacrime.htm, accessed March 29, 2023.

51 "Homicide in San Francisco, 1849–2003," Criminal Justice Research Center, Ohio State University. https://cjrc.osu.edu/research/interdisciplinary/hvd/united-states/san-francisco, accessed March 29, 2023.

52 Barmann, Jay "Despite Violent Year Around the Bay and the Nation, SF Is Set to Record Similar Homicide Rate to 2019," SFist, December 31, 2020.

53 "Crime rate in San Francisco, California (CA): murders, rapes, robberies, assaults, burglaries, thefts, auto thefts, arson, law enforcement employees, police officers, crime map, " https://www.city-data.com/crime/crime-San-Francisco-California.html,

accessed March 29, 2023, and Office of the Attorney General, California, https://oag.ca.gov/sites/all/files/agweb/pdfs/cjsc/prof10/1/38.pdf, accessed March 29, 2023.

54 Murphy, George, "Nelder Can't Be Renamed Chief," *San Francisco Chronicle*, December 30, 1975, 2.

55 Lenn, Ernest, "Gain appointed new police chief," *San Francisco Examiner*, January 12, 1976, 1, parentheses mine.

56 Interview with Rich DeLeon, George Moscone Oral History Project, March 30, 2011.

57 Interview with Lois Salisbury, George Moscone Oral History Project, undated circa 2010–2012.

58 Turner, Wallace, "Job-Bias Lawsuit Settled by San Francisco Police," *The New York Times*, January 28, 1979, 24.

59 Interview with Duffy Jennings, George Moscone Oral History Project, May 10, 2011.

60 Interview with Barbara Taylor, George Moscone Oral History Project, undated circa 2010–2011.

61 DeLeon, George Moscone Oral History Project, March 30, 2011.

62 Interview with Jim Molinari, George Moscone Oral History Project, undated circa 2010–2011.

63 Cleve Jones, interview with author, March 9, 2021.

64 Press release, Office of the Mayor, December 15, 1976.

65 Press release, Office of the Mayor, January 28, 1977.

66 Plaque on the Haight-Fillmore building. Noted San Francisco raconteur John Yelding-Sloan brought this plaque, and this event, to my attention.

67 Editorial board, *New York Post*, July 6, 2020.

68 Press release, Office of the Mayor, August 10, 1978

69 Deleon, George Moscone Oral History Project, March 30, 2011, 46.

70 Hartman, Chester, *City for Sale*, 31–32.

71 Hartman, 61.

72 Hartman, 60.

73 John Elrick, "Yerba Buena Center: Revelopment and a Working Class Community's Resistance," Found SF, undated.

74 Hartman, *City for Sale*, 138–139.

75 San Francisco Voter Information Pamphlet, November 2, 1976.

76 Draft unpublished letter from George Moscone to the *San Francisco Chronicle*, November 16, 1978.

77 Corey Busch, interview with author, October 29, 2021.

78 In the summer of 1984, I was preparing for my senior year in high school and was not able to attend any part of the official convention. However, I was able to time my lunch break from my summer job South of Market to make it to the parking lot of the Moscone Center to attend a Rock Against Reagan concert where I saw, among other bands, Dead Kennedys.

79 Chamings, Andrew, "The Bizarre Tale of the world's last lost tourist, who thought Maine was San Francisco," *San Francisco Chronicle*, February. 10, 2021.

80 Barnes, W. E., "Moscone quits law firm to avoid 'conflicts,'" *San Francisco Examiner*, February 10, 1977, 5.

81 Busch, interview, October 29, 2021.

82 Jonathan Moscone, interview with author, November 6, 2021.
83 Jonathan Moscone, interview, November 6, 2021.
84 Chris Moscone, interview with author, November 4, 2021.
85 Chris Moscone, interview, November 4, 2021.
86 Mayor's schedule, December 10–11, 1977.
87 Jonathan Moscone, interview with author, November 6, 2021.
88 Form 721 "Statement of Economic Interests," George Moscone, February 8, 1977.
89 Johnston, David, "The Curious Questions About Moscone's New House," *Bay Guardian*, October 12, 1978.
90 Johnston, David, "Moscone Erects the Stonewall Defense, *Bay Guardian*, October 19, 2021.
91 David Johnston and Bruce Brugmann "KNBC-TV in Los Angeles Names Mayor Moscone as a 'Principal Target' in the FBI Probe," *Bay Guardian*, September 28, 1978, 3.
92 Johnston, David, "Was the Alleged $10,000 Hughes Bribe Merely A Down Payment to Influence Moscone on Airport Expansion?" *Bay Guardian*, October 5, 1978.
93 Johnston, "Moscone's Top Aide Doesn't Properly Report $8,000 from Joe Cerrell," *Bay Guardian*, October 12, 1978.
94 Johnston, *Bay Guardian*, October 12, 1978.
95 Austin, Edith, "Bay Bits," *Sun-Reporter*, October 12, 1978, 9.

Chapter 12. The Changing Board of Supervisors

1 Jennings, Duffy, "Passage of Prop. T Jolts Supervisors," *San Francisco Chronicle*, November 4, 1976, 28.
2 Jerry Carroll and Dale Champion, "Prop T—It's a Whole New Ball Game," *San Francisco Chronicle*, November 4, 1976, 4.
3 Interview with Josh Getlin, George Moscone Oral History Project, May 22, 2009.
4 Interview with Barbara Taylor, George Moscone Oral History Project, circa 2010.
5 "Opponents Say Prop. T Will Kill Recall Moves," *San Francisco Chronicle*, September 25, 1976, 12.
6 Mellinkoff, Abe, "Instant Democracy," *San Francisco Chronicle*, October 25, 1976, 40.
7 Cone, Russ, "The Propositions: what they mean," *San Francisco Chronicle and Examiner*, October 31, 1976, 29.
8 "Dividing the City," *San Francisco Chronicle*, October 29, 1976, p. 42. Grammar in original.
9 "Districting Is Not for San Francisco," *San Francisco Chronicle*, October 8, 1976, 42.
10 "Kopp calls Prop.T a petty power ploy," *San Francisco Examiner*, October 12, 1976, 4.
11 "Prop. T: Prescription for chaos," *San Francisco Examiner*, October 13, 1976, 36.
12 "Prop. T dilutes voter power-vote No," *San Francisco Examiner*, October 27, 2976, 32.
13 Citizens for Representative Government, June 18, 1974, meeting minutes.
14 Interview with Jerry Roberts, George Moscone Oral History Project, April 26, 2011, parentheses mine.
15 Lone Mountain College is now part of the University of San Francisco.
16 Community Congress, 1.

17 Brahinsky, Rachel, "Rise and Fall of the Black Fillmore," in Carlsson, Chris *Ten Years that Shook the City: San Francisco 1968–1978*, 151.

18 San Francisco Voter Information Pamphlet, October 1976, 18.

19 San Francisco Voter Pamphlet, October 1976, 18. Capitals in original.

20 "Political Quake," *San Francisco Chronicle*, November 24, 1976, 30.

21 "No on Prop. T," Channel 7, San Francisco, October 22, 1976.

22 "Repeal Prop. T," Channel 7, October 2–3, 1977

23 Harvey Milk, letter to the editor, *San Francisco Examiner*, November 11, 1976, 38.

24 Roberts, Oral History Project, April 26, 2011.

25 Roberts, Oral History Project, April 26, 2011.

26 Barbagelata, John, "Supervisor Barbagelata Speaks," Why Yes on B, campaign flyer spring/summer 1977.

27 Wright, Gale W., "Special S. F. Election," *The San Francisco Policeman*, May 1977.

28 George Moscone, No on A and B undated 1977 statement. Grammar and italics in original.

29 Getlin, Oral History Project, May 22, 2009.

30 "Fairness," No on A and B campaign flyer, undated 1977.

31 Campaign flyer, "It's Simple: No A, No B" San Francisco Labor Council, AFL-CIO, International Longshoremen's and Warehousemen's Union, Joint Council of Teamsters, 1977, bold in original.

32 Caen, Herb, "View From the Middle," *San Francisco Chronicle and Examiner*, June 12, 1977. Grammar in original.

33 Caen, *San Francisco Chronicle and Examiner*, June 12, 1977. Spelling in original.

34 Davis, Mike, "New Alliance Tackles Old Power Centers," *Common Sense*, July-August 1977, 10–11.

35 George Moscone, Office of the Mayor, August 2, 1977.

36 *San Francisco Chronicle*, August 3, 1977, 1.

37 Roberts, Oral History Project, April 26, 2011.

38 George Moscone schedule, week of July 18–24, 1977.

39 George Moscone schedule, July 5–8, 1977.

40 Larry Griffin, interview with author, July 24, 2021.

41 Roberts, Oral History Project, April 26, 2011.

42 San Francisco Board of Elections Summary Report, November 8, 1977.

43 San Francisco Board of Elections Summary Report, November 8, 1977.

44 "Dan White A Democratic Candidate for Mayor," Campaign Flyer, 1977.

45 "Unite and Fight with Dan White," campaign flyer, 1977.

46 *San Francisco Chronicle*, November 4, 1977, *San Francisco Progress*, November 1977 and Federation News, October 1977.

47 Interview with Rich DeLeon, George Moscone Oral History Project, March 30, 2011.

48 Interview with Larry Del Carlo, George Moscone Oral History Project, circa 2011

49 DeLeon, George Moscone Oral History Project, March 30, 2011.

50 I first learned of Bella Abzug in the summer of 1977 because my grandparents were supporting her for mayor. Twenty years later, I campaigned on the Upper West Side alongside Abzug in support of C. Virginia Fields whose successful campaign for Manhattan borough president I was managing.

51 George R. Moscone schedule, September 1, 1977
52 Letter from George Moscone to Ruth Shack, March 30, 1977.
53 Press release, Mayor George Moscone, June 21, 1977.
54 Mastrangelo, Greg, "Statement of Opposition to the Youth Campus Project," December 1977.
55 Robinson, Eugene, "The Controversial S. F Youth Campus wins and OK," *San Francisco Chronicle*, December 1, 1977, 30.
56 Dianne Feinstein, letter to the editor, *San Francisco Chronicle*, December 1, 1977, 30.
57 Benet, Tom, "Supervisor Reject Teen Care Center," *San Francisco Chronicle*, December 6, 1977, 1.
58 "Youth Campus," *The Monitor*, December 15, 1977.
59 "The Case for a Youth Campus," *San Francisco Chronicle*, December 2, 1977, 62.
60 Mayor George Moscone, press release, December 13, 1977.

Chapter 13. Moscone's Last Year

1 Jonathan Moscone, interview with author, November 6, 2021.
2 Ledbetter, Les, "Bill on Homosexual Rights Advances in San Francisco," *The New York Times*, March 22, 1978, 22,
3 Ledbetter, "Bill on Homosexual Rights," *The New York Times*, March 22, 1978.
4 "Board Unit Backs Youth Campus Plan," *San Francisco Chronicle*, March 1, 1978, 9.
5 Tom Benet, "Board OKs Youth Contract," *San Francisco Chronicle*, March 14, 1978, 4.
6 Geluardi, John, "Dan White's Motive More About Betray Than Homophobia," SF Weekly, January 30, 2008.
7 Geluardi, "Dan White's Motive," *SF Weekly*, January 30, 2008, parentheses mine.
8 Generally, baseball teams wear their team name at home and their city or state on the road, so Moscone wanted their uniforms to say "Giants" at home and "San Francisco" on the road.
9 For more on this, see my two books *San Francisco Year Zero: Political Upheaval, Punk Rock, and a Third- Place Baseball Team* (Rutgers University Press, 2019), and *The Giants and Their City: Major League Baseball in San Francisco, 1876–1992* (Kent State University Press, 2020).
10 Noted San Francisco Giants fan Charles A. Fracchia Jr., who was the subject of Jon Leonoudakis's 2020 film *The Adventures of Superfan!*, credits his lifelong passion for the Giants to that 1978 team.
11 California Voters Pamphlet, June 6, 1978, compiled by March Fong Eu, June 6, 1978.
12 Mayor's remarks, May 15, 1978.
13 Ballotpedia, https://ballotpedia.org/California_Proposition_13,_Tax_Limitations_Initiative_(June_1978), accessed March 29, 2023.
14 Jim Jones, letter to George Moscone, August 3, 1977.
15 "Accusation of Human Rights Violations by Rev. James Warren Jones Against our Children and Relatives at the Peoples Temple Jungle Encampment in Guyana, South America," Concerned Relatives, April 11, 1978.
16 "Affidavit of Deborah Layton Blakey," July 15, 1978, 9,
17 "California Voter's Pamphlet," November 7, 1978, 28.

18 Reagan, Ronald, "Two Ill-Advised California Trends," *Los Angeles Herald Examiner*, November 1, 1978.

19 "Anti-Prop. 6 Fund-Raiser," *San Francisco Chronicle*, September 29, 1978, 2.

20 "Final Results County by County," *San Francisco Chronicle*, November 9, 1978, 6.

21 Carroll, Jerry, "Gay Happy Days Are Here Again," *San Francisco Chronicle*, November 8, 1978, 3.

22 Moscone Administration Accomplishments, 1978.

23 Mayor George Moscone press release, March 14, 1977.

24 Mayor George Moscone press release, May 24, 1978.

25 Chignell, Paul, "Moscone Must Go," *Police Officers Association Notebook*, June 1977.

26 San Francisco Police Officers Association press release, undated circa 1977.

27 San Francisco Police Officers Association, survey results, undated circa 1977.

28 In addition to my own writing about those weeks in chapter eight of my book *San Francisco Year Zero: Political Upheaval, Punk Rock, and a Third-Place Baseball Team* (Rutgers Universithy Press, 2019), see also Talbot, David (2013), *Season of the Witch: Enchantment, Terror and Deliverance in the City of Love*, New York: Free Press or Weiss, Mike (1984) *Double Play: The City Hall Killings*, Boston: Addison-Wesley.

29 This is still the case in San Francisco.

30 Jones, op. cit.

31 Javers, Ron, "Angry Meeting in Guyana," *San Francisco Chronicle*, November 17, 1978, 1.

32 Liebert, Larry, "What Politicians Say Now About Jim Jones," *San Francisco Chronicle*, November 20, 1978, 2, parentheses mine; brackets in original.

33 Liebert, *Chronicle*, November 20, 1978, 2, parentheses mine.

34 "Kopp Votes on Jim Jones," Memo from Josh Getlin to Mel Was, circa November 21, 1978.

35 Caen, Herb, "In This Corner," November 24, 1978, 43, parentheses mine.

36 Mayor George Moscone, press release, November 27, 1978.

37 Jon Rubin, interview with author, October 29, 2021.

38 Art Agnos, interview with author, November 11, 2020.

39 Willie Brown, interview with author, September 15, 2020.

40 Rudy Nothenberg, interview with author, November 17, 2020.

41 *Milk* (2008), Dustin Lance Black.

42 Talbot, David, *Season of the Witch*.

43 Shilts, Randy, *The Village Voice*, July 4, 1979.

44 Rubin, interview with author, October 29, 2021.

45 Burton, interview.

46 Chris Moscone, interview.

47 Saslafsky, interview with author, November 10, 2020.

48 Official Program, George Moscone and Harvey Milk Memorial, City of San Francisco.

49 Talbot, *Season of the Witch*, 329.

50 "Daniel White was always serving people-in various capacities," *Palo Alto Times*, November 27, 1978.

51 Reinka, Janet, "White: 'The brightest thing on the (political) horizon,'" *Palo Alto Times*, December 1, 1978.

52 Dolan, Maura, "Dan White in jail: it's a family affair," *San Francisco Chronicle*, December 17, 1978.
53 Willie Brown, interview with author, September 15, 2020,
54 For a discussion of this, see Pogash, Carol "Myth of the Twinkie defense/The verdict in the Dan White case wasn't biased on his ingestion of junk food," SF Gate, November 23, 2003.

Epilogue.

1 For an excellent literary treatment of this idea, see Joe Eskenazi, "The Day Harvey Milk Didn't Die," *San Francisco Magazine*, May 24, 2016.
2 Curry, George, "Run, Jesse, Run," *St. Louis American*, February 26, 2014.
3 I worked for David Dinkins during his unsuccessful reelection campaign in 1993 and graded papers for the class he taught at Columbia University when I was a graduate student there in the fall of 1994. We were not close but had a good relationship. The one time I sought to discuss George Moscone with him was in 1996 while I was a visiting professor at Brown University, the name did not seem to resonate much with him.
4 George Moscone, *San Francisco Magazine*, October 23, 1978.
5 Jonathan Moscone, interview with author, November 6, 2021.
6 Larry Griffin, interview with author, July 24, 2021.
7 Jon Rubin, interview with author, October 29, 2021.
8 Arnold Townsend, interview with author, March 11, 2021.
9 Ellipses in original.

Bibliography

Agee, Christopher Lowen, *The Streets of San Francisco: Policing and the Creation of a Cosmopolitan Liberal Politics, 1950–1972*, Chicago: University of Chicago Press.

Agee, Christopher Lowen, "The Emergence of the North Beach Beat Scene," FoundSF, undated.

Alioto, Joseph L., "Inaugural Address by the Honorable Joseph L. Alioto: Mayor of San Francisco," January 8, 1968.

Alioto, Joseph L., "For American Cities—A Declaration of Independence," inaugural address, January 8, 1972.

Alioto, Joseph L. (1999), "Changing the Face of San Francisco: Mayor 1968–1976, and Antitrust Trial Lawyer," an oral history conducted in 1991 by Carole Hicke, Regional Oral History Office, The Bancroft Library, University of California, Berkeley.

American Community Surveys (2019), "San Francisco Neighborhoods: Socio-Economic Profiles."

American Institute of Architects (1961), Board of Directors of the Northern California Chapter, Statement at City planning Commission Hearing on Trafficways Report.

American War Library, "Vietnam War Allied Troop Levels 1960–73," undated.

Anderson, Patrick (1981), *High in America: The True Story Behind NORML and the Politics of Marijuana. New York: The Viking Press.*

Anderson, Totton J.; Lee, Eugene C. (June 1967). "The 1966 Election in California," The Western Political Quarterly. 20 (2): 535–554.

Ansolabehere, Stephen, James Snyder, and Jonathan Woon, (1999), "Why did a majority of Californians vote to limit their own power?" Presentation at meeting of American Political Science Association.

Anspacher, Carolyn, "Cop Cleared in Slaying at Hunters Pt.," *San Francisco Chronicle*, October 21, 1966, 1.

Austin, Edith, "Demos Failed To Tell It Like It Is," *Sun-Reporter*, April 19, 1969, 2.

Austin, Edith, "Bay Bits," *Sun-Reporter*, November 25, 1972, 6.

Austin, Edith, "Bay Bits," *Sun-Reporter*, October 12, 1978, 9.

Austin, Edith, "Bay Bits," *Sun-Reporter*, November 30, 1978, 9.

Ballotpedia (1972), "California Marijuana Legalization, Proposition 19," undated.

Barbagelata, John (1969), "For Supervisor, John Barbagelata," *Statements of Qualifications of Candidates and Propositions*, 9.

Barbagelata, John, "Businessman mayor needed to run City," *San Francisco Examiner*, November 29, 1975, 37.

Barbagelata, John (1987). *Homeward*, self-published.

Barmann, Jay "Despite Violent Year Around the Bay and the Nation, SF Is Set to Record Similar Homicide Rate to 2019," SFist, December 31, 2020.

Barmann, Jay, "SF Sees Exact Same Number of Homicides In 2022 As Previous Year, While Burglaries Are Down," SFist, January 3, 2023.

Barnes, W. E., "Moscone quits law firm to avoid 'conflicts,'" *San Francisco Examiner*, February 10, 1977, 5.

Bay Guardian, "SF Election Intelligencer: 'Feinstein's ahead, but . . .'" October 10, 1975.

Belcher, Jerry, "Gov. Brown Walks On Riot Street," *San Francisco Examiner*, September 29, 1966.

Belcher, Jerry and Rich Jordan, "S. F.'s Young Rising Politicians," *San Francisco Chronicle*, November 7, 1963, 68.

Belmonte, Peter (2001), *Italian Americans in World War II*, Chicago: Arcadia Publishing.

Benet, Tom, "Supervisors Reject Teen Care Center," *San Francisco Chronicle*, December 6, 1977, 1.

Benet, Tom, "Board OKs Youth Contract," *San Francisco Chronicle*, March 14, 1978, 4.

Benoit, Monique, "On the Side of the Underdog," *San Francisco Chronicle*, March 9, 1965.

Black, Jason Edward and Charles E. Morris, eds., *Milk, Harvey. An Archive of Hope: Harvey Milk's Speeches and Writings*, Berkeley: University of California Press, 2013.

Blumenfeld, Sam, "Moscone Campaigns With His Heart and Sole," *San Francisco Examiner*, May 19, 1966, 32.

Booker, Matthew Morse (2013), *Down by the Bay*, Berkeley and Los Angeles: University of California Press.

Brahinsky, Rachel, "Rise and Fall of the Black Fillmore," in Carlsson, Chris, *Ten Years that Shook the City: San Francisco 1968–1978*, 151.

Brooks, Stephen C. (1980), "Politics of Crime in the 1970s: A Two-City Comparison," Reactions to Crime Project.

Burns, Jerry, "Morning Line On Next Mayor," *San Francisco Chronicle*, November 25, 1974, 6.

Butler, Katy, "S. F. mayor's race in the stretch," *Bay Guardian*, October 10, 1975.

Caen, Herb, "All the News That Fits," *San Francisco Chronicle*, November 14, 1969, 25.

Caen, Herb, "About This Town," *San Francisco Chronicle*, August 6, 1973, 24.

Caen, Herb, "Pocketful of Notes," *San Francisco Chronicle*, August 16, 1973, 33.

Caen, Herb, "From Here to Absurdity," *San Francisco Chronicle*, November 8, 1973, 30.

Caen, Herb, "One Thing After Another," *San Francisco Chronicle*, November 29, 1974, 31.

Caen, Herb, "This Old Town," *San Francisco Chronicle*, October 24, 1974, 27.

Caen, Herb, "Pocketful of Caenfetti," *San Francisco Chronicle*, February 10, 1975, 17.

Caen, Herb, "One Thing After Another," *San Francisco Chronicle*, July 17, 1975, 23.

Caen, Herb, "The Rambling Wreck," *San Francisco Chronicle*, December 4, 1975, 25.

Caen, Herb, "One Man's San Francisco," *San Francisco Chronicle*, January 15, 1976, 25.

Caen, Herb, "View From the Middle," *San Francisco Chronicle and Examiner*, June 12, 1977.

Caen, Herb, "In This Corner," *San Francisco Chronicle*, November 24, 1978, 43.

Caen, Herb, "'Twas the Day After," *San Francisco Chronicle*, December 26, 1995.

Campbell, Bruce J., "Millionaire Lawyer Aims for Top," *San Francisco Chronicle*, September 9, 1967, 8.

Carlsson, Chris, *Ten Years that Shook the City*, San Francisco: City Lights Books, 2011.

Carlsson, Chris, "Hunters Point Uprising," Found SF, undated.

Carlson, Peter (2009), *K Blows Top: A Cold War Comic Interlude, Starring Nikita Khrushchev, America's Most Unlikely Tourist*, New York: Public Affairs.

Carlson, Richard, and Lance Brison, "The Web that Links San Francisco's Mayor Alioto and the Mafia," *Look*, September 23, 1969, 17.

Caro, Robert (1974), *The Power Broker: Robert Moses and the Fall of New York*, New York: Vintage Books.

Carroll, Jerry, "Milk, Agnos Slugging It Out for the Assembly," *San Francisco Chronicle*, June 1, 1976, 5.

Carroll, Jerry, "Gay Happy Days Are Here Again," *San Francisco Chronicle*, November 8, 1978, 3.

Carroll, Jerry, and Dale Champion, "Prop T—It's a Whole New Ball Game," *San Francisco Chronicle*, November 4, 1976, 4.

Chamings, Andrew, "The Bizarre Tale of the world's last lost tourist, who thought Maine was San Francisco," *San Francisco Chronicle*, February 10, 2021.

Chignell, Paul, "Moscone Must Go," *Police Officers Association Notebook*, June 1977.

City and County of San Francisco, "Voter Handbook, General Municipal Election," November 6, 1973."

City and County of San Francisco, "Voter Handbook," November 2, 1975.

City and County of San Francisco, "Voter Information Pamphlet," October 1976, 18.

City and County of San Francisco, "Voter Information Pamphlet," November 2, 1976.

Clendinen, Dudley, and Adam Nagourney (1999), *Out For Good: The Struggle to Build a Gay Rights Movement in America*, New York: Touchstone.

Cone, Russ, "Morrison Backs Two for Board," *San Francisco Examiner*, October 31, 1963, 6.

Cone, Russ, "New Study of the Parkway," *San Francisco Examiner*, May 19, 1964, 1.

Cone, Russ, "The Propositions: what they mean," *San Francisco Chronicle and Examiner*, October 31, 1976, 29.

Cone, Russ, "Shelley Concedes It's Over for Freeways," *San Francisco Examiner*, March 22, 1966, 12.

Coulthard, Cheryl (2018), "The Peoples Press: The Evolution of the Media's Treatment of Jim Jones and the Peoples Temple," *Communal Societies*, Vol. 38, No. 2.

Criminal Justice Research Center, The Ohio State University, "Homicide in San Francisco, 1849–2003," undated.

Curry, George, "Run, Jesse, Run," *St. Louis American*, February 26, 2014.

Dance, Gabriel, and Tom Meagher, "Crime in Context," The Marshall Project, August 18, 2016.

Davies, Andrea Rees (2012), *Saving San Francisco: Relief and Recovery after the 1906 Disaster*, Philadelphia: Temple University Press.

Davis, R. B., "Bawdy Bravado in City Parks," *San Francisco Chronicle*, June 21, 1964, 149.

Davis, Mike, "New Alliance Tackles Old Power Centers," *Common Sense*, July–August 1977, 10–11.

DeLeon, Richard (1992), *Left Coast City: Progressive Politics in San Francisco, 1975–1992*, Lawrence: University of Kansas Press.

Delgado, A. J., "The Unburied Truth About Jim Jones," *National Review*, May 6, 2014.

Detrick, Rod, "Player Sketches of Basketball Tigers," *Pacific Weekly*, December 7, 1951, 4.

Dispatcher, "Why the ILWU Backs Moscone for Mayor," November 28, 1975, 1.

Dispatcher, "He's Labor's Choice," November 28, 1975, 1.

Dolan, Maura, "Dan White in jail: it's a family affair," *San Francisco Chronicle*, December 17, 1978.

Doty, Richard, "George Moscone: A visit with the mayor of San Francisco, class of 1953," *Pacific Review*, November 1977, 2.

Doyle, Jackson, "Reagan Funds for 'Campaign Lies,'" *San Francisco Chronicle*, November 1, 1978, 14.

Draper, George, "Thousands at City Hall Tribute," *San Francisco Chronicle*, April 6, 1968, 1.

Drewes, Caroline, "The Dedicated Dianne," *San Francisco Examiner*, March 9, 1969, 111.

Dushek, George, "The Early Days of Cow Hollow," *San Francisco Chronicle & Examiner*, February 6, 1966, Section 11, 2.

Elrick, John, "Yerba Buena Center: Redevelopment and a Working Class Community's Resistance," Found SF, undated.

Eskenazi, Joe, "The Day Harvey Milk Didn't Die," *San Francisco Magazine*, May 24, 2016.

Feinstein, Dianne, letter to the editor, *San Francisco Chronicle*, December 1, 1977, 30.

Fichera, Sebastian (2011), *Italy on the Pacific: San Francisco's Italian Americans*, New York: Palgrave Macmillan.

Finefrock, James, and Robert Hollis, "Closeup: The Candidates, Part Three: Their style and stands," *San Francisco Examiner*, December 3, 1975, 9.

Fleming, Thomas, "Thomas Fleming's Weekly Report," *Sun-Reporter*, January 12, 1974, 7.

Fleming, Thomas, "Political Potpourri: Moscone Almost Announces for Mayor," March 23, 1974, 11.

Flynn, Daniel J. (2018),
Cult City: Jim Jones, Harvey Milk, and 10 Days That Shook San Francisco, Wilmington, DE: Flynn ISI.

Flynn, William, "My secret ambition . . ." *San Francisco Chronicle & Examiner*, December 31, 1976.

Freeman, John, "War Anxiety in San Francisco's Western Neighborhoods," *Outside Lands: San Francisco History from the Western Neighborhoods Project*, Vol. 13, No.1, 2017, 7.

Flynn, Daniel (2018), *Cult City: Jim Jones, Harvey Milk, and 10 Days That Shook San Francisco*, Wilmington. DE: Intercollegiate Studies Institute.

Garratt, Robert F., *Home Team: The Turbulent History of the San Francisco Giants*, Lincoln: University of Nebraska Press.

Gay Crusader, "Dianne: First Woman Mayor of San Francisco," 1975 Election Special, 5.

Geiger, A. W. and John Gramlich, "6 Facts About Marijuana," Pew Research Center, November 22, 2019.

Geluardi, John, "Dan White's Motive More About Betray Than Homophobia," *SF Weekly*, January 30, 2008.

Gilliam, Harold, "Many Seeds of Rebellion," *San Francisco Chronicle*, October 14, 1964, 1, 14.

Godfrey, Brian (1997), "Urban Development and Redevelopment in San Francisco," *Geographical Review*, Vol. 87, No. 3 (309–333).

Goodfellow, James, "His Beloved City Mourns Gene McAteer," *San Francisco Examiner*, May 27, 1967, 5.

Graham, Bill, letter to George Moscone, December 4, 1975.

Grieg, Michael, "George Moscone—Who He Is, What He's Like," *San Francisco Chronicle*, January 8, 1976, 6.

Grieg, Michael, "Moscone's Self-Appraisal," *San Francisco Chronicle*, January 9, 1976, 4.

Guinn, Jeff (2017), *The Road to Jonestown: Jim Jones and Peoples Temple*, New York: Simon and Schuster.

Gumina, Deanna Paoli (1978), *The Italians of San Francisco 1850–1930*, New York: Center for Migration Studies.

Gunn, Jeff (2017), *The Road to Jonestown: Jim Jones and Peoples Temple*, New York, Simon and Schuster.

Haight Ashbury Neighborhood Council, dear neighbor letter, March 23, 1961.

Hamilton, Mildred, "Gina Moscone: The private first lady," *San Francisco Chronicle and Examiner*, November 19, 1978, Scene section 1.

Hamlin, Jesse, "How Herb Caen Named a Generation," *San Francisco Chronicle,* November 26, 1995.

Harris, Michael, "Reagan's Views of Riots," *San Francisco Chronicle,* September 30, 1966.

Harris, Michael, "Feinstein Ahead in S. F. Poll," *San Francisco Chronicle*, October 9, 1975, 1, 30.

Hartman, Chester (2002), *City for Sale: The Transformation of San Francisco,* Berkeley, University of California Press.

Hatfield, Larry D., "Cow Hollow—Chic New Tourist Mecca," *San Francisco Examiner*, August 3, 1970, 38.

Henderson, Jason Mark (2013), *Street Fight: The Politics of Mobility in San Francisco*, Amherst: University of Massachusetts Press.

Hirsch, James (2010), *Willie Mays: The Life, the Legend,* New York: Scribner.

Hoppe, Art "GOP Ousts Tuna—No Surprise," *San Francisco Chronicle*, May 16, 1960, 32.

Issel, William, "Land Values, Human Values, and the Preservation of the City's Treasured Appearance," Environmentalism, Politics, and the San Francisco Freeway Revolt, *Pacific Historical Review*, Vol. 68, No. 4 (November 1999).

Issel, William, "'The Catholic International' Mayor Joseph L. Alioto's Urban Liberalism and San Francisco Catholicism," *U.S. Catholic Historian*, Vol. 22, No. 2, Urbanism and American Religion (Spring 2004), 99–120.

Issel, William and Robert W. Cherny, (1986), *San Francisco 1865–1932: Politics, Power, and Urban Development*, Berkeley and Los Angeles, University of California Press.

Jacobs, John (1995), *Rage for Justice: The Passion and Politics of Phillip Burton*, Berkeley: University of California.

Javers, Ron, "Angry Meeting in Guyana," *San Francisco Chronicle*, November 17, 1978, 1.

Jennings, Duffy, "Passage of Prop. T Jolts Supervisors," *San Francisco Chronicle*, November 4, 1976, 28.

Johanesen, Harry, "W. Brown Upsets Gaffney," *San Francisco Examiner*, June 3, 1964, 1.

Johanesen, Harry, "Moscone's ties to the Burtons," *San Francisco Chronicle*, November 23, 1975, 4.

Johnson, Katherine M, "Captain Blake versus the Highwaymen: Or, How San Francisco Won the Freeway Revolt," *Journal of Planning History*, Vol. 8, No. 1, February 2009, 56–83.

Johnson, Victoria L. *How Many Machine Guns Does It Take to Cook One Meal?: The Seattle and San Francisco General Strikes*, Seattle: University of Washington Press, 2008.

Johnston, David, "Was the Alleged $10,000 Hughes Bribe Merely a Down Payment to Influence Moscone on Airport Expansion," David Johnston, *Bay Guardian*, October 5, 1978.

Johnston, David, "The Curious Questions About Moscone's New House," *Bay Guardian*, October 12, 1978.

Johnston, David, "Moscone's Top Aide Doesn't Properly Report $8,000 from Joe Cerrell," *Bay Guardian*, October 12, 1978.

Johnston, David, "Moscone Erects the Stonewall Defense, *Bay Guardian,* October 19, 1978.

Johnston, David and Bruce Brugmann, "KNBC-TV in Los Angeles Names Mayor Moscone As A 'Principal Target' in the FBI Probe," *Bay Guardian*, September 28, 1978, 3.

Jones, Jim, letter to George Moscone, July 12, 1976.

Jones, Jim, letter to George Moscone, August 3, 1977

Kilduff, Marshall, "Moscone Names New Permit Appeals Board," *San Francisco Chronicle*, January 30, 1976.

Kilduff, Marshall and Phil Tracy, "Inside Peoples Temple," *New West*, August 1, 1977, 30.

Kramer, Larry, "Tampering charges in mayor race," *San Francisco Examiner*, December 14, 1975, 1.

Kossen, Sydney, "Bitter S. F. Battle for State Senate Seat," *San Francisco Examiner*, June 1, 1966.

Lai, Clement (2012), "The Racial Triangulation of Space: The Case of Urban Renewal in San Francisco's Fillmore District," *Annals of the Association of American Geographers*, Vol. 102, No. 1, 157.

Lakeside Property Owners Association, letter to San Francisco City Planning Commission, March 24, 1961.

Lathrop, William, "The San Francisco Freeway Revolt," *The Transportation Engineering Journal*, (1971) 97/1, 133–144.

Ledbetter, Les, "Bill on Homosexual Rights Advances in San Francisco," *The New York Times*, March 22, 1978, 22.

Leip, Dave, "1960 Presidential General Election Results—California," Dave Leip's Atlas of U.S. Elections, undated.

Lenn, Ernest, "Gain appointed new police chief," *San Francisco Examiner*, January 12, 1976, 1.

Lewis, Jason, "Black History: Jackie Robinson excelled at a higher level in other sports," *Los Angeles Sentinel*, July 14, 2011.

Liebert, "What Politicians Say Now About Jim Jones," *San Francisco Chronicle*, November 20, 1978, 2.

Lombardo, Timothy J. (2018), *Blue-Collar Conservatism: Frank Rizzo's Philadelphia and Populist Politics*, Philadelphia: University of Pennsylvania Press.

Los Angeles Times, "Pot and the Law," March 5, 1975, B6.

Maciag, Mike, "Vehicle Ownership in US Cities Data and Map," *Governing*, December 9, 2014.

Marcus, Bob, "Lowell, Sacred Heart Draw Cage Inaugural," *San Francisco Chronicle*, January 6, 1946, 28.

Marinucci, Carla, "Alfred J. Nelder / 1915–2002 / Former S. F. police chief a lifelong public servant," *San Francisco Chronicle,* January 31, 2012.

Marks, Milton (1996), "State Government Oral History Program, Oral History with Milton Marks."

Mastrangelo, Greg, "Statement of Opposition to the Youth Campus Project," December 1977.

Malcolm, Andrew H., "Police Out, San Francisco Faces Fire and Transit Strikes," *The New York Times*, August 20, 2975, 1.

McCarthy, Leo (1996), interview, California State Archives, State Oral History Program.

McDowell, Jack S., "Has Moscone Changed His Views," *San Francisco Chronicle*, September 10, 1967, 12.

McGloin, John Bernard (1978), *San Francisco: The Story of a City*, San Rafael, CA: Presidio Press.

McGruder, Robert, "Alioto's Spirit is Catching in San Francisco," *Cleveland Plain Dealer*, February 20, 1969.

McKinney, Joan, "A Pretty Expert on Crime," *San Francisco Chronicle*, July 11, 1965, 4.

Mellinkoff, Abe, "Instant Democracy," *San Francisco Chronicle*, October 25, 1976, 40.

Melnick, Norman, "Riot Cop Back on New Beat," *San Francisco Examiner*, October 22, 1966.

Milk, Harvey letter to the editor, *San Francisco Examiner*, November 11, 1976, 38.

Mitchell, Lincoln, "Ruby the Pizza Guy" in John van der Zee, *San Francisco Childhood, Memories of a Great City Seen Through the Eyes of Its Children* (2011), Kensington, CA: Grizzly Peak Press.

Mitchell, Lincoln, "Towards Land's End" (2014), *Roads & Kingdoms*.

Mitchell, Lincoln (2018), *Baseball Goes West: the Dodgers, the Giants and the Shaping of the Major Leagues*, Kent, OH: The Kent State University Press.

Mitchell, Lincoln (2019), *San Francisco Year Zero: Political Upheaval, Punk Rock, and a Third-Place Baseball Team*, New Brunswick, NJ: Rutgers University Press.

Mitchell, Lincoln (2020), *The Giants and Their City: Major League Baseball in San Francisco, 1876–1992*, Kent, OH: The Kent State University Press.

Moore, Percy, "The Kind of People We Are," letter to the editor, *San Francisco Chronicle*, October 31, 1963, 38.

Morch, Albert, "Lee Moscone: Every son's dream of the perfect mom," *San Francisco. Examiner & Chronicle*, May 14, 1978, Scene, section 3.

Moscone Democrat, "Moscone bid for Governor opens with statewide tour," 1973, 1.

Moscone Insider, "The Jeep Trip: Bit! By a Pig! Where?!" Issue 2, 1973, 1.

Moskowitz, Ron, "Harvey Milk Blames 2 Factors for Defeat," *San Francisco Chronicle*, June 10, 1976, 7.

Moynihan, Daniel Patrick, speech opposing UN Resolution 3379, November 10, 1975.

Mullaney, Alexander, "Look: San Francisco Mayor Joseph Alioto and the Press," e-scholarship, undated.

Murphy, George, "Moscone's Hat First in Ring," *San Francisco Chronicle*, December 20, 1974, 2.

Murphy, George, "The New Milton Marks," *San Francisco Chronicle*, October 2, 1975, 22.

Murphy, George, "Kopp Backs Barbagelata for Mayor," *San Francisco Chronicle*, December 8, 1975, 5.

Murphy, George, "Nelder Can't Be Renamed Chief," *San Francisco Chronicle*, December 30, 1975, 2.

Northern California Historical Records Survey Project, Service Division, Work Projects Administration, *A Guide to Church Vital Statistics Records In California, San Francisco and Alameda Counties: Six Denominations*: San Francisco, May 1942.

Oak Leaf, "Surprise Party Announces Friberg, Moscone Betrothal," March 22, 1950, 7.

Oakdale Leader, "Large High School Class Graduates," June 17, 1926, 1.

Oakdale Leader, "Monge Pleads Guilty," June 17, 1926, 2.

Oakdale Leader, "Local Girl Weds S.F. Man Sunday," February 14, 1929, 4.

Oakdale Leader, "We Wonder Why," November 29, 1978.

Organized Labor, "Backed by Labor," May 23, 1966
Osman, Suleiman (2011), *The Invention of Brownstone Brooklyn*, London: Oxford University Press.
Palo Alto Times, "Daniel White was always serving people—in various capacities," November 27, 1978.
Pawel, Miriam (2019), *The Browns of California*, New York: Bloomsbury.
Peoples Forum, November 2, 1086, 2.
Pepin, Elizabeth and Lewis Watts (2006), *Harlem of the West: The San Francisco Fillmore Jazz Era*, San Francisco: Chronicle Books.
Pimsleur, J. L., and Kevin Leary, "S. F.'s 'Uncle Miltie' Dies—Inveterate Campaigner/Milton Marks served 4 decades in office," *San Francisco Chronicle*, December 5, 1998.
Pogash, Carol, "Myth of the Twinkie defense/The verdict in the Dan White case wasn't based on his ingestion of junk food," SF Gate, November 23, 2003.
Potrero Boosters and Merchants Association, letter to Mayor George Christopher, April 19, 1961.
Prokes, Michael, letter to George Moscone, July 13, 1976.
Reagan, Ronald, "A Time for Choosing," October 27, 1964.
Reagan, Ronald (1966), Morality Gap Speech.
Reagan, Ronald, "Two Ill-Advised California Trends," *Los Angeles Herald Examiner*, November 1, 1978.
Reinka, Janet, "White: 'The brightest thing on the (political) horizon,'" *Palo Alto Times*, December 1, 1978.
Reiterman, Tim and John Jacobs (1982), *Raven: The Untold Story of the Rev. Jim Jones and His People*, Boston: E. P. Dutton.
Rexroth, Kenneth, "Revolt: True and False," *The Nation*, April 26, 1958, 379.
Richards, Rand, "Neighborhood Historic Sites," *The Marina Times*, January 2003, 8.
Richardson, James, (1996) *Willie Brown: A Biography*, University of California; Berkeley.
Roberts, Jerry, "Who gets the Feinstein/Ertola/Marks vote?" *Bay Guardian*, November 28, 1975.
Roberts, Jerry, "The first glimpses of the New Mayor," *Bay Guardian*, December 24, 1975, 3.
Roberts, Jerry, "City Strike: yellow dogs, red herrings and blue munis," *The Bay Guardian*, April 9, 1976.
Roberts, Jerry (1994), Dianne Feinstein: Never Let Them See You Cry, San Francisco: HarperCollinsWest.
Robertson, Bob, "Dobbs Says Picket Plan Has Political Motive," *San Francisco Chronicle*, October 18, 1963, 4.
Robertson, Bob, "The Board, GIs and the Dentist," *San Francisco Chronicle*, June 11, 1965, 4.
Robinson, Eugene, "The Controversial S. F. Youth Campus wins an OK," *San Francisco Chronicle*, December 1, 1977, 30.
Robison, Jennifer, "Decades of Drug Use Data from the '60s and '70s," Gallup, July 2, 2002.
Rosenbaum, Art, "A Picnic at Candlestick Park," *San Francisco Chronicle*, April 10, 1976, 1.
Rosenbaum, Jack, "Silent Treatment," Jack Rosenbaum, *San Francisco Examiner*, May 6, 1966, 35.
Sacramento Bee, "Sensible Pot Laws Change," March 11, 1975.
Sacramento Bee, Gloria Wernsman Glyer obituary, July 2017.
Saint Ignatius College Prep, "George Moscone Wins Frosh Elocution Medal," *The Red and*

Blue: Official Organ of the Student Body, March 1944.
San Francisco Chamber of Commerce (1959), *The Downtowner.*
San Francisco Chamber of Commerce (1961), Report to the San Francisco Planning Commission.
San Francisco Chronicle, "5 S. F. Winners Fail to File Campaign Fund Reports," July 14, 1960, 26.
San Francisco Chronicle, "The Chronicle Recommends," November 2, 1960, 1.
San Francisco Chronicle, "California Legislature," November 9, 1960, 1a.
San Francisco Chronicle, "S.F. Vote For All Offices," November 9, 1960, 1a.
San Francisco Chronicle, "Final S.F. Vote," November 8, 1961, 1.
San Francisco Chronicle, "Parting Advice from Mumford," January 16, 1962, 2.
San Francisco Chronicle, "Lawyer Arraigned As Bookmaker," April 7, 1962, 3.
San Francisco Chronicle, "Burton Acquitted In Bookie Charge," November 30, 1962, 3.
San Francisco Chronicle, "Moscone Blast at Billboards," October 20, 1963, 23.
San Francisco Chronicle, "Melee at S.F. Drive-in," November 4, 1963, 1.
San Francisco Chronicle, "Day of Secret Talks by Brown, UC Brass," December 7, 1964, 1.
San Francisco Chronicle, "A Petition to Bay Area Congressmen," December 28, 1964, 14.
San Francisco Chronicle, "Labor Group Backs Moscone, December 17, 1965, 19.
San Francisco Chronicle, "A Roundup of Political Activity," April 27, 1966, 21.
San Francisco Chronicle, "A Roundup of Political Activity," May 9, 1966, 50.
San Francisco Chronicle, "The Mayor's Message," September 30, 1966.
San Francisco Chronicle, "Proclamation," April 6, 1968, 1.
San Francisco Chronicle, "Dianne Chooses Her Committees," January 9, 1970, 4.
San Francisco Chronicle, "Gay Voters Endorse Seven Candidates," October 27, 1973.
San Francisco Chronicle, S. F. Vote Tally, November 7, 1973, 4.
San Francisco Chronicle, "Race for Mayor: Moscone to Announce," December 6, 1974, 5.
San Francisco Chronicle, "Barbagelata Files to Run For Mayor," June 11, 1975, 2.
San Francisco Chronicle, "Sensibly Easing Penalty for Pot," March 24, 1975.
San Francisco Chronicle, "Feinstein Ahead in S.F. Poll," October 9, 1975, 1.
San Francisco Chronicle, "Rally Against U.N on Zionism," November 17, 1975, 8.
San Francisco Chronicle, "Barbagelata Tells his Supporters 'We Won," December 12, 1975, 2.
San Francisco Chronicle, "Unhappy Incident in Moscone's Past," January 9, 1976, 4.
San Francisco Chronicle, "Opponents Say Prop. T Will Kill Recall Moves," September 25, 1976, 12.
San Francisco Chronicle, "Districting Is Not For San Francisco," October 8, 1976, 42.
San Francisco Chronicle, "Dividing the City," October 29, 1976, 42.
San Francisco Chronicle, "Political Quake," November 24, 1976, 30.
San Francisco Chronicle, "The Case for a Youth Campus," December 2, 1977, 62.
San Francisco Chronicle, "Board Unit Backs Youth Campus Plan," March 1, 1978, 9.
San Francisco Chronicle, "Anti-Prop. 6 Fund-Raiser," September 29, 1978, 2.
San Francisco Chronicle, "Final Results County by County," November 9, 1978, 6.
San Francisco Chronicle, Charles O. Morgan obituary, June 10, 2012.
San Francisco City Planning Commission (1961), Hearing on Trafficways Report.
San Francisco Board of Elections, Summary Report, November 8, 1977.
San Francisco Examiner, "Prep Rivals Vie Tonight," February 4, 1946, 18.
San Francisco Examiner, "Moscone Seeks Office," March 29, 1960.
San Francisco Examiner, "Moscone To Run for Board Seat," March 21, 1963, 9.

San Francisco Examiner, "Union Body for Shelley," August 27, 1963.
San Francisco Examiner, Political Notes," September 5, 1963, 19.
San Francisco Examiner, "George Moscone," October 11, 1963.
San Francisco Examiner, "Moscone To Run for State Seat," January 18, 1964.
San Francisco Examiner, "Chamber To Boost Panhandle," July 8, 1964, 8.
San Francisco Examiner, "Pay Hike? Don't Give a Hoot," August 25, 1964.
San Francisco Examiner, "S. F. Lawyer Squad Returns from Miss." January 27, 1965.
San Francisco Examiner, "Eastland Blasts S. F. Supervisors," February 4, 1965, 1.
San Francisco Examiner, "Burton Cash for Moscone," June 5, 1966, 1.
San Francisco Examiner, "How S. F. Voted," November 9, 1966, 6.
San Francisco Examiner, "Moscone Involved in Auto Mishap," April 14, 1970, 12.
San Francisco Examiner, "Barbagelata files as mayor candidate," June 10, 1975, 6.
San Francisco Examiner, "They Were a Couple of Sweethearts," November 15, 1975, 1.
San Francisco Examiner, "Recount over—no change," January 18, 1975, 3.
San Francisco Examiner, "Kopp calls Prop. T a petty power ploy," October 12, 1976, 4.
San Francisco Examiner, "Prop. T: Prescription for chaos," October 13, 1976, 36.
San Francisco Examiner, "Prop. T dilutes voter power—vote No," October 27, 2976, 32.
San Francisco News & Call Bulletin, "Atty. Moscone Will Seek Post As Supervisor, March 21, 1963.
San Francisco Planning Department, "The Tentative Plan for the Redevelopment of Western Addition Project Area Number One," undated.
San Francisco Planning Department (2022), "Industrial Land in San Francisco: Understanding Production, Distribution, and Repair."
San Francisco Police Department (1966), 128 Hours: A Report on the Civil Disturbance in the City & County of San Francisco."
Saxon, Wolfgang, "George Moscone, A Firm Mayor Who Stressed Anticrime Effort," *The New York Times*, November 28, 1978.
Schaefer, Hal, "The Owl Steps Out," *San Francisco Chronicle*, September 28, 2963, 28.
Schaffer Library of Drugs, "A Fiscal Analysis of Marijuana Decriminalization," undated.
Schoenwald, Jonathan M., *A Time for Choosing: the Rise of Modern American Conservatism*, e-book, New York: Oxford University Press, 2003.
Scott, Joe, "The Political Animal," newsletter, December 24, 1975.
Scott, Mel (1959), *The San Francisco Bay Area: A Metropolis in Perspective*, Berkeley: University of California Press.
Shilts, Randy, *The Village Voice*, July 4, 1979, untitled.
Shilts, Randy (1982), *The Mayor of Castro Street: The Life and Times of Harvey Milk*, New York: St. Martin's Press.
Sobredo, James, "The Battle for the International Hotel," FoundSF, undated.
Song, Oral History Interview (1986), by Raphael J. Sonenshein, Oral History Program, History Department, California State University, Fullerton, for the California State Archives State Government Oral History Program.
Sports Illustrated, "Popup," August 21, 1967, Volume 27, No. 8, 11.
SPUR, "Report on the Proposed Freeway and Trafficways Plan for the City and County of San Francisco," April 1961.
Starr, Kevin, "The show-biz campaign," *San Francisco Examiner*, June 3, 1978.

Starr, Kevin, "Two traditions," *San Francisco Examiner*, April 3, 1980, 24.

Sun-Reporter, "Moscone for State Senator," Primary Election Special, May-June 1966, 2.

Sun-Reporter, "Moscone Begins Early Campaign," February 5, 1972, 4.

Sun-Reporter, "Moscone To Honor Aaron," September 1, 1973, 4.

Sun-Reporter, "'One Brotherhood': Muslims, People's (sic) Temple Get It Together in L.A.," June 5, 1976, 4.

Sun-Reporter, "Supervisor's Barbagelata's Self-Deception," January 24, 1976, 7.

Sundahl, Carl, "Tile Layers 19 Notes," *Organized Labor*, August 12, 1963.

Talbot, David (2013). *Season of the Witch: Enchantment, Terror and Deliverance in the City of Love*, New York: Free Press.

Time magazine, "Crime: Stirrings on Death Row," April 21, 1967

Trimble, Peter ,"Burton Is Off and Running," *San Francisco Examiner*, November 7, 1963, 1.

Turner, Wallace, "Magical, 'Happy' San Francisco Also Has Problems and Tears," *The New York Times*, December 11, 1975, 47.

Turner, Wallace, "Job-Bias Lawsuit Settled by San Francisco Police," *The New York Times*, January 28, 1979, 24.

Ungaretti, Lori, "The Sunset District: From Dunes to Cityscape," undated, FoundSF.

Veronico, Nicholas (2007), *Images of America: World War II: Shipyards by the Bay*, San Francisco: Arcadia.

Waite, Elmont "City Vote: Prop. A 'in'; Underwood Ahead," *San Francisco Chronicle*, June 8, 1960, 11.

Waugh, Dexter, "Butterflies . . . dashed hopes," *San Francisco Examiner*, November 2, 1975.

Wax, Mel, "Voice In Nowhere Mississippi," *San Francisco Chronicle*, January 21, 1965, 22.

Wegars, Don, "Feinstein Announces She's Running for Mayor," *San Francisco Chronicle*, April 23, 1975, 2.

Weiss, Mike (1984), *Double Play: The City Hall Killings*, Boston: Addison-Wesley.

Weisser, Peter, "Senate Oks Sex Bill: Liberalized Law for State Adults," *San Francisco Chronicle*, May 2, 1975, 24.

Welter, Jack, "A Moscone contributions tangle," *San Francisco Examiner & Chronicle*, November 23, 1975, 4.

Wernsman, Gloria, "Buzz of the Hornet," *Sacramento State College Hornet*, February 8, 1952.

Wright, Gale W., "Special S.F. Election," *The San Francisco Policeman*, May 1977.

Yglesias, Matthew, "America's 10 biggest cities, in every decade going back to 1790," Vox, July 5, 2015

Yollin, Patricia, "A Secret History / The harassment of Italians during World War II has particular relevance today and serves as a warning of what could happen," *San Francisco Chronicle*, October 21, 2001.

Author Interviews

Art Agnos, November 11, 2020.

Willie Brown, September 15, 2020.

John Burton, September 11, 2020.

Corey Busch, October 29, 2021.

Jeannette Etheredge, January 13, 2022.

Cleve Jones, March 9, 2021.

Joe Kelly, October 10, 2021.
George Miller, November 5, 2020.
Christopher Moscone, November 4, 2021.
Jonathan Moscone, November 6, 2021.
Rudy Nothenberg, November 17, 2020.
Jon Rubin, October 27, 2021.
Sharyn Saslafsky, November 10, 2020.
Larry Simi, October 28, 2021.
Arnold Townsend, February 24, 2021.

Interviews from the George Moscone Oral History Project (2009–2012)
Jerry Adams, undated.
Phil Bronstein, undated.
Willie Brown, undated.
Gordon Brownwell, June 15, 2011.
Bruce Brugmann, undated.
Joe Cotchett, August 26, 2009.
Vince Courtney, January 10, 2011.
Belva Davis, May 4, 2011.
Larry Del Carlo, undated.
Richard DeLeon, undated.
John De Luca, August 24, 2011.
Derrald Etheley, May 4, 2011
Dianne Feinstein, undated.
Josh Getlin, undated.
Sue Hestor, July 20, 2009.
Agar Jaicks, undated.
Duffy Jennings, May 10, 2011.
Marshall Kilduff, August 2010.
Cappy Lavin, July 2, 2011.
Jim Molinari, undated.
Jenifer Moscone, undated.
Jonathan Moscone, undated.
Rebecca Moscone, November 30, 2009.
David Nelson, November 2012.
Nancy Pelosi, undated.
Jerry Roberts, April 26, 2011.
Hadley Roth, July 19, 2011.
Frances Park-Li Rothman, October 18, 2011.
Yvonne Ryzack, undated.
Lois Salisbury, undated.
Larry Simi, undated.
Barbara Taylor, undated.
John Vlahos, January 24, 2011.

Index

About the Author

Lincoln Mitchell teaches in the School of International and Public Affairs and the political science department at Columbia University. He has written numerous books, scholarly articles, and opinion columns on American politics, foreign policy, the history and politics of San Francisco, and baseball. In addition to his academic interests, Mitchell has worked in domestic political campaigns and on foreign policy projects in dozens of countries, particularly in the former Soviet Union. Mitchell earned his bachelor of arts degree from the University of California, Santa Cruz, and his PhD from Columbia University. He lives in New York and San Francisco.